YO-CBU-428

ENERGY OPTIONS

REAL ECONOMICS
AND THE
SOLAR-HYDROGEN SYSTEM

ENERGY OPTIONS

REAL ECONOMICS
AND THE
SOLAR-HYDROGEN SYSTEM

J. O'M. BOCKRIS

The Flinders University of South Australia
Adelaide, Australia

Texas A & M University
Texas, U.S.A.

AUSTRALIA & NEW ZEALAND BOOK COMPANY
SYDNEY MELBOURNE BRISBANE AUCKLAND

First published in Australia in 1980 by
Australia & New Zealand Book Co Pty Ltd
23 Cross Street Brookvale NSW 2100 Australia

National Library of Australia Cataloguing-in-Publication Data

Bockris, John O'Mara.
Energy options.

Index
Simultaneously published, New York:
Halsted Press and London: Taylor & Francis.
ISBN 0 85552 088 4

1. Power resources. 2. Solar energy.
3. Hydrogen as fuel. I. Title.

621.4

Typesetting by Dalley Photocomposition, Sydney
Printed in Australia by
Hogbin, Poole (Printers) Pty Ltd, Redfern NSW Australia

CONTENTS

PREFACE

This book is a successor to *Energy: The Solar-Hydrogen Alternative*. At first, the intention was to create a second edition of this book, essentially updating it. However, it became clear that the energy scene had changed so much since the first book was written (1973-74), that the writing of a new book became desirable.

The first book consisted of an isolated scientific inquiry: would it be feasible to avoid the health hazards of low-intensity radiation by the massive collection of solar energy in desert areas, its transfer to cities in hydrogen, and the use of this as a fuel, along with electricity?

What technology has developed has often less to do with its scientific feasibility, or the optimization of public need, and is more dependent on political and commercial advantage. Hence, attention is given in this book to economic and, occasionally, sociological factors. The idea of *real costs* of various forms of energy, i.e. the *net* cost to buyers, of the use of the particular form of energy, as apart from the price charged by the seller, is developed for one unit of a given form of energy.

For whom is this book intended? For engineers and scientists, primarily, and above all for technocrats (are there many?) who are planning the energy future.

Watertight compartments to knowledge are dangerous. This is not yet taken into account sufficiently in practice by scientists engaged in energy work. Economics, sociology, political science, are fields of knowledge with which those who consider energy options must be conversant. Woe to him who devises a process for coal gasification without accounting for the climatic influences of its use two to three decades away.

John O'M. Bockris
January, 1980

The Flinders University of South Australia

Texas A & M University

ACKNOWLEDGEMENTS

I wish to acknowledge the liberal support of the Flinders University of South Australia, where the majority of the work of writing this book was carried out, and the enthusiastic collaboration of Mr James Kelly and Dr David Lawson, of the Jet Propulsion Laboratory, Pasadena, who facilitated a three-month sojourn at this institution, where about one-quarter of the book was written.

I also wish to acknowledge the help of Mr M. S. Tunuli in the editing of chapters, and of Dr J. Tendys and Mr G. Durance of the Australian Atomic Energy Commission in discussions of the chapters on fusion technology; Dr Robert Zweig, for discussion of the medical aspects of pollution; and Professor C. J. Smith of the University of California at Berkeley, for discussions of systems for the massive collection of solar energy and its economical conversion to electricity on a very large scale.

Many thanks are due to Mrs Dorothy Hampton who typed most of this book, often under some tension, and made many helpful contributions to my peace of mind. I would also like to record my thanks to those many who have contributed to this book in answering my letters of enquiry, and my indebtedness to my colleague, Dr Nejat Veziroglu for encouragement and help.

1

PERSPECTIVES OF
THE ENERGY SITUATION

The origins of classical energy policy

Students of Energy may think of energy policy as a topic exemplified by concern with, e.g. the number of wind generators which should be installed in windy areas. Such a concern would be associated with an energy policy which had as its goal the provision of energy in a way which would optimize the satisfaction of public needs in a time scale greater than that (several decades) needed to change to the use of renewable resources. In fact, the principal well-springs of policy in the United States are oriented towards relatively short-term considerations of the optimal vending of the residual non-renewable resources. Thus, the policy is effected by considerations of the present. It works so as to optimize the use of existing capital.

For example, the concept of diminishing the rate of the disbursement of gasoline by methods which could probably be made palatable to the electorate (e.g. negative and positive taxes to bring about the use of cars which consume less gasoline per unit distance) was not found acceptable to the Congress in its rejection of much of the first Carter energy programme. Such moves would diminish the sales of oil.

A result of having such a basis to energy policy—treating energy as though its main aspect were that of a commodity to be sold—is preoccupation with the remaining non-renewable sources (oil, natural gas, coal, uranium), whilst energy conversion from the renewable resources (gravitation, wind, solar, fusion) as main supply sources remains less discussed, except by engineers and by the public; and their development, and hence cost reduction, is less supported by government research funds than, say, the conversion of coal to oil.

Two other aspects of the present U.S. energy policy may be mentioned.
1. It seems little occupied with *context* on the time axis—how far we are from the end of the use of fossil fuels, and how will the present policy affect the public's position towards the end of that time—and afterwards. How long will it take to *build* the new converters? At what cost? To whom?
2. It is much preoccupied with the direct, *apparent* cost to the consumer, without concern with the ancillary costs, a kind of material silent majority. For example, present fuels pollute. Reversing this pollution is very costly. They cause illness. It will be shown below that the order of magnitude of such costs is that of the price at which the oil is being sold. This cost is borne, unconsciously, by the buyer, who does not identify the source of his illness. Were it placed properly and publicly onto the price of the present fuels, their cost would increase, thus changing the comparative

position with respect to alternate fuels which do not provoke the hidden costs.*

Some difficulties of classical energy policy

The classical energy policy may not be that leading to the public's greatest long-term advantage. Does the choice of what fuel for transportation is supported, in respect to research and development funds, depend on the feasibility of its high price/cost ratio, rather than upon relative cost, including the ancillary social cost, at the time the fuel may be needed? If so, this may be an advantageous policy for the corporate vendor, but less helpful to those whose jobs and comforts depend on the price and availability of energy in suitable forms after 1985. As evidence of this, one difficulty of the present coal-uranium energy policy is its unpopularity, as measured by the active protest groups.

However, there is a more pressing difficulty in the present energy policy. By having a view-ahead range of a few years, and not the time it will take to build the necessary new energy-conversion equipment (15-50 years), continuation of the present policy may lead to social suffering (lay-offs, cold houses).

Further, the present policy places on a largely unconscious public, and its descendants, significant future costs, the bearing of which will be irreversible if capital investments continue in machinery, the use of which implies such future costs. Thus, atmospheric pollution and emphysema, brought about by the use of coal products, is a social cost.[1] The cost of the social damage, pollution, illness and death, will not, however, be borne by the manufacturers of the fuels which will cause such damage. Guarding the plutonium wastes, which present policy has the United States producing to give its citizens a few generations of plentiful energy, will have to be shared by several hundreds of generations in the future.

Many would agree that the present policy lacks wisdom. It can have political viability only in the absence of realisation among voters that alternative paths to energy for transport and industry, which could permanently underlay the economy, exist.

A general solution to the energy question

The question is: what system of energy conversion, using inexhaustible sources, will provide energy in suitable media at the least cost, including the social costs of pollution,[1] at the time it is needed?

Prolonged consideration shows that few solutions are available. The source had better be renewable. Consideration of the technical aspects (Chapters 2, 4, and 5) show that the development of coal and uranium are fraught with both pollutional and investment hazards of great magnitude. The conversion of tidal and gravitational energy does not seem to offer significant scope for development due to the lack of magnitude.[†] Solar energy could contribute sufficient energy for the present population.[‡] It would provide energy with

---

* Conversely, in a sense reminiscent of Orwell's well-known *Double Speak*, the renewable-resource energy options are sometimes referred to as 'high risk'.
† However, there may be possibilities in the development of an Archimedean Generator.[2]
‡ This assumes a 10% efficiency collection from 1% of the earth's land area.

(after construction) complete absence of pollution. Of its supposed fundamental defects—diluteness, sporadicity and high cost—the first is a myth[3] (see Chapter 7); and the second is overcome by arranging for the energy collected at the site to make a storable fuel. As to the last, in terms largely of the systems analyses of the late 1970s, the impression of high costs appear to have been largely an inheritance from the early applications of solar energy in space technology, where costs are not the first consideration.[4] The cost of a unit of energy in commercial applications for the massive provision of solar energy, look as though they could be competitive with those of breeder reactors,[5] the most relevant comparison.

A solar-hydrogen-based economy would have sufficient energy, be inexhaustible, and relieve the concern for pollutional damage such as is being done by the present systems, and which would be increased, it seems dangerously, by the proposed breeder programme. The most important need in respect to the solar-hydrogen system of energy development is support by funds from the U.S. Department of Energy such as are being at present given more to the development of modes of energy conversion aimed at making vendable the remaining coal and uranium.

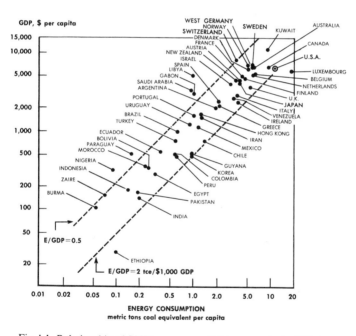

Fig. 1.1. Relationship of GNP to energy available per capita in 1974.[7]

The relation of the energy supply to the economy

There are now fifty-one countries on the famous relation of G.N.P. per capita to energy consumption per capita. The relation seems linear (but see Chapter 16), and is shown in Fig. 1.1.

The graph establishes the portentous connection between the degree of use of energy in a community and the material living standard of the population.

The efficiency of energy use

An interesting ratio is the energy per unit of Gross National Product. This obviously represents the efficiency of energy use, and is shown in Fig. 1.2.

It is not surprising to note that the most efficient country is Switzerland and the least efficient the United Kingdom.

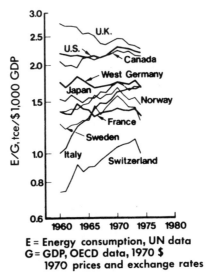

E = Energy consumption, UN data
G = GDP, OECD data, 1970 $
1970 prices and exchange rates

Fig. 1.2. Efficiency of energy use in various countries as a function of time.[7]

Employment and energy

H. R. Lyndon, J. D. Parent and J. G. Sahe have pointed out that the post-war energy-consumption patterns in the United States are related to changes in the deflated price index.[6] Civilian employment rises or falls with the change in the rate of energy use. For every 10% increase in real energy costs, consumption decreases by 2%, and unemployment increases by 1%.

These statements mean that a 1% increase in employment causes an increased energy consumption in the United States by 758,000 barrels of oil per day, and a 1% increase in the price of fossil fuels causes a decrease in energy consumption (and hence an increase in employment of 0.1%) by the equivalent of 81,700 barrels of oil per day.

There are important conclusions to be made from these statements. One is that conservation—one of the main, and, for the immediate future, the only, weapon in the energy situation—would give rise to social suffering by means of unemployment. A substantial cut in energy use (say 20%) would increase unemployment by several per cent of the civilian work force.

The second one is that the needed raising of the price of fossil fuels would be helpful only to the longer-term interests of the public. It would damage the vendor, for it would give rise to a drop in sales. It would damage the buyer because it would bring unemployment.

The insignificance of uranium, without breeder reactors

Low cost uranium would only make a minor impact on energy resources if it is used up in fission reactors. Thus, in units of 1 ton of coal equivalent ($27.7.10^6$ BTU or 7.10^6 k cal), one has:[6]

Natural gas	76-93
Crude oil	114-135
Coal	497
Uranium oxide in fission reactors	34.6

Coal and energy from breeder reactors

The use of both these methods of providing energy is fraught with pollutional and other difficulties, which will be discussed in Chapters 4 and 5 respectively. However, it is interesting to note that the coal which seems to be recoverable would be equivalent to about one-fifth of the energy which might be obtainable from uranium oxide at less than $30 per ton in breeder reactors.[7]

The central role of hydrogen as an energy medium

From earlier considerations of a large number of fuels,[8] the fuels which are considered viable in the post-oil era, have now been reduced to methane, methanol and hydrogen.

Among the advantages pertaining to hydrogen is that it is the only substance which can both be produced from the remaining fossil fuels, and also, by means of water-splitting, from atomic and solar sources. The advantage would be felt in the coming decades whilst coal, solar and breeder reactors compete to give energy.

The spending of the energy capital and the gaining of energy income

It is conceptually important to see the use-up of the fossil fuels and uranium oxide as a spending of basic capital.

Correspondingly, it is clearly invalid to compare the price of energy obtained by the spending of this energy capital with the price of energy obtained from energy income—namely, energy conversion of renewable resources. However, capital is exhaustible and, therefore, the use of part of its remainder to build the means to obtain income upon its exhaustion is necessary.

The counter case: no conversion of renewable resources

The arguments against immediate investment in energy-conversion machinery using renewable resources are important to consider. They are evaluated in Table 1.I.

Among matters mentioned in Table 1.I which seem to have the greatest importance is the concept that the law of supply and demand will hold. This seems to have limited validity when one is talking about the end of supply.

That no change can be made whilst such a large investment is in the present technology is the essence of the difficulty: the energy policy works

TABLE 1.1: The Case Against Conversion to the Use of Renewable Energy Resources

Statement	Description of degree of truth	Discussion
World has enormous untapped resources of fossil fuels	True	Only a small percentage of these resources are useful with present technology (Chapter 2)
There is no shortage of oil or natural gas	True	However, a shortage will be felt in the mid-1980s. The supply of liquid and gaseous fossil fuels will peak in the early 1990s (Chapter 2). Lead time in building new plants will be decades
There is a huge potential for additional resources in oil shale and tar-sands	Not true	The description 'huge' must be comparative. Resources in tar-sands and oil shale are quite small compared with resources in coal, and much more expensive to convert to useful energy (Chapter 2)
We shall find twice as much oil as we have used in the past	Not untrue	However, energy is used at an increasing rate each year. The total amount of available oil has been taken into account in calculation of the peaking period—the early 1990s (Chapter 2)
World petroleum resources represent at least another 30 years' supply	The degree of truth in this depends upon semantics	The oil reserves-production rate ratio published by P. E. Playford in 1977 extrapolates to zero about 1990[9]
The law of supply and demand will work: as the price rises, the fuel will become available	This statement would only be true if reserves and resources could be identified as the same; and then only in practice, until the price rise is too much	The oil reserves are roughly one-third of resources: coal reserves are roughly one-twentieth of resources. To convert resources to reserves needs new technology. If such technology is invented, it is likely to be expensive. At present this technology (e.g. in underground gasification) is not visible (Chapter 4)
The alternatives to fossil fuels are all much more expensive that the fuels they seek to replace	True	The present prospect shows hydrogen from renewable resources at 2-3 times (1978 $) the 1978 price of gasoline. A comparison of fuels from renewable resources with those from fossil-fuel capital whilst it lasts is incorrect
Oil from coal needs vast amounts of coal	True	1 ton of coal gives 1 barrel of oil
The capital to convert the non-renewable to the renewable systems will be immense	True	What if the converters are not built before the peaking of the production rate of fossil fuels?
No change can be made whilst we have such a high investment in the present technology	Questionable.	More capital available *after* exhaustion??

out as though it were more concerned with the realisation of the capital in remaining oil and coal than with a policy which will result in the new energy-converter equipment being ready in time.

The need for a new attitude in the relation of economics to energy policy

There is a more general matter to be brought out. It is the relation of economic thinking to thinking on how to create the future energy supply.

At present, *economics* determines energy policy (the economic benefit to what has been indicated).[10] However, *energy* is the basic commodity of an industrial society. Economics is a rationalisation of the facts of demand and supply—when there is something to supply. The degree of supply of energy is basic to the conditions under which economic considerations can be made. Energy determines our lives in an industrial society in the same way as the supply of oxygen determines the life of the biological organism. *It is necessary to reverse the relative importance given to the science of economics, and energy science.* Economics should be called upon to implement an energy policy which is related to the needs of supplying consumers. The energy policy should be made and based primarily upon the future needs of the society, not the preservation of present capital, and hence present machinery. Thereby, the economic policy should be used to achieve the necessary goals for a time, say, 30 years ahead.[11] (The choice of 30 is arbitrary. Lead times are 15-50 years.)

Thus, at present there is much overproduction of material goods; there is unemployment which arises because it is cheaper for a manufacturer to use mechanisation and computerisation rather than a force of highly-paid human operatives. Hitherto, the displaced workers have been taken up by expansion—and the use of more energy. It is no longer satisfactory to continue to expand society to provide jobs for those displaced by machines. The alternatives are:

1. An unstable situation which would arise were sufficient persons put into the lower-income group, of those no longer needed to operate automated machinery.
2. Provide the unemployed with sufficient compensatory income from taxes of those working so that they are not materially deprived.
3. Changing economic policy to provide labour-intensive means of production (i.e. tax the use of job-removing technology).

Labour-intensive means of production may not lead to a reduction of average living standards.[12] It depends upon how much energy per head is available. Sufficient displacement of persons by mechanisation without compensatory expansion is likely to decrease average living standards. An increased degree of labour intensification in industry will not lead to increased production costs, because energy costs will rise to a degree such that it will be cheaper to employ people than to mechanise.[13] Tax allowances for depreciation of machinery at the present time work in an anti-job manner, and encourage a too-rapid rate of use-up of the remaining fossil fuels. This typifies the situation where a change in economic policy is necessary: where energy facts are primary to economic theory based on the tacit assumption of limitless energy resources.

At present, large-scale advertising encourages people to purchase what they do not need. When the encouragement is towards energy-consuming goods, the advertising should be very highly taxed so that the use-up of the remaining reserves is slowed, and allowance made for that needed in the conversion to renewable resources.[14]

Changes in technology to those which use less energy can be encouraged by tax credits[15]—the use of heavy tax against the energy-using machinery, and a negative tax in favour of job-producing technology.[16]

It is the conventional wisdom which must be changed. What is that wisdom? It could be described roughly as 'It is good to have high production which gives a cornucopia of material goods (and uses a great deal of energy)'. The high-energy-using society must be modified, utilising directed economic policy to do so, into a society which uses less energy.

The present situation, as Zelby points out,[10] is putting the cart before the horse. It is no use economic theory deciding the use of energy, and the production of more energy-converting machinery. Energy is the vital underlay of society. On the present modes of obtaining it, it is exhausting at a rate which is too fast for us to have time to form the capital to build the renewable resource-conversion equipment before energy exhaustion overtakes us.

To prevent this, economics should become the hand-maiden of energy policy[17] until capital has been created to purchase equipment for the conversion of renewable energy resources, and thus avoid a significant decline in the energy per head.*

About the effects of the continued absence of executive decisions in energy policy

Kursted and Nachlass point out that the absence of decisions in energy policy towards the building of new energy equipment in the United States is tantamount to a decision: that society will wind down with the exhaustion of the fossil fuels.[18]

The success of an economic policy based upon maximum production of everything which people can be stimulated to work to purchase, has been great. It does not work, however, in respect to the exhausting phase of the fossil fuels. The present policy would result in the use-up of residual fossil fuels until nothing is left. There is no incentive for corporate executive bodies—groups who have a political influence more than proportionate to their numbers—to reduce selling, and use their capital to finance the construction of plants which will not be profit-making for decades. It is not a matter of *lesser* profit: executives who advocated such a policy would ruin their companies.

Energy production needs to be taken over essentially by the Government. Nor need this mean a change in the way of life of citizens. We do not *organise* the size and activity of our armed forces by considerations of the market, although we use private enterprise in the competitive letting of contracts for weapon manufacture. We must regard having the right kind and degree of

---

*In a minor sense, the Carter-proposed 1979 tax on oil profits, some of which would be used to support energy research, illustrates the energy-oriented use of economic policy.

energy-production facilities as somewhat in the nature of the way we regard our armed forces: basic to survival.

What this adds up to in practice would seem to be the need for a new *authority* in the United States, the principal characteristic of which, at least for the next generation, should be dynamic. It should be the Energy Executive Authority (EEA). It would buy the residual fossil fuels and uranium resources, and control the rate of supply of these to the economy in a way which assures that priority is given to their use in building the *New Energy Producing Systems*. It would control the capital formation necessary thereto.

We have around one decade in which not only must such an Energy Executive Authority be formed, but actually accomplish the building of a significant amount of machinery; for after 1990, the oil and natural gas supply will no longer keep pace with demands (see Table 1.II).

TABLE 1.II: Some Options in Energy Policy

Policy	Good	Bad
Continuation of growth till 1990s.	Political stability till 1990s.	By starting capital investment in new plant only when economy forced to turn down by lack of fuel, particularly difficult situation created. A threat of gross catastrophe (never enough capital investment to make up decline caused by the decreasing energy supply.)
Reduce energy use (say) 5% per year (i.e. vigorous, enforced conservation) for (say) 10 years.	Time at which liquid and gaseous fossil fuels would decline delayed. Rate of needed capital investment in new plant reduced: coal could then last $\sim$ 100 years.	Unemployment would grow, prosperity drop. Political stability? Climatic changes due to CO_2?
Introduce gigantic ($50B/yr) U.S. energy R & D program. Otherwise, continue normal economy.	Would reduce costs of devices. Faint hope abundant energy from fusion. Fair hope acceptably priced clean energy from solar.	Although needed capital investment likely to be reduced, oil and gas will still turn down so soon that capital investment needed to maintain energy supply remains potentially devastating.
Directed 'wartime' economy. Strict rationing decreases use-up remaining resources. Directed government building programs coal < atomic < solar. Temporary cessation of increased automation.	High employment. Boom economy in engineering, building. Prospect continued growth living standards.	Inflation 10s%. Restrictions might last more than a decade.

SUMMARY OF CHAPTER

1. The present energy policy treats energy as if it were a commodity to be sold, like any other. Such a philosophy does not optimize the long-term prospects for the consumer.

2. Part of the present energy policy has given rise to much public protest. It heaps major costs onto future generations.

3. Material welfare is proportional to the energy per head.

4. There are substantial differences in energy efficiency among nations.

5. Employment in the civilian work-force rises and falls in a way parallel to the energy being consumed.

6. Uranium in non-breeder reactors will contribute unimportantly to the future. It is worth developing only in connection with plutonium production.

7. One advantage of hydrogen as a fuel is that it could interface with all the three energy sources of the coming decades: coal, breeder-atomic and solar.

8. It is important conceptually to realize that the present energy supply is tantamount to a consumption of capital. The cost of fuels from renewable resources (income) should not be contrasted in price with that of fuels derived by using up the now-scarce energy capital. The use of the residuum of this should be increasingly directed towards the building of plants for renewable resource conversion.

9. The absence of building of such machinery at present is due not only to a misapprehension in respect to valid price comparison, but also to an inertia connected with capital invested in present plant.

10. Economic laws, nurtured within a society illusionally conscious of a limitless flow of energy, may have to be suspended: classical economics should not govern energy policy. Economics should become the hand-maiden of energy policy.

11. There seems a need for the treatment of the future energy supply as the central concern of government, somewhat as (but in priority to) defence. The considerations should be shielded from the influence of the owners of the residual fossil fuel.

12. It is not rational to continue an economy we call normal until after we have found the capital to build the plants to convert renewable resources to a practical energy form, before the exhaustion of the present non-renewable resources.

AUTHOR'S CHOICE OF THE SINGLE MOST IMPORTANT CONCLUSION FROM CHAPTER

Present economic thinking (maximization of immediate societal benefit) will inexorably lead to the exhaustion of the non-renewable energy resources before the machinery for converting the renewable ones can be built.

REFERENCES

1. R. Zweig, World Hydrogen Energy Conference, Miami, 1976.
2. J.O'M. Bockris, disclosure to N.A.S.A.'s Jet Propulsion Laboratory, 1 March 1978.
3. J.O'M. Bockris & L. Handley, *International Journal of Energy Research*, 1978, **2**, 295.
4. J. E. Parrott, Conference on Solar Energy, Royal Institution, 1977.
5. *Nuclear News*, June 1975.

6. H. R. Linden, J. D. Parent & J. G. Sahe, Internal Report of Institute of Gas Technology, 1977.

7. *ibid.*, Table in Section 15.

8. J.O'M. Bockris, *Environmental Chemistry* (Plenum Press, New York, 1977), pp. 583-604.

9. P. E. Playford, *Oil & Natural Gas*, 1977, **23**, 8, 9.

10. L. W. Zelby, Alternative Energy Sources Conference, Miami, 1977.

11. P. F. Drucker, *The Age of Discontinuity* (Harper & Rowe, New York, 1978), p. 142.

12. R. L. Heilbroner, *The Worldly Philosophers* (Simon & Schuster, New York, 1964), p. 156.

13. M.A. Adelman *et al., No Time to Confuse* (Institute of Contemporary Studies, San Francisco, 1975).

14. E. F. Schumacher, *Small is Beautiful* (Harper Torch Books, New York, 1973), p. 50.

15. J. C. Fisher, *Energy Crises in Perspective* (J. Wiley, New York, 1974).

16. K. E. F. Watt, *The Titanic Effect* (Sinauer Associates, Stamford, 1974).

17. G. M. Brannon, *Energy Taxes and Subsidies* (Ballinger Publications, Cambridge, Mass., 1974).

18. R. Kursted & N. Nachloss, Alternative Energy Sources Conference, Miami, December 1977.

2

TIMES OF EXHAUSTION OF
THE FOSSIL FUELS

The dominating influence of the subject

For some time after a nuclear reactor had been demonstrated as feasible, in Chicago in 1942, it was thought that nuclear energy would be available relatively quickly, e.g. in the 1950s. It was thought that it would be extremely cheap. Neither the expectation of the ready availability nor the promise of price has been maintained. Four decades later, the prospect is for another four decades in which the supply of fossil fuels is an important determinant in the standard of life. It is true that the prospect of electric power from breeder reactors is present, though the development is far behind what is necessary, because of fears connected with radioactive-waste disposal. However, the development of electricity from solar energy is only at pilot plant stage.

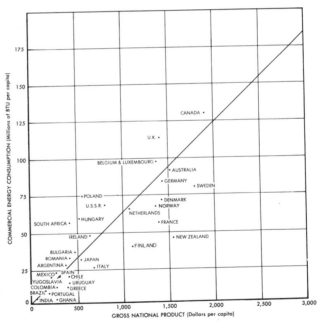

Fig. 2.1. Per capita consumption of energy and per capita gross national product (1971).

It is known that the material standard of life is linearly dependent upon the energy per person being used in the society (Fig. 2.1). It follows then, that (as far as fossil fuels are concerned) we look forward to some further years (1-2 decades) of a continued upwards movement of living standards (see Option 1, Table 2.I), though at a lesser pace than before, and then, after the mid-1990s, to a decline.

TABLE 2.I: NON-COMMUNIST WORLD (OUTSIDE U.S. AND CANADA)
EXPLORATORY WELLS COMPLETED[6]
(Data are from Foreign Developments Issues of the Bulletin of the American Association of Petroleum Geologists, vols. 36-60 [1952-1976]. Names of countries listed in the footnotes are as of 1975. Former colonial names of these countries are not listed in the footnotes, but the wells drilled in these countries before they changed their names are included in the totals.)

	South, Central America & Mexico[1]	Europe[2]	Africa[3]	Middle East[4]	Far East[5]	South Pacific[6]	Total
1975	408	296	209	144	284	28	1369
1974	503	243	191	80	279	51	1347
1973	489	216	153	98	251	67	1274
1972	549	219	223	77	194	99	1361
1971	539	199	251	69	186	76	1320
1970	520	166	263	73	115	122	1259
1969	499	240	248	49	129	65	1230
1968	522	196	251	62	125	95	1251
1967	516	171	233	99	98	88	1205
1966	552	216	219	90	99	105	1281
1965	503	228	279	66	128	163	1367
1964	428	221	288	71	137	145	1290
1963	428	285	348	63	96	111	1331
1962	503	279	338	62	137	56	1375
1961	532	267	273	73	128	18	1291
1960	607	307	227	54	123	30	1348
1959	455	372	185	40	121	58	1231
1958	466	402	148	26	102	35	1179
1957	468	339	87	24	85	55	1058
1956	423	262	94	24	41	68	913
1955	439	190	90	23	64	52	858
1954	498	214	99	19	53	33	916
1953	442	175	92	8	39	7	763
1952	399	221	77	16	24	9	746
1951	324	180	85	26	31	6	652

1. *South America, Central America and Mexico:* Argentina, Bahamas, Barbados, Belize (British Honduras), Bolivia, Brazil, Chile, Colombia, Costa Rica, Dominican Republic, Ecuador, Guatemala, French Guiana, Guyana, Haiti, Honduras, Jamaica, Lesser Antilles, Netherlands Antilles, Nicaragua, Panama, Paraguay, Peru, Puerto Rico, El Salvador, Surinam, Trinidad, Tobago, Uruguay, Venezuela, Mexico.

2. *Europe:* Austria, Denmark, Belgium, Eire, France, West Germany, Greece, Italy, Netherlands, Norway, Portugal, Spain, Sweden, United Kingdom, Malta, Switzerland.

3. *Africa:* Algeria, Angola, Cameroon, Central African Republic, Chad, Congo Republic (Brazzaville), Dahomey, Egypt, Equatorial Guinea, Ethiopia, Gabon, Gambia, Ghana, Guinea, Guinea Bissau, Ivory Coast, Kenya, Lesotho, Liberia, Libya, Malagasy Republic, Mali, Mauritania, Mauritius, Morocco, Mozambique, Niger, Nigeria, Sao Tomé and Principe, Senegal, Seychelles, Sierra Leone, Somalia Republic, South Africa, South West Africa, Spanish Sahara, Sudan, Tanzania, Togo, Tunisia, Uganda, Zaire, other areas including Botswana, Burundi, Malawi, Rhodesia, Rwanda, Swaziland, Upper Volta, Zambia.

4. *Middle East:* Iran, Israel, Kuwait, Neutral Zone, Saudi Arabia, United Arab Emirates, Bahrain, Qatar, Oman, Cyprus, Jordan, Lebanon, Turkey.
5. *Far East:* Bangladesh, Brunei, Burma, Indonesia, Japan, Kerguelen Islands, South Korea, Malaysia, Republic of Maldives, Pakistan, Philippines, Portuguese Timor, Sri Lanka, Taiwan, Thailand, South Vietnam, Fiji, Tonga, New Hebrides, Solomon Islands.
6. *South Pacific:* Australia, New Zealand, Oceania, Papua New Guinea.

This prospect could be overcome were it possible greatly to increase the rate of building of solar and atomic replacements for the fossil fuels. However, neither with the breeder reactor, nor with potential solar-hydrogen plants, are we at a production position (rather a pilot plant position in both cases); and the capital investment needed in such plants would be too high to be acceptable to the population, for it could only be raised by abnormal devices such as greater taxation.

Incredulity in the face of evidence

Were realisation of the exhausting position of the fossil fuels widespread among the bulk of consumers, and its relation to the time and money needed to replace such sources understood, political action (e.g. formation of a war-time type of economy) could be undertaken. In this way, the necessary capital formation for the construction of the machinery to obtain fuels from renewable resources could be financed. However, there is a psycho-social barrier: elected representatives with a dismal platform of facts concerning fossil fuels remaining, the long lead times to build new conversion equipment, with super-massive capital investments needed, face the danger of loss of their seats. A further difficulty is that when, in selected audiences of specialists, statements are made concerning the fact that less than two decades of increasing production of liquid fossil fuels remain, the reaction is incredulity. Such statements were made in earlier decades and proved untrue. For this reason, a presentation of the evidence concerning the imminent exhaustion of liquid and gaseous fossil fuels,[1] on the one hand, and the more distant exhaustion times of coal will be made in this chapter.

Oil and its recovery

It is a popular misconception that oil is found in underground pools. It is often thought that oil is obtained by pumping out tank-like spaces until they are empty. The reality is different. Oil exists interstitially among the pores of rocks, and it is best to picture it as analogous to a liquid in a sponge. The oil is usually under pressure. When a well is bored, the oil therefore flows into the well and in some cases has sufficient pressure initially to spurt into the air.

The recovery of oil under these pristine conditions, when there is sufficient oil pressure for the oil to tend to remove itself spontaneously, is called primary production.

Secondary production is achieved when the pressure is too low for the spontaneous removal to take place, but oil can be obtained by pumping water or gas into the reservoir to increase the pressure (Fig. 2.2).[2] One sometimes refers also to 'tertiary' recovery—not yet widely applied—when an attempt is made to lower the viscosity of the oil (to increase its ease of flow) by injecting steam or chemicals into the well.

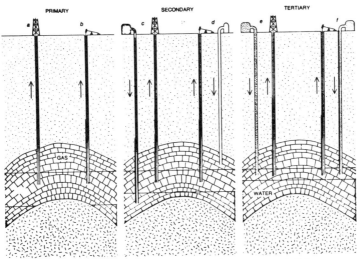

Fig. 2.2. Primary, secondary and tertiary recovery of oil.[2]

The average amount of oil removable in terms of primary production is only 25% of that remaining in the well. The secondary and tertiary methods, however, by no means lead to complete recovery. In fact, in the U.S. at this time, such methods have increased the removal from about 25% to about 32%.

Another factor in the recovery of oil concerns the maximum *rate* at which it is possible to remove it from a field, at the current price and with the current technology. The rule is that it is not feasible to produce more than 10% of oil recoverable in a field in any one year without reducing the amount of oil that can be recovered. The ratio of the reserves ('that which can be recovered with the given technology at the given price') and the yearly production is about 10, although it may be as high as 15, and is sometimes less than 10. If, therefore, one estimates that there is a certain amount of oil in a field below the ground, it is reasonable to divide it by about 4 and then to take 1/10th of this as the yearly maximum production.

Allowing for the discovery of oil and natural gas in the future

One of the misunderstandings which bedevil acceptance of the estimates made concerning the exhaustion of the fossil fuels is that no allowance for discoveries in the future has been made. However, the estimates are composed of two different components. New discoveries are discounted by utilising data on the rate of discovery, which allows one to get an idea of what will be available from the on-going exploration. Secondly, the ability of wells discovered earlier to give rise to further oil is constantly reassessed.

The very large Middle East resource was discovered in the 1930s, and the average rate at which reserves were added to in the past would be much lower had it not been for that discovery.

It is important to consider whether it is likely that another region of the world will be found in which such large deposits of oil may be found. It is not likely (*cf.* Flower).[2] Thus, seismic exploration has been carried out over

much of the surface of the world. The most likely place in which new discoveries can be made is in the Middle East itself. There is a factor which
makes it likely that discoveries in the future will decline: the most likely areas
for oil exploration (which can be geologically identified) have already been
examined, so that the incentive for further exploration is dropping. At
present the discovery rate is some 15 billion barrels per year (1 barrel = 42
gallons) and it is reasonable to conclude that this discovery rate will gradually
decline as the years continue.

However, one factor is more positive: and it may be possible to increase
the recovery rate from each well beyond the approximately 30% which is now
recovered. Indeed, according to Moody and Geiger of the Mobil Oil Corporation, it might be possible to increase the yield to about 40%.[3] However,
such increases are not to be taken as pure good news, because the machinery
needed to achieve them would make the oil arising available only at a greater
price than present ones, in constant dollars.

A decline in the rate of finding new oil as times goes on can be seen if
one plots the discovery rate per unit of drilling as a function of time (Fig.
2.3; see also below).

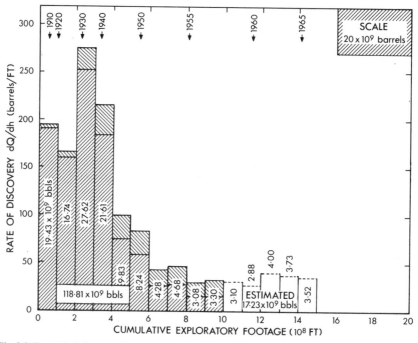

Fig. 2.3. Rate of oil discovery has been declining since 1930 if plotted as oil discovered per unit of
ground drilled.

Undiscovered, total, and available oil and natural gas

The estimates of the oil available are made on the basis of past discoveries,
estimates of what each well is worth (see below), and judgment about the
probability of new discoveries based upon the data of the past. The main

sources in the West of such data are the *Oil and Gas Journal; The 20th Century Petroleum Statistics;* and *World Oil.*

There is agreement within some ± 8% of the estimates for world proven reserves. As of 1976, these were about 600 billion barrels.

One of the difficulties is the variation in the range of estimates for the sub-economic resources. The difficulty is less in the degree of certainty of the geological estimates of the existence of these resources, and more in the ease (this means the cost) of recovery. Thus, according to Duncan and Swanson,[4] the total amount of shale oil with a limit of 10 gallons per ton could be as high as 28,000 billion barrels, but only 80 billion of this is *recoverable*. New technology might increase that degree but that new technology would increase cost.

A similar situation exists for natural gas. According to Papadopulos *et al.*,[5] the resources of natural gas are one hundred times the known reserves. This does not mean that we can recover this gas at acceptable prices, or indeed perhaps at any price.

An extreme example of the ratio between the total amount known and the amount available is for uranium and gold in the sea.* The total amounts present are exceedingly large. However, the availability in the case of uranium is often described as 'marginal', because of the amount of mechanical work which would have to be done in pumping the necessary volume of sea water.

The dominating role of the one area in the world in the supply of oil

The important character of the region of the world surrounding the Persian Gulf can be seen by reference to Fig. 2.4. Europe and Japan depend entirely, and the U.S. increasingly, upon this area of the world, only 500 miles square. The vulnerability of such a supply is clear.

Discovery-rate analysis

One means of predicting the future amount of oil likely to be discovered is to plot discovery-rate as a function of time. This would be expected to decline because all areas of the world have been (or are being) studied seismically by oil companies (Table 2.I): they will undertake the expensive operation of drilling (more than 1 million dollars per bore) only in regions where the seismic indications are good, i.e. indicate *large* deposits. This expected fall-off of the rate of discovery as a function of time is as the less-good areas are examined, and is indicated in Fig. 2.3.

---

* Thus a preliminary discussion could be as follows. Let the concentration of Ur in sea water be c moles l^{-1}, so that c^{-1} litres has to be treated to give 1 mole. the weight of this water is $10^3/c$ grams and to lift it a height h costs $10^3/c$ g h ergs, or 981 10^{-4} h/c joules $= \dfrac{981\ 10^{-4}}{3.610^6}\dfrac{h}{c}$ kwh $= 10^{-7}\dfrac{h}{c}$ kwh. 1 mole of Ur gives c. $\left[\dfrac{0.3}{100}\right] 10^6$ 23 4.2 10^3 Joules $= c.\ 10^8$ Joules at 30% efficiency.

Hence if $\qquad\qquad 10^{-7}\dfrac{h}{c} << 10^8$

there may be point in trying to extract Ur from the sea.

Take c $= 10^{-9}$ moles l^{-1}, $\qquad\qquad$ h $< 10^6$ cm

∴ the water containing one mole of Ur could be lifted 10,000 metres with the fission energy in it, and hence the necessary pumping through, say, 1000 metres would not be economically unfeasible.

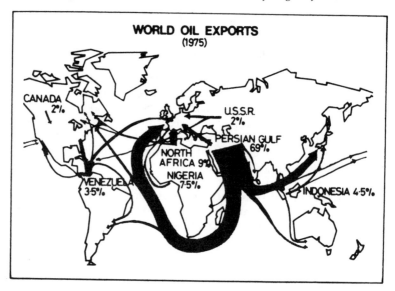

Fig. 2.4. Over-dependence of the world energy supply upon one area of the world.[7]

However, another way of indicating the future is in discovery-rate analysis which takes the number of barrels of oil per well as a function of the number of wells drilled.

As can be seen from Fig. 2.5., the amount to be discovered per well is declining, i.e. the incentive for exploration is declining as the number of wells examined increases.[6] When no virgin areas remain, the quality of the remaining wells can be expected to drop more rapidly.

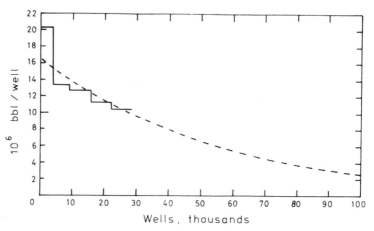

Fig. 2.5. Barrels per well as a function of the cumulative number of wells drilling is getting less worth-while.[6]

The world-wide character of oil exploration

Seismic drilling, carried out world-wide, is followed by the drilling of oil wells

if the expectation looks good. It does not mean that the well will be a successful one (Fig. 2.5).

In Table 2.I the number of wells drilled, divided into six areas, are given
as a function of time. A *small* number of wells have been drilled in the fertile
Middle Eastern area. The greatest number have been drilled in America. The
South Pacific area, essentially Australia, has received the smallest number
of drillings, owing to the small expectations there, as indicated from seismic
exploration of that continent.

Deductions of the year in which the rate of production of oil will maximise

The estimation of when the maximum rate of the production of oil will occur
is the essential datum in considerations of building machinery for extraction
of energy from alternative resources. It is the essential datum in the present
economic prospect of the world because the economy is now so much dependent upon the rate of production of oil that a decline in production (in the
absence of the build-up of compensating energy-conversion devices) will give
rise to economic decline (see Chapter 1).

It is possible to estimate the date of the maximum, using two facts and
one assumption. The facts are the amount of oil in reserve (at present price,
with current technology) and the indication of future discoveries from the
extrapolation of the discovery-rate function of Fig. 2.5. The assumption concerns economic activity during the coming two decades, and it is usual to
consider that the use of energy will grow at 2, 3 or 4% (in the late 1970s it
is growing at 3%).

It is interesting to apply such analysis to American oil. One obtains Fig.
2.6. For U.S. crude oil production, the maximum occurred in the early 1970s.
By 2010, the production rate will be one-third the maximum.[6]

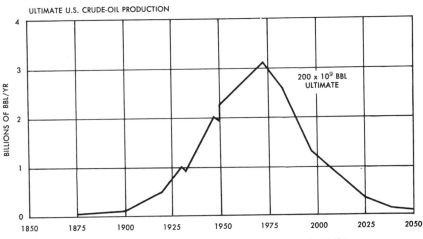

Fig. 2.6   U.S. crude oil production began to decline in 1968.[8]

One of the more important relations to be published in this book is the
relation derived by Root and Attanasi in 1978, concerning the production

of crude oil in the non-Communist world outside the U.S. and Canada.[6] They project three possibilities in consumption (Figs. 2.7 and 2.8). Curve A represents a 7% per year growth in production, and a zero growth in drilling rate. The ratio of reserves to production declines below 15 in 1987, and to 10 in 1992. Production then declines.

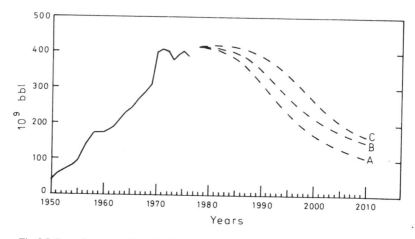

Fig. 2.7. Proved reserves of crude oil in the non-Communist world including Mid East.[6]

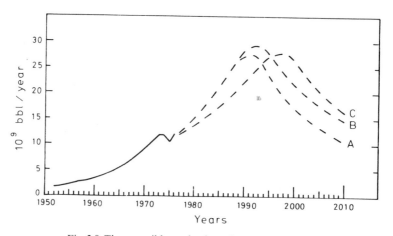

Fig. 2.8. Three possible production schedules world oil.[6]

In the second graph, B, of Fig. 7, the drilling rate was assumed to increase at a rate of 3% per year, and the production growth was assumed to be 7% per year, whereupon the reserves divided by rate of production ratio will fall below 15 in 1988 and production would peak in 1983 (curve B).

Finally, if drilling were increased by 3% per year and production growth were restricted to only 5% per year, the reserve production ratio of 15 would be attained in 1991 and production for the area would not peak until the year 1998 (curve C).

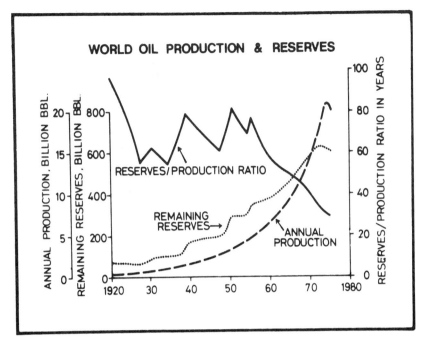

Fig. 2.9. Reserves to production ratio for world oil, as seen in 1977, extrapolates to zero by 1990.[7]

Thus, a reasonable conclusion to be made from these projections is that the non-Communist Western world production of oil outside the U.S. will peak in the 1990s. As the production in the U.S. will have peaked well before this,* world production is likely to come to a peak in the early 1990s.

There is another way to illustrate somewhat similar thoughts. It comes from the work of Playford.[7] The extrapolation of the reserves-production ratio to zero occurs about 1990 (Fig. 2.9).[7] Such a figure is pessimistic because it neglects the extra oil which could be obtainable at higher prices.

These estimates tend to be more pessimistic than earlier ones. Thus, Parent and Linden, who earlier (1973) calculated various cases as shown in Fig. 2.10 and found a maximum for a world crude oil production by 2005.[8]

The conclusion is that it is not reasonable to expect world oil production to increase after the mid-1990s.

These conclusions would only be altered by the application of special methods for the raising of capital, and thus the building of atomic and solar converters in great numbers so that less oil is used; or by a reduction of economic activity, the so-called depression induced by, for example, sufficiently high interest rates.

The conclusion that the maximum of production of the Western world's oil will occur around 1995 does not mean that in the 1980s the rate of production will keep up with needs. This depends upon the rate of economic growth.

---

*The fact that U.S. oil production is declining supports Root and Attanasi's use of a 7% growth figure for the production of foreign oil.

Even with the lessened rate of economic growth, the production of crude oil will not keep up with needs after 1985.

In summary, Western economies have less than one decade to go before they will feel the shortage of oil, and less than two decades to go before there will be a turn-down in the production rate of oil, with the ancillary social effects.*

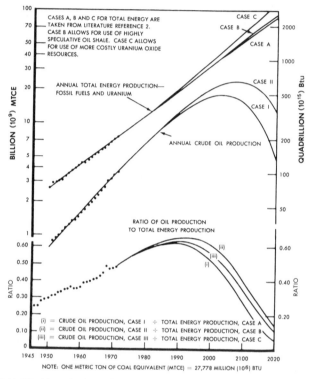

Fig. 2.10. World crude oil production rate, as seen in 1973, maximises around 2005.[8]

The relative agreement among various authors

Parent and Linden give the estimates made of *resources* of crude oil from conventional sources from 1942 until 1972.[9] There was an increase in the estimates for roughly the first 20 years of this period, but since the middle 1960s, the estimates have been reasonably constant. Thus, the last twelve estimates give a value of 1,900 ± 200 billion barrels (Table 2.II). (Reserves would be about one-third of this.) Change in this estimate seems unlikely

---

* Such statements are applicable only in the absence of the compensatory building of conversion plant from other sources. However, in view of lead times of more than twelve years for breeder reactors, and the very large capital investment needed for any of the three general approaches to new equipment, there are now doubts as to whether there will be sufficient time and/or capital to affect that building. If the capital is not available before decline, it is less likely to be available once decline has commenced.

at this time *at the present price.* Substantial increases in price (hundreds of per cent) could justify the machinery for improved secondary and tertiary recovery and give rise to an increase of as much as 10% and conceivably 20% on the above figures. Even this increase is not likely to shift greatly the date at which the maximum in oil production would occur, because any increase in the production rate before the maximum would cause an increased rate of expansion, which would tend to bring the maximum production at an earlier date, and hence compensate the increased oil available.

TABLE 2.II: ESTIMATES OF WORLD ULTIMATE RESOURCES OF CRUDE OIL
FROM CONVENTIONAL SOURCES, 10^9 bbl

1942	Pratt, Weeks and Stebinger	600
1946	Duce	400
1946	Pogue	555
1948	Weeks	610
1949	Levorsen	1500
1949	Weeks	1010
1953	MacNaughton	1000
1956	Hubbert	1250
1958	Weeks	1500
1959	Weeks	2000
1965	Hendricks (U.S. Geological Survey)	2480
1967	Ryman (Esso)	2090
1968	Shell	1800
1968	Weeks	2200
1969	Hubbert	1350-2100
1970	Moody (Mobil)	1800
1971	Warman (British Petroleum Co.)	1200-2000
1971	Weeks	2290
1972	Warman	1900
1972	Bauquis, Brasseur and Masseron (Inst. Franc. Petr.)	1950

The possibility that significant errors exist in the estimates of the exhaustion time of oil*

Oil will be a *component* of our energy resources for many decades after the maximum which will be reached in the 1990s. However, it will be a decreasing component, and will reach around one-quarter by 2010. From the time of the maximum, we must either bring into service other methods of obtaining energy, or suffer a decline in economic activity.†

The question whether the projections made in the present literature of the date of down-turn are pessimistic can be given a scientific discussion. For example, it might be thought that the additions to the reserves which have been assumed are conservative because they are less than the total resources present in the earth. It is certainly *possible* that break-throughs in techniques for secondary and tertiary production will give rise to significantly more oil than had been assumed.

For example, suppose there were no constraints upon OPEC production

---

*'Exhaustion time': This phrase is used here to refer, perhaps without a desirable degree of precision, to the maximum in the production rate.

†The difficulty of needing a vastly inreased rate of capital investment just at the time wealth (this is proportional to fossil fuel *spending*) begins to decline will be noticed.

and 30 billion barrels per year were added to reserves between 1975 and 2000 instead of 20 billion barrels, which are the highest estimate assumed in the forgoing. If we continue to limit the reserves-production ratio to 15, the oil supply would then continue to meet demands until somewhere between 2005 and 2010. The situation is sketched in Fig. 2.11.

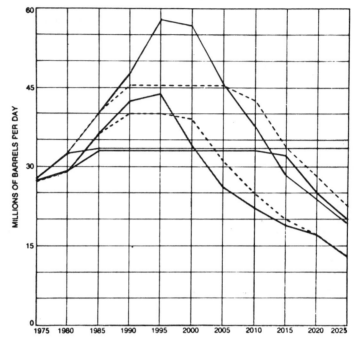

Fig. 2.11. OPEC production. Various speculative scenarios with government controls (plateaus) or growth (sharp maximum) possibilities with additions to reserves from resources.[2]

Alternatively, suppose there were a discovery rate outside OPEC of 15 billion barrels per year, the OPEC production limit would be reached—and a restraint on the total supply would occur—soon after 1990.[2]

This would still be less by some 15 million barrels per day then the demand projected for a reasonable growth rate. Thus, *even the most optimistic projections of additions to reserves cannot make really significant* (more than fifteen years) *differences in the estimate for the topping out of oil production.*

Tar sands and shale oil

Many persons assume that there are vast amounts of tar sands and shale oil which could give a surfeit of oil once more. Indeed, large sources of these sands do exist in Venezuela and Colombia, as also in the U.S., Canada and China.

The Athabasca tar sands in Alberta are being processed at present. Thus, there is a plant there which is producing 45 thousand barrels per day. The point is, as before, the *availability* of these resources *at a certain price.* The obtaining of oil from shale is a difficult matter: it requires a technology in which the oil, adherent to tiny particles of sand and rock, is removed.

An example quoted by Playford refers to a Syncrude plant in Canada, which was estimated in 1972 to cost 500 million dollars.[7] One of the major participants, the Atlantic Richfield Corporation, withdrew when the cost estimate had increased 400% to 2 billion dollars, and their interests were taken over by the Canadian and British Governments. The present projected price is 2.5 billion dollars, but, for all that, the production is to be only 125 thousand barrels a day. Even this is based upon the earlier and more easily mined surface sands.*

What are the difficulties of extraction of oil from shale? They are, as indicated, the large capital costs. However, they also involve environmental problems in large-scale strip mining and waste disposal. Further, they have huge water requirements. Shale oil plants need 3.5 barrels of water for each barrel of oil. The oil shale deposits in the U.S. are in places where it would be difficult to secure large volumes of water.

As with coal, the main hope for the economic development of oil shale deposits on a large scale is in underground gasification, a subject discussed elsewhere in this book, and one which has no prospects of making progress at substantial speed.

It is interesting to compare the total world energy reserves and those given at a World Energy Conference in 1974 as shown in Table 2.III.[7]

TABLE 2.III: WORLD ENERGY RESERVES
(WORLD ENERGY CONFERENCE 1974)

	10^{18} *Joules*
Coal	15.1
Tar sands	5.6*
Oil shale	5.3*
Oil	3.9
Gas	1.9
Uranium, Non-breeder fission	0.8[†]
Uranium, Breeder fission	49.5[†]

* Largely resources rather than reserves.
† Excludes Communist Bloc.

The values for tar sands and oil shale are resources (not reserves), and how much of them can be turned into reserves is doubtful. Oil and natural gas form about 7% and uranium less than 1% of the total non-renewable reserves.

Coal: world reserves

Before discussing this subject, attention must again be drawn to the difference between resources and reserves. Resources, which geologists are able to deduce lie in the earth, represent the amount down to a certain depth, without reference to whether it can be recovered. Reserves represent that which can be extracted with present technology at the present price. The following discussion is about reserves, though it will mention resources from time to time.

---

*The extraction of oil from shale is not new. Playford notes that it was a new technology in Sydney, Australia, in 1860 and was closed down there (superseded technology) in 1952.

Another general statement needs to be made. The so-often repeated indication that *'coal would last for centuries'* is not acceptable, because it refers to *resources* rather than *reserves*; and at the present rate of use rather than the rate of use which would be needed in the future, after the exhaustion of the oil (if coal fluidization plants do get built in time).

TABLE 2.IV: Coal Resources According to W.E.C., 1974, 10^9 t_m

	Recoverable Reserves	*Total Reserves*	*Total Resources*
U.S.A.	181.781	363.562	2,924.503
Canada	5.537	9.034	108.777
Latin America	2.803	9.201	32.928
Europe	126.775	319.807	607.521
Africa	15.628	30.291	58.844
U.S.S.R.	136.600	273.200	5,713.600
China, Mainland	80.000	300.000	1,000.000
Rest of Asia	17.549	40.479	108.053
Oceania	24.518	74.699	199.654
	591.191	1,420.273	10,753.880

t_m = metric ton = 1.1023 short ton

The difference between total *resources,* total *reserves* and then recoverable reserves is marked (only 6% of U.S. coal).

Heating values of the fossil fuels

To get from the fossil fuels in terms of cubic feet or barrel to some thermal quantity we need to have conversion factors. In the case of coal, the value, of course, is somewhat variable and represents a mean value. The values are shown in Table 2. V.[9]

TABLE 2.V: Heating Values Used in Converting from Conventional
Quantities to Energy Units

	Heating Value
Natural Gas	1031 Btu/cf (1024 Btu/cf for the U.S.)
Crude Oil	5.8 x 10^6 Btu/bbl
Syncrude from Shale Oil and Bitumens	5.8 x 10^6 Btu/bbl
Natural Gas Liquids	4.1 x 10^6 Btu/bbl
Coal	20 x 10^6 Btu/short ton (22 x 10^6 Btu/short ton for U.S. proved reserves)
Uranium Oxide, U_3O_8	
In burner reactors without Pu recycle	400 x 10^9 Btu/short ton
In breeder reactors	30 x 10^{12} Btu/short ton

One metric ton of coal equivalent (tce) = 27.778 x 10^6 Btu

The life indices for the total fossil fuel

Introduction

The construction of a production-time code is a matter of judgement, as well as research and facts.

Thus, firstly, an estimate of the total resources must be made. This is not an absolute amount, for there is usually some statement of the type, 'down to 3000 feet', or etc. Thereafter, there is a definition of the reserves and this has a definite meaning, though it may change with time. At any given time it means what can be obtained with the present technology at the present cost. The technology and cost (dollars of a given year) are bound together: unless the technology changes, or there is a significant change in depth, the cost of recovering the fuel will not change significantly in constant dollars.

Having decided upon what value of reserves one is going to draw—what can be recovered at the given time at the given price—one then has to decide the more doubtful matter of what kind of economic expansion should be assumed. As we are dealing, at least for oil and natural gas, in exhaustion times which are relatively near, and as the effect of exhaustion without replacement with alternative energy sources would be catastrophic, a zero rate of expansion should be induced. However, pressure from corporate interests is so great for economic expansion whilst that is still possible (i.e. by using up the reserves faster then many consumers might regard as necessary), that the figures which are discussed in calculating the future production rate assume 1, 2, 3 and 4% growth per year.

Any change in the expansion rate and the growth rate will change the year at which passage through the maximum occurs. Prosperity can be maintained by keeping up growth (keeping fuel prices low), and then fossil fuel exhaustion will occur earlier. Economic depression can be created by a zero growth rate, and the time of the more fundamental decline can be postponed (or, better, compensated by the easier capital investment for new plant if more time is available).

Growth equations

The energy problem—finding the maximum of the production rate—is only one of the growth problems. There are several of these and they have been fitted by equations which have been reviewed by Linden.[10] He points out that the exponential, the Gompertz and the logistic equations are the most important or at least the most popular. Thus, Hubbert pointed out that world coal between 1860 and 1913 increased at about 4.4% per year, 0.75% for the next period and 3.6% from World War II to the present.[11]

Putmann[12] pointed out the fitting of the logistic equation to population growth in various countries by Pearl and Reid.[13] Exponential trends have been observed to apply for periods of 20-50 years in the consumption of non-renewable resources. Finally, the costs increase and the production rate will drop. The Gompertz and logistic equations on the other hand have assymptotes.

According to Elliott and Turner[14] (*cf.* Hubbert),[11] the rate of production of natural resource as a function of time for the resource, and the quantity remaining, may be expressed as:

$$\frac{dP}{dt} = f(D) \cdot f(S) \tag{2.1}$$

in which P = cumulated production of the resource; t = time, calendar years; $\frac{dP}{dt}$ = annual rate of production; f(D) = function of demand; f(S) = function of remaining supply; but the supply is a function of the fraction of the resource remaining, so that one gets:

$$\frac{dP}{dt} = \frac{b'P}{U}\left[1 - \frac{P}{U}\right]$$ (2.2)

in which U = ultimate resource and b' = a constant.
Integration of equation (2.2) gives:

$$-\ln\left[\frac{U}{P} - 1\right] = \frac{b't}{U} + n = bt + n$$ (2.3)

in which n = constant of integration and $b = \frac{b'}{U}$.
Thus:

$$P = \frac{U}{1 + \exp(-bt)-n}$$ (2.4)

One may then take the second derivative of equation (2.4), equate it to zero, and let t_m be the time at which the maximum rate of production occurs. The solution is that:

$$n = -bt_m$$ (2.5)

Combining equations (2.4) and (2.5), we have that:

$$P = \frac{U}{1 + \exp[-b(t-t_m)]}$$ (2.6)

This equation (2.6) is that derived by Elliott and Turner,[14] and is similar to that of Hubbert, in which:

$$P = \frac{U}{1 + A\exp[-b(t-t_r)]}$$ (2.7)

where t_r = a reference calendar year and A = a constant, when the substitution, $A = \exp b(t_m - t_r)$ is made. It is $\frac{dP}{dt}$ which maximizes.

The Elliott and Turner equation has the limitation that 50% of the resource is produced at the time of maximum rate of production. Other more complex relations remove this limitation, which does not seem to be important for the present calculations.

Hald has shown that a number of growth equations can be derived from the form $\frac{dy}{dt} = f(y)g(t)$, where t is time, and y is a variable such as the cumulative production or discovery rate.[15] If $f(y) = y(U-y)$, the rate will depend on time, the magnitude of y, and the total amount present, U.

The estimates of Turner and Elliott

Turner and Elliott made certain estimates and these are shown in Fig. 2.12.[14] They are noteworthy by the fact that they were the first estimates to take into account the effect of the taking over from oil and natural gas by coal, and the first to show that the probable maximum rate of the use of coal, at expansion rates of 3% per year, does not take place in 'several hundred years', but in less than a century, in fact *as soon as 30 years after the oil has turned down.*

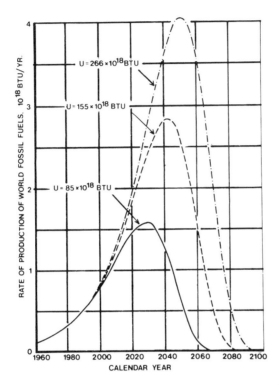

Fig. 2.12. Effect of the value of the resource base assumed upon the production rate of fossil fuels.[14]

The life indices calculations of Parent and Linden

Life indices mean the time between the present and the year in which no more of the resource at the given price will be available, i.e. the division of the amount left by the use rate in a given year.

Parent and Linden gave the life indices for the total fossil fuels (essentially, however, for coal) assuming an annual growth rate of 1, 2, 3 and 4%, using a basis of proved reserve;[9] total recoverable resources (B); and finally doubling of B. The really important value is, therefore, the A value, and if we look at Table 2.VI we show that for a growth rate of 3%, we would have only 10 years more of coal at 2010 world-wide and about the same for the U.S.A.

These results indicate the need for considerable conservation, i.e. zero or negative growth rates, because, if one continues to use fuels at the projected rates, it will be difficult to build sufficient atomic and solar collectors in the short time before oil and gas begin to decline in production rate (whereafter it will be much more difficult).

TABLE 2.VI: LIFE OF WORLD FOSSIL FUEL RESOURCES AT VARIOUS
DEMAND GROWTH RATES
(Based on 1975 Year-End estimates)

Annual Growth Rate, p	Date When Remaining Reserve/Consumption Ratio Drops to 10 Years		
	A	B	C
4	2005	2050	2067
3	2010	2067	2090
2	2018	2098	2131
1	2031	2166	2229

A. Proved reserves: 0.751 to 0.790 x 10^{12} tce; mean = 0.7705 x 10^{12} tce
B. Total remaining recoverable resources (5.066 to 5.695 x 10^{12} tce; mean = 5.38 x 10^{12} tce)
C. Effective doubling of B resources
    tce = metric tons of coal equivalent

The limit to growth

The material of this chapter has significance for the future of the world economies and, therefore, for the political systems. *It seems necessary to decline the growth rate* until after the use of non-renewable energy resources have been replaced by machinery to convert the renewable resources. The argument may be spelt out. Insofar as we continue to grow in energy need (i.e. economic activity), at around 2 or 3% per year, we should come to an insufficiency in liquid and gaseous fuels which would give rise to a need for energy-producing plant building in a time period shorter than would be economically possible.

If, however, we decrease our growth rate to zero, then our energy resources will continue to be there for a longer time, and the amount of money we have to spend building renewable resource machinery would be reduced. An unpopular hold-up of the economy would make the time over which the capital investment in energy conversion equipment could be made much longer, and hence the needed inflation less.

However, at the present time our economic system is built in such a way that we must expand. The reason for this is that increased computerisation and mechanization removes jobs, so that if we do not expand the economies, the rate of job loss is about 4% per year (Commoner[16]). There would arise an unacceptable degree of unemployment.

Hence, the implication of the present chapter can be simply stated: it is essential that we reduce economic growth until the plant has been built which will supply the necessary energy from sources which will not exhaust. Correspondingly, during the interim, until the plant is there to allow expansion, we must either cease further displacement of jobs by mechanization or compensate equally the workers displaced.

The necessary changes in economic policy would cause inflation and depression. The alternative is catastrophe. The limit to growth is the availability of that capital, rather than engineering concepts.

Inappropriate economic behaviour

At the present time there is no rational government energy policy in any of the countries of the Western world. By 'rational' is meant a policy aimed at the long-term optimization of the prospects of the bulk of the consumers in view of the situation presented in this chapter. The energy policies of many countries with faith in U.S. technology follow that of the U.S. But these are not policies based upon the facts of downturn in the supply of gaseous and liquid hydro-carbons, in a time of 1 to 2 decades, but policies based upon short-time considerations of the economic advantages of the leading international (mostly U.S. based) companies.

The main objective in these policies is the converse of what is needed from a longer-term viewpoint. It is *growth*. It is not the accepted economic doctrine that growth has a limit, because when those doctrines were formed, there was no concept of resource exhaustion. Government policy is to make things grow: each product should be sold at a higher rate, etc. To attain such a goal, the path of least resistance is to produce more oil, spend more energy, increase personal income, and thus prosperity. Such a policy is backed by the electorate (where there is no realization of its consequences), and the electorate would get rid of its representatives were they to pursue any other policy, which would, by definition, lower real income (as would conservation). When one understands it, one can see that the present public philosophy is inimical to a successful longer-term (2 decade) outcome of the situation. The more the oil is used up, the earlier the time of exhaustion will arrive and the greater the difficulty of achieving the rate of capital investment necessary for building the new energy conversion machinery.

What should be done (for future security) is to reduce normal economic activity, decline its growth rate to zero or negative, and invest in the building of energy machinery for energy conversion using renewable resources worldwide. The dilemma is that this would produce depression and, within our present social system, unemployment. However, we are the victims of the effects of old words, no longer appropriate to our socio-economic prospects. 'Depression' can be 'safe rate of economic activity'. Unemployment is ruinous because it brings the image of rejection (the suggestion of incompetence); and the reality of reduced living standards. If it becomes socially important to reduce the numbers working so much that the number no longer in the work force pushes 'unemployment' above historic norms, then a new name, indicating the acceptability of the position (e.g. being a 'conservational' would clearly be *good*) could be introduced. Negative economic consequences could be reduced towards zero by the magnitude of conservationals' (untaxed) government minimum monthly income. Alternatively, instead of a right to sharing in the income of the economy, without working, citizens could have a right to a job, and the work week could be adjusted to the acceptable energy outgo, which would depend on the degree of capital investment in appropriate new energy conversion machinery.

Assuming the possibility of capital formation rate in the order of $100B per year, for new energy plant, the necessary time would be a half century. Growth could be continued when the machinery for energy production was available, though there are other reasons why growth cannot continue indefinitely.*

---

* Eventually the energy production would cause a temperature increase in the earth's atmosphere.

Difficulties in attaining corporate goals under conditions of exhausting fuel reserves

Consider a corporation which is weighing the building of an oil-from-coal plant. What is desirable is to catch the rising price of fuels, produce expensive oil from coal, but at the right time—when a market is ready for oil at that price. If conventional oil production is increased, for example, by some advance in the technology of tertiary recovery, so that the rate of oil production does not peak for a further two years, the company's directors may have the new plant on their hands, paying interest on the money with which it has been constructed, but not receiving income from it. They will, therefore, choose the later date among two possible dates at which oil production is predicted as passing through the maximum production rate, i.e. when the new plant will be needed.

From the consumer's point of view, the considerations are different. If the plant is not there, there will be lay-offs, cold houses, closed schools. These social costs will not appear on the balance sheet of the company, but could give rise to resentment among consumers, and, if prolonged, unrest.

One may correspondingly consider the conservation situation (Root & Attanasi).[6] Consider a company which undertakes converting of some of their machinery from oil to coal-burning with advantage to the community because the oil production peak will thereby be reached at a later time. However, there is no incentive for the company to do the conversion. It is only after a strict government regulation is made which forces it to change (or, oil prices per unit of energy have been raised above coal) that there is incentive to make the conversion.

If there is to be a peak in oil production between 1985 and 1990, the consumer's interest is to be sure that building the machinery is started in time so that, if it is needed in 1985, it will be there. But the corporate interest is served by waiting till 1990.

This can be generalised. From the point of view of the long-term interests of the consumer, the best policy would be to conserve now, i.e. to cut growth to zero, and invest at once in the construction of new energy conversion machinery, thus expending the oil over longer times. From the corporate view, it is best to continue to vend till the cost of producing it is more than the cost of some alternative resource which can be sold at better profit.

The free enterprise system goes back to the Hobbsian idea of defining good as that which brings the most happiness to the greatest number of people. It has correspondingly been assumed that the pursuit of individual prosperity (assumed the same as happiness) improves the general welfare. There are no incentives in terms of improvement of material welfare to encourage conservation or the development of an alternative energy source at all. This is one reason for the absence of a rational energy policy. It is difficult for a free enterprise economy to prepare for a decline in conventional fuels and the building of an alternative energy system, because such action implies temporary (but lengthy) decline in 'prosperity'. (That the alternative is permanent continued decline is not always brought out.)

There is an international version of the conflict between corporate and consumer interests. Suppose a country exists which is willing to embark on a national policy of conservation, then the rest of the countries have more oil available. This will decline their wish for conservation and they will increase prosperity by using up the remaining oil at a greater rate. Their citizens will become more well-to-do whilst those of the conservational country will decline. Therefore, there is no *national* incentive for any country to conserve.

SUMMARY OF CHAPTER

1. Even expert audiences are sceptical when confronted with statements concerning the imminent decline of oil and natural gas. One possible origin of such incredulity is the magnitude of the consequences.

2. Secondary and tertiary recovery could not add much, perhaps ten years, to the oil reserves. These are about one-third of the oil resources.

3. It is unlikely that a second gigantic oil area such as that in the Middle East exists: most of the planet has been subjected to seismic exploration.

4. There is a great difference between fuels which are present ('resources') and what is available ('reserves'). The ratio is 1:3 for oil; 1:20 for coal.

5. The amount of oil discovered per year is steadily declining.

6. Root and Attanasi, of the U.S. Geological Survey, conclude that the maximum of world oil production will occur in the 1990s.

7. Since 1965, there has been concurrence about how much oil is present among many independent analyses.

8. It is unlikely that whatever (small) uncertainty exists in these estimates will alter the time at which world oil production will reach its maximum, by more than fifteen years.

9. Tar-sands and shale oil are more difficult to make useful than coal.

10. The confusion about the amount of coal which could be used arises because of the small amount *available* with current technology, among plentiful total resources and the time it will be reached.

11. There are a number of equations which allow prediction of the maximum use-rate of a resource.

12. Parent and Linden estimate coal use could reach its maximum as early as 2005; and it is unlikely to last past 2100.

13. The essential conclusion is that economic growth should be limited until energy conversion from renewable resources has been set up.

14. The economic philosophy of the Western world is growth. This philosophy is based on the assumption of plentiful available energy. Its continuation greatly increases the needed capital investment rate for building machinery for energy conversion from renewable energy resources.

AUTHOR'S CHOICE OF A MORE IMPORTANT CONCLUSION FROM CHAPTER

The capital investment needed for the building of coal-conversion plants (and in particular for atomic and solar conversion equipment) will be very great (see Chapter 16). Such capital investment will have to be spread out. Consequently, to stretch out liquid and gaseous fossil fuels, economic growth will have to be restricted until the economics of renewable-resource conversion have been satisfactorily embraced in the context of 21st century development—ecological, as well as economic.

REFERENCES

1. J. D. Parent & H. R. Linden, Institute of Gas Technology, January 1977.
2. A. R. Flowers, *Scientific American*, 1978, **238**, 42.
3. J. D. Moody & Robert E. Geiger, quoted by A. R. Flowers, *loc. cit.*
4. D. C. Duncan & V. E. Swanson, *U.S. Geological Survey Circular* 523, 1965.
5. S. S. Papadopoulos, R. H. Wallace, J. B. Wesselman & R. E. Taylor, in D. E. White & D. L. Williams, Assessment of Geothermal Resources, in the U.S., 1975; U.S. Geological Survey, 1975; U.S. Geological Survey Circular, **726**, 125-146, Fig. 15-16.
6. D. Root & E. Attanasi, in *The American Association of Petroleum Geologists Bulletin*, 1978, in press.
7. P. E. Playford, *Oil & Gas*, 1977, **23**, 9.
8. J. D. Parent & H. R. Linden, Institute of Gas Technology, 6 April 1973.
9. J. D. Parent & H. R. Linden, Institute of Gas Technology, 23 February 1977.
10. H. R. Linden, *World Energy Conference, 1974*, p. 18.
11. M. K. Hubbert, 'Energy Resources', in *Resources & Man* (National Academy of Sciences, 1969) pp. 15, 42, 72.
12. P. C. Putman, *Energy for the Future* (van Nostrand, New York, 1953).
13. R. Pearl & L. J. Reid, *The Growth of Human Populations* (Williams & Wilkins, Baltimore, 1924).
14. N. C. Turner & M. A. Elliott, American Chemical Society Meeting, Boston, Mass., April 1972.
15. G. Hald, *Statistical Theory with Engineering Applications* (Wiley, New York, 1952).
16. B. Commoner, *The Poverty of Power* (Alfred Knopf, New York, 1976).

3

THE TIME NEEDED TO REALISE A MAJOR TECHNOLOGICAL CHANGE

Introduction

In considering the options for the new types of plants which have to be built in readiness for the energy insufficiency expected around the mid-1980s, it is important to have some ideas about the time which has been needed for major technological changes in the past.

There are several orders of importance in technological change. For example, the introduction of electron microscopy had far-reaching consequences in basic chemistry and physics, the results of which only faintly as yet affect innovative technology.

The introduction of video tape-recorders is an advance of a different character, less important in its far-reaching implications, but significant in affecting the standard of life.

Lastly, among these examples is the contraceptive pill. Research leading to its development has had obviously civilisation-affecting consequences.

The change of energy source from the fossil fuels to the extraction of energy from renewable resources will be the most far-reaching technological change hitherto made. The present materially-affluent civilisation has been made possible by applications of pre-twentieth century to make machines driven by the fossil fuels. The extraction of energy from the fusion process, either from solar energy or from a controlled fusion reaction on earth, will determine the standard of life in the coming centuries.

In view of the evidence given in Chapter 2, a down-turn in liquid and gaseous fossil fuels from the 1990s, it is important to have some idea of the time between research and practical commercialisation.

Previous work

Examinations of the origins of innovations in scientific research has not been greatly investigated. In Project 'Hindsight' of the American Department of Defense of 1965, the view backwards into innovations was only 15 years, and thus diminished the part played by fundamental research as a basis to the innovations examined. However, the National Science Foundation initiated an investigation in 1967, which had the objective of investigating the relation of previous research efforts to innovation. The work, carried out at the Illinois Institute of Technology, is called 'Technology in retrospect and critical events in Science'.[1]

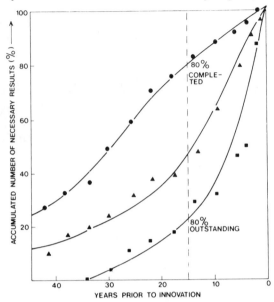

Fig. 3.1. Time before innovation at which various kinds of research began.
—●— = Fundamental work; —■— = Engineering work; —▲— =
Commercialization work.

Corrections were made to take into account the work done before the innovation could be made commercially available.

The essence of these results is shown in Fig. 3.1.[2] The fundamental work is about 80% complete some 15 years before the innovation is introduced to the public, but at that time the engineering work is only about 40% complete, whereas commercialisation is some 20% complete.

Thus, commercialisation takes place largely in the last 15 years, although its research can be traced to some 35 years before the innovation.

These results are shown in Table 3.I.

TABLE 3.I. Times Needed for Research, Development and Commercialisation Work Prior to an Innovation

Origins	Years before
Scientific work	> 75 years
Engineering and development work	∿ 60 years
Commercialisation work	∿ 35 years

It is interesting to look at other recent developments from those used by the National Science Foundation in this context. Thus, the beginnings of work on atomic fission can be seen in the work of Rutherford in 1922. Commercialisation 75 years later (1997) may indeed represent the time at which widespread atomic energy technology will be said to have become effective. If we take the Chicago experiments of Fermi in 1942 as indicating the beginning of the engineering work, then we conclude that 2002 would be the beginning of the general innovation of atomic energy. Finally, if we take the first practical working fission reactors as having begun functioning in 1953, and regard this as the beginning of commercialisation, then we get 1988 as the beginning of the general innovation of atomic energy utilising the general rules derived above. The average from these three dates is 1995 ± 5 years, remarkably in the middle of the range of predictions for the turn-down of oil and natural gas production rates!

Another example which can be taken concerns space flight. Thus, here the basic investigation was carried out by Tsiolkovskii in 1883.[3] The first orbited space flight was in 1958—precisely 75 years from the beginnings of fundamental work.

Another application on which these equations could be used is the photo-voltaic cell, the Si p-n junction, discovered at the Bell Telephone Laboratory by Chapin, Fuller and Pearson.[4] On this basis, one would expect practical innovation to be made around 2029. Work on the commercialisation of massive solar farms would not begin, then, until about 1994, which seems later than the present trend suggests. Corresponding to the above approximate rules, the engineering work should have begun around about 1969, and in fact, an intense development effort in photovoltaics can perhaps be seen as beginning around 1972, with the TYCO work on the ribbon method on the massive production of cheap Si of photovoltaic grade.

Thus, the past history of the development of technologies suggests that atomic and solar sources will be introduced on a commercial scale between around 1995 and around 2030, respectively.

Relevance of previous investigations to the development of a new energy technology

The examinations carried out by the National Science Foundation of the relation of research to innovation, based on investigation of the contraceptive pill, video tape-recorders, and electron microscopes etc., may have a limited relevance to the development of new energy technology. These earlier developments were carried our under the stresses and resistances associated with the attractiveness of the project, opposed by the inertia of the existing situation, and the lack of consciousness of the innovation which implies absence of initial consumer demand. However, for a change of energy technology, the stakes are higher than for the developments mentioned above. The introduction of new energy technology, involving the use of new fuels, will mean a transformation in many technologies; and the greater the degree of disturbance of old technology, with its associated capital investment, the greater is the degree to which the situation will be resisted.

However, once a sufficient degree of consciousness spreads among the electorate, concerning the need for a change in energy technology within the lifetimes of voters, political advantages may at last accrue to Congressmen who force developments in this direction.

Incentives

The usual incentive to fundamental research is curiosity, but this can be directed and stimulated enormously by appropriate financial reward. It is the direction in which the researcher applies his creativity which can be guided by the appropriate monetary gradient. Such a situation should be applied to researchers in universities and research institutes, as well as in commercial groups.

The development work which is the main activity of corporate groups is less easily applied to research for new energy technology. Thus, the normally valid cycle of a market becoming visible, and this stimulating research to supply it, is less applicable in the case of the energy situation, because of the long lead times, and the uncertainty of the time at which a market may arise.

Thus, economics should be aggressively used to serve the energy policy (Chapter 2) in the provision of guarantees to corporations so that were they to produce energy devices which could not be profitable for a gap of a certain number of years, such losses should be covered by government-backed insurance.

Alternatively, instead of government intervention into the corporate economy in this indirect way, it can intervene directly by nationalising the activity of assuring an adequate energy supply, as with the organisation of defense; with use of the services of the corporations in the same way as in the Space Programme, and in the work of the Department of Defense.

Defensive research

Defensive research is carried out by corporations. Thus, automotive manufacturers who work on, for example, electric cars, do so partly so that they may be ready to defend their investment in the fossil-fuel-using technology or be ready for government legislation which might make it mandatory, for environmental reasons, to produce electric cars outside of the (stimulated) demands of the market.

A well-financed corporate research programme which leads at the applied research level to significant innovative technology, will not lead to commercialisation by the corporation of the new venture until the market shows a probability of a profitable return on the capital invested. This rational, capitalistic approach has produced the living standards known principally in the United States. It is not necessarily the background condition appropriate to the research and development of devices to produce energy from renewable resources, because such devices will at first produce expensive energy which will not be marketable unless the energy from the residual fossil fuel capital is sufficiently highly taxed. As this would mean an overall increase of energy price to the population, and would depress the economy, it could be, only with difficulty, a part of the policy of a democratic government.

The result of 'defensive research' is that some corporate research is carried out without serious intent at new product information. It has sometimes more the goal of maintaining present product manufacture, i.e. defending invested capital.

'Totally free' research

Although a stress in this book is on capital investment, the time aspects of the energy situation, and the environmental situation which join to make the basis for the advocacy of a solar-hydrogen economy, there must be some 'totally free' discussion about the extraction of energy from renewable resources; and some more far-out thinking concerning the obtaining of energy in usable forms. Support for such more novel research is difficult to find, owing to the fact that the Government agencies have programmes with defined aims, and the research worker can mostly apply for contractual support of work in the direction of these aims. Such programmed work is the necessary basis and centre of any government research programme, but a degree of support, perhaps 0.1% of the effort, should be put into new energy-conversion concepts based on totally free thinking which may occasionally lead to significant new concept formation.

Lack of consciousness in the electorate of the relevant material

There is a lack of consciousness in the electorate in respect to the order of magnitude of the expenditures which are needed to build sufficient energy-conversion machinery for solar, wind and gravitational sources to make up for the exhaustion of the fossil fuels. Correspondingly, there is a lack of consciousness of the nearness of the time in which there will be no more energy capital to spend, and the relationship between the energy supply and the economy. These lacuna in electoral consciousness could be remedied by appropriate Government use of the media. These would have to return to the 1930s for precedents—but the situation of energy exhaustion is more threatening than that of 1930.

Imagination and the limits to growth

The two limits of progress consist of insufficiencies in imagination, and available energy. In this book, there is an advocacy of limits to growth as something inevitable, but this may be in the short term of, say, 100 years. Thus, were it possible to find a method whereby one could obtain much greater amounts of energy per head of population, economic growth could continue, although population growth would have anyway to be checked.

At present, the only concept by which such an increase could occur is in terms of the potential fusion technology (Chapter 7). Science fiction has often been the forerunner of real scientific developments. A futuristic concept concerns the possibility that atomic explosives could be used to break up a planet and that its parts be placed in a solar orbit somewhat outside that of the earth. Then, it would be in principle possible to reflect onto the earth a very much greater degree of solar energy than the earth receives at present. Were this energy beamed to certain receiving areas, it could be converted to usable energy. A final limitation is related to a significant temperature increase which would occur at sufficiently high energy use.

However, at this time, the possibilities of growth lie beyond the transfer of energy technology to the renewable resources, and it is with this transfer that this book is principally concerned.

Doom?

With all exponential growth curves associated with the use of limited resources, sufficiently rapid and continued growth of production brings a point at which a sudden turn-round in production rate occurs, followed by a rapid decrease if use is continued. If a slow-down in the use-up rate of the resource occurs before the maximum, the availability of the resource for further use is stretched out and the maximum of the use-rate is put off, whilst action can be taken to build a renewable supply of the resource. If the Western economy is run at full rate, expanding and using the maximum amount of fuel available per year up to the downturn point in the 1990s, it is probable that the accretion of the capital necessary for building the new energy-conversion machinery will not be possible.

Successful formation of the capital needed appears to imply a cutback in spending and hence consumer prosperity. It is not psycho-socially possible for politicians to contemplate proposing such an action during a time in which the living standard is kept high by the spending of the residual fossil fuel capital. However, after the commencement of down-turn in the 1990s, when the spending of this capital will slow, it will certainly be much less possible politically to propose a cut-back *greater* than will arise from necessity, i.e. from diminished fuel production. Thus, one might say that reining back the economy is essential for survival; but that, were it brought about, the electoral process would act to eject the government which legislated the slow-down.

Spreading of consciousness of the situation throughout the electorate might be possible. Although a small degree of this has already occurred, those who pursue a low-energy life style have, necessarily, separated themselves from the rest of the community. Indeed, the reaction of many consumers appraised of the situation is to suggest an increase of spending in their present lifetime in terms of achieving extravagant goals in a 'last chance' situation. Expectation of a concerted effort by leading corporate groups, in terms of self-preservation, to take actions which would give rise to a decrease in consumer spending (i.e. reduction of energy use) is not reasonable. Thus, the corporations are locked into elective processes involving their shareholders. The intense capital formation needed would demand a very substantial decrease in dividend payments, and the shareholders would then change the composition of the Directorial Board until dividends were reinstated.

The threat to the technological societies in fossil fuel exhaustion is less in a lack of the necessary innovative concepts or technology, or even in a lack of capital and time. The threat is in the absence of a requisite societal mechanism to spread realization of the options within the electorate.

SUMMARY OF CHAPTER

1. In technological developments, the fundamental research must be started more than 75 years before the commercial situation is achieved.

2. Engineering of a new development takes some 60 years.

3. Commercialisation work starts about 35 years before sales are being made to the public. However, 80% of this work is done in the last 15 years before sales.

4. The statements made in points 1, 2 and 3 are based upon an investigation of the development of technologies less vital than that of an energy technology to replace the fossil fuels. If and when consciousness of the need reaches the public, there could be a vast democratic pressure for rapid development to occur.

5. Energy technology developments may not be suitable objects for the present Energy (e.g. Oil) Companies. Thus, the lead time for building is 1-2 decades and the time of profitability cannot be foreseen with definition at that distance. Hence, the risk is too high as a business venture.

6. Only government can undertake the risk of developing plant which may be ready before its time.

7. Some corporate research occurs with the object of protecting an existing technology.

8. In assessing whether technological development of solar energy upon a massive scale can be carried out in time (before decline of fossil fuels makes the financing impossible to get within a democracy), the barriers are less technological than sociological.

AUTHOR'S CHOICE OF SINGLE MOST IMPORTANT CONCLUSION FROM CHAPTER

The lead time for a new technology is some 75, 60 or 35 years depending upon whether reference is made to fundamental, engineering or commercialisation aspects of the development. The oil supply will turn down in the 1990s.

REFERENCES

1. Technology in retrospect and critical events in Science, National Science Foundation, C535–1969.
2. R. Forskning, *Tidskrift Svenka Ges.*, 1064, **14**, 1.
3. K. Tsiolkovskii, *Free Space, 1883, begun on 28th February, 1883, and completed on 13th April, 1883;* first published in *Molodoya Gvardiya*, 1940, p.45.
4. D. M. Chapin, C. S. Fuller & G. L. Pearson, *J. Appl. Phys., 1954,* **25**, 676.

4

THE FLUIDIZATION
OF COAL

Introduction

In the previous chapter, it has been assumed that, in terms of decades, natural gas and oil are virtually exhausted (that is, they will be available in the U.S. predominantly from O.P.E.C. countries as from the mid-1980s), and the major discussion concerned coal. It was learned that coal will *not* last in great abundance for hundreds of years, but that if its presence in the ground is the point, it could act as a replacement energy source till the end of this century, and probably for a few decades more, variously estimated at one (if there is no new technology for mining coal) up to ten, if the total known and projected coal (as distinct from the *available* coal) is taken as an energy base.

However, the considerations of Chapter 3 neglected all those connected with the actual process of mining and extraction of energy in the form of some suitable fuel, from coal.

The conversion of coal to a form of natural gas and oil has been examined and practised for decades, and plants have been built to carry out such a conversion. Thus, coal gasification could be carried out without much development work, except for the sulphur removal which is not yet practical. That a process can be made to work economically is not necessarily an indication that it should be developed. The post-1980 sort of question must now be asked and answered—what are the long-term ecological consequences? What amount of sulphur-containing compounds would be injected into the atmosphere in the gasification of coal? What of dust and aerosols similarly injected? What of the carbon dioxide content of the atmosphere and the climatic consequences of its steadily increasing concentration? There are a number of less obvious questions. They concern, for example, the rate at which coal mines could be built and that at which a great number of new miners could be trained. Considerations of these matters are relevant to a book on a Solar-Hydrogen Economy: they relate to estimates of the time at which achievement of the latter will be necessary.

What is coal?

What is the composition of coal? The briefest answer is: $CH_{0.8}O_{0.1}$. Coal is not a simple substance: it resulted from complex organic processes, which took place on and in the ancient earth. There are many different coals, with a changing scale of C content. The main ones are called lignite, sub-bituminous, bituminous and anthracitic. Apart from being a dehydrogenated hydrocarbon, coal contains other elements in small concentrations, like chlorine, sulphur and traces of several metals.

Coal is not only chemically variable: it is a complex sort of solid. Thus, a reason why oil is preferred to coal as a fuel—and natural gas preferred to oil—depends on the greater difficulty of handling and manipulating the complex solid.

Coal *is* the 'Ugly Duckling' of fuels. Its products corrode and foul the plant. A plant built for use by one coal may be fouled by the use of another.[1] Coal is gritty. It must be mined and then pulverised. The prospect of its re-introduction as a main source of energy clashes with environmental considerations, in terms of pollution by ash, sulphur and CO_2.

The fluidization of coal

One of the reasons why oil, and latterly natural gas, have been fuels much preferred to coal is that they can be transmitted more readily than coal. It follows that if we can obtain liquids or gases from coal, these fuels will be more acceptable than coal in solid form.

The production of gaseous products from coal (mostly methane) is easier than the production of liquid ones (alcohols, fuel, oils). Thus, basically, the production of methane from coal can be represented by the simple reaction:

$$C + 2H_2O \rightarrow CH_4 + CO_2$$

The production of liquid fuels from coal is a more difficult task. It occurs by passage over a catalyst of the products of the reaction of coal with steam, and this gives rise to a large number of products, some of which may be saturated hydrocarbons with a useful number of carbon atoms, i.e. a number large enough to make the substance a liquid oil. Gasoline can be made by a refinement of the mixtures of oils.

The technology of the fluidisation of coal has been predominantly a German science, and was first developed in Germany in the 1920s, and particularly in the 1930s. South Africa has been the principal country to practise the liquefaction of coal in recent times—as from 1955.[2]

Coal gasification to Methane ('Synthetic Natural Gas', S.N.G.)

There are two main approaches to the gasification of coal at this time. One is called the Synthane process,[3] and the other, Hygas.[4]

The Synthane Process

Introduction

The Synthane process is relatively advanced, and has given rise to a pilot plant at Bruceton, Pennsylvania, upon the performance of which the following discussion is based.

Technical Operation

The Synthane pilot plant at Bruceton runs at about 600 psi, and the temperatures are 1300-1500°F. The coal is introduced to a gasifier dry, but previously has been powdered so that it will pass through a 20-mesh screen and less than 20% of it through a 200-mesh screen.

In Fig. 4.1 is a diagram of the Synthane process operation. Coal which has been powdered and dried is introduced into the gasifier. At first it was introduced near the top of the reactor and allowed to fall down towards the fluidised bed (Fig. 4.1). More recently, the coal has been fed right into the fluidised bed. The fluidised bed injection gives better results.

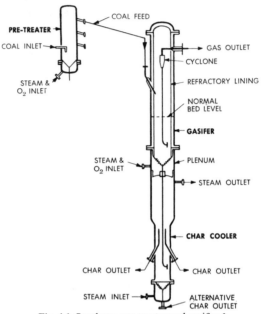

Fig. 4.1. Synthane pre-treater and gasifier.[3]

The so-called gasifying agents, steam and oxygen, are introduced into the coal bed through nozzles, and attached to a cone which forms the bottom of the gasifier. A cyclone is present to reduce entrainment of fine particles of coal into the raw gas stream. Between 65% and 80% of the carbon in the coal is converted to methane; the rest is discharged towards the lower part of the gasifier in the form of a char.

The char is cooled with de-superheated steam, and then is taken to a slurrying system and rejected from the system. It could perhaps be sold as a by-product fuel.

One of the problems which occurs in this operation is the formation of a vitrified brick which clinks on being struck in the cone of the gasifier. 'Clinker' is formed because of high local temperatures in the bed.

The gas which is obtained in the Synthane process is treated by a gas-liquid separation, CO shift conversion, acid gas removal, and methanation.

Environmental considerations in coal gasification

Along with the production of methane in coal gasification, there are significant side reactions which produce condensable hydrocarbons, but these do not occur in the Synthane process. The condensate obtained from cooling the gas stream is low in contaminants, and contains, e.g. phenols. These should not be a serious problem.

There is the hydrogen sulphide formed from the sulphur present in most coals. Both hydrogen sulphide and carbon dioxide are acid, and can be taken from the gas stream by passing it through a solvent. Later, the solvent is regenerated in a pure form by releasing the gases separately from the fuel gas stream. The hydrogen sulphide can be chemically removed from the carbon dioxide and the latter is released into the atmosphere.

The hydrogen sulphide must be eventually oxidised to sulphur, and the question then becomes where to put that.

Let us consider a plant which produces, say, 250×10^9 Btus per day. This is equivalent to about 1.6 thousand MW of thermal power, or around 500 MW electric, i.e. it is a fairly small plant.

The amount of sulphur produced per day in tonnes is

$$\frac{250.10^9.250.32}{20.212.10^3.10^6}$$

$$\simeq 466 \text{ tonnes per day}$$
$$\simeq 170,000 \text{ tonnes of sulphur per year}$$

where 212 kcals mole^{-1} is the heat of combustion of methane per mole and 32 is the atomic weight of sulphur.

Thus, were this sulphur compressed into a cubical object, the yearly production from the one small plant would be equivalent to a cubic block of sulphur 60,000 cubic metres in size and therefore having a side of c. 40 metres in length, height and breadth.[5]

This difficulty applies not only to the Synthane process, but to all processes which attempt to make fuels from sulphur-containing coal.

Economics

The economics of coal gasification plants are dependent on how much capital investment is needed. About 70% of the cost of the gas depends on the capital investment, and this stresses the need for abnormally careful judgment about the details of the manufacturing plant.

The economics given by Weiss and Lummus concerning the Bruceton plant are as follows:[3]

	$ Million
Total installed cost of coal gasification plant	850
Contingency, 15%	129
Total plant investment	987
Initial charge of catalysts and chemicals, royalties, allowance for funds during construction, start-up costs, working capital	211
Total plant investment	1,198
Total net operating cost	135
Annual gas production, 1 trillion Btu	82

Average cost of methane, based on utility financing method: $3.40 per MBTU (1977 dollars).

Such estimates sometimes prove optimistic in practice. However, it seems likely that synthetic natural gas could be produced by coal gasification for less than, say, $4.00 per MBTU in 1978 dollars. This shows the difficulty of using hydrogen from water splitting ($5-9/MBTU) as a fuel *unless* the environment damage caused by burning coal (CO_2,S) is added to the price of its products instead of being met from taxes used to support environmental protection measures necessary mainly because carbonaceous fuels are being used as the energy source.

The Hygas process[4]

Introduction

The Hygas process is one developed largely at the Institute of Gas Technology. The Hygas process, as also the Synthane process, represents a second-state technology compared with the original German coal gasification technology of World War II.

The Hygas process can deal with all types of coal from lignite to bituminous. The Hygas process uses non-slagging fluidised-bed gasification stages and is shown in Fig. 4.2.[4]

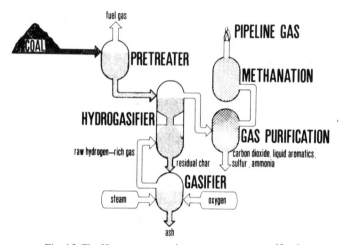

Fig. 4.2. The Hygas process using a steam-oxygen gasifier.[4]

There are no tars or complex heavy hydrocarbons produced in the Hygas process. The main product is clean, pipeline-quality gas and the by-products include light oils, elemental sulphur (see above), and ammonia.

The situation with the Hygas process in the late 1970s is that the pilot-plant programme is obtaining data upon which a commercial plant design will be built.[5]

The conversion of coal to hydrogen

It has been outlined above how synthetic natural gas could be obtained from coal at a price around $4.00 per MBTU.

Production of hydrogen from coal could be carried out by two methods.[6]

There is a Synthane process and the CO_2 acceptor process. When coal is reacted with steam at 450 psi and 800-900°C, the gaseous products are CO, CO_2 and H_2. Small amounts of methane are produced. The methane becomes a major product as the pressure is increased to 1000 psi. The CO_2 gas is removed from the final gas by washing by monoethanomine or potassium hydroxide. The final gas is only 97-98% pure. CO_2 is a by-product.

The alternative process, called the CO_2 acceptor process, involves lime which is introduced with coal when this is reacted with steam. The CO_2, the reaction product gas, is removed by the lime as calcium carbonate. With the CO_2 removed, the shift reaction occurs in the main reactor, and this eliminates the need for an external shift reactor and the washing to remove CO_2. Heat must now be applied to drive the coal-steam reaction, and this is given by the shift reaction, but also by the reaction of lime with the CO_2. In a separate reactor, the calcium carbonate can be heated to give off CO_2 to the atmosphere and reproduce lime. More coal is used for this process.

A flow sheet has been produced by Kincaid. Thus, the fuel is ground up in both processes. Lignite (preferred for both processes) is dried. If bituminous coal is used, it has to be heated to remove volatile hydrocarbons. Gasification is done for both the steam-oxygen and the CO_2 acceptor processes in fluidised beds at 450 psi. If lignite is the fuel, 1600°F is acceptable, but bituminous coal has to go to 1800°F. In the steam-oxygen process, 12 lb of lignite, 8.8 lb of steam and 5.2 lb of oxygen produce 1 lb of hydrogen.

The price of H_2 produced from large-scale coal gasification is a hypothetical quantity for no plants as yet produce it. There are two ways in which to obtain estimates. We know that the estimated Synthane price for CH_4 is about \$4.50 per MBTU. The essential difference in the manufacture of H_2 from coal, rather than CH_4, is that the pressure is around 250 psi and the temperature 800-900, whereas with CH_4 the pressure has to be *raised* above that for H_2. Hence, H_2 from coal by reacting it with steam ought to be somewhat cheaper per unit of energy than CH_4, i.e. less than the conservative \$4.50 per MBTU, estimate for CH_4 based on the Synthane projection.

However, a detailed estimate of the cost of H_2 from coal was made by Kincaid in 1973. It is shown in Table 4.I, but the values therein have been revised to 1978 values assuming a C.P.I. value for 78 to 73 to 1.90; and taking coal costing \$25 per ton one obtains much lower estimates than if one began with

TABLE 4.I: Economics of Coal to Hydrogen

	Steam-oxygen process Bit. coal (10^6 Btu)	CO_2 acceptor process (10^6 Btu)
Fixed charges (15%)	54.5	70.5
Oxygen	52.1	
Power	29.6	72.4
Direct labour	1.9	2.5
Materials	34.9	81.1
Maintenance	28.9	39.0
Other utilities	4.9	2.9
Operating allocation	8.2	10.2
General and administrative	8.4	10.6
	2.24	2.90

the price for CH_4. The average price from this base would be around $2.50. Another estimate,[7] without the detailed accounting of Kincaid, gives $4.50 for H_2 from coal at $25 per ton. H_2 from coal at about $3.75 seems a feasible price for H_2 from coal at this time (late 1970s).*

Coal gasification to produce both synthetic natural gas and hydrogen

Foh and Gahimer have recently described an integrated coal gasification-water splitting process.[8] Coal gasification processes produce relatively high-temperature heat as a by-product, and this heat is normally turned into electricity by a steam cycle.

Foh and Gahimer suggest that hydrogen and oxygen are produced via water electrolysis. The coal gasification-water splitting process is integrated together to produce both methane and hydrogen.

Another concept is to use the steam-iron process to produce hydrogen.[8] A by-product for methane production from coal can be CO, and this can be used to carry out the reaction

$$Fe_3O_4 + CO \rightarrow 3FeO + CO_2$$

Steam can then be reacted with FeO. Thus,

$$3FeO + H_2O \rightarrow Fe_3O_4 + H_2$$

Thus, in the first concept, called the U-gas process by Foh and Gahimer,[8] one has a gasifier section which includes coal storage and preparation, coal feed systems, gasification, etc. One then has a gas purification system which includes waste-heat recovery and sulphur removal, and gives rise to the production of methane, and finally one has a pure recovery section which includes gas turbines, boilers, and electric generators, which in their turn give rise to electrolytic hydrogen.

The alternative is to use a steam-iron process as outlined above, whereupon one has a reducing gas generator which includes coal storage and preparation for gasification with a steam-air mixture. There will be an oxide reductor which will include the first oxide and electric power generation, and finally the hydrogen production stage which includes the steam-iron reactor and product up-grading. Methanation is added to remove the carbon monoxide and carbon dioxide and compression to 1,000 psi is carried out.

Some of the results in terms of 1977 prices are shown in Fig. 4.3. This estimate for hydrogen (electrolytic) is about $5 per MBTU.† The real price of the hydrogen is reduced by its having been obtained from coal with its burden of S deposits and the portentous implication of deleterious climatic change.

---

*There would be advantages of using H_2 from coal rather than CH_4. Firstly, the CO_2 problem could be solved (injection into sea). Secondly, the coal-based fuel could be mixed with that from atomic and solar sources (H_2 from water). Thirdly, fossil-fuel air pollution (and its costs) would be eliminated.

†Electrolysers with an efficiency of near 100% are regarded as feasible. The price would then be about $3.75.

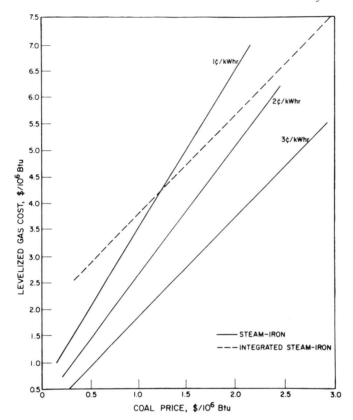

Fig. 4.3. Fuel gas cost sensitivity to coal price and by-product credit for the steam-iron and integrated steam-iron processes suggested by Foh and Gahimer.[8]

These processes are not yet fully worked out. For example, acyclic DC generators are less expensive than AC generators plus rectification, and as DC power is required for electrolysers, it makes sense to make hydrogen directly. However, the steam-iron process produces electric power as well, and could be used in conjunction with acyclic DC generators.

Electrolyser oxygen could be used in the process by cycling it back to replace 26% of the gasified air requirement.

Integrated processes are less sensitive to coal price fluctuations than the non-integrated ones. Thus, non-integrated processes produce cheaper fuel gas with a combination of low coal price giving a high electric power by-product credit; the integrated process produces cheaper fuel gas with a high coal price but gives a low electric by-product credit.

The liquefaction of coal

The basic process in the liquefaction of coal is the contacting of the powdered coal with a catalyst, and this is generally powdered iron. Carried out at tem-

peratures in the region of 300°C in steam, this process gives a series of substances, which include light and heavy oils, as also alcohols, acetaldehyde,
acetone, and other ketones. About one barrel of oil is obtained from each
tonne of coal.

The South African Government's process at Sasolburg is an example.[9] At
Sasolburg, two types of processes are operated, both of which use the Fischer-
Tropsch synthesis. One process is called ARGE. It uses a precipitated iron
catalyst in pelletised form to which promoters have been added in a fixed-
bed, tubular reactor system. Another process, called Synthol, uses a promo-
ted iron catalyst powder which is entrained in a circulating bed.

The first, or ARGE process, has now been dropped in favour of the
Synthol process which produces several thousand barrels of oil per day.*

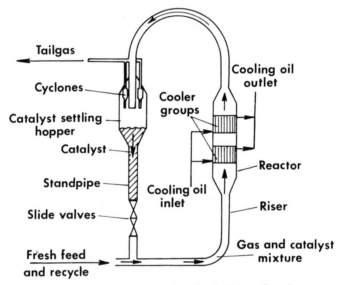

Fig. 4.4. The synthol reactor of the South African plants.[9]

The powdered coal feed arrives at 160° and 21.5 bar. The type of apparatus is shown in Fig. 4.4. When the coal flows down through the side valves
and is brought into contact with the gas, the temperature is 335°C. A mixture
of the iron catalyst and the coal is at about 315°C. The temperature of the
mixture increases as the heat from the Fischer-Tropsch synthesis and the
water-gas reaction gets into it.

These reactions are:

$$nCO + (2n+1)\, H_2 \rightarrow C_nH_{2n+2} + nH_2O$$

$$nCO + 2nH_2 \rightarrow C_nH_{2n} + nH_2O$$

There then follows the water shift reaction, which is:

$$CO + H_2O \rightarrow CO_2 + H_2$$

---

*There exists an impression that the South African petroleum supply is largely from coal. In
fact, only a few per cent comes from coal and the rest is from the refinement of Middle East
oil.

The gas steam enters the scrubbing tower, not shown in Figs 4.4 and 4.5. The heavy hydrocarbons are condensed out, and the lighter ones sent back again.

The light hydrocarbons are used for production of power and gas.

In respect to the catalyst preparation, this occurs from the iron ore and

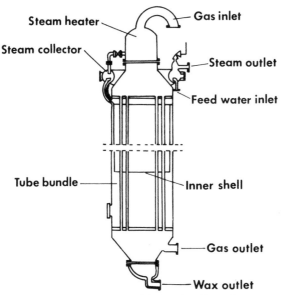

Fig. 4.5. The arge reactor of the South African plant.[9]

takes about two days for combination. It is important to get a constant feed for the reactor. Slight changes in the catalyst give considerable changes in the mix of the products.

In Table 4.II is shown the hydrocarbon mix obtained at Sasolburg in respect to light hydrocarbons, and the mix in respect to the heaviest is shown in Table 4.III showing that heptane is the main product, followed by octane.

These are among the light oils, whereas among the heavy oils those with carbon atoms in the 21-25 group are the heaviest.

Apart from this, Sasolburg produces also non-acid chemicals, largely ethanol, as are shown in Table 4.IV. About 35% of the produce is crude oil.

Many other products are synthesised in the Sasol process.

Economics of oil conversion processes

It is difficult to state at this time what the cost of oil from coal would be. A guesstimate made in 1978 suggests that it would be in the region of $20-$30 per barrel, and the resulting gasoline would cost around $2 per gallon.

However, these guesstimates may be too low: thus coal in 1978 is around $25 per ton—and a ton of coal has to be used to make a barrel of oil.

TABLE 4.II: The Light Hydrocarbon Mixture at Sasolburg

| | COMMERCIAL RUN | | | PILOT PLANT | | |
	Start	End	Average	a	b	c
CH_4	7	13	10	30	50	70
C_2H_4	4	3	4	15	17	12
C_2H_6	3	9	6			
C_3H_6	10	13	12	15	11	6
C_3H_8	1	3	2			
C_4H_8	7	9	8	16	13	6
C_4H_{10}	1	2	1			
$C_5 +$	6	9	8			
l.o	40	30	35	22	8	6
d.o	14	2	7			
n.a.c.	6	6	6	2	1	0,2
acids	1	1	1	0,05	0,05	0,01

Selectivity is C-atoms converted
l.o = light oil
d.o. = decanted oil
n.a.c. = non-acid chemicals
acids = water-soluble acids

TABLE 4.III: The Carbon Atom Distribution at Sasolburg[2]

Carbon Atoms	Light oil	Decanted oil
4	3,4	
5	7,7	
6	14,3	
7	16,3	
8	14,5	
9	13,1	
10	8,2	1,9
11	6,8	1,2
12	6,5	2,3
13	5,0	2,7
14	2,1	3,2
15	2,1	3,7
16-20		23,2
21-25		28,0
26-30		19,9
31-35		9,5
35+		4,4
mono olefins	75%	75%
paraffins	10%	
oxygenates	8%	
aromatics	7%	

Post-Sasolburg work on coal liquefaction

The Sasolburg plant with catalytic conversion, using the Fischer-Tropsch synthesis, is not economic, and other ways of converting coal to a liquid fuel have been devised. These may be placed under the following headings:
1. Carbonation;
2. Non-catalytic hydrogenation;
3. Indirect catalytic hydrogenation;
4. Direct catalytic hydrogenation.

TABLE 4.III: Non-Acid Chemicals from Sasolburg

Non-acid chemicals	Wt%
Acetaldehyde	3,0
Propionaldehyde	1,0
Acetone	10,6
Methanol	1,4
Butyraldehyde	0,6
Ethanol	55,6
MEK	3,0
i-Propanol	3,0
n-Propanol	12,8
2-Butanol	0,8
EEK-MPK	0,8
i-Butanol	4,2
n-Butanol	4,2
n-Butylketone	0,2
2-Pentanol	0,1
n-Pentanol	1,2
C_6t alcohols	0,6

Acids	Wt%
Acetic acid	70,0
Propionic acid	16,0
Butyric acid	9,0
Valeric acid and higher	5,0

One of these processes, the so-called H-coal process, involves a catalytic hydrogenation and operates at 300 psi and 850°F.[10] It involves a moderately severe hydrogenation.

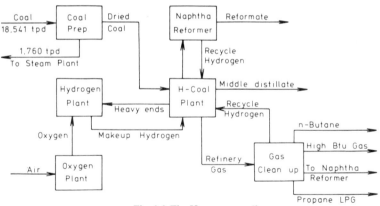

Fig. 4.6. The H gas process.[10]

The H-gas process is shown in Fig. 4.6. The process produces not only liquid hydrocarbons, but also a number of gaseous hydrocarbons as well.

The hydrogen plant gasification of the vacuum tower bottoms is based on an entrained unit followed by two stages of shift conversion and two stages of acid gas scrubbing to produce hydrogen at better than 95% purity.

The economics of the process can be seen from Table 4.V. The table was based upon $20 per ton coal price, and the price in mid-1978 is above $25 per ton. Taking it as $28 per ton, the Syncrude cost would be about $32 per barrel. There are 42 gallons per barrel, so that the cost of crude per gallon will be about 76 cents; this would result in a refined gasoline at less than $2 per gallon.*

TABLE 4.V: Economic Summary Of H Gas Coal Liquefaction Process[10]

Capital Investment	$650,000,000
Syncrude value (Arab light @ $14.50/bbl)	$16.69
Syncrude cost @ 15% DCF ROR*	$22.78/bbl

*Based on $20 per ton coal price, Illinois No. 6 coal and product gas @ $2.00/M BTU.

The production of methanol from coal

It is possible to produce methanol from coal by operating at 3,000-4,500 psi, using a $ZnO-Cr_2O_3$ catalyst. Lurgi has developed a 700-1200 psi process for the copper catalyst. The efficiency is about 59%.[11]

The difference between available coal and total coal

When coal resources have been stated, it is often said that 'not all this coal will be available', and a figure of a half or a quarter is usually quoted. However, according to Westmoreland, Forester and Sikri such an estimate would be much too optimistic.[12]

To understand this in respect to United States coal, it should be comprehended that a variety of different types of coal is present. Among the names given to these are: lignite, sub-bituminous coal; high, medium, and low volatile bituminous coal; volatile bituminous coal; semi-anthracites; and anthracite. Coals are usually distinguished by their heat of combustion, the degree of volatile matter, and the structural swelling tendency. Other parameters which are important, are the moisture content and the chemical nature of the inorganic material, and also the hetero-atom content (e.g. Cl, etc.).

It is important to differentiate between what are called resources—'a concentration of naturally occurring solid, liquid or gaseous materials on the earth's crust in such a form that extraction of a commodity is potentially feasible'—and reserves, which are 'that portion of the identified resource from which a useful mineral and energy commodity can be economically and legally extracted at the time of determination'. Reserves can be recovered at the time considered. Resources may be recoverable, some time, at some cost.

Some 400 billion tons of coal are economically recoverable in the United States by deep-mining and strip-mining techniques.[13] However, the total amount of coal is about 6,400 billion tons. Thus, the extractable amount at present is about 6%.

It is important to realise why 94% of U.S. coal is at present not available for use in future energy programmes. Much of it is contained in seams which are too thin to be mined economically, e.g. less than one metre thick. However, other coal seams are too thick to be efficiently deep-mined—a thickness exceeding 5 metres—since the mine roofs cannot be supported.

---

*1979 *estimates* of the cost of synthetic gasoline from coal suggest around $6 per MBTU. This is less than the cost of the actual product made at Sasolburg. Among uncertainties are the financial implications of the sale of side products.

Most deposits are too deep for strip mining (about 60 metres is the maximum depth).

Much other coal is too deep for mining at all, since the worth of the coal depends on the cost of the manpower needed to obtain it from the depths of the mine. Other coal seams dip steeply, or are highly faulted, or lie under land which is not available.

If in-situ gasification were ever practicable—see below—about 30% (rather than the present 5%) of the total U.S. coal resources would be available.

Occupational hazards of coal recovery

Even at the present time, underground coal mining is plagued by health problems. Methane gas is trapped within many seam structures, and this gives rise (apart from asphyxiation of workers) to a tendency to explosions within the mine. If the mine is washed out with ventilating air, these pockets may be removed, but the technique increases the price of the coal. The pervasive dust gets into the miner's skin and his clothes, but more importantly into his respiratory system, causing the disease known as 'black lung'. The collapse of mine roofs and the sudden flooding of areas of a mine occupied by workers are every-day happenings.

Could undergound gasification make the availability of coal above 6% of the total resources?

The concept that some chemical reaction may be begun within the coal body and that some useful gas may arise from this, rise to the surface, and be trapped, is an old one, and was suggested by Sir William Siemans in 1868. It was latterly taken up by Mendeleev in the U.S.S.R.; and in the United States, Ensen G. Betts was awarded a patent in 1907.

The first actual experimental work was carried out by Ramsay in the U.K. in 1912.

Since this time, extensive research and development work has been carried out in underground gasification. The work has been stronger in Russia than elsewhere because of the great influence of Lenin in that country, and because he advocated that the U.S.S.R. establish a State Trust for the development of in-situ gasification. As many as six locations were at one time active in the U.S.S.R., but only three are active in the late 1970s.

In-situ gasification was carried out in many countries, though in the U.K. and U.S. the work was brought to a halt round about 1960. Seams were not thick enough, there was unreliable control of the reaction zone, and there was excessive water influx, etc.

Since about 1971, activity has started in the United States again, and this is based on a Review published by Arthur D. Little in that year.[14]

Between 1972 and 1977, considerable activity has occurred, with underground gasification processes being tried out in various places.

The principles of underground gasification

A good way to show this is illustrated in Fig. 4.7, which represents the Morgantown, Virginia, development. Thus, in the pre-treated seam, the injected gases flow through an area which has been burned out, and feed thereby a combustion-gasification flame front. The combustion forms CO_2, and also

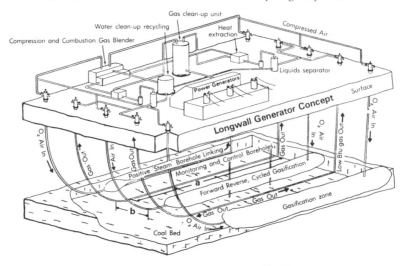

Fig. 4.7. Longwall generator in-situ coal gasification concept.[12]

the combustible fuel gas CO, but the most important aspect of it is that it generates heat. The steam gasification which follows thereby forms both hydrogen and CO, and also some methane at the leading edge of the front where coal pyrolysis takes place. The in-situ gasification products are swept out into the production well, and this leads to the surface and various production areas.

In Fig. 4.8, aspects of in-situ gasification are shown.

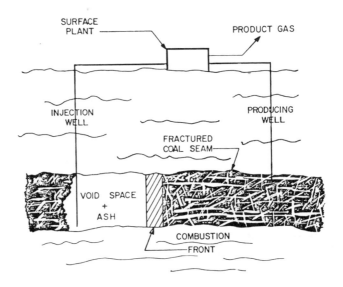

Fig. 4.8. Schematic on coal gasification.[12]

The potential advantages of in-situ gasification

Apart from the fact that it could increase the availability of U.S. coal resources from 6% to 30% of the total, in-situ gasification would give rise to an improvement for the workers, i.e. it would remove the need for miners. Moreover, the degree of air pollution which is associated with strip mining, and even underground mining, is reduced; the occupational hazard aspect of the situation would be reduced.

The greatest advantage, however, would be economic. Because there is no mining, and vast amounts of coal could be tackled at one time, some extremely low predictions for the cost of synthetic natural gas from in-situ gasification have been made, and values as low as $3 per MBTU have been quoted in the late 1970s.

The difficulties facing the successful development of underground gasification

It must be stated that if coal is to be used as a *massive* source of energy after 2000, then it will only be so if underground gasification, or some as-yet-unseen technological alternative, is achieved. A tiny fraction of U.S. coal is actually available to strip-mining and deep-mining techniques, and without underground gasification, coal as the major source of liquid fuels would not be a reasonable alternative.*

It is all the more disquieting, therefore, to learn that there are considerable difficulties to overcome in respect to underground gasification.

1. Underground gasification generally causes a land subsidence. Although a gentle subsidence is perhaps tolerable, if underground gasification were to become general, the constant consequence of the subsidence of land above the areas undergoing gasification would clearly not make the process any more acceptable to the community.
2. There is a basic trouble of surface-to-volume ratio. The volume of the coal bed which is being attacked is great compared with the surface area which the attacking gases (oxygen, steam) can compact. Hence, the actual calorific value per unit volume of the gas which comes out is not great. There has to be a large excess of air (or oxygen) and steam to get methane or hydrogen, and as, in practice, it is the net Btu per thousand s.c.f. which matters, this is clearly not likely to be one comparable, say, with methane. Thus, underground gasification yields of the past have been around 50-100 Btu per thousand s.c.f. (compare methane: 900). Some recent experiments have given rise to gases which have a calorific value of about twice this.[12] Although low Btu gases are of value, their large-scale use would bring about changes in the distribution system, and probably of systems which burn it.
3. A difficulty arises in the size of the coal bed which it is necessary to have to make the setting up of the plant worthwhile. Thus, to run a small 500 MW electric plant for 25 years, it is necessary to have a coal bed of 30 million tons of coal. A dense coal bed of this size may not be easily found— the coal may be in seams which are thin and deep, etc.

---

*This statement refers to the logistic difficulties of building enough mines, and training enough miners.[15]

4. In proposing new methods of coal gasification, it must be recalled that one is looking at a field in which research and development has been active for about 70 years, and very intensive in the U.S.S.R. for the last 50 years. It is significant that the direction in this last country (where there are essentially never research cut-backs caused by budgetary reduction) has been to reduce research in coal gasification rather than to increase it.

The use of conventional explosives in underground gasification

According to G. H. Higgins,[15] it may be possible to shatter and then powder the coal with conventional explosives, sending steam down at 700-1300°K. Reactants would be pumped out at 500-1000 psi, and the CO_2 and methane removed.

Higgins considers even brackish water would be acceptable, and under these conditions he estimates about 100 years supply of natural gas at about $2 per MBTU.

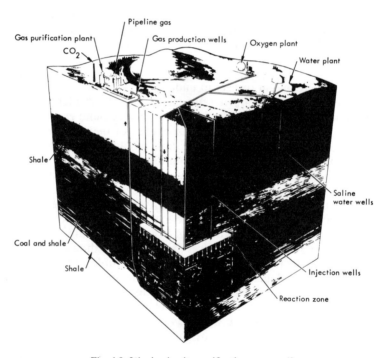

Fig. 4.9. Higgins in-situ gasification process.[15]

The steam would be pushed down slowly (Fig. 4.9). A thermally-stable hot zone advances and is kept hot by the reaction.

The reactions which would take place in the coal bed (as conceived by Higgins) are shown in the Table 4.VI.

The concept has not yet been proved. The difficulties which are attached to it are:

1. It may be necessary to have so much explosive to put the coal into a sufficiently powdered state that it would become uneconomic and impractical.
2. The ground would still subside in the same way as in conventional coal gasification. Subsidences of about 200 ft could occur.
3. It is as yet not known whether the coal bed would be sufficiently permeable so that the gases could rise. For a relatively impermeable mass, the reactants could not be successfully injected (Table 4.VI).

TABLE 4.VI: ΔH AND ΔF FOR REACTIONS IMPORTANT TO THE GASIFICATION PROCESS AT TEMPERATURES OF 500 AND 1000°K

	Reaction	ΔH_{500}	ΔH_{1000}	ΔF_{500}	ΔF_{1000}
			(kcal mole^{-1})		
(1)	$CH_{1.16}O_{0.35}$ $0.35\ H_2O(g)$ $+0.115\ CH_4+0.885\ C$	+ 9.304	+11.134	+2.159	− 0.997
(2)	$CH_{1.16}O_{0.35}+0.535\ H_2O(g)$ $0.557\ CH_4+0.443\ CO_2$	+ 10.526	+12.026	+ 2.896	− 3.234
(3)	$CH_{1.16}O_{0.35}+1.77\ H_2$ $CH_4+0.35\ H_2O(g)$	− 7.884	− 8.884	− 4.124	− 1.364
(4)	$CH_{1.16}O_{0.35}+1.115\ O_2$ $CO_2+0.58\ H_2O\ (g)$	− 98.637	− 97.112	− 103.687	− 107.212
(5)	$C+1/2\ O_2 \rightarrow CO$	− 26.30	− 26.77	− 37.18	− 47.94
(6)	$C+2\ H_2 \rightarrow CH_4$	− 19.30	− 21.43	− 7.84	+ 4.61
(7)	$C+H_2O \rightarrow CO+H_2$	+31.98	+32.47	+ 15.18	− 1.90
(8)	$CO+H_2O \rightarrow H_2+CO_2$	− 9.51	− 8.31	− 4.85	− 0.63
(9)	$CO+3\ H_2 \rightarrow CH_4+H_2O$	−51.28	−53.87	− 23.02	− 6.51
(10)	$2\ CO \rightarrow C+CO_2$	−41.49	−40.78	− 20.03	+ 1.27
(11)	$CO+1/2\ O_2 \rightarrow CO_2$	−67.79	−67.55	− 57.21	− 46.67

4. Would the product gases be easily withdrawn from the lower part of the bed?
5. What of the removal of carbon dioxide and water?

Logistical difficulties in the development of coal as a main source energy supply

As it now appears that underground gasification is the only hope for a massive use of the coal as *resources,* then the question now becomes how long it may take to build plants of this kind.

Although this cannot be answered until one knows more of the final form of practical underground gasification plant, the logistical difficulties with conventional mines suggest that it might be difficult to build sufficient equipment in the time available,[16] i.e. before the production rate of oil turns down in the 1990s.

The pollutional consequences of coal becoming a main source of energy

It is improbable that coal could become the main source of energy because of the lack of availability of about 94% of U.S. coal to deep-mining and strip-mining techniques; and the difficulties in progress on underground gasification. Apart from this difficulty, however, there would exist a greater one: had it been possible to recover sufficient coal to make it worthwhile trying to set up large-scale coal liquefaction industries. The difficulties are pollutional and consider:

1. The sulphur problem; and
2. The carbon dioxide problem.

The problem of pollution potentially caused by sulphur depends upon the origin of coal, and tends to be worse in United States coal than, for example, Australian coal. On the other hand, the carbon dioxide problem is a universal one and will occur however fossil fuels are burnt.

The sulphur problem

There is between 1% and 6% sulphur in most American coal, and the majority of it contains the higher limit. Let us assume as a first approximation that it all contains 5%, and that all of this is rejected into the atmosphere as SO_2. We further assume (for simplicity) that the SO_2 remains in the first 10,000 metres of the atmosphere, and that all energy-producing equipment is running on coal. A calculation shows that the amount of sulphur dioxide in the atmosphere is then, after one year's emission without removal by other reactions, about 200 micrograms per m^3. This is equivalent to very polluted air, only observed in highly industrialized zones (the amount of sulphur found in rural atmospheres is in the region of 1-10 micrograms per m^3).[17]

Let it be assumed now that we remove 99% of the sulphur, then there will be about 2 micrograms per cubic metre up to 10,000 metres (neglecting photo-chemical removal processes), and this would be tolerable (for even air above the oceans has up to 4 micrograms per cubic metre).[17]

There are, of course, removal modes for sulphur dioxide in the atmosphere. There is a photochemical oxidation which goes:

$$2SO_2 + O_2 + h\nu \rightarrow 2SO_3$$

In fact, such a reaction produces ozone as a by-product, and is one of the mechanisms whereby ozone can exist at higher concentrations in the lower atmosphere. Of course, the SO_3 gets converted with the moisture of the atmosphere to sulphuric acid. Sulphate particles, presumably of this origin, have been found over the Atlantic Ocean by Cadle *et al.*[18]

The chemical removal of some 99% of the SO_2 is well-assured, but the question now becomes where the resulting sulphur will be kept and in what form. A calculation shows that a 1,000 MW plant produces sulphur of volume 10^5 cubic metres in size per year.

This mass (from one small plant) would amount to a block around 10^5 cubic metres per year, i.e. a city block in length and breadth and some 10 metres in height. The entire energy supply for the U.S. would produce about a million such blocks per year. Another way to get some idea of the magnitude of the problem is to assume that sulphur in the form of a powder were distributed over the entire United States. It would form a visible dust layer about one micron thick.

There does not appear to be an easy solution to the problem of what to do with the sulphur removed from coal. Reburial in the mine is a possibility—

and would add proportionately to the cost of coal-derived fuels.

The carbon dioxide difficulty

It has been known for a long time (for history, see Plass[19]) that the apparent steady state between the photosynthetic production of oxygen from carbon dioxide and water as a by-product of the photochemical synthesis of hydrocarbons, and those other processes which added carbon dioxide to the atmosphere, including metabolism, are no longer in balance. This process must have been, at least as a time average, in balance over many hundreds of millions of years,* but the disturbance which has arisen from Man's un-ecological behaviour has altered the natural situation during the last 100 years. Thus, in 1850, the amount of carbon dioxide in the atmosphere of the world was 290 parts per million. About a quarter of the increase has come during the past decade. By the year 2020, if present trends continue, the amount of carbon dioxide in the atmosphere will be about 350 parts per million.

It is essential to take notice of this increase, although the reason is not obvious. Carbon dioxide appears at first to be a benign pollutant, and as it is only at 0.03% by volume in the atmosphere, its presence there might be thought at first to be one of our lesser concerns. It turns out, however, that, in planning a new energy system, it should be our greatest. The reason concerns the temperature equilibrium of the earth. This is partly connected with the radioactive material inside the earth, but is mainly affected by the amount of solar radiation being absorbed by the earth. That which is not absorbed is reflected into space, and the amount which escapes the earth's atmosphere depends upon the concentration of CO_2 (and water) in the air, for this absorbs radiation in the infra-red. After the absorption, the excited vibrational levels de-activate to produce heat, and there is a rise in the temperature of the atmosphere.

The rise of temperature, as calculated, will not be a negligible one, and there is evidence to show that the average mean temperature of the world has already been affected by an amount of the order of 1°C, due to the increase in CO_2. The world-wide rise of temperature by 2070 would be about 9°C, if we continue to burn fossil fuels as the main energy source.

This kind of temperature rise would have substantial effects upon the ecology of the earth; for example, they would make the American wheatgrowing areas too arid, whilst creating zones of fertility in other parts of the world.[20]

Moreover, the situation is not only a threatening one, but both actions which might correct it are destructive to our present social organisation. Thus, there are only two possible causes of the carbon dioxide increase:
1. Because we are injecting into the atmosphere more carbon dioxide than the green plants can deal with, owing to the fact that we base our economy upon energy from the combustion of hydrocarbons;
2. Because we are clearing the forests.

To remedy these causes, we can stop clearing the forests, decreasing the

---

* Perhaps over billions of years. However, in the first billion years of the planet, the atmosphere was largely CH_4.

amount of agriculture or decrease the amount of energy we obtain from oil and coal. Neither of these courses is welcome. At the same time, as will be shown in this section, the continuation of cause (1) or (2) will, in time, bring uncomfortable consequences.

Carbon dioxide has not only had a long-range trend to increase since 1900, but it also cycles on a yearly basis, as shown by the measurements in Fig.4. 10.[21]

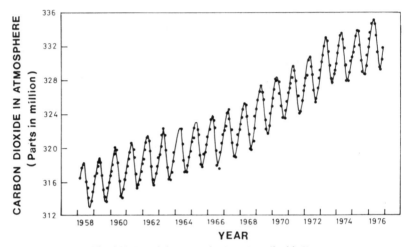

Fig. 4.10. Trends in atmospheric carbon dioxide.[21]

The cause of the long-term increase in carbon dioxide content

This has usually been ascribed to the accelerating release of carbon dioxide through the combustion of fossil fuels.

On the other hand, more recently, a counter-view has arisen from workers at the Marine Biology Laboratory in Woodshole. Thus, Woodwell, Whittaker and Lykens have suggested that there is a substantial release of carbon dioxide from plant and animal life, which is not compensated by being used up again in the formation of further hydrocarbons.[21] Thus, the essential reason for this release has been the distribution of forests and oxidation of humus.

The question of whether the biotic pool is getting larger or smaller did not become a question of controversy until 1976, when papers published in Berlin challenged the normal oceanographic model of the atmosphere. The present situation is that instead of acting as a sink of carbon dioxide and removing it from the atmosphere, many forests are being denuded of the biota and become a net source of carbon dioxide.

Only about half of the CO_2 introduced into the atmosphere remains there, whilst the rest is absorbed in the sea or otherwise removed.

The CO_2 increase in the atmosphere comes certainly from *both* the decrease of green plant area and the increase in CO_2 injection. The C^{14} data suggests that the greater contribution has been from the latter cause.

Agricultural effect of greenhouse warming

It appears that the earth will be warmed *differentially*, with temperatures increasing towards the Poles.[21] Thus, the desert zone will move poleward and enlarge the area of aridity, thus reducing the area suitable for agriculture. This is not a helpful tendency in view of the fact that no social control mechanism exists which can reduce or reverse the increase of the world's population which will collide with the decreasing area available for agriculture.

The Greenhouse Effect[22]

The average albedo of the earth (including clouds, surface of land, and water, and the atmosphere) is 29%. Theoretical calculations show that the average temperature of the atmosphere should be 254°K. If, on the other hand, the earth is considered as a black box having an albedo of zero, then there should be an equilibrium temperature of 277°K. These temperatures are 34° and 11°C respectively less than the average real temperature of the earth, which is about 288°K. The reason for this difference is the greenhouse effect of the atmosphere, caused partly by water and by CO_2. Because CO_2 does not absorb the high-frequency spectrum of sunlight, but only absorbs the infrared radiation, which is the reflection of sunlight from the earth's surface, an increase in its concentration will lead to a further increase in temperature.

Many persons have attempted, since the realisation of the possible effects by Raleigh, to make calculations of what kind of temperature increase would arise if the carbon dioxide was not stationary in the atmosphere. A review of these calculations[22] is given by Niehaus.[23] The most recent calculations have been carried out by Mannabe and Strichler,[24] and these take into account the feedbacks which will occur if the temperature is increased, namely an increase in cloud concentration. Mannabe and Weatherald[25] found that 2.4° was the increase in the world temperatures if carbon dioxide was doubled.

Model calculations by Niehaus[26]

Niehaus's first calculation assumes what he calls an optimistic equilibrium strategy. He is referring to the energy distribution in the world, and assumes the full use of nuclear reactors as soon as possible. It is assumed that the population is stabilised at 8 billion by 2050, all persons having on average a material standard of living equal to that at present in the U.S.A. The assumption is made that by 2100 the percentage of nuclear power will be 90%.

It is important to notice that in spite of the assumptions made, which are optimistic in respect to coal use (i.e. assume that less coal will be burned than is probable), the carbon dioxide concentration still rises to 500 parts per million by about 2050, and the temperature change at that date will be about 1.5°C (Fig. 4.11).

One difficulty in the calculations reported by Niehaus is the lack of accounting for a dust-level change during this time.[26] An increase in the dust level would counteract the increase of temperature which is being discussed.

Influence of the surface ocean layer

The ocean has plenty of capacity to absorb CO_2, and indeed the whole fossil-

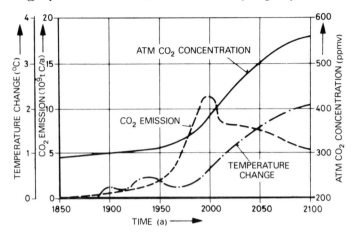

Fig. 4.11. Atmospheric temperature change due to CO_2.[26]

fuel load could be burnt and all the resulting CO_2 absorbed into the sea. The difficulty is that, if the CO_2 is in the atmosphere, this equilibrium would not come for a time of more than 1,000 years. Thus, carbon dioxide easily dissolves in the surface of the sea. However, the temperature gets lower as one goes downwards, so that there is no convectional driving force, and it has to diffuse slowly downwards.

Important changes occur in the absorption of CO_2 by changing the temperature of the surface water, and fluctuations (of duration a few months) in the carbon dioxide concentrations in the atmosphere, as are observed, are probably due to these effects.

Behaviour of Niehaus' model if no nuclear energy is used

The basis of this calculation assumes that in some way the coal which appears to be so difficultly available, is made available (e.g. underground explosions, making underground gasification possible), and then the situation is as given in Fig. 4.12, and shows that the temperature will rise by some 5° at about 2050, and finally to about 8.8° by 2100. The resulting atmospheric concentration of carbon dioxide will be about 1500 parts per million.

Thus, it is clear that *we cannot depend upon coal to replace oil into the next century, even if our resources could be turned into our reserves,* i.e. the unavailable coal became available, unless CO_2 is prevented from reaching the atmosphere (Fig. 4.12).

Can the CO_2 effect be dealt with?

It would be possible to build new coal-burning plants on the sea-board, taking the exit gas from conversion plants deep into the ocean, where the CO_2 would dissolve. This would be an extreme strategy, for it would take away from us that part of the use of coal—had coal been as available as has often been assumed—which would be most useful: a source of synthetic gasoline.

We could run a totally electrical economy, based upon coal, delivering the CO_2 into the oceans and running cars on batteries; or produce H_2 and use

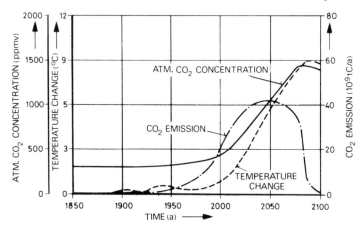

Fig. 4.12. Atmospheric concentration of carbon dioxide as a function of time: the result of using coal as a fuel.

that as the distributed fuel (no CO_2 injection into the atmosphere). This suggestion depends for its practicality upon satisfactory underground gasification because of logistic difficulties of mining coal.

Summary of reasons for the non-viability of coal as a massive energy-source after 2000

1. *Availability.* Coal cannot be considered as a massive resource if the coal available at present prices is that considered.
2. The comparison of the price of nuclear and coal-derived electricity is already in favour of nuclear, particularly in respect to 1985 and beyond (Chapter 5).
3. In respect to automotive fuel, nuclear electricity will be convertible into hydrogen at an efficiency approaching 100%. Hydrogen-fuelled cars have a range of speed equivalent to those of gasoline-fuelled cars. *Per unit distance,* the economics of hydrogen use in transportation would be some 25% more favourable than that of synthetic liquid methane or synthetic gasoline (Chapter 12).
4. The massive use of coal would cause a severe problem in respect to the disposal of sulphur.
5. The massive use of coal as a fuel would threaten dislocation of the world agricultural system some 2-3 decades into the next century.
6. The success of underground gasification would solve some problems. It has been a field of intensive research in Russia and other lands for more than 50 years. Success has been minimal.
7. In the absence of underground gasification, the building of the necessary mines by 2000 would need an impossibly high building rate.[16] To be 'all-coal' by, say, 2030, implies opening a new mine about every day until that time.

APPENDIX

Simplistic illustrations on the lastingness of coal

It is easy to calculate how long the coal supply would last with certain gross simplifying assumptions. The first one is that the rate of consumption of energy stays constant at its 1975 value. By doing so we bring in one kind of difficulty (no growth in the economy), but by assuming there will be growth we are threatened by exhaustion before enough renewable-resource conversion technology can be built.

It is better, therefore, to assume, for the moment anyway, that there is no growth from the 1975 level. Now at that time the entire economy was running at 10.4 kilowatts per person. Taking a population number as 250 million, we have therefore that the joules per year is:

$$250.10^6.10.7.10.3.8,760.60.60$$

At the same time, a reasonable value for the calorific value of coal in lignite would be about 2.6 x 10^{10} joules per ton.

If we assume no underground gasification, we have about 400 billion tons of coal available in the U.S. in deep mining if (as seems improbable)* we could mine coal at a rate needed to replace oil *in time,* then the lastingness of the coal available with present technology would be given simply by dividing one figure by the other. The result is around 100 years, the exact figure being affected by the assumed efficiency of conversion to usable energy (it is 60 years at 33%).

There will never be a time at which we would ever 'run entirely on coal'. There will be continued oil production for many decades after the beginning of decline in the 1990s. Breeder and solar contributions will be there. However, for a vivid impression of the relatively small amount of coal we have (compared with the gross overstatements so often made), let us suppose that we ran entirely on coal from 2000.

If the energy needs are to grow between 1975 and 2000 at 3% (but remain constant after 2000), then the need for energy at 2000 would be 2.09 times higher than that at 1975, and the number of years of coal we would have left from 2000 would be about 62 years at 100% efficiency of conversion or some 20 years at 33%.

Trivial calculations of this type are, of course, not accurately applicable to any real situation. The truth is more complex because we shall have a multi-determined energy situation past 2000: coal and declining oil and natural gas will contribute, as well as solar and atomic. However, the point is that such simplistic calculations do show the illusional nature of the supposition that we have 'a thousand years of coal'. This widespread impression arises because it is not realized what a small fraction of coal resources is available; and the effect of growth on need. The results quoted above assume that growth ceases at 2000. If one continues to grow at 3%, and then 'switches in' coal as the total provider at 2025, then the 400 billion tons of coal would

---

* Because of the difficulty of building so many new mines; in training the necessary two million miners in time, etc.

be equivalent not to 62 but to about 30 years of coal supply, or just 10 years at 33%!

It seems reasonable to see that supply alone (apart from CO_2 and S) would limit coal to around 2030 in the absence of satisfactory coal gasification.

SUMMARY OF CHAPTER

1. Coal is a complex solid C-H compound of variable composition and is difficult to handle.

2. Coal gasification is easy and cheap; liquefaction is more difficult and expensive. The liquid fuel from coal would be some 50% more expensive than the gaseous.

3. The two main American processes for coal gasification are called Synthane and Hygas. Fundamentally, each is a technology for the large-scale reaction of coal with steam to give CH_4 and CO_2. The price of the product would be around $4 per MBTU, assuming that the environmental damage costs are subsidized by using taxes to pay for the environmental damage they cause.

4. Coal can be gasified to hydrogen and not to CH_4 by choosing specific conditions for the steam-coal reaction. The (1st Law) cost of the hydrogen would be slightly less than that for methane. Although the hydrogen thus produced would thereafter do no more environmental damage, the latter comes from the CO_2 and S resulting from coal. The S difficulty would be undiminished by the use of H_2 as the fuel from coal. The CO_2 difficulty might perhaps be removed by building plants situated near the shore, and piping CO_2 into the deep water. The (2nd Law) cost of H_2 would be substantially less than that of methanol in transportation (Chapter 12).

5. The Fischer-Tropsch coal liquefaction plant is the basis of what is now in practice in South Africa. It involves an iron catalyst working on the products of the steam-coal reaction.

   Modern versions would produce oil at $20-30 per barrel and gasoline at perhaps $2 per gallon, or around $14 per MBTU, assuming the true cost is subsidized out of taxation by means of payments to counteract the resulting environmental damage done by releasing the products of the fuel-making processes into the environment.

6. About 400 billion tons of coal (only) are available in the U.S.A. at present prices. The difficulties of recovering the rest ($\equiv 94\%$ of the total) are complex and varied.

7. Underground gasification has been much researched, but with little success. The use of large quantities of conventional explosive seems to give some prospect, though would cause subsidence of the surface land.

8. The disposal of the several per cent sulphur in most U.S. coal provides a difficulty in the large-scale use of coal. Reburying it in the mine would seem necessary. This is one of the costs neglected in the price estimates at present given for oil from coal.

9. The CO_2 difficulty of the massive use of carbonaceous fuels into the next century is sufficiently great so that such fuels could not continue to be used in transportation and industry past around 2020. However, H_2 from

coal *could* be used, with shore-line CO_2 injection into the sea. (Though there is still the S difficulty.)

10. Coal is hence not a viable source of energy to replace oil on a longer scale, if the fuel proposed from it is a hydrocarbon.

AUTHOR'S CHOICE OF THE MOST IMPORTANT SINGLE CONCLUSION FROM CHAPTER

Because of CO_2 and other difficulties, coal could not be used as a main source of energy unless it were to give H_2 as a fuel, with CO_2 injection into the oceans. Such a conclusion decreases the applicability of successful underground gasification, where the fuel must be processed over the coal field.

REFERENCES

1. L. Lessing, *Fortune* (November 1972), p.210.
2. J. C. Hoogendoorn, publications and reports of South African Coal, Oil & Gas, 1974.
3. A. J. Weiss & C. E. Lummus, Alternative Energy Sources Conference, Miami, 1977.
4. B. S. Lee, Alternative Energy Sources Conference, Miami, 1977.
5. J. L. Johnson, *Advances in Chemistry*, 1974, **131**, 192 *cf.* the *A.G.A. Monthly*, 1977, **59**, 12.
6. W. Kincaid, Hydrogen Economy Meeting, Cornell University, Ithaca, 1973.
7. K. Cox, private communication.
8. S. E. Foh & J. S. Gahimer, Alternate Energy Sources Conference, Miami, 1977.
9. J. C. Hoogendoorn, *The Sasol Story* (South African Coal, Oil & Gas Corporation, 1976); *GAS*, 1972, p.32.
10. A. Wellman, Alternate Energy Sources Conference, Miami, 1977.
11. P. F. H. Rudolph, Lurgi Company, Publication 24072, 1974.
12. P. C. Westmoreland, R. C. Forrester III & A. P. Sikri, Alternate Energy Sources Conference, Miami, 1977.
13. Quoted from statement of Division of Oil, Gas & Shale Technology, ERDA, Underground gasification programme, ERDA 77-51, March, 1977.
14. Arthur D. Little, Bureau of Mines Report OFR 11-72, NTIS No. PB-209, 274, 1971.
15. G. H. Higgins, Lawrence Livermore Radiation Laboratory, Atomic Energy Contract, No. W-7405-ENG-48, 1972.
16. J. O'M. Bockris, *Energy: The Solar-Hydrogen Alternative* (Australia & New Zealand Book Company, Sydney, 1975), pp.51-54.
17. C. F. J. Brickard, in J. O'M. Bockris (ed.), *Environmental Chemistry* (Plenum Publishing Corporation, 1977).
18. R. D. Cadle, W. H. Fischer, E. R. Frank & J. P. Lodge, *J. Atmospheric Science*, 1968, **25**, 100.
19. G. Plass, in J. O'M. Bockris (ed.), *The Electrochemistry of Cleaner Environments* (Plenum Publishing Corporation, 1977).
20. A. Flowers, *Scientific American*, 1978.
21. G. M. Woodwell, *Scientific American*, 1978, **238**, 137.
22. K. Sekihara in J. O'M. Bockris (ed.), *Environmental Chemistry* (Plenum Publishing Corporation, 1977).
23. F. Niehaus, Report of the Nuclear Center at Juelich (JUEL, 1975), pp.11-65.
24. S. Mannabe & R. F. Strichler, *J. Atmospheric Science*, 1964, **21**, 361.
25. S. Mannabe & R. T. Weatherald, *J. Atmospheric Science*, 1967, **24**, 241.
26. F. Niehaus, Report of Nuclear Science Center at Juelich (JUEL, 1976), pp.76-35.

5

FISSION

Introduction

The processes of atomic fission are well known, and discussed in so many books that a detailed presentation of the principles here would be superfluous.[1]

Suffice to say that uranium ores occur particularly in Africa and Australia, and that these ores contain uranium oxide, U_3O_8, the uranium atoms therein consisting of two isotopes, U^{235} and U^{238}, only the former one of which is fissile. About 0.3% of uranium atoms are, in fact, U^{235} and therefore undergo fission, and the rest of the uranium is not active.

The discovery of the energy which could be obtained from atomic fission was made accidentally. Researches which were going on simultaneously in the late 1930s, by Fermi and his associates in Rome, and by Hahn, Meitner and Strassman in Berlin, had as their objective the formation of transuranic elements. The research involved the bombardment of uranium with neutrons. The neutrons were to enter the nucleus of uranium and form a new heavier element.

An unexpected result was found: an inert gas was evolved, and a new element formed which was found upon chemical analysis to be barium, atomic number 56—not a transuranic element.

Thus, the *fundamental fission reaction* was found to be:

$$^{235}_{92}U + ^{1}_{0}n \quad ^{139}_{56}Ba + ^{94}_{36}Kr + 3^{1}_{0}n$$

Now, in 1939, Frisch, who was Luise Meitner's cousin, discovered that the energy released in this reaction was stupendous in comparison with energies released in chemical reactions. Thus, as the energy of binding of neutrons to protons in the nucleus is much larger than that between nucleii and extra-nuclear electrons in chemical bonds, any difference of the sum of the binding energies of nuclei on the two sides of a nuclear reaction will give rise to net energies of reactions which will be enormous compared with the net energies of chemical reactions.

Soon after the realisation of Frisch, the military possibilities were foreseen. The key point is that, in the above reaction, one neutron gives rise to the fission products plus *three* neutrons. Now, under circumstances in which all these three neutrons collide with the 235 isotope of uranium again, there would be nine neutrons produced, then twenty-seven, and so on. This type of happening is a branching chain reaction, and is the mechanism by which chemical reactions become explosive. Here, however, we are faced with energy changes which are of the order of 10^6 times greater than the energy changes in chemical reactions, and so the idea arose—the basis of the atomic bomb—that explosions of the order of one million times greater than the ordinary explosions, per unit mass of explosive involved, could be carried out by utilising uranium, appropriately enriched in U^{235}, as the explosive.

The branching chain reaction is not possible unless the concentration of the U^{235} in the natural uranium (the mixture of the U^{235} and the U^{238}) is increased above that in the naturally found ore. Thus, if the neutron flux in the above reaction is made infertile by collision with atoms which do not undergo fission, i.e. the three neutrons produced in the above reaction do not strike other atoms of uranium 235 but strike atoms of uranium 238 etc., then there will not be three neutrons produced for every one used, and the chain reaction will not occur. Hence, the first necessity in the making of the mixture which gives rise to the very large energy release involved in an atomic explosion, is to increase the concentration of the U^{235} above the natural 0.3%.

Another condition is necessary: apart from the concentration of the uranium 235 necessary to make an explosion, there is a matter of the actual mass of it. If the mass is too small, many of the neutrons which are released in the fission-type reaction above do not collide with other uranium atoms but simply escape from the mass. Thus, to bring about an explosion there is a *critical minimal mass* of uranium 235.

In a reactor, where it is desired to produce a steady amount of heat, the point is to damp down the branching chain reaction which causes the explosion. This is done by adding cadmium rods to the mass of uranium ore, enriched to the extent of 2-4% of uranium 235. What the cadmium rods do is to absorb many of the neutrons. If sufficient neutrons are absorbed, then the reaction which occurs is slowed down, i.e. is not explosive, but a very interesting amount of heat will be produced. This can then be removed by some heat-exchange system and brought into contact with some energy-conversion system, normally the steam cycle, which then gives electricity, etc.

Around 100 fission reactors of this type exist in the world today. However, they still supply only very small fractions of the electricity (and no other kind of energy) in the leading technological countries.

Exhaustion of the uranium supplies

If atomic fission energy—without breeding—were to be used as a basis in the future energy system, i.e. the present known uranium ores were the only source of our uranium, then it is often stated that the supply would fuel those reactors which are planned until about 2000 only.

As of 2000, the planned reactors would still supply less than half the electricity of the countries involved, and this electricity is only one-quarter of the total energy needed. Fission alone, therefore, without breeding, cannot be the main energy source of the future.

This generally-held view does seem essentially true. However, there is probably a good deal more uranium in the earth than is often assumed.*

---

* There are very large total amounts of uranium in the sea, but in extremely dilute quantities (see following).

Thus, the amount of an ore which is 'available' depends upon how much one is willing to pay for the greater trouble of extracting an ore which is, e.g. deeper in the ground or, e.g. present in much more dilute concentrations. There is a great deal of uranium in granite rocks at a few parts per million.

Now the prospect of an increase of the price of uranium is not such a serious one as one might at first think because the major cost of nuclear electricity would be the cost of the plant (i.e. the cost of the money needed to build it), and the cost of the fuel could be increased several times, even ten times, whilst affecting the cost of the electricity by, say, only 25% or so. Such an increase is small at a time when there are prospects of increases in fossil fuel energy costs of several hundred per cent.

There is merit in attempting to remain with fission rather than breeders, because the fission reactor has the advantage that, although it involves dangers—to be discussed below—it does not involve the production of plutonium. It is the storage of the plutonium wastes which is the quintessential difficulty of the breeder, and this would be avoided by staying with the fission reactor. As the available ores would run out in a few decades, it is worth considering whether uranium could be extracted from the sea.

Although estimates of the concentration of uranium in sea water vary from measurements in different parts of the world (as they do with gold), the order of magnitude figure for the concentration of uranium is $4 \ 10^{-9}$ mole per litre. this means $5 \ 10^8$ litres (or $5 \ 10^5$ cubic metres) of water for 1 lb of U.

There is no doubt *chemically* that uranium in the very small concentration of 0.004 ppm (which is another expression of 4.10^{-9} moles l^{-1}) could be removed from water. It would be possible to complex it with some organic material, perhaps contained in a membrane.

However, the work done in dealing with the $5 \ 10^8$ litres of water may be too large to make the removal worthwhile. Without proposing detailed schemes for the engineering of the extraction, it is not possible to make a precise calculation. In most arrangements, the sea would have to be pumped up some gradient. Suppose that this involved a lifting of the water through 10 metres, the work done would be $5.10^{11} \ 981 \ 10^3$ ergs $= 1.2 \ 10^4$ kwh. At 4 cents kwh^{-1}, this means that the pumping work done would cost $480 per lb of U. At present, the price is in the region of $30 per lb. Of course, much would have to be added to the hypothetical cost of pumping water 10 metres because of the membrane costs, cost of extraction from the latter, and finally recovering U from the extraction solution, etc.

One approach which avoided this difficulty would involve places in the world where natural forces cause the sea to move, often at several kph, constantly in one direction. An appropriate membrane, suspended in this flow, might extract uranium with no pumping work and the costs would be reduced. However, there would be counter costs concerned with removing the membrane periodically to extract uranium from it.

Let the membrane have an area A. At k kph, the number of ccs sec^{-1} passing through the space formerly occupied by the membrane is $\dfrac{A \ k \ 1000.10^2}{60 \ 60}$ ccs sec^{-1}. If it is arbitrarily assumed that 90% of the water which would have passed seeks another path, i.e. 10% passes through and half of the U is extracted, then the membrane gathers U at the rate of $\dfrac{A\,k\,10^2}{3.6}\left[\dfrac{4.10^{-9}}{2.10^3.10}\right]$ 238

grams sec^{-1}. The amount per year works out to be about 10^{-3} A k lbs and the return at \$30/lb is 10^{-3} Ak.30. If the membrane costs \$2 per ft^2, the membrane pays for itself in about $\dfrac{1}{10k}$ years or if k is 5kph, about one week.

Of course, this calculation neglects all the ancillary costs, in particular the cost of dealing with an enormous membrane. But the method now seems worth real investigation.

The safety of fission reactors

The safety of nuclear reactors is mostly discussed in terms of the breeders, and stresses the difficulties of plutonium. A discussion of this situation is below.

However, there are significant dangers connected with the fission reactor alone. One fairly important concern is the possibility of a break-down in containment.

Supposing that containment of the material within a reactor producing one gigawatt (1000 megawatts) were broken by an accident arising from a human chance miss-action, or maliciously.[2] Then, about one-quarter of the ^{131}I content of the reactor would be distributed up to 10,000 metres over 48 of the United States at about twice the allowed dose of iodine; and about one-half of the ^{90}Sr inventory would get around into the fresh water run-off of the country to a concentration of six times more than the allowed dose.

The likelihood of such an event is low in peace time. However, the number of civil disorders which are occurring in the world is increasing; apart from civil disorders, widespread wars occur every few decades. One of the best things an enemy could do as a beginning to any war would be, instead of bombarding a country with hydrogen bombs, to have placed relatively small bombs to blow up several nuclear reactors on the first day of war. Were even one attack successful in blowing open the containing dome, the population of the country would be little concerned with their country's ability to withstand attack for some time thereafter.

What is little discussed, is the ultimate disaster connected with an atomic reactor—that it could undergo an atomic explosion. This is called the Bethe-Tait accident or critical reassembly.[3,4] It has been discussed by McCarthy and Okrend.[5] Thus, if the cooling system in a reactor failed, and the temperature rose sufficiently, the cadmium rods would melt and there is a *possibility* of the mass becoming critical in the sense that the nuclear chain reaction would begin. The likelihood of this is low, even in the case that the reactor was blown up by chemical explosion, but a low-yield disassembly—'a nuclear fizzle'[6]—would be enough to break open the steel container around the reactor, and burst the contents into the atmosphere. This would result in a catastrophe and its results in numbers of deaths is difficult to calculate, for it would be necessary to continue to consume water, and this would have six times the allowed dose of ^{90}Sr.

An argument occasionally proferred is that atomic reactors have existed for some years and that no disaster of the kind envisaged has occurred. However, 4000 atomic reactors are planned for the U.S. within the next generation, and this is approximately 100 times more than that which has existed in the past decade. An increase in the chance of a happening will thus occur. The damage to the country, and indeed to the world, from *one* such disaster would be great. It is usually suggested that with extreme precaution the chain of circumstances leading to such a disaster could be always avoided. However, this does not apply to situations arising from internal violence, or from war.*

The breeding process

The amount of uranium 238 to that of 235 is some 140 to 1, so if it were possible to transmute the 238 isotope into some other nucleus which itself is fissile, then there would be a possibility of increasing the amount of available active atomic fuel by more than 100 times. In this case, Ur could be an energy source for around one millenium.

Two kinds of reactions are used for breeding. One is based upon uranium 238:

$$U238 + n \rightarrow U239$$
$$U239 \rightarrow Np239 + \beta$$
$$Np239 \rightarrow Pu239$$

Uranium 238 can be turned into plutonium 239, and *this is fissile.*

Thus, plutonium 239 is fissionable by neutrons. By capturing one neutron, the infertile 238 has been transmuted into fissionable 239.

The second breeding cycle is based upon thorium and gives:

$$Th232 + n \rightarrow Th233$$
$$Th233 \rightarrow Pa233 + \beta$$
$$Pa233 \rightarrow U233 + \beta$$

Uranium 233 is fissile and could be used to give energy.

Under technological conditions, the plutonium formed in the first cycle would be a mixture of isotopes of plutonium, Pu239, Pu240, Pu241 and Pu242.

Uranium and thorium resources in reference to the breeder processes

The amount of uranium and thorium at various price levels is shown in Tables 5.I and 5.II.

TABLE 5.I: US Uranium Resources (ERDA [II-5]) (1000 t U)[7]

Cost Range[a] ($/lb U_3O_8)	Identified	Potential	Total
0-15	400	1200	1600
15-30	140	930	1070
at 100	Chattanooga shales 60-80 ppm		4000
at 150	Chattanooga shales 25-60 ppm		6000

[a]*Costs*, not prices.

---

*The accident at Three Mile Island, Pa., in April, 1979, was associated with the generation of a huge hydrogen bubble. The lesson is that unforeseen events supersede expectations.

TABLE 5.II: Thorium and Uranium Resources (World Energy
Conference of 1974, [II-4]) (1000 t U)[7]

		Identified	Potential	Total
USA[a]	Thorium[c]	320	?	—
	Uranium	730	1300	2030
World[b]	Thorium[d]	800	1960	2760
	Uranium	1960	2080	4040

[a] Data from Bureau of Mines, Bulletin 650, 1971;

[b] Total of 28 non-communist countries in the case of U, and a total of 14 non-communist countries and the USSR in the case of Th, including the US;

[c] Only up to $10/lb;

[d] Cost range mostly unknown.

If the cost of the uranium is allowed to rise to $200 per kilogram, the amounts of uranium available would be in the tens of megatons.

Belostotsky suggested that the amount of uranium and thorium has been under-estimated.[8] He points out that during the energy crisis of 1973/74, following the 400% increase in crude oil prices, there was a considerable stimulus to finding new nuclear fuels. Estimates are based on an earlier date and might now be considerably increased.

However, even the most optimistic estimates on uranium ores make it clear that breeder reactors are necessary if non-fusion atomic energy is to be a massive source of energy to replace fossil fuels.*

In conclusion: breeders would make a base to our energy and, with hydrogen as the intermediate fuel, could make a possible world.[9] The counter-argument is connected with the health hazards which plutonium brings. It does not seem that there can be any answer to the danger of such hazards in a civil disturbance or war. A solar source would remove such perils. If its cost is competitive, and its feasibility proved by the use of H_2 as a medium, it makes breeders *unnecessary*.

Breeders and fission reactors

The breeder is a fission reactor but, because of a different disposition of the cadmium-absorbing rods which are inserted to modify the chain reaction occurring among the U^{235}, the neutrons are used to act on the surrounding mass of U^{238}.

The U^{238}, when irradiated, does not undergo fission (thus producing a large amount of energy) but a nuclear reaction, to form transuranic elements (the aim of the original work which was being carried out by Hahn and Meitner, and by Fermi, when they discovered that U^{235} undergoes fission to barium and krypton, giving out a large amount of energy).

The principal product of the breeding process is plutonium. Plutonium is like U^{235} in that it can be induced, under bombardment, to undergo *fission*, and thus produce a large amount of energy per act.

---

*Such a conclusion involves the assumption that extraction of uranium from rocks, or from the sea, makes fission-based energy using such materials more expensive than breeder energy. However the final price of breeder electricity is not precisely defined, because of hard-to-estimate final safety costs.

The efficiency of breeding turns out to be less good than was expected in the original plan on this concept, which supposed that each U^{235} could produce more than 100 Pu atoms.

Breeder reactors

To get breeders to breed has been the main difficulty of breeder technology to date. A breeder reactor which does not breed is still a useful atomic reactor.

What are actual breeding ratios?

The amount of data on this point is small, because few breeders have been built. Carle,[10] a spokesman for the French Phoenix breeder reactor, says that the early experiments with this reactor have shown a breeding ratio of 1.1. This means that each U^{235} creates not one atom of plutonium but, on average, 1.1. However, Carle states that a ratio of 1.2 and perhaps even 1.4 may be obtained from the next development of the Phoenix reactor, Super Phoenix.

The importance of breeder reactors

There can be no future in atomic energy without successful breeder reactors, unless Ur could be economically extracted from the sea or granite rocks. Ordinary fission reactors would burn up the available land-based uranium ores in some 20-30 years.

Negative aspects of breeder reactors

There has been much that is negative stated about the breeder and, in fact, President Carter has reduced the American breeder effort, rather than speeded it up, which one might have thought the situation demanded (if there is not yet to be building of solar collectors on a massive scale).

The following matters are difficulties in respect to the breeder:

1. The amount of money which has been invested on research in breeder reactors. This is about 6 billion dollars, taking into account all world research. Only one billion dollars has been spent in developing the light-water fission reactor.
2. In spite of the development costs, few breeders have been built. The number which have been attempted since 1953 is less than ten: only two remain working. When one takes into account the advantages of a successful breeder, and looks at the development expenditure so far, one becomes receptive to the view of E. Teller, the former director of the Livermore Laboratory, who has stated that 'breeders don't work'.*[11]
3. Even after the 6 billion dollars, engineers say that the breeder reactor will not be ready for mass production until the end of the century.
4. The low breeding ratio is disappointing. If it is not possible to go above 1.2, the lasting time of Ur fuel would not be hundreds of years.
5. Apart from the development costs of breeders, the final costs will be more than that of a fission reactor. The electricity developed will be greater than the several cents per kilowatt hour which is the projection for the fission

---

* It seems that the 'don't work' refers to the low breeding ratio or to the poor economics.

reactor. The original promise of cheap electricity from atomic energy has not been fulfilled. Much of the cost of the breeder reactor comes from the safety precautions which become more, rather than less, with time.

6. Finally, breeder reactors produce *plutonium* as a waste product and this has a half-life of 25,000 years. There is fear about the development of massive quantities of plutonium.

If the breeder reactor is so doubtful after so many years, costs so much, and is uncertain in respect to breeding ratio, why is it necessary to develop it when massive solar collection is relatively simple, and the price of electricity (therefore hydrogen) would be competitive with that from breeder reactors?[12]

The development of breeder reactors involves a dangerous technology, involving commitments to future generations. Is it a *necessary* technology in view of the potential availability of massive solar power?

What kind of breeder reactor?

Hitherto only one kind of breeder reactor has been discussed. It is called the liquid-metal-faced breeder reactor. However, Weinberg has pointed out that it is unwise to develop only one type of model,[13] whereas in fission reactors, there are six types of models (the pressurised water reactor; the boiling water reactor; the Canadian thorium cycle CANDU reactor; the steam-generating heavy water reactor; the high temperature reactor; the graphite moderated reactor) in current use.

Weinburg's idea is that we need to experiment with different types of breeder reactors—Weinberg stresses the molten salt breeder. He points out that there is as yet no successful processing.

The breeder reactor programme is in trouble, though there is enthusiasm for it in France and the U.S.S.R. One reason for the poor American contribution is commercial: if breeders were built massively now, as their electricity is more expensive than that of fission reactors, they could not make a profit. Companies build reactors in the U.S.—in Europe the research is government based. But companies cannot build until the market for the more expensive product is there. And, after that, it will take a decade to build one reactor.

There is little time left before we feel the energy turn-down from the oil and gas exhaustion. Normal market conditions should be replaced by the functioning of an Executive Energy Authority and its building of appropriate energy converters in time to meet the down-turn in available oil and natural gas, expected in the 1990s.

Pollution from fission and breeder reactors

Introduction

It seems likely that if there had not been such a large capital investment already made in breeder research, they might by now have been abandoned, in view of the difficulties anticipated from the large stores of plutonium wastes which would build up throughout the world.

However, a commitment has been made, and it is necessary to show that it has not been a good one and that, from the point of view of consumers, it is advisable to tread water before going rapidly in another direction.

Claimed emotional content of reactions against nuclear energy

Many who support the use of nuclear energy claim that action groups which have been formed to combat the promulgation of nuclear energy have an emotional content in the basis of their action.

Whatever the degree of emotional content of some group efforts by lay individuals, there is a solid scientific basis to objections to nuclear energy. These scientific objections will be presented, following the work of F. P. J. Robotham.[14]

GROUPINGS OF SCIENTIFIC OBJECTIONS TO THE DEVELOPMENT OF NUCLEAR ENERGY

The objections may be put under three headings:

1. Mining, milling and fuel production: Here the objection pertains to the release of radioactive gases into the atmosphere.
2. Reactor operation: Some dangers which are associated with the operation of a massive number of reactors: a sufficient basis for judgment does not yet exist because of the small number of reactors hitherto built.
3. Fuel processing and waste management: This refers to both radioactive wastes and to the stage in which recycling of the fuel occurs. Difficulties arise from accidental venting to the atmosphere.[15]

The situation of actions connected with the production of atomic energy can be looked at in two ways:

1. Those relevant to an ideal situation in which human failure is eliminated;
2. Those likely to occur in view of the fact that machines break down, and the humans who operate them, and who have to carry out specific operations in emergencies, are fallible.

Estimates must obviously be based upon the latter situation. Most unfortunately, the estimates of the Atomic Energy Commissions of the world have been based upon scenarios of the former situation.

There is an insidiousness about the dangers from the development of atomic energy. The automobile kills about 100 people per day in the U.S., a greater rate of killing than that which occurred during the Vietnam War. However, no objection is issued against the automobile: it is vital to our existence. Furthermore, it can be stated the automobile chooses its victims randomly over the population, whereas those going to war feel picked upon.

When a person is killed by a traffic accident, there is no doubt of the immediate cause of the event. The difficulty with deaths due to nuclear air pollution is that they occur by means of cancer, several years after the person has been exposed (mostly unconsciously) to the radiation which causes them. It is seldom clear that an individual has died as a result of nuclear radiations. All that is clear is that a certain increase in the number of deaths occur in correlation with the presence of a reactor. The spread of nuclear energy would cause a creeping-up of the death rate, especially for those living near reactors and processing plants.

MINING AND MILLING

All uranium ores slowly produce the radioactive gas radon. When uranium ores are mined, the earth over the ores is removed so that radon is brought into contact with the miners. The U.S. Environmental Protection Agency has estimated that 1,000 miners have developed lung cancer because they have worked on uranium mining.

After the uranium has been mined, the residual ore is in the form of a sand called 'tailings'. These contain thorium 230, the half-life of which is 76,000 years. The tailings continue to let out radioactive radon during this time.

The effects of the release of radon 222 on the American population have been calculated by Pohl as being equivalent to 400 deaths per gigawatt year.[16] As the population is 250.10^6 and the use per person about 10,000 watts, the total use 2.5×10^{12} watts or 2.5×10^3 gigawatts, the deaths per year would be 800,000 from radon, far more than the deaths from cars (but see below).

Pohl's estimate is greater than the estimate quoted for nuclear energy deaths of 0.01 deaths per gigawatt year, and one death per gigawatt year among workers in the nuclear industries.[13] Comparable deaths from electricity reduction from coal are estimated to be about 10 deaths per gigawatt year.

The mining and milling dangers could be reduced: tailings could be reburied, and the radon escape reduced. The radon exposure to the workers could be reduced by a Code of Practice.

DANGERS ARISING DURING REACTOR OPERATION[14]

In considering what can go wrong in reactor operation, it is appropriate to recall that the reactors we are considering are mostly the boiling water reactor and the pressurised water reactor. The stress upon water and its cooling action will be clear as we go on.

One of the points concerning the operation of a reactor is its *cooling*. As the reaction produces heat, were it not cooled, the core—where the heat is produced—would heat up the surroundings and disastrous things would occur (see below). Therefore, one of the points of safety is the continuation of cooling.[9]

The abbreviation LOCA is used for the discussion, and these letters refer to what is regarded as the maximum credible accident which is a *Loss Of Cooling Accident.*

The steel domes around atomic reactors are meant to contain the steam from a LOCA, which would be radioactive, but their integrity is based upon calculation. It is simply not known whether a dome would really hold after a LOCA.

The temperature of operation of a nuclear reactor is some 330°C in respect to the cooling water, which is therefore under pressure.

It is necessary to follow what would happen were a LOCA to occur and the core to heat up. The first thing would be that the moderator would be burnt and this would stop the nuclear reaction occurring, because the appropriate distance between the rods would no longer be maintained. This would reduce the heat production from the reactor by about 94%. However, there would be a remaining 6% of heat which would come from the fission products themselves. Considering then a 1000 MW_e reactor, which would therefore be approximately 3000 MW_{th} reactor, there would be 180 megawatts of heat coming out of the core, after a LOCA.

What would happen in a highly specialised structure—made indeed for such accidents—if one happened? The core would fall to the bottom of the container. The container, however, is 15 centimeters thick steel and it would contain the core for some time, about half an hour.[14] The core, with its 180 megawatts of heat production, would then fall to the bottom of the second containment vessel, and would heat this up and pass through in about one day.

If it continued to heat, then the core would end up about 100 metres underground, having sealed itself into the surroundings.*

There would be a release of radioactive gases including xenon, krypton, and radioactive iodine. We have been considering what would occur with a reactor melt-down and core-release if no auxiliary cooling were brought into play, but if cooling were played on to the core after the melt-down, i.e. an attempt were made to cool down a 180 megawatt source, then strontium 90 would be released, and would come into the atmosphere inside the dome. The great question is—would the dome hold?

If the dome did not hold, then 3000 people would be killed in the first week, due to radiation sickness, and 30,000 people would die over the next 20 years, as a result of cancers which could not, of course, be identified directly as being due to the accident.[14]

We now have to discuss whether a LOCA is likely. We shall discuss a famous near-miss of a LOCA and refer to other possibilities. As the causes of LOCAs are human failures, it seems likely that a LOCA will occur. Thus, no company in the U.S. will bear the risk of insuring an atomic reactor.

Correspondingly, the Swiss Government, in 1973, contemplating buying reactors from the U.S., demanded experimental proof for the fact that the results of a LOCA could be contained within the steel dome. This could not be given.

There is weakness in estimating the likelihood of dome failure, because an experimental test of a LOCA would be so expensive to carry out, and therefore mathematical models have been used to estimate the accident situation. However (*cf.* Kendall & Monglewar[17]), the difficulty in relying on the mathematical model is that they do not take into account the human element; nor do they take into account gaps in engineering knowledge, particularly in the break-down probability of materials under abnormal conditions.

The situation projected by the American A.E.C. (therefore by all other A.E.C.s) may be unduly optimistic. Karl Hocevar, an expert in reactor safety, an author of the THETA code which has been used in the analysis of the emergency application of cooling in light-water reactors, left the U.S. Atomic Energy Commission, Idaho facility, in 1974, and his resignation letter referred to what he considered to be the 'hood-winking of the public' by the Commission.[14]

THE RASMUSSEN REPORT
The most famous report which considers reactor safety and operation is the Rasmussen Report. What this said, essentially, is that the probability of accidents is negligible.

---

* This situation is called 'The China Syndrome'.

The following criticisms have been made of the Rasmussen Report:
1. The base of some 60 reactors in the U.S.—some of which have been only operative for a few years—is too small a sample upon which to base statistics for the likelihood of operational disasters.
2. The systems considered in the report were those of simple reactor systems, whereas future reactor systems will be complicated.
3. The report assumes that many things which do happen in reactors cannot go wrong. However, there is a possibility that anything may go wrong. There are many happenings in the reactor, so that, even if the probability of each malfunction is very small, the large number of things gives rise to a significant probability of failure. This is neglected in the Rasmussen Report.
4. Speed has criticised the probability statistics used in the Rasmussen Report and considers the report, on this ground, to be fallacious.[14]
5. The Rasmussen Report neglects the probability of human error. However, it is this which is the greatest danger in reactor safety.

An example of the inapplicability of the Rasmussen approach is given by the functioning of the Apollo engine in the space programme. The Apollo engine is a simple device compared with an atomic reactor. Applying the Rasmussen statistics, Robotham reports that the Apollo engine would have had a failure rate of 1 in 10,000 missions.[14] However, the actual failure rate was 4 in 100. In the ground failures, 20% of them occurred from functions, the failure of which would have been considered impossible in a Rasmussen analysis. 35% of the failures in flight occurred due to failures which would have been regarded as impossible in the Rasmussen approach. More impressive still is the numerical application of Rasmussen analysis to reactor function. For example, Rasmussen considers multiple fractures would occur in boiling water reactors with a probability of 2 for 10^{18} reactor years. In fact, 15 failures have occurred in 10^3 reactor years.

THE BROWN FERRY INCIDENT

The effect of human error is well shown by the Brown Ferry Incident in Dakota, Alabama. This occurred because a technician was measuring the flow of air from one room to another, using a candle to indicate the direction. The candle flame set fire to some urethane insulation. The urethane set fire to the insulation around some cables. This set fire to the mechanism which controlled the cooling of the reactor core, and destroyed vital equipment which should have come into operation when the cooling mechanism failed.

Because the cooling of the reactor core was destroyed or damaged, the water which was around the reactor fell from 200 inches above the core to 48 inches from the core. It was stopped by an emergency arrangement.

The candle and the urethane is an example of human error. However, several other things occurred which would not be taken into account in Rasmussen analysis. The fire extinguishers turned out to have been filled with a liquid inappropriate to fighting the kind of fire concerned; the threads on the hoses would not match each other.

The stark point is that were an accident to occur, the deaths would be so bad that it is difficult to contemplate them. But the present prospect is of construction of several thousand reactors, compared with the 60 or so now in operation. The chance of an accident occurring will be increased by one order of magnitude.

DANGERS ARISING FROM INCREASE IN RADIOACTIVITY OF THE ATMOSPHERE

According to Robotham,[14] the average figure for the time 1969-1974 in the U.S. for the increase in radioactivity is: 1.275 MAN-REM. The MAN-REM measures the dose received by a population multiplied by the number of people within that population.

Let us suppose that by the year 2010, there would be 2000 reactors, each of 1000 megawatts. Then, the total dose would be $1.275 \times 1000 \times 1000$. Each plant would operate at about 70% capacity so that the number of MAN-REMs would be $1.275 \times 1000 \times 1000 \times 70/100 = 890 \times 10^3$ MAN-REM, or about 4-5 milli REMs per person in the U.S.

The average natural background is 100 milli REMs per year and the exposure due to X-ray examinations and so forth may be as high as 60 milli REMs per person/year. Hence, the situation does not look bad but there are two caveats. Firstly, there will be significant numbers of cancers caused by this extra radiation and we can take the estimate made as about one cancer death per 0.5×10^3 MAN-REM if irradiation occurs when a person is 25 years old, and one death per 2×10^3 MAN-REM if the person is aged 45.

The number of deaths caused by radiation would then be between about 450 and 1800, nearer the latter, as the average age in the U.S. is nearer 25 than 45.[18]

However, this estimate is based upon experiments on damage which have arisen from doses of radiation injected into people for short times when the radiation intensity is strong.[19] It is now known that the radiation damage is greater, per dose, if the dose is absorbed slowly (as it is under natural conditions), and it may be that the deaths per person to be expected from the above amount of increase in radiation would be greater than calculated.

BIOLOGICAL DAMAGE ARISING FROM RADIATION FROM RADIOACTIVE SUBSTANCES

After the discovery by Becquerel that some kind of radiation was coming from uranium contained in minerals, it was assumed that deleterious health effects were associated with a relatively high level of radioactivity, and that there was no detectable effect on human health below a certain critical level of radiation, measured by the amount which entered the body per unit times.

One argument in favour of this concept was the fact that life had evolved in the presence of a low level of environmental radiation; and the diagnostic X-rays did not seem to give any overt effects.

The present position is that, during the 1970s, evidence has developed which seems to undermine the basic postulate of a lower level of radiation intensity under which no damage occurs. It is now suggested that all radiation damages cells. The presence of atomic reactors will cause a very slight increase in radioactivity in the atmosphere. If there is no lower limit to biological damage, even such slight increases in the background radiation will cause some health risks. This conclusion has influence upon our concepts of the likelihood of being able to utilise atomic energy successfully.

NUCLEAR RADIATIONS

There are two basic forms of nuclear radiation, wave and corpuscular. Gamma rays represent the former and alpha particles represent the latter. Neutrons are the most important example of this class.

Another type of corpuscular radiation is the fission fragments, isotopes of former chemical elements such as barium and strontium.

The wave and corpuscular forms of radiation are absorbed in matter through collision with electrons in the atoms of molecules and these collisions in turn give rise to fast-moving electrons which cause ionization and excitation. The actual biological damage in the cells is due to these rapidly moving electrons. The spatial distribution and density of the energy per unit distance will be different depending upon which kind of radiation originally produced the electrons.

Thus, heavy particles produce a region of high ionization in their wake, but do not travel far. Gamma rays produce a low density of ionization but over a larger distance.

MECHANISM OF BIOLOGICAL DAMAGE[20]

One kind of damage is of a bullet-like type. Molecular bonds are broken by the electrons. This is the principal cause of the DNA damage in the nuclei of cells—genetic damage—which may be transmitted to future generations if it is not repaired before the cell reproduces itself.

The second type of damage is indirect. It occurs by the production of highly reactive chemical species in the aqueous fluids between the cells and then this chemical species diffuses to the cell surface. This indirect action is, for example, involved if either the dissolved oxygen in the cell fluid captures an electron to become O_2^-, or the water in the cell is reacted upon by the electrons to give rise to the negative oxygen ion.

Thereafter, the oxygen ion causes oxidation of phospholipid cell membranes. As will be seen below, one of the most important points is that *biological damage is different, for the same dose, depending upon the rate at which this dose is delivered.* Until recent time, this fact had not been known. It was thought that the particles taken into the body per year, independent of the intensity at which the body had collected them, was the important quantity.

Damage to cells is not only proportional to the amount of energy pushed into them. Much depends on the type of particle which is doing the damage. Thus, a massive densely-ionizing particle, such as an alpha particle, plowing into the nucleus of a cell, is more likely to break strands of DNA molecules, thus causing genetic damage, than is a beta ray. This is shown in Fig. 5.la.[19] Such particles of course come from uranium, radium and thorium and these are elements, some of which are in atomic reactors.

Now, in respect to the indirect chemical type of biological damage, a different picture occurs. The molecule which does the damage has to diffuse from the point at which it is produced, some hundreds of Angstroms from the cell surface which it may damage. The chance of it being able to reach the cell surface *and then adsorb on it* is affected by the local concentration of excited molecules.

Thus, if excited molecules are high in concentration near the cell-surface-solution interface, they are repelled by each other, and do not settle down

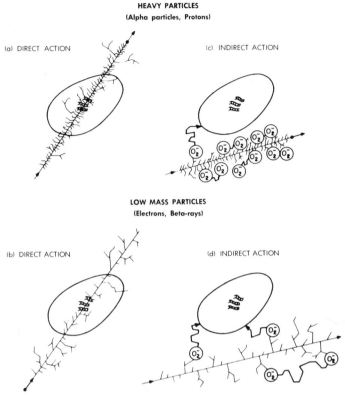

Fig. 5.1. Basic Modes of Action of ionising particles from radioactive substances on living cells.[19]
A larger fraction of O_2^- reaches the cell surface in (d) than in (c).

on the cell surface. Hence, a high flux of radiation, carrying out damage by the chemical mediation method, does less damage than a low flux of this radiation when the O_2^- molecules diffuse to the cell surface, and are not repelled by other molecules, thus settling onto the cell surface and being then in a position to cause chemical destruction of elements in cells.[19] When the dose rate is high, there are, at a given time, competitor ions at the interface and hence each given ion has less chance of adsorption because of the repulsion offered by the other ions (Fig. 5.1).[20]

We can now begin to understand that medical diagnostic X-rays can be biologically less damaging, because they consist of a rapid pulse of high dose than the same total amount of radiation produces by low-level background radiation.

THE FUNDAMENTAL WORK OF PETKAU[19,20]

In radio-chemical studies of the action of radiation of synthetic phospholipid membranes immersed in water, Petkau uses a diagnostic X-ray machine operating at 26 rads per minute.[19] He found it took the enormous dose of 3,500 rads to break his phospholipid membranes, about 35,000 times the annual dose from the normal background radiation, which is about 0.1 rads in most parts of the world. Thus, the phospholipid membranes were unlikely to be damaged by the typical diagnostic X-rays.

However, when Petkau substituted a very small amount of radioactive sodium salt in the water instead of the external X-ray beam, and the dose-rate was reduced to only one millirad per minute, he found it took only 0.7 rads to rupture the membrane, or some 5,000 times less than with the high-intensity medical X-rays.

Distinction has first to be made between the two types of radiations, the X-radiation and the beta particles from the Na^{22} in the radioactive salt. This could give rise to a factor of 10-20 difference and the rest had to be accounted for in terms of dose rate.

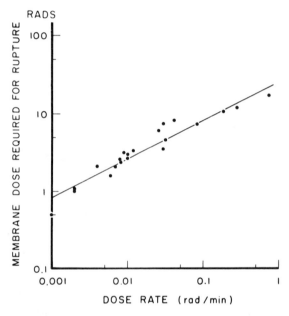

Fig. 5.2. Effect of dose rate on the total dose required to rupture a cell membrane.[19]

Fig. 5.2 shows the effect of dose-rate and *there is a decrease in the absorbed dose (needed to cause detectable damage) measured in rads, as the dose-rate is reduced.*

This is a fundamental result. It has bearing on the danger of radiation from radioactive substances. Thus, if experiments are done in the laboratory with a high dose-rate, and it is found that no damage can be measured with a certain total dose, delivered at this high dose-rate, it does not mean that the same dose delivered at a lower dose-rate will also not cause damage.

This discovery leads to a modification of the previous viewpoint on the danger of radiations from radioactive substances.

Somewhat later, Petkau and Chelack were able to show that it was indeed the presence of O_2^- radical which was involved in causing biological damage.[21]

IMPLICATIONS OF THE PETKAU WORK FOR RISKS ARISING FROM
VERY LOW DOSES OF ENVIRONMENTAL RADIATION

The increase in the concentration of radioactive substances which would arise from a full nuclear economy is a very small one—in fact, the increase is less than that of the background radiation. Therefore, if Petkau's work is to be significant, it is important to show[22] that the decrease in the dose-rate needed to produce biological damage holds down to the small dose-rates of 10-100 millirads per year produced by global fall-out and the release from nuclear facilities.[23,24]

This appears to have been done by two different types of analysis, one of which involved the precursors of blood cells in the bone marrow of rats,[25] and the other of which dealt with the permeability of human red cells exposed to X-rays a few times above the background level.[26]

Thus, with the experiment with rats, it was found that when the animals were taken in pairs and exposed to strontium 90, *with equal doses*, the damage was worse the *lower* the concentration (i.e. the lower the *rate* at which the particles were received). This is the same indication as that of Petkau.[21]

Correspondingly, in the work with X-rays, the permeability of the erythrocyte membranes of those exposed was compared with that of other individuals with no X-ray exposure. A plot of the percentage increase in per-

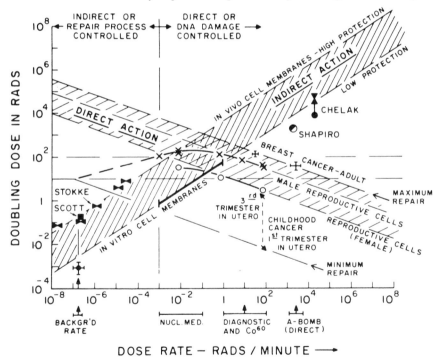

DOSE RATE — RADS / MINUTE →

Fig. 5.3. Effect of dose rate on total dose needed to produce a given amount of damage.[19] The indirect action causes the critical *dose* required to cause biological damage to *decrease* as the dose *rate* declines towards those of the background radiation. This means that the dose needed to cause a given degree of damage when it is administered quickly in the laboratory tests will be much bigger than the dose needed to cause damage when this is taken in slowly as in actuality.

meability showed that there was a more rapid rise for the lowest exposure and a levelling out of the highest exposure in consistency with the Petkau work.

Thus, at very low dose-rates, it is the indirect chemically mediated damage to cell structure such as the phosfilibrium membrane which dominates. The situation is summarized in Fig. 5.3.

The reverse occurs with the genetic damage experiments, and this suggests that genetic damage arises from the direct hit type of process, and not from the indirect chemically-mediated damage. At low dose-rates below, say, 10^{-4} rads per minute (natural background dose 10^{-7} rads per minute), the indirect chemically-mediated damage has the lower doubling rate (Fig. 3). Thus, *in a population exposed to background radiation, it would be the chemically mediated rate which would give rise to the health damage.*

Such damage would include diseases normally associated with ageing, such as diseases of the lungs, heart and circulatory system, for these would be expected to increase as the production of free radicals leads to an increased deficiency of free radical damage to cell membranes.

It seems likely that ageing effects arise from radiations by a mechanism of this type. This alters the significance of the low-dose increases which would occur were atomic reactors used as a main source of energy.

Thus, work on increased biological damage from slowly received small doses of radio-active materials casts doubt upon previous conclusions which have been made on the safety features from atomic reactors. *Small increases in the dose-rate, even smaller than that of background, may have an effect upon health.*

The medical evidence for damage by low-level radiation

This has been obtained in several cases—for example, that of uranium miners.[27,28]

Developmental defects in new-born children exposed to high background radiation from local rocks and soils has also been noted.[29]

Thorium-bearing sands, for example the monasite sands in Brazil, have been shown to give rise to chromosome abnormalities.[30] Intrauterine exposure of a developed infant has been studied by Alice Stewart at Oxford.[31] Stewart's work was the first to show that total doses from background radiation in one year can produce health effects in man. She found that mothers who had been exposed to three X-ray films had twice the likelihood that their children would develop leukemia before the age of 10 than those who were exposed to no X-rays during pregnancy. Correspondingly, there has been evidence that fall-out from radioactive testing has given rise to congenital anomalies. This was described by Le Vann,[32] who showed that for children born in Alberta in 1959 there was a low rate of anatomically recognisable birth defects. However, a second survey carried out in 1962 for children born the previous year showed a greater incidence of such defects. Le Vann found that the greatest increase took place for children born closest to the Arctic Circle, where the long-lived high altitude fall-out from the large series of 22 nuclear tests carried out by Russia at Novaya Semelya in 1958 would affect children born in that region more than those born in southern Alberta.

The net result of the dose rate-radiation-damage work

The basic result of work on the relation of dose-rate to health damage has been to make us realise that we must take into account effects of small doses of natural and man-made background radiation, because they are received very slowly by the body.

This new concept explains fetal leukemia deaths, and their correlation with radio isotopes in milk during nuclear testing. It enables us to understand the efficiency of radicals in damaging phospholipid membranes: the high concentration near the interface produced by the high dose-rate does not allow adsorption of so many oxygens as a low dose-rate, when the oxygens do not repel each other, because fewer arrive at the surface per unit time.

Ageing is partly related to the free radicals which are produced by radioactive substances.[33]

The implication of these results is against the use of atomic energy, because, whatever precautions are taken, there will be some small increases in the background radiation of the atmosphere—but those increases now seem likely to have an effect on *ageing and debilitation.*

Disposal of waste products[34]

1. General

Of the difficulties of nuclear energy, that concerned with waste products is the most well known. A practical solution has not been found.

2. The origin of the wastes

When a reactor operates, it burns only one-third of its uranium before the fuel element must be removed. The element is then taken to a processing plant and dissolved in acid. The solution obtained thereby is chemically divided into three parts:
(a) the part containing uranium;
(b) the part containing the fission products from uranium;
(c) the plutonium.
The first stream, the uranium, will be concentrated, then recycled back into the reactor and used again.

The second stream, the fission products from the uranium, contains mainly strontium 90 and cesium 137. The active life is in the region of 1000 years.

At present the products are kept in solution. The solution boils and water has to be added. The metal vessels corrode and tend to crack. Thus, 450,000 gallons of liquid have entered the soil around Hanford, Washington. Such leakage eventually reaches the water table.

The idea proposed by the U.S.A.E.C. (therefore, all other A.E.C.s) is to wait for 5-8 years after the second stream fission products have been produced in any given year, and then *glassify* them. This means introduce them into a glassy material, and cool the glass so that products may be taken away in glass bricks.

These bricks would be placed in salt mines, in regions not subject to earthquakes, and the radiation from them would then be negligible.

The objections here are two:
(a) The idea has not yet been implemented over 25 years of operation of atomic reactors. Why not?

(b) The glassy material in which the fission products will be placed is not stable and would decompose and devitrify,[35] thus freeing the radioactive materials. However, were they by then sufficiently deeply in the salt mines, perhaps this would not matter. Transporting glass bricks to the mines gives rise to some anxiety, for accidents (road, train) will certainly occur.

Dealing with the third stream

The third stream contains the transuranic elements, the new elements produced in the reactor, among which are plutonium 239, which represents the most important waste material; plutonium 238; and neptunium 237.

What order of magnitude of these wastes do we have to deal with? A single 1000 megawatt (e) reactor produces 230 kg of plutonium per year. Even if we suppose that there were only 1000 reactors operating by the year 2000, we would be producing from this alone 230,000 kg of plutonium and world-wide the production would be about 700,000 kg per year.

The separation of plutonium from the rest of the wastes would occur at a processing plant and at the moment this is only 98.5-99% efficient. Let us be hopeful that the efficiency can be raised to 99.9%. We would then have about 700 kg per year which will have to be stored because it cannot be processed back to the reactor.

This is 700×10^9 micrograms, and by the year 2000 the world population may be as much as 7.10^9 people, whereupon the amount of plutonium per person would be 100 micrograms, stored somewhere.

The difficulty is: where? All answers (e.g., that in terms of salt domes) involve transportation over long distances, and the dangers of accidental spillage and hijacking.

Hijacking

It is easy to make an atomic bomb. With 700,000 kg of plutonium per year being made, it is difficult to avoid the conclusion that some amount will be stolen. Unaccounted losses have already occurred. For example, 200 tons of uranium have disappeared at sea.[14]

The introduction of hijacking has led to certain possibilities in respect to the presence of enormous quantities of plutonium. The protection measures (several hundred soldiers surrounding each reactor; shadowing persons who have had an opportunity to steal plutonium), promises a nightmare world.

Experience of processing plants to date[14]

The fuel reprocessing (taking the plutonium back to the reactor, etc.) was tried at West Valley, N.Y. between 1967 and 1972, where 600 tons of fuel was processed. In 14 separate incidents, 39 workers were exposed to excessive levels of fission products and plutonium. In the last year of operation the company running the plant lost 7 million dollars. It would cost 600 million dollars to improve the plant, and it has been abandoned. It still contains 2 million litres of high level waste.

The G.E. Company has spent 5 years and 64 million dollars developing a plant at Morris, Illinois: this has now been abandoned.

One plant is building at Barnwell, South Carolina. The estimate in 1974 was 100 million dollars. The plant is now expected to open in 1985 with a cost of 850 million dollars.

The views of scientific groups outside the Atomic Energy Commissions

Several scientific groups have made statements criticizing development of a plutonium economy. The Margaret Mead statement summarized the views of a Committee of 21 persons during three Nobel laureates. The final paragraph reads:

> The unprecedented hazards of a plutonium economy demand an unprecedented political response. These are hazards so grave that every citizen should have a voice in deciding whether this is the road to energy independence we, or anyone, should take. All who believe the technology which serves human values should join in opposing the plutonium economy and in seeking to divert into safer and more constructive channels the vast resources being devoted to nuclear power. The responsibility of these decisions cannot be delegated to nuclear experts, for the key issues are not technical or economic but social and ethical, and in a democracy these issues should be resolved in political processes.

The Flowers Report from Britain—a Standing Royal Commission on Environmental Pollution: its 6th Report on Nuclear Power and the Environment—has a statement which includes the following:

> Plutonium appears to offer unique potential for threat and blackmail against society because of its fissile properties. The construction of a crude nuclear weapon by an illicit group is credible. We are not convinced that the government has fully appreciated the implications of this possibility. Given all existing kinds of security measures, the risks from illicit activities at the present level of nuclear development are small; the concern is with the future. The unquantifiable effects of the security measures that might become necessary in a plutonium economy should be a major consideration in decisions on substantial nuclear developments.

In summary, the dangers of the plutonium picture are so great that their acceptance would only be justified if there were no alternative. But, if a plutonium economy is not possible, an atomic base to the economy is less credible, for then its achievement as a long-term replacement for oil and natural gas would depend on Ur recovery from granite rocks or from the sea.

Summary of the difficulties of a nuclear economy

Mining and milling operations give dangers to miners—would, and do, cause cancers among the miners. The reactor-operating situation at present is threatening. With sufficient precautions, increased costs and enormous care, these difficulties could probably be overcome.

Plutonium manufactured and stored in large quantities is too dangerous to accept. A future nuclear economy based upon breeders hence appears socially undesirable.

The major political question at the time is why research and development of alternatives to such a dangerous path are being funded by the Department of Energy at less a level than those of coal and nuclear, where the risk factors seem much higher than with alternatives utilising renewable resources.

The projected economics of fission reactors

There have been many accounts of the costs of electricity from fission reactors, and some of these reports are referenced here.

It now appears certain that the costs of electricity generated from nuclear power plants will be lower than the costs of electricity generated from coal, and one-third the cost of electricity generated from oil (see Table 5. III).[36]

Thus, for 1975 operation, the ratio is approximately 1.3, i.e. the coal costs are about 30% more. The 1975 nuclear costs were in the region of 1.3c per kw hour and the fossil fuel costs were in the region of 1.7c per kw hour.[37]

Of course, the most important thing is to project the future and the reports which have been quoted above[38] suggest that the nuclear generation of electricity will continue to have an economic advantage through the 1980s, with the exception of the areas of the U.S. where low-cost coal is available (see Table 5.IV).

TABLE 5.III: Nuclear and Fossil-Fuel Generating Costs (Mills/KWh) Averages for 1975 Operation

| | REPORT | | | | |
| | ERDA | | | AIF | |
Costs	Nuclear	Fossil-fuel (predominantly coal)	Nuclear	Coal	Oil
Capital	7.85	6.11	—	—	—
Fuel	2.72	9.59	2.67	10.59	21.70
O&M	2.38	1.47	—	—	—
Total (Generating)	12.95	17.17	12.27	17.54	33.45

Notes: 1. ERDA Generating costs correspond to average capacity factors (C.F.) of 63.6% for nuclear and 52.5% for fossil-fuel (predominantly coal). AIF costs to C.F. of 64.4% (nuclear), 54.8% (coal) and 42.5% (oil).
2. ERDA costs are based on utility data reported to the FPC on 33 nuclear plants (totalling 43 units) and 13 multi-unit fossil-fuel plants. AIF costs are based on data reported directly to AIF by 34 utilities (TVA not included).

It is the flue gas de-sulphurization which accounts for the difference. Where no de-sulphurization is necessary, as would be the case with Western Coal in the U.S., the electricity costs may be lower from coal.*

In the studies of the 1985 situation, largely carried out by Reichle[39] (*loc. cit.*), the projected generating costs for nuclear electricity are not thought to vary with the part of the country, though it will have gone up to about 5c per kw hour in 1985 [sic].

The costs of reactors starting in 1985, but in 1976 dollars, are shown in Table 5.V.[38] In these calculations it is assumed that a plutonium recycle is taking place, i.e. that the plutonium produced in the first cycle of the uranium 235 is recycled back into the equipment. This is not yet occurring.†

It seems as though the nuclear situation shows advantage over the coal situation so long as no precautions have to be taken in addition to those of 1977. However, there may have been an over-optimism in this because of

---

*The currencies in the present discussion concern the year at which the estimate is made, i.e. the 1985 costs are projected to 1985 money by taking into account the expected escalation in costs of the various components of the cost estimate.
†This is perhaps the nearest one comes to Weinberg's Faustian bargain: *relatively* cheap energy could be got from nuclear reactors (compared with that from coal) but the dangers are great.

TABLE 5.IV: Nuclear And Fossil-Fuel Generating Costs (Mills/KWh)
Projected Costs From Various Sources

	FPC[1] (12/76) 1-1000 MWe 1982 U.S.			ERDA/CEP[1] (11/76)			S&L (Brandfon)[1] (9/76)		
Report (date) Units Initial Service Year Region				1-1100 MWe 1984 Eastern U.S.	2-550 MWe 1984/85 Eastern U.S.		1-1100 MWe 1985[2]	2-550 MWe 1984/85[2] Upper Middle West	
Fuel	Nucl.	Coal (with FGD)	Coal (no FGD)	Nucl.	Coal (with FGD)	Coal (no FGD)	Nucl.	Coal (with FGD)	Coal (no FGD)
Costs									
Capital	22.51	17.56	14.21	31.8	26.5	22.4	30.7	26.2	22.2
Fuel	5.40	14.60	11.79	8.0	18.9	20.7	18.4	27.0	31.1
O & M	1.92	3.92	1.92	4.0	6.1	3.5	2.5	6.4	2.7
Total (Generating)	29.83	36.08	27.92	43.8	51.5	46.6	51.6	59.6	56.0
C.F./F.C.R. (%)	60/15.75				60/15		70/18		

[1]Based on data in Table A-1, FPC 12/76 report 'Factors Affecting the Electric Power'.

[1]From ERDA critique of 11/76 CEP report 'Power Plant Performance'.

[1]'An Analysis of Power Generation Costs 1985-2000' in Electric Light & Power, 20th September, 1976.
[2]Levelized costs over 1985-2000.

TABLE 5.V: Regional Generating Costs as Presented in ERDA Publication 76-141 'Comparing New Technologies for the Electric Utilities', 9 December, 1976

For 1985 Startup National Electric Reliability Council Region	*Coal-Fired Plant Costs (Mills/KWh)*			
	Capital	*Fuel*	*O&M*	*Total*
ECAR	7.90	9.60	2.70	20.2
ERCOT	6.80	9.20	2.80	18.8
MAAC	7.60	10.60	2.70	20.9
MAIN*	6.30	11.60	1.80	19.7
MARCA*	6.20	9.50	1.90	17.6
NPCC	7.70	11.90	2.80	22.4
SERC	6.70	10.60	2.60	19.9
SPP*	6.50	9.90	1.80	18.2
WSCC*(SW)	5.80	8.80	1.90	16.5
WSCC(MT)	6.80	4.50	2.80	14.1
	LWR Plant Costs (Mills/KWh)			
ECAR	9.00	6.10	1.30	16.40
ERCOT	7.70	6.10	1.30	15.10
MAAC	8.70	6.0	1.30	16.0
MAIN	8.70	6.0	1.30	16.0
MARCA	8.70	6.0	1.30	16.0
NPCC	8.80	6.10	1.30	16.20
SERC	7.70	6.10	1.30	15.10
SPP	9.0	6.0	1.30	16.30
WSCC	8.0	6.10	1.30	15.40
WSCC	8.0	6.10	1.30	15.40

* Low Sulphur Coal (no FGD scrubber used)

the fact that the plutonium cycle is accepted although it is not yet ecologically acceptable; and because the objections made to storage of plutonium wastes may increase the costs given. The wastes are at present stored in steel canisters and not yet placed in brickettes, moved to mining shafts, etc. If anti-hijacking precautions are brought in, there may be substantial increases in costs in the nuclear case.

Breeder and solar as main source energy

Characteristic	*Breeder*	*Massive Solar*
First demonstration practical power	1953	1978
Prospect for massive technology	>2000	<2000
Environmental hazards	Great: Wastes. Hijacking. Possible health hazards of increase in background	After construction, zero
Practical fuels	Electricity and H_2	H_2 and electricity
Storage	In H_2 and batteries	In H_2
Transmission	Electricity < 1000 km; H_2 > 1000 km	H_2. Collection of energy on stationary satellites and energy beams to local sites.

Land area needed	Negligible	On earth *c.* 50sqm/kw for photovoltaics to 2 sqm/kw for OTEC. In space, 10sqm/kw.
Technology	High	Low except for orbiting satellite collector method
Potentiality	Could supply world > 100 years to present U.S. living standards	Could supply world for all time to present U.S. living standards
World research funding to date	6B	*c.* 500 m, but this mainly for minor appliances in household. OTEC not even tried as pilot plant by 1979.
Remaining R & D necessary before commercialization only dependent upon capital made available	>25 years	∿ 10 years
Degree of certainty of attainment	High in respect to low breeding ratio. Teller says: 'After 20 years' research, breeders do not work'.	Photovoltaic and solar thermal proved. Biomass does not need proof. OTEC?

SUMMARY OF CHAPTER

1. Uranium available to fission reactors from U_3O_8 ores at $30 per lb would exhaust by *c.* 2000. It *might* be economically extracted by using sea currents to press the sea through membranes, or from low concentrations in granite rocks.

2. Fission reactors are dangerous in the sense that human failings in their operation can easily be seen potentially to cause disasters and because they could be blown up by saboteurs in a civilian disturbance or war.

3. The development of a future atomic energy base is strongly dependent upon breeders. Danger apart, the breeder could make an energy base for hundreds of years.

4. Actual breeding to date is poor compared with the ideal aim.

5. Six billion dollars have been spent on breeders: this is six times more than what was spent on the development of light-water fission reactors. Teller says: 'Breeders don't work'. He refers to the low breeding ratio and poor economics. Costs of electric power from breeders will be greater than that from fission reactors. The breeder produces plutonium wastes.

6. Considerations of danger in atomic energy is based on ideal functioning. The accidents occur from human failures.

7. Mining and milling is at present dangerous: it releases radon.

8. The Loss Of Cooling Accident during reactor operation has not yet been tested. It is likely to occur sometime. The steel dome is supposed to contain the radio-active products but its efficacy is based only upon calculations.

9. The Rasmussen report (upon which much discussion of Atomic Safety is based) includes a number of instances of inapplicable logic.

10. The Brown-Ferry incident, in which a LOCA almost occurred, was due to a succession of chance failures, most of which would have been accepted as 'impossible' in an estimate of danger.

11. Estimates of deaths which will be caused at year 2000 by present-planned atomic reactors vary from around 1000 to around 100,000.

12. The work of Petkau suggests that the damage done by low-intensity radiations to biological organisms depends greatly upon the time over which the dose was received by the body. The testing done in laboratories administers small doses in short times. The same dose, delivered over a year, may be much more damaging. On this basis, the increase in background radiation arising from the presence of a large number of reactors could give rise to the indirect and delayed death of a larger number of people than has heretofore been supposed.

13. Satisfactory disposal of waste products has not yet been engineered: for 20 years schemes have been proposed but nothing realized. It does not seem possible on any scheme to allow for hijacking plutonium; or destruction of plants by attack in wartime.

14. Fission reactors will produce electricity more cheaply than coal in an estimate up to 2000. The reason is the cost of the sulphur removal, which does not include the sulphur re-interment. However, future electricity costs could be raised by increasing costs of satisfactory waste disposal and re-processing.

AUTHOR'S CHOICE OF SINGLE MOST IMPORTANT CONCLUSION FROM CHAPTER

There seems to be no practical way to forestall the plutonium involved in the breeder process passing into the hands of subversives. Plutonium is the active material in atomic bombs.

REFERENCES

1. A. B. Lovins, *World Energy Strategies* (Friends of the Earth International, London, 1975).
2. J. P. Holdren, 23rd Pugwash Conference, Aulenko, 30 August-1 September 1973; *Bulletin Atomic Scientists*, 1974, **30**, 8.
3. A. B. Lovins, *New Scientist*, 1974, **61**, 693.
4. J. Jackson & J. E. Boudreau, internal document, Argon National Laboratory, December 1972.
5. W. J. McCarthy & D. Okrendy, in D. J. Thompson & J. G. Beckerley, *The Technology of Nuclear Reactor Safety* (M.I.T. Press, 1964/70).
6. A. B. Lovins & J. H. Price, *Non-nuclear Futures* (Friends of the Earth International, 1975).
7. W. Häffle, J. P. Holdren, G. Kessler & G. L. Kulcinski, in D. Faude & M. Helms (edd.), *Fusion and Fast Breeder Reactors*, first IIASA Conference on Energy Resources, Austria, **7** (1976), pp. 23-52.
8. A. M. Belostosky, in W. Häffle, J. P. H. Holdren, G. Kessler & G. L. Kulcinski, *Fusion and Fast Breeder Reactors* (1976), **7**, 13.
9. G. M. K. Goldstein, International Conference—Energy Resources, Miami, 5-7 December 1977.
10. M. Carle, quoted by G. Vandryes, *Nuclear News*, April 1975, p.82.
11. E. Teller, after-dinner speech at Miami THEME Conference on Hydrogen Energy, 1974.

12. J. E. Perrott, Economic Assessment of Solar Energy Conversion, International Solar Energy Society, Conference C12 at the Royal Institution, July, 1977.
13. A. Weinberg, *Nuclear News,* June 1975, pp. 78, 96.
14. F. P. J. Robotham, presented to the Australian-New Zealand Association for the Advancement of Science, Melbourne, 1977.
15. H. A. Kurstedt, J. A. Nachless & P. S. Kurstedt, paper at the Alternate Energy Conference, Miami, 5-7 December 1977.
16. Quoted by Robotham, *op-cit.*
17. H. W. Kendall and S. Moglewar, Joint Review Committee, Sierra Club, Union of Concerned Scientists: 'Preliminary Review of the A.E.C. Reactor Safety Study', U.C.S., November 1974, pp. 24-35.
18 A. B. Lovins & J. H. Price, *Non-Nuclear Futures* (Friends of the Earth, San Francisco, 1975).
19. E. J. Sternglass, in J. O'M. Bockris (ed.), *Environmental Chemistry* (Plenum Publishing Corporation, New York, 1977), p.477.
20. ICRP Report of Committee II on Permissible Dose for Internal Radiation (Pergamon Press, London 1959); A. Petkau, *Canadian Journal of Chemistry,* 1973, **49**, 1187.
21. A. Petkau & B. Chelack, *International Journal of Radio-Biology,* 1974, **25**, 321.
22. V. Brodie, *Radio-active Contamination* (Harcourt Brace Jovanovich, New York, 1975).
23. Radio-active Waste Discharges to the Environment from Nuclear Power Plants, U.S. Environmental Protection Agency, Washington, D.C. (BRH/DER, 70-2).
24. National Technical Information Service, Springfield, Virginia, 22151, ORP/SID 71-1.
25. T. Stokk, F. Oftedal & A. Pappas, *Acta Radiologica* 1968, **7**, 321.
26. K. G. Scott, E. T. Stewart, C. D. Porter & E. Sirafinejad, *Arch. Envir. Health* 1973, **26**, 64.
27. Report of United Nations Committee on Effects of Atomic Radiations, Annex G., United Nations, Annex G, New York, 1962.
28. F Lundin, J. C. Wagoner & V. E. Archer, U.S. Dept. of Health, Education & Welfare, 1971 (PB-204-871), National Technical Information Service, Springfield, Va., 22151.
29. J. T. Gentry, E. Parkhurst & G. V. Bulin, *Am. J. Public Health*, 1959, **49**, 497.
30. M. Barcinski, *Am. J. Human Genetics* 1975, **27**, 802.
31. A. Stewart, J. Webb & D. Hewitt, *Brit. Med. J.*, 1958, **1**, 1495.
32. L. J. Le Vann, *Can. Med. Assocn. J.*, 1963, **89**, 120.
33. D. Harman, *J. Gerontol*, 1956, **11**, 298.
34. A. B. Lovins & J. H. Price, *Non-Nuclear Futures* (Friends of the Earth International, 1975), p.33.
35. Rustum Roy, private communication, April 1978.
36. Atomic Industries Forum INFO., 19 March 1976.
37. Federal Power Commission Report 1976, 1 December, Appendix A, Table A-1.
38. Department of Energy Report, 'ERDA Review of Recent Report on Economics of Nuclear and Fossil Fuel Electricity', 20 May 1977.
39. L. F. C. Reichle, Ebasco Services Inc., Public Utilities, Fortnightly 1977, 2 February.

6

FUSION

Introduction

In atomic fusion, nuclei of heavy elements break up to give nuclei of more stable lighter elements and release much energy. In fusion, the nuclei of 2H atoms combine to give the more stable nuclei of He—and evolve much energy.

It is often stressed that, in fusion, mass is annihilated. This is true. However, mass is annihilated in every reaction in which energy is given out. In chemical reactions, the amount is infinitesimal, and in nuclear reactions, with an energy change a million times more, it is less infinitesimal. The origin of the greater energy change is the tighter binding in the nucleus than among the extra-nuclear electrons of chemistry.

There is no doubt that, were it possible to engineer *practical* controlled fusion at an acceptable price, this would be the most advantageous source of energy. The continuous fusion of hydrogen nuclei to form helium upon an astronomical scale is the principal energy-producing process occurring in the sun. Fusion reactors would occupy a negligible space compared with that needed to be exposed to the sun to obtain the same amount of energy from the remote source.

Thus, the main question with energy from the fusion of nuclei is its attainability. No *net* energy from fusion experiments has been obtained, although neutrons from the fusion process have been produced on a millisecond scale, and in the present chapter we shall describe the principles of its probable eventual attainment, and discuss questions dealing with the difficulties which will influence whether the process may give energy more cheaply than it could now be obtained from the massive collection of the solar energy which constantly reaches the earth, and is at present allowed to flow away without collection and conversion to a storage medium.

As to whether fusion energy is to be regarded as renewable energy or not—in the literal sense it is not renewable, because one is using up tritium and deuterium (see below). The amount of tritium which could be made from lithium would give about 100 years of world energy at present rates. Deuterium obtained from the sea would last a time so long that a deuterium-based fusion source (however, the *least* attainable one in the projected thinking about fusion energy) could be regarded effectively as a renewable source energy.

The plasma, and the basic concept of attaining fusion[1]

The fundamental concept of bringing about conditions whereby hydrogen nuclei fuse to helium nuclei is to utilise the kinetic energy of translating nuclei to overcome the electrostatic repulsion which exists between protons.[2]

To achieve the situation in which kinetic energy can overcome the large energy of repulsion set up between two nuclei near enough to combine in a nuclear sense, it is necessary to raise the temperature to an astronomical magnitude.

The order of magnitude the temperatures would have to become can be obtained by regarding the necessary temperature as

$$kT > e^2/r$$

From this, one gets that

$$T > 1.8\frac{10^5}{r_o}$$

where r_o is the *distance* between the approaching nuclei in Angstroms.

The distance at which the attractive force of the nuclear reaction to form helium starts to become active is about $10^{-3}°A$, and the temperature is therefore in the vicinity of 10^8 °K.

At such super-enormous temperatures—ten times greater than the temperature at the centre of the sun—atoms consist entirely of nuclei, together with the electrons formerly attached to the nuclei. Matter consisting of ions and the electrons produced therefrom is a plasma, and one of the methods of obtaining fusion—the method upon which most of the research has so far been done—utilises plasmas of the hydrogen isotopes.

The basic idea of the technique of reaching fusion utilising plasmas is, then, that one attains the plasmoid state by applying a sufficiently large potential across a dilute hydrogen gas. Electrodes are not placed in contact with the gas, for this cools it—the current is induced by external windings. The gas becomes ionized and the current then passes through it, causing ohmic heating. Supplementary heating is employed, e.g. by means of radio-frequency heating, or by injecting particles into the gas. This gas becomes a plasma, and by increasing the current sufficiently, so principle indicates, one may attain a temperature of 10^8 °K, or whatever temperature is necessary to cause nuclei to fuse together to form new nuclei.

Chemists will realise that the super-enormous temperature gives rise to a super-enormous difficulty in finding a material of containment. From the first ideas of controlled fusion as an energy source, physicists have had to answer this obvious difficulty. The plasmas which they envisage would be very dilute so that it is not a question of a *substantial* (in the mass sense) chunk of glowing sun having to be held within the laboratory; and, secondly, there has been in the forefront of concepts in fusion research the idea of 'material-less containment', i.e. the plasma, at 10^8 °K, has been thought of as being contained inside a 'magnetic bottle'. This is a cage of magnetic field lines which would act on the + ve ions and electrons which make up a plasma to push it into a certain shape and keep it there. A material container or crucible retains a gas or liquid by means of intermolecular forces which come into play upon collision and give the appearance of 'solidity'. There is, in principle, no fundamental difference between attaining this containment by having a visible solid material repelling oncoming atoms by electrostatic forces, and having a plasma contained by magnetic forces which are invisible.

Finally, if a magnetic bottle could, in practice, rather than in terms of a calculation, contain a 10^8 °K plasma, one would then be able to have some way (several have been suggested, see below) of extracting the kinetic energy from the very energetic neutrons of the glowing plasma, and transducing this to a practical form of electricity, which in turn could split water to form a practical medium for long distance transmission and storage of hydrogen.

The big concept behind all this is that, once the plasma has been struck into life, i.e. the fusion reaction started to occur, it would have a tendency to be self-perpetuating (so long as the physical arrangement could be maintained). However, it is not the thought that there would be a steady-state system. Fusion would be carried out in *pulses*.

One would be burning hydrogen, but in the nuclear sense, i.e. *nuclear* reactions would be occurring, and because the nuclear binding forces are of the order of magnitude 10^6 times more than the chemical ones, vast amounts of energy in the form of neutron kinetic energy would be released.

The eventual question—in the end, the greatest question in energy policy—in our decision as to what our future energy source will be, is: can energy in a usable form be extracted from the fusion process more cheaply than energy can be extracted from the more dilute (on earth) solar source?

The nuclear reactions in fusion[2]

It would be ideal if one could just simply take ordinary hydrogen containing very largely the hydrogen of nuclear mass one, and fuse that. However, the probability of attaining fusion with hydrogen of mass one is lower than the probability of attaining it with heavier hydrogen isotopes, and for this reason the fusion of ordinary hydrogen is not considered. However, even with the hydrogen isotopes, the situation is not simple. The most obvious fusion reaction after the rejected $H^+ + H^+$ is the fusion of deuterons, D, or ^2H. However, the temperature at which the fusion of deuterium isotopes begins is five times higher than the temperature at which another nuclear reaction involving hydrogen isotopes begins, namely the fusion of the very rare tritium isotope, Tr, or ^3H, with the less rare D or ^2H. The fusion of the ^3H with ^2H occurs at 10^8 °K, whereas the fusion of the deuterium ions would occur at 5.10^8 °K. The attainment of these astronomical temperatures represents a very considerable difficulty in the attainment of fusion. Hence, the experimental work and the potential first plants will be made with the deuterium plus tritium fusion reactions rather than the deuterium plus deuterium fusion reaction. Deuterium is plentiful compared with tritium, so that it is desirable indeed that, eventually, when controlled fusion is attained, and if the energy from it is competitive with the price of solar energy collected on earth,* or from satellites, one would use deuterium.

---

*It might be thought to be an incredible proposition that the complex technology of fusion could give energy cheaper than the simple technology of solar collection and conversion to H_2. Simple though the solar collection might be, it would involve *vast areas* of collectors and it is the material costs of these which could make the smaller, if much more complex, fusion technology cheaper.

The nuclear reactions to which we are referring can be written as follows:

The deuterium one can be written:

$$^2H + {}^2H \rightarrow {}^3He(0.82) + n(2.45)$$
$$\rightarrow {}^3H(1.01) + p(3.02)$$

As stated, this reaction will not occur until 5.10^8 °K. Furthermore, the average energy which would be given out per unit occurrence of it is twenty times smaller than the energy gained in the alternative reaction with tritium.

This reaction in the deuterium plus tritium reaction is:

$$^2H + {}^3H \rightarrow {}^4He(3.5) + n(14.1)$$

and this commences at 1.10^8 °K.

The figures in brackets refer to the energy associated with the reaction products and the unit used is mega electron volts, i.e. 10^6ev. This means that if we could recapture the total kinetic energy of the neutrons after they come out of the nuclear reaction, as indicated above, we should be able to recover 14.1 mega electron volts per mole of helium produced.

Another piece of terminology must be explained, and that is the method of representing temperatures in plasma physics. This is not in terms of degrees Kelvin, but in terms of kilo electron volts. This is a number of electron volts in energy which equal to the kT corresponding to T, and so if one says that one has a temperature of 10keV, one means that one has a temperature such that kT would be equal to 10 thousand electron volts. Electrons in the plasma are then travelling at 1/10th the velocity of light.

It can be seen from the above that the reaction of deuterium with tritium ions is favourable compared with the reaction of deuterium ions together. The better quality comes out of two aspects. First of all, the energy produced is greater per unit of reaction and the temperature at which the fusion reaction would start is lower. Of course, using tritium has a considerable disadvantage: there is no source of tritium in significant amounts—the amount of tritium in water is too small to be of interest. Tritium has to be *made,* and this can be done by means of a nuclear reaction involving lithium.

The production of the tritium is planned by nuclear physicists to occur within the reactor itself, and according to current concepts, there would be two nuclear reactions of lithium which would be induced by neutrons. The one reaction would be:

$$^6Li + {}^1n \rightarrow {}^4He + {}^3H$$

The other one would be:

$$^7Li \rightarrow {}^4He + {}^3H$$

The first of these reactions gives out 4.8 Mev, and the second one is endothermic and gives -2.5 Mev.

The tritium released in these reactions would then be led to join with deuterium, and a concept often stated by physicists is that this deuterium would

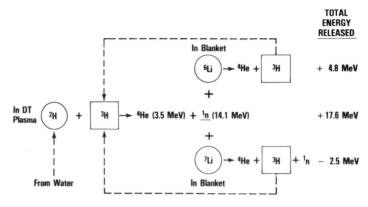

Fig. 6.1. The deuterium-lithium-hydrogen fuel cycle.[3]

be readily available from water.*

These processes are shown in Fig. 6.1.[3]

The Lawson Criterion and containment[3]

The requirement for fusion in the process described above is not only that the temperature shall be high enough so that the approaching nuclei overcome the coulombic repulsion between positive ions with sufficient energy to fuse. In addition, we must confine the hot fuel free from contact with material walls or from contamination with impurities for a significant fraction of the fuel to react. This requirement can be reduced to a quantitative relation known as the Lawson Criterion. It relates the density of the fuel (n particles per unit volume) to the minimum time during which they are confined together, τ.

The order of magnitude of these two quantities which some think are most desirable are, respectively, [†] 10^{14} per cc, and 1 sec.

Multiplied together, these quantities make the Lawson Criterion for the commencement of fusion:

$$n\tau > 10^{14} \text{ cm}^{-3} \text{ sec}$$

The present main aim of fusion physics, as the basis to the possible future fusion technology, is the attainment of conditions which correspond to the Lawson Criterion. In Table 6.I some of the values of τ, $n\tau$ and t are tabulated.[4]

One of the ways in which we can show the degree of progress towards fusion technology is to portray the degree to which the Lawson condition

---

*However, as the deuterium is present in water at a mole fraction of the order of magnitude 10^{-3}, and as the probability of its reaction at the electrode is much less than that of a proton, the extraction of HD by electrolysis from water would take about 10^4 times more energy per atom than the production of H_2 from water.

†The value of the product $n\tau$ is more important than the individual quantities.

TABLE 6.I: Plasma Parameters in Toroidal Pinches[3,4]

Year	r_e (s)	T_i (K)	$n\tau$ (cm^{-3}.s)	Sustainment time (s)
1955	10^{-5}	10^5	10^9	10^{-4}
1960	10^{-4}	10^6	10^{10}	3×10^3
1965	2×10^{-3}	10^6	10^{11}	2×10^{-2}
1970	10^{-2}	5×10^6	5×10^{11}	10^{-1}
1976	5×10^{-2}	2×10^5	10^{13}	10^0
Reactor requirements	10^0	10^8	10^{14}	10

has been met with time, and one of the methods of portraying this, with the code names of the various reactors which have been used, is shown in Fig. 6.2.

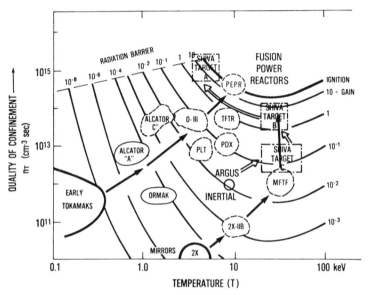

Fig. 6.2. Fusion physics progress and expectations.[3]

It seems to be a matter of the temperature to which the situation is raised, and there is an exponential relationship between the temperature of the plasma and the 'quality of confinement', namely the $n\tau$ of the Lawson Criterion.

The situation in 1978 was that the highest Lawson Criterion attained is around 7.10^{13}, and more than 10^{14} would give fusion.

In respect to the other necessary criteria in 1978, the time of containment is about one-fiftieth of that necessary, sustainment time is about one-tenth of that necessary, and the temperature is about one-fifth of that necessary.

One of the questions which has to be looked at is whether the progress of attainment of conditions for fusion as a function of research time is a linear one or whether it is becoming asymptotic, i.e. that we are getting less and less quickly towards the attainment of fusion.* Such plots are shown in Fig. 6.3.

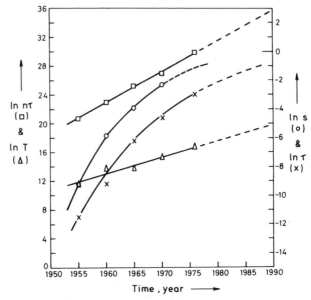

Fig. 6.3. Containment time, sustainment time and plasma temperature as a function of time of experiment.

Fig. 6.3 suggests that the Lawson Criterion will be attained some time in the 1980s. However, confusingly, the plots of Fig. 6.3 shows that the attainment of the appropriate τ and the appropriate temperature is becoming more difficult as the attempts continue. On this basis, attainability is not yet certain. Is extrapolating of the plot of the Lawson condition criterion with time a misleading generator of projections for the date of the attainment of fusion?

Confinement[4]

There are two ways whereby it is hoped to obtain confinement, and as already stated, the magnetic bottle method is the most researched. The other method, which we shall discuss in detail below, is the so-called inertial method. What is hoped for here is that the heating necessary to achieve fusion is sought by striking a solid hydrogen particle with a series of very large laser photons. The impacts are planned to be so large that the hydrogen nuclei within the D-T molecule compress themselves together with an enormous force, and fuse. The momentary neutron pulse which arises from this latter process, carried out many thousands of times as a result of many laser pulses (in fact, a series of small explosions), is seen as being taken away and turned into useful heat.

---

* Indeed, the attainment of fusion sustained would not necessarily bring us to a useful energy conversion device. Much energy has to be put *in* to reach fusion. Getting a *net* gain in energy is at present a difficulty.

The concept of magnetic pressure has to brought in here. The pressure due to a magnetic field can be written as $\dfrac{B^2}{2\mu_o}$, where B is the magnetic field and μ_o is the magnetic susceptibility. This field, acting upon the charge particles in the plasma as a result of the application of the well-known formula, $He_o v$, for the force of a magnetic field upon a charge, e_o, travelling at a velocity, v, is that which is intended in the magnetic field method to keep the plasma in balance. Against this is the plasma pressure, which is nkT, where n is the number of particles per cc.

In reality, $\dfrac{B^2}{2\mu_o}$ does have to be not equal to, but greater than, nkT, because of the complex field configurations, and the ratio may be about an order of magnitude whereupon, B is some 15 Tesla (∴ 150,000 gauss).

The various schemes of confinement

There are several schemes of confinement, and one is called the Z pinch. A large, rapidly rising current is carried by the plasma, and this current serves both to heat and confine the plasma. The heating arises from the compression which arises because of the magnetic field produced by the current in the plasma and the friction produced by that current. The magnetic force compresses the plasma.

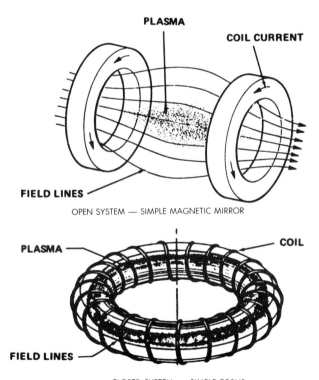

OPEN SYSTEM — SIMPLE MAGNETIC MIRROR

CLOSED SYSTEM — SIMPLE TORUS

Fig. 6.4. Magnetic confinement configurations.[1]

This system was found in earlier experiments to be *unstable,* but various attempts have been made to get it stable by adding extra fields.

Another method is called the *magnetic mirror* method. This is shown in Figure 6.4.[1] The ions and electrons of the plasma particles can be 'reflected' by magnetic mirrors, and therefore should not escape from the end.

Extra heating of the plasma in the mirror can be achieved by injecting particles into the plasma, by radio-frequency heating, or by compressing the plasma with a magnetic field.

The most successful method is called the Tokamak method, the name arising from the Russian word for magnetic bottle. The plasma is contained in a torus, and a toroidal field is given by coils which pass a current outside the torus. However, the system then contained in a *simple* toroidal field is not stable because the field is stronger on the inside of the torus than on the outside. In addition, ions drift in opposite directions, setting up an opposing field, and this causes the plasma to drift outside the torus. In the *Tokamak method*—one of the more successful at the present time—stability *is* attained by a suitable arrangement of the magnetic field, the magnetic field lines are arranged to cancel the electric field which arose earlier from the magnetic field heterogeneity, and appropriate adjustment had led to the holding of a plasma for 10^{-3} sec.

The present position in the achievement of the Lawson Criterion[4]

The relative attainment of the various quantities in plasma, such as the confinement time, the critical temperature, etc. have been plotted in Fig. 6.3.

A more positive way of showing this is to illustrate the Lawson Criterion as a function of the temperature, rather than the date at which these were attained.

This is shown in Fig. 6.2.

The transfer of the neutron energy from inside the fusion reactor to the outside[3]

The usual thought is that the neutron energy should be utilised to obtain heat by impact on a refractory and eventually be led to form steam and work a turbine, etc. Fig. 6.5 shows one method which is considered.

The liquid to be heated is passed through a hot refractory.[5] In the conventional energy supply concepts, heat is conducted across the surface, but in the present concept the heat energy comes from the heat of the high-energy neutrons within the energy-conversion region.

One advantage which could arise from this approach is that the neutron stream could heat a sink to very high temperatures, limited only by the sink's melting point. 1,000-2,000° for producing steam is practical. Under such conditions, steam is more effective in the thermodynamic sense (Carnot efficiency) than it would be if it were used at lower temperatures. Thus, if one transferred heat by conduction (not by direct neutron heating) across surfaces the temperature would be lower and the Carnot efficiency less.

The Inertial Confinement Concept

The beginning of this concept was at KMS Industries in 1969, and the Principal Investigator was Keith Bruchner who filed a patent which concerned

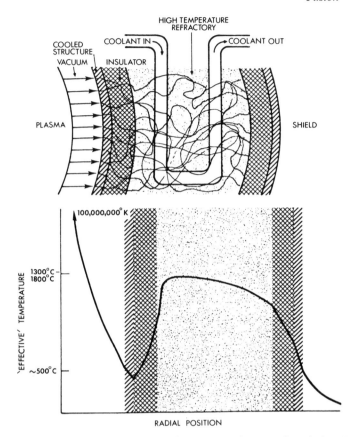

Fig. 6.5. High temperature fusion blanket concept: a heat transfer technique.[3]

a new process for controlled nuclear fusion.

The Inertial Confinement Fusion is brought about by using highly energetic beams, e.g. laser beams, electron beams, and ion beams, to deliver energy in giant pulses, each very short, to the surface of a small mass of the potential fuel. This may, for example, be a mass of solid deuterium-tritium, present in drops, and resting on a platform at the top of a stem.

Laser beams strike the drop from many directions simultaneously and hence compress it. A shock wave passes through the drop. It is claimed by the authors of the method that the remarkable degree of compression of 'several thousand times' (*sic*) should theoretically occur.* Were this to happen, fusion should occur.

There would be a series of momentary fusion reactions taking place which would give out neutron streams, which could then be transferred to an outside system which would be heated to containable temperatures.

---

*The compressibility of liquids is net linear with the pressure, and hence the supposition that a drop can be compressed to 10^{-3} of its original volume may be regarded as a matter which would have to be proved.

Eventually, the pellets would be fired in great numbers into a container, and repeated pulses of a laser would strike them in flight. One of the difficulties up to the present time has been to get the laser beams actually to hit the hydrogen droplets. Another difficulty is that, so far, the energy to drive the laser has been more than that obtained from fusion.

At the present time, the size of the pellets is 50-500 microns.

The arrangement in inertial confinement[5]

The essence of this is shown in Fig. 6.6. There is an oscillator on the left, which shapes the pulses and triggers the system for releasing the laser energy. There is a series of low power-level rod amplifiers, and then several higher-power disc amplifiers.

A major object in illuminating the pellet is to provide a uniform flux density. This helps the pellet implosion. In Fig. 6.7 we show the lens mirror system. The first momentary thermonuclear reaction from mechanically derived implosion from a laser driven apparatus was observed on 1 May 1974.

In Fig. 6.8, fusion is occurring. The dramatic Fig. 6.9 shows an implosion effect, i.e. a successful collision between a laser pulse and the hydrogen-tritium droplet.

The present position in laser fusion[5]

It is claimed that momentary laser fusion has been obtained in the laboratory and in individual examples. One difficulty is that the laser systems have not yet been sufficiently powerful. The direction of the work is to make bigger drops and increase the laser power. The aperture of the laser beam will be increased to more than 14 cm (*sic*). One of the matters to investigate is coupling of the laser light and the hydro-dynamics in respect to frequency.

No *net* energy has hitherto been produced from laser fusion. The laser pulses have been too small. If inertial confinement for civilian use is to become feasible and economic, there will have to be multi-pulsing of gigantic lasers. Of course, the energy to operate these has to be less than that of producing pulses in fusion.

Methods of conversion of laser fusion energy to useful energy

One of the advantages of potential fusion plants is that they could be small, say 100 MW. One could nestle inside a small town. Electrochemical conversion of the energy (once some has been obtained) to molecular hydrogen from water would be easy, and would produce the deuterium needed for further energy conversion.

There could be some radiolytic cycles, in which, for example, CO_2 is split and then the water-gas-shift reaction takes the resulting carbon monoxide with water to hydrogen and reproduces CO_2.[6]

The environmental impact of possible fusion reactors

Although fusion reactor design is as yet only at the conceptual and theoretical stage, an assessment as to the dangers of this possible form of energy production have been made. This is important because opposition to the breeder programme arises largely because of the difficulties of storing plu-

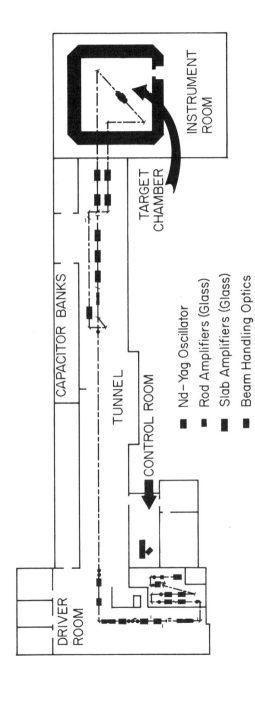

Fig. 6.6. Inertial confinement: laser floor plan at the K.M.S. Company.[5]

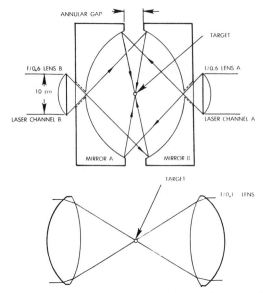

Fig. 6.7. The lens mirror system used in inertial containment to give the compressing pulses to the drop.[5]

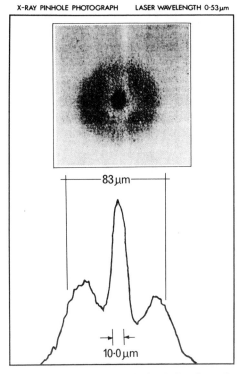

Fig. 6.8. This is an X-ray pattern of the imploding drop. The original diameter is 63 μm and the drop is compressed to 10.0 μm.[5]

Fig. 6.9. Photograph of an imploding drop from K.M.S. Laboratory.[5]

tonium without danger to the population. In fusion there are no liquid radio-active wastes; and there are no reprocessing plants which can leak biologically dangerous materials into the atmosphere.

Dangers from the operation of the reactors[4]

The most significant hazard generated on a potential site of a practical reactor during normal operation would be from leakage of tritium to the external atmosphere. This substance is a low-energy Beta emitter with a physical half-life of 12.3 years, and a biological life of 12 days.

Calculations show that if less than 0.03% of the tritium per year leaks into the atmosphere, there is a negligible danger. It is not yet known whether such a small leakage rate can be achieved.[2,4]

Another difficulty is that the components which make up the fusion reactor would suffer from radiation damage and would have to be replaced. This replacement might have to be frequent. Where will such radio-active materials be placed? What degree of environmental hazard in respect to air pollution would they represent as the centuries continued and the (buried) debris built up?

Biological effects of the great magnetic fields involved have to be investigated.[7] Qualitatively, there are many and varied effects. Screening would be needed.

Possible accidents[2]

It is as yet difficult to know what the accident situation in the possible fusion reactors would be because the cause of such accidents, materials difficulties with the container, have not been researched. It is indeed not yet known where *any* materials will withstand the neutron flux in a fusion reactor.

What would happen if there were a fire or a chemical explosion in a nuclear fusion plant, and the tritium were released into the atmosphere? Such a possibility would have less bad consequences than would be the case with breeder reactors, because of the less dangerous character of tritium when compared with plutonium. Further, DT would tend to rise rapidly once it escaped into the atmosphere, whereas Sr^{90} and etc., would tend to contaminate the atmosphere at ground level.

The weapons implication

Plutonium could be used to make atom bombs by dissidents who would probably from time to time do this. No such danger exists in respect to tritium from fusion reactors.

On the prospects for success in fusion

A number of research milestones have to occur before fusion can be regarded as a feasible competitor for the massive collection of solar-fusion energy on earth:[4]

1. The Lawson Criterion must be reached, and doing this may take another decade.
2. A continued burning of the hydrogen (though in pulses) must be achieved, and attaining this may take two further decades.
3. Thereafter, towards 2010, it may be possible to attain conditions which allow examination of material effects of practical high-energy neutron fluxes on components which could be used in a demonstration plant. At this time the rate of production of oil and natural gas will be one-third that of the early 1990s.

Some estimates of time and cost have been made in the United States to set up a demonstration plant.[4] If the effort continued at the billion dollar level as at present, a demonstration plant could be set up around 2030, when oil and natural gas from wells will be a small component of our energy supply.

If a crash programme were initiated now, a demonstration plant might be attainable in only fifteen years after controlled fusion has been demonstrated. It is obvious, therefore—and admitted by those who think of fusion as a main source of energy in the future[2,4]—that fusion cannot solve the problems associated with the decline of the oil and natural gas supply in the 1990s.

It is not useful to give a systems-analysis version of the cost of fusion energy until some net energy has been obtained from controlled fusion. However, although in the 1950s and 1960s, cheap energy from breeders was promised, there is no projection which suggests that energy from fusion will be cheap.

Funding of fusion research

The total world expenditure on fusion in 1970 was about $100m. At present, the U.S. research programme is about $250m, and world wide, about $1B.

Although research support in Japan has increased, funding of fusion research in the Soviet Union and Western Europe has remained static over the last quarter-century.[1] If research on fusion is going to lead to a practical technology during the next 100 years or so, a considerably increased research tempo has to be obtained—above all, research in blanket design and coolants, and materials research into substances (if any) which can withstand neutron fluxes of super-astronomical energy and density.

The main research problems in nuclear fusion
The following are foreseen in the 1980s:[4]

1. *The nature of the reactor blanket*

   In the magnetic variation of the fusion reactor, the plasma is confined by the magnetic lines of force, but there must be a material region somewhere to, e.g. shield the magnetic coil system from nuclear radiation, as well as to convert the kinetic energy of the neutrons produced in the plasma to energy which can be used. One of the blanket materials foreseen is liquid lithium. This could breed tritium when the neutrons from the plasma strike it, as well as becoming hot. On the other hand, lithium is not an easy material to handle from the point of view of corrosion resistance. A better alternative would be lithium oxide or a molten salt involving lithium. However, the temperature would then be not much more than 1000°C. No blanket material has yet been evaluated, because of the lack of an adequate intensity of sufficiently energetic neutrons.

2. *The processing of the lithium*

   About 10 kilograms of lithium per gigawatt of power will have to be processed to produce the necessary tritium, and there have as yet been no design studies as to how such a huge quantity of intensely radio-active material could be safely stored. However, accidental release into the atmosphere of tritium would be far less dangerous than a liquid containing, say, plutonium salts in solution. Any tritium evolved in combination with H or D would rapidly dissipate upwards.

3. *The containing wall*

   Somewhere in the reactor there must be a wall exposed to the thermo-nuclear plasma. Such a wall will be exposed to about 50MW year m^{-2} of radiational energy from neutrons.
   So far there have been no significant flux of 14 MeV produced.* The highest neutron flux to which a material has ever been exposed under experimental conditions is 5 MeV. Damage would not be linear with energy. Relevant experiments have not, therefore, been possible. Finding of materials which can withstand the neutron flux *with suitable economics* may prove to be difficult.

---

* *Producing* 14 MeV neutrons is not difficult. It has not yet been possible to get a flux of them which simulates that in fusion.

4. *Radioactivity*

The residual radioactivity of the parts of the reactor is a difficulty. One suggestion is to use vanadium, titanium and aluminium alloys, because these would have a low radio-activity after neutron bombardment.

5. *Magnetic fields*[7]

To obtain sufficiently strong magnetic fields, it will be necessary to use super-conducting magnets, and these would have to be large and complex. They would need niobium-titanium alloys because this is one of the better alloys in which to produce the super-conductivity effect. Better still is a niobium-tin alloy, but there may be difficulties because of the effect of the stresses at the high magnetic fields concerned.

6. *Energy storage*

The fusion reactor concepts provide special difficulties in energy storage because in some designs there will be a discharge of many gigajoules in fractions of a second, and the feasibility of receiving and storing energy of the hurricane variety has not yet been solved conceptually.

Would fusion be an inexhaustible energy source?

It is usual to regard fusion as an ultimate energy source. Tritium from lithium would be consumed in about 100 years if fusion were the main source of energy, and thereafter deuterium could be used and 'deuterium is easily extracted from the sea'.

There is no doubt there is enough material in the sea for a supply of deuterium which would last for hundreds of millions of years, but there are two questions which need to be answered if we are going to plan in the future for a deuterium-based economy.

1. It has been shown in Table 6.1 that the temperature needed for the fusion of deuterium is greater than that for the tritium-deuterium fusion, and in Fig. 6.3 that there is a suggestion of an asymptotic character in some quantities with increase of time. Will the temperature to fuse deuterium in a controlled way ever be attained? Thus, if kT is to reach 5.10^4 kev, the corresponding electron velocity would be about one-third of the velocity of light.

2. Another aspect of the use of deuterium (essential if fusion is to be regarded as inexhaustible) is its extraction from water in the sea. 'It is there in huge abundance'. In fact, it is there to the extent of 5.10^{-2} moles of HOD per mole of water, i.e. about 10^{-3} in respect to mole fraction.

If the discharge of hydrogen and deuterium had the same probability as electrodes in electrolysis, we would separate, therefore, one deuterium atom for every 1,000 hydrogen atoms. However, the situation is not like that because of the 'separation factor', i.e. the deuterium is less easily evolved than the hydrogen in solution. Calculations and measurements[8] show that this separation factor varies (according to the material used for the electrodes), but is around 10, so one has that one deuterium atom will be evolved for each 10,000 hydrogen atoms. The cost of obtaining 1 atom of D from water would then be some 10^4 times the cost of obtaining one atom of hydrogen.[8]

One has to add to this the cost of the design of the plant, and the processing of very large quantities of seawater.

Calculation suggests that the cost of the deuterium from sea-water by electrolysis would be at least 10% of the cost of the energy produced from it at 100% efficiency.

Fusion as a main energy source

1. The concept of a technology of controlled thermo-nuclear fusion remains —whatever its present difficulties of attainment—the greatest concept of applied physics, and it could be argued that is is a greater concept than that of electro-magnetism, the heart of the engineering of the present. Thus, some of the concepts of science-fiction, particularly those concerned with travel outside the solar system, could become scientifically reasonable prospects if the fusion of nuclei could become controlled, and the immense energy produced therefrom obtained.

2. Correspondingly, it is agreed by all in the field that, on the present graph of progress, we are *at least fifty years away from the beginning of a technology* of the production of energy by means of nuclear fusion. Building the plant thereafter would take, on the grounds that a capital investment of the order of magnitude 10^3 kW^{-1} is involved, about a further half-century. As with other aspects of the matter of providing another source of energy to supplant that of the chemical reaction between fossil fuels and oxygen, the first prediction could be improved (perhaps halved) were sufficient monetary investment placed in the area.[4] It is worth raising the question as to whether it is probable that nuclear fusion will be *engineered economically* even fifty years from now. Thus, there is a suggestion of an asymptotic character (Fig. 6.3) to the progress of the present leading characteristics in the ascent towards the critical conditions for fusion.

3. If thermo-nuclear fusion in the laboratory is attained—and sustained—there remain materials problems which may not be surmountable at costs which are consistent with an overall energy cost of fusion less than that of simple, massive, energy collection from desert and sea. It is unfortunate that at present there are no machines which produce neutrons at a flux which imitates that which they would have in a reactor, so that experiments on materials problems in this field cannot yet be done.

It is not a prospect that fusion could be ready for building by the turn-down of oil and natural gas. It is questionable whether a fusion technology could be built to meet the turn-down of the coal, even if this source can be made to last until 2050. Finally, supposing that a fusion technology is eventually shown to be feasible, the hydrogen fuel which it will supply will have to be in competition with that which will come from the simpler solar technology which would be in competition with it. This technology, which can be built now, and systems analysis gives an excellent prospect of producing hydrogen from it at a cost less than that from, e.g. breeder electricity, or from coal in the later 1980s.[9]

It is true that the solar collection would use up a lot of desert or ocean surface (though less, in terms of energy per unit area and time than oil fields). For what else could these desert spaces be used? Is fusion a *necessary* technological aim?

Fusion and solar as main source energies

Characteristic	Fusion	Massive Solar
Laboratory demonstration of *sustained* energy production	2000?	1954 (photovoltaics)
Prospect for first practical technology	2030?	IMW, Albuquerque, N. M., 1978; 10 MW Barstow, California, to be attained in 1982
Systems analysis of large scale price of energy per kW	No prospect of cheap energy offered	Solar-thermal and OTEC $\sim$ \$3,000 per kW. Photovoltaic, with mirror concentrators $\sim$ \$2,000 per kW (amorphous silicon)
Environmental hazards	Much less than breeders, but tritium escape must be less than 0.03% per year. How to dispose of rejected solid material from reactor?	After construction—zero
Practical fuel to be produced	H_2	H_2
Materials problems	Potentially severe: uninvestigated owing to lack of neutrons of suitable flux density	Silicon and degradation from sand abrasion? OTEC: biofouling? Solar- thermal: thermal stability?
Storage aspects	Special problems due to development of very large surges of power	H_2, stored underground or in hydrides
Transmission of energy, distances greater than 1,000 km	Hydrogen? Transmission via satellite in stationary orbit	Hydrogen. Collection of solar energy *on* stationary satellites and energy beams to local sites
Land area needed	Negligible	On earth from *c*.50 sq.m/kW for photovoltaics to *c*.2 sq.m/kW for OTEC. In space, 10 sq.m/kW
Classification of technology	Extremely high	Low (except for orbiting satellite collector method)
Potentiality	If deuterium were fused, could be base for higher energy civilization than that of the 20th century	Could provide entire population of planet with living standards of affluent countries in the late 20th century
World Funding, 1978	*c*.\$1B	*c*.\$200 million, but this mainly to develop secondary applications in households. OTEC not even tried.
Duration of research effort on > \$10M scale	25 years	3 years
Degree of certainty of attainment with sufficient research	Improvement of some criteria asymptotic with duration of effort	Photovoltaics and solar thermal proved. Biomass does not need proof. OTEC?

SUMMARY OF CHAPTER

1. The D-T reaction in fusion would yield 14 ev neutrons and starts at 1.10^8 °K. The reaction between D atoms does not start till 5.10^8 °K and yields 2 ev neutrons. Only the latter would give an inexhaustible source.

2. Fusion has not yet been maintained in the laboratory for significant times. There is a hint of asymptotic character about the approach of vital criteria to the needed value for sustained fusion, as a function of the years of research.

3. The main criterion to be attained is that of Lawson. It relates the concentration of reactants to the time of containment. It must be that:

$$n\tau > 10^{14}\,\text{cm}^{-3}\,\text{sec}$$

for sustained fusion.

4. Attainment of the necessary temperature ($\sim 10^8$ °K) is one problem in fusion; after this, sustainment of the plasma. Magnetic field line ('Tokamak') confinement is one concept. Inertial confinement is another.

5. Were fusion to be attained, the heat would be transferred through a sustaining wall, separated from the plasma by means of a vacuum. A heat transfer system would work within the heated wall material.

6. In inertial confinement, laser beams strike a drop. It is hoped that they will compress it until it fuses.

7. Environmental dangers from fusion would be less than those from breeders. Tritium escape must be less than 0.03% per year. Decommissioning of neutron-irradiated plant would be a danger.

8. A major uncertainty in the prospect of fusion technology is that, hitherto, there has not been a sufficient flux of neutrons of 14 mev available to ascertain what substance will be stable in such a flux.

9. The attainment of the Lawson criterion is expected in the 1980s. After perhaps 2010, testing of materials might begin. A beginning of useful technology in 2030-2040 might be possible. The cost prospects are not estimable yet.

10. Tritium-based fusion depends on Li supplies and would last 100 years. Deuterium fusion would be a much more difficult task. Moreover, the concept that deuterium is available in vast abundance in the sea is diminished in positive significance by the estimate that the cost of recovering it would be some 10^4 times more than that of recovering H from the same source.

AUTHOR'S CHOICE OF MOST IMPORTANT CONCLUSION FROM CHAPTER

Even if sustained fusion is ever attained, its economics as a main energy supply is in doubt, partly because of the energy needed to extract sufficient deuterium from the sea.

REFERENCES

1. M. H. Brennan, in *Physics and the Energy Industry* (Flinders University of South Australia 1974), p.120.
2. M. O. Hogler & M. Kristiansen, *An Introduction to Controlled Nuclear Fusion* (Lexington Books, New York, 1977).
3. J. M. Williams, J. R. Airey, S. L. Bogart and H. S. Cullingford, Alternate Energy Sources Conference, Miami, 5-7 December, 1977.
4. International Fusion Research Council, Report on Nuclear Fusion, 18-1-1978.
5. H. J. Gomberg, Developments in Inertial Confinement at K.M.S. Fusion, Report of 7 November, 1977.
6. C. Willis, A. W. Boyd & P. E. Bindner, *Canadian Journal of Chemistry* 1970, **48**, 1941.
7. W. Pressmann, *Electro-magnetic Fields and Biological Phenomena* (Plenum Publishing Corporation, New York, 1967).
8. J. O'M. Bockris, D. B. Matthews & S. Srinivasen, *Discuss Faraday Soc.* 1965, **39**, 239.
9. J. E. Parrott, Economic Evaluation of Solar Energy Conference C12, Royal Institution, July 1977.

7

SOME DIFFICULTIES OF THE AMERICAN ENERGY POLICY IN THE LATE 1970s

Introduction

One difficulty in discussing this topic arises from the fact that, although there are many scientists and engineers who are familiar with the technology of fossil and atomic fuels and the associated energy prospects, few have a professional knowledge of the prospects for the renewable energy source which must replace them. None of the few hundreds of people who do have such knowledge has any power directly to affect the course of events— essentially the direction of capital investment of many billions per year in new machinery. At present, the direction of flow of research funds, and the intended direction of flow of plant-building funds, is overwhelmingly for coal and nuclear development (see Chapters 4 and 5).

Another difficulty of discussing the American energy policy in the late 1970s is that a country's stance in respect to how it will face energy exhaustion is an intensely political matter. There is the direct link between the energy per head in a population, the price of that energy, and the standard of living of the people (Chapter 1). On the other hand, profits are being made by organisations which are selling at a high rate the exhausting material by which the technology is run, although at present there is no assured connecting supply for continuation after the oil supply begins to decline. Consequently, a discussion of the rate at which such non-renewable sources are being sold may give rise to hostility from those who have the monopoly of these sales. The persons who are profiting by the commercial sale of fuel are, *ipso facto*, powerful politically. Clearly, it is not in the short-term interests of these individuals (nor of the many hundreds of thousands who own shares in the corporations concerned) to hasten the realization by the electorate of the time-scale of approach to the maximum production rate, or to the connection between energy per head and living standard. The matter of how much fuel remains is sometimes trivialized by publication of statements of the kind: 'It is important that the United States cuts back its imports of oil'. Reading such a statement, a consumer might well believe that a cut-back would be possible and that it is due to simple extravagance that so much oil is being imported. Correspondingly, an attempt to raise the price of oil (the only way, outside unpopular rationing, to slow its use) is met by opposition, for it would cut sales and increase activity in the development of methods of conversion of the renewable resources. When these become competitive (which is a function of the R & D investment), the value of the remaining fossil fuel capital will be reduced.

The third difficulty is that, if one did nothing about the situation, but encouraged the continuation of the selling off of oil at the same rate, or encouraged an increase in the rate of sales still taking place [*sic*], nothing untoward would happen for about a decade except that there would be an even greater affluence in the countries with a living standard (a rate of expenditure of fossil fuel capital) greater than the average, which we now have. The deluge of the 1990s would indeed be a greater deluge, but nothing around us would be visible to indicate its coming, and, as a man can drive a car with perfect function until the last of the gas, so we would continue to exist as though our prospects were good. Nor is it a case of the smallness of the number who can read the charts. For, were one such reader to become Captain, and slow down the ship, there would be a devastatingly negative reaction from the passengers who, according to the rules by which the biggest and best ships are run, have power to fire any Captain who does not please them *at the time.**

The present energy situation, and energy policy, is, as no other matter, a topic where the long-term view must be taken: a perspective of thirty years is a minimum, and detailed planning through 2050 and even 2100 is desirable. The first of these two latter dates is that at which persons who understand the situation think we might come out once more into a situation where free, liberal spending of energy (even economic expansion), i.e. an increase in energy per head, could again take place.

Much of advocated energy planning over what would be called by some, 'long times' into the future, runs counter to the attitude of the established thinking in the United States. Essentially, this is for expansion and growth at the highest rate: the information concerning exhaustion and economic and logistical difficulty of the replacement of oil with coal-derived synthetic fuels, has either not penetrated, or been ignored. The persons who are regarded publicly as governing the United States—the Congressmen and Senators in the Federal Government, and the lesser politicians in the State Governments—are, by the nature of the elective process, naturally interested in the view their voters take of them at the *next* election. To be re-elected, they must not only please the people but the groups who contribute to their election expenses and hence determine their chance of being elected by the voters: the corporations, etc. But the corporations are not interested in altruistic acts, in giving up expansion and growth, i.e. in decreasing their profitability. They are interested in their advancement in terms society regards as virtuous: making money (i.e. conniving at spending the fossil fuel capital at an *increased* rate). Any hint of cut-back in energy per head (i.e. in the rate of using up the reserves) will be opposed, not by attacking the cause of the early fossil fuel decline (expansion)—for expansion is a good word—but by obfuscating the situation by, for example, publishing true but incomplete statements ('this Company will be able to supply America with coal for hundreds of years on into the future') and discouraging the man who

---

*It is essential to keep in mind the equivalence between the standard of life and the energy per head—often pushed into the background of discussion—because of the unpleasant nature of what is associated with the concept of lessened energy per head, which would result in 'Depression'.

reports unpleasant energy facts (the spread of realization on the times of exhaustion would tend to promote conservation and reduce the apparent prosperity).

The only *immediate* path which can be taken in American energy policy *is* severe conservation, and it must again be re-asserted that that conservation is synonymous with lowered real income, lack of growth, and therefore lowered profit in business enterprise. As this could bring with it, given the nature of U.S. society as one which stresses individualism, unemployment beyond earlier experience, one can readily understand that the viewpoint of company directors, their employees, and all whose job security is not independent of the state of the economy, will be that conservation (which must always, of course, be publicly praised) is to be in reality avoided by every reasonable political means.

A minor example of this trend is the penalty exerted upon house-holders who introduce solar panels to produce hot water. In order to make this difficult, so that no decrease in the rate of selling fossil fuels shall occur, the tariff of electricity for the solar user is raised.*

There is a psychological point which must be brought out. There is a number of things which are not mentionable in society. *What* is not mentioned varies with time. One of the 'un-subjects' of the present is the estimated time (e.g. from insurance statistics) of one's personal death. Behind the question of cutbacks, and the need for Draconian conservation, is the fact that the rate of production of oil and natural gas (on a world scale) will pass through a maximum as early as 1990, and that, in effect, is a kind of death sentence, unless Draconian conservation puts the date off. The analogy to a personal death is clear, and it may be this which sometimes makes it difficult to make people discuss the energy exhaustion situation calmly. Attempts to discuss the inevitable reduction of high living standards sometimes bring opposition to facts, but usually with an attitude of embarrassment.

'Prosperity' and the using-up of non-renewable resources

There has been, during the last 100 years or so, an element of falseness concerning living standards. Thus, income is proportional to energy per head, so that by giving away the oil capital at greater or lesser rates, 'prosperity' can be made greater or lesser. It is necessary to have machinery to convert the energy into some useful movement, but this is secondary. The primary determiner is the rate of distribution per person of the non-renewable fuel.

This gives a false basis to recent prosperity, viewed from the longer term. In personal terms, it is analogous to looking rich by spending one's capital. The good effects are temporary. Spending all the fossil-fuel capital to bring about good living decreases the possibility of investing in machinery to con-

---

* An extreme example of hanging on to the wealth of the present for short-term gain and thus hurrying the End is the action of the business community in China in the civil war fought between them (led by Chiang Kai Schek) and the community led by Mao. The industrialists of the bigger cities did not want the war brought near the cities—it would have interfered with business in that year—although assured by Chiang that it would improve the chance of final victory.

vert the renewable energy sources to useful energy (income) for the long term.

What is the United States energy policy?

It is difficult to find out whether the United States has an energy policy, because it sometimes seems that persons whom one might expect to be eager to discuss it are shy of discussing what they think the policy may be. If one asks an energy scientist, one of the few who has a grasp of the whole area of non-renewable and renewable resources and the economic relation between them, what the U.S. energy policy is, he will usually refer to persons 'higher up in the hierarchy'. If one asks such persons, they tend to opine that the matters are technical and should be referred to the scientists below. Another difficulty of finding out what is the U.S. energy policy pertains to the fact that there is little written about a policy for times later than about 1985. However, most of the changes which threaten, occur shortly after 1990. It is not difficult to give a picture which is entirely true and quite tranquil so long as one does not look beyond 1990, and particularly past 2000 (where most of the discussions stop).

One of the matters seldom discussed is the rate and magnitude of capital investment needed to build the new energy-conversion machinery, and from where these amounts—several Gross National Products—would come from, and *over what time.* Another undiscussed matter is whether we have the energy from the last remains of the liquid and gaseous fossil fuels still even now being used to fuel *expansion* [sic] to build the machinery for the recovery of energy from renewable energy resources. What does such a calculation show? At what rate *may* we spend energy now? What level of G.N.P. will be acceptable in view of the necessity of such gargantuan capital formation within the next few decades?

President Carter's plan, April 1977

1. To increase energy conservation and fuel efficiency.
2. To raise the price of oil and natural gas.
3. To encourage conversion to coal.
4. To promote the development of nuclear power.
5. To stimulate the long-term development of renewable resources.

Specific goals for 1985 are:

1. To reduce the annual growth of energy demand to below 2%.
2. To reduce gasoline consumption to 10% below its current levels.
3. To reduce oil imports from a potential level of 16 million barrels per day to 6 million, which would then be one-eighth of the energy consumption. At present the United States import half its oil. (There is no statement of where the rest would come from. U.S. production of oil is falling at about 10% per year).
4. To establish a strategic petroleum reserve of 1 billion barrels (4 weeks' supply!).
5. To increase coal production by two-thirds, to more than one billion tons per year.
6. To bring most American homes to a minimum standard of efficiency in

respect to heat insulation.

7. To use solar energy to give some 2.5 million homes hot water.

After this fairly mild Energy Plan had been announced, it was attacked and watered down because it hinted at conservation, i.e. of recession and the beginning of decline.

It is better to regard it as the National Energy Plan—although in reality it has been emasculated—and to follow Naill and Backus[1] in analysing whether it would have been possible to achieve it whilst continuing to have a society regarded as normal—in the absence of consciousness that the production rate of oil and natural gas is to turn down in the 1990s.

The analyses which these workers made of the Carter National Energy Plan show that, although the demand and coal production goals set by the NEP (National Energy Plan) may be thought as achievable by 1985, the Plan would have fallen short of attaining its more important goal: the reduction of oil imports. In fact, oil imports would have risen to 27 quads (one quad equals 10^{18} BTU) by 1985, instead of dropping to 12 quads as the Plan attempts to achieve. Such a rise will bring into focus the world oil shortage and begin to affect the economic functioning of the United States.

The United States National Energy Plan after 1985[1]

Naill and Backus find that the National Energy Plan after 1985 will mean more and more imports of oil for the United States.[1] The National Energy Plan, however, does do something towards improving the long-term energy prospects for the United States.

Thus, projections of demand show that gross energy demand will go up to 143 quads per year in the year 2000 if no plan were taken into account, whereas it would be 118 quads with the plan. The energy demand will grow 2.5% until 2000 under 'business as usual', but would have grown only at 1.8% per year under the plan.

Oil

The National Energy Plan reduces demand for oil by 20 quads in 2000. The benefits of the reduced oil demand are reduced by the Plan's depressive effect on domestic oil production. This is dependent upon the world oil price, and the conservation programme will lower U.S. demand for foreign oil and therefore reduce the world price.

Natural gas[1]

Because of the declining availability of gas in the United States, there would be a major gas shortage over the next 25 years with 'business as usual', but the National Energy Plan cuts down the severity of the shortage through conservation.

As the United States is such a large oil importer, reduction in U.S. imports would produce a significant repercussion in the world oil market. If the Carter National Energy Plan had not been emasculated by the representatives of the people, the plan would have put off the beginning of overt oil shortage from about 1983 to 1993, and bought the country 10 years in which to form capital to buy plants for the conversion of the renewable resources.

It is a reasonable conclusion that the National Energy Plan, had it not been emasculated, would have given rise to some good results, but it *is* only a slow-down and weak energy-conservation plan, and does not recognise the severity of the long-term problem, with its potential for Gross Catastrophe. It is too optimistic. The Plan is a plan for living on coal, and it has been seen in Chapter 4 that a coal-based plan—one which uses a substantial fraction of existing coal—would give rise to grave pollutional and ecological difficulties.

The basic difficulty of the National Energy Plan, therefore, is that it is a plan with too short a range and that its effect, had it not been weakened, at the best, would be to postpone the commencement of overt Decline for some ten years. It does not tackle the nucleus of the problem: that we have to pay for a gigantic investment in the machinery for conversion of renewable sources from the fossil fuels before they are exhausted (see Chapter 16).

A major lesson to be learned from the fate of the Carter 1977 National Energy Plan[1]

The NEP was heavily attacked in the Congress (the Congressmen stressing the viewpoint of the corporations among their constituents), and some of its weak provisions were torn down because they would have given rise to a beginning of the decline in living standards, and hence a slackening of the economy.*

This brings into focus the question of whether a *voluntary* (temporary) giving up of a high standard of living to build the conversion machinery is too much to expect: U.S. life is a matter of striving to get it. The only possibility would be by means of the imposition of laws by Congress. But the election of U.S. Congressmen is made possible by the payment of the expenses involved. And the payers are mainly those whose financial status depends upon a satisfactory prosperity in business. Indeed, if the board of a corporation were to vote for measures to allow for the future by reducing *present* earnings, their own stock-holders, some of them living on the income from the company's shares, would doubtless dismiss the Board and set up one which gave the best dividend the short-term situation would allow.

Some doubtful concepts which may obfuscate the present energy policy

1. Conservation can be pleasant. (There is a linear relationship between energy per head and income. Conservation means less income per head within the present social system. Conservation means increased unemployment.)
2. Energy is a commodity like any other. If one form gets too expensive, some other form will replace it.
3. The introduction of the use of the renewable energy resources is a matter for research, and when 'the problem has been solved' there will be

---

*It is always assumed that this is Dreadful. However, this may have to become an outmoded concept. It is only thought dreadful by the population because it threatens individuals, not with the few per cent decline in living standards corresponding to that of the economy, but the devastating decline resulting from loss of employment; not because of unsatisfactory performance but because of the Laws of the Economy working like a Russian roulette machine upon those who have a good income, and are suddenly deprived of the means of good living. The terror would disappear if the reduction were spread evenly over the population.

no further difficulty.
4. We need a new method of making electricity, e.g. atomic power. (Electricity is only some 20% of the present energy supply.)
5. It is satisfactory to analyse and plan the situation until 2000. (Inflection and considerable perturbation will occur about then.)
6. Scarcity of oil will be resolved in the normal market way by price rises. (This becomes inapplicable when the price becomes impossible, or when there is an 'absolute' exhaustion—no more oil at *any* price.)
7. There must be plenty more oil available if one looked for it, as, for example, off-shore oil. (This may be true: but such oil is likely to be more expensive than alternatives.)
8. If we are going to run out of oil, then we shall have to 'switch over to some other source of energy' (without recognition of the lead time of many decades; or the gigantic capital investment needs).
9. Nuclear energy is an acceptable option (reactor breakdowns; exhaustion of uranium ores by 2000; sabotage; hijacking; waste disposal; poor breeding efficiency).
10. Coal is plentifully available. (It does not seem possible to use coal to replace oil on a massive scale because of sulphur pollution and carbon dioxide-caused climatic change.)

Topics of importance[2]

The importance of enforcing a reduction in growth of demand

Demand *reduction* (conservation) should be *legislated.* A comprehensive programme is needed. Among the matters which should be legally enforced are the use of heat pumps, better home insulation, more efficient furnaces, transportation at minimal horsepower (e.g. no passenger car of more than 50 hp, falling to 20).

After energy constancy has been obtained by, say, 1983, a reduction in demand of, say, 5% per year should be enforced until the demand for energy has been reduced and supply *from renewable resources* has been increased to be equal to demand. (At present, the only renewable resource in use is the hydro-electric one, of which about one-tenth has been tapped.) A reduction in demand within the present system will mean a proportionate increase in unemployment, with the draconian and socially unreasonable effects on individuals.

Should synthetic fuels be developed from coal?

This is a more difficult discussion because making methane and oil from coal is something we know how to do. However, the capital investment would be the same order as that for making the machinery to convert the *renewable* resources. The construction of one large plant would take about six years. Moreover, the degree of the coal supply available is doubtful. Although the total coal present in the earth could *perhaps* be stretched to support us until 2050, the difficulty of removing it from the ground at sufficient speed and dealing with the sulphur and fly-ash is large, so it is very difficult to see how the large-scale development of coal could be a solution to our problems.[3]

It seems that the answer to fuels from coal is that some increase (say from the region of 20% as now, to the region of 30%) could be expected.

It would be better to get hydrogen from coal, not methane. This could be obtained as easily as synthetic natural gas (CH_4) and could be mixed with the hydrogen from the decomposition of water from nuclear and solar plants.[4] *Oil* from coal is more difficult to obtain (and therefore more expensive) than methane. However, it might be more profitable for energy companies to make expensive oil and not sell cheap synthetic natural gas, or the corresponding liquid natural gas.

3. The de-regulation of oil and gas

It has been shown by Naill that de-regulation makes little difference in eventual resource availability.[5] It is possible that it would stimulate new searchings to some extent.

4. The counter-advantages of sulphur

There must, of course, be enforced stack gas control. Stack gas collectors could utilise a certain amount of SO_2 to depolarise hydrogen air electrolysers in the production of hydrogen, and electrolysis of water to produce transmittable hydrogen fuel. The use of the SO_2 roughly halves the cost of the hydrogen. Such a solution to the S problem would lead to excess sulphuric acid by-product.[6]

5. Abandonment of nuclear power?

The difficulties of the development of breeder reactors are large, and there is a case for closing down atomic energy plants and abandoning development except for research on fusion. Thus the problem of the storage of high-level wastes may be unsolvable because it involves the design of social as well as technical systems, and our present system has too low a degree of hegemony by the government to allow the required social engineering. Is our energy situation, time-wise, so threatening that it seems that the dangers from nuclear plants represent the lesser of two evils and that nuclear reactors may only be abandoned *after* alternatives have been built?*

6. The vulnerability of the United States' energy supply at present

Saudi Arabia, on which country the United States depends increasingly for its fuel, is a country ruled autocratically by about 100 princes of the Saudi family. A revolution could bring restriction in delivery of some 35% of the United States' energy supply. Counter-invasion and military action are not likely to be successful. They could bring foreign retaliation—and destruction of the refineries.

A nuclear weapon exploded on the large Saudi Arabian oil refinery at Rostranavor would destroy it and shut off Saudi-Arabian shipments. It would take much more than one month to rebuild. But one month is the duration of the U.S. *intended* reserve. At present, *a few days* without the arrival of the tankers from Saudi Arabia would bring catastrophe to the United States. The shipments go by sea. The Soviet navy could present a challenge to that of the United States in the Indian Ocean, into which the tankers must proceed from the Persian Gulf.

---

*It is a difficulty of any system that once sufficient capital is in a certain kind of plant, change will be difficult.

7. *A misplacement of priorities*

There is at present overstress on short-term issues, such as the price of natural gas or the licensing of nuclear plants.

This concentration on short-range matters takes away attention from the speed of approach to a downturn of the world supply of oil and removes attention to the need to make provision for the necessary capital investment in the building of the New Energy Conversion System.

Policy matters needing increased stress

1. *The spreading of realization of the time aspects to the people*

The degree of energy available per head is an essence of politics. Some persons do not understand realistic time scales in respect to the energy situation. The world supply of oil is going to peak (maximum of production per year) in the 1990s. It must be understood what this means, in particular, *how long it will take and how much it will cost* to build a new energy system—*any* new energy system. Whatever organisation is necessary to use the media to impart this knowledge to the people should be formed and become active rapidly. The Exhaustion of the Fossil Fuels is the most important fact since the Industrial Revolution, which marked the beginning of the use of fossil fuels.

2. *Time needed for building a sufficient number of mines to provide us with a replacement by coal in 1995*

The number of coal mines which would have to be opened every day until 2000 must be calculated and stated, and the national effort that this would mean made clear, with the starting date.[3]

The difficulties of working with coal, in particular the heavy metal emissions from coal-fired power plants, must be clarified; and the predicted deaths compared with those from breeder reactors made a matter of public debate.

3. *The alternative renewable resources*

A building schedule for the conversion of these resources, particularly the solar ones, is needed. It should be *regarded as having a status higher than that of defense,* which depends on it, and be implemented by an Energy Executive Authority, an analogue of the Department of Defense.

4. *Time and capital needed*

Above all, the time and capital investment scales should be investigated, and the results published in the media. What it means for *living standards* must be spelt out and communicated by a courageous President.

5. *The Energy Executive Authority*

This should be set up and put into action, building. Its budget will have to be greater than that of the Department of Defense, for defense depends on energy availability.

6. *The influence of the democratic process*

This has held back the building of the atomic energy plants, and must be brought into accordance with reality. Energy exhaustion is *bound* to occur unless dynamic and far-reaching actions are taken in time. It would not be appropriate, with so few years left, that the building of the National Energy Conversion System should be subject to harassment by those who do not understand the dangers from *not* building whatever is necessary. Further, every path is associated with *some* danger. But the greatest of these dangers arises from an absence of building new energy-conversion plants at such a late date.

The present direction of U.S. Government research funding

1. *In respect to policy*

The main stress in policy of the Department of Energy seems to be in the direction of aiding optimal conversion of the coal and uranium to supplant oil and natural gas.

Is this policy a realistic one? Should the emphasis be on this or on the conversion of the renewable resources?

2. *In respect to relative values*

In U.S. Government circles, the options available for the use of the massive conversion of renewable resources have been termed 'high risk' and the development of atomic breeder reactors described as 'low risk'.

Is this a reversal of the situation looked at by persons not in control of the funding policy? Does the description of solar conversion as high risk and plutonium producing breeders as low risk reflect a logic which has become out-dated with increase of knowledge?

The funding of options for 1978 show a tilting towards the continued development of nuclear energy, at the expense of the development of truly renewable resources, in particular massive solar and solar-connected fuels. Is this a rational weighting?

3. *In respect to timing*

It may be that no particular timing for the building of sufficient elements of the New National Energy Conversion System has been set up. It is possible that the time scale of consideration is one which is consistent with the view to 1985. There is as yet no public discussion of the peaking of the world oil supply in the 1990s. Some of the goals (i.e. that for the cost reduction of photovoltaic converters) to commercialisable values are for dates like 1986. However, the systems have to be built extensively after this, and this building will take *decades* (on grounds of capital investment), so that with a downturn of the fossil fuel supply in the 1990s, there will be difficulty with a time scale implied by such a date as 1986 for the beginning of building.

4. *In respect to personnel*

Does the fact that some of the personnel deciding energy funding were earlier part of the former Atomic Energy Commission imply that there could be an underlying (if unconscious) bias towards continued stress on the nuclear developments (see Chapter 5)?

5. *In respect to basic tilt*

The strongest tilt in the U.S. Energy policy is nuclear. Is this emphasis consistent with the slow and extremely expensive development of breeder reactors; the exhaustion of uranium ores at low prices within two to three decades; and the fact that fusion is still laboratory-bound after 25 years of attempts to get started?

6. *Effects of Department of Energy funding on research in other countries*

Does the nuclear tilting make U.S. Energy research support policies a good model to be followed in respect to research policies in other countries which must develop new energy sources? Most countries (including the Soviet Union) *follow* American actions in technological matters. In devising the machinery for conversion of the renewable energy resources to useful energy, may it not be that to follow the nuclear and coal-wedded United States is unwise? Does this wedding derive less from technological considerations than from those of capital investments made when the technological considerations were different?

Some directions of a rational energy policy

1. *The need for a setting up of a time dependence of priorities*

The major lack in the energy policy is an out-of-kilterness of statements with the reality of the time of a downturn in the production of the fossil fuels (1990s).

There must be a calculated rate of building of new plants which will meet the predictable rate of down-turn in fossil fuel production.

2. *A fast decision as to where the major policy is going to go*

A large-scale development of coal as a replacement for oil is an unfavourable solution for logistic, pollutive and social reasons. The long-term development of atomic energy seems hardly feasible without breeder reactors. The dangers of the associated plutonium economy have been described by many independent persons of authority and intelligence to be unacceptable in respect to massive development.

A fast decision has to be made as to which of the *renewable* resources should be developed; by what approach, at what cost, and when (all with attention to the date of 1990)?

3. *The capital investment*

The problem in the building of the new energy systems is in the capital investment needed. Such matters have to be brought out clearly before the Congress. Do the consequences of their non-solution constitute a greater threat than does atomic warfare?

4. *The need for a fast education of the electorate*

By the use of the media, the people should be brought into contact with the concept of Energy Exhaustion and an understanding of Renewable Energy Resources. At present, few people understand that the end of an era (dominant reliance on a spending of fossil fuel 'Capital') is at hand. They do not understand the idea of 'Energy Income', energy from renewable resources.

5. *Focusing on a realistic time scale*

The focus should be on 1990 and particularly in the years beyond 2000. The next few years will look after themselves. Discussions which show that all will be not too bad till 1990 are true but tend to mislead. A lack of realisation of the many years lead-time prevents spread of the concept of 'starting now' on building machinery for the conversion of the renewable resources.

6. *Conflict of interest*

Those who sit upon Committees implementing energy policy should not have financial connection with companies still selling the non-renewable resources of a country. At present, some important government Committees, including those of the Office of Management of the Budget, are influenced by such persons. They control the degree of funding in research in the U.S. National Laboratories.

7. State Energy Research Laboratories should be set up throughout the country.

8. A calculation should be made of what rate of energy expenditure in the economy is necessary, and over what time, to extend the non-renewable resources until the capital for building the machinery for obtaining energy from the renewable sources can be formed.

9. The beginning of the building of the national energy conversion system (for renewable resources) should not be delayed after 1983.

10. Whatever modifications in the economy are necessary for achieving the economic goals for the capital investment will have to be made in the 1980s.

A difficulty little discussed

Scientists are educated with certain ingrained 'No-nos':
1. A scientist must present facts and theories but not express concern in respect to the social consequences thereof. Such expression may be termed 'hysterical' and the scientist will lose face among his peers. The social consequences of technological developments are the concern of, e.g. sociologists.
2. Scientists must serve the corporations and help them sell at the maximum rate. They are not expected to lie, but public stress upon something unfavourable to the employer of most scientists—the corporations—will not add to career growth.
3. If a man is, e.g. a biochemist, his area of expertise is biochemistry and no other. If he publishes in another area, he will be criticised by his colleagues, above all should these utterings touch on the sociological or economic. He must not integrate. Only philosophers do that and philosophy as a discipline is not taken seriously by scientists.

These ingrained inhibitions in scientists, aided and abetted by the salary gradients of the 'system,' have importance in respect to the direction of energy policy within the U.S. Thus, any person who carefully studies, e.g. publications by scientists of the U.S. geological survey; and who understands some elementary facts concerning lead time and financing of the building of plants, will find himself full of concern for his own later years, and for the children's lives. In the system of his training, he fears ridicule for expression of that concern.

Correspondingly, it is undeniable that, as the present prospect is one of a shortfall of oil before substitute equipment can be built, it would have a long-term improved effect to slow down the economy. Yet, implementing such thoughts would 'damage' the economy, but it is obviously necessary to increase the probability of its survival. Most scientists are insufficiently secure to point this out in published work.

Utilising knowledge from fields in which one does not have a formal training can have its dangers. This does not mean that one should not practise a measure of it. On the contrary, a subject such as the future of the energy supply involves many disciplines outside engineering, in particular economics, but also sociology, national and international politics, and even the psychology of the reaction of masses of people to certain perceptions of danger, versus the attractions of temporary comfort.

There are few scientists qualified in all these areas. However, it is they who are most likely to give answers which should prove most advantageous for the greatest number over the shortest time. Such considerations weigh in favour of the interdisciplinary government-funded research institute; and for the collaboration of persons from different departures in universities.

However, it also encourages scientists who have a formal qualification in one field to *think* and study *widely*, and that is one reason why the increasing modification of university courses into mixes containing various degrees of interdisciplinary character is good.

SUMMARY OF CHAPTER

1. The affluent countries exist at present under a misunderstanding: they can go on somewhat as before. This is not possible. The affluent world has to pass through a difficult period of adjustment analogous to that of living on disbursements from capital to living on earned income. *This cannot be done voluntarily,* and an organisation to coordinate this change (the Energy Executive Authority) should be set up, as an analogue to the Department of Defense.

2. The United States depends for a substantial part of its oil supply on the sea-borne passage through an ocean in which the U.S. does not have unchallenged naval power. This principal supply country is ruled by about 100 persons from a single family, and is, therefore, obviously subject to revolution and take-over, with uncertainty of the direction of oil policy thereafter.

3. The central difficulty is not the scientific and technological one. It is the degree of capital investment needed over a relatively short time, some three to five decades.

4. Is the direction of U.S. Government funding of energy associated with limitations in conceptualization which arise because of the origin of a number of the personnel who make it in the former Atomic Energy Commission? It seems intellectually clear that its policy of giving priority to supporting research on coal and uranium should be modified in the direc-

tion of the massive support of the development of means for converting the renewable resources to useful energy forms.

5. The element of *time* should be brought to the foreground in discussion and related to the rate of capital investment and living standards.

6. One difficulty is the limitation on the Executive Branch of the U.S. Government exerted by the elected politicians, sensitive to short-term election prospects, and wedded to attempting to maintain living standards which are inconsistent with the prospects of energy exhaustion. A *calculated* path towards the building of a New Energy System is necessary. The fuels we use are no longer going to meet our needs as from a certain time, which depends on the rate at which the economy is run. The higher that rate (the greater our spending of energy capital), the sooner will the point of down-turn be reached. The longer we leave it to begin the building of the new energy system, the higher the rate of capital investment will have to be when we do start to build it, and the less possible the building before the non-renewable fuels necessary for that building are exhausted.

AUTHOR'S CHOICE OF SINGLE MOST IMPORTANT POINT EMERGING FROM CHAPTER

The central difficulty of present energy policy is the lack of widespread realisation of the essence of the situation: that it is dominated by a competition between the time at which the present fuels will exhaust and our gathering the capital to construct the renewable-resource converters before that happens.

REFERENCES

1. R. F. Naill & E. Backus, *Technological Review* 1977, **79**, 1.
2. D. L. Meadows, F. Andrew-Ford & R. F. Naill, 'Critical Post-1985 Energy Policy Issues', Dartmouth System Dynamics Group, 1975.
3. J. O'M. Bockris, *Energy: The Solar-Hydrogen Alternative* (Australia & New Zealand Book Company, 1975).
4. M.I.T. Policy Study Group, 'Energy Self Sufficiency: an economic evaluation,' *Technological Review* **76** (May 1974).
5. R. F. Naill, Transition to Coal, Second Annual Report, 'Projects on the dynamics of long-term resource availability,' Thayer College of Engineering, Dartmouth College, Hanover, 1974.
6. J. O'M. Bockris & R. F. Fredlein, *A Workbook of Electrochemistry* (Plenum Publishing Corporation, 1974).

8

THE PRACTICALITY OF SOLAR ENERGY CONVERSION TO ELECTRICITY AND HYDROGEN ON A MASSIVE SCALE

Introduction

The future sources of *massive energy supply* have for long been regarded as nuclear; and solar sources have been regarded as principally for household energy. However, the prospect of the exhaustion of uranium ores not long after those of oil and natural gas, and the difficulties with breeders, have made a re-think necessary.

At present, the major American research investment for future energy supplies is in the high-risk nuclear sources, and coal with its difficulties of carbon dioxide and sulphur. These programs were devised before it was found that economics for photovoltaic, solar-thermal and OTEC projects are competitive with projections for breeder-nuclear reactors; and before there was knowledge that breeder reactors would be associated with striking hazards (Table 8.I).

Thus, in 1978, the funding for solar energy requested by the Department of Energy is in the region of $200 million (mostly for secondary and household solar), whereas the funding for research into nuclear energy is over $2 billion.

This smaller support for solar energy conversion may reflect earlier thinking, according to which photovoltaics was the main solar conversion mode seen for solar and this was decisively more expensive than the nuclear sources. The picture has changed because concentrators have made solar-photovoltaics cheaper;[1] and because there are now new prospects (solar-thermal and OTEC) for the conversion of solar on a massive scale. The arrival of H_2 as an energy intermediate in prospect has made the concept of a general supply of solar energy for everything more credible. Simultaneously, stress on environmental protection has increased, and the Three Mile Island accident diminished the credibility of coal-based and nuclear futures (Table 8.I).

Doubtless these changes in the scientific and technological picture will eventually be reflected in the funding situation. However, investment-inertia is bound to slow down the change which eventually has to follow a change in knowledge.

The amount of solar radiation striking the earth

The solar spectrum is shown in Fig. 8.1. The solar energy which reaches the

131

TABLE 8.1: CHANGES IN REALIZATION DURING THE 1970s NOT YET FULLY REFLECTED IN GOVERNMENT RESEARCH SUPPORT PROGRAMMES

Coal	Nuclear	Solar
Large ratio of resources to reserves (20:1) implies not enough available coal supplant oil > 50 yrs.	Production of fissionable Ur may maximize soon after oil and natural gas.	The use of concentrators gives prospect of 4 cents kwh^{-1} from photovoltaic.
If available coal used as fuel, CO_2 would give serious climatic changes next century.	Prospects for the realization of fusion as a practical technology are more than 50 years distant.	Solar thermal and OTEC methods give prospects of economics which are better than those of photovoltaic.
S purifications stage makes electricity from U.S. coal more expensive than that from nuclear.	The only massive, long-term atomic energy in prospect is the breeder. Less than ten breeders have been built during 20 years and $6B.	Some OTEC analyses suggests LH$_2$ cost competitive with gasoline.
Replacing extracted S in mines is step so far neglected in economic analysis for coal products.	Breeders produce plutonium. Plutonium storage problems involve great hazards.	High-technology satellite collecting solar would become economic if orbiting costs dropped to $100 per lb. This *is* a prospect for < 2000. (Space Shuttle.)
Gasoline from coal more expensive than H$_2$ from atomic and solar, if second law and environmental damage cost accounted.	Hijacking has become a prevalent and increasing social phenomenon. A schoolboy has constructed an atomic bomb. Atomic bombs are fuelled by plutonium.	Interfacing with water-splitting technology to H$_2$ eliminates solar difficulties such as sporadicity, storage and transmission from good collecting areas to major use areas.
Gaseous H$_2$ from coal would be cheaper per km of travel than LNG from coal. LH$_2$ from coal equal in cost per km of car travel to synthetic LNG. (CO_2 difficulties diminished if fuel from coal is H$_2$.)		

earth's surface is about $\sim 33\%$ less than that entering the atmosphere owing to scattering and selective absorption at certain wavelengths by water and carbon dioxide molecules in the atmosphere.

If the sun is directly overhead, on a cloudless day, the rate of energy arrival on the earth is about 1 kW m^{-2}. Thus, if the efficiency of the collector is 10%, there would be needed (for the above condition) 10 sq. metres to collect energy at a rate of 1 kW. Several factors reduce this amount for the usual practical situations which are not those of the ideals stated above:

1. *The latitude.* This may be compensated for by orientating the collectors appropriately.
2. *The rotation of the earth.* This may be compensated for by making the collectors track the sun.
3. *Clouds: diffuse insolation.* Fig. 8.2 exemplifies the variation of solar radia-

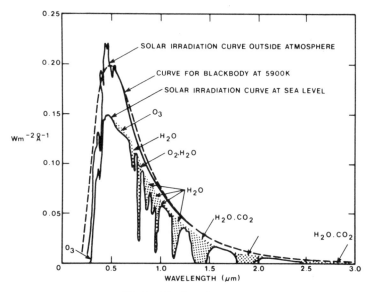

Fig. 8.1. The Solar Spectrum.

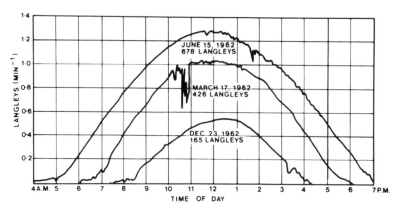

Fig. 8.2. Solar radiation at Madison, Wisconsin, latitude 43°N. (1 Langley
1 caloric $cm^{-2} min^{-1}$)

tion in Madison, Wisconsin. The average 14 hours of sunlight for the latitude 43 was 3.5 times less for 23 December, 1962, than for 15 June of that
year. The maximum between 10-12 p.m. was about 1.25 kW per sq. metre.
Averaged over a 24 hour period, the results of Fig. 8.2 suggest figures of
0.24 kW m^{-2} for the June and 0.08 kW m^{-2} for the December data.

Thus, a calculation of the energy which could be collected in a given location must refer to data for insolation per year at the area. It must use average
annual incidence figures. It is important to know how much of the light is
diffuse (as on a bright but cloudy day). Thus, devices in which solar energy
is collected through a lens-focusing system are dependent upon visibility of
the solar disc. Information on the total light flux is not sufficient. Hence, the

advantage of cloudless skies may be greater than is indicated by information given by the total solar energy lines as a function of latitude.

A world map of solar insolation (but not of visibility of the disc) is given in Fig. 8.3.

TABLE 8.II: SOLAR-ELECTRIC ENERGY FROM EARTH'S HIGH-INSOLATION AREAS[2]

Desert	Nominal Areas		Nominal Annual Thermal Energy Flux		Percentage of area assumed usable	Electric energy extracted at 25% efficiency (Gwhe/year)
	Sq km	Sq mi	(Gwh_{th}/km^2)	(Thousands of Gwh_{th})		
North Africa	7,770,000	3,000,000	2,300	17,870,000	15*	670,000,000
Arabian Peninsula	1,300,000	500,000	2,500	3,250,000	30†	244,000,000
Western & Central Australia	1,550,000	600,000	2,000	3,100,000	25	194,000,000
Kalahari	518,000	200,000	2,000	1,036,000	50	129,000,000
Thar (NW India)	259,000	100,000	2,000	518,000	50	65,000,000
Mojave, S. Calif.	35,000	13,500	2,200	77,000	20	3,900,000
Vizcaino, Baja, Calif. (Mexico)	15,500	6,000	2,200	34,000	25	2,100,000
Total/ Average	11,447,500	4,419,500	2,190 ave	25,895,000	31 ave	1,308,000,000

*   Parts of Arabian and Lybian deserts.
†   About 60% of Rub' al Khali desert.

The solar-electric energy available from the most energy-rich parts of the world is shown in Table 8.II. North Africa (particularly the Sahara), most of Saudi Arabia, more than 50% of Australia and parts of South Africa and India *are the great energy-rich land areas of the world.* Australia combines the properties of a high degree of education among the population, and the second-largest amount of solar energy falling on one nation. The energy collectable at 1% coverage of land is that needed for a world population of 4 billion to have an energy per head equal to that of the United States. On the South Australian town of Adelaide, for example, the average solar energy per day—taken to be collectable at 10% efficiency—is equivalent to about 50,000 barrels of oil per day. Unfortunately, the Australian Commonwealth Government has a budget for solar energy research which is small in comparison with the per capita research budgets in solar energy of countries where the resource is not so abundantly available. It is principally the biocatalytic route which has attracted interest there. No building of solar energy conversion plants is as yet proposed. Energy Committees of the Australian Federal Government are made up of financiers, with few scientists—and these are coal/nuclear persons. They lack representatives of massive solar conversion.

It is important to distinguish the intensity of insolation from the area of useless (i.e. cost-free) desert space on which it falls. Some regions in the world

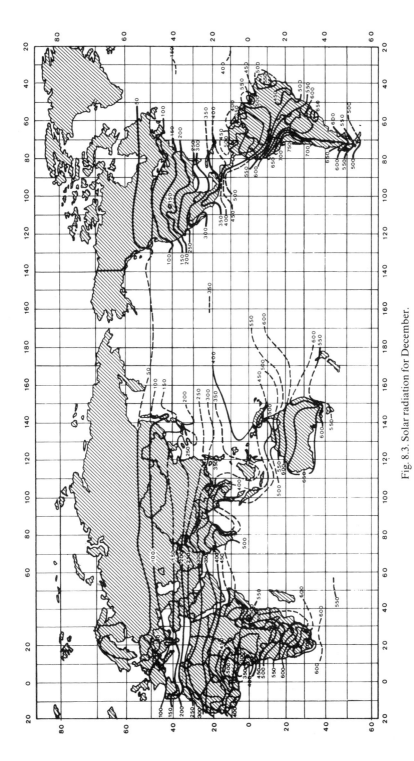

Fig. 8.3. Solar radiation for December.

receive a greater yearly average intensity than does the Australian Continent. However, 59% of the Australian Continent is a desert, mostly flat. It is this property, combined with the intensity of insolation, which makes Australia so attractive for the development of land-based solar-energy collection on a very large scale. Australia could be the Energy Depot for the Far-Eastern countries—particularly were Japanese initiative and capital to lead the development.

Population and living standard, supportable by solar energy

The sun radiates 1.7×10^{17} watts onto the earth continuously. 10% of this on 1% of the earth's surface is 1.7×10^{11} kW. A world population of 10 billions, with a total power need per person of 10 kW (including all industry, transportation, etc.), needs 10^{11} kW, i.e. all could be supplied by 10% efficient collection on *c*. 1% of the earth's surface. Were this energy use to be exceeded by introducing substantial new heat (e.g. from fusion) then the earth's temperature would rise; i.e. there is no *feasibility* of producing a *much* greater amount of usable energy on earth than could be converted from a 1% coverage of the earth by solar collectors, or by collection from a large fraction of the present deserts.

Uses of small-scale solar energy[3]

If roof-top collectors could contribute to the residential energy supply, particularly in the sunny areas of the world, the amount of energy from central sources which would have to be transferred over long distances would be reduced. When excess household energy can be collected from roofs, the possible storage modes are as hydrogen or in electrochemical batteries. Local transportation could be fuelled by energy so obtained.

The main uses of small-scale energy are as follows:

1. *Cooking*[4]
Solar energy for remote areas was developed in Mexico in the 1950s. It could not compete with oil, at that time cheaply available from the Middle East.

2. *Use for household heating*[4]
Black-sheets, with copper pipes containing water soldered onto the back, are manufactured in Israel, Japan and Australia (Fig. 8.4).

Solar space-heating of houses is incipient (Figs. 8.5 and 8.6). Air can be forced past the back side of the roof-top heat collectors, which could house photovoltaic cells. Duct work takes the air to a storage system (a molten salt, rock pile, or a large water reservoir), and cold air from the house is circulated over the storage system.

3. *Household cooling*[4]
In one concept for solar space-cooling, there would be two connected vessels, one containing liquid ammonia, and the other a concentrated solution of salt in ammonia. The latter solution has a lower vapour pressure than has pure liquid ammonia, and the latter vaporises to the compartment containing a solution of the salt in liquid ammonia. The vaporisation causes cooling. On the reverse cycle, solar heat is focused on the solution and liquid ammonia is made to evaporate back to the first compartment, where high pressure and

lower temperature cause condensation. The cycle is repeated.

Another concept, as yet to be applied, would use radiation to the night sky. There are IR windows in the atmosphere. If the object to be cooled (a house roof for example) contains a surface made of material which radiates in the wavelength range of the windows, it will cool air in contact with it. Silicon or iron has been suggested.

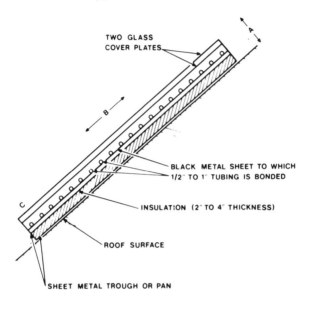

NOTES: ENDS OF TUBES MANIFOLDED TOGETHER
ONE TO THREE GLASS COVERS DEPENDING
ON CONDITIONS
DIMENSIONS: THICKNESS (A DIRECTION) 3 INCHES TO 6 INCHES
LENGTH (B DIRECTION) 4 FEET TO 20 FEET
WIDTH (C DIRECTION) 10 FEET TO 50 FEET
SLOPE DEPENDENT ON LOCATION AND ON
WINTER-SUMMER LOAD COMPARISON

Fig. 8.4. The roof-top solar heat collector.

Solar desalination[5]

The utilisation of solar energy to produce potable water from brackish or sea water is becoming attractive. Solar desalination has been in use at various arid locations for several years.

There are three types of solar or part-solar stills:
1. Black-bottomed basin type stills in which solar energy is the direct source of energy for evaporation.
2. Humidification-dehumidification plants, in which solar energy could be re-used one or more times in multiple effects in flash-evaporation devices. Helium is used to transport the vapours so that no vacuum pump has to be used.
3. Solar-assisted plants, in which solar radiation is the source of heat, but which have vacuum pumps to provide for liquid and vapour circulation.

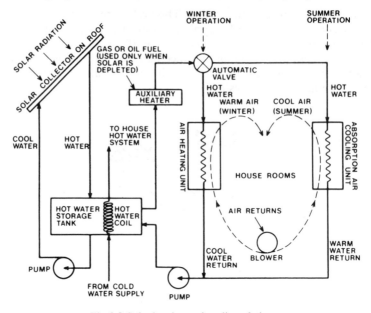

Fig. 8.5. Solar heating and cooling of a house.

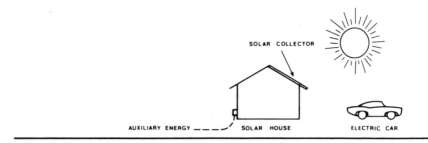

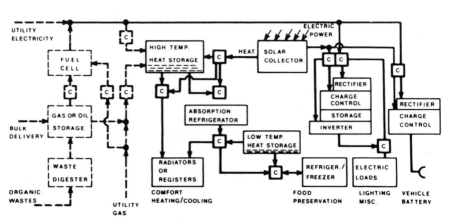

Fig. 8.6. Solar energy for housing.

The cost of these plants in 1978 dollars runs to 2 cents per gallon, at 50,000 gallons per day. This is cheaper than the flash-evaporation plants which are usually used for desalination, although of course the comparison depends upon the cost of fuel and the place where the desalination is to take place. The further one is away from a fuel centre, the better solar evaporation looks.

Another concept, hypothetical as yet, proposes the extraction of moisture from the atmosphere. Even over the Western Australian desert, there is a relative humidity of 10%, i.e. about 0.2% of the air mass is, in fact, water vapour. If such air were passed through a tower containing calcium chloride (during the night), the water in the air would be retained in the solid. During the day, the solid could be heated by the use of tracking mirrors and could be made to give up the water, which would be condensed and collected. The method could have value in hot, dry areas with local populations of a few hundred.

If one accounts for drinking, cooking, laundry, bathing, sanitary and primary production (but not industry and commerce), about 300 litres per person per day are needed. For a community of 1,000 persons, a chimney 300 feet high and 6 feet in diameter would have to have air containing 0.1% of water passed through it about twice per minute (assuming a 12-hour day) to provide the necessary water (assuming 100% efficiency of water absorption, recovery and condensation). The order of the cost per person per year would be tens of dollars.

Costing of massive solar sources

It is erroneous to cost solar sources in a simplistic way—by taking the cost per kilowatt hour. One should not neglect the cost of the absence of the pollution, which comes from the use of fossil fuels, and at present is subsidised by payments out of taxes. Such costs may be estimated to be as much as 50% of those of a unit of fossil fuel.

Comparison of the costs for solar energy must take into account the following:
1. The cost of pollution of fossil fuels.
2. The costs for decommissioning atomic plants.
3. Differences in efficiency of energy conversion in the use of solar-based fuels such as hydrogen compared with conventional fuels.

Correspondingly, the cost per kilowatt of solar plants and of the plants for the use-up of non-renewable resources cannot be compared, because to the costs of amortization of the latter must be added the fuel costs.

The solar and nuclear sources for massive energy production

The situation in this respect is shown in Table 8.III.

The apparent possibilities of massive solar have improved during the 1970s: but the realization of this is not yet widespread.

The solar-thermal method[6]

The solar-thermal method is the simplest method for collecting solar energy. It is also called the 'mirror' method, and the 'power tower' method. There

TABLE 8.III: Nuclear and Solar as Main Sources of Energy

Nuclear as Main Source	Solar as Main Source
1. Has grown up as an appendix of the weapons industry and receives thereby much tacit subsidy	1. Systems analyses of several schemes show costs in the region of $3,000 per kW; and 4-5 cents kwh^{-1}
2. Research: has always been very well funded—several national laboratories	2. Has had, hitherto, less than 1% of the research funds given to nuclear
3. Involves substantial health and hijack hazards	3. Low Technology: no doubts as to feasibility
4. Would only be commercial in competition with coal if regulatory agencies relaxed their safety demands	4. Building time $\leqslant$ 10 years per plant
5. Takes > 10 years to build one plant	5. Totally environmentally clean
6. Only Breeder System worth considering for post 2000 atomic energy: electricity produced from breeders costs more than that from fission. Could not compete with coal	6. No worries to future of manufacturing from environmental lobby
	7. Relative easy technology: could be built world-wide, including 3rd World indigenous engineering, with acceptable environmental effects.

is a tower, on the top of which is a receiver for heat, basically a water boiler. The tower is surrounded by a number of mirrors, called heliostats, and these orient with the sun, focusing their solar light upon the receiver surrounding the boiler.

A simple design of solar-thermal plant is in Fig. 8.7, and one out of many heliostat possibilities is in Fig. 8.8.

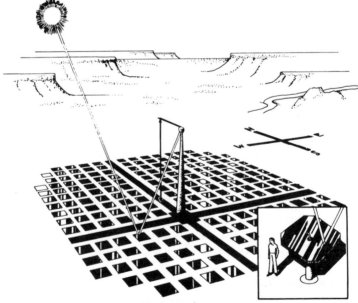

Fig. 8.7. Central receiver (solar-thermal) power plant (Davidson & Grether).

RECEIVER ASSEMBLY

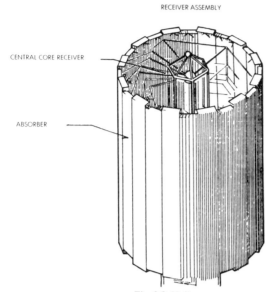

Fig. 8.8. Heliostat concept.

Concerning the top of the tower, it is intended to turn the solar heat into mechanical power which could give rise to electricity; there are several possibilities. Basically, some thermal engine is intended, a Rankine-cycle engine is one of several under funding.

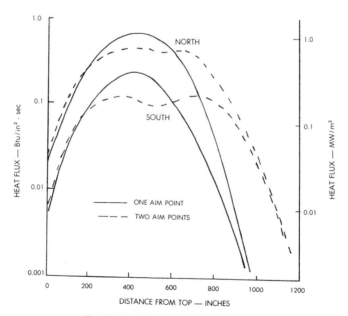

Fig. 8.9. Possible layouts in solar-thermal.

Several choices exist in respect to the field geometry. These are shown in Fig. 8.9. The central receiver refers to a tower located at the centre of the field. It may be better to have the tower placed south of the field's centre.[6] An individual tower would be used to generate about 100 MW, electric. In another design, smaller towers would be used. Tower height varies as the square root of the output of the field feeding the tower. If the amount to be collected is 100 MW, the tower has to be 300 m high.

The energy to be collected is sporadic, so that a storage system has to be involved. One of the possibilities for this is to split water and store hydrogen. Another idea would be to dissociate SO_3 with heat to SO_2 and oxygen. Were these two cooled and separated (*if* that is feasible), the SO_2 would be a suitable storage medium, and could be regenerated in the form of electricity via a fuel cell.

An artist's impression of a layout of mirrors and tower can be seen in Fig. 8.10.

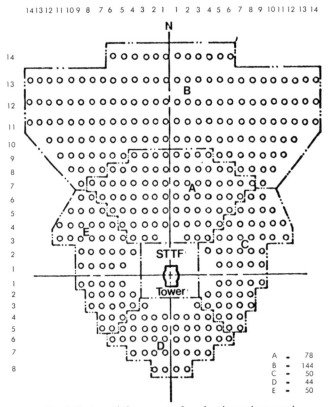

Fig. 8.10. An artist's concept of a solar-thermal proposal.

The tower construction has variants. The generation of steam may take place at the top of the tower, or at the bottom.

Space requirements for the solar-thermal plants are large. One square kilometre of mirror area gets about 100 MW_E of sporadic power. The plants are material intensive. For the 100 MW electric, one needs about 4.10^4 tons of steel and about 2.10^5 tons of concrete. The heliostats must survive severe winds: about 8 tons of concrete goes into one heliostat.

What makes up the cost of 1 kW of a plant is given in Table 8.IV.

TABLE 8.IV

	$
Land	2
Structure and facilities	44
Heliostats	300
Central receiver, tower, heat exchanger	95
Storage tanks	90
Turbine plant equipment	80
Electric plant equipment	24
Miscellaneous plant equipment	4
Cooling towers	20
Contingency allowance	39
Spare parts	3
Indirect costs	78
Escalation to start of construction	296
Interest during construction	199
Escalation during construction	169
Total, in 1990 dollars	*$1,440*

The cost given here assumes large-scale mass-production. A one-off plant built today would cost far more. It is not known, of course, whether the costs listed above can actually be attained.

In Table 8.V it is seen how the projected costs of various solar-thermal (sometimes called 'power tower') units vary.

TABLE 8.V: COMPARISON OF PROJECTED COST OF POWER TOWERS OR SOLAR THERMALS[6]

Martin-Marietta (\$ per kW electric)	McDonald-Douglas (\$ per kW electric)	Aerospace (\$ per kW electric)
1,685	1,210	1,440

All these costs are projected and consider that a large mass-production effort is underway. They are serious estimates, however, and simulate the situation which, should it arise, would reduce costs to the amounts shown.

The 5 MW solar-thermal test facility at the Sandia Laboratories[7]

The first solar-thermal test facility capable of delivering 5 MW has been built at the Sandia (U.S. Government) Laboratories, and started producing power at about 1 MW in 1978. The tower rises 61 m and extends about 15 m into the earth.

Four primary experimental locations are in the tower top.

The tower interior contains an elevating module about 9.1 m x 7.6 m, and 13.1 m high. This can be placed anywhere in the distance between ground level and 61 m level. It will lift 90,700 kg and is a workshop. The heat-rejection system supplies cooling fluids to experiments to dissipate collected energy. It supplies boiler-quality feed water at a rate of about 3.16 litres per second at a temperature of 288°C.[7]

The energy collection field consists of 222 heliostats. Provision for heliostats to an original plant total of 312 has been made. The heliostat field can concentrate 5 million watts, and produce an intensity of 2.5×10^6 watts per m^2 under a favourable sun. The reflector surface of one heliostat is made up of 25 back-silvered glass mirrors, and these total $37.2m^{-2}$.

The facets are assembled into a mirror module and the module is moved by an azimuth and elevation mount and drive system. The position is known by a digital output optical encoder. The heliostats focus by mechanically warping the mirrors.

The alignment is accomplished by using a laser-like beam the size of a facet, and this is directed to the facet of interest and the reflection is returned to the target.

The heliostat characterisation system is used to evaluate individual facets, and also the overall heliostat performance. Heliostat reflectivity is important. Preliminary results indicate that the average reflectivity can drop as much as 15%, from about 80% to 65%, in a month. Natural cleaning by rain improves the reflectivity by about 5%. Cleaning techniques will vary from annual cleaning to automated techniques. High-pressure water and detergent sprays indicate that 80-90% of the normal reflectance losses due to dirt can be recovered.

The Sandia solar-thermal is being used as a general test facility and a picture during building is shown in Fig. 8.11.

Fig. 8.11. Central tower at Albuquerque during building.

Otto J. Smith's Design, or a Solar-Thermal Facility[7]

In the Otto J. Smith design for the production of electricity from solar-thermal plants, the tower surrounded by heliostats is short. The sun shines on heliostats and the heat is collected by high-boiling liquids and taken to a heat exchanger. The plant can be built immediately, would be easy to erect, and uses conventional engineering techniques and materials.

In the 100 MW module system, the electric generator is driven by a conventional steam turbine: heat is obtained from heat exchange fluids collecting energy from the solar farm.

The solar farm area is 2.4 km², and is divided into 1100 identical modules. Each module area is 2175 m², and contains 312 small mirrors of 2 m² area, each reflecting sunlight; it concentrates the latter through the window of a receptor on a short tower, 20 metres high at the site of the mirrors.

Each receptor takes up 5 kW of thermal power from its mirrors. The receptor is an insulated cavity containing pipes through which heat exchange fluids are pumped. The fluids leave the receptor at high temperatures and are collected in the power-house, where they pass through heat exchangers and are cooled off, being pumped back to the solar field.

Each module has a hexagonal ground plan for the best utilisation of the land. The hexagon shapes are interlocking like a honeycomb, and the tower for the mirrors in one hexagon has its base in the middle of a different hexagon to the south. This field pattern minimises the cost of piping, and reduces losses due to the angle of the mirror with respect to the incident sunray, and due to reflection at the cavity receptor window.

Maintenance would be done at night.

Cost of an Otto J. Smith plant[7]

The mirrors and other controls would cost 59% of the power plant cost. The solar energy receiver, tower, and piping cost is 11%. The power-house and heat exchanger, turbine, generator, and switch-yard, 15%. The efficiency of the mirror system is 84%, that of the receiver and heat transport 89%, and that of the power-house 37%.

The mirror plate is fibreglass epoxy, 2 metres wide by 1 metre high, over a paraboloid mould. The mirror surface is metallised polyester, which is held down on the plate electrostatically. With this construction, the mirror surface can be replaced if damaged by sand storms. Suitable surfaces are silver polyester. The mirror is mounted on a 5 ft high pedestal, with motor controls to adjust the angle of elevation.

Each receptor has a double-paned window which is cooled by triethylene between the panes. The cool glass minimises heat loss by convection. The triethylene glycol is circulated at the power-house and provides pre-heat for the boiler feed heat water.

In the centre of the receptor cavity are black pipes at 400°C with a heat exchange fluid, and at the back of the cavity are additional black pipes at 600°C. Heat is brought to the central power house at 550°C.

Comparisons of the Otto J. Smith Module Solar-Electric System with others

The low optical-concentration ratio in the Smith design permits a relaxed requirement on the mirror surface and controls. The hexagon field boundaries for the heliostat fields minimise piping and costs.

The design distinguishes itself from those elsewhere funded by the fact that the mirror surfaces are easily replaced; the metallised polyester film with an electrostatic hold-down is inexpensive; and the mirror focal length is short to produce a good image and concentrate the reflected light to the receptor. Short tower heights reduce the long-term maintenance and repair costs.

Costs of electricity from the Otto J. Smith Plant

The cost of the 1,000 MW unit would be about $1.3 billion, and the initial electricity generation cost would be 3.1 cents per kW/hr, in 1978 dollars.[8]

Building is labour intensive.

Pollution from solar-thermal plants[6]

Pollution with solar-thermal plant in action would be zero, but during the making of a plant the effluent will be considerable and will consist of particles, sulphur oxides, nitric oxide, hydrocarbons, and carbon monoxide.

According to Davidson and Grether,[6] the effluents from the corresponding coal and oil-fired plants would be an order of magnitude greater than that associated with the building of the solar-thermal plants.

Strain on engineering and manufacturing trades in the building process

There would have to be increases in trades in the region of 10-40% in regions where plants were being built.[7]

Land requirements

The requirement is about 3 km^2 of land per 100 MW. At least 55,000 km^2 of land is suitable in the SW part of the United States for solar-thermal plant.

The amount which would supply the entire electric demand for the United States would be about 11,800 km^2.

Penetration by solar-thermal plants into the energy market[6]

The degree to which the solar-thermal plants will be able to take over from other plants depends on their making a fuel, most obviously hydrogen. This was not appreciated by Davidson and Grether,[6] who regard their solar-thermal plants only as electricity providers. They suggest that by the year 2000 about 100 GW_E plants could be built.

This is a small amount of solar plant, compared with what is needed. Thus, the energy needed by 2000 will be (assuming continued expansion to that time at 2% per year) about twice that needed at present, which is about 2.5 10^6 MW (or about 2.5 10^3 GW). In view of the expected turn-down in oil and gas supplies by the early 1990s, it would seem reasonable to have solar and atomic plants provide one-quarter of the needed load at 2000.

Socio-economic effects of building solar-thermal plants[6]

Davidson and Grether made an analysis of the effect of building solar-thermal plants upon employment.[6] They found that building a solar-thermal plant causes much more employment than the building of a coal plant. The number of man-years needed to build a coal plant with an energy equivalent of 100 MW$_E$ over its lifetime was 3,900. The corresponding number for the equivalent solar-thermal plant was 10,000.

Putting this another way, the number of man-years per million dollars of investment for the solar plant was 60.6 man-years, and for the coal plant, 51.7 years. However, the assessments made at this time are labile because of the fact that, as the solar-thermal plants become better understood, the degree of mass production will increase.

Ecological effects of solar-thermal plants

The present energy consumption in the United States is 10 kW per person. During the 21st century, the world's population may rise to 10 billion. We let it be assumed that the standard of living will be equal to the standard of living of Americans in the 1970s.

To generate 100 MW of base load power, about 2-3 km^2 of reflector surface would be required. The area affected by support personnel would be about 1 km^2 per 100 MW. Thus, to meet the demand we should need 10^6 plants, and these would take up 2.10^6 km^2 of mirror area. If we took the ground cover ratio for the plants as one-third, the area needed would be 6.10^6 km^2.

Let us estimate the effects on the albedo of the above. Let us follow Davidson and Grether[6] in assuming that an area equal to the total mirror area of the plant becomes black, and an area equal to 1.10^6 km^2 for the support personnel also becomes black. Thus, 3.10^6 km^2 is darkened, and this area is spread over an area of 9 10^6 km^2, corresponding to the ground cover ratio of one-third for the support personnel. We assume that the new albedo would be two-thirds of the old. The distribution is that of the Table 8.VI. The radiation temperature of the earth is defined by the following equation:

$$S4\pi R_e^2(1-\bar{\alpha}) = \sigma 4\pi R_e^2 T_R^4$$

where σ is the Steffan-Boltzmann constant, T_R is the radiation temperature, S is the solar constant (1.4 kW)m^{-2}, R_e the radius of the earth, and $\bar{\alpha}$ its mean albedo.

The left-hand side of the equation is the radiation absorbed by the earth per unit time. Only half the area will be tracking the sun and the other half will be on the dark side of the earth.

TABLE 8.VI: Mirror and Land Areas for Scenario by Rough Location
(Davidson and Grether)

Region	Percentage	Total Mirror Area (km^2)	Land Area (km^2)
N. America	15	4.5x10^5	13.5x10^5
S. America	10	3.0x10^5	9 x10^5
Europe	<5	1.5x10^5	4.5x10^5
Sahara	15	4.5x10^5	13.5x10^5
Arab. Penin.	10	3.0x10^5	9 x10^5
India	15	4.5x10^5	13.5x10^5
China	15	4.5x10^5	13.5x10^5
Australia	5	1.5x10^5	4.5x10^5
S. Africa	5	1.5x10^5	4.5x10^5
USSR	5	1.5x10^5	4.5x10^5
Total	100	3 x10^6	9 x10^6

The tracking mirrors are normal to the sun. The cross-sectional area of ½ A_d of the deserts of the world become absorbing for direct radiation.[9] The earth's radiation gain is therefore:

$$\tfrac{1}{2}\ SA_d(1-\alpha_d)$$

where α_d is the albedo of the desert.

Values of this vary from about 0.2 to 0.4.

Using the above equations, one finds that the temperature increase would be:

$$\delta T_r = \frac{1}{8}\ \frac{\alpha_d}{1-\bar{\alpha}}\ \frac{A_d}{TR_e^2}\ T_r$$

where T is the original temperature before introduction of the solar-thermal system.

In using a value of 0.3 for α_d and 285°K for T_r, Davidson and Grether found:

$$\delta T_r = 0.2°K$$

Further discussion by Davidson and Grether suggests that, if one takes into account desert area taken up by buildings for the support personnel, the rise in the earth's temperature could be as high as 0.4°.

Summary on Solar Thermal[6,7,10]

The cost would be $1,400 per kW; and 10,000 man-years would be spent in building a 100 MW_E plant, 2.5 times more man-hours than the same energy production by a coal plant. There is pollution in building a plant, but the pollution is less than that which would arise from building a coal plant, and there would be no long-term CO_2 pollution.

The production of a large number of solar-thermal plants would significantly affect industries and occupations. Water would be required in great amounts. Changes in micro-climate would not be great, e.g. less than 0.5° increase in temperature, and precipitation changes in cm per day would be less than .01 cm. Water requirements seem to be the greatest difficulty to be faced in the building of solar-thermal plants.

Ocean-Thermal Energy Conversion[8,9,11]

Introduction

Ocean thermal energy converters (OTEC) utilise the temperature difference between the top and bottom of the sea to cause a thermal engine to work. The warm sea at the surface acts upon a working fluid which boils at low temperatures, and then after the vapour from this fluid has evaporated and passed through a heat engine, producing mechanical energy, the vapour is returned to the condenser which draws up cold water to condense the liquid, whereupon the cycle starts again.

History of OTEC

The idea was proposed by D'Arsonval, a French scientist, in 1930; George Claude took his self-funded project to Cuba and set up a device which produced 22 kW but which was, after 2 weeks' functioning, ruined by a hurricane. Designs were made in the late 1950s in France, but did not prosper because of the low price at which the oil capital was being given out at that time.

A significant amount of American work took place in the late 1940s and in the 1950s, under Howe and Beorse.[12]

In the mid-1960s, the Andersons, a father and son engineering team in Pennsylvania, redesigned OTEC plants, but once more the low cost of oil kept interest low.

The present situation is that no OTEC pilot plant has been built* whereas photovoltaics are routinely used in space vehicles, and a solar-thermal plant has begun to function in Albuqerque. What the OTEC plants have lost in realisation hitherto, however, they have made up in the large number of Systems Analyses (twenty-six of them!).[14] Everything is known about OTEC which can be known without putting equipment in the water and proceeding to try it out. This has been planned and promised for 3-4 years but it does look as though it might occur in 1985. It is interesting to note that, meanwhile, very large research support is being given to develop the production of fuels from coal already done in Germany in the 1930s.

Heat exchangers

The temperature difference in which OTEC is to work would be between some 80°F and 40°F, i.e. it is useful only in tropical waters. As the heat passes through the heat exchangers, there would be roughly a 50% temperature drop. This would leave 20°F out of the initial 40°F temperature difference for conversion to useful work. Of these 20°F, about 25% of the electricity generated by the turbo-generator would be consumed to pump water through the heat exchangers. Hence, OTEC plants are left with only about 15°F of effective temperature difference to work on. This is equivalent to around a 2% Carnot efficiency.

Why do these losses occur, and can anything be done to stop them? Heat encounters resistances, rather like electricity. Materials resist having heat transmitted through them. To increase the rate of heat flow one must increase the temperature driving force or decrease the resistance along the path of heat flow.

In an OTEC system, the available temperature difference is limited. An engineer must resort to increasing the surface area in the exchangers. At the present time, three mechanisms for evaporation are being considered for OTEC plants: pool boiling, forced convection, and film evaporation. Once the evaporation has taken place, the vapour escapes from the liquid-vapour surface and builds up a pressure on the evaporator. This vapour pressure, moderate in comparison with steam pressure, must build up high enough so that it can exert the force needed to turn the turbine shaft.

---

* Although the Andersons have privately funded a tiny demonstration model, producing 200 watts, in a swimming pool.[13]

Heat exchanger calculations

The heat transfer is calculated using the basic equation

$$Q = uA\Delta T_m$$

where u equals the overall heat transfer coefficient, A equals surface area, and ΔT_m equals the mean temperature difference. The heat transfer coefficient is calculated assuming a thin tube wall.[15]

The equation for the overall heat transfer coefficient for a circular pipe is represented by Eckert as:[16]

$$U = \cfrac{1}{\cfrac{1}{h_i} + \cfrac{T}{k} + \cfrac{1}{h_o}}$$

Here, h_i is the heat transfer coefficient between seawater and the outside tube well; T is the tube well thickness; k is the thermal conductivity of the tube well; and h_o is the heat transfer coefficient between the fluid and the outside tube well.

According to McAdams,[17]

$$h_i = 0.023 \left[\frac{DG}{\mu}\right] 0.8 \left[\frac{C_p\mu}{k}\right] 0.4 \left[\frac{k}{D}\right]$$

where D is the diameter of the tube, G is the mass flow rate of the seawater, μ is the bulk viscosity of the seawater, C_p is the specific heat of the seawater, and k is the thermal conductivity of the seawater. Nelson[12] chose a laboratory value of 5,000 for the Reynolds number for the seawater, taking the rate of flow as equivalent to four feet per second.

The heat transfer coefficient for the condenser working flow was calculated using the relation suggested by McAdams;[17] the equation is recommended for condensation in horizontal-tube exchangers and given by:

$$h_o.C = 0.725 \left[\frac{k_f^3 \rho_f^2 g h_{fg}}{ND\mu_f \Delta T}\right]$$

Here, k_f is the thermal conductivity of the working fluid condensate; ρ_f is the density of the working fluid condensate; g is the acceleration due to gravity; h_{fg} is the latent heat of the working fluid; N is the number of tubes in the vertical stack; D is the tube temperature; μ is the viscosity of the working fluid; and ΔT is the difference in the well and saturation temperature.

The heat transfer from the boiler to the working fluid interface was broken into two parts by Nelson.[12] One part covered the surface-to-liquid transfer in the cycle range, and the second in the two-phase region where boiling is supposed to nucleate and where transfer is increased by the stirring action of the bubbles on the tube surfaces.

This is the basis of the heat transfer calculations which are carried out and which are the centre of the OTEC concept.

The best working fluid for OTEC

Any liquid which is stable, cheap, and which will boil at 25° or less is worth considering for OTEC, but its condensation properties must also be examined. Working fluids which have been proposed are ammonia, water (boiling at reduced pressure), butane, propane, freon-12, carbon dioxide, ethane, and hydrogen sulphide.

Ammonia is the best: it is probably of little point to pursue others. Ammonia can be produced as a by-product of the OTEC station; it has the least ecological dangers compared with the other system; and the processes go well with the submerged heat exchanger so that pressure differences can be reduced, allowing a low-cost heat exchanger design.

OTEC machinery

There must be a start-up machine to set the pilot plant in motion. A diesel generator would do. Heavy-duty pumps would be necessary and it may be that they could be copied from pumps which are used in dykes and reservoir systems at the present time.

The modular concept

An advantage of OTEC is that it could be modular, and added to from time to time. Thus, small systems for heat exchangers could be started with, and gradually expanded as the need grew.

What kind of ship-like platform?

Several platforms are under consideration: they could either be disc-like in shape, or semi-submersible cylinders, or like a ship.

Transport of energy from OTEC

If the plant is near shore, there would be every possibility of transferring the energy to land via cables. If it is far away from shore, it would be better to make liquid hydrogen and transport this to land by tug.

Bio-fouling

Bio-fouling will tend to occur when marine life attaches itself to the heat exchangers. It is a slime formation on the water side of the heat exchanger surface. It is essential to involve in every OTEC design, effective suggestions for the counteracting of bio-fouling.

According to Nath, Ambler and Hansen,[18] the most common method for controlling bio-fouling is cleaning with high-pressure sprays. Other methods include heat treatment, chlorination, toxic coatings, etc. High water velocities will reduce fouling. Another method of bio-fouling cleaning suggested by Perrigo and Jensen[19] would involve soft rubber balls that are frequently fed into various tubes in the heat exchanger to wipe undesirable substances from the surface. Another method uses cavitation in a hydraulic system to remove these materials.

An experimental study of bio-fouling has been carried out by Fetkovich, Grannemann, Mahalingam, Meyer and Muchmeyer.[20] They conclude from experiments that the bio-fouling rate was slow for a few weeks, but increased after a few months. Bio-fouling increases with pumping velocity; on the other hand, the surface roughness may significantly affect the bio-fouling rate. A polished surface does not bio-foul as easily as a rough surface.

There is a strong depth-dependence of the bio-fouling rates in the sense that when the substances are immersed, the bio-fouling rate is less, i.e. bio-fouling is a phenomenon which takes places near the surface.

Bio-fouling experiments should be carried out for various types of waters and electrochemical chlorination of the surface with occasional pulses should be tried as a main method of permanently stopping fouling.

An elegant method has been proffered by Nubel.[21] Each tube of the cooler or condenser is equipped with a cylindrical basket at either end and a nylon bristle brush. Under normal operating conditions, the brushes rest on cages beyond the downstream tube sheet. Periodically, the flow of cooling water is reversed. This causes the brushes to travel through the tube to the opposite end, where they are captured by the baskets, held briefly, and, upon return to the standard flow direction, shuttled through the tubes to assume their starting position. On the trip through the tubes the brushes loosen sediment, which is flushed out ahead of the brushes.

Other methods include the use of chemical cleaners, flow-driven brushes, the recirculating rubber balls, the ultrasonic cleaning, and water jet cleaning. There is no method as yet known which would give a guaranteed cleaning of the OTEC situation. It is one of the earliest items which needs investigation on an experimental basis.

Corrosion

Copper and aluminium are considered good thermal conductors, whereas titanium is poor. However, aluminium tends to corrode when exposed to seawater: copper and titanium corrode less. The cost of an aluminium heat exchanger would be lower than that of a copper unit. Titanium, however, is compatible with ammonia as a working fluid. However, titanium is still too expensive for large-scale application.

It is better, from the point of view of getting cold water, to make the pipe long enough to reach the deepest water. But it is more expensive to make a long pipe. The optimum condition may be with a pipe 1,000 ft long.

Mineral-rich ocean water[22]

Water taken up from the depth is mineral rich. Brought to the sea surface by OTEC circulation, a fish catchment area could be started near each plant.

Storms[22]

There are two options for positioning or station-keeping: the plant could be moored to the seabed or it could navigate itself like a ship and drive into the storm. Dynamic positioning with thrusters, perhaps the thrust put out from the condensers, could position the plant in stormy weather.

Sites for OTEC

The Gulf Stream, where the water moves past the site, would be suitable. Another site would be in the Gulf of Mexico, 50-100 miles from the Louisiana coast. There is the possibility of putting an early plant near an island, such as Hawaii or Puerto Rico, because with islands the land slopes rapidly away and the plant could be as near as two miles to the shore.

Industrial production on the site[22]

Electrochemical processes could be utilised at sea with OTEC electricity. The electricity at sea would be cheaper than that piped to land. It would be better to move the industries to the OTEC plants, e.g. aluminium or ammonia manufacture at the sites.

The electrical power could be used for deep mining of minerals, and for the manufacture of hydrogen, which could be sent back to shore. Desalinated seawater could be utilised.

Economic evaluation of OTEC

About twenty-six systems analyses have been made of OTEC.[13]

Cost of OTEC plants

This must be a systems analysis matter, in the absence of the will to experiment, but several analyses have a variation between them of 300 and 1,266 in 1977 dollars — *the cheapest projected cost of all solar possibilities.*[13]

A detailed breakdown of one plant is shown in Table 8.VII.

A comparison of OTEC costs with those of nuclear and coal may be made, and the electric power component is shown in Table 8.VIII.

TABLE 8.VII: CALCULATION OF ENERGY COST OTEC PLANTS
(G. H. Levi)

Source		*TRW* *1975 Baseline Design*	*Improved heat transfer* *Aluminium heat exchangers*	
Capital Cost $/kW		$2100	$1040	$1040
ANNUAL OUTLAYS				
Return Rate	11%	$231.2	$114.4	
Depreciation/				
Amortization	1%	18.5	9.2	
Administrative	1% = 18%	21.0	10.4	
Taxes (local)	3%	63.0	31.2	
Insurance on				
Capital Cost	2%	42.0	20.8	
SUBTOTAL		$375	$186	$156*
OPERATING EXPENSES				
Protection		1.5		
Crew		6.7		
Logistics		2.6		
Maintenance		15.4		
Miscellaneous		2.8		
Overhead		4.2	33.2	33.2
TOTAL		$408.9	$219.2	$189.2

Busbar Cost in Mills/kwh = Annual Outlay/(8760 x Capacity)

Capacity			
80%	59	31	27
90%	52	28	24
100%	47	25	22†

* 15% of capital cost based on more conventional fixed utility charge.
† This lowest estimated cost would be equivalent to a gaseous Hydrogen cost of around $9 per MBTU and LH$_2$ ≏ $12 per MBTU.

Price comparisons arising from OTEC

Talib, Knopka, Biederman, Vlazeka and Yudow have analysed the current energy prices from OTEC.[23] One has the following comparison:

Synthetic natural gas from coal	$2.50-$4.00
Synthetic natural gas from naphtha	$3.96-$5.38
Methanol from coal	$6.00-$7.50
Liquid natural gas from coal	$3.00-$4.50
Estimated cost of OTEC electricity in 1978 dollars for 1985	3.75-4.00 cents kwh
OTEC-based liquid hydrogen after passage of 100 miles	$12.52 per MBTU
Hydrogen gas at 100 miles	$8.44-$10.08 per MBTU
Electricity from OTEC on-shore made by 33% efficient conversion process *(it could be made at double this efficiency in a fuel cell)*	7-9 cents per kwh (4-5 cents per kwh)

Ammonia could be obtained at a competitive cost by OTEC even at present and is hence *the potential subject of commercial development.*

TABLE 8.VIII: PROJECTED ELECTRIC ENERGY COST COMPARISONS—80% CAPACITY
(G. H. Levi)

	Oil	Coal	Nuclear	Nuclear	OTEC
Capital Cost $/kW	600	700	1200	55% capacity	1400
Energy Cost					
Fixed Charges	12.8	15.0	25.7	37.4	
Fuel Cost	29.0	17.3	5.4	5.4	
Operating/Maintenance	2.0	3.0	2.5	2.4	
Total mills/kWh	43.8	35.3	33.6	45.2	35

Some of these prices are shown in Fig. 8.12.

It is interesting to note that the costs estimated by Talib *et al.*[23] are above other estimates of Dugger and Francis.[24]

OTEC costs would not compete with residual oil and natural gas. Could OTEC compete with coal? Liquid H_2 from coal would be about $7-8 per MBTU. According to Talib *et al.*,[23] OTEC could not compete with this. According to Dugger and Francis it could.[24] As in previous comparisons of solar prices with those of fossil fuels, the environmental damage done by mining these, and expelling their complex polluting materials into the atmosphere, should be accounted for. It does not represent the actual situation if the one kind of fuel (e.g. oil from coal) is produced, subsidized—whilst a similar subsidy is not given to the solar product.

OTEC and nuclear plants

An analysis has been given by Larvi and Zener of OTEC systems in comparison with nuclear systems.[25] They have plotted the original utility announced costs against the actual final costs of nuclear plants. The real costs are twice the apparent cost announced when the plant was planned.

Thus, the real cost figure for nuclear plants in 1978 is about $3,000 per kW; with breeders it would be substantially greater.

However, the most important aspect is to be brought out. When one buys

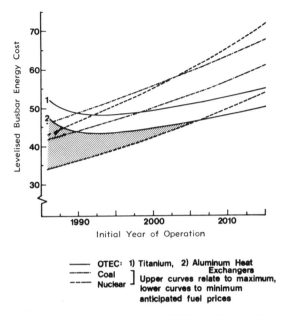

Fig. 8.12. Economic competitiveness of OTEC (Milles & Washom).

a plant, one assumes that it has a certain capacity factor and this factor has been assumed to be about 80% for nuclear plants. Larvi and Zener have plotted the actual use rate of nuclear plants and the use factor turns out to be 54%.[25]

On this basis, the figure for nuclear plants of $2,600 for the mid-1980 plants, in 1977 dollars, is deduced.

Compared with this, *the OTEC plants would be relatively cheap,* being cost-estimated in the range $1,200-$1,700. However, the realisation of this does depend upon whether the Government is willing to develop what seems to be the strongest competitor to the nuclear plants, in the development of which much capital has been invested.

The economic competitiveness of OTEC compared with
nuclear and coal energy

A study of the central topic has been carried out by Milles and Washom.[26] They took the Lockheed study of OTEC and made a comparison of it with coal and nuclear possibilities, shown in Fig. 8.12. The cost differential is highly favourable to OTEC for the years after 2000.

Several other things come out from this study. For example, it is clear that the investment needed for the development of OTEC, as with solar thermal, is *too great for private industry,** and that the rate of progress depends entirely upon government funding. However, hitherto, the really large funding for development has been in the direction of the high-risk options of nuclear and coal.

---

*On the other hand, the profit-making potential of an ammonia plant from OTEC is to be noted.

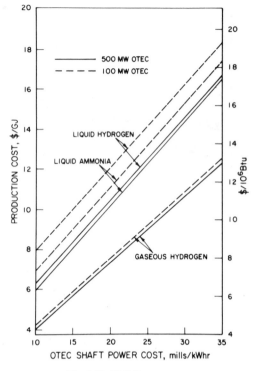

Fig. 8.13. OTEC power costs.

Points in favour of the development of OTEC are pointed out by Milles and Washom.[26] The learning experience from the first few units will clarify the market potential (see Fig. 8.13).

The return on investment, as shown by Lindal, Hornberg and El-ramly,[27] would be 25%, based on power costs of 25 million per kW/hr for sea chemicals. Organic chemicals and plastics could be produced competitively with land-based ones, even at present. Gaseous and liquid hydrogen, liquid ammonia, methanol, hydrazine and other organics could be made by OTEC and used as chemical energy-carriers.

The ecological effects of OTEC

It is important to be sure that OTEC plants do not have ecological difficulties by disturbing the vertical distribution of heat as they graze the seas. Thus, Martin and Roberts compared OTEC operation on the thermal structure of the Gulf of Mexico.[28] They used a one-dimensional heat conservation equation to predict the horizontal mean temperature; the surface heat fluxes were parameterised in terms of the observed variables; and the sea surface temperatures.

The operation of 1,000 OTEC plants in the Gulf of Mexico is parameterised by the the addition to the model of a mean vertical velocity profile. The result is a surface cooling on the warming of the depth. The sea surface temperature drops about 3° during the first two years, and then remains constant. However, the deep water in the region above the cold water intake re-equilibrates the result to 4°C.

The missed-flow OTEC plant

There have been so far two basic ideas in OTEC. The first one was the original idea of D'Arsonval. Some liquid, such as ammonia, is boiled on contact with the warm water at the surface at one pressure and, after passing through a heat engine, where it does work, condenses at a lower pressure with the help of cold water.

Designs of most OTEC plants so far work like this.

The second French physicist who worked with OTEC, George Claude, attempted to avoid heat exchangers, and the bio-fouling difficulties, by using water as a working fluid. The warm water was sprayed into one chamber which had been evacuated. Here, because it was warm, steam evaporated from the drops and went to a turbine to do work, and was condensed in a second chamber by cold water spray. This is called an open-cycle system. The low density of the steam required, of course, a large turbine to absorb the work, and the large size has discouraged people pursuing this path.

Inventors have been seeking a way around the mechanical design difficulties of the steam turbine in open cycle processes. Beck suggested that the vapour generated from the warm water should be used to lift that water against gravity.[29] Bubbles of steam would be nucleated in the water and would lift it in a manner similar to that which occurs in the air or gas lift pump of the chemical industry. Zener and Fetkovich[30] supported the two-phase mixture of Beck[29] and thought a foam structure would be effective.

When the water had been lifted in this way it would fall down in hydraulic tubes and provide the power.

Ridgeway,[31] in 1977, suggested an open cycle system similar to these, but a mist of water is lifted against gravity by the flow of steam from a high-pressure region to a low-pressure region. The warm water from the surface would fall, doing external work, then be made into a mist and be lifted back to the surface of the ocean from where it would be discharged.

The centre of this system is the large duct preparation to accommodate upward flow of the mist of small water droplets in the steam. The bottom of the duct is below the ocean and the duct is above it. Warm water is taken from near the surface, filtered, and allowed to descend. The water then passes through a hydraulic turbine, where most of the pressure energy is removed. By means of the pressure remaining, the water is sprayed into tiny jets into the bottom of the duct, where the ambient pressure is below the saturation vapour pressure of the injected warm water. Some of the water evaporates and forms steam, and this steam raises the water droplets to the top of the duct again, against the force of gravity. The droplets are small enough so that the viscous friction is sufficient to enable the steam to carry them up, in Ridgeway's process.

When the flow has reached the top, it is turned outwards towards the condenser. After condensing the steam, the mixed waters are returned to the ocean. Electrical generators could be connected to the hydraulic turbines. The essence of the concept is the generation of the steam-water mixture and its survival for a few seconds.

There is enough energy to lift the water to interesting heights, even if its temperature is 20°C, when 4°C cold water is available to establish the final temperature.

The advantage of this process is the avoidance of heat exchangers and bio-fouling.

Undue delay in the OTEC development?

There has been hesitation in funding real pilot plants with OTEC, in spite of the advantages which systems analysis indicate. The Solar Energy Division of the Department of Energy asked for $178 million in 1978, but for the nuclear budget the request is $2.3 billion.

Recent progress in OTEC is as follows:

1. A programme plan aimed at OTEC demonstration at the 100 MWe level by 1985 (still paper studies) in steps 1-5-25 MWe.
2. The construction at Argonne Lab of a heat exchanger test facility to test evaporators and condensers at the level of 1 MW. Five exchangers have been designed, built and delivered to Argonne. The aim is to provide industry with proven alternate heat transfer technologies.
3. The government has issued an RFP for the conversion and operation of a platform (ship, barge, . . .) with 6-foot diameter, 3,000-foot-long cold-water pipe to test heat exchangers in the ocean at the level of 40 MWe or 1MWe. A turbine may be added later. Work should be completed in the early 1980s. This is called the OTEC-1 project.
4. TRW has a contract to build for the government the first 1 MWe heat exchangers to be tested on OTEC-1.
5. Lockheed, TRW and Westinghouse are designing heat exchangers for testing on OTEC-1; a 10 MWe power plant is to be located off a tropical island; and a 100 MWe commercial plant is under design.[32]

It seems clear that with OTEC one needs to have a ban on any more paper studies and simply build some pilot plants.

Criticisms of the OTEC concept

The concept is only usable in warm water. The question of storms will be with us until solved by practical tests.

Will the bio-fouling problem be overcome?

Some basics of photovoltaic couples

Principles

When radiation of frequency exceeding a critical value strikes a solid, it may cause positive and negative carriers in excess of equilibrium to be generated. One of these must collect on a surface of the system, so that an excess inter-facial charge develops, and therefore a potential difference is built up be-tween the phase containing the excess carriers, generated by the solar pho-tons, and that which is not so insolated, and hence contains no corresponding excess carrier concentration. The carrier generated by light must live for τ secs, where τ is the time to diffuse to the boundary.

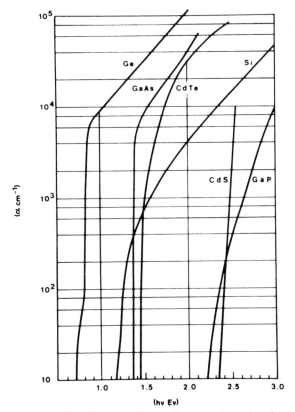

Fig. 8.14. The absorption coefficients and wavelength.

Generation of carriers

The number of photons in a beam which has traversed a distance x of material is

$$N_{ph,x} = N_{ph,x=0}e^{-\alpha x}$$

α being a function of wavelength. Fig. 8.14 shows how α depends upon frequency or wavelength. Thus, at frequencies less than the critical value, α tends to zero and there is no absorption. ν_{crit} is given by $h\nu_{crit} = E_{gap}$ where E_{gap} = the energy gap of the semiconductor. The importance of E_{gap} is that it determines whether solar radiation (which exists largely between 0.5 and 2 eV) will cause charge generation in a given semiconductor. Any semiconductor with an energy gap greater than about 1 eV is of lesser—and if greater than 2 eV, very little—use as a solar energy converter. The thickness needed to absorb 90% of the incident radiation is:

For, e.g. GaAs: $x_{min} = 2.10^{-4}$ cm

$\alpha x > 2.3$

Thus: $x_{min} > 2.3/\alpha$

Larger thicknesses are dead weight.

There are two kinds of behaviour for the α-x relation. That typified by GaAs has $\alpha > 10^4$ for most of the range above 1.3 eV. Another behaviour (Si) shows that a slow increase of α with v is also possible. Materials of the first type are called 'direct' and of the second type 'indirect'. The first type is more desirable, if available, because the needed thickness is less and the amount of the material is smaller. Hence the term 'thin-film photovoltaics'.

The dependence of efficiency of conversion on energy gap is shown in Fig. 8.15.

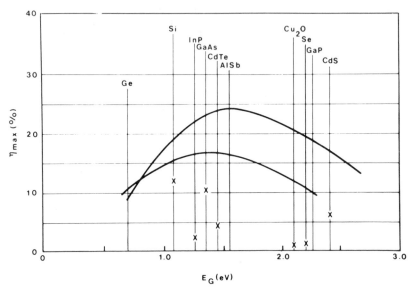

Fig. 8.15. Conversion efficiency and energy gap.

Types of photovoltaic junctions

There are two types of p-n junctions, homo and hetero. Silicon is the classic example of the first type, copper sulphide-cadmium sulphide a well-known example of the second type. Organic materials may also be considered.

One possibility is to make a metal on one side and a semiconductor on the other: little knowledge of such couples exists at present.

Diffusion to the boundary

Recombination of carriers is a principal cause of loss of efficiency. The direct gap materials, such as GaAs, have a short lifetime for carriers ($c.$ 10^{-8} sec). The lifetimes of indirect couples are longer, e.g. 10^{-3} sec for silicon. This has important consequences. Thus, the indirect gap materials (thicker, longer lifetime) are more affected by the presence of recombination centres (impurities), for, when the carriers live for a longer time, they are more likely to collide with impurity atoms and thus undergo hole-electron pair recombination. Thus, for thin-film photovoltaics, less purification is necessary, the requirement of single crystallinity is less, and thus the cost of a unit quantity of the semiconductor concerned (and the cost of unit energy produced) is reduced.

The central property of lifetime is not only affected by recombination in the semiconductor, but also by recombination on the surface. To raise the efficiency of a collector from 10%, often quoted for silicon, to, say, 20%, one would need in a material, 100μ thick, and $\rho =$ approximately 0.01 ohm cm, a surface recombination velocity of less than 100 cm sec^{-1}.[33]

What materials are sufficiently available for the massive conversion of solar energy?

The rate of use of energy (both as electricity and in other forms) in affluent societies is about 10 kW per capita. Let it be assumed that this is to be supplied by photovoltaic collection of solar energy at 10%. If the collectors were made 10μ thick, the mass of the substance required would be in the order of tens of millions of tons. This would be reduced by ten to one hundred times if the material concerned was not Si, but a thin-film photovoltaic, e.g. cadmium sulphide-copper sulphide. This large quantity of material needed reduces the possible choices: it is met, among present photovoltaics, only by silicon. The production of materials such as Ga, Sb and Te is tiny by comparison with that which would be needed were they to be used on a massive scale: and it seems very unlikely that it could be increased by the necessary several orders of magnitude. Thus, cadmium had a production in 1968 of 15,000 tons.

One substance, the elements of which are plentifully available, is aluminium. AlSb is a substance which is a possible candidate (production of antimony 68,000 tons in 1968).[33] Its energy gap is suitable for solar energy collection. Other details, such as surface recombination rate, are not known. AlSi may also be a photovoltaic of future importance.

Suitability as a photovoltaic, and E_{Gap}

What is the relationship between the efficiency of conversion and the energy gap? The current-voltage relation across a small p-n junction is similar to that across an electrodic junction. Thus, following a formulation made by Loferski:[33]

$$I_{sc} = e_o \int_{E_G}^{\infty} Q(h\upsilon)N_{ph}(h\upsilon)d(h\upsilon)$$

where I_{sc} is the current density across the couple, N_{ph} the number of incident photons of frequency υ; and E_G the energy gap.

However,

$$V_{oc} = \frac{kT}{e_o} \ln\left[\frac{I_{sc}}{I_o}\right]$$

where V_{oc} is the open circuit voltage, I_o the equal and opposite current in either direction at equilibrium and

$$I_o \alpha \exp\left[-\frac{E_G}{kT}\right]$$

The above equations show that V_{oc} increases with increase of E_G. Correspondingly, I_{sc} decreases with increase of E_G. The product of I_{sc} and V_{oc} (namely, the power per unit area produced by the photovoltaic device), plotted against E_G, passes through a maximum. Fig. 8.15 shows the actual efficiency of a number of couples as a function of E_G. The efficiency maximum occurs for E_G in the region of 1.2 to 1.5 eV and the maximum theoretical efficiency is 25%. It decreases with increase of temperature, and this reduces the advantage of using optical concentrators of solar energy, which, when used to increase the intensity of solar radiation reaching the photovoltaic several times, heats this up.[33]

Silicon is the best prospect. Its E_G value means it is sensitive to most of the solar spectrum.* Silica is available in very large quantities. A negative aspect is that it is an indirect semiconductor and cannot be made into thin films. Further, its carriers have a relatively long lifetime, so that it has to undergo super-purification, and must be highly single crystalline. Few alternatives exist. AlSb and AlSi are prospects.

The photovoltaic known as 'cadmium sulphide' requires some explanation. It is the hetero-couple Cu_2S-CdS and the energy gap which determines the activity is that of cuprous sulphide, 1.1 EV, near to that of silicon. (This contrasts with that of cadmium sulphide itself, 2.3 EV, higher than that of silicon.) The maximum efficiency of cadmium sulphide-cupric sulphide junctions should theoretically be 20%, as for silicon. However, the maximum efficiency observed for the sulphide couple is 8%.

Directions of fundamental research in silicon[34,35]

The main direction is in controlling non-radiative recombination. Impurity and defect levels in the forbidden gap may be responsible. Auger effects may be present. Even very highly purified silicon contains a sufficient concentration of impurities to lower the lifetime. These do not affect *transistor* performance, but may affect lifetime relevant to photovoltaic use, so that the manufacture of photovoltaics is a more demanding technique than for transistors. Could materials be obtained which would tolerate higher doping? If so, this would achieve a higher output voltage, yet maintain lifetimes enough for efficiency in collection.

There are many questions which have to be tackled before progress can be made with silicon; for example, by what mechanism do doping elements contribute to recombination? Technology to obtain large-area p-n junctions must be improved, with respect to impurity pick-up, whilst remaining highly single crystalline. Vacancies, and other defects, must be reduced; annealing techniques must be examined. Could surface recombination be counteracted with an applied potential difference to reduce diffusion of undesirable centres?

The attainment of 10% efficiency for the conversion of light to electricity in silicon is 20 years old and the theoretical maximum is 20%. Striving for an increase in efficiency may not be the most economically effective research goal. Lower production costs of highly single crystalline and pure materials are needed to transform the prospect for commercialisation. What of cheaper techniques for polycrystalline junction formation? Can large *strips* of semiconductor material be grown in single crystal form, but remain uncontaminated? How is it best to keep the temperature of the cell low in high insolation?

---

* 0.5 to 2.0 eV.

What of cheap mirror systems, and tracking mechanisms for increasing the light falling upon the cell? What about the join-up of solar collectors with storage systems?

Organic semiconductors, such as pthalocyanines, have several positive and negative characteristics when compared with Si. They often have greater values of α so that the thickness required is less. They do not need to be made in single crystal form. The disadvantage is their relative lack of efficiency (about 1%).[36,37] On the positive side, there is a loose coupling, whereas in the inorganic systems there is less trapping of the photo-produced electrons in the lattice, and this should lead to higher efficiencies: this is one reason why, as with the work of Lyons,[37] there is interest in organic semiconductor research for solar energy converters. However, organic materials are poorer in the transport of excitation energy, involve higher effective masses, lower carrier mobility and sharper absorption bands. These factors tend to reduce efficiency for the intake of radiation.

Long lifetime cadmium sulphide photovoltaics

These have been reviewed by Boer.[38] He reports that CdS/Cu$_2$S layers might be made in which the lifetime is more than 10 years, so long as the films are encapsulated. The conversion factor is 5%. Encapsulation is between two glass sheets, with hermetic sealing. They may be filled with N_2. Two copper foils protrude to provide electrical contacts. The cells would be mounted on roofs of houses, over parking lots, roadways and particularly in desert areas.

TABLE 8.IX: SUMMARY OF CADMIUM SULPHIDE CELL LIFETIME[41]

(Calculated from [extrapolated] rates of decay measured at higher temperatures)

Conditions	at 25°C	at 50°C
1. Air, continuous light	2.1 years	.67 year
2. Air, cyclic light	5.4 years	1.2 years
3. Argon, continuous light	8.0 years	1.5 years
4. Argon, cyclic light	38.0 years	3.2 years
5. Nitrogen, continuous light	32.0 years	3.2 years
6. Nitrogen, cyclic light	60.0 years	5.1 years

Lifetime of cadmium sulphide components

Ten to twenty years' life is the aim (Table 8.IX). The criticism of CdS/Cu$_2$S cells is that they have a shorter life than is acceptable for practical purposes. Cadmium sulphide degrades under insolation in moist air. However, after encapsulation against moisture, and if an inert gas such as nitrogen is circula-'ted over the cells,[39] life testing and extrapolation on a log (rate of decay) basis, predicts a rate of loss of efficiency which would give a life of up to 20 years.[40] Bismuth doping has indicated an increased high-temperature stability. Part of the degradation arises from ion migration and diffusion which can be reduced by doping near the p-n junction.

Examples of degradation when the cells are encapsulated in nitrogen is given in Fig. 8.16. In the absence of O_2 and water, one can anticipate usable lives of greater than 20 years at 50°C and greater than 100 years at 25°C.

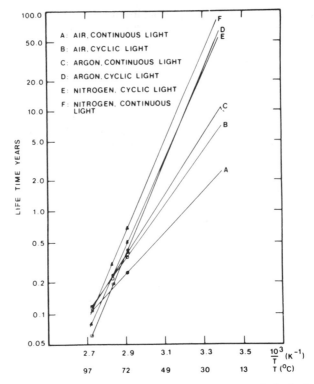

Fig. 8.16. Effect of ambient gas on lifetime. Lifetime of CdS/Cu$_2$S cells.

Cost estimate for cadmium sulphide cells

Alternatives have been described for the mass fabrication of solar cells, e.g. photo-etching of grids or using glass shingles of about 1 cm thickness. The deposition rate of cadmium sulphide layer occurs at about 1μm per sec, and Table 8.X gives a variation in costing due to Aaron and Isakoff.[41]

TABLE 8.X: Projected Costing for the Production of CdS/Cu$_2$S Solar Cells*[41]

	Concept 1 (film)	Concept 2 (film)	Concept 3 (glass)
Essential materials $/ft^2	1.65	1.45	1.69
Labour and supervision	0.89	0.40	0.75
Maintenance, utilities, taxes, insurance, depreciation, ($/ft^2)	0.21	0.21	0.58
	2.75	2.02	3.02
Mill Cost			
Total investment ($/ft^2/yr)		(2.44)	(4.67)
Selling, administration, research	0.37	0.29	0.45
Operating earnings (10% on working capital)	0.27	0.21	0.31
Operating earnings (10% on perm. investment)	0.27	0.31	0.67
$/ft^2	3.67	2.83	4.45

* The evaluation is based on an assumed volume of production of 100 million sq. ft./yr and the figures are corrected to 1978 money.

Boer[42] considers that it will be possible to reduce the costs below those of Aaron and Isakoff.[41] They would come to $1.61 per square foot (c. $40 10⁶ per square mile, i.e. about $320 per kW).* The cost of a fault indicator and short protection system might be $64 per kW, equivalent to adding 44 cents per square foot. Amplification by focusing has not been taken into account.

The overall costs, including installation, are shown in Table 8.XI.

Using the installation costs, fixed charges and other financing charges, it is possible to evaluate (Boer)[42] the cents per kWh. It is about 4.3 cents per kWh (1978).

TABLE 8.XI: TOTAL COST OF ELECTRIC POWER INSTALLED USING CdS-Cu_2S PHOTOVOLTAICS

System	A Sc	B Sc	C Sc	D Sc	A S	B S	C S	D S
Total costs $/kW	387	457	585	617	516	597	724	756

	$/kW for Total System Continuous
	Shingle	Sheet
A. Use of d.c. only	(AS)	(ASc)
B. Use of 115 Volt a.c.	(BS)	(BSc)
C. Use of 115 Volt a.c. with some storage	(CS)	(CSc)
D. Use of phase controlled synchronous d.c. to 115 V a.c. inversion	(DS)	(DSc)

Use of combined systems

Boer has suggested solar panels, which are also heat collectors.[38] There would be a network of CdS/Cu_2S thin-film solar cells between two glass plates. This sandwich is cemented to a plexiglass plate and backed-up with a styrofoam profile. Panels about 3 ft x 4 ft will produce about 110 volts at 0.6 amps in full sunlight. Were the cells sealed in inert gas, a 20-year lifetime is predicted by Boer.[38]

Photovoltaics: higher efficiencies

The presentation made in this chapter on photovoltaics has been concerned hitherto with costs and lifetime. Efficiency increase has been less stressed, because theory indicates (Chapter 7) that an increase in efficiency of more than twice times those commonly obtained with photovoltaics is not to be expected, whereas cost reductions for Si cells of several orders of magnitude seem possible. However, a doubling of the efficiency from the 5-8% of CdS and the 10% of Si would clearly be of great interest.

Woodall and Hovel have reported efficiencies of 16% for heterojunction solar cells containing Ga, Al and As.[43] Twenty per cent would be obtainable in space. The authors attribute the higher efficiencies of these couples to a lesser surface recombination, which occurs as a result of the influence of heavily doped layers. Open circuits give up to 1.0 volts. When the solar input

---

* In photovoltaic and photothermic solar energy collecting devices, the cost in $ per kW cannot be compared directly with that of fossil fuel or nuclear devices. The final cost of a unit of energy, delivered to the consumer, is more important (and the most important is the total net cost including environmental damage costs, together with an allowance for the efficiency of conversion to a useful fuel). Nuclear and fossil fuel devices can be worked 24 hours per day and solar only during the sunlight hours; the variation due to weather must be taken into account. Conversely, solar devices have no fuel costs.

is 98.3 mW cm^{-2}, the current density is 18-21 mA cm^{-2}. Couples are 6-7μ thick.

Large-scale use of Ga would not be feasible because of a lack of the material.

Similarly, Loferski, Crisman, Chen and Armitage tried to obtain improvements in efficiency by covering the cell with fine collector junctions, separated by a distance small compared with the minority diffusion length.[44] n-Si wafers were used and onto these a grating pattern of Al was introduced. Results were not improved compared with the conventional Si cells but the response was 'blue-shifted'.

Thin-film solar cells for terrestrial application

The development of the cuprous sulphide-cadmium sulphide thin-film solar cells by Shirland and Brody at the Westinghouse Research Laboratory has gone apace.[45] Thus, for example, Shirland, Greenieck, Symond and Brody report on their latest work with cuprous sulphide–cadmium sulphide films.[45] The plastic substrate has been replaced with a metal foil which is impermeable, and the plastic cover has been replaced by an integral glass layer. These provide a hermetic seal for the active cuprous sulphide region which is otherwise attacked by moisture.

They have developed a new grid system which consists of a fine-space metal pattern applied with vacuum deposition.

A laboratory-scale fabrication system has been set up for making cadmium sulphide thin-film solar cells. The facility has been operating for two years. The average efficiency of the cells is 4.9% and the yield of acceptable quality is 81%. Recent efficiencies have been 5.2%.

The stability studies are important for cadmium sulphide, and they have been carried out by encapsulating cells behind glass, and accelerating degradation by high-temperature operation. After 20 months of accelerated operation no loss of output was experienced in cells at 40°, 60° and 80°C. There was, however, an 11% loss on the cells operated at 100°C.

TABLE 8.XII: POSSIBLE MARKET GROWTH: U.K. ASSESSMENT

Phase	Applications	Power Range	Viable Array Cost per Peak Watt
1	Small power applications in remote or difficult sites with no mains supply; battery charge maintenance on boats, caravans and emergency equipment.	Up to 100 W	$40
2	Water pumping; power for remote dwellings, hospitals and schools. Cathodic protection for pipelines.	100 W to a few kilowatts	$2-5
3	Large scale power generation either in centralised installations or on the roofs of dwellings, hospitals, schools, offices and factories.	A few kilowatts to several megawatts	About 50c
4	Large solar farms; satellite solar power stations.	Thousands of megawatts	About 30c (Glaser)

Market growth of photovoltaics

A summary of the various phases of market growth during the next 50 years and some estimates on pay-back times are shown respectively in Tables 8.XII and 8.XIII.

TABLE 8.XIII: The Time Required for a Cell to Generate the Energy Needed for its Production: (U.K. Assessment)

Author	Reference	Annual production capacity (peak watts)	Energy consumed in production of 1 peak kW (kWh)	Time required to recover energy (in years)		
				Satellite solar power station	Desert solar farm	UK
A: Silicon cells						
1. Wolf	16	Present production capacity $\sim 5 \times 10^4$	62,500	5.1	29	71
2. P. N. Reynolds	Private communication	Present production capacity $\sim 5 \times 10^4$	30,000	2.4	14	34
3. Glaser	17	10^{11}	12,500	1.0	5.6	14
4. Wolf	16	10^{10}	6,250 represents a reasonable goal	0.51	2.9	7.1
5. Currin *et al.* (coupled with results from Wolf)	14	10^{11}	$\sim 1,500$	0.12	0.70	1.7
B: Cu$_2$S/CdS cells						
1. K. W. Böer	18	5×10^8	$\sim 1,000$*	0.08	0.46	1.1
2. R. J. Mytton	19	1×10^8	240*	0.02	0.11	0.27
3. J. F. Jordan	20	2×10^9	$\sim$ 240	0.02	0.11	0.27

*These figures are increased above those derived from the respective papers to include 100kWh/kW capacity for the production of CdS powder from Cd metal, the extraction of Cd metal from zinc ore, and the production of plastic film encapsulant.

Projected cost reduction in solar photovoltaics[46]

There is a limitation to the cost reduction of a silicon wafer. The starting point in the manufacture is sand. This is reduced to metallurgical silicon, from which purified trichlorosilane is synthesised. The trichlorosilane is reduced with hydrogen in a reactor to form high-grade polycrystalline silicon. A large cylindrical crystal, 50 cm in diameter, is pulled from the molten polycrystalline silicon by rotating a small seed crystal in the surface and withdrawing it under closely controlled conditions. These crystals are then sawn into wafers which, after lapping, polishing and etching, are processed to silica cells.

The time required for a cell to generate the energy needed for its production is shown in Table 8.XIII. As the plants pay for themselves within the lifetime of their use, the immediate cost of their initial manufacture is less important.

Approaches to the practical attainment of sufficiently cheap photovoltaic energy

The slow development of the massive use of solar energy arose out of cost considerations. The success of the use of solar collectors in photovoltaic energy in NASA space vehicles has in fact been a difficulty, because the silicon photovoltaic cells used on these vehicles were costed at 10^5 dollars per kilowatt of conversion power. The corresponding price of electricity would have been 10^3 too high. A three orders of magnitude cost reduction was not thought possible.

However, there have been improvements, and in two ways.

For some time in the beginning of the 1970s, it was thought possible so much to lower the cost of production of silicon that, when the reduction of cost allowed for in mass production was brought into the calculation, the material would be cheap enough without concentrators.

In the manufacture of Si, a cylindrical crystal up to 15 cm in diameter is pulled out of the molten polycrystalline silicon by radiating a small seed in the surface. The crystal is then sawn into wafers. This is the basic way of making the type of silicon which has been used in the NASA space vehicles.

A substantial saving would be possible if a monocrystalline silicon wafer is produced directly from the melt in the form of a continuous closely controlled strip.

This 'edge-defined-film growth' process (EFG) is under development at Mobil, Tyco and IBM. Tyco reports ribbons 25 mm wide, 0.2 mm thick and up to 20 m long. One foresees here the possibility of long planks of silicon photovoltaics of sufficient purity.[47] The possibility of silicon in the region of $300-$400 per kW of conversion power (including auxiliaries) has been foreseen by this method by Currin et al.[48] Currin assumed a conversion efficiency of 0.1, metres long ribbon, and a polycrystalline silicon production corresponding to 100,000 MW per annum. The EFG silicon ribbon would cost $250 per peak kilowatt.

Another approach to the low-cost silicon route is to prepare a polycrystalline ribbon of the required thickness, and pass this through a furnace to transform it into single crystals.[49]

A third approach is the polycrystalline one—the efficiency of the silicon conversion drops to 5%, but the cost also drops to something like $100 per peak kilowatt.

Apart from obtaining the photovoltaic Si, one has to inter-connect and assemble the cell, obtain support for the structure, have power conditioning equipment built, and arrange storage.

During the later 1970s, the concept of photovoltaics without concentrators, competitive with solar-thermal or OTEC has faded.

The necessity of pre-concentration before photovoltaics

In a zeroeth approximation, the cost of all auxiliary photovoltaic equipment, including the lens concentration system, is considered to be zero: the cost of the photovoltaic itself is high.

Then, if one achieves a concentration power of R, the cost of the photovoltaic is reduced by this factor. If, further, the concentration power can be of the order of 1,000 (claimed by some workers), then the cost of a unit of power would decrease by 1,000 times, the needed figure.

The apparently astounding nature of such cost-reduction factors (a more realistic first approximation analysis is given below) would seem to have induced such a negative reaction as to have put off possible development for some time, and until 1975, photovoltaics struggled along by utilising the sun without concentrating it on expensive photovoltaic crystals. There was a more scientific reason for the rejection of the mirror concentration method, because, as the conversion efficiency of photovoltaics to electricity is only of the order of 10%, much energy gets converted to heat, and such concentration would cause an increase in the photovoltaics temperature. This increase gave a decrease in the efficiency of conversion and if this was reduced sufficiently, the point of concentration was removed. Difficulties were foreseen. As the temperature increased, the lifetime of the photovoltaic would decrease, due to an increase of combination with the surroundings.

It is now seen as essential to use photovoltaics *with* concentrators.

Martin Wolf thinks that the slow progress with concentrators arose out of commercial rivalry between the semiconductor industry and the optical components industry.[50] Foreseeing a $20 billion per year business, the semiconductor industry was eager to keep the business entirely to itself. One needs contributions from both industries.

The cost of electric power for photovoltaics with lens concentration

The following analysis is from the work of Perrott.[51] Other calculations have been published recently.[47]

Consider a static flat-plate system, exposed to a total irradiance, Q_0, on a plane normal to the sun's direction. The power output will be

$$W_f = Q_0(1\text{-}g)A\eta$$

where g is the loss due to the fact that the flat plate system is not accepting the entire solar irradiation, A is its area, and η is the efficiency of conversion. The capital cost will be Ap_{fc}, where p_{sc} is the price of solar cells per unit area.

If we assume a useful life of τ, and a real interest rate of r,* then the cost per unit of energy will be

$$\text{Cost} = \frac{p_{sc}r}{Q_0(1\text{-}g)\eta(1\text{-}e^{-r\tau})}$$

The power output of the concentrating system is:

$$W_c = QA\eta(1\text{-}f)$$

where A is now the aperture of the collecting lens or mirror, and f is the fraction of solar energy which is diffuse.

---

*The real interest rate is the apparent interest rate, minus the rate of inflation.

The efficiency will depend on the flux because of the rise of temperature in the cell.*

The flux of energy with the lens system will be

$$Q_o R_c (1-f)$$

where R_c is the concentration ration, A/a, a being the actual cell area.

The cost of the concentration system can be written as

$$p_c A + p_{sc} a,$$

where p_c is the cost per unit area of the aperture of the whole cell, apart from the solar cell.

The cost per unit of energy will then be:

$$\text{Cost with lens system} = \frac{(p_c R_c + p_{sc})r}{Q_o(1-f)R_c\eta(1-e^{-r\tau})}$$

We first of all get rid of the expression $e^{-r\tau}$, because even if the net r is only 1%, τ will be 20-30 years, and the value of $e^{-r\tau}$ will be negligible.

Looking at the final expression, the following is clear:

1. The cost of the concentrator per unit area needs to be less than that of the solar cell. This condition is usually easily obtained.
2. The climatic factors $Q_o f$ and g must be helpful: the sun must shine for long times in the districts concerned; the diffuseness, f, must be small, and the loss due to the fact that the flat plate is not tracking the sun must be kept small.
3. The efficiency must be good at high radiance, not only when the cell is cool, or there must be a method of keeping the cell cool.

Perrott gives a table (8.XIII) which shows the values of R which have been suggested, and some other factors.[51]

The absolute limit of R is 10^4, so we can safely assume a value of 1,000.

TABLE 8.XIV (PERROTT): CERTAIN DATA ON LENS SYSTEMS PERTINENT TO THE COST OF A PHOTOVOLTAIC WITH LENS CONCENTRATION

Reference	Upper limit of concentration ratio of R	Cost p.c. in $1m^2$
Beam & Hansen,[52] Conference Rec. 11th IEEE Photovoltaics Specialists' Conference, page 32.	80	250
Slater & Gauradi,[53] Conf. Rec. 11th IEEE Photovoltaics Specialists' Conference, page 356, 1975.	1,000	60
Evans & Florscheutz,[54] ISES Conference, Los Angeles, 1975.	1,200	60
Burgess,[55] 12th IEEE Specialists' Conference, 1975	1,600	250
Mash,[56] J. E. Perrott, 1976	?	100-150

* The cell can be kept cool by use of a heat exchanger, taking off hot water from its back. The heat in the water can be transferred elsewhere.

The equations show that it is necessary to get a high degree of insolation during the day, i.e. desert regions are helpful. This will make f small and Q large.

The values used by Perrott have costing estimates which are as follows:[51]

p_c, the cost of the lens system: $200/m^2$

Using gallium arsenide as the solar cell, and an R_c value $= 10^3$, the p_{sc} at this time would be $30,000 per m^2, with an efficiency of 20%. Perrott thinks that favourable desert conditions for $Q_0(1-f)$ would be 3.10^3 kWh/yr/m^2. With the pessimistic interest rate of 10%, the cost is 4 cents per kilowatt hour.

Readers of this book will realise that 4 cents per kilowatt hour is a reasonable figure for comparison with nuclear and coal. The comparable costs of electricity from these sources are given by Moore[33] and are 4c per kWh for 1975 (increasing in the future), and 5-15c per kilowatt hour for electricity from diesel generators.

The use of Perrott's analysis is that it shows that *photovoltaic electricity with concentrators* would be cheaper in desert areas than projected breeder electricity but—and this is the point—without accounting for the considerable cost items of the social difficulties projected for the breeder reactors and other pollutional difficulties, and without the cost of decommissioning atomic plants. The discussion is therefore not yet realistic in respect to the comparative cost advantages of photovoltaic energy, in the sense that the real cost analysis accounting for these points would favour the photovoltaic collection more than would appear at present. (Conversely, transport of electricity from desert areas will weigh against the solar source.)

With an advanced electrolyser using a potential of 1.6 volts, and taking the amortisation, insurance and maintenance as $1 per MBTU, one would get gaseous H_2 at about $16, and liquid at about $19. This contrasts poorly with the present projected cost of LH_2 from coal at $7-8 per MBTU; and the projected costs of LH_2 from OTEC which are in the range of $7-14.

Future energy prospects of interest to consumers (the electorate) lie between OTEC, solar-thermal and photovoltaics, rather than with nuclear or coal. But the situation with coal products depends so much on problems of pollution, logistics of being able to mine so much extra coal so quickly, and the possibilities of dealing with CO_2, e.g. by rejection to the ocean.

LH_2 from coal would still be cheaper than LH_2 from the best projections of photovoltaic and solar-thermal. OTEC could *perhaps* produce LH_2 at a cost competitive with the apparent costs of coal. But what of the cost of sulphur pollution with coal? The costs quoted for LH_2 from coal ($7-8 MBTU^{-1}) are without accounting for the final disposal of the sulphur (reburial?); without accounting for the costs of dealing with the long-term CO_2 problem by leading it into the deep ocean; and without accounting for the probable residual pollution (less studied) from the combustion products of CH_4 if LNG is the general fuel for transportation and not the cheaper (in costs per km) stored gaseous hydrogen.

The projected development of solar energy from satellite collectors in space

The advantages of going to space for solar energy collection

One of the difficulties of the situation with collecting solar energy on the earth is that it is only reasonable to collect it in certain areas—roughly the area of 2000-3000 km north and south of the Equator, and in desert areas where the land—which has to be so large in area—is effectively zero in costs, for it is useful for little except solar-energy collection.

This collection, far from the points where the energy is needed, increases costs because of the necessary conversion to electricity or hydrogen, and piping. Further, there is the diurnal character of solar energy on earth.

To avoid these terrestrial objections, a proposal has been advanced by Peter Gläser for a satellite solar power station in geosynchronous earth orbit.[57] The solar energy is there available 24 hours a day during most of the year.

In the Satellite Solar Power Station (SSPS), the electricity produced by solar conversion would be fed to microwave generators which would form part of the transmitting antennae. The antennae would direct the microwave beam to the receiving antennae on the earth, and the energy would be re-converted to electricity and hydrogen for storage and transmission to places more than 1000 km away (at closer distances, some energy would be transmitted in the form of electricity).

In the geosynchronous earth orbit (GEO), the SSPS would receive four, and up to eleven, times the solar energy available on the earth (because of the absence of diurnal variation, absorption in the atmosphere, and cloud cover). This energy would be available continuously, except around the equinoxes when the SSPS would be eclipsed for about 72 minutes per day.

The SSPS would also be eclipsed by the moon for about 90 minutes at infrequent intervals. The value per square metre of insulation would be $1.3-1.4 \text{kW m}^{-2}$.

Photovoltaic collection of energy on satellites[52]

The satellite could utilise either a photovoltaic, a thermo-electric, or a thermionic method of collecting energy. The photovoltaic option is to take silicon cells or gallium arsenide cells and then to use these on the satellite. The advantage of the gallium arsenide would be the lower weight, because they have to be only one-tenth as thick as the silicon solar cell. Another possibility is cadmium sulphide.

Alternatively, mirrors would focus solar radiation onto a cavity where the heat would be absorbed by a working fluid and transferred to heat-engines coupled to electric generators. The electricity would then be supplied to the microwave power transmission system and sent to earth. Here, the situation would be similar to that of the solar-thermal method. Rankin-cycle engines would be used.

An alternative possibility would be a device analogous to OTEC. On the hot side facing the sun, there would be distillation of a liquid under pressure and in this situation it seems likely that water would be suitable. Condensation could occur in a condenser placed upon the shadow-side of the satellite where the external temperature would be near to 0°K. One advantage of this concept would be the great decrease of area (and hence mass) which would need to be orbited. The presence of vacuum conditions would be helpful.

TABLE 8.XIV: Microwave Power Transmission Efficiencies[57]

| | | Efficiency | |
| | | | |
Characteristic	Presently demonstrated*	Expected with present technology[+]	Expected with additional development[‡]
Microwave power generation efficiency	76.7[+]	85.0	90.0
Transmission efficiency from output of generator to collector aperture	94.0	94.0	95.0
Collection and rectification efficiency (rectenna)	64.0	75.0	90.0
Transmission, collection and rectification efficiency	60.2	70.5	85.0
System	26.5[‡]	60.0	77.0

* Frequency of 2450 MHz (12.2cm wavelength).
[+] This efficiency was demonstrated at 3000 MHz and a power level of 300kW CW.
[‡] This value could be immediately increased to 45% if an efficient generator were available at the same power level at which the efficiency of 60.2% was obtained.

Microwave power generation

The frequency selected by Gläser would be in the region of 3.3 GHz.[58] Dickinson and Brown showed, in 1963, that microwaves could transmit much power.[59] The reception has to be, for the main lobe, 90% of the power, and the side lobes can be controlled.

The ionosphere only slightly absorbs microwaves (0.1%). Troposphere absorption would be 1%. Rainfall attenuates microwave radiation about 3%. Overall efficiency, including some rain, would be > 75%.

Microwave generator would be a cross-field device. A pure metal, self-starting, secondary, emitting cold cathode gives broad band gain. Use of samarium-cobalt alloys would reduce weight, but perhaps introduce problems of availability. The individual microwave generator would weigh fractions of a kg per kW of power output.

The space antenna would be about 1 km in diameter and the receiving antenna should be 7 km in diameter for 90% transmission. Very important would be a master phase-control to keep the beam on target.

Keeping station[60]

For an orbited satellite collecting 5,000 MW at 1 kW per sq m, the area would be about 4.10^7 sq m, and could consist of two panels each 4.3 by 5.2 km. It would have to keep station exactly and would need fuel to do this. The propellant needed would weigh about 30,000 lb per year.

Economics[57]

An economic analysis for the orbited satellite depends much more upon future projections than with other solar collectors. Gläser gives the following suggestions for a 1990 projection (re-calculated in 1978 dollars):

Solar cells and solar collector array	499 dollars per kW generated by the prototype
Microwave generators and transmitting antennae	208
Rectifiers and receiving antennae	161
Transportation to orbit and assembly	2221-1288

The projected value of about $2,600 per kW *assumes* a reduction of about one order of magnitude in the cost of putting substances into orbit. The projection is more favourable than at first sight because of the absence of diurnal and weather factors.

The main doubts depend on the reduction of the cost of putting materials into orbit; and the availability of sufficient thin-film photovoltaic materials. It seems that at present the first hurdle might be less of a problem than the second. However, as has been shown above, there are two alternative possibilities for transduction of power: a solar-thermal; or an OTEC analogue.

Present development programme

It is planned to have test satellites operational by 1992.

Larger aspects of the satellite solar power station

The satellite solar power station represents an opportunity to make space useful, and the prospect which we have had for years of factories in space, zero gravity points, and space hooks—which at first sound science fictional, but which are likely to be realised within a century—attract one towards the SSPS. The prospects here depend entirely upon the economics of orbiting. It seems that the prospect of reaching $100 per lb (1978 currency) within 20 years is good. If the space shuttle, using chemical fuels, does not allow attainment, it seems probable that manless atomic-powered orbiting, with remote control, of a space freighter might be realizable in this time frame.

Wet photovoltaics

Introduction

The basic idea of wet photovoltaics is to have an n and p type semiconductor separated by an electronically conducting wire, the surface of each semiconductor being in an ionic solution. The electrodes are duly irradiated. An electrode reaction takes place at each and produces products which may be hydrogen and oxygen.

A basic advantage foreseen for wet photovoltaics is the presence of charge acceptors in solution at a short distance from the point of production of charge within the semiconductor by the absorption of photons. Thus, $1/\alpha$ is generally of the order of one micron, where α is the absorption coefficient. If we use semiconducting electrodes, as with silicon, the thickness of which is greater than one micron, the path length of the carriers to the contacts attached to the electrodes is longer than it is in the case of an electrode where the charge carrier has to flow only to the electrode-solution interface, i.e. about one micron.

Thus semiconducting electrodes used in wet photovoltaics might not have to be as pure as silicon in dry photovoltaics. Other possible advantages are pointed out below.

The history of this subject, briefly, is concerned largely with the work of Fujishima and Honda.[61] These workers, whose initial aim was to examine the catalytic properties of titanium dioxide surfaces, noticed that a gas was evolving from the surface during the washing of TiO_2 crystals. Subsequent experimentation brought them to join the TiO_2, irradiated, to a platinum electrode in the form of an electrochemical cell. They found that a current flowed and reported that hydrogen was being evolved from the platinum, and oxygen from the titanium dioxide. This turned out to be erroneous and, in fact, oxygen was being reduced in one electrode and evolved at the other.

The first time these workers observed the evolution of hydrogen from platinum and oxygen from titanium was in an experiment in which they utilised a pH gradient of 14 to facilitate the cell's functioning.[62] This would not be a practical arrangement because of the production of an alkaline environment near an electrode where hydrogen is evolved and an acid one near an electrode at which oxygen is being evolved.

The independently-working hydrogen-oxygen cell

The realisation of wet photovoltaics has been devised in two parts, largely work which has been led by Gerischer, Bard, Heller, Nozik and others who have concentrated on the functioning of redox electrodes.[63, 64]

The work of Ohashi, McCann and Bockris was the first in which stable self-driven cells producing hydrogen and oxygen were realized.[65] The apparatus is shown in Fig. 8.17.

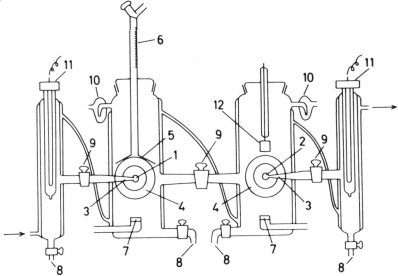

Fig. 8.17. Schematic of a photo-electrochemical cell. (1) p type CdTe electrode; (2) n type TiO_2 electrode; (3) Luggin capillary; (4) window of quartz-optical flat; (5) gas collector; (6) gas burette; (7) frit; (8) drain; (9) stop cock; (10) gas outlet; (11) reference electrode; (12) Pt electrode.

In this cell, each electrode can be examined separately whilst it is controlled by a potentiostat and the current-potential curves examined.

At the same time, there is a possibility of electrodes driving each other to pass a spontaneous current and evolve hydrogen and this, too, was examined.

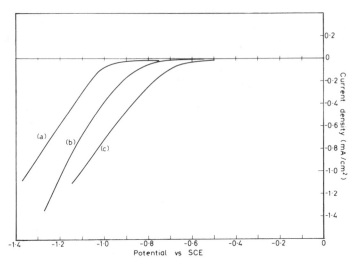

Fig. 8.18. Photocurrent-potential curves of p-type CdTe electrode in 1M NaOH. Sweep rate 10 mv/second. (a) First curve obtained by potential sweep; (b) Stable curve after 4 sweeps; (a) and (b) at 25°C; (c) at c. 18°C. Light intensity $\cong 0.05$ watt cm^{-2} for (a) and (b); 0.1 watt cm^{-2} for (c).

Typical results are shown in Fig. 8.18.

The individual electrodes are shown in individual performances as a function of wavelength of the electrodes as shown in Fig. 8.19. Quantum efficiencies to 90% are realised at certain wavelengths.

The quantum efficiency relationships for strontium titanate electrodes are shown in Fig. 8.20, and the relationship of potential to current is shown in Fig. 8.21. Time dependence of cells is in Fig. 8.22 and the total power in Fig. 8.23.

If a reasonable overall quantum efficiency for the conversion of solar light to electricity and hydrogen plus oxygen could be carried out in a type of cell represented by the work of Ohashi, McCann and Bockris above,[65] both the hydrogen fuel and electricity could be produced in the same plant. There would not be need for difference in apparatus between the light-collecting apparatus, the hydrogen fuel-producing apparatus, and the electricity producer. Two plants (that of the hydrogen electrolysis device, and that of the electricity-producing device) would thus be replaced by one plant. The cell solution itself is a cooling device which would allow highly concentrated solar radiation to be utilised, if used at the same time.

If one assumes, in a zeroeth approximation, that the unit cost of the equipment is equal in all three of these, then this cost could be reduced by some twice times.

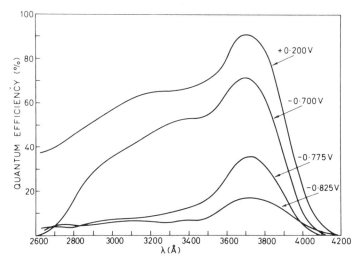

Fig. 8.19. Quantum efficiency-wavelength relation for TiO_2 in 1M NaOH at fixed potentials.

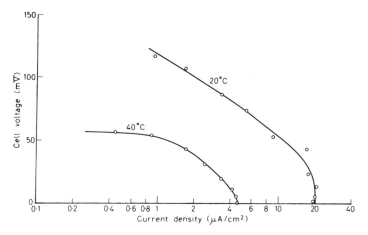

Fig. 8.20. Light-driven cell ($nTiO_2$ + pCdTe) in 1M NaOH with no bias potential.

However, there is a probability that in the more complex processes occurring in photoelectrochemical generators, efficiency would always be less, as is indeed the counterpoint if the wet photovoltaic devices are compared with the classical dry photovoltaic device in a competition between reduced efficiency in the wet photovoltaic against the reduced cost of plant which would be likely were the wet photovoltaic to function at a technologically interesting level of efficiency.

The efficiency to date is disappointing, but has amounted to about 2% maximum overall energy conversion efficiency for solar light using GaP as cathode and TiO_2-$LaCrO_3$ as anode.

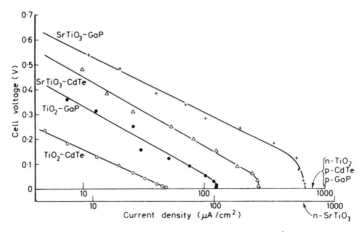

Fig. 8.21. Light-driven cells. Xenon radiation 0.05 watt cm^{-2}; 25°C; Area 0.05 cm^2, 1M NaOH.

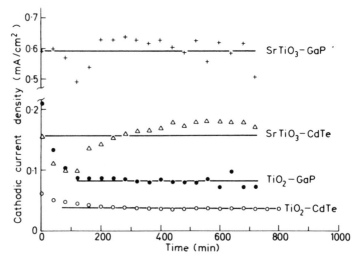

Fig. 8.22. Current density-time curves for 1M NaOH at 25°C. External resistance: 1 kilo-ohm; pCdTe, pGaP; and TiO_2 $\cong 0.05$ cm^2; nSiTiO_3 $\cong 0.06$ cm^2. Xe irradiation is 0.05 W cm^{-2}

Mechanism of photoelectrochemical hydrogen generation

The general principle is that of a fuel cell which is light-driven mechanistically, for electrons enter the anode and activate electrons from the valency band. This frees holes to transport themselves to the interface and to receive electrons from OH⁻ ions. The freed electron then goes round the circuit until it finds the cathode, and emits to the solution to neutralise protons there.[66]

The most important element of the cells is the energy gap of the electrodes. If the energy gap is less than about 0.5eV, the electrons fall back from the conduction band into the valency band and become deactivated. The semiconductor is too much like a metal. For energy gaps of more than about

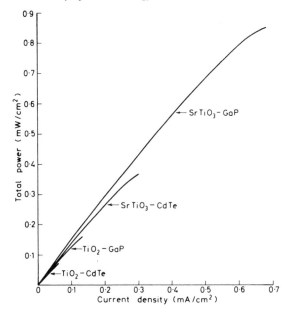

Fig. 8.23. Total power-current density relationships. 1M NaOH 25°C. Xe, irradiation 0.05 watt cm^{-2}.

2eV, the degree of the solar spectrum which is absorbed is too small to be of interest. Hence the essential point is to obtain electrodes which have energy gaps between 0.5 and 2eV.

Few such electrodes are available. One is cadmium telluride with an energy gap of 1.6eV.

There are three other properties which are important in the possible formation of electrochemical energy-producers. One of them is the relation between the flat band potential and the critical potential, namely that at which the current becomes significant. The flat band potential is therefore important, and one reason for this is seen if a cathode is functioning under situations in which the flat band potential is more negative than that of the energy level of the electrons in the electrode, the field gradient for electrons to attain the surface is in the wrong direction. Although the electron is impelled under $\partial\bar{\mu}/\partial x$ ($\bar{\mu} = \mu + nF\psi$), an unfavourable sign for $\dfrac{\partial\psi}{\partial x}$ (the potential gradient) will be important.

Electron affinity has an important influence upon the functioning. When the electron affinity changes, the relative positions of the acceptors change. The smaller the values of the electron affinity, the larger are the calculated quantum efficiencies for cathodes.

The major difficulty of the work, however, is the third requirement, namely that the corrosion situation be a satisfactory one. This is not straightforwardly determinable in the thermodynamic sense because this may give unnecessarily pessimistic results.[67] However, it is difficult to deal with because it is not a purely thermodynamic matter, the corrosion being stimulated by the photochemical situation. Many anodes, in particular cadmium sulphide, dissolve readily in the solution, making initially for an apparent strong quantum efficiency, but only because the photoelectrochemical reaction is dissolving the surface.

The needs of photoelectrochemical hydrogen-electrical energy generators

The first thing which is needed is an anode which has the properties of an energy gap of $0.5 < E_g < 2eV$. It may be not so difficult to get such a substance, but will it be possible to get one which is stable and does not dissolve? $LaCrO_3 - TiO_2$ looks a reasonable candidate for this possibility, although its identity is as yet unclear.

One method which might succeed, but is difficult experimentally, would be to put very thin layers of platinum or gold, or some non-attachable semiconductor, upon the surface of the electrode. This has already been done by Bockris and Uosaki who plated cadmium sulphide with titanium dioxide and found the dissolution reduced.[67]

Among the possibilities of a future project in such a situation would be silicon. The n silicon—the anode—might then be stable, whilst the p silicon would be stable under cathodic conditions.

Apart from this, the forward look is towards anodes such as the lanthanum chromite which have good energy gaps—for example 1.6eV—but which do not at the present time seem to be easily dopable and to give reasonable conductances.[68]

In addition to this there would be a number of substances, the ferrites, which could have suitable properties.

The photo-electrochemical converter has an interesting potential and awaits further research. The union of an energy gap of ~ 1.5 with a stable surface would have many consequences.

Biocatalytic production of hydrogen

There has been interest in living and non-living systems which cause the breakdown of water to form hydrogen.

Such processes are analogous to the electrolysis of water, but use sunlight to catalyse by a chlorophyll-containing membrane system and an iron–sulphur-containing enzyme called hydrogenase.[69]

Algae contain hydrogenase which causes hydrogen gas to be evolved from water by photosynthesis instead of $NADPH_2$, which fixes carbon dioxide to the level of carbohydrate.[70]

Thus, with a hydrogenase enzyme, any plant-type system might have the ability to produce hydrogen. This has been demonstrated in the laboratory using components extracted from leaves and bacteria (Neal).[71]

The potential of the system can be realised if the stability of the biological components can be improved. The chloroplast membrane and the enzyme-hydrogenase are sensitive to prolonged incubation. However, it may be possible to eliminate the biological components completely by synthesising model components which copy the biological compounds, e.g. iron-sulphur catalysts, instead of the hydrogenase and chlorophyll layer.

One would require a manganese catalyst to evolve oxygen from water by the action of sunlight, corresponding to the work carried out by Calvin.[69] Such a semi-synthetic system could be a three-layer arrangement which would produce oxygen on one side and hydrogen on the other. Alternatively, one could evolve hydrogen and oxygen in a single compartment using micro-encapsulation technology corresponding to the suggestions of Butler and Kitajima.[72]

An alternative would be to place the chloroplast in one compartment which would evolve oxygen on illumination, and the hydrogenase in another compartment (dark, hydrogen evolved). The economics of hydrogen and oxygen separation would be important.

An economic assessment has been carried out with a 10% energy conversion efficiency factor assumed. Hydrogen production in the South-West United States could be achieved at about 10 moles per square metre per day: cost projections are less than $3 MBTU^{-1}.[73]

A basic difficulty is that the systems are not yet stable, and have been operated hitherto for only a certain number of hours.[73]

Wind as a massive source of energy

Introduction

The solar-gravitational source, wind, was the first energy harnessed by man, windmills having appeared in England and France in the 12th century. The use of small aerogenerators in remote areas, particularly in Australia, is well known, the machines producing 1-2 kW in a 20 mph wind and becoming energy-producing in winds above 4 mph. Storage of electricity is usually made in lead-acid batteries.

Aerogenerators have seldom been considered as a massive source of power because: (i) wind is generally regarded as sporadic and unreliable; (ii) if strong winds exist, they are in remote areas (Alaska), and were formerly of little interest as a power supply; (iii) the equation which connects the dimensions of a rotor to the wind velocity is little known, and so trial calculations of what might be in relatively high mean annual winds are seldom made.

The relevant equation for instantaneous power is:[74]

$$\text{Power} = \frac{16}{27} \cdot \frac{1}{2}\rho v^3$$

per unit area swept out by a rotor, where ρ is the density of the fluid and v the velocity of the wind. $\frac{1}{2}\rho v^2$ is the kinetic energy of the wind per unit volume and $\frac{16}{27}$ a hydrodynamic factor for the extraction of energy. The empirical equation is:

$$\text{Power} = \frac{16}{27} \cdot \frac{1}{2} c\rho v^3$$

where c is a parameter, generally about $\frac{1}{2}$. The dependence of v is noteworthy.

It should be noted that the wind equation requires the mean of the cubes of the instantaneous wind velocities over the year. *If the mean of the velocities is cubed, results are 2 to 3 times too small* (Bockris, 1975).

Winds

Winds are in fact constant, that is, the pattern of their velocities as a function of time repeats itself year after year. Thus, Fig. 8.24, from the work of Mullett,[75] shows the mean wind velocity at the Adelaide Observatory, Australia, from 1878 to 1954. After 1900, the effective mean variation is 1.4%, i.e. the wind velocity over the 54 years was 98.6% constant. The winds in towns are diminished; they are about half the velocity in open areas.

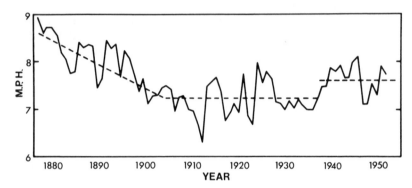

Fig. 8.24. Annual mean velocities in Adelaide. 1870-1900: building growth. 1900-1940: roughly constant. 1940: change of position of anemometer.

South of the 30th parallel of latitude, there is a system of anti-cyclones, a group of vortexes of subsiding cold air, drifting constantly around the planet. The group travels west to east at 40-60 km/h. It travels across the coast of South Australia, New Zealand, Chile and the Cape of Good Hope. It is the presence of this kind of high-velocity wind system over the sea which makes the massive use of wind energy feasible. This Great Southern Wind, which blows constantly round the world with a breadth of about 1,000 km, is identical with that known to mariners as the Roaring Forties, and is unique in constancy of velocity and breadth. However, there are many other regions of the world where the wind at ground level averages more than 25 km/h around the year, and mountain areas where greater velocities are frequently continuously available for the transduction of energy.

Apart from global factors,* there are local ones. Strong winds are found on hill crests. Nellie Carruthers derived an equation for the dependence of velocity on height.[76] It is:

$$\frac{v_1}{v_2} = \left\{\frac{h_1}{h_2}\right\}^{1/5}$$

Table 8.XV shows results obtained by Mullett for South Australia.[75] A hill of over 200 feet in open country is a good site. Flat country sites must not

---

*The Great Southern Wind arises from the heat at the equator. Air massess rise there, then later cool and fall, to become the origin of the wind described.

TABLE 8.XV: Wind Velocities Measured by Mullett in South Australia[75]

Site No.	Measured mean speed (mph)	Measuring height (ft)	Height factor (100 ft)	Adjusted speed for 100 ft (mph)	Site description
101	17	30	1.18	20	Sea level
102	12	30	1.23	15	Flat country
103	16	30	1.18	19	130 ft hill
104	16	30	1.20	19	Sea level
105	15	30	1.23	18	Flat country
106	17	30	1.10	19	600 ft ridge
107	22	30	1.10	24	800 ft ridge
108	13	30	1.23	16	Flat country
201	17	10	1.30	22	Sea level
202	21	10	1.15	24	400 ft hill
203	17	10	1.30	22	Sea level
204	16	10	1.40	22	Flat country
206	18	10	1.30	23	800 ft hill
207	20	10	1.15	23	1,200 ft hill
208	17	10	1.20	20	400 ft hill
209	17	10	1.30	22	Sea level
210	14	10	1.30	18	Sea level
211	14	10	1.30	18	Sea level
212	19	10	1.25	24	Sea level
213	16	10	1.40	22	200 ft hill
214	16	10	1.30	21	Sea level
215	15	10	1.30	21	Sea level
216	18	10	1.30	23	100 ft hill
217	17	10	1.20	20	1,200 ft range
218	20	10	1.15	23	1,200 ft ridge
219	12	10	1.40	17	Sea level
220	17	10	1.25	21	200 ft hill
221	18	10	1.20	22	300 ft hill

Note: 'Sea level' refers to coastal sites less than 100 ft above sea level.

be more than a few miles from shore. Vegetation does not occur in windy areas.

A typical velocity and frequency graph is shown in Fig. 8.25.

Aerogenerators

With the ideal equation for an aerogenerator, using $\rho = 1.4 \ 10^{-3}.g.cc^{-1}$, R being the radius of the rotor in metres, v in km per hour:

$$Power = 2.7 \ 10^{-5} v^3 R^2 \ (kW)$$

The equation is illustrated in Table 8.XVI. In practice, one can expect a power of ⅓ to ½ of that given by this equation.

The 'all or nothing' character of wind power is clear from Table 8.XVI. For wind velocities below 20 km/h, there is little to be collected. Above 30 km/h, a rotor of 50 metres radius would in practice deliver about 1 MW. 50 metres is too large for a practical rotor, the weight of which goes on an *axis*. Other designs are possible. One, due to Mullett, is shown in Fig. 8.26. The objective is to reduce the weight on a central axis. It consists of a ring spinning on an axis normal to its plane and resting on a number of rollers. Generators are coupled to the axes on which the rollers rest.

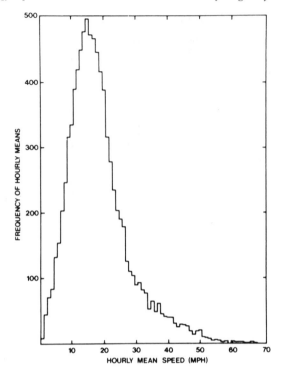

Fig. 8.25. Annual velocity—frequency for South Australia.

TABLE 8.XVI: THE IDEAL WIND ENERGY EQUATION
(Radius of rotor: 50 metres)

Average wind velocity in km (hr)$^{-1}$	Power in megawatts (approx., rounded off)
10	0.1
20	1
30	2
40	4
50	8

The total potential energy in certain stable wind currents[75]

At 30 km/h, wind contains more than 1000 MW per cubic km. A wind such as the Great Southern Wind contains a very large amount of energy indeed. If the current were only 100 km wide, the world round, the energy in it up to 0.1 km could support the entire present population at a 10 kW per person level. In fact, the zone in which such winds exist is between latitudes 30° and 40°S., about 1000 km wide and up to an undetermined height. Thus this current has more than 10 times the entire needed world supply of energy if collected up to a height of 0.1 km.*

---

* Collection of only a very small fraction would ever be feasible. However, the illustration indicates, at 1% collection efficiency, a greater *energy density* than does solar energy. It seems reasonable to predict a more economic attainment than that of fusion.

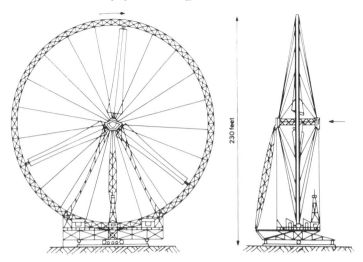

Fig. 8.26. One possibility for an air-turbine (Mullett).

There are probably other circulating systems of the same kind, as well as some places where coastal and particularly sea-borne winds average near to 30 km/h. For example, much of the Western Coasts of Ireland and Scotland have mean annual coastal winds of 28 km/h. The Western Islands of Hawaii are in a similar situation. Greenland and Alaska have a high *average* wind velocity.[77]

Storage and transportation
Storage of wind energy is as essential as that of solar. The winds discussed are averages and the velocities quoted are of mean annual winds in which there are periods of quiescence. Storage in low-pressure gasometers on land or in high-pressure gasometers on the sea-bed would be two options for storage.

The distance of the cities to be supplied from the location of the wind belt would be of diminished importance in a Hydrogen Economy.

Economic competitiveness of wind energy
An analysis has been made of this by Lapin.[78] Windmills become competitive if the full costs of ordinary fuels rise four times above those of 1973. In the case of crude oil, this has already happened. The difficulty for private enterprise is that there is no guarantee that the market would be stable. Better devices could be developed. Government finance or guarantees would be used in the construction of early wind-energy grids.

According to Serdensen,[79] wind energy is less expensive than solar devices in Denmark.

The spacing of wind turbines in large arrays
Newman has worked upon this important question.[80]

How far behind a windmill can the next wind turbine be placed by taking into account the effect of the increase in roughness of the earth's boundary layer due to the drag of the turbines? The thickness of the boundary layer changes in proportion to the square root of the skin friction which is appropriate for a turbulent layer.

The equations given by Newman relate the spacing to the diameter of the wind wheel and to the velocity of the wind at ground level and at a height corresponding to the middle point of the wind wheel.[80] A typical value is 15 diameters between turbines. This clearly is an important limitation on the area aspects of possible wind farms, and once more stresses the sea as the best locale for wind turbines.

Possibility of very high altitude wind energy conversion

There are several regions of the world where winds blow more than 160 km/h, in a west to east direction (the so-called jet stream). It is tempting to suggest the possibility that means might be found to tap the vast energy resources in such winds. Suppose it were possible to maintain a turbine at an altitude of, say, 10,000 metres (hydrogen balloons?), application of the above equation shows that the necessary radius for 1 MW of power would be reduced 17 times, e.g. from 50 metres to about 3 metres.

Perhaps such a scheme will never be feasible. However, buildings up to 1600 m in height have been proposed and wind turbines erected at heights of 1000-2000 metres would be feasible. According to Carruthers' formula, however, the gain at such heights compared with that at 100 ft would be about five times.

Cost of wind generators

Estimates by Otto J. Smith suggest that in a 32 km/h wind, the cost of wind-generated electricity could be as low as 1.5 cents per kwh.[81] Taking the mean annual wind as 25 km/h makes the cost about 2.1 cents per kwh, only equalled by hydro-electric sources. With E = 1.6 volt and the amortisation and insurance + maintenance at $1MBTU^{-1}, one obtains a gaseous H_2 cost of $6 and hence an LH_2 cost of about $9.

Low-head hydro-electric power: a realisable alternative

Utilisation of hydro-electric power has been limited to big hydro-electric situations. An alternative involves the use of the potential energy in hydro-electric heads of less than 20 metres to generate hydro-electric power. The technology is referred to as low-head hydro-electric power.[82]

About 105 million kilowatts of hydro-electric capacity would be available for future development. This is about 5% of the needs of the country.

The advantage of the hydro-electric development would be that it would provide extremely *cheap* electric power—much cheaper than electricity from coal or nuclear sources.

A comparison of figures appears in Table 8.XVII.

TABLE 8.XVII: Cost of Delivered Electric Power[82]

	Electrical energy delivered at mils. per kW/hr
Low-head hydro power	10-20
Oil	25
Coal	26
Nuclear	40

The low-head hydro-electric would be half the mean cost of the other sources.

At present, hydro-electric power amounts to 13% of the generating capacity of electricity in the United States. However, it is liable to drop to 10% in the next 20 years. The projected hydro-electric capacity, which excludes potential low-head hydro power resource below 5 MW, could generate between one-quarter and one-half of all U.S. electricity requirements.

There are areas where the cost of hydro-electric power could be reduced below those in Table 8.XVII.

Hydro-electric power on a large scale

Introduction

Only one-tenth of the hydro-electric resources are exploited. The rest has been thought too far away.

La Roche has been considering the potentialities of Greenland.[83] It has an ice volume of 2.6M.km³, and contains 8% of the world's fresh water. Water accumulates inland, and is precipitated on the ablation zones towards the coast, by ice movement. Ablation in the summer is greater than the accumulation and is equal to the sum of the melted water from icebergs.

The melting water of the peripheral ablation flows through an ice-free coastal zone which has the characteristic of an Alpine plateau, and is 400-800 m above sea level.

Thus, in Greenland a unique situation occurs. Much ice has a surface melting characteristic, and a convenient situation for collecting this water at 600 m above the sea exists.

Assessment of the potential of the Greenland hydro-electric resource[84]

The volume of water flowing to the sea should be separated into the melting water from the Greenland ice cover, and precipitation on the ice-free coastal zone.

The water of the ablation ice is about 120-315 km², and the volume of precipitation on ice-free coastal zones is 105 km².

It is possible to conclude from a study of the lake-like structures up to 76° latitude North that the volume of water is as in Table 8.XVIII, namely the

TABLE 8.XVIII: SITE PRE-STUDY RESULTS FOR GREENLAND HYDRO-ELECTRIC SOURCE
(La-Roche)

Site		G1	G2	G3	G4	G5	G6
Horizontal distance storage to power station	m	11.750	100	12.000	13.000	2.250	3.750
Head	m	680	75-90	450	320	432	210
Distance to Head ratio		17.3	1.3-1.1	26.7	40.6	5.2	17.8
Power capacity	MW	110	40-48	110	110	110	110
Investment cost Mio $		46	22-42	54	67	33	44
Energy production GWh		965	350-420	965	965	965	965
Energy cost mills/kWh		6	8-11	7	8.5	3.7	5.5

head at 400 m gives us 50 GW at least. With a head of 200 m, there is another 6.7 GW and 105 km³. .

Propositions exist to exploit the increased head in the mountain range protruding through the ice at 1,000-2,000 m above sea level. The head would double to a potential between 22-85 GW for annual exploitation. (This is still only 2-3% of the U.S. need around 1990.)

Glacier storage

According to Stauber, it should be possible to exploit the additional head from the high mountain level downwards.[85] Thus, there should be storage of the ablation water on the inland ice; and some tappings of natural water channel systems on the ice surface could take place.

Summary of available power from Greenland

It seems that 15-39 GW is proved, and 60 GW reasonably assured. 100 GW could be then eventually obtainable.

Cost of electricity from the hydro-electric resources

The cost would vary between 5 and 10 mills per kW hr.

The possibility of the export of energy from Greenland

This would be carried out via water electrolysis. Let us assume a mean of 5 mill power. Utilising the formula with the value of E as 1.6, c as 0.5, and with the amortisation factor at $1 per MBTU, one gets about $2.72 per MBTU for the hydrogen in Greenland.

Liquefaction at $3 per MBTU gives us liquid hydrogen in Greenland at about $5.72 per MBTU, and the transport to the United States can be assumed to add another 50 cents, so that the delivered value would cost about $7 per MBTU (gasoline from coal $6/MBTU; LNG $5.50/MBTU).

Hydrogen sea-cities?

Hansen has suggested that cities on the ocean may be a part of near future development.[86] 'The seaward advancement of industrial societies' was discussed in December, 1974, in the National Academy of Sciences. The Ecofisk in the North Sea is an off-shore city. If big nuclear plants are to exist, they should be far from the people they are supplying. OTEC manufacture of H_2 would be off-shore.

One of the energy future scenarios is that of a situation in which energy will be mined at large OTEC platforms, and tugs pushing barges containing liquid hydrogen will supply the world with fuel just as oil is now taken from the wells.

The energy of the future comes from the deserts and tropical seas, and that is where the cities should develop.

We may move entirely towards the sites where this energy is largely available, and where—as in the middle Pacific—there is the most equable climate in the world. An early version of this would be based upon an OTEC plant. Recycling would be carried out, mariculture used, and seaborne transport would be driven by hydrogen. Ammonia, liquid hydrogen and aluminium would be produced at sea.

On the selection of an energy source to replace oil and natural gas

At present, the main research effort in all western countries in respect to future energy sources is concentrated upon the fluidization of coal and the development of breeder reactors. Fusion is seen as an eventual hope and solar energy is to be developed for house heating.

In this chapter, facts have been presented which mainly originated in the later 1970s, and hence after the policies which gave rise to the 'coal-nuclear club' description of the Department of Energy had been founded.

It is clearly very difficult to change the policy directions of the U.S. Department of Energy, or that of any other major power, because of the inertia attached to research funding contracts, apart from the disentropic energy which must be put into changing opinions and outlooks among the few who exert powerful leadership in any organization. Thus, it is naive to imagine that the decisions made are simply the result of applying technological and economic reasoning to the tasks at hand. Politics (the influences exerted in the interests of powerful groups, one of which is the public) will play a dominating role, and the direction of that role will always be for a continuation of the same, with great doubt, and even ridicule, thrown at concepts which would necessitate change.

In this section, the case is made that, at the technical and economic level, a grave error is being constantly made by most of those who publish work concerned with the evaluation of new energy systems. This error is the assumption that the First Law Cost of energy is the function which has to be minimized. The net good, it is assumed, will be from a system which gives energy from one source at a lower cost than that from another. It is not this First Law, but rather the corresponding Second Law Costs which should be counted in evaluating one energy source against the other (Table 8.XIX).

A second error is to take the time frame of the considerations as here-and-now. This is an easier error to confute than the first. The energy systems recommended for funding must, it seems obvious, be those, the relevant characteristics of which (see below) are germane, not to the here-and-now, but to a situation when such new energy sources will be needed—as soon as 1985—in terms of the maintenance of the present U.S. living standards (and even earlier if the oil supply of Iran is interrupted); and no later than 1995-ish if the situation is particularly favorable in respect to new discoveries. Thus, the *present* price of the present energy sources is largely irrelevant, though the timing of the considerable price escalation they will undergo as exhaustion nears is supremely relevant in estimates of the time left for research, development and building. An anticipatory policy is of the essence. It must be entirely different from the normal basis to commercial development because of the large lead times involved in the necessary research and development, and also the very large time (a half century?) over which the conversion to the future sources will be accomplished. Further, the main time-determining factors are economic.

That estimates to be made one decade, and even five decades, away are very, very uncertain, does not in any way justify the simplistic attitude of

TABLE 8.XIX: AN ATTEMPT TO ESTIMATE THE RELATIVE-REAL-COSTS OF THE NEW ENERGY SYSTEMS

	Resource availability supply all needs (0-10)	Labour intensivity in construction	Raw materials to construct machinery	Environmental damage, etc.	Feasibility technology	Product in first 5 columns = 'Desirability'	$ cost/1 MBTU fuel	Factor attempting represent cost damage and efficiency relative gasoline	Relative real cost (RRC) (Coal to gas=1)	Desirable RRC with coal to gas RRC =
Coal to gasoline	4	4	10	1	8	1280	7	1	28	1
Coal to LNG	4	4	10	3	10	4800	6	0.6	0.6	0.2
Coal to gas H_2	4	4	10	5	10	8000	5	0.3	0.3	0.1
Coal to LH_2	4	4	10	5	10	8000	8	0.3	0.4	0.1
Breeders to H_2	8	1	10	0	5	0	>20	0.3	>0.8	∞
OTEC to H_2	10	2	10	10	5	10000	11	0.3	0.4	0.1
Solar-thermal to H_2	10	8	9	9	7	45360	15	0.3	0.7	0.01
Photovoltaic to H_2	10	8	5	9	10	36000	16	0.3	0.7	0.01
Bio-mass to LNG	3	10	3	5	4	1800	?5?	0.5	0.4	0.02
Wind-H_2	5	3	6	10	8	7200	9	0.6	0.7	0.04
Hydro-electric to H_2	0	3	10	8	10	0	6	0.6	0.6	∞

* The factor of desirability is obtained by multiplying together the numbers in the first five columns. 0 represents the view that lack of suitability in a factor considered makes the source unacceptable. For example, it seems that hydro-electric sources are not sufficient to provide a general source of energy.
⁺ Where cost estimates cover a wide range, as with OTEC, the mean has been taken.

comparing new energy source cost estimates with the price of fossil fuels at present, whilst oil, gas and coal are still available. For such comparisons are much worse than uncertain: *they* are certain—certainly *wrong*.

Now, to return to the first error, the use of the First Law Efficiency costs, e.g. comparing the cost of 1 MBTU of gasoline from coal with that of 1 MBTU of (e.g.) hydrogen gas from wind power: this is certainly wrong because it is centered on the view of the seller, not upon that of the buyer. As the founding stone of western political thinking is that the good of the majority must be optimized, policies which are largely to the advantage of the 10% who are company shareholders versus those of the 90% (it is really much more) who do not gain or lose directly depending upon corporate profits, are obviously socially inconsistent with the democratic theme. Their viability as policies would depend on lack of feedback from the electorate, and hence would not be a safe basis for, sooner or later, the electorate does get the big picture and, thereafter, duly exerts the influence corresponding to what is its image of Reality.

If one pays X_A for a unit of fuel A and ⅔ X_B for a unit of B, but if fuel A is twice as efficient in conversion to the useful form of energy required, the expensive A is the cheaper fuel. This does not have to be argued, though it must be said that there will be a different relative efficiency of the conversion of A and B to the various forms of useful energy, and even different in different converters. For example, hydrogen is converted to mechanical power more efficiently than methane in an automobile engine, but not in an aircraft engine. A difficulty is that we do not *at present* know the relative efficiencies of conversion in many cases—as we do not know with greater precision than a few years when new energy sources will be needed—but this does not change the clear conclusion that Second Law costs represent more accurately than First Law costs, the relative economic preference of one fuel, or source of energy, over another; and hence (for the differences are often great) should always be used in comparing the relative advantages of energy policy A with all the alternatives. However, hitherto, this has not been done.

Lastly, environmental and health hazards have to be expressed in terms of cost per unit of fuel, and the net cost used as criterion of excellence (Table 8.XIX).

SUMMARY OF CHAPTER

1. During the 1970s the relative prospects of Solar Energy as a massive source of energy have been improved (Table 8.I), partly because of the decline in the prospects of breeders.

2. OTEC, solar-thermal and photovoltaic with concentrators are projected as giving electricity cheaper than the cost at present projected for breeder electricity.

3. The *concept* of combining H_2 with solar improves the prospects for massive solar source because it makes possible the storage and transmission of solar energy (in gaseous H_2) over long distances.

4. The greater efficiency of H_2 than of gasoline in internal combustion engines helps the solar-hydrogen fuel to be competitive in cost with other possibilities.

5. The world's greatest solar-absorbing areas are within 3000 km of the equator and more than 3000 km from the places where large amounts of energy are needed. A medium of transmission cheaper than that of electricity is needed.

6. Large-scale solar desalination would cost about 2 cents per gallon.

7. Costings of solar sources are usually carried out unrealistically. They neglect the costs of pollution caused by atomic and fossil fuels and this is an implicit subsidy to these sources. They neglect the large costs of decommissioning atomic plants; they neglect the differences in energy conversion which are attached to the different fuels (e.g. H_2 is some 1.5 times more efficient in conversion to mechanical energy in automobiles than is gasoline).

8. A comparison of nuclear (breeder) and solar sources for a massive energy supply is in favour of solar so long as the cost of making breeders safe is taken into account.

9. Solar-thermal plants are at the pilot plant stage, and would cost $1000-2000 per kW if made in large mass-production facilities. According to one cost projection, electricity from solar-thermal would cost 3.5 cents per kWh.

10. Solar-thermal plants, world wide, as the total world energy source, would cause an acceptable world temperature increase of 0.4°C. Building solar-thermal plants would be much more labour intensive than would be the building of comparable coal plants. Pollution during building would be less than that during coal plants.

11. OTEC plants have been subject to twenty-six system analyses and, according to these, give the cheapest prospects for the production of a fuel from solar energy.

12. Ammonia would be the working fluid for OTEC. Ships would graze the seas and tugs pull barges containing LH_2 to shore. LH_2 price estimates vary from $7.50 to $16.50 per MBTU.

13. OTEC seems significantly cheaper in prospect (after 2000) than coal, nuclear, solar-thermal and photovoltaic. The slow development in terms of funding in the U.S. and the zero funding elsewhere has been interpreted by some as evidence of a nuclear-coal tilt in government policy. Present U.S. Government plans call for a 100 MW_e plant but only by 1985.

14. Photovoltaic substances seem to be limited to those containing Si (or Al and Si) were they to be used massively.

15. It is essential, if photovoltaics are to be accepted as the basis of the large-scale energy source of the future, that they are used with concentrators. In such a case 4 cents per kWh electricity from photovoltaics is foreseen (but this would be dearer than solar-thermal).

16. The under-developed wet photovoltaics offer the possibility of producing H_2 and electricity from the same thermal plant.

17. The satellite solar-collecting scheme would be practical if the cost of orbiting were reduced to $100 per lb: this is in prospect with the space shuttle, and before 2000.

18. Bio-catalytic production of hydrogen could still be the cheapest of all approaches. However, at present the reactions concerned function for only a few hours. Little research has been done.

19. The massive collection of wind energy would give electricity more cheaply than solar energy, so long as wind turbines were placed in areas where the mean annual wind velocity is at least 20 kph. One turbine of 50 m radius would then support around 1000 people and the associated societal and industrial machinery. However, the area needed is sufficiently large so that ocean-based plants would be desirable.

20. Hydroelectric electricity would be cheaper than solar or wind and far cheaper than nuclear energy. Gaseous hydrogen fuel from low-head hydro-power would cost about $6 per MBTU. H_2 from coal would be still cheaper, only so long as the costs of atmospheric damage and S and CO_2 pollution are neglected.

21. Large-scale hydro-electric power, particularly from Greenland, seems to offer the cheapest hydrogen fuel, about $2.75 in Greenland and about $6 as liquefied in the U.S. This would be about the same cost as LH_2 from coal, but would avoid environmental damage and health hazards.

22. In respect to magnitude, the low-head hydro-electric power could give about 0.3 of the U.S. electrical energy need (or some 0.2 of the automotive load). Greenland's maximum potential is about 0.1 of the U.S. automotive load. Hence, cheap hydro-electric power (and H_2 fuel) is not a general solution to energy prospects, though it may often be worth developing where it exists. The transport of energy at low cost over large distances in hydrogen may make hydro-electric power from remote areas accessible. It is not yet clear how much hydro-electric sources could contribute: at present it seems that the amount would not be more than 5% of total need.

23. In an attempt to find what energy source should be developed, accounting for initial cost, second law efficiency, and some factors representing social costs (these subjectively estimated), the first three are: solar-thermal to H_2; photovoltaic to H_2; and coal to H_2, with CO_2 rejection to the ocean (however, the coal estimate neglects the sulphur re-burial cost).

AUTHOR'S SELECTION OF A MORE IMPORTANT CONCLUSION FROM CHAPTER

OTEC, solar-thermal and photovoltaic with concentrators all offer projected costs of electricity at values less than the projected costs of electricity from breeder reactors. The solar source from which the projections of First Law costs are nearest to the *apparent* price of L.N.G. from coal is OTEC.

The relative desirability of the competing new energy sources could be represented by taking the reciprocal of the values in the last column of Table 8.XIX.

	Figure of Merit *(Rounded off)*
Solar thermal to H_2	100
Photovoltaic to H_2	100
Bio-mass to H_2	50
Wind to H_2	25
OTEC to H_2	10
Coal to LH_2 (CO_2 to sea)	10
Coal to gas H_2 (CO_2 to sea)	10
Coal to L.N.G.	5
Coal to gasoline	1
Breeders to H_2	0
Hydro-electric to H_2	0

The figure of merit is based on an objective estimate of the unit cost of the fuel; an objective factor for the second law of efficiency of its use (taken for urban motoring); and subjective judgements on five social desirability factors. The figures are intended to give some indication of the *relative qualitative* desirability of developing the source. The non-appearance of breeders arises from the subjective judgement that the hazards are unacceptable.

REFERENCES

1. J. E. Perrott, 'Economic and Commercial Assessment of Solar Energy', Conference C.12, Royal Institution, July 1977; C. E. Backus, *J. Vac. Sci. Technol.*, 1975, **12**, 103; K. Kreb, *Proc. International Conference on Solar Electricity*, Toulouse, 1976.
2. K. A. Ehricke, 'The power relay satellite concept of the framework of the overall Energy picture', North American Aerospace, Rockwell International, E-73-12-1, December 1973.
3. D. Watson, *Solar Houses*, Gardenway Publishing, 1977.
4. B. E. Swardan, Alternate Energy Sources Conference, Miami, 5-7 December 1977.
5. M. Davidson and Donald Grether, 'The central receiver power plant', Lawrence Berkeley Laboratory, University of California, Berkeley, ERDA Contract No. W-7405-ENG-48.
6. 'The U.S.A. 5MW Solar-Thermal Test Facility', International Solar Energy Conference, Vigyan Bhawan, New Delhi, India, 16-21 January 1978.
7. Otto J. Smith, Meeting on Solar Supply for Towns, Palm Springs, 6-8 April 1978.
8. 'Ocean-thermal energy conversion, programme survey', October 1976, Division of Solar Energy, ERDA, Washington, D.C., 20545.
9. Gay Heit Larvi, Alternate Energy Sources Conference, Miami, Florida, 5-7 December 1977.
10. Second Ocean Thermal Energy Conversion Workshop, 26-28 September 1974, Washington, D.C., published by the Clean Energy Research Institute, School of Engineering, University of Miami (H.P. Harrenstein, ed.).
11. A. Talib, A. Knopka, N. P. Biederman, C. Vlazek & B. Yudow, 'Alternative Forms of Energy transmission from OTEC plants', International Solar Energy Conference, Vigyan Bhawan, New Delhi, India, 16-21 January 1978.
12. M. I. Nelson, Alternate Energy Sources Conference, Miami, Florida, 5-7 December 1977
13. L. Akobjanoff & E. D. Howe, *Research* (June 1956), pp. 220-226.
14. Fritz Haber, *New Scientist*, 13 December 1977.
15. E. A. Eckert, in *Heat and Mass Transfer* (McGraw Hill, 1963).
16. W. McAdam, *Heat Transmission* (McGraw Hill, New York, 1954), 3rd edition.
17. J. G. McGowan & W. E. Heronemus, Workshop Proceedings, Second Ocean Thermal Energy Conversion Workshop, 26-28 September, 1974, p.80.
18. J. H. Nath, J. W. Ambler & R. M. Hansen, Proceedings of the Fourth International Conference on Ocean Thermal Energy Conversion, New Orleans, 22-24 March 1977, p. V-56.
19. D. Perrigo & G. E. Jensen, Proceedings of the Fourth International Conference on Ocean Thermal Energy Conversion, New Orleans, 22-24 March 1977, p. VII-3.

20. J. G. Fetkovich, G. N. Grannemann, L. M. Mahalingam, D. L. Meyer & F. L. Munchmeyer, Proceedings of the Fourth International Conference on Ocean Thermal Energy Conversion, New Orleans, 22-24 March 1977, p. VII-15.
21. E. D. Nubel, Proceedings of the Fourth International Conference on Ocean Thermal Energy Conversion, New Orleans, 22-24 March 1977, p. VI-61.
22. See Proceedings of the Fourth International Conference on Ocean Thermal Energy Conversion, New Orleans, 22-24 March 1977.
23. A. Talib, A. Knopka, N. Biederman, C. Vlazek & B. Yudow, International Solar Energy Conference, Vigyan Bhawan, New Delhi, India, 16-21 January 1978.
24. G. L. Dugger & E. J. Francis, First World Hydrogen Energy Conference, Miami, Florida, 1976, 3A-63.
25. A. Lavi & C. Zener, Proceedings of the Fourth International Conference on Ocean Thermal Energy Conversion, New Orleans, 22-24 March 1977.
26. J. M. Milles & B. J. Washom, Proceedings of the Fourth International Conference on Ocean Thermal Energy Conversion, New Orleans, 22-24 March 1977, p. III-3.
27. B. Lindal, C. D. Hornburg & N. El-Ramlay, Proceedings of the Fourth International Conference on Ocean Thermal Energy Conversion, New Orleans, 22-24 March 1977, p. III-34.
28. P. J. Martin & G. O. Roberts, Proceedings of the Fourth International Conference on Ocean Thermal Energy Conversion, New Orleans, 22-24 March 1977, p. IV-26.
29. J. Beck, *Science,* 1975, **189,** 293.
30. C. Zener & J. G. Fetkovich, *Science,* 1975, **189,** 294.
31. S. L. Ridgeway, Proceedings of the Fourth International Conference on Ocean Thermal Energy Conversion, New Orleans, 22-24 March 1977, p. VIII-7.
32. We are indebted to G. Heit Larvi for providing us with a summary of the plans for OTEC, visible in Washington around June, 1978.
33. J. J. Loferski, 'The principles of photovoltaic solar energy conversion', Brown University, Rhode Island, March 1972.
34. Report of the Australian Academy of Sciences on Solar Energy Research in Australia, No. 17, 1973, p. 22.
35. J. Stackhouse, 'Solar Energy' in the *Financial Review,* Sydney, January 1974.
36. 'Solar cells: outlook for improved efficiency', National Academy of Science, Washington 1972.
37. L. Lyons, private communication.
38. K. Boer, 'Direct solar energy conversion for terrestrial use', Proceedings of the Ninth IEEE Photovoltaic Specialists' Conference, Silver Springs, Maryland, May 1972.
39. F. Schirland, Third Conference on Large-Scale Solar Energy Conversion for Terrestrial Use, Delaware, October 1971.
40. L. Partain & N. Sayed, 'Accelerated life tests of cadmium sulphide-cuprous sulphide solar cells', NSF Grant No. G134872, May 1973.
41. H. A. Aaron & S. E. Isakoff, Third Conference on Large-Scale Solar Energy Conversion for Terrestrial Use, Delaware, October 1971.
42. K. Boer, private communication.
43. J. M. Woodall & H. J. Hovell, *Appl. Phys. Letters,* 1972, **21,** 379.
44. J. J. Loferski, E. E. Crisman, L. J. Chen & W. Armitage, 'Methods of improving the efficiency of photovoltaic cells', Seventh Semi-Annual Report on NASA, Grant No. NGR40-002-093, 1973.
45. B. Brody, private communication, 1978; F. Shirland, G. Greenieck, H. Symond & B. Brody, as quoted by F. Shirland, May 1978.
46. *cf.* 'Solar Energy: A U.K. Assessment', prepared by the U.K. Section of the International Solar Energy Society, May 1976, Table 8.2, p.241.
47. K. V. Ravi, H. V. Serreze, K. Bateshe, A. D. Morrison, D. N. Jewett & J. Ho, Eleventh IEEE Photovoltaic Specialists Conference, Phoenix, Arizona, May 1975.
48. C. G. Currin, K. S. Len, E. L. Ralph, W. A. Smith & J. Sterner, Ninth IEEE Photovoltaic Specialists Conference, Silver Springs, Maryland, May 1972.
49. 'Solar Energy: A U.K. Assessment', prepared by the U.K. Section of the International Solar Energy Society, May 1976.
50. M. Wolf, *J. Vac. Sci. Technol.,* 1975, **12,** 984.
51. J. E. Perrott, 'Economic and commercial assessment of solar energy conversion', U.K. I.S.E.S. (Royal Institution, London, W.1., 1977), p.49.
52. A. Beam & J. Hansen, Eleventh IEEE Photovoltaic Specialists Conference, Phoenix,

Arizona, May 1975, p.32.
53. S. Slater & G. Gauradi, Eleventh IEEE Photovoltaic Specialists Conference, Phoenix, Arizona, May 1975, p.356.
54. E. Evans & F. Florscheutz, ISES Conference, Los Angeles, 1975.
55. E. Burgess, Twelfth IEEE Photovoltaic Specialists Conference, 1975.
56. J. Mash, quoted by J. E. Perrott,[51] *loc. cit.*
57. P. E. Gläser, Proceedings of the IEEE Conference, 1977, **65**.
58. P. E. Gläser, *Astronautics and Aeronautics*, August 1973, p.60.
59. R. M. Dickinson & W. C. Brown, Technical Memorandum No. 83-727, Jet Propulsion Laboratory, California Institute of Technology, Pasadena, May 15th, 1975.
60. Special issue on Active and Adaptive antennae, IEEE, Transactions of Professional Group of Antennae and Propagation, March 1964.
61. A. Fujishima & K. Honda, *Nature*, 1972, **238**, 37.
62. A. Fujishima, K. Kohayakawa & K. Honda, *Journal of the Electrochemical Society*, 1975, **122**, 487.
63. A. J. Bard & M. S. Wrighton, Symposium on the physical prop. of liquid semi-conductors, by the Electrochemical Society, 1978; H. Gerischer, M. T. Spitler & F. Willig, Extended Abstracts, Electrochemical Society, May 1979.
64. B. Miller, S. Menezes & A. Heller, Symposium on the physical prop. of liquid function semi-conductors, by the Electrochemical Society, 1977; P. A. Kohl & A. J. Bard, *J. Electrochem. Soc.*, 1979, **1261**, 603; A. J. Nozik, Extended Abstracts, Electrochemical Society, May 1979.
65. K. Ohashi, J. McCann & J. O'M. Bockris, *Energy Research*, 1977, **1**, 259.
66. J. O'M. Bockris & K. Uosaki, *J. Electrochem. Soc.*, 1978, **125**, 223.
67. J. O'M. Bockris & K. Uosaki, *Energy* (1976), vol. 1, pp.95-96.
68. L. Handley, Report to Flinders University, School of Physical Science, 1978.
69. N. Calvin, *Science*, 1973, **184**, 375.
70. M. Gibbs, Proceedings of the Workshop on Bio-solar conversion, National Science Foundation, Bethesda, Maryland, July 1974; K. Mitsui, in N.T. Verisoglu (ed.), *Hydrogen Energy Fundamentals* (University of Miami, 1974), S2-13 and S2-48.
71. G. Neal, D. Nicholas, J. O'M. Bockris & J. McCann, *Heliotechnique & Development*, 1976, **1**, 481-487.
72. W. L. Butler & M. Kitajima; Proceedings of the Conference, U.K. I.S.E.S. (London, June 1975), pp. 13-15.
73. J. M. Noel, 'Energy conversion systems', Workshop Proceedings, NSF/RA/W-73-006, 1973, p.186.
74. J. O'M. Bockris, *Environmental Conservation* 2, 4 (1975).
75. L. F. Mullett, 'Wind as a commercial source of energy', Engineering Conference, Canberra, 1956.
76. N. Carruthers, *Quart. J. Roy. Met. Soc.*, **69**, 1943.
77. A. H. Stodhart, in 'Energy Conversion Systems', Workshop Proceedings, NSF/RA/W-73-006 (1973), p.62.
78. P. Lapin, *Energy Conversion*, 1977, **16**, 213.
79. B. Serdensen, *Energy Resources Science*, 1975, **189**, 255.
80. B. G. Newman, *Energy Conversion*, 1977, **16**, 169.
81. Otto J. Smith, Meeting on Alternate Energy Sources, Palm Springs, California, 6-8 April, 1978.
82. J. Mills & G. L. Smith, Alternate Energy Sources Conference, Miami, 5-7 December 1977.
83. K. Laroche, First World Hydrogen Energy Conference, Miami, 1976, 2C-33.
84. F. Gutmann, private communication, 1978.
85. H. Stauber, private communication, 1972.
86. J. Hansen, Report to National Academy of Sciences, December 1974.
87. V. Guruswamy & J. O'M. Bockris, *J. Solar Energy Materials*, 1979, **1**.

9

COMPARISON OF FUELS

Various aspects of a Hydrogen Economy have been presented. The advantages of hydrogen, in respect to a common medium for coal-nuclear and solar sources seem significant and, in some areas, essential. One should not, however, present hydrogen as a fuel without presentation of the strengths of alternative and competing fuels.

Alternatives to a Solar-Hydrogen Economy are time-dependent in strength. Thus, fossil fuels *will* run out: it is not controversial to state that it would be better to change away from them as soon as is economically possible. Such a change will be forced by uncompetitive costs resulting from exhaustion, and hastened by increasing air pollution. It should be encouraged by the desirability of having a supply of fossil fuels left for the synthesis of petrochemicals.

The necessity for a fuel

In some discussions of new energy sources, there is unclarity between the energy source and the fuel from it. The solar energy which gave rise to the photosynthesis of the present fuels in earlier times is forgotten, so that fossil fuels are naively regarded as energy sources. In fact, they are solar-based media of which the storage has been made over aeons, in a form almost ready for direct use.

The need for a fuel, in addition to electricity, is manifest when we consider our present system.[1] This is one which runs on two main fuels, electricity and gasoline, as also on natural gas, fuel oil and coal. If we were to attempt to run on electricity derived from renewable resources alone, a modification in much of technology, particularly in transport and industry, would have to occur. Much which is now chemical would then better become electrochemical. This would add to the capital investment programme needed during the coming decades. As the main difficulty in developing renewable energy sources is the degree of capital investment needed,[2] it will be better to introduce a new fuel for transmission from central sources, analogous to natural gas, and confine the use of electricity to its present purposes.

In considering environmentally clean fuels which are consistent with the new energy sources, it is principally electricity, hydrogen and the alcohols (methanol and ethanol) which rate (Fig. 9.1). Liquid synthetic natural gas from coal will certainly be a fuel to be considered by some, but reliance on it as a long-term fuel for the future would give rise to a major development of coal, with the considerable climatic consequences of injecting too much CO_2 into the atmosphere.

It might be thought that ammonia or hydrazine could be considered. Ammonia is rejected because it is expensive to make, and starts with

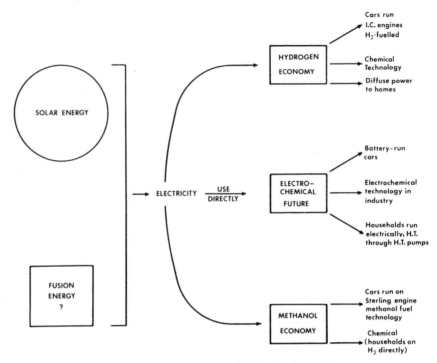

Fig. 9.1. The three main possibilities for future fuels.

hydrogen. A fuel made from hydrogen by an endothermic reaction must cost more to make than hydrogen, although one must weigh the higher cost of storing gaseous hydrogen against the costs of storing liquid ammonia.

Another substance which might be considered is hydrazine, the advantage being that it consists of easily available elements. However, hydrogen is in it, and the synthesis of hydrazine is expensive, mainly because of the recrystallisation of the hydrate from solution for storage. It is not practical to store hydrazine in solution because of the volume involved (e.g. in on-board storage in a car).

Alternative fuels

All energy considerations depend upon the time-frame for use, to which reference is made, and all are dominated by questions of economics (Fig. 9.2). It must be recalled that preparation and construction must commence *several decades* before use.

The present fuel distribution system will have to be rebuilt as the sources of energy change. In practice, the change will spread over several decades, for reasons of the limits on capital investment. Hence, a comparison of costs assessing the likely fuels of the post-1990 future should consider the relative costs at that time, not the relative costs at present. This seems obvious. However, comparisons made by engineers and economists are still with *present* costs. The case is because 'future costs are not known'. This is not really a valid statement because, although future costs must necessarily be

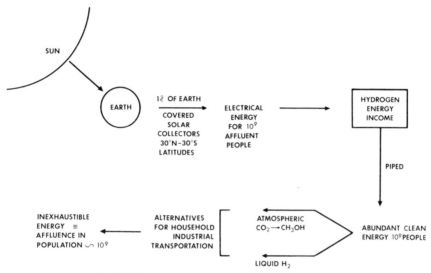

Fig. 9.2. The price of energy and the level of affluence.

estimates and—all question of inflation apart—therefore doubtful, the most important relevant aspect is clear: when the oil and natural gas fuels can no longer supply total (expanding) need, costs will rise. Further, the date of the beginning of this insufficiency is predictable to ± 2 years as occurring around 1992. It is, therefore, acceptable to foresee a cost increase of present fuels in constant dollars during the 1980s, and a particularly enhanced rise during the 1990s.

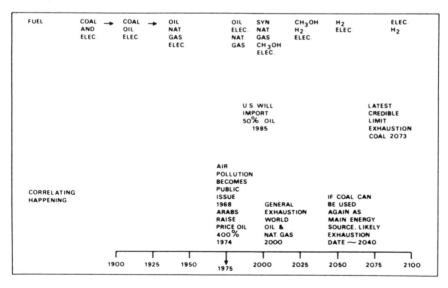

Fig. 9.3. The time of dominance of various fuels.

Gasoline will certainly continue as the major fuel for 10 years, and be still an important (perhaps still the most important) component of our fuels even 20 years from now (Fig. 9.3). After the maximum of oil and natural gas production, gasoline will have to be gradually displaced. On the way, materials will be mixed with it, probably ethanol, or methanol.

Methanol is an attractive component of such mixtures because of its ease of storage and transmission. Methanol does not have the same status as hydrogen or electricity because of the difficulty of coupling it with the future solar or atomic sources.

1. *Availability*

The fuel must be *permanently* available: a change in the fuel system, once around 2000 and then around 2030, would seem poor economics.

2. *Economics*

In so far as cost is low and price is high—as in the present situation for oil—price is a political matter: cost and price will come nearer as resistance to selling increases.

3. *Other sociological factors*

The choice of the fuel to succeed gasoline will be affected by compatibility of the fuel with the present capital investment in certain machinery. The change will be forced in so far as cost catches up with price for the old fuels, due to the fact that liquid and gaseous fuels will eventually not meet demand, a condition anticipated as early as the mid-1980s.

4. *Compatibility with solar and atomic sources*

Would it be good economics to introduce methanol production on a large scale if it would not mesh with hydrogen and electricity from solar sources?[2]

Hydrogen can be produced from coal, solar or atomic: it can be the common medium from all of them.

A Methanol Economy

Methanol is a possible fuel for the phase between the end of oil and natural gas and the primary dependence on atomic and solar energy.

A methanol fuel base to the economy (founded on coal) would have several advantages:

1. Natural gas has a lower pollution index than does methanol, but it is a gas and it would be more convenient (i.e. more applicable to plant now owned) if the new fuel were a liquid at room temperature and pressure.
2. Methanol can be produced from coal, but it can also be produced from vegetative materials and this makes it a possibility as a medium of solar energy. It could also be a medium of atomic energy in the sense that CO_2 could be extracted from the atmosphere and used with hydrogen from nuclear-based electrolysis.
3. Internal-combustion engines may probably be run on methanol with few changes in the present engines.
4. Storage could be more convenient than that of gaseous hydrogen, and cheaper than that of liquid hydrogen.

5. Transmission could be slightly cheaper than that with hydrogen.
6. Safety would be better than that of hydrogen.
7. It could leave the capital invested in the fossil-fuel technology less disturbed than movement to a technology of the other two fuels, hydrogen and electricity.

To balance against these positive aspects of methanol is the CO_2 difficulty after 2000. Some alleviation would be obtained by using methanol in fuel cells. Thus, methanol transduces fairly well (though not as well as hydrogen) to electricity in fuel cells, whereas methane and hydrocarbon oils are not good fuels for such cells.[3] The lack of mutual compatibility of a fuel consistent with solar and atomic sources would be a difficulty. Continued pollution with some degree of hydrocarbons and with NO would result.

Transduction possibilities with hydrogen are superior to those of methanol. Hydrogen makes a pollutionless fuel (negligible NO) in internal-combustion engines.

Liquid hydrogen is inevitable for post-Concorde aircraft (their range will be otherwise too small), and it would be advantageous to have the same fuels for land-based and air-based transportation.

In a sense, methanol is a fuel only, whereas hydrogen could be the fuel, storage and transmission medium, and principal chemical for the entire economy. Thus, all the pollutional advantages of running factories and industry on hydrogen; the advantages of having cheap excess hydrogen in metallurgy and for recycling; the side effects of fresh-water production; and the synthesis of proteins from hydrogen, nitrogen, CO_2 and enzymes, are lost if methanol, rather than hydrogen, were the general medium of energy.

The prospective price of methanol from coal in 1978 dollars is around $10 per MBTU.

Gaseous hydrogen from coal would be $3-$4 and LH_2 from coal would

TABLE 9.I: Pure Methanol Vehicle Performance Record[4]

Vehicle	Use:
1972 Plymouth Valiant	Operated by Meter Readers
Owner:	Service Time and Mileage:
City of Santa Clara	30 months and 20,000 miles

Best Anti-pollution Performance

	HC Gr/Mi	CO Gr/Mi	NO Gr/Mi
City vehicle:			
Air Resources Board*	0.0	0.42	1.30
Santa Clara University (CVS-1)	0.026	1.42	0.67
1976 Standards:			
California State (CVS-2)	0.9	9.0	2.0
Federal (CVS-2)	0.41	3.4	2.0

Principal problems:
Cold start, fuel system materials, sluggish performance when set at minimum pollution levels.

*The test by the Air Resources Board was the 7-mode test with the results converted to CVS-1.

be around $6-$7 MBTU^{-1}. After coal is no longer sufficiently plentiful, methanol will have to come from (the necessarily cheaper) hydrogen produced by water splitting.

Methanol as a fuel for the internal combustion engine

There is a difference in the octane values between methanol and gasoline which would need minor alterations being made to engines intended to run on methanol. Studies carried out by Pefley, Adelman and McCormack on methanol-fueled internal-combustion engines are encouraging.[4] The emissions are less than in gasoline-fueled vehicles. Part of the work was carried out on what was called 'dissociated methanol,' i.e. hydrogen.

Cars were run on pure methanol for 20,000 miles with no unusual difficulties in performance. Some results are shown in Table 9.I.

Such vehicles have been placed first in clean air tests. Emissions from methanol-driven cars are shown in Fig. 9.4. NO is about the same as with gasoline (Table 9.I).

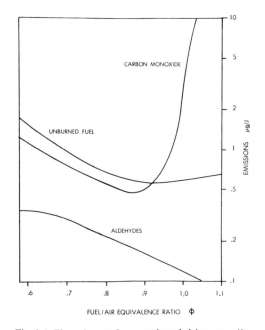

Fig. 9.4. The exhausts from methanol-driven cars.[11]

One of the difficulties is holding methanol and gasoline in solution in the presence of traces of water. Excess aldehyde and NO production are others.

Preparation of methanol[5]

The price of methanol from water and carbon dioxide would be c. $10.00 per MBTU, and cheaper than gasoline from coal. Methanol could be obtained in three ways:

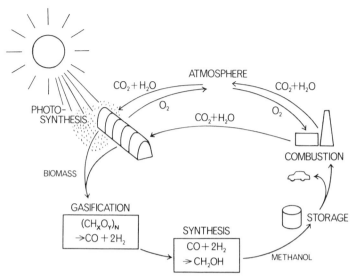

Fig. 9.5. Methanol from photosynthesis.[5]

1. From plant growth, cane sugar or beets[5] (Fig. 9.5). This process uses atmospheric CO_2 and avoids the greenhouse problem.[6]
2. Using carbon dioxide from carbonate rocks and hydrogen from water via nuclear or solar energy and electrolysis (Fig. 9.6).
3. From the ingestion of carbon dioxide from the atmosphere and the corresponding hydrogen from water.

No. 2 would be the most economic. However, the greenhouse difficulty reappears.[6]

The extraction of carbon dioxide from the atmosphere[7] would need a work of

$$2.303 \; RT\ln 10^6/4.10^2 \simeq 4.6 \; \text{k.cal per mol}$$

Assuming that the total cost is five times the amount for this work, that of the CO_2 should be $1.50 per MBTU equivalent, and this would have to be added to the cost of gaseous hydrogen from water at, say, $9 per MBTU. There would be plant costs and this would add about $1 per MBTU, so that $10.50 per MBTU for methanol from this route might be a rough estimate.[8]

The cost of methanol from atmospheric CO_2 and water would be about the same as the cost of liquid hydrogen, more expensive than hydrogen but cheaper than gasoline from coal (Fig. 9.7).

The hazards of methanol

Emissions on burning methanol are less than those with gasoline. It produces no soot, no sulphur. Pb emissions would be eliminated if mixed with benzene.

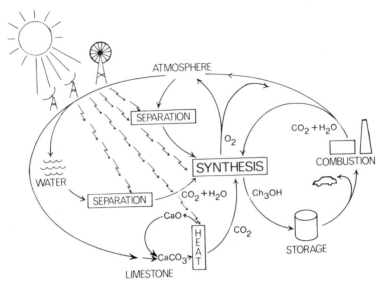

Fig. 9.6. Methanol from collection of CO_2.[5]

However, ingestion of methanol is much more toxic than that of gasoline. Lethal doses may be as low as 0.1 gm/kg.[9,10]

Table 9.II shows the toxicity of the three fuels.

TABLE 9.II: COMPARATIVE TOXICITY RATINGS[11]

	Eye Contact	Inhalation	Skin Penetration	Skin Irritation	Ingestion
Methanol	2	2	2	1	1
Benzene	2	4	2	2	2
Gasoline	(2)	(3)	(3)	(1)	(2)

1 = mild; 5 = extreme toxicity; ( ) = estimated—depends on composition

Source: Chemical Rubber Company

Corrosion occurs easily with methanol in contact with Pb plated fuel tanks and synthetic gaskets. Water content must be removed.

Synthetic natural gas

Gaseous or liquid methane could be used in internal-combustion engines: there is some use in the late 1970s. Methane burns cleanly to CO_2.

The production of natural gas will peak world wide around the century's end. However, it could be obtained from coal at around $4.50 per MBTU (Chapter 4).

To regard synthetic natural gas as a fuel to replace gasoline one would have to foresee a very large building of mines, the training of an immense number of miners (2,000,000 for the U.S.), take into account the costs of desulphurisation and then the reburial of the S; and estimate the environmental damage due to the CO_2 climatic problem. These costs should be added to the present apparent cost of the fuel (i.e. to the $4.50 per MBTU).

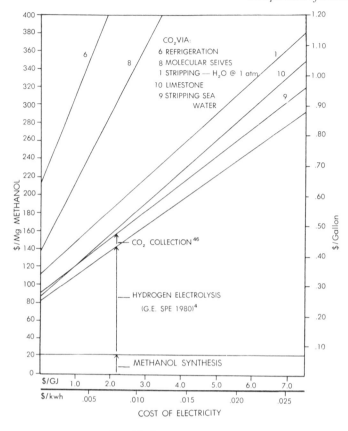

Fig. 9.7. The methanol cost.[8]

Hydrazine

Hydrazine as a fuel is a liquid at room temperature, colourless and odourless. It has been used in fuel cells to drive trucks, and has powered villages in Vietnam.

Hydrazine has a high price and carcinogenic properties. An ammonia smell often accompanies hydrazine because of dissociation.

Electricity

Electricity has excellent environmental properties and can be transmitted economically up to 1000 km. A negative feature is the cost of transporting it to further distances. Such costs are unimportant now because the electricity generally comes from generating plants running on oil or coal and it is these fuels which are transported to the plants. The electricity in grid wires travels only a few hundred miles at most. However, with atomic sources, the economy of large scale will be important, and pollutive dangers will encourage the keeping of such equipment in remote areas. In solar generation, it will be better to use the desert regions of the world and these are clearly far (i.e. > 1000 km) from the sites of energy use.

Our present economy interfaces with liquid or gaseous fuels and this is negative for electricity as is the fact that it is difficult to store in bulk quantities.

Hydrogen

General

An advantage of the hydrogen path as a fuel is the small degree of alteration which would be needed in the internal-combustion engine, now used with gasoline, to make it compatible with hydrogen. The completely clean nature of hydrogen and the benign product of its combustion is attractive.* It is the only ecologically sound fuel in the sense that its formation and use returns the environment to the same state as before.

The use of hydrogen in automotive transportation is attractive in respect to its consistency with the use of hydrogen for other purposes. It is the clean alternative to natural gas and does not create CO_2 nor have to bear the heavy environmental damage costs of other fuels.

On negative aspects of hydrogen as a medium of energy

Although acceptance of, and enthusiasm for, the proposition that hydrogen should be the general medium of energy has been shown by engineers and scientists, particularly those in the fields of energy conversion, aeronautics, pollution control, the gas industry, the atomic energy industry, etc., there are those—mainly from the oil industry—who are negative to the concept. It is essential to weigh the validity of the criticisms.

Before they are listed, however, it is desirable to make several statements:

1. Most of the considerations associated with a Hydrogen Economy depend on the time frame in which it is purported to play a role in energy technology. Those who advocate the change to hydrogen view the present Fossil Fuel Economy as already in its terminal stage: the time scale for the end of fossil fuels is 'near' (by which is meant short compared with the time needed to research and build a new energy system), and so they do not consider competition between a Hydrogen Economy and one based on oil or natural gas. Coal is clearly a temporary stop-gap, to be used if its apparent cost PLUS the cost of reburial of sulphur, atmospheric pollution from its combustion products and world climatic change from CO_2 are less than those of competing fuels from atomic or solar sources. The latter are those for which hydrogen is to be a medium. The cost estimates which are made are for massive-use projections, and these are projections in the sense of time, and technology.

On the other hand, those who criticise a Hydrogen Economy usually see it as a direct and immediate competitor to natural gas and oil. For them, the time scale is 'now', the ending of the useful price range for fossil fuels is 'far off' (they mean beyond their career times) and, if coal is

---

*A widespread image is that the very large German Airship, HINDENBURG, hydrogen lifted, *exploded* with loss of all life. In fact, the gas bags were slashed and set on fire whilst the vehicle was moored at Lakehurst, N.J., but contained disembarking passengers. It burned and sank a few tens of metres to the ground over several minutes. Of those who died, nearly all were killed by jumping from too great a height.

included, 'hundreds of years' away (compare the material of Chapter 4).

The merits of hydrogen look different if seen from this short-term point of view. If, in a thought experiment, one changes to a Hydrogen-run Economy, in 1970s technology and costs, the gains would be in the elimination of the health hazards, the allowance to function of plant being phased out because of pollution, and the giving to advanced aircraft a greater payload. The first of these would be a boon to consumers, but it would be balanced by disadvantages, the disruption of the present system, and (if obtained via electrolysis or nuclear heat) the greater cost of the fuel. The only supporters of the introduction of a Hydrogen Economy 'today' (were this conceivable) would be environmentalists, city planners, ecologists, and those who look at real rather than apparent costs, i.e. take into account the cost of pollution from those whose plants are losing capital value because they pollute. Simplistic First Law (apparent) economics would win.

The reason for considering the Hydrogen Economy *now* is that the time for change to it is long compared with the time at which oil and natural gas will begin to become scarce (10-15 years). As far as synthetic fuels from coal are concerned, its lifetime and pollutional difficulties are such that conversion 'as soon as possible' to hydrogen becomes a rational goal: the new fuel from coal should be hydrogen. Indeed, the production of hydrogen fuel from coal, rather than LNG, would allow a diminution of some environmental difficulties of coal—if plants were shore-built and CO_2 were injected into the oceans.

2. Another dividing line—not the same one as that discussed in (1)—is whether consideration should be given to the need for coupling the new fuel with solar and nuclear sources, or not. If yes, the claims of hydrogen are increased. Then, indeed, even with present technology, they look good, and hydrogen becomes a strong contender as the future fuel. The pros and cons are laid out in this chapter. The nearest competitor is methanol. But methanol would have to come increasingly from hydrogen after 2000, and the pollutive products of its combustion are as threatening as those of gasoline.

3. All depends on the time period considered. If these are those over which a change from oil and gas will have to be made (50 years), hydrogen becomes a likely medium, with electricity the alternative, dependent for its competitive power on the development of electrochemical technology. But it is possible to take individual points—important points—in which hydrogen offers a disadvantage compared with other possibilities. If these points are examined, within the present time frame, it is possible for an anti-hydrogen case to be presented, using facts and without making any false statements.

The main criticisms of the use of hydrogen are:

1. Making hydrogen is too expensive

It has been shown elsewhere in this book (e.g. Chapter 8) that this assertion can be rebutted, so long as one has not to compete with the solar-originated store of oil and natural gas. A new technology of energy conversion could only be economically feasible when these are exhausting; therefore, the rightful comparison is carbonaceous fuels from coal, or electricity from atomic or solar sources, etc.

When these comparisons are made, even when the simplistic measure of price of the same energy unit is the measure, the result is not unfavourable to hydrogen. Indeed, in the simplest comparison, gaseous H_2 and gaseous CH_4, both from coal, H_2 is slightly cheaper. But comparison in this way is simplistic. One must know the Second Law use-factor, in the use for which the fuel is applied; and one must know the cost of the environmental damage and other societal factors which affect the real total costs of each fuel. One estimate of such matters is in Table 8. XIX.

2. 'It is better to produce methane from coal, not hydrogen'

This was indeed a criticism of weight whilst the possibilities of hydrogen from coal were not known and whilst the Second Law efficiencies, and environmental consequences, were not accounted for. One cannot compare the price of hydrogen, in dollars per unit of energy, with that of methane without accounting for the long-term effects of CO_2 released into the atmosphere, which hydrogen production could diminish; or the higher efficiency of using hydrogen from coal in land-based transportation.

3. The double Carnot difficulty

Were it possible to use fossil fuels without pollutive difficulty, this objection would have to be weighted seriously in automotive applications. It neglects the Second Law efficiency of the use of hydrogen. It does not apply to some of the proposed future methods of making hydrogen, e.g. its creation from coal, or by photosynthesis (Chapter 8). However, the criticism is, in any case, in the wrong time scale. Double Carnot simply ends up as a price per ton-mile in transportation. The correct question is: Would the price per ton-mile using hydrogen be less than that using methanol, or using electricity; and what are the environmental relative weights? These questions are considered, e.g. in Chapter 8.

4. Energy can be transmitted over long distances more cheaply in hydrogen than in wires. But the electricity at the other end will be more expensive

Whether this criticism is true depends on the distance from source to sink; and the efficiency of the reconverter fuel cells. Up to 800 miles for 700 kilovolts transmission, with a fuel cell efficiency of 60%, the criticism is true. Fuel-cell efficiencies for hydrogen as a fuel of 66% are acceptable. But the most important fact is the distance. Transmission lines of several thousand miles are expected, particularly with solar sources. There is no doubt about the favourable economics of hydrogen in such situations. In any case, the criticism is weak because it implies that much hydrogen will be converted to electricity. This is unlikely: hydrogen is to be used as a universal *fuel*, taking over from natural gas and oil.

5. 'Hydrogen is dangerous'

Hydrogen is in some comparisons a more dangerous fuel than natural gas. The situation is weighed in Chapter 15.

6. *Difficulties of introducing hydrogen as a fuel in transportation would be great*

This criticism is true of the storage of gaseous hydrogen at this time. It is compensated by the new knowledge that the efficiency of conversion of hydrogen in an automotive engine is greater than that of gasoline.[12] However, only if a pollutive damage cost is added to the LNG costs does *liquid* hydrogen from coal become cheaper than LNG from coal. Advances in the storage of gaseous hydrogen in fibreglass and other plastic-type substances could change this situation.

TABLE 9.III: Electricity, Methanol and Hydrogen Compared as Fuels

Property	Electricity	Methanol	H_2 Liquid	H_2 Gas
Methods of preparation	Photovoltaic; or heat engine etc.	Photosynthetic; or CO_2 from rocks + H_2 from water	$H_2O \xrightarrow{\text{heat}}_{\text{elec}} H_2$ Liq. N_2 $\to H_2$ (Low T) Expansion $\to H_2$ (Liquid)	$H_2O \xrightarrow{\text{heat}}_{\text{electric}}$ H_2
Mixes with water	Not applicable	Complex; but in gasoline forms two immiscible layers if water present	Not applicable	Not applicable
Corrosion	Zero	Significant problem	Zero	Zero
Flame speed	Not applicable		306 cm sec^{-1}	306 cm sec^{-1}
Flame temperature	Not applicable	2900°C	2050°C	2050°C
Luminosity	Not applicable	Fair	Poor	Poor
Production of pollutants on combustion	Zero	CO + Aldehydes worse than gasoline $\sim$ NOX worse than H_2	Zero	Zero
Use in fuel cell	Not applicable	Poor compared with H_2; better than oil	The best	The best
Compatible present IC Engine	Not applicable	Good. Some redesign necessary	Good. Fuel injection needed	Good. Gas storage difficult > 100 miles[7]
Storage	Difficult in large amounts	Easy	Liquefaction costs $2-$3 per MBTU	Compressed gas in tank; hydride
Transmission	Too expensive > 1000 km	Costs slightly less than H_2 in pipeline	Costs 25% > methanol	0.2 cents per 1000 km
Biological hazard	Safety preventions well practised	Very toxic; air pollution caused by large spills	Zero	Zero
Consumer acceptance before facts realised	Excellent	Very good	Fairly poor	Poor

Economic comparisons

One has to compare the fuels–electricity, hydrogen and methanol–upon the same energy basis, and then to take into account ancillary costs, such as storage, efficiency of conversion to some other kind of energy in end use; and the cost per unit of fuel of the environmental damage which the use of some fuels cause. On an energy scale, without dealer profit and taxes, U.S. gasoline is about $3 per MBTU *at the present time.* Such a price hides an environmental cost which would be between 25% and 50% of the present cost of gasoline, were coal the future source of the new fuels.

The 1st Law cost of fuels near to atomic or solar plants would be: electricity, less than hydrogen and less than methanol; and, far from the plant: hydrogen, less than electricity, less than methanol, depending upon distance.[12]

SUMMARY OF CHAPTER

1. It is not advisable to advance into the time past 1990, when oil and natural gas will be in decline, without decision on a single fuel to couple with the renewable energy resources, as well as with coal.

2. The three fuels to be considered as replacements for oil, gasoline and natural gas are: electricity, methanol and hydrogen. Liquefied synthetic natural gas is a possible competitor, whilst coal is regarded as an admissible fuel (i.e. whilst the environmental damage from its use is neglected).

3. Methanol has the advantage of consumer-taste compatibility and the disadvantages of continuing the pollution of the atmosphere if used to fuel cars. It would be more expensive than liquid hydrogen from coal. However, methanol from atmospheric CO_2 and H_2 would be cheaper than LH_2 from electrolysis.

4. The chief factors which influence the choice of a fuel are: non-exhaustibility; economics; can the new fuel fit the machinery of the old technology and thus preserve its capital value?; would the new fuel interface with the new atomic and solar sources?

5. Liquid synthetic natural gas provides a good fuel option to replace gasoline. The major disadvantage is the necessary origin—coal. Sufficiently large scale coal production would pollute with sulphur and CO_2.

6. Hydrogen has the advantage of inexhaustibility (solar$\rightarrow$ electricity; water + electricity$\rightarrow$ hydrogen); fair economics on a second law efficiency basis; reasonable compatibility with fossil fuel technology; excellent interfacing with the future energy technologies and an optimal character in respect to the absence of pollution.

7. At more than 1000 km from an atomic or solar plant, the relative fuel costs would be hydrogen < electricity < methanol. Gaseous hydrogen from coal would be significantly cheaper than synthetic natural gas on a Second Law basis.

8. The pros and cons of hydrogen as a fuel depend on the time scale considered, in particular whether coal is to be used as a main energy source whilst the conversion of the renewable resources is being developed. Were hydrogen to be the fuel from coal, CO_2 injection into the ocean would

be possible and the damage from using coal would be diminished.

9. Hydrogen is not proposed for massive use until oil and natural gas are in decline, because it is not till then that the real hydrogen price will be less than the real price of oil products. It *is* proposed as the fuel to interface with coal, solar and nuclear sources. But the time at which these sources will have to be building is in the order of one decade distance. Construction of a hydrogen-orientated technology would take a greater time than this.

AUTHOR'S CHOICE OF A MORE IMPORTANT CONCLUSION FROM CHAPTER

Were hydrogen, instead of synthetic natural gas, to be used as the fuel from coal, the difficulties of developing coal as a major interim source would be diminished: its economics are better than that of S.N.G. for some purposes. Hydrogen would be the one fuel which would interface compatibly with coal, solar and (the possible) atomic sources of energy.

REFERENCES

1. J. O'M. Bockris (ed.), in *Environmental Chemistry* (Plenum, 1977), chapter 18, p.583.
2. B. H. Klein, in J. O'M. Bockris (ed.). *ibid.*, chapter 22, p. 749.
3. J. O'M. Bockris & S. Srinivasen, *Fuel Cells* (McGraw Hill, New York, 1969).
4. R. K. Petley, H. G. Adelmann & M. C. McCormack, presented at the Conference on Methanol, Henniker, New Hampshire, June 1974. See also: J. W. Michel, ORNL-TM-4461, Oak Ridge, Tennessee, June 1973.
5. D. L. Hagen, in *Methanol* (ERDA, December 1976), p.I-27.
6. K. Sekihara, *Environmental Chemistry*, chapter 10, p.285.
7. E. Hietbrink *et al.* (in J. O'M. Bockris ed.), *Electrochemistry of Cleaner Environments* (Plenum, New York, 1972).
8. M. Steinberg, M. Beller & J. R. Powell, Brookhaven, 1974.
9. B. J. Berger, Lawrence Livermore Laboratory, UCRL, 76076, 1974.
10. H. S. Posner, *J. Toxicology & Environmental Health*, 1975, **I**, 53.
11. ERDA Handbook on Methanol, 1976, p.I-27.

10

TRANSMISSION OF ENERGY OVER LONG DISTANCES

Introduction

The concept of a Hydrogen Economy (Chapter 2) originated in the realisation that, if hydrogen were the medium of energy, its transmission over long distances would be cheaper than the transmission in wires of an equivalent amount of energy. The advantages of hydrogen as a fuel for cars, for aircraft, for general use in industry, and the solution to the air and water pollutional problem, were pointed out independently.[1-4]

The need to have long-distance transmission of energy is shown in Fig. 10.1 and Table 10.I. Thus, Alaskan coal would be uneconomic because of the cost of transporting it to centres of use. Were the coal gasified, and the gas sent to use centres, the difficulty would be overcome.

The energy sources of the future are likely to originate far from the centres of population. This is so in respect to coal, because the large undeveloped

TABLE 10.I: SUMMARY OF REASONS FOR REMOVING POWER PLANTS FROM POPULATED AGRICULTURE-INTENSIVE AND INDUSTRY-INTENSIVE AREAS WHICH IMPOSE A HIGH INTRINSIC BURDEN ON THE LOCAL/REGIONAL AIR-WATER-LAND ENVIRONMENT

Electric power stations	For environmental burden reasons				For hazard reasons	For other reasons
	Air	Water	Land	Thermal		
Low-sulphur coal power stations		*	*		Solid waste	
High-sulphur coal power stations*	*	*	*		Solid waste	Remote geographic location of large bituminous coal reserves
Oil-fired power stations		*				
Nuclear converter power stations		*		*	Nuclear waste	Public fear of power plant failures
Nuclear breeder power stations*		*		*	Nuclear waste; Pu-239 shipping over highways and by rail	Public fear of power plant failures
Solar power stations*						Remote geographic location of most of world's choice solar energy regions

*Asterisks indicate particularly strong reasons for remote siting.

212

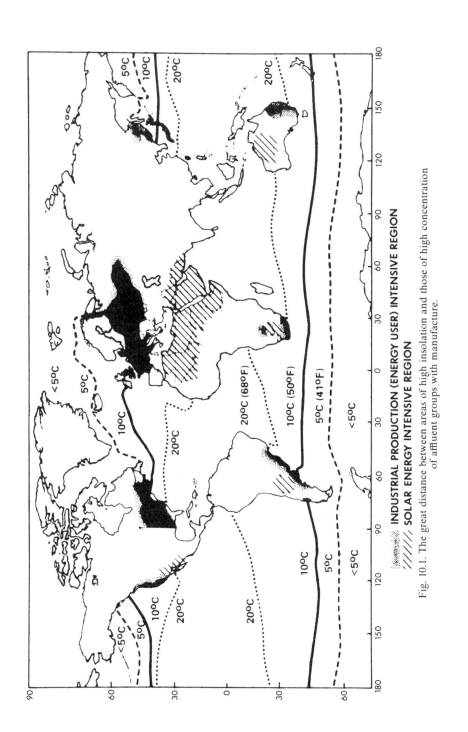

INDUSTRIAL PRODUCTION (ENERGY USER) INTENSIVE REGION

SOLAR ENERGY INTENSIVE REGION

Fig. 10.1. The great distance between areas of high insolation and those of high concentration of affluent groups with manufacture.

coal deposits (Alaskan, Australian and Siberian) will be far from population centres. For nuclear energy, a large distance from use centres would reduce pollutional difficulties. For solar energy, areas of maximum insolation are in North Africa, Saudi Arabia, Australia, the Kalahari Desert in South Africa, and on the tropical seas.

There are three methods to be considered for energy transportation over 500 miles. They are:

Direct electrical transmission

The cost of transmission through cables depends on the transmission voltage. Potentials above 1 million volts are not feasible. Costs are cheaper in unsightly overhead electric cables. Underground passage of power involves a large increase in cost. The possibility of superconductivity will be discussed.

Space relay of beamed power

It would be possible to beam from, say, Central Australia to parts of the United States, via satellites.[5]

Transmission of hydrogen through pipes

In the non-pollutional technology which must be built, electrical energy arriving from a distant region of the world (or directly from space), via microwave beams from a satellite, will probably be converted to hydrogen for storage before diffusion to industry, households and for use in transportation. Its *arrival* near the site of use in this form would be consistent with convenience in use, but also, as will be shown, under certain conditions, more economic than alternate possibilities, so long as the accounting includes Second Law efficiencies and environmental costs.

Direct electrical transmission

A typical loss in power in a cable 3,000 miles long, consisting of copper, is 55% if the voltage of transmission is 600,000 volts.

As the loss is I^2R, it can be diminished by the use of higher voltage transmissions at lower currents for the same resistance. 700 kV can be used. 1000 kV is discussed and experimental set-ups exist. The difficulty is the corona discharge, which is dangerous in the vicinity of buildings, and electromagnetic effects on mechanisms in the neighbourhood.

One may consider lowering the temperature to reduce the resistance. Were it economic to reduce the temperature to liquid hydrogen values, one could obtain super-conductivity, and the difficulty of losses in electrical transmission would be resolved.[6]

In the U.S. there are about 3,000 electricity-producing plants. These may evolve to some 300 super-large plants, with a capacity of 2000-3000 MW each.[7] According to Meyerhoff, it will not be possible to carry the electrical output from these plants in the normal way.[8] Cables could perhaps be immersed in liquid nitrogen, or LNG[9] could be run through a pipe, keeping it at low temperatures, and the electricity passed through the pipe.[10]

These possibilities are left to the references given and the use of superconductive cables considered. There are two types of superconductors, I and II. Type I superconductors are exemplified by lead, tin and indium. Their very low critical temperature makes it unlikely that they will be practical. Type II superconductors consist of alloys, typified by NbZr, NbTi. These have relatively high critical temperatures, are hence more acceptable. They suffer high losses in an a.c. field. Niobium is little available; however, a cable would consist of only .005 cm of Nb on a 1 cm copper tube.

There are problems connected with the passage of a cable underground, although there is pressure on the utilities to increase the amount of underground transmission because of the poor public reaction to overhead lines. The increase in cost for underground transmission is shown in Fig. 10.2.[11] An underground superconducting power line is indicated in Fig. 10.3.[8]

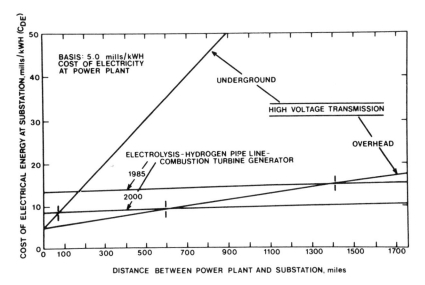

Fig. 10.2. Comparison of cost of electrical energy at distribution substation for electrical transmission in hydrogen.

Difficulties of progressing towards superconducting transmission are various.

Line termination

When the superconducting line meets up with another conductor, it is carrying very large power per sq. cm. The technique of a connection to a non-superconductor is unclear.

Dielectric strength

Materials which have sufficient dielectric strength to be in contact which superconducting cables are difficult to obtain. Pressurised helium or a vacuum have been suggested: their use over very long distances may not be economic.

Thermal contraction

A method which allows for thermal contraction between conductors and the

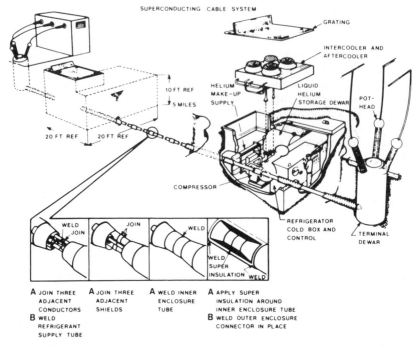

Fig. 10.3. Superconducting line.

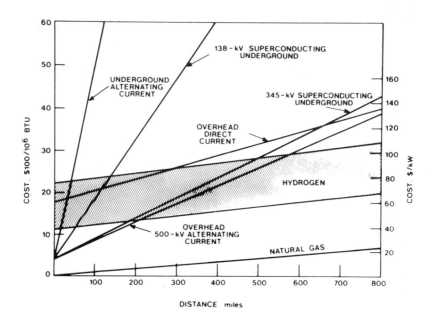

Fig. 10.4. Cost of energy transmission.

cryogenic envelope when the line is cooled has yet to be published.

Cryogenics

A cryogenic capability which would cool lines with acceptable economics over very long distances has to be developed.

The cost of introducing superconductors seems prohibitive. They are summarised in Table 10.II (Fig. 10.4).[13] The case for transmission with superconducting cables, on technical grounds, is weak compared with that of transmission in hydrogen; and the economic aspects prohibitive. Of course, this would change if higher temperature superconductivity becomes practical.

TABLE 10.II: ELECTRICITY TRANSMISSION COSTS[12]

Data	Value Assumed	Ref. source
Average cost of five 500-kV lines built since 1969—includes right-of-way, excludes cost of one urban line	$182,000/mile	20
Cost of d.c. line at 0.65 times the cost of comparable a.c. line	$118,000/mile	20
Typical power capability of 500-kV line	900,000 kW	20
Typical a.c. terminal cost	$11/kW	20
Typical d.c. terminal cost	$42/kW	20
Average 500-kV overhead line cost	$0.144/kW-mile	20
Average 500-kV overhead line cost	$59.25/10⁶ Btu-hr-mile	20
Average d.c. overhead line cost	$0.130/kW-mile	20
Average d.c. overhead line cost	$38.50/10⁶ Btu-hr-mile	20
Cost of two terminals for a.c.	$22/kW	20
Cost of two terminals for a.c.	$6,561/10⁶ Btu-hr	20
Cost of two terminals for d.c.	$84/kW	20
Cost of two terminals for d.c.	$24,612/10⁶ Btu-hr	20
Cost ratio of underground to overhead power transmission	10:1 to 40:1	20
Cost of underground line	$2.01/kW-mile	20
Cost of underground line	$592/10⁶ Btu-hr-mile	20
Total overhead line plus terminal costs for 200 miles	$0.158/kW-mile	20
Total underground line plus terminal costs for 200 miles	$2.35/kW-mile	20
Projected cost for 138,000-V super- conducting line for 10 miles	$1.23/kW-mile $0.92/kW-mile	20 20
Projected cost of 345,000-V superconducting line for 10 miles	$0.28/kW-mile	20

Transmission through directed microwave radiation

Gläser has suggested that there should be space platforms which receive energy directly from the sun and beam it to earth (Chapter 8).[14] An analysis of this system leads to a relatively expensive way of obtaining solar energy. Thus, a mid-1970s space shuttle can lift about 28 tons into earth orbit, and is planned to fly 60 times per year. To put up a 10,000 MW system, weighing about 10,000 tons, would take, then, about 6 years. To put up a *relay* satellite system which relays power from one continent to another would take less than one year on the same basis. It is desirable to keep the heavy and complex parts of the system on the ground—the lighter parts in space. Such considerations will apply particularly to the cost per kW, for, in the orbiting solar *collector* system, this is overwhelmingly the cost of putting the collector into orbit.

Because of the higher insolation of latitudes between 30°N and 30°S, and the availability of relatively calmer seas and very much flat desert there, it may become economically attractive to transfer massive quantities of solar energy over many thousands of miles. Ehricke suggests that ground-level collected solar energy could be beamed up to a satellite, and then down to a use centre, several thousands of miles distant.[5] The general concept of a world supply based on collectors in Australia, South Africa, Chile, etc. (see Figs. 10.1 and 10.5;[5] see also Tables 10.III.[16] and 10. IV) becomes reasonable to analyse.

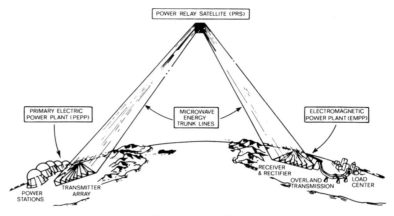

Fig. 10.5. Power relay satellite concept.

TABLE 10.III: POWER RELAY SATELLITE CONCEPT—PERFORMANCE AND COST DATA

Power generated	13,800,000 kWe	Maximum values.
Power delivered	9,000,000 kWe*	Beam power
Energy delivered over 30 years	2.1 trillion kWhe*	can be less.
Transmitter array:		
Construction cost	$4.3 billion	$56/kWe*
Maintenance cost (30 years)	$17 billion	
Overall cost	$21 billion	10mil/kWhe*
Power Relay Satellite		
(1 kW²; 300 tons)		
Construction/delivery/erection	$1.05 billion	$119/kWe*
Maintenance cost (30 years)	$2.1 billion	
Overall cost	$3.15 billion	1.4 mil/kWhe*
Electromagnetic power plant (EMPP)		
Construction cost	$2.1 billion	$232/kWe*
Maintenance cost (30 years)	$1.33 billion	
Overall cost	$3.43 billion	1.61 mil/kWhe
Grand total		
Construction cost	$7.4 billion	$826/kWe*
Maintenance cost (30 years)	$20.2 billion	
Overall energy transmission cost	$28 billion	13.0 mil/kWhe*†

* Power delivered.
† According to a newer analysis, taking into account the lessened maintenance cost caused by the development of platinum-coated amplitrons—this cost goes down to about 7.2 mil/kWh^{-1} (but this does not include the capital cost, which puts the figure up to 10 mil/kWh^{-1}).

The transmission of energy by microwave beam from a terrestrial source to a load centre, via a relay satellite, should offer a more economic system of·using the transfer of energy through space than that which places the collector in orbit. Ehricke's sketch is shown in Fig. 10.5. The primary electric power plant (PEP) is on the left and would perhaps be a solar collector station in Australia, near Alice Springs. The satellite would be in geosynchronous orbit over the equator, and the receiver would be a few tens of miles out to sea from, e.g. Osaka. The transmission 'line' would be a microwave beam.

In Ehricke's plan, transmitting and receiving antennae would consist of very many individual elements. He suggests a helix antenna 1.4 in. in diameter, 14 in. in length. Modules would measure 8-12 metres and hold 12,000 helices. A square antenna with a side of 10 km and an aperture of 100 km^2 would contain 1.25 modules or 1.6 helices. Each module would be powered by a microwave power generator and have a phase shifter, to keep the beam focused on the power relay satellite (PRS).

TABLE 10.IV: Characteristics of Microwave-PRS Energy System

Microwave Energy (point-to-point transmission via power relay satellite).
Note:
MW = microwave
PRS = power relay satellite
kwb = kilowatt beam power; as used in (C), kwb refers to the beam power at transmitter aperture
kwe* = d.c. electric kilowatt as delivered at the busbar of the receiver power plant.

A. *General*
   Avoids questions of engineering overseas pipeline; building tanker fleet. Because of high cost of the transmitter, is economically important to use energy sources lasting at least 30 years, i.e. largely for transmission solar energy from high insolation areas or exporting fusion energy.

B. *Processing*
   Conversion to MW energy at high efficiency ($\gtrsim$ 90%) in microwave power generators at the expected state of the art at mid-1980s. Transmission efficiency over several thousand miles 50-60%.

C. *Loading*
   As phase-controlled MW beam in transmitter antenna. Antenna size large, but not prohibitive ($\gtrsim$ 138,000 kwe*/km^2). Relatively high construction cost, due to stringent engineering requirements ($\sim$\$3/ft^2; $\sim$\$43M/km^2; $\sim$\$413/kwb; $\sim$\$476/kwe*).

D. *Shipping*
   Power Relay Satellite (PRS) in geosynchronous orbit needed for beam redirection. Stringent PRS engineering requirements. But moderate construction cost ($\sim$\$117/kwe*) due to small size ($\sim$1 km^2) and to shuttle, which keeps maintenance low. Environment effects of beam on atmosphere are small.

E *Unloading*
   Receiver-rectifier system (rectenna) of 85% conversion efficiency to d.c. current. Therefore, little thermal load. Environmental burden? Receiver size is larger, but not prohibitive ($>$ 90,000 kwe*/km^2). Receiver power plant construction cost is small ($\sim$\$232/kwe*). Operating costs low. Operation is simple, making system suitable for export and use in developing countries.

F. *Storage*
   Has no storage capacity, would need to convert to hydrogen anyway.

G. *Conversion to electricity*
   In rectenna, conversion to a.c. after electric transmission close to load centre.

H. *Transmission to user*
   Receiver power plant can be located near load centres, due to its low socio-environmental burden quotient. D.c.-power transmission yields superior efficiency to a.c.-power transmission.

A number of influences tend to de-focus the beam, so that the outgoing microwave beam would bypass the PRS. One is roughness on the surface of the antenna. Irregularities must be measured and compensated for by phase shifts, whose value would be computer determined. Clouds would decrease the efficiency of transmission only a few per cent, but hail and snow could offer greater attenuation. However, feedback signals between the satellite and the transmitter could be used to compensate negative effects rather completely.

For a small roughness tolerance of 1 mm, required to achieve only 2% scattering loss, the size of the modules in the Power Relay Satellite would have to be reduced, and made adjustable. Precise mechanical pressure could be exerted on the corners of the modules, using electrically powered gear-drive actuators, to bring about phase shifts. Several options for surface to control are available.

TABLE 10.V: AUSTRALIAN ENERGY EXPORT POTENTIAL

Alternatives	Domestic energy supply	Energy Export Suitability
Coal —direct use	**Envir.	† Transp./Environment
—gasification	*	*
Oil shale/Tar	**Envir.	**
Local nuclear power—direct	**Envir. Safety	† Complexity/Pu-239 profile
Remote nuclear power		
—direct	*	
—hydrogen	*	*
—microwave	*	*If distance > 4,000 miles
Solar power		
—direct		*Power plant equip. export
—hydrogen	*	*
—microwave	*	*If distance > 4,000 miles
—artificial		
hydrocarbons	† Energy requirement	† cost

*Promising
**Conditionally promising
† Not promising

The overall transmission efficiency would be 60-65%. This would correspond to a 600,000 volt line, 4,000 miles long. 9 million kW could be transmitted by a 10 by 10 km transmitter array and a 1 by 1 km PRS.* Calculated basic performance data and costs are shown in Tables 10.III and 10.IV.

The dollars per kW for the PRS plant would be $840. The corresponding figure for the hydrogen synthesis plant would be $140. The cost of the power generation system would be in the same range as that of a non-breeder nuclear plant. The cost is less than that of putting a solar collector into orbit (at present $14,000 per kW with future projections down to $1,400 per kW). Some characteristics are shown in Table 10.IV. An export profile for Australia is shown in Table 10.V.

---

*Development of amplitrons with platinum-coated cathodes will improve the cost picture.

Transmission in hydrogen

Introduction

The origins of the concept of reliance on hydrogen as a general replacement for oil, gasoline, and natural gas lies in the note by Bockris, of December 1971.[4] However, the concepts of this time lacked a quantitative foundation. An important element was provided at Bockris' suggestion by Gregory, Ng and Long.[17] A comparison was made of the costs of transporting energy in hydrogen over distances up to one thousand miles with that needed to transport the same energy in electricity. As there is energy needed for the splitting of water, transport in hydrogen is more expensive than transport in electricity up to a certain distance. As the distance increases, the smaller energy needed to push a certain amount of energy in a gas through a pipe, than to push the same energy through a wire in the form of electricity, will give a distance at which the transport of hydrogen becomes cheaper than that of electricity. With the economics used by Gregory, Ng and Long in 1972, the cross-over point was around 500 kilometres, depending on the transmission voltage.[17]

With atomic and solar energies, the cost of energy transport over long distances has an importance not present for fossil fuels. The need to transfer energy from solar sources over distances of 3000 km is clear from Fig. 10.1. With breeder reactors, the economics of scale will mean that individual plants tend to be big ($\sim$ 10,000 MW), and their location far from large cities would seem advantageous. The figure of Gregory, Ng and Long is one of the legs upon which the Hydrogen Economy is based.

However, the figure is less simple now than in 1972. The cross-over is the distance at which energy in the form of H_2 gas becomes cheaper than energy in the form of electricity. If hydrogen has to be reconverted to electricity at the receiving end, i.e. pass through a fuel cell and undergo a further loss of 25%, the cross-over would come at larger distances than those of Figs. 10.2 and 10.4. Conversely, if electricity has to be converted to a fuel, for example, for transportation, and for industrial needs, there is no point in transmitting the energy electrically. The implications of Gregory's diagram are then too pessimistic, for hydrogen is preferable at all distances. In many instances, with the solar source, hydrogen is basically necessary for storage.

Another aspect which diminishes the clarity of the implication of Fig. 10.4 is the fact that the break-even point for transport in the form of hydrogen depends upon the transmission voltage. In so far as this is raised towards the practical maximum of 10^6 volts,* the distance at which the use of hydrogen becomes advantageous in transmission gets extended to higher distances than those of Gregory, Ng and Long, whose maximum transmission voltage was 700kv.

Equations for the cost analysis[18]

The types of equations used for calculation of the cost of gas flow are shown in Table 10.VI.

Equations 3 and 4 of Table 10.VI suggest that the compression ratios of

---

*The use of higher voltages seems improbable due to effects of the field surrounding the wire.

TABLE 10.VI: Gas Flow Equations

Inputs

Q = pipeline energy flow (MMBtu/hr)
T_1 = flow temperature (°R)
P_1 = initial pipeline pressure (psia)
C = compression ratio
d = pipe outside diameter (in)

Equations

$$m = \frac{Q}{3.6 \times 10^{-3} (LHV)} \qquad \text{mass flow rate (lb}_m/\text{sec)} \qquad (1)$$

$$M = \frac{m\sqrt{RZT_1/k}}{144\pi r^2 P_1} \qquad \text{initial Mach number in pipe} \qquad (2)$$

$$\frac{L}{D} = \frac{1}{4f}\left[\frac{C^2-1}{kC^2M^2} - ln\, C^2\right] \qquad \text{pipeline length to inside diameter ratio} \qquad (3)$$

$$(HP) = \frac{m}{550\eta}\left[\frac{k}{k-1}\right] RT_1 C^{k-1} \qquad \text{compressor power per length L (hp)} \qquad (4)$$

where

LHV = low heating value of gas (Btu/lb$_m$)
R = gas constant (ft. lb$_f$/lb$_m$ °R)
Z = compressibility factor
k = C_p/C_v, ratio of specific heats
r = inside radius of pipe (in)
4f = friction factor
η = compressor efficiency

TABLE 10.VII: Liquid Flow Equations

Inputs

Q = pipeline energy flow (MMBtu/hr)
P_1 = pipeline pressure at pump output (psia)
P_2 = pipeline pressure at pump input (psia)
d = pipe outside diameter (in)

Equations

$$m = \frac{Q}{3.6 \times 10^{-3} (HHV)} \qquad \text{mass flow rate (lb}_m/\text{sec)} \qquad (5)$$

$$V = \frac{m}{\pi r^2 \rho} \qquad \text{flow velocity (ft/sec)} \qquad (6)$$

$$\frac{L}{D} = \frac{1}{4f}\left[\frac{288\,(P_1-P_2)}{\rho V^2}\right] \qquad \text{pipeline length to inside diameter ratio} \qquad (7)$$

$$(HP) = \frac{144m(P_1-P_2)}{550\eta\rho} \qquad \text{pump power per pipeline length L} \qquad (8)$$

where

HHV = high heating value of fluid (Btu/lb$_m$)
r = inside radius of pipe (in)
ρ = fluid density (lb$_m$/ft^3)
4f = friction factor
η = pump efficiency

hydrogen to another gas with which a comparison is sought may be an important factor. In the pressure regions of 1000 psi, and for ratios up to about 1.5 in compression ratio, there is little difference in the energy lost in pushing gases containing the same amount of energy over a given distance. There is a balance between the (more expensive) increased pipe diameter, having a reduced number of compressors; against the cheaper, smaller pipes, having the need for more expensive compressors.

Reynolds and Slager were interested in liquids too,[18] not only because of liquid hydrogen but also because of liquid ammonia as a transportation medium. For the liquid situation, the equations are given in Table 10.VII.

The equations for the cost analysis are then shown in Table 10.VIII.

TABLE 10.VIII: Cost Equations

$$C_{PIPE} = 200W + 1300d + 70d + C_{ROW} \ (\$/mi) \tag{9}$$

where

pipe weight, $W = 28.2t \ (d - t) \ (tons/mi)$ (9a)

pipe thickness, $t = 0.7P_1d/60,000 \ (in)$ (9b)

$$C_{PUMP} = [230(HP) + 15,000d]/L \ (\$/mi) \tag{10}$$

$$C_{TRANS} = 10^4 \left[\frac{0.15 \, (C_{PIPE} + C_{PUMP})}{(0.90) \, (8760) \, Q} + \frac{2546(HP)}{0.40LQ} C_{FUEL} \right]$$
$$(cents/MMBTU/100 \ mi) \tag{11}$$

In the Reynolds and Slager work, the cost of the fuel is taken as $0.4 per MBTU, less than one-tenth of what is anticipated for hydrogen at this time. However, the fuel cost does not have much great effect upon the cost of transport per unit of energy and distance. An increase of an order of magnitude in energy costs would increase the cost of transmission by about two times. Gas line pressure also has only a small effect on the transmission cost.

Some costs as a function of flow are seen in Fig. 10.6.

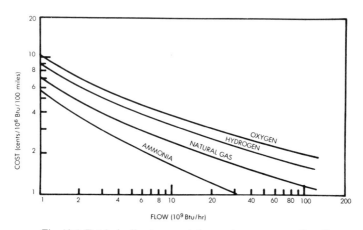

Fig. 10.6. Total pipeline transportation cost versus energy flow.[18]

Results of calculations on the cost of hydrogen transmission

There is an increase in the cost of transporting energy in the form of hydrogen, rather than in the form of natural gas, by 30-50%. The optimum distance between compressor stations is higher for hydrogen. The cost of hydrogen increases by 5% per 1000 km. As the maximum distance over which hydrogen transport in pipes will be likely is 5000 km, transport costs for hydrogen in a pipe will be less than half the cost of the fuel on arrival.

Beghi and de Jace calculated the cost of transport of oxygen.[19] It is better to combust hydrogen with pure oxygen rather than with air, because of the diluting effect of the nitrogen in air, but the oxygen costs to transport, and this increases linearly with increase of distance. There must be an upper distance in which it is no longer worth bringing oxygen along. It is surprising that Beghi and de Jace found this to be as high as 1000 km.

The principal results of de Beghi and de Jace calculations are shown in Figs. 10.7 and 10.8.[19]

The calculations of Beghi and de Jace can be compared with those of Reynolds and Slager, but by taking into account the larger flow-rates. Up to 2.10^{11} BTU $(\text{hr})^{-1}$ were considered by Reynolds and Slager compared with a maximum of $0.5 . 10^{11}$ BTU $(\text{hr})^{-1}$ considered by Beghi and de Jace.[19]

At this flow rate, the cost of 1 kWh of hydrogen at K thousand km from source = cost 1 kWh of H_2 at source + 0.08K (cents).*

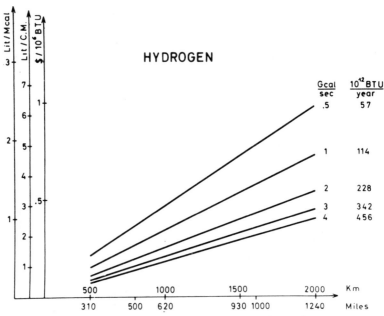

Fig. 10.7. Cost of transmission as a function of distance for different flows of hydrogen.[19]

---

*This formula has been derived from Beghi and de Jace by assuming an inflation rate of 10% per year.

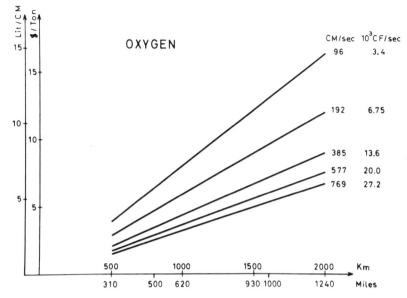

Fig. 10.8. Cost of transmission as a function of distance for different flows
of oxygen.[19]

Thus, if the cost of hydrogen at source is $9 per MBTU, the cost at a distance of 3000 km would be around $9.75.* For comparable conditions the results calculated by Reynolds and Slager[18] are 25% lower than those of Beghi and de Jace.[19]

Over- and under-sea transmission of energy

Introduction

The calculations reported in the last section referred to over-land transmission in pipes. They cannot be applied to under-sea transmissions. Thus, for inter-continental export of hydrogen over long distances such as Darwin-Australia to Yokohama-Japan, there are several alternatives. The simplest, a pipeline on the ocean floor, would not be acceptable cost-wise (see below). A buoy-supported pipeline may be economically acceptable (its economics have not been calculated) but it would be open to interference in wartime, and hazard shipping.

Lastly, liquefaction and shipment may be considered.

Transmission of energy over distances of more than about 5000 km may be do-able more economically by power-relay satellite, than by the transfer of hydrogen in pipes.[20]

Underwater pipelines

Knopka, Talib, Biedermann and Yudow calculated the underwater pipeline based on the known cost of laying natural gas pipelines in 1500 feet depth of seawater.[21] The differences which have to be introduced for hydrogen are taken into account in the calculations.

---

*'Around' because the cost depends on, e.g. the flow rate, etc.

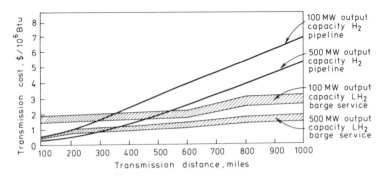

Fig. 10.9. Transmission cost of hydrogen gas by underwater pipeline and liquid hydrogen by barges for 100 and 500 MW plant output capacity.[21]

Among assumptions of the calculation (Fig. 10.9) are that pressures will not be above 1500 psi; no pipes over 16″ diameter are used; and the cost of electricity feeding the compressors would be 2c per kwh. A facility of 500 MW was assumed. No rising pipes to shore or to the OTEC stations were calculated.

Shipment in ocean-going barges

Barges pushed by 1700 hp ocean-going tugs were thought to be better than tankers. The cost of the tug was taken to be $1.5 M. The cost of the cryogenic barges is uncertain. There is an established technology for cryogenic river-barges which carry liquid hydrogen. NASA made the calculations of the ocean-going barges.[22] The range is $200-300 per barrel. 25% was taken as the cost of money and maintenance. On-site storage must be taken into account. Terminal facilities assumed in the calculation included tanks, unloading arms, pumps, etc. The terminal unit could deal with one week's output from an OTEC plant.

The results are incorporated in Fig. 10.9.

Over-sea and under-sea costs

The results of the calculation are stark. About 500 km is the break-even point for under-sea transport in a pipeline, and at longer distances it is better to refrigerate the hydrogen and send it by cryogenic barge. The cost of energy landed does not depend greatly upon the distance which the barge has to travel.

The costs of about $15 per MBTU for liquid hydrogen are not *so* prohibitive.*[21] They are four times the 1978 basic U.S. gasoline costs, and also above the price of gasoline in Japan. Methyl alcohol from 1975 coal should cost $7.50 per MBTU, and the coal to be compared with OTEC in, say, 1990 is likely to have more than doubled in constant dollars, owing to the exhaustion of competing liquid gaseous fossil fuels. But OTEC costs in constant dollars may fall with improving technology and scale-up.

---

*Knopka *et al.*[21] (Institute of Gas Technology) show calculations which are about twice as large as the costs obtained by the calculations of Dugger and Frances[23] who come from the Johns Hopkins University.

It is noteworthy that Knopka *et al.* calculated ammonia price from the OTEC cryogenic barge was $277 per ton in 1976[21]—to be compared with an actual ammonia price in 1975 of $200 per ton, which would clearly escalate with the natural gas price. The calculated ammonia cost of Dugger and Frances from OTEC is below that of the commercial price of 1978 and hence suggests a commercial opportunity at this time.[9,23]

Pumping up to pressure

In discussions of pipeline transmission, the assumption is made that the pressure will be *c.* 100 ats. Higher pressures would be possible but involve more expensive steels. Further, the cost of reaching the higher pressure (*cf.* Dickson, Ryan & Smulyan[24]) may be considerable. Basically, the work to be done is $RT \ln p_2/p_1$. If $p_2 = 100$, and $p_1 = 1$, the work done at 298°C is about 6 cals per mole, i.e. about 10% of the heat energy potential in 1 mole of hydrogen. The increase in the price of hydrogen because of this factor could be as great as 20% (around $1.50 per MBTU). An advantage of the electrochemical method arises: water electrolysers work at *c.* 30 ats. It would seem easy to bring them to work at 100 ats, by increasing the voltage about 60 mv. Changes in overpotential would also be present. Conversely, many hydrogen-oxygen cells demand a potential above that expected because of increased IR drop between their electrodes owing to bubbles, and this component would be decreased at the increased pressure. A 100-ats cell would work at a potential increase of less than 30 mv, i.e. a cost increase at 2-3%.

Such an advantage does not pertain to the cyclical chemical method of obtaining hydrogen, because a separate mechanical pumping stage would have to be involved. This partly explains why there would be less cost in increasing the pressure in a water electrolyser to that in a thermo-chemical cycle reactor.

Could the present natural gas transmission system be used for hydrogen?

The system of natural-gas pipelines which exists in the United States at this time means a large investment is associated with the present system. There is a tendency to want to continue to use it when the energy medium becomes hydrogen.

Basically, there are no qualitative scientific reasons (e.g. no embrittlement of the present lines upon the use of hydrogen) to suggest that the present lines will not carry hydrogen at a pressure of up to, say, 1000 psi. However, the present system will make only a small contribution to the eventual hydrogen-carrying lines of future technology.

1. The present American natural-gas lines originate on the Gulf Coast of the U.S. and the South-West. There is no reason to suspect that the possible breeder reactors and likely solar collectors of the new energy system will be placed so that this direction will be important (Dickson, Ryan and Smuylan[24]).
2. Embrittlement is unlikely to be severe for pipes. However, for pumps and valves, the situation is questionable and the necessity of renewing these, and increasing their number, would have to be taken into account in judging the contributions which the old system would make.

3. The volumetric loss would be three times greater for hydrogen than for natural gas, but hydrogen has a volume energy density of one-third that of methane so that the energy loss due to leakage would be the same. Were the hydrogen leakage situation significant, the insertion of a plastic sleeve would be sufficient to reduce the leakage rate below that acceptable with natural gas.
4. The present lines will make a small contribution to the needed energy system of 2000 and beyond. Thus, the small volume density of hydrogen means that a section of pipeline would have to have hydrogen pumped through it four times faster than for natural gas. Then, the leak problem might become significant (Dickson *et al.*[24]). A large increase in pipeline would be needed in a Hydrogen Economy at 2000, so that the present system, even if it could take hydrogen, will become irrelevant.

Thus, whatever capital is in the present system will not lose its value, but the present pipeline system would support only the beginnings of a Hydrogen Economy.

Liquid hydrogen in transmission

Hitherto, transmission as a gas has been considered in the Hydrogen Economy, and shown to be a cheaper way of transmitting energy than is transmission through wires or satellite over certain longer distances. If the hydrogen is first liquefied, this cost difference would be decreased (with electricity at 4 cents/kWh, liquefaction would cost \$3.30 per 10^6 Btu). Apart from these costs, there is a problem in the insulation of the pipelines. A number of factors involved in hydrogen transportation are shown in Table 10.IX. However, liquid transmission could have applications:
1. There may be situations where hydrogen would arrive in a tanker already liquefied. It would then be practical to transfer it in pipes to refuelling stations as a liquid. (See also Table 10.IX.)
2. Cryogenic superconductivity. There is the possibility of carrying electricity through pipes which contain liquid hydrogen. There could be a dual

TABLE 10.IX: Rough Estimates of Costs Involved in LH_2 Transportation by Cryogenic Tankers[5]

Item	Liquefied Natural Gas	Liquefied Hydrogen	Comments
Temperature (1 Atm)	−259°F	−423°F	
Gas-to-liquid volume reduction	625	800	
Pounds/cu. ft.	36.2	4.37	
Volume required for equal heating value	∿1.64	∿4.5	Crude oil = 1.0
Refrigerated tanker cost (\$/cu. ft. storage volume)	850	800-1,200	Based on \$182 m per tanker with 2-2.3 10^6 cu. ft.
Tanker fleet investment	\$6.6	\$31B	For 1,800 B cu. ft. gas equiv./year
		\$910B	For 9B barrels crude oil equiv./year
Amortisation and running operating cost of world-wide energy distribution in hydrogen economy (mils/kWh)		6.4	30-year operating period. 66% energy utilisation. Annual operative cost of 3% of initial investment.

hydrogen and electric economy in which liquid hydrogen was passed through pipes and used for various purposes, but the pipes were also used to pass electricity under superconducting conditions. There may be certain distances in which the dual passage of hydrogen and electricity is economically attractive.

Liquid hydrogen has been transported on rail and road for more than a decade. Truck drivers on the road are instructed for three days before being allowed to drive tankers containing hydrogen (Dickson *et al.*[24–26]). They do not have to have a special background. Batch deliveries of liquid hydrogen are regularly made to Cape Canaveral.

The cost of a cryogenic pipeline to pass liquid hydrogen was quoted by Dickson *et al.* as being $100 per foot for a 5″ pipeline:[24] it is one-third of the cost of building a turnpipe and indicates why, for distances over one kilometre, hydrogen will be transported in gaseous form whilst the liquid will go to tankers, rail, road or sea-going.

Transmission of energy by means of a heat pipe

Introduction

Schulten introduced the concept of a heat pipe in 1974.[27] The idea is shown in Fig. 10.10.

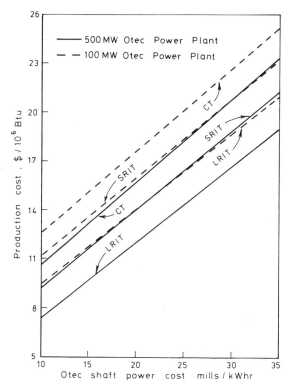

Fig. 10.10. Chemical heat-pipe energy transmission.[27] The EVA-ADAM system.

The energy source is in the form of heat. It is used to drive some endo-thermic reaction, e.g. $CH_4 + H_2O(g) \rightarrow 3H_2 + CO + 49.4$ Kcal per mole of CH_4. The H_2 and CO are then cooled and stored. They are transmitted through a pipe and when heat is required the mixture is warmed and an exothermic reaction occurs. The heat is set free from about 800°K. Ninety per cent 1st law conversion is achieved at 1300°K at 40 ats.

The part of the cycle into which the heat is put is called EVA, and the part which gives out the heat is called ADAM. The reverse, or ADAM, part of the cycle, in which hydrogen combines with CO to give CH_4 and steam, is 90% complete at 800°K.

There are other reactions which could be used. For example (Carden[28]),

$$2NH_3 \rightarrow N_2 + 3/2 + H_2$$

$$SO_3 \rightarrow SO_2 + 1/2\ O_2$$

The latter (Chubb[29]) is favourable because the SO_2 can be stored as a liquid and is easily transportable.

These ideas are valuable in respect to heat storage in chemicals and trans-mission of energy in pipes containing cooled chemicals which would later react. Two pipes are necessary, because the chemical product of the heat-giving reaction would have to be piped back to the heat source.

Two types of efficiencies

Is it better to use the available heat to cause a heat-pipe cycle to function, or is it better to use it to make hydrogen from water and transmit hydrogen (to combine, later, with atmospheric oxygen or O_2, which is co-piped)?*

Two types of efficiencies can be considered. The usual definition of what is called a first law efficiency is:

$$\varepsilon = \frac{\text{amount of energy transferred}}{\text{energy put into the system as heat}}$$

However, there is a certain degree of deception or irrelevance about a first law efficiency. It deals with energy as such, without involving itself in the issue of whether the energy is *available* in a form in which one can do work, the only worthwhile energy.

One therefore determines another kind of efficiency:

$$\varepsilon_2 = \frac{\text{work transferred}}{\text{work available at the beginning}}$$

Such 'Second Law' efficiencies implicitly account for the loss of heat as entropy, i.e. the unavailable energy (Denbigh[30]), but also for other inefficien-cies in going from heat to work.

Although we may bring heat energy at various temperatures from solar or atomic sources, there will be only one sink to which it must go. We say this has a temperature T_0 and it is the earth's heat reservoir temperature at 290-300°K.

---

*This is a cheaper option up to 1000 km.

The Second Law efficiencies of thermochemical hydrogen cycles and chemical heat pipes.

Funk[31] has shown that the efficiency of a chemical cycle is given by

$$\varepsilon_1 = \frac{\Delta H^\circ_{298}}{\Delta G^\circ_{298}} \frac{T - T_o}{T}$$

where T is the temperature in which the system gives heat to the reactors, and T_o is that of the surroundings.

Cox[32] maintains without proof that the efficiency of a chemical heat pipe is given by

$$\varepsilon_2 = \varepsilon_1 \frac{\dfrac{T_2 - T_o}{T_2}}{\dfrac{T_1 - T_o}{T_1}}$$

where T_2 and T_1 are entry and exit temperatures respectively.

TABLE 10.X: Second Law Efficiency for Thermochemical Cycles[32]
Basis: Input Thermal Energy, $Q_t = 100$ Kcal
$T_1 = 1300$ K, $T_o = 298$ K

ε_1	ΔH_1 (Kcal)	ΔG_1 (Kcal)	ε_2
0.9285	92.85	77.1	1.0 (Upper Limit)
0.50	50	41.5	0.54
0.40	40	33.2	0.43
0.30	30	24.9	0.32
0.20	20	16.6	0.22

TABLE 10.XI: Second Law Efficiency for Chemical Heat Pipe Systems[32]
Basis: Input Thermal Energy, $Q_t = 100$ Kcal
$T_1 = 1300$ K, $T_o = 300$ K

ε_1	Q_2(Kcal)	W_{max} (Kcal)	W_{act} (Kcal)	η_2 max	ε_2
1.0	100	62.75	30.0	0.81	0.39
0.9	90	56.48	27.0	0.73	0.35
0.8	80	50.20	24.0	0.65	0.31
0.7	70	43.93	21.0	0.57	0.27

It is seen in Tables 10.X and 10.XI that using heat to generate hydrogen gives rise to more available work than putting the heat into a heat pipe, and this seems to be a fundamental result. It is based upon the energy efficiency, and a more meaningful result is that based on the final cost of the available energy at a certain distance in a certain form. For example, if the second law efficiency for a system which produces hydrogen is 0.4, and the corresponding heat pipe efficiency is 0.3, but the corrosion and plant amortization costs of the hydrogen production for a hypothetical thermochemical plant are greater than those of the simpler plant for the heat pipe, the latter may still be a preferable way of transferring heat.

Finally, however, using heat to bring about a dissociation reaction, and not to produce hydrogen, reduces the availability of hydrogen as a chemical reactant and clean household fuel.

SUMMARY OF CHAPTER

1. Various kinds of d.c. power transmission, use of a 'power relay satellite', and hydrogen pipeline transmission are the three most likely ways of sending solar and atomic-based energy. Each method would have its place, depending on distance. Superconductivity is not practical.

2. Transmission in H_2 becomes cheaper than transmission in electricity at distances which vary with circumstance from 300 to 1000 km.

3. The incremental cost of transferring energy in the form of H_2 is about 0.1 cents per kWh per 1000 km on land.

4. Underwater pipe transmission is not economic for distances above around 500 km. Barges pulling liquid H_2 are considered: they deliver liquid hydrogen for transmission costs of around $15 per MBTU without much dependence on distance.

5. Bringing H_2 pressure up to *c.* 100 atm for pipeline transmission could be done relatively cheaply in the original electrolytic cell.

6. The present natural gas pipelines *will* be usable for the transmission. However, it will be inadequate for a general Hydrogen Economy.

7. Transmission in liquid H_2 in pipes is generally too expensive. However, combined with superconductivity, use might be made of such systems over distances of a few km.

8. For a given amount of heat, it is cheaper to convert it to hydrogen and reject the water after formation than push it through a heat pipe, in the form of chemicals, with return of the original chemical.

AUTHOR'S ARBITRARY SELECTION OF A MORE IMPORTANT CONCLUSION FROM CHAPTER

For distances between 1000 and 4000 km on land, transmission of H_2 through a pipe is the cheapest mode of transmitting energy. Transport of liquid hydrogen in barges for oversea distances > 500 km depends little on distance but would cost $15 $(MBTU)^{-1}$.

REFERENCES

1. R. A. Erren & W. A. Hasting-Campbell, *J. Inst. Fuel*, 1933, **VI**, 277.
2. R. O. King, *Can. J. Res.*, 1948, **26F**, 264.
3. R. Wittkofski, paper presented to American Chemical Society Symposium on Non-fossil Fuels, Boston, 1972.
4. J. O'M. Bockris, *Environment*, 1971, **13**, 51.
5. K. A. Ehricke, The Power Relay Satellite, North American Space Group, Rockwell International, December 1973.
6. R. P. Feynmann, R. B. Leighton & M. Sands, *Lectures in Physics* (Addison-Wesley, 1964).
7. A. Kusko, *IEEE Spectrum*, 1968, **5**, 75.
8. R. A. Meyerhoff, *Cryogenics* (April 1971), p.91.
9. P. Graneau, IEEE Trans. Power Apparatus and Systems, PAS-89, 1 (1970).
10. A. Pastuhov & F. Ruccia, Conference on Low Temperatures and Electric Power, IIR, London 1969.
11. J. H. Russell, L. J. Nuttall & A. P. Fickett, paper presented at the American Chemical Society Meeting Hydrogen Fuel Symposium, Chicago, Illinois, August 1973.

12. D. P. Gregory, assisted by P. J. Anderson, R. J. Dufour, R. H. Elkins, W. J. D. Escher, R. B. Foster, G. M. Long, J. Wurm & G. G. Yie, 'A Hydrogen-Energy System', prepared for the American Gas Association by the Institute of Gas Technology, Chicago, August 1972, p.X-22.
13. R. A. Erren & Hastings-Campbell, *loc.cit.*, p. X-23.
14. P. Glaser, *Astronautics and Aeronautics* (August 1973) p.60.
15. K. A. Ehricke, 'The Power Relay Satellite—A Means of Global Energy Transmission through Space—Part I', North American Space Operations, Rockwell International Corporation, El Segundo, California, March 1974.
16. K. Ehricke, Statement before the Committee on Aerospace Stations, U.S. Senate, 31 October 1973.
17. D. P. Gregory, D.Y.C. Ng & G. M. Long, in J. O'M. Bockris, *The Electrochemistry of Cleaner Environments* (Plenum Press, New York, 1972).
18. R. A. Reynold, W. L. Slager, THEME, 1974, S2-1.
19. G. Beghi & J. de Jace, THEME, 1974, S2-11.
20. J. O'M. Bockris, *Energy: The Solar-Hydrogen Alternative* (Australia & New Zealand Book Co., Sydney, 1975), p.1151.
21. A Knopka, A. Talib, N. Biedermann & B. Yudow, 1st World Hydrogen Energy Conference, Miami, 1976, Vol. II, 1B-19.
22. N. Breit & A. Garcia, private communication, October 1975.
23. G. L. Dugger & E. J. Frances, World Hydrogen Energy Conference, 1976, I, 3A-33.
24. J. Dickson, P. Ryan & T. Smulyan, *A Hydrogen Economy* (Stanford Research Institute, 1976).
25. Idem, *ibid,* p. 85.
26. S. Linke (ed.), *A Hydrogen Energy Economy* (Cornell University, 1973), p.25.
27. R. Schulten, C. B. von der Decker, K. Kugeler & H. Barnett, Proceedings of the British Nuclear Society International Conference, London, England, 38, 1, (November 1974).
28. P. Carden, Canberra, Australia, private communication, 1975.
29. T. A. Chubb, *Solar Energy*, 1975, **17**, 129.
30. K. Denbigh, *The Principles of Chemical Equilibria* (Cambridge University Press, 1971).
31. J. Funk, Proceedings of the U.S.A-Japanese Joint Seminar on Key Technologies for the Hydrogen Energy System, Tokyo, Japan, July 1975.
32. K. E. Cox, R. H. Carty, W. L. Conger, M. A. Solomon & J. E. Funk, World Hydrogen Energy Conference, Miami, 1976, II, 1B-4.

11

STORAGE

Introduction

There is a daily and a seasonal variation in demand for energy. If the post-2000 supply of energy is to come substantially from solar sources, there will be diurnal variations in supply. Further, there will be times at which the sun is obscured by cloud, with known probabilities of this being for several days in succession.

Whereas for atomic energy a storage system is desirable, for solar energy one is essential. In addition to the storage forced by the out-of-phaseness of supply and demand, there should be attention to storage of very large amounts of hydrogen for possible export (shipping or piping) from, for instance, Australia to Japan.

Storage of solar energy in hydrogen will probably be preferable to other methods of energy storage because it lends itself easily to transmission and does not need special geographic features, e.g. suitable formations for pumped storage, etc. Nevertheless, other methods, except pumped storage,* will be discussed for comparison.

Thermal energy storage

Storage in eutectics is a method to be considered, both for the storage of solar energy and nuclear energy—so long as one refers to those energy sources and methods of transduction (e.g. solar-thermal or fission reactors, respectively) where heat is the form of energy produced or demanded.

The method depends upon the latent heat of the liquid concerned. During freezing, the liquid undergoes solidification at a constant temperature, whilst the latent heat of fusion is given out.

Other phase changes such as the crystallisation of Glauber's salt, $Na_2SO_410H_2O$, are used.[1] This stores 1.7 times the amount of energy per unit volume that water does, but near the transition point—not over a large temperature range.

A high latent energy of fusion, coupled with a low price per unit volume, would be the principal criteria to be used. Other criteria, stability and lack of corrosive properties in contact with relatively cheap container materials, are important.

Most of the materials used are eutectics of simple inorganic salts, e.g. alkali and alkaline earth metal fluorides, such as $NaF-MgF_2$. The temperature range at which the storage occurs for various eutectics is between

---

*Pumped storage is the oldest method of storing large amounts of energy.[1] However, it depends upon pumping water up to fill a reservoir and thus is limited to a few parts of most countries.

150°-850°C. In Fig. 11.1 are shown systems which have been stressed in the work of Schroeder, at Philips.[2]

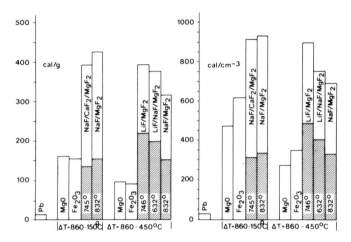

Fig. 11.1. Molten salt heat storage.

Thus, calories per gram are in the region of a few hundred and the calories per cc approach 1,000. This may be compared with the lead-acid battery, where the energy in calories per gram is 20-30. These storers of heat have an energy capacity per unit weight several times greater than that of even modern electricity storers such as Na-S. They store, however, about half the energy per unit weight of a hydrogen-air battery.

The heat storage method has difficulties in the insulation and lifetime of the storer. Corrosion of steel vessels by molten salts at the temperature concerned is a difficulty. Its removal depends upon the removal to a high degree of water and air from the salt. This can be done; it is a matter of trade-off between the cost of removing water and oxygen versus the cost of shorter life for the steel vessel. Addition of Al also reduces corrosion.

Among the classical work in this field is that of Telkes[3] and among the more recent that of Schroeder.[2] The cost of these molten salt storers involves a number of factors which are difficult to estimate. It may be as low as $0.7 per kWh (year).

The method is an easy one. It improves on scale-up, because the heat per unit volume escapes more slowly as the surface area of the storer increases.

The negative aspects of the storage of energy as heat are the difficulty of heat loss; the material problems associated with situations at high temperatures; and the fact that heat is not a good form in which to transport energy over long distances. The method is not one for long-term storage.

Storage in steam seems to have prospects, because of a possibility of transmission of energy in well-insulated steam-containing pipes.

Electrochemical energy storage

The principles are well known. If the energy source produces electricity directly, storage in electrochemical energy storers—batteries—is particularly acceptable. Thus, batteries do not need any special site, emit no noise, have no pollutants, are modular in nature, and hence have no problems about size. The requirements are 50 watts per kilogram, 200 watt-hours per kilogram, 4 years' life and a cycle-life of at least 1,000. The first two requirements are met by several batteries of Table 11.I.[4] The cycle and total life are not yet clear. A 100 megawatt-hour store would be contained in a space of 8 metres cubed.

The lead-acid battery is suitable for the purpose for which it is used— starting up internal-combustion engines. The amount of energy needed is small. The fact that the lead-acid battery has *the poorest energy density of all used batteries* is of little importance. What is necessary is a high power-density, and the lead-acid battery does have a good power-density, compared with other batteries. The misunderstanding is that the lead-acid battery is typical of other batteries. The facts are shown by the parameters in Table 11.I.[5]

TABLE 11.I: BATTERY PARAMETERS*,4

	W/kg	Wh/kg
Zinc-air	100	100
Ni-H$_2$ (compressed)	300	80
Ni-Fe	132	50
Zn-O$_2$	300	160
Aluminium-air	150	240
Sodium-sulphur	100	100
Sodium-air	200	400
Li-Cl$_2$ (liquid storage)	300	500
H$_2$-air	100	2000
Pb-acid	200	20-30

*The figures given are in the middle range in terms of the effect of rate of discharge. As the *rate* of discharge increases, the storage per unit mass decreases.

An attractive possibility is the hydrogen-air battery.

Costs of lead-acid battery storage are $1-5 per kWh (year).[5]

Realistic costs of developing battery systems of lower weight (e.g. zinc-air, and hydrogen-air) are unavailable, because such systems have not been commercialised.

In recent times most development money has been put into the sodium-sulphur battery. Costs of sodium-sulphur battery storage are *c.* $1 per kWh (year).[6]

The sodium-sulphur battery has an energy density of 3 to 5 times greater than that of the lead-acid battery. The working temperature of 350°C is a less desirable feature.[7] It has reached a level of reliability which allows it to be part of a scheme for electrification of British trains. The main difficulty has been the cracking of the β-A1$_2$O$_3$ membrane. Development of a cheap iron-air battery, which has characteristics which are 2 to 3 times better than that of lead-acid for energy density, looks promising.[8]

The pros and cons of electrochemical storage are easy to discern. Among the advantages are the consistence with photovoltaic power, or with thermo-electric conversion, for here electricity is produced. Relatively high power-densities (100 watts per lb) are obtainable. Although there is a gradual loss of energy in electrochemical batteries when they are not discharged, the problem is negligible compared to the rate of loss of energy to the surroundings in modern heat storers (Table 11.II).[9]

A disadvantage of electrochemical systems for massive storage lies with the amount of material which would be needed. There is not enough lead to supply lead batteries for cars, were their use to become widespread.[6] Conversely, iron-air cells, and perhaps the sodium-sulphur cell, would be free from difficulties of material scarcity.

On a smaller scale, for cars and railway engines, electrochemical storage has great (and probably unique) advantages.[10] Battery storage would seem limited to about 1,000 megawatt-hours.

One of the more underdeveloped parts of electrochemical storage seems to be shown by the hydrogen-air fuel-cell battery. The fuel cell is well developed. Hydrogen liquefaction or gaseous storage, with coupled electrochemical regeneration, is a promising avenue.

Kinetic energy storage

Introduction

Early fly-wheels had a storage capacity of 3 watt hours per lb (lead-acid battery, 10-15 watt hrs per lb) and were not attractive. There were two difficulties to be overcome in refurbishing the fly-wheel. Firstly, the low energy-density; secondly, the danger of the fly-wheel breaking loose.

These difficulties have been reduced by work at the John Hopkins University laboratory under Rabenhorst.[11]

TABLE 11.II: Some Approximate Estimates on Rate of Loss on Storage[9]

Type of system	Rate of loss % per day	Remarks
Pumped water storage	Negligible	Needs special geographic features
Thermal	5 to 10	This with conventional insulation (fibreglass). Losses could be used in space heating
Battery	0.1-0.2	For lead-acid battery. Varies greatly with type of battery
Inertial	0.5	About 2 kW continuous dissipation from a 10 MWh store
Chemicals	zero	
Pipes	zero	
Hydrogen (liquid)	0.3-0.8	But boil-off can be used
Underground (gas)	Not known. Probably negligible	

The super fly-wheel

The principal concept in the improvement of the fly-wheel is the replacement of a massive metallic wheel by certain configurations consisting of anisotropic materials, such as glass, graphite and boron. These materials are stronger for their weight than isotropic materials, so long as they are used in certain shapes. This will give rise to an increase in energy density, but, in particular, a diminution of danger.

One of the new configurations is a thin solid bar of composite material with a concentration of high-strength filaments, all running in the same direction. Alternatively, a number of brush-like rotors consisting of thousands of thin rods, bonded to a hub ('whirling spaghetti'). The stress is along the direction of maximum strength (Table 11.III[10] and Fig. 11.2[10]).

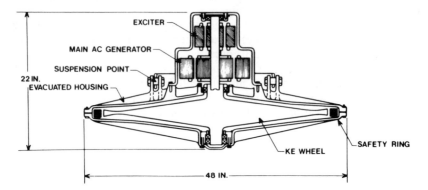

Fig.11.2. A new type (conical) flywheel. The vacuum reduces friction. Magnetic levitation reduces this toward zero.

TABLE 11.III: Strength-to-Density Ratios for Fly-Wheel Materials[10]

Material	Ultimate tensile strength (ksi)	Density (lb/in³)	Ultimate strength-to-density ratio (10⁶ in-lb/lb)
S glass	260	0.072	3.61
E glass	200	0.075	2.67
Maraging steel (18Ni-400)	409	0.289	1.41
Sitka spruce	19	0.015	1.27
Philippine mahogany	24	0.019	1.26
Hickory	32	0.028	1.14
Redwood	16	0.014	1.14
Titanium (6A1-4V)	150	0.160	0.94
4340 steel	260	0.283	0.92
Aluminium (2024-T851)	66	0.100	0.66
Cast iron	55	0.280	0.19

Energy density of super fly-wheels[11]

This is up to 30 watt hours per lb—at the maximum when the rotation begins—but if one takes into account retardation, an average of 12 watt hours per lb is found. This improvement of several hundred per cent on the 1950 fly-wheels is of great interest. However, although equal to a lead-acid battery in energy density, that of the super fly-wheel is some 3-5 times less than that of, e.g. the sodium-sulphur battery (see Table 11.I).

Materials[12]

The material factors have been reviewed by Rabenhorst,[12] and some of the materials which he states would be suitable for the fly-wheel construction are fibreglass, epoxy, wood, carbon fibres and some special organics, e.g. a du Pont product called Kevlar. Bulk glass may also be suitable. It is unclear where the optimal trade-off would be between price and the properties of these materials.

Advanced engineering concepts[13]

Magnetic suspension giving zero contact between solids, and hence diminished friction, has been proposed.

Pros and cons

The concept of using anisotropic spaghetti-like rods in the fly-wheel has led to an improvement in the energy density for fly-wheels, a diminution in the danger of their use. There is no indication that super fly-wheels are likely to approach electrochemical power sources in respect to energy density. They may well exceed them in respect to power density. The cost of short-time storage in dollars per kWh-year may well be cheaper than that for batteries.

There may be some cases where the fly-wheel concept has advantages. Indeed, Gorman has discussed the possibilities of fly-wheels in respect to solar energy.[14] One of the difficulties is the necessity of charging the fly-wheel through the medium of mechanical energy.

Thus, in spite of the enthusiasm shown by the originators of the super fly-wheels, it is unlikely that they would be important for the large energy-storage plants which are needed for the storage of solar and nuclear energy.

In respect to their potential use in transportation, the nearest competitor would be the H_2-O_2 battery with energy densities about 1,000 watt hours per lb. One use of fly-wheels might be in conjunction with fuel cells in cars. Thus, the fuel cell has a lower power density and the fly-wheel has a higher power density than batteries (even the new ones). Fuel cell-energised fly-wheels could provide the accelerative surges needed in starting and overtaking.

Storage in chemicals

Introduction

A compromise between storage in inertial systems and storage in hydrogen is storage in hydrides. This would avoid the expense of liquefaction, and the bulk involved in gaseous storage. In particular, hydrides have been suggested for automotive applications by American workers at Brookhaven[15] and by Dutch workers at Philips.[16]

The attraction of the storage in hydrides is that it gives a higher density than liquid hydrogen without the difficulties of liquefaction. Correspondingly, there is no safety problem. The disadvantage is the weight of the metal involved, and some doubts concerning the life time.

Intermetallic compounds and their high degree of absorption

Workers at Philips were the first to discover that AB_5 intermetallic compounds (A = a rare earth, and B = Ni or Co) absorbed and desorbed large amounts of hydrogen at small pressures and near to room temperatures.[16]

Examples are LaNi$_5$ and SmCo$_5$. The equilibrium pressures are shown in Table 11.IV.[16]

In SmCo$_5$ – H and LaNi$_5$ – H, there is a two-phase region in which hysteresis occurs and the magnitude of this hysteresis is related to the expansion which accompanies formation of the hydride.[17] The La-Ni system shows compounds with lattice constants, which define the compound concerned, e.g. LaNi$_2$.[18]

TABLE 11.IV: EQUILIBRIUM PRESSURES (AT ROOM TEMPERATURE) FOR SOME AB$_5$ COMPOUNDS AT HALFWAY SATURATION WITH HYDROGEN[16]

Compound	Pressure (atm)
PrCo$_5$	0.6
NdCo$_5$	0.8
SmCo$_5$	4.0
GdCo$_5$	20.0
LaNi$_5$	2.5
PrNi$_5$	12.0
NdNi$_5$	20.0
SmNi$_5$	60.0

Prospect of use of hydrides in transportation[19]

The positive aspects are the up-take of hydrogen and its reproduction upon gentle heating. The volume taken up for the large amount of hydrogen stored would be small. The negative aspects are the high price of such rare materials, corresponding to the small amounts available of, e.g. lanthanum and samarium.

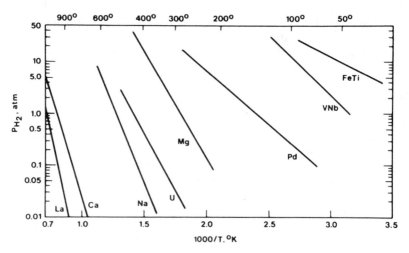

Fig. 11.3. Dissociations pressure with metal hydrides.[27]

Use of cheaper materials for storage as hydrides[20]

Magnesium hydride, MgH$_2$, is the most promising of these. It contains 7.6% of hydrogen. It decomposes at 1 atm at a temperature of 287°C. It is cheap.

There are possibilities with magnesium-nickel alloys. Fig. 11.3 shows the dissociation pressure of several hydrides.[20] The process is being developed for storage of roof-collected solar heat.

Economics of storage in cheap hydrides

There seem to be discrepancies in the estimate of this. According to Savage *et al.*,[21] the price would be between $6 and $46 per MBTU per year, compared with about $3.50 per MBTU per year for liquid hydrogen storage.* In Fe-Ti-Mn, the cost is around $4 per MBTU per year.

Further information on hydride storage

There are interesting documents by Lynch[17] and Kuijpers.[18,22]

Summary of hydride storage

In spite of the attractiveness of this method, because of its safety and small volume, the economics, and the scarcity of the really attractive metals, make it questionable that it will be used on a large scale. Long-term stability of the hydride may also be in question.

A general survey of the possibilities for storage in gases

Introduction

During the last several decades, natural gas has been stored in mines, caverns in impermeable limestone, and in shale. Cavities of rock salt have also been used.

Several other techniques are possible and have been surveyed by Eakin.[23] Natural gas is soluble, e.g. in liquid propane. At 600 psi, the volume of natural gas soluble in propane is 39 SCF per cubic ft at 104°F. Absorption in solids is a possibility, not a good one.

Reversible chemical combination: this would refer to the formation of a hydride, and can be considered. The possibilities of liquefaction are obvious.

The difficulties with liquefaction are the energy needed to reach the low temperatures at which hydrogen condenses, and the expense of the container. Chemical storage needs a cheap substance. Water would be the only one cheap enough. The solubility is insufficient and needs a low temperature for absorption, whilst regeneration provides difficulties. One of the difficulties with absorption in a liquid is the huge quantities required.

As to tanks, mines and quarry pits, it is a matter of costs. Mine cavities would seem the cheapest. Too much heat would probably be absorbed from the surroundings and there is much work to be done on the properties of rocks before the parameters are well enough known to be the basis of engineering calculations.

Depleted gas fields[24]

If reservoir size and characteristics are suitable, this is a good method because: (a) the reservoir has already been made, which reduces costs; and (b) the reservoir is known to be gas-tight (Fig. 11.4).[24]

---

* This is about $0.01 per kWh year. It is about 10^2 times less than storage in batteries.

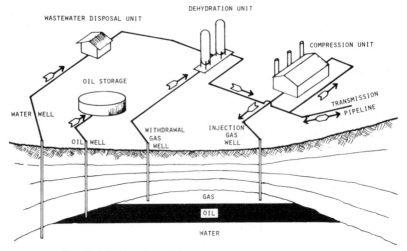

Fig. 11.4. Depleted gas field as reservoir for hydrogen storage.

Aquifers

The relevant considerations are the characteristics of the aquifer, what pressure would be needed to get the gas in, etc. Each case must be evaluated by itself.

Liquefaction

The present concepts envisage liquefaction largely for holding hydrogen energy for peak shaving rather than for dealing with the enormous quantities involved in diurnal swings. Costs are reviewed below.

Salt cavities

These have been, and will be, used for gas storage. The economics of the salt cavities relate to their location with respect to the transmission centre and the location of the demand centre. Gas storage in salt cavities is cheaper storage than that in liquid form.

Gasometers

Pressure vessels, e.g. 3 to 6 metres in diameter, and 100 metres long, are often used for the storage of gases.

Storage in pipes[25]

One of the advantages of storage in gases in the possibility that, when the system involves a large distance between the transmission centre and the user centre, there is substantial storage in the pipe.

The number of days' supply for a city of 10 million people which could be kept in a pipe 5,000 km long, 2 m in radius and 100 atm in pressure can be calculated thus:

$$n = \frac{PV}{RT} = \frac{100 \times 3.1 \, (2 \times 10^2)^2 \, 5 \times 10^3 \times 10^2}{0.08 \times 298} \tag{11.1}$$

$$= 3 \times 10^{11} \text{ moles of hydrogen} \tag{11.2}$$

The amount of energy in this quantity is obtained by recalling that 1 mole of hydrogen gas gives 58 k cal per mole upon burning. Hence, the number of moles of hydrogen in the pipe would give $6.9 . 10^{13}$ BTU. New York contains about 10^7 people, each equivalent in overall energy need per unit time to 10 kW, and, on this basis, there would be up to around one week's supply of energy for the city in the pipe. Perhaps about half of this would, in practice, be easily available because, as the pressure drops, so the same work of pumping will pump half as much energy per unit of time.

If the pressure of the gas in the pipe is cycled between about 75 and 125 atm, its fatigue life should be about 50 years.

Storage in air

Oil-driven turbines would compress air and force it into caverns. The air would be compressed to about 40 atm. Little development has been made.[1]

The existing natural-gas system

In the present natural-gas system, transmission of gas over distances up to 3,200 km through pipes takes place and the pressures used are 5 to 75 atm. Storage aspects are important because of the variation in demand, e.g. in the Eastern U.S. there is a 5 times variation between winter and summer.

Local storage in low-pressure tanks is possible to about 1 million cubic feet.

Pipeline storage (line-pack storage) is used. Underground storage capacity in the U.S. has some 325 underground pools in 26 States (Table 11.V).[25]

TABLE 11.V: NATURAL GAS SYSTEM DATA (U.S. 1970)[25]

Consumption:	
63.8 x 10⁹ cu. ft./day	23.34×10^{15} Btu/yr
Storage capacity:	
Underground gas reservoirs	5,178 x 10⁹ cu. ft.
Liquefied natural gas (SCF)	15 x 10⁹ cu. ft.
Total	5,193 x 10⁹ cu. ft.
Length of pipeline:	
Field and gathering main	66,556 mi
Transmission main	252,621 mi
Distribution main	595,653 mi
Total	914,830 mi
Number of customers (meters):	
Residential	38,097,000
Commercial	3,131,000
Industrial	199,000
Total	41,427,000

Underground storage for hydrogen

General

Compared with natural gas which is extensively stored underground, hydrogen will be more expensive to store there because its energy per unit volume is less than one-third that of natural gas. With pressures limited to, say, 200 atm, the storage capacity may be as low as one-third that of natural gas. There may be further increases in cost arising from the probable provision of higher-quality piping in view of the hydrogen environmental embrittlement problem. Embrittlement problems are not expected at pressures less than 100 atm, so there is a trade-off situation between the lessened cost achieved if one increases the gas pressure in the reservoir *vs* the added cost of higher quality (chromium containing) steels at higher pressures. At first, at least, whilst there will be plenty of exhausted fields to use, pressures over 100 atm will not be attempted, because of embrittlement possibilities (Fig. 11.4).

Pressure in reservoir and withdrawal rate[26]

The major contenders in the early years of the Hydrogen Economy will be reservoirs which were the natural gas fields, so that a comparison of the behaviour of hydrogen on exit from such a reservoir to that of natural gas is in order.

Firstly, the pressure may be assumed to be the same (100-200 atm) with a tendency to the lower value because of embrittlement dangers at greater pressures.[26]

It is in respect to the release-rate that there will be a difference. The relevant rate is in energy (not in volume) per unit time. For a given pressure differential, the flow rate is inversely proportional to the viscosity. The viscosity of methane is about twice that of hydrogen in the pressure region concerned. Hence, hydrogen will flow about twice as fast for a given Δp (the pressure difference within the reservoir to that without). As the energy density of hydrogen is 1/3.8 that of methane, the rates of delivery of energy from a reservoir having a Δp the same as that of natural gas would be one-half that observed when natural gas was the energy storage medium. Hence, if the energy output rate is to be the same as with natural gas, either the pressure or the number of outlet tubes must be doubled compared with the natural gas case. It seems likely that the latter would be the mode accepted.

In the same-pressure-twice-the-outlet situation, it must be recalled that a given reservoir will still contain only 1/3.8 times the energy which it would have had when filled with natural gas to the same pressure.*

Compressors

The compressing and withdrawal equipment would have to handle four times greater gas volume with hydrogen. Walters[26] points out that there would be no need in the hydrogen compressor facilities for heat exchangers or cooling towers such as those required for the natural gas situation—a cost saving to be laid against the increase for the larger pump. Injection wells will be twice, not four times the size, because of the roughly twice faster flow for hydrogen compared with that of natural gas.

An added methane difficulty and a frequent trouble with natural gas pipes is the formation of solid hydrates which block the line. The absence of such possibilities with hydrogen would allow a greater flow rate at the reduction

---

* Pressure must be maintained in the reservoir to keep up the flow of hydrogen at a certain energy per unit time. To maintain this pressure, considerable amounts (say one-third of the total capacity) of hydrogen will have to be injected into the reservoir and maintained there throughout the life of the reservoir. This hydrogen will then not be able to be withdrawn during the life of the reservoir, and must be considered a part of the capital investment of the reservoir.

valve, another factor to lay off against the added cost of hydrogen stored.[26]

Impurities introduced into hydrogen on the use of natural gas reservoirs

There will be some contamination of hydrogen stored in a former natural gas reservoir. No description can be made about this: it will depend on the field. Water vapour will be present.

Costs

The cost of storage will be four times greater for hydrogen stored in reservoirs than for natural gas thus stored. Comparisons are shown in the Table 11.VI.

TABLE 11.VI: COMPARISON OF ESTIMATED NATURAL GAS AND HYDROGEN STORAGE CAPITAL COSTS[26]

	Capital costs per million Btu, 1975 dollars	
	Natural Gas	Hydrogen
Gaseous, underground	$1 to $1.5	$3 to $6
Gaseous, high-pressure bottle	$180	$864
Gaseous, low-pressure holder	$272	$1044
Liquid, vacuum-Perlite insulation vessel	$36 ($26)	$90 ($50)
Liquefaction and vaporisation	($10)	($40)

$6 per MBTU at 10% is, then, $0.60 per MBTU-year for 10% money. This is about one order of magnitude less than the cost of liquid hydrogen storage. However, two points must be laid against this. Firstly, there is the fact that liquid hydrogen storage has aspects (i.e. a higher energy-density) which cannot be rivalled with underground storage. Secondly, the cost of gaseous hydrogen storage is too low because it neglects, e.g. purification if the hydrogen is to be used in the situation in which a methane impurity would not be acceptable.

All these considerations assume the reservoir to be available. If it has to be created, e.g. by excavation, or even by means of underground explosion, added costs will have to be borne. The costs per MBTU-year depend, then, on the financing method, i.e. the years allowed for amortisation.

The development of granular-iron-titanium as a hydrogen storage medium

Introduction

It has been shown in Fig. 11.3 that of all the hydride systems known there is advantage in MgH_2 because of the temperature (287°C) to which it has to be raised to release hydrogen; and because of the relatively favourable weight fraction of hydrogen which is contained in the hydride (*c.* 10%). However, iron-titanium (or Fe-Ti-Mn) has some counter-advantages to allay the lesser weight (*c.* 2%) of hydrogen which can be contained within it. One does not need to heat it: at room temperature the dissociation pressure is a manageable 5 ats. The components are abundant, and hence cheap. Above all, the material has been taken up in intensive work at the Brookhaven National Laboratory at first by Strickland, Reilly and Wiswall,[27] whose work is summarised in the following.[5]

Reilly and Wiswall found the basic data which are shown here in Fig. 11.5.[28]

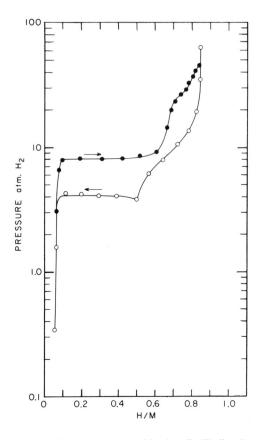

Fig. 11.5. Pressure-composition in a Fe-Ti alloy.[28]

Thus, in the plateau, the alloy is represented roughly by FeTi + FeTiH and on the ascending section by FeTiH + FeTiH$_2$.

Vessel and alloy preparation[27]

The Brookhaven workers evolved a complex design which involves cooling devices to carry away the exothermic heat absorption. The vessel wall is $\frac{1}{4}''$ thick for pressures of 50 ats. Normal steel is used. In a typical exercise, 839 lb of FeTi alloy, containing 10 lb of hydrogen, was contained in a tube 6 ft long and 12 in. in diameter.

The alloy is made in an induction furnace lined with alumina in an inert atmosphere. It is crushed into small pieces and granulated to 4-100 mesh and the presence of small quantities of oxygen decreases the capacity of the material, because of the formation of passive layers which are not reduced by hydrogen at room temperature.

It is not possible to absorb hydrogen first: an activation procedure is needed. One heats and pumps out gases at 600°F and then brings into contact H_2 at 20 psi.

Thereafter (i.e. after O-layer reduction), the temperature is reduced to room temperature and then the pressure is increased.

The purpose of the activation is not only to bring about a cleaning of the surface, but also to cause micro-fissuring, and hence to increase the real area available for the adsorption, which is preliminary to the absorption.

Other methods of increasing area are known but would be expensive.

Charging time

This is of the order of one hour.

Cost

The cost of such a system has been computed by Salzano, Isler and Yu.[29] For example, the alloy needed in a medium-sized car would cost *c.* $2,000.

The liquefaction of hydrogen

Introduction

Were hydrogen to be available in liquid form, its use in vehicles, particularly in aircraft, would be practical with little modification of the vehicle. The availability of liquid natural gas may tempt one to think lightly of hydrogen storage in liquid form. However, the liquefaction of hydrogen is a far more difficult task than the liquefaction of methane, and the reasons for this are not only that the boiling point of hydrogen is 20.4°K, whereas the boiling point of methane is 109°K. A number of special difficulties are associated with the liquefaction of hydrogen and these will be discussed below.

Nevertheless, on the positive side, helium (boiling 4.2°K) is even more difficult to liquefy than is hydrogen, yet its liquefaction is routinely carried out in low-temperature physics laboratories. Since liquid hydrogen became the principal fuel for space vehicles, the development of its technology has been immensely furthered during the last two decades. Of the advances in technology thereby achieved, the more important is the simplest: the application of the fact that the difficulties of storage of something far away from the ambient temperature are reduced greatly as the size of the vessel increases (i.e. the volume to surface ratio increases). Thus, the largest storage vessels used by NASA for liquid hydrogen contain 900,000 gallons. This is equivalent to an energy in the order of 10 million kWh (30 billion BTU).

That the manufacture of large quantities of hydrogen can be carried out and hydrogen stored is established. What remains to be shown is whether the advantages of stored liquid hydrogen can be had at an acceptable cost.

Amounts of liquid hydrogen stored so far compared with amounts stored by other methods.

10 million kWh has meaning only in comparison with the amounts available in other energy stores. Thus, Walter gives Table 11.VII.[26]

Thus, the liquid hydrogen store, though apparently big, is only within the order of magnitude needed for a central energy storage facility. Some 50 of the largest NASA tanks would be necessary to equal the typical liquid-methane storage-tank in peak shaving.

TABLE 11.VII: The Relative Sizes of Various Types of Energy Storage Facilities[8,26]

	Billions of BTU
LH$_2$ Tank, NASA	38
L.N.G. Peak shaving tank	2000
Pumped hydro-electric storage, largest	51
Underground reservoir, typical	20,000

The difficulties of liquefaction

There are four difficulties:

1. The depth of the temperature makes all the operations more difficult than those with methane. Thus, all materials (water, oxygen) gaseous or liquid at high temperatures, freeze. The fall in temperature of gas brought into a cold tank tends to form a cryogenic pump which may introduce impurities.

2. The usual method of liquefying gases depend on the fact that the inversion temperature (that at which expansion causes a fall in temperature) is above room temperature. For hydrogen it is 204°K. Hence, to liquefy hydrogen, one has to have an auxiliary liquefaction plant, e.g. nitrogen, or perhaps a halogenated hydrocarbon, firstly, to bring the temperature of the gas below the inversion temperature. This two plants-in-one necessity gives rise to an increased cost.

3. The energy needs in refrigeration are subject to Carnot-like considerations. Thus, the efficiency with which a mechanical engine can extract heat to a temperature of 0°K is zero, and decreases as this temperature is approached (Fig. 11.6).[30]

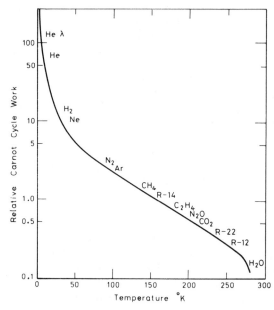

Fig. 11.6. The efficiency in refrigeration.[31]

4. Hydrogen molecules consist of two types in respect of nuclear spin. The first, the orthotype, has nuclear spins in the same direction. The second, or para type has the nuclear spins in the opposite direction. At room temperature, hydrogen is 75% ortho in form. As the temperature falls, the equilibrium form becomes increasingly para and that at $0°K$ extrapolation shows a 100% para form (Fig. 11.7). The change from ortho to para gives out heat and hence the energy to liquefy is greater than that calculated by the normal equations involving a specific heat.[31]

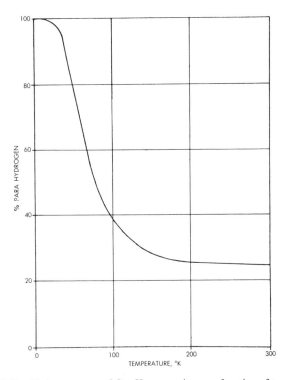

Fig. 11.7. Equilibrium amount of O-p H_2 conversion as a function of temperature.

The technique of liquefaction of hydrogen

It is necessary to bring the hydrogen temperature to below $204°K$ by the use of liquid nitrogen, or etc. Thereafter, centrifugal turbines can be used to cool the liquid and the work can be partly recovered from the heat evolved. An important matter concerns the degree of ortho-to-para conversion which is undertaken during the liquefaction process.[32] Spontaneous conversion is slow at the low temperatures involved. If no catalysis is used to accelerate conversion during liquefaction, it takes place during the following day or so, and heat is then evolved because the para form is more stable than the ortho, and boil-off is caused. Hence, if the hydrogen concerned has to be stored for more than a few hours, it is necessary to spend the extra energy to deal with the heat evolved and liquefaction with conversion to the equilibrium p/o ratio. If, however, hydrogen is to be liquefied for only a few hours, it may be more economic to withstand this small loss due to the boil-off associated with partial conversion of ortho to para after liquefaction and save on the energy needed to bring about change to the equilibrium o/p ratio, i.e. to deal with the entire heat of evolution. The work necessary to convert to 95% p is 18-36% of the total work necessary to liquefy, and it depends upon the rate at which it is done.

Storage of liquid hydrogen

General

The technique of storage of liquid hydrogen was advanced greatly during the last two decades. In 1952, the technique was only highly evacuated dewars with silvered walls. Then, anti-radiation baffles were introduced. Improved insulation—the use of perlite—was started. A technique described as 'quilted super insulation' is used (Fig. 11.8).

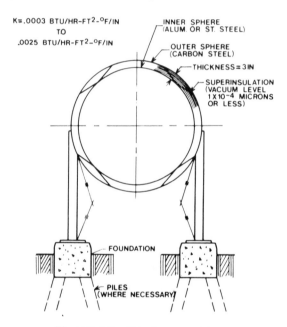

Fig. 11.8. A liquid hydrogen container.

Energy in liquefaction

Owing to the large energy used in liquefaction because of the low efficiency of conversion, it is worthwhile asking what fraction of the chemical energy available in the hydrogen-oxygen conversion is used up in the liquefaction process. Although the theoretical minimum energy is 1.3 kWh lb^{-1}, the actual amount is 5.6 kWh lb^{-1}. This is $\frac{5.6.2}{485}$ kWh per mole or $\frac{5.6.2 \ 10^3.3.6.}{485.4.18}$ k cal mol^{-1} = 22.5k cal $mole^{-1}$. The reaction of 1 mole of hydrogen with oxygen gives 58k cal mole so that about 39% of the energy available by combustion of gaseous hydrogen from a liquid store has to be expended in liquefying it. It is probable that some of this could be recovered. It is a guess-timate to suggest 25% as a net loss of energy on liquefaction.

The cost of the energy used in liquefaction, related to 1 MBTU, can be calculated. It is 110 kWh, so that, if one takes the cost of massive low use-period electric power at the site of use as 1.5¢ per kWh (reasonable in 1978 for massive use of power *at* a power station without transmission costs, and using low use-period power) the cost of energy used in liquefaction is about $1.65 per MBTU. In addition, there is amortization, maintenance and insurance. In the parallel case of the manufacture of hydrogen gas from water to electrolysis, the total cost (1978) is (229 Ec + 70)¢ per MBTU where 229Ec is the cost of the electrical energy and 70 is the cost in cents of the other matters itemised above. With E = 1.6 volts and c = 1.5¢ kWh^{-1}, the amortisation, maintenance, manpower and insurance as a fraction of the total cost is about 12%.

Assuming that this figure applies to the plant for liquid hydrogen manufacture, the total cost per MBTU of H_2 is $1.65 + 0.19 = $1.84. This is an optimistic figure. Thus, the energy costs taken under the defined circumstances are real, but costs of maintenance of the complex liquid hydrogen plant are likely to be much greater than those of an electrolysis plant. It seems reasonable to increase these by 100%, i.e. to 38¢ per MBTU, so one gets a total cost for liquefaction of 1 MBTU of about $2.03.* The middle range of 1 MBTU of hydrogen from water in 1977 dollars for a 1985 technology is about $7.50,[33] so that it is reasonable to state that liquefaction increases the cost of hydrogen by about 25%.

However, significant amounts of energy from the heat evolved in liquefaction could be recovered. This is shown in Table 11.VIII

TABLE 11.VIII: THE ENERGY DENSITY OF LH_2 COMPARED WITH THAT OF OTHER FUELS[34]

Fuel	kWh kg^{-1}	kWh L^{-1}
Iso-butane	11.6	9.3
LH_2	33.0	2.3
Metal hydride 7.6% H_2	2.6	3.7
FeTiH$_{1.0}$	0.5	1.8

LH_2 is therefore the most energy-dense liquid medium available for *weight*, although it is interesting to note that greater energy density upon a *volume* basis is available from iso-octane (essentially, gasoline) and some hydrides.

Small containers for liquid hydrogen

A number of cryogenic storage tanks suitable for vehicular use have been tried out (Tables 11.IX and 11.X).[34]

A storage period of 10-24 days is possible. Longer periods may reasonably be envisaged. Further, pressure may be built up without venting for after three days. In a typical tank, discussed by Peschka and Carpetis,[34] the pressure mounts to 4.5 ats. An increased capacity for boil-off can be attained by the use of, for example, magnesium to absorb hydrogen.

---

*The actual *price* (not cost) offered by a company in 1978 is about $3 per MBTU.

TABLE 11.IX: TANK-WEIGHT AND STORED ENERGY[34]

	Capacity	Overall volume	Material	Empty weight	Max. weight	Stored energy		Max. operation pressure
	(l)	(l)		(kg)	(kg)	(kWh/kg)	(kWh/l)	(bar)
Isooctane[1]	50	55	steel	∿10	∿55	8,5	9,3	—
MMMC-tank[2]	189	210	Al	∿40	∿53	8,5	2,18	∿2,5
Tank in A.F. study[3]	150	220	Al	∿55	∿61	6	1,67	2,5
DFVLR-tanks[4] I) in operation	120	140	stainless steel	∿75	∿83	3,5	2,1	8
II) planned	120	140	Al	∿40	∿49	6	2,1	8

[1] Equivalent to 1892 of LH_2.

[2] Tested on hydrogen powered vehicles. Manufacturer: Minnesota Mining and Manufacturing Company. Spherical shaped tank with neck. Maximum permissible acceleration in every direction 30 g.[33,35]

[3] Flat tank.

[4] Flat tank without neck. Armatures, including heat exchangers for warming up of hydrogen, integrated with the tank. Maximum permissible acceleration in every direction about 10 g for the stainless steel tank, about 30 g for the aluminium tank.

TABLE 11.X: CHARACTERISTIC DATA OF DIFFERENT VEHICLE TANKS[34]

See table 11.IX	Capacity	Heat leak	Hydrogen boiling rate		Pressure buildup rate bar/h		Maximum permissible operating pressure	Normal operating pressure
	(l)	(W)	g/day	l/day	100% capacity	50%	(bar)	(bar)
MMMC-tank	189	∿2,9	∿555	∿7,8	∿0,35	∿0,069	∿3	∿24
DFVLR tank I	115	3,5[+]	∿665	∿9	1,1	0,125	8	13,5
DFVLR tank II	115	2,0	380	5,2	0,4	0,072	8	23

[+] measured with liquid nitrogen. The corresponding values are calculated from the liquid nitrogen boiling rate.

Cost of LH_2

The cost,* in 1977 dollars, of 1985 technology for LH_2 would be around $10 per MBTU if the H_2 originated in electrolysis, compared with the gasoline price (commercial price diminished by dealer mark-up, tax and transportation from the refinery) of about $2.75. Liquid hydrogen from coal would cost around $8 per MBTU. The price ratio gasoline: LH_2 of about 3.4 is relatively encouraging put in the context of the exhaustion of oil and natural gas which seems certain to raise by several times the cost of gasoline in constant dollars during the next one to two decades. As the sort of time for important elements of our technology to become solar-hydrogen would be three decades (due to a limit in the rate of capital investment possible), there is no difficulty in respect to price competition of liquid hydrogen with gasoline. Conversely, in the short term, it must be recalled that the $2.75 quoted for the New York gasoline, although shorn of dealer mark-up, tax and transpor-

---

*The actual commercial *price* as supplied to NASA in 1978 is about $22 per MBTU.

tation costs from the refinery, is still a price, and not a cost. Thus, the pump price of U.S. gasoline has remained constant in dollars with *decreasing* real cost since 1975, i.e. there is a substantial difference between price and cost for gasoline, so that an 'exhaustion increase' of cost of gasoline may not be allowed to show until the last few years of the availability of the fuel. The situation pertains to the lack of warning to the public arising from the price insensitivity due to the cushion of the high price-to-cost ratio. As the cost of operating goes up, there can be a decrease in price-to-cost ratio so that the price does not go up as much as the cost.

There is another comparison which could be made, namely to the cost of gasoline from coal at a future time. Estimates (see Chapter 4) of this vary (1978 dollars) from $5-6 per MBTU. This cost should be compared with the cost (1978 dollars) of H_2 at a time when gasoline may be available from coal; and hydrogen from solar-derived electricity via water splitting. The cost of solar electricity (solar-thermal) will be around 4 cents kWh $^{-1}$ and the corresponding cost of gaseous hydrogen should then be about $16. The cost of the liquefaction process should (1990s, in 1978 dollars) be about $3, suggesting a price of liquid hydrogen (1990s, in 1978 dollars) of about $17 per MBTU. Liquid hydrogen from solar sources would be about three times more expensive than gasoline from coal, neglecting the environmental damage and advantage in Second Law efficiency, and environmental damage.* Taking these matters into account makes the ratio about 1.5 times in favour of (synthetic) gasoline.

Hydrogen storage in chemical media

The storage of hydrogen in simple metallic hydrides formed from Mg and particularly in FeTi has been discussed. These metals absorb hydrogen which enters the alloy and is rejected again at, e.g. a lower pressure or a higher temperature, etc. In the chemical sense, the concept of a stoichiometric hydride formation is not stressed in these associations.

Another concept to be considered is to use straight-out chemical combinations, as in the union of hydrogen with B to form B_2H_6. Whether this is a useful way of storing hydrogen depends on the ease of reversing simple reactions for decomposition to the original store substance, plus hydrogen. There is significant inorganic chemical work still to be done here.

The following compounds contain more hydrogen than FeTi and are less expensive than rare earth compounds.

Solid-like forms of hydrogen[36]

Some potential may lie in storage in forms of hydrogen at temperatures lower than the melting point ($-253°C$).

Hydrogen slush may be a method which is of value, a mixture of solid and liquid hydrogen. Metallic hydrogen has been discussed. It is hypothetically

---

*An estimate of 25 cents/gallon for this assumes the value of 1 pollution-caused death to be $1 million.[35]

TABLE 11.XI: Some Hydrogen-Containing Compounds of Interest

Compound	Weight % H_2
$LiAlH_4$	10.5
$BaBH_4$	10.6
$LiBH_4$	18.3
B_2H_6	21.0

formable at a pressure of several megabars. Were it to be stable at room temperatures, it could be a super conductor and would have metallic strength with a density several times less than that of aluminium. It could possibly become a convenient energy storer.

There are reports which suggest that metallic hydrogen has been formed.[36] The density has been reported to be 1 to 1.3 g cc^{-1}.

Storage in super-conducting wires

In an electromagnet, the passage of electricity causes a power loss, and power must be constantly supplied to maintain the field. If the wire is superconducting, the magnetic field—once set up—would remain and could give back energy by drawing current from the magnet.

Such a scheme might be feasible for a large store, e.g. 1,000-10,000 megawatt hours. One would need a solenoid with a radius of 50 metres and a height of 50 metres. Nb-Ti would be used. Such technology may be useful before 2000.

Under-water storage

A schematic for this is shown in Fig. 11.9.

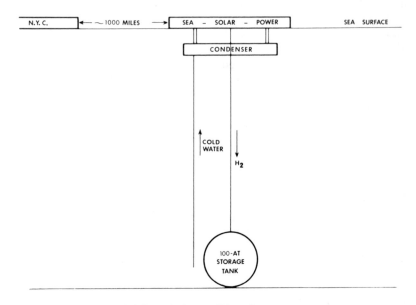

Fig. 11.9. Schematic for possible under-water storage.

SUMMARY OF CHAPTER

1. Molten salts, batteries (particularly the high energy-density ones), fly-wheels, and storage in chemicals, are all general methods of storing energy which have their place, depending on the original form of the energy and how long it has to be stored.

2. In respect to gases, depleted gas fields, liquefaction, salt cavities, gasometers, storage in pipes, and under compression in caverns, are all possibilities, depending on the amount to be stored.

3. Underground storage of hydrogen (Fig. 11.4) involves pressures in the order of 100 ats. The rate of outflow from a field filled with H_2 would be about half that observed when natural gas is being stored. Compressors would have to be larger and natural gas impurities would be present, while costs would be some four times more.

4. Iron-titanium alloys have become a possible H_2 storage medium for some situations, e.g. in electricity storage using H_2. Charging time is 1 hr. Initial cost is high. Weight in transportation may be compensated by air-conditioner removal, as cooling can be achieved by passing gas over FeTiMn.

5. Liquid H_2 storage became practical on a large scale because of the use of H_2 as a space-vehicle fuel. Although NASA tanks hold *c.* 1 million gallons, they are still small compared with LNG tank quantities.

6. H_2 is difficult to liquefy because of the low efficiency of refrigeration at low temperatures and because of the energy used in o-p conversion. As it does not cool on expansion at $> 204°K$, it is necessary to refrigerate it firstly in liquid N_2.

7. About 39% of the energy of H_2 is taken up by the liquefaction process. Conversely, LH_2 has the highest energy density of any liquid. Storage for 10-24 days is possible. LH_2 from coal should cost around \$8 per MBTU at this time (its commercial price is around \$22). In a projection to 1990, LH_2 using H_2 from a solar source would be around three times more expensive than that from coal on a First Law basis, but only 1.5 times more accounting for Second Law costs and pollution.

8. Hydrogen storage in chemicals (B_2H_6?) does not look encouraging.

AUTHOR'S ARBITRARY CHOICE OF A MORE IMPORTANT CONCLUSION FROM CHAPTER

The cost of H_2 from coal stored in FeTi or light metal cylinders would be less than synthetic liquid methane from coal for unit distance in driving a vehicle. LH_2 from a solar source in a 1990 projection compared with gasoline from coal (taking account of Second Law and pollution costs) could be around 50% more expensive, i.e. could become cheaper, were the cost of coal to increase (non-inflationally) by more than 50%.

REFERENCES

1. A. L. Robinson, *Science*, 1974, **184**, 784-5.
2. Philips Research Press Release No. 724/1230/108E, 1974; 735/1011/122E.
3. M. Telkes, Storage of Solar Heat, Institute of Energy Conversion, 27 June 1974.
4. *Technology of Efficient Energy Utilization*, Report of NATO Science Committee, Conference in Les Arcs, France, 8-12 October 1973.
5. G. Brown, St. Joe's Minerals Corporation, private communication, October 1973; see also

reports from Ford Scientific Laboratory, 30 June 1974, TNSF Contract C805.
6. K. G. Pankhurst, British Rail Research, private communication, October 1974.
7. J. O'M. Bockris & A. K. Reddy, *Modern Electrochemistry*, Rosetta Edition (Plenum, New York, 1974), chapter 11.
8. Numerous announcements by Westinghouse Company, 8 October 1973 onward.
9. Table constructed partly from data given by J. McAllen, C.S.I.R.O., private communication, 12 July 1974.
10. R. T. Dann, *Machine Design*, 16 May 1973, p.130.
11. D. W. Rabenhorst, Intersociety Energy Conversion Engineering Conference Proceedings, 1971, p.38.
12. D. W. Rabenhorst, presented 14 Symposium, American Society for Mechanical Engineers, Albuquerque, N.M., 1974.
13. N. V. Guila & L. D. Linkin, *Russian Engineering Journal*, **52**, 12 (1973), 3.
14. R. Gorman, 'Solar-Cells', Flywheel Storage, Bell Co., Report TM-70-1012-3, 15 September 1970.
15. K. C. Hoffmann, W. E. Winsche, R. H. Wiswall, J. J. Reilly, T. V. Sheehan & C. H. Waide, presented at International Automotive Engineering Congress, Detroit, January 1969.
16. J. H. N. van Vucht, F. A. Kuijpers & H. C. A. M. Bruning, Philips Research Report 25, 113-140 (1970).
17. F. E. Lynch, 'Metal Hydrides: The Missing Link in Automotive Hydrogen Technology', Energy Research Corporation, Provo, Utah, 18 August 1973.
18. K. H. J. Buschow & H. H. van Mal, *Philips Research Report*, **29**, 203 (1972).
19. P. Hill, *The Engineer* (July 1972), p.3.
20. R. H. Wiswall, Jr., & J. J. Reilly, presented at the 7th Intersociety Energy Conversion Engineering Conference, San Diego, California, September 1972.
21. R. L. Savage, L. Blank, T. Cady, K. Cox, R. Murray & R. D. Williams (edd.), *A Hydrogen Energy Carrier*, Vol. II—Systems Analysis (NASA-ASEE, 1973).
22. F. A. Kuijpers & H. H. van Mal, *J. of the Less-Common Metals*, **23**, 395 (1971).
23. B. E. Eekin, paper presented to the A.G.A. Operating Section, Conference, 1960.
24. D. J. Clarke, G. S. Crib & W. J. Walters, presented at the 108th Annual Meeting of the Institute of Gas Engineers, Salihull, May 1971.
25. R. A. Reynolds & W. A. Slager, THEME Conference, Miami, 1974, S2-1.
26. A. B. Walters, World Hydrogen Energy Conference, Miami, 1976, 2B-65.
27. G. Strickland, J. J. Reilly & R. H. Wiswall, THEME Conference, February 1974, Miami S4-9.
28. R. H. Wiswall & J. J. Reilly, *Chem. & Eng. News*, 16 September, 1974.
29. E. J. Salzano, R. I. Isla & W. S. Yu, First World Hydrogen Energy Conference, Miami, 1976, 8B-89.
30. C. R. Baker & B. Spencer, 1st World Hydrogen Energy Conference III, Miami, 1976 2B-99.
31. J. Dixon, R. Ryan & T. Smulyan, Stanford Research Institute, February 1976.
32. C. R. Baker & R. L. Shaner, World Hydrogen Energy II Conference, Miami, 1976, 2B-17.
33. J. O'M. Bockris, *International Journal of Energy Research*, 1978, **2**, 9-17.
34. W. Peschke & C. Carpetis, First World Hydrogen Energy Conference, Miami, 1976, 2B-43.
35. R. Zweig, First World Hydrogen Energy Conference, Miami, 1976, IV, C-49.
36. F. V. Grivorev, S. B. Kormer, O. L. Mihailova, A. P. Tolochko & V. D. Urlin, *ZhETF Science* 294 (25 February 1974).

12

ASPECTS OF A HYDROGEN ECONOMY

The origin of the concept of a Hydrogen Economy

Jules Verne, in 1869, made Captain Nemo somewhat ambiguously indicate water as a fuel of the future.[1] J. B. S. Haldane, in 1923, made a clear suggestion that the future fuel would be liquefied hydrogen obtained by the electrolysis of water, with the energy source being wind.[2] In a little-known paper of 1927, A. T. Stuart saw hydrogen from hydro-electric sources as a fuel[3] (and developed the idea further in an inter-office memo of 1934). Erren and Hastings-Campbell came into the picture in 1933 with work about the use of hydrogen in internal-combustion engines.[4] Sometime in the 1930s, according to Justi,[5] Lawaczek was the first to point out that hydrogen pushed through pipes would be a cheaper way to send energy from one place to another than electricity through wires. Niederreither, 1937, suggested storage and the re-creation of electricity through fuel cells.[6] Sikorski, in 1938, thought hydrogen to be a good fuel for helicopters.[7] The Australian, Just, in 1944, encouraged the use of hydrogen during a shortage of gasoline.[8] In 1948, King published his well-known work on the use of hydrogen to drive cars.[9]

Bacon and Watson[10-12] began the present era of suggestions in favour of hydrogen by their 1950 suggestion which united those of Haldane[2] and Niederreither.[6] Weinberg, in 1959, was the first American author to propose hydrogen as a fuel for cars.[13] In 1961, Lessing wrote an article in *Fortune* magazine which talked of hydrogen as a general fuel but it seemed that he was talking mainly about the fusion program.[14] Bockris,[15] in 1962, proposed photo-electrochemical cells, floating on sea-borne platforms, electrolysing seawater and supplying cities with hydrogen for all purposes. Lindström, in 1963, stressed the Lawaczek suggestion.[16, 17] Justi, in 1965, presented the concept of hydrogen from land-based solar farms, supplying far-off cities.[18] Bockris, in 1969, in a talk with Linden,[19] suggested that an Institute of Gas Technology team should examine piped hydrogen transmission. The phrase 'A Hydrogen Economy' was used for the first time by Bockris and Triner, 3 February 1970. They had been discussing fuels in transportation. The discussion suggested that hydrogen would be the best fuel there, but developed to apply it to other areas of energy use. It was suggested that we should be living in 'A Hydrogen Society', and then that this would in fact be 'A Hydrogen Economy'. Bockris described this most general concept of the use of hydrogen (nuclear or solar based) in an article in 1971.[20] About the same time, Dean and Schoeppel lauded the use of hydrogen in transportation and also used the phrase 'A Hydrogen Economy'.[21] Bockris and Appleby,[22] in 1972, suggested that the Hydrogen Economy could be an ultimate mode of distributing energy, be the energy source coal, nuclear or solar. Gregory, Ng and Long,[23] in 1972, published a quantification of Lawaczek's suggestion, that Bockris had requested from Linden in 1969. Marchetti supported these ideas.[24] Lessing lauded them in a *Fortune* article.[25]

From 1972, the Hydrogen Economy concept can be said to be well known and, in 1974, Veziroglu, Bockris, Billings, Kelley, Escher, Martinez and others formed the Hydrogen Energy Society.*

The medium of future energy

The likely sources of energy for the future are atomic and solar. Atomic reactors can provide electricity which would become cheaper as the reactors increase in size, but with size there comes the difficulty of thermal pollution, so that large atomic reactors, which would give relatively cheap electricity at source, would have to be placed either on the ocean, far from population centres, or in remote areas, such as Northern Canada, Siberia or Central Australia.

Correspondingly, massive solar collectors are likely to be far from the population centres which need them, for they would be most advantageously situated in North Africa, Saudi Arabia and Australia (see Chapters 8 and 13). Hence, the electricity to which they would give rise is liable to have to travel at least 1,000 miles, and, in some situations, as much as 4,000 miles, to go from the site of production to the site of use (Figs. 12.1 and 12.2).

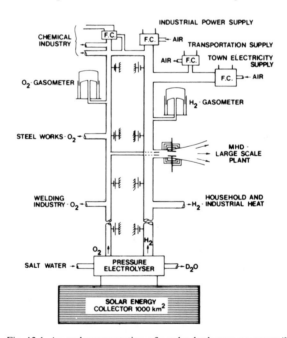

Fig. 12.1. An early presentation of a solar-hydrogen economy.[18]

*This sought to be the official body of the concept. An earlier body, called 'The Hindenburg Society', was organized by Escher.

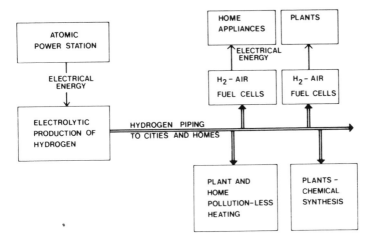

Fig. 12.2. A hydrogen economy.

The likelihood of this situation, and the energy loss in conduction, gave rise to the concept of a 'Hydrogen Economy'.[20] Thus, it could be cheaper to convert electrical energy, which will be a product of solar and atomic reactors, to hydrogen at the energy source. Thereafter, the hydrogen would be transmitted through pipes—the pumping energy being relatively small—and converted back to electricity at the site of use (fuel cells), or used in combustion to provide mechanical power.[26]

The distance at which it becomes cheaper to transmit energy by hydrogen rather than in the original electrical form, depends upon the voltage of transmission, and the dependence as shown in Fig. 12.3.[23] For situations in which there are distant energy sources (the typical energy source of the future), therefore, hydrogen is likely to be the medium of energy (Fig. 12.4).

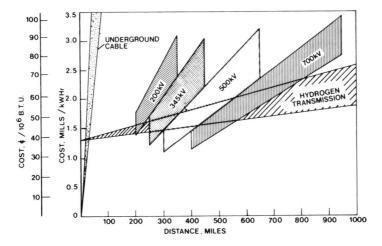

Fig. 12.3. The basic diagram of Gregory, Ng and Long.[23]

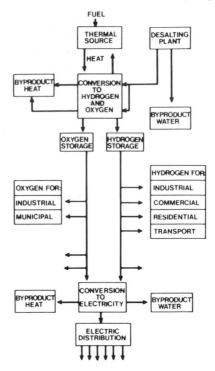

Fig. 12.4. Another conception of a hydrogen economy.[27]

Consequences of a Hydrogen Economy

At present, some 10% of energy is provided by the transmission of electricity through wires. Hydrogen would not only fulfil this requirement, but the other major energy requirements:

1. *Chemical technology:* Sufficiently cheap hydrogen could be used in a large number of reduction reactions, with cheapened costs and pollution greatly reduced, or negligible.

2. *Metallurgy and refining:* A number of processes may be carried out more cheaply with hydrogen than by using reducing agents such as carbon. Another reason for increasing the use of hydrogen is to reduce air pollution at present associated with metallurgy and refining.

3. *Effluents:* The upgrading of effluents could occur more easily with cheap electricity and/or oxygen available via a Hydrogen Economy. An in-house treatment of sewage through its electrolytic oxidation to carbon dioxide, or its chemical treatment in a molten salt at high temperature (producing CO_2) may become practical.

4. *Water:* A fraction of drinking water needs could be met by the use of hydrogen as the medium of energy. The end reaction involved is the production of liquid water. For a community at 10 kW per person, there could result about 14 gallons per person per day of fresh water, of which about 3 would be produced in the house.

5. *Transportation:* Hydrogen could be used in internal-combustion engines,

which run well on hydrogen after only small modification. Fuel cells would probably eventually be used because of their greater efficiency. Trains, likewise, could be driven from fuel cells running on gaseous or liquid hydrogen.

SEA TRANSPORTATION: Large freighters will be necessary in the foreseeable future. They could run on hydrogen-oxygen fuel cells with liquid hydrogen storage. They would use energy islands in southern seas, at which the hydrogen could be produced, as refuelling centres.

AIR TRANSPORTATION: Independently of the more general concept of the Hydrogen Economy, subsonic, supersonic and hypersonic aircraft would all run with advantage on hydrogen.

The use of hydrogen as a fuel in transportation would allow attractive concepts to be realised. One of these is economic hypersonic flight. Single-seat individual helicopters would become feasible and perhaps economic.

The transduction of hydrogen in a Hydrogen Economy

Introduction

In a Hydrogen Economy, the hydrogen is likely to come from a distant highly-insolated source, in pipes as a gas, or perhaps in tankers in a liquid form, and be transduced locally to mechanical or electrical energy.

There are three ways in which this could be achieved:

1. In an extension of the present system, hydrogen may be used to fuel internal-combustion engines. Only minor changes are needed in petroleum-fueled engines to make them run on hydrogen. An evolution within the automotive industry via internal-combustion to hydrogen as a fuel seems a likely path for the development of a Hydrogen Economy. The disturbance of the industry would be less, and therefore more economically attractive, than if the other non-polluting option, that cars run on electrochemical power sources (which would mean largely rebuilding the means of production) were adopted. For household electricity, one could continue the present system, distributing electricity (produced from hydrogen introduced to a central point in a town) to points of use in houses by means of cables. However, one would lose the total energy concept made possible by a Hydrogen Economy, accompanied by the in-house production of heat and electricity. In our present system, electricity-producing stations are cooled by water which is then discarded, that is, the system gratuitously heats rivers and the sea instead of houses and people. Rationality must not be sought in our present energy system, because this grew up in an era in which fossil fuels were cheap and seemed inexhaustible.

2. Secondly, one could develop advanced modifications of combustion engines. These include the Wankel and Sarich rotary engines which have the advantage of high power-to-weight ratios (their tendency to pollute more than classical chemical transducers would no longer be important if they were fueled by hydrogen). One of the disadvantages of the internal-combustion engine, its tendency to have an efficiency below 30%, is unchanged with new power plants, with the exception of the rocket engine, which needs hydrogen and pure oxygen.

3. Alternatively, hydrogen could be used to produce electricity in fuel cells at local sites. How local the site would be is a matter for systems analysis: for instance, for household energy, it might be better to have substations for every few hundred houses, rather than in each house. The advantage would be that of ease of maintenance, and the total energy concept could be preserved by piping heat to the surrounding buildings. Mechanical energy would arise from electric motors. Running on hydrogen, fuel cells show efficiencies up to 75%, easily greater than 60%. A catalyst may not be necessary in hydrogen–air fuel cells.

The chemical converter

The internal-combustion engine running on hydrogen is examined in this chapter. The principal advantage of continuing to use it is that it allows continuation of the amortisation of the capital invested in the means of production in the present transportation industry. Further, internal-combustion engines have higher power-to-weight ratios than electrochemical engines at present developed, and this balances their poorer performance in respect to energy density and efficiency. The power per unit weight with internal-combustion engines is about 0.5 hp per lb, whereas for the best hydrogen–air fuel cells it is about 0.1 hp per lb. The capital cost of an internal-combustion engine is said to be smaller than that of fuel cells, but this is because of the present mass production facilities available for the former transducer, and the absence of any for the fuel cell. In fact, the fuel cell is simpler in mechanism than the combustion engine, particularly if the latter is driving a generator; it has few parts, none moving, and seems likely to be producible more cheaply if the same numbers per plant are considered. Correspondingly, the electric motor which would transduce the fuel cell energy to mechanical power is a far more rugged mechanism than the combustion engine. On electric railway engines, a million miles between major overhauls is commonplace.

Continuation of the use of internal-combustion engines in a Hydrogen Economy depends less on technological factors, and more on the socioeconomic one of existing technology and the necessity of protecting capital. On the scientific side, the absence of a substitute for noble-metal electrocatalysts is important. Catalysts are desirable for the air electrode in fuel cells. Noble metals are unacceptable, not only because of price considerations, but owing to the lack of a sufficient supply. The lifetime problem still poses difficulties.

The principal disadvantage associated with internal-combustion engines, the fact that they are the primary sources of air pollution, is removed by the use of hydrogen. (Though NO remains a pollutant, it is produced in smaller quantities from hydrogen combustion compared with those of the gasoline-driven engines.) Noise pollution, however, would remain and also the vibratory properties of internal-combustion engines, leading to a more rapid erosion-corrosion factor among vehicles driven by them as opposed to the vibration-free functioning of electrically powered vehicles, the latter resulting in useful lives of 20 to 30 years (another powerful disadvantage from a corporate standpoint).

The balances which will determine the optimal mode of transduction depend upon the application, with the following factors:

1. What is the importance of high power-density (chemical engines best) versus high energy-density (electrochemical engines best)?
2. Is fuel cheap enough so that high efficiency of conversion (electrochemical best) is not important?
3. For the application in question, is the need for electricity (many metallurgical applications) or mechanical power (transportation)?
4. To what degree are economic factors (electrochemical best) important? Thus, for space flight, capital costs are of minor importance, although the weight of fuel is of supreme importance.

Some minor factors, for example, novelty, availability of experience among engineers for chemical engines, and their lack of availability for electrochemical ones, will be factors which will diminish in importance with time, but lack of electrochemical engineers will be of decisive importance until sufficient engineers with *practical* electrochemical background are available.

Other chemical engines

Several heat engines exist, apart from the internal-combustion engine, in particular: modifications of reciprocating engines, such as the rotary engine; the Sterling engine, in which an external combustion heats a gaseous working substance; the jet; and the rocket motor.

Rotary engines such as the Wankel have a higher power-density than have piston engines. The diesel and Sterling engines are less bad polluters than petrol internal-combustion engines, and hence provide a lesser advantage upon conversion to hydrogen fuel. The jet engine works well on hydrogen. It does not have a competitor in respect to aircraft in electrochemical engines, because here the power-to-weight ratio is of dominating importance and is much higher (20 kW kg^{-1}) in a jet engine than in an electrochemical engine (which does not at present have the prospect of > 1 kW per kg in power).

The Aphodid steam engine

The use of pure oxygen with hydrogen greatly improves the prospects for steam engines. The Carnot efficiency will be greater (perhaps over 50%) because of the lack of heat removal by nitrogen. One would use the steam onto turbine blades. The problem of the temperature which these could withstand whilst remaining economical would be the main one.

Another advantage would be the reduction in size. There is no boiler in this steam engine (Fig. 12.5). The reduction in size could be *c.* 100 times. Pollution would be only NO.

Rocket engines

Spacecraft fly on rocket engines fuelled by H_2 and O_2. Their application on the ground is, in prospect, particularly for electricity production. Liquid hydrogen is pumped to 1000 psi and brought into a thrust chamber, where its temperature is increased sharply. It is then brought into a turbine which produces the pressure both for the H_2 and the O_2 (i.e., the liquid hydrogen expansion provides the pump energy). The hydrogen–oxygen combustion provides the thrust which can generate the power.

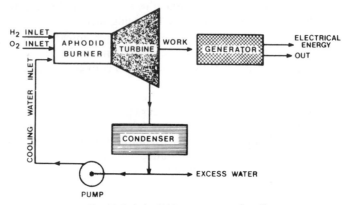

Fig. 12.5. Aphodid burner steam plant.[28]

Pollution would be only NO, and the efficiency would be far above class-ical air-operated engines.

The functioning of an electrochemical energy converter

Although 'fuel cells' have become a newspaper topic, there are many engineers who do not appreciate the mode of operation of an electrochemical converter, so that some statements will be made here with the aim of chang-ing that situation. A full account of the theoretical basis of the converters will be found in Bockris and Srinivasen,[26] and an elementary account in Bockris and Nagy.[29]

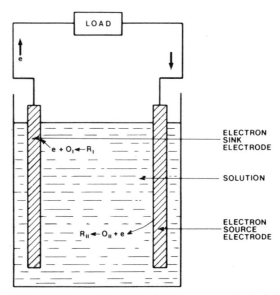

Fig. 12.6. Schematic of an electrochemical converter: chemical fuels produce electricity and a new product.[29]

A very simple diagram which illustrates the basic steps in the work of an electrochemical converter is shown in Fig. 12.6.[30] The overall reaction (say, the combination of hydrogen and oxygen to form water) must go spon- taneously at the temperature and pressure concerned. Hydrogen is brought into contact with one electrode, and oxygen (it may be air) in contact with the other. There are numerous ways of doing this, they will not concern us at present. The hydrogen—in general 'the fuel'—will undergo some preliminary reactions on the electrode, e.g. hydrogen molecules will dis- sociate and give rise to adsorbed hydrogen atoms, after which there will be ionisation on the surface (the electrochemical step) and the electrons therefrom will contribute themselves to the circuit, flow through the load (e.g. an electric motor) and end up at a lower potential, in the oxygen electrode, where they will donate themselves to oxygen in the solution. This is a simple description of an electrochemical converter. In the case of hydrogen and oxygen, the electrode reactions are:

$$2H_2 \rightarrow 4H^+ + 4e \tag{1}$$

and

$$O_2 + 4H^+ + 4e \rightarrow 2H_2O \tag{2}$$

Water is thereby formed in the overall reaction and, with appropriate tem- perature control, this evaporates, condenses, and may be used as potable water.

Many other fuel cells may be envisaged, e.g. natural gas may be a fuel, with oxygen at the counter-electrode. If the hydrocarbon is cracked beforehand, the reactions at the electrodes will be as above.

Pollution and electrochemical conversion

Electrochemical converters can work at relatively low temperatures. There is no heat pollution. In a fuel cell which oxidises hydrocarbons, CO_2 and H_2O are the only products, there are no unsaturated hydrocarbons to cause pollu- tion, and no NO.

Thus, the fuel cell represents a completely ecologically acceptable energy source and can be considered, when run on hydrogen fuel, as zero polluting. In contrast with the hydrogen combustion engine, no NO is produced.

Heat generation in fuel cells: qualitative

In a chemical converter, the essential way in which energy is produced is that the chemical reaction gives rise to products which have a lesser potential energy than the reactants. The maximum amount of energy which may be obtained ideally (neglecting the practical Carnot factor) from a chemical reaction is the free energy.

In an ideal electrochemical converter the major part of the heat, which would be produced in a chemical converter, is eliminated. There is no collision between reactants to give heat as the difference between the poten- tial energy of the product and reactants. The corresponding energy (diminished by the entropy loss) appears directly as electricity.

Thus, one could refer to electrochemical conversion as 'cold combustion'.[31] The heating or cooling which may accompany the action of an electrochemical converter is connected, on the thermodynamic side, with the $T\Delta S$ heat of the reaction; and with the existence of certain kinetic hold-ups, see below. The unavoidable $T\Delta S$ component usually amounts to less than 10% of the ΔH component in a reaction, so that there is very little heat given out in fuel-cell action from the thermodynamic aspects of its activity.

That there is, in practice, some heat produced in fuel cells—so that, in the 'total energy concept', they may also be used as heat sources—is because kinetic inefficiencies (associated with the electrochemical concept of overpotential, and the ohmic loss in the solution) enter into the total practical heat production of the cell.[32]

The Electrochemical Engine

This term, first used by Henderson,[33] is that given to the fuel cell-electric motor combination.

In the electrochemical engine, the stress would be upon power per unit weight, rather than efficiency per unit weight. At present, the electrochemical converter can do as well as a diesel heat engine, and the lower power per unit weight which it represents compared with other heat engines is compensated by its freedom from pollution, and greater energy efficiency.

Advantages and Disadvantages of Electochemical Transduction

1. No moving parts, and hence potentially a longer life than that of combustion engines. The actual life of fuel cell electrodes at the present time is short. The cause is partly due to poisoning of the electrode and the resultant decrease of catalytic properties on its surface. Another, more important, cause is recrystallisation. Overcoming the former difficulty can be expected, but the reduction of recrystallisation rates by an order of magnitude may be more difficult.
2. High efficiency.
3. No noise pollution.
4. Electrochemical transducers can be made in any size and modules assembled to give any power. There is only a small scale-up factor. Internal-combustion engines are not satisfactory at < 1 hp and cannot be scaled up by module addition.
5. Chemical engines need starting by electrochemical sources, and waste fuel on idling. Electrochemical engines switch on and off without the need of auxiliary power sources; they have no warm-up period and do not need to idle.

The negative aspects of an electromechanical transducer centres on its lower power-density (and, at present, its shorter lifetime). It will not be easy to obtain electrochemical transducers with power densities greater than 1 kW per kg, because the factor is limited by diffusion *in solution*, which must be less in velocity than diffusion in the gas phase. Even with excellent electrocatalysis, there will always be a greater diffusional barrier to high rates in a solution-phase reactor.

Secondly, negligible capital is as yet invested in fuel cell plants, so that they do not have this considerable influence encouraging their use: the capital is in the older, competing devices. That is a principal reason why conversion to the non-polluting electrochemical devices will be difficult.

Thirdly, the only period of continued and significant support fuel cells have had (with the exception of the strong effort of the United Technologies Company) is that between 1962 and 1968, when some $20 million per year of U.S. Government funds was spent on research and development in fuel cells in the U.S. From about 1969, this (space-oriented) programme was curtailed: government support of electrochemical energy conversion and storage was removed, just as chemical reactors as a main cause of air pollution came into public consciousness.

Fourthly, few engineers understand the mechanism of electrochemical engines, whereas all engineers understand chemical engines in principle, and hundreds of thousands of engineers and mechanics have real experience of them. What seems right to nearly all engineers are systems which contain pistons, produce heat and noise and have moving parts. Silent, motionless, electrochemical systems have a strangeness factor.

The last three difficulties are worth overcoming. The efficiency, potential life, and absence of noise and moving parts, give such great advantage to fuel cells that the transducer eventually used for hydrogen is likely to be the electrochemical one. Most of the non-space oriented researches in fuel cells in the American programmes carried out during the 1960s were attempts in laboratories of oil corporations to transduce hydrocarbons by means of fuel cells to electricity. However, hydrocarbon fuels give low rate constants, and, therefore, high overpotentials. Efficiencies were hence not much better than those of internal-combustion engines. With hydrogen as a fuel, the advantages of the electrochemical transducer is realisable, because hydrogen reacts rapidly at an anode, causes little overpotential and hence has a low efficiency loss.

Situations where electrochemical transducers would have the advantage, compared to chemical transducers, would depend upon the net indications among the following:

1. What is the relative importance to the applications of high energy-density (electrochemical engines best) compared with high power-density (chemical engines best)?
2. Is the cost of fuel sufficiently high so that a doubling of the efficiency of its conversion to useful energy would be sufficiently attractive to make it economically better to buy the new technology?
3. Is the application one in which *electricity* is needed (electrochemical conversion is direct) or *mechanical energy* (chemical conversion direct)?
4. Economic factors. These are more difficult to estimate, because electrochemical engines are not yet in mass production. The lifetime of the converters is the key point of the reality of this figure. The gain in efficiency, and absence of noise pollution and vibration, are to be laid against possible increases of initial cost.

Uses of electrochemical converters in the pre-hydrogen-economy time

Although the first uses of hydrogen as a fuel may well be in the internal-combustion engines, with fuel cells developing finally as the main transducers because of their higher efficiency, it is possible to see contemporary use of fuel cells, in special-purpose applications. There are some areas where their application has no rival, e.g. auxiliary power in lunar missions.

Another aspect of fuel cells which might seem right for immediate exploitation is in portable generating sets, where the lesser weight of the fuel cells for the unit of energy transported would be of great advantage.

A third example would be for power sources for isolated centres. Here, the main cost of the power is the cost of transportation of the fuel. Directly fuel becomes expensive, the fuel cell with its greater efficiency, becomes a more desirable transducer.

Indoor vehicles, too, would be an immediate application for fuel cells, for the reason of the lack of pollution, and they would then give a much longer range than the present used battery vehicles. In shunting-engines, where a great deal of idling wastes fuel if they are powered by diesel engines, fuel cells would show an advantage.

There are two immediate applications in naval affairs. Smaller submarines, where atomic power may be uneconomic, would be possible subjects for fuel cells. Absence of noise would decrease detectability. Deep submergence vessels at present use batteries, and would have a longer range on fuel cells.

In the Army, infra-red detection of tanks and other transport would be avoided by fuel cell power. Lastly, recreational applications in campsites, road carriers, scuba-diving, etc., would prove a fertile area for the development of fuel cells before they become of general use in a Hydrogen Economy.

Other devices needed during the use of hydrogen

Apart from the actual transduction of hydrogen to energy by chemical or electrochemical means, many new devices will be necessary. One of these will be the burners to use hydrogen. Thus, if hydrogen burns in oxygen, the reaction is a straightforward formation of water. If hydrogen combines with oxygen in air, 3.76 molecules of nitrogen are mixed with 2 molecules of water, 1 of oxygen and 2 of hydrogen. The nitrogen absorbs a portion of the combustion energy and this results in a lower flame temperature. Thus, in pure oxygen, the burning temperature is about $3080°K$, whilst for the burning in air it is about $2400°K$.

The formation of NO_x has to be taken into account. The lower combustion temperature in the presence of nitrogen will decrease the Carnot cycle efficiency.

Catalytic burners may be of interest. Hydrogen reacts with oxygen in air whilst in contact with the catalyst, and heat can be produced without flame.[34] Very thin catalytic layers, perhaps palladium, would be suspended on a ceramic substrate. The operating temperature is under $750°C$. No nitric oxide is formed. The burner is inherently safe for use in houses without flues. It could form the basis of a non-polluting space-heating system.

Flame burners will have to be different for hydrogen. There are at present two types of combusters, the catalytic type and the flame combuster, the latter being, of course, the usual type. Its satisfactory performance depends upon the stability of the flame and its lack of flash-back. If the fuel velocity is too high, the flame advances away from the burner and is extinguished. If it is too low, it enters the burner and tends to flash back.

Thus, hydrogen burners must be produced which allow for these conditions. The flow rate of hydrogen through the air must be about three times that for methane. A larger flame stability range must be allowed for. A thermal sink could be used to extinguish the flame.[35,36] Pilot ignition lights would be easy to arrange.

Natural gas burners will have to be replaced because their port size will be too big, their air mixing devices will be unsatisfactory, and because the flame temperature will be higher.

Metallurgy and hydrogen

Ferrous metallurgy[37]
There is interest in non-polluting iron production, i.e. ferrous metallurgy which avoids CO and CO_2 injection into the atmosphere. Reduction of Fe_2O_3 with H_2,

$$Fe_2O_3 + 3H_2 \rightarrow 2Fe + 3H_2O \tag{3}$$

is well known and there are various processes by which it can be carried out.[27] Among these is the H iron process, the Hygas process and the Purofer process. 1 kg of iron needs about 1 cubic foot of hydrogen for its reduction. The temperature of the fluidised bed in which the reduction is carried out ranges between 500 and 800°C. Water in significant quantities would be the condensable product.

The difficulty of changing from the normal reduction to hydrogen is that the capital in present blast plants could not be recovered once the swing to hydrogen reduction sets in.

The stimulus for change to a hydrogen reduction process for iron is the decrease in pollution, but this is not a factor from which an increase in profit can easily be made. It is important not to use the process:

$$Fe_2O_3 + CO \rightarrow 2Fe + CO_2 \tag{4}$$

Marchetti quotes 2,500 megawatts as the necessary energy to give 3.5 million tons per year of iron in sponge form from a hydrogen reduction plant.[27]

The achievement of widespread hydrogen reduction in ferrous metallurgy will affect the geography of the ferrous industry: it will avoid the necessity of having a plant at a point which takes account of the availability of both the ore and coke. Hydrogen will arrive in pipes from the distant nuclear or solar stations. Alternatively, a nuclear reactor may be associated with large steel production plants and produce hydrogen directly at the plant, by electrolysis. Cost savings should arise from the elimination of the costs of the transportation of coke.

Other metallurgical processes
The possibilities of a future hydrogen technology for iron production infer similar possibilities for other technologies which at present pollute the atmosphere. Copper, zinc, nickel and lead are metals where the technology of production could be achieved by a hydrogen reduction to give H_2S and then a reaction of this substance to give sulphur and water. (Other possibili-

ties, e.g. molten salt electrolysis, exist for the pollution-free production of these materials.)

Chemical technology[38]

Hydrogen is extensively used in chemical technology now, e.g. in the production of oil and fats (Table 12.I). The use for these is about 48%; 38% is used in fertilizer production and 14% in methanol production. An expansion in the use of hydrogen in chemical technology would follow a reduced price of hydrogen, in constant dollars, which can be expected either from research on new methods or as a result of reasonably declining energy costs or as a result of breeder or solar technology.

With the rising price of natural gas supplies, resulting from the approaching exhaustion of that resource, there will be an expansion of the need for hydrogen as the replacement. Organic chemical technology will face a future without oil or natural gas as base products. For some 50 years it may be possible to use organic chemicals from coal. After this, the production of organic chemicals will involve hydrogen because much of it must start with carbon dioxide (from carbonate rocks and the atmosphere) by the process of reduction:

$$CO_2 + H_2 \rightarrow HCHO \tag{5}$$

Alternatively, such reduction of carbon dioxide could be carried out using electrochemical reduction.[39,40]

The use of H_2 from electrolysis to produce CH_3OH at \$7-8 per MBTU (1978) has been proposed and analysed by Steinberg, Beller and Powell.[41]

TABLE 12.I: CONTINGENCY FORECASTS OF DEMAND FOR HYDROGEN BY END USE, YEAR 2000[38]
(billion standard cubic feet)

End use	Estimated demand 1968	U.S. forecast base 2000	Demand in year 2000			
			United States		Rest of world*	
			Low	High	Low	High
Anhydrous ammonia	872	3,060	2,460	4,490	7,200	12,700
Petroleum refining	775	4,580	2,340	32,640	6,000	36,000
Other uses†	413	1,450	1,450	24,660	2,000	25,000
TOTAL	2,060		6,250	61,790	15,200	73,700
Adjusted range			15,500 (Median	52,530 34,015)	24,950 (Median	63,950 44,450)

*Estimated 1968 hydrogen demand in the rest of the world was 2,995 billion cubic feet.
†Includes hydrogen used in chemicals and allied products, for hydrogasification of coal and oil shale, in iron ore reduction, and for miscellaneous purposes except plant fuel.

Other industrial applications

The largest single area of energy consumption (30% of the whole) is in the processing of materials: heating, mechanical drive; primary metal industry;

chemicals; petroleum refining; food, stone, clay and glass products; and paper and allied products. The 1970 distribution of energy to these suppliers is shown in Fig. 12.7.[42] Natural gas supplies about half of these energy needs and, thus, many products of industry will be directly affected by natural gas price rises.[42]

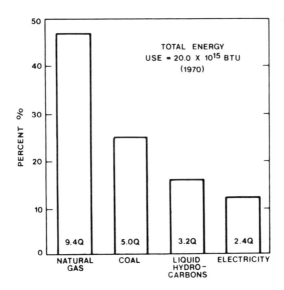

Fig. 12.7. Amounts used among fossil fuels and electricity. The latter was only 12% of the total in 1970.[28]

The growth pattern here is 3% per year and it is estimated that conservation efforts will reduce the demand by only 5 to 8%.

Hydrogen could be used in many of these processes, where natural gas is used at present. Hydrogen could be used in internal-combustion engines, so that it can be used for the working of these in industry. Gas-turbine power plants, at present fuelled by natural gas, could be fuelled by hydrogen without significant problems. The hydrogen could be used for blade cooling. Much depends upon the fuel cell: improvement in this would lead to a takeover of many of the tasks carried out in industry by natural gas and internal combustion.

Hydrogen for food production[43,44]

Hydrogen can be combined with carbon dioxide to produce formaldehyde and methanol, and combination with nitrogen in the presence of enzymes can produce proteins and other foods. From carbon dioxide, food production is possible.

In terms of animal food, this has been done. The synthesis of proteins and hydrocarbons is possible with an efficiency of 50%.

Schlegel in particular, has developed the concept of electrolysis and the production of hydrogen thereof, giving rise to food.[43] The basic reaction would be to use the aerobic hydrogen-utilising bacteria called 'Knallgasbacteria'. These are suited to the transformation of the energy of molecular hydrogen to organic material. The reactions can be summarised by:

$$6H_2 + 2O_2 + CO_2 \xrightarrow{enzyme} (CH_2O) + 5H_2O \qquad (6)$$

Up to now, only a few chemolithotrophic hydrogen-oxidising bacteria have been isolated from enrichment of cultures. The main direction of the research is seeking new strains of the Knallgasbacteria.

Schlegel and Lafferty have developed methods of production of 'Biomass' for the union of hydrogen with carbon dioxide and discuss the enrichment in growth, the basic metabolism and the way in which internal generation of a hydrogen-oxygen mixture can occur.[45]

It appears that a reasonable research expectation is the large-scale synthetic production of food from carbon dioxide and hydrogen. The former would be recovered from the atmosphere and the latter produced electrochemically from water.

Sewage and trash[44]

The Pittsburg Coal Research Centre of the Bureau of Mines has reported on the pyrolysis of trash in hydrogen to give methane and ethylene. These materials could be used as source materials for plastic manufacture. Glass and metals settle out of the reactor for further use.

Uses of oxygen on a massive scale[46]

A massive use of oxygen takes place now in the steel industry. In the following, a few newer ideas are suggested:

1. *Aerobic sewage treatment*

At present, sewage treatment involves air oxygen. However, emphasis is increasingly placed upon pure oxygen. This would enable a plant for sewage purification to be 3 to 4 times smaller than that at present, with gains in the cost of plants.

2. *The reversal of pollution*

A clean-up of many areas of the world is now necessary, for example, river areas such as the Rhine in Germany and the Hudson River in the U.S.

These waters decay because the biological organisms which give rise to normal ecological balance and lead to the destruction of pollutants have themselves decayed through lack of oxygen. This is because pollutant and organism compete for oxygen. If the pollutant wins, the organism dies.

The Union Carbide Corporation has developed a high-pressure oxygen treatment for lakes.[46] Lake water is passed through a pipe and oxygen is injected at high pressures therein. The oxygenated water is re-introduced into the lake and its oxidifying properties revivify the latter. With surplus cheap oxygen available in a Hydrogen Economy, such a process might become economic.

Injection of ozone breaks up detergent materials.

3. *Trash*[47,48]

If incinerators were fed with pure oxygen, instead of air, there would be a higher flame temperature, the plants would burn the trash more efficiently, CO would be eliminated, and smog rising from trash combustion reduced.

Metals would be produced in oxide form as a residue from the combustion of the trash, e.g. zinc, tin and aluminium could be recovered as oxides.

4. *Other uses*[49]

The widespread use of oxygen in industry in processes which now use air would reduce the size of plants, and thus reduce fixed costs. The elimination of NO as a pollutant from internal-combustion engines would occur if they were run on hydrogen-oxygen mixtures.

Much *speculative* thinking needs to be done in respect to the application of pure oxygen when better estimates of its price as a function of distance are available.

Transportation

Introduction

Transportation is beset with the difficulty of the *rising price* of fossil fuels, together with that of the atmospheric pollution, of which it is the largest cause. Air transportation suffers from the first two, but also from the need of a lighter fuel for future high-performance aircraft to increase their range, and hence commercial viability.

The use of hydrogen as a fuel for internal-combustion engines solves the difficulties of pollution and weight.* It seems likely that hydrogen from coal will be cheaper than gasoline long before a Hydrogen Economy could be implemented. The use of hydrogen in transportation may form its first large-scale application.

Relevant properties of hydrogen and other fuels

This is shown in Table 12.II.

TABLE 12.II: COMPARATIVE FUEL PROPERTIES[51]

Property	Hydrogen	Other Fuel
Heating value, Btu/lb	53,000	20,000 (gasoline)
Minimum ignition temperature, °F	1065	1000 (butane)
Theoretical flame temperature in air, °F	3887	3615 (butane)
Flammability limits, % by volume in air	4.0-74.2	1.9-8.6 (butane)
Maximum flame velocity ft/sec	9.3	1.03 (butane)
Specific volume liquid litres/kg	14.3	1.33 (gasoline)
Energy density: Btu per cu ft	2.50×10^5	9.38^5 (gasoline)

Hydrogen-based Transportation

The kWh/mile for various types of vehicles is shown in Fig. 12.8. The results show the energy requirements as a function of vehicle range and speed with zero grade road load.[53] With such data, Hietbrink *et al.* calculated the effect on the electric utilities of the introduction of a substantial degree of electrification of cars by 2000.[54] The basis of the results are the projected car registrations in the U.S.A., and estimates of future electric generation.[55] Other

---

*Eckland & Kestner make a clear comparison of the battery-driven and hydrogen-propelled car, coming out strongly in favour of the latter.[50]

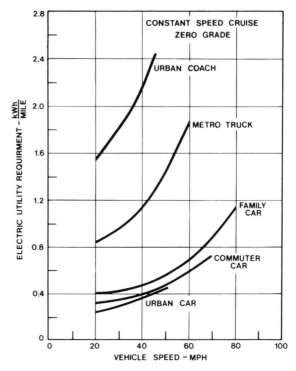

Fig. 12.8. Energy requirements for various kinds of vehicles, as a function of speed.[52]

assumptions which Hietbrink *et al.* made are that cars average 8,000 miles per year; 1 kWh/mile; the diurnal load pattern will be the same at 2000 as in 1972; and battery charging (correspondingly, hydrogen production) at night.

Fifty-two per cent of the generating capacity is in use all the time. It is reasonable to expect at least 20% of the total power load could be available for the production of hydrogen. *The complete automobile load could be obtained from low-use-period power at 2000.* (For 1969, 28.5% of the automotive load could have been supported.) This battery-oriented calculation is conservative and would apply with little change to a situation in which cars were hydrogen driven, the low-use-period electricity being used to generate hydrogen at, say, 75% efficiency. Schoeppel calculates that about half the total automotive fuel needs could have been obtained from hydrogen from night-time power in 1972.[56]

The hydrogen could be carried in cylinders, or liquefied. More space (3.75 times more) would be needed for the containment of liquid hydrogen than for the gasoline.

Four advantages would accrue from the introduction of hydrogen as a fuel for transportation.

1. It could be developed now, on the basis of low-use-period power and classical hydrogen generators. The cost at which hydrogen could be expected therefrom (~$7-8) would be substantially above the price of gasoline but

when the efficiency of use of hydrogen compared with that of gasoline is taken into account this difference is reduced. If the environmental cost of gasoline is accounted for, hydrogen is already cheaper. And it is clearly synthetic fuels from coal, rather than residual gasoline for oil, with which H_2 should be compared.

2. It would eliminate more than half of present air pollution.
3. Conversion could be carried out gradually, gas stations would carry both gasoline and hydrogen until the changeover was complete.
4. The energy sources would be at first coal, and later increasingly nuclear and solar. Continuity would be preserved.
5. If the development of coal as a temporary energy source is to be pressed more than nuclear or solar sources H_2 could come from coal at a price of ∿$4.50 per MBTU.

History of hydrogen-based transportation

The Rev. W. Cecil proposed the application of hydrogen to produce moving power in machinery to the Cambridge Philosophical Society of 1820.[57]

Ricardo noted that, if the hydrogen-air mixture was rich, there was violent ignition and backfiring.[58] A basic advance was made by Burstall of Cambridge University.[59] He pointed out that the chief difficulty was the rapidity with which hydrogen burns. *If a small ignition advance was used,* satisfactory burning could occur. Erren's is the most well-known name associated with the advance of the hydrogen engine.[60,61,62] He worked with dirigibles, and used hydrogen normally vented in flight to run their engines during descent. He used improved cylinder-wall hydrogen injection techniques, which reduced the possibility of backfiring. There was controversy between Erren and King. King stated that, if weak mixtures are used, it is not necessary to use the special injection technique suggested by Erren.[63,64] According to King, backfiring was due to the aggregation of carbon particles in the cylinder.[64] King thought it might be acceptable to use carburetted hydrogen engines, so long as they were frequently cleaned.[64] Fig. 12.9 shows that the backfire regions depend upon the equivalence ratio. A lean mixture is satisfactory, the displacement must be more than about two-thirds.[65,66,67]

These works of the 1930s were the basis of the hydrogen engine and the work has come alive again with the contributions of Schoeppel and Murray.[68] They started where Erren had stopped. They have found that high-pressure injection of hydrogen near the top centre of the cylinder causes ignition to occur immediately, injection being continued during a portion of the power stroke. The injection technique used by Schoeppel and co-workers gets away from the carbon nucleation problem observed by King. Ignition is caused to occur as soon as enough hydrogen is in the cylinder to support combustion. This is at the beginning of injection.

An attempt was made by the Perris Smogless Automobile Association to build a vehicle in which hydrogen and oxygen were both used.[69] However, the oxygen dewars are too weighty. Billings and Lynch used metal hydrides for storage in vehicle propulsion by hydrogen in the 1970s.[65]

Swain and Adt developed, at the University of Miami, a method of port injection which utilises the manifold side of the intake valve heads to face the injectors.[70] Their work resulted in a 1970 Toyota running 22 miles on one

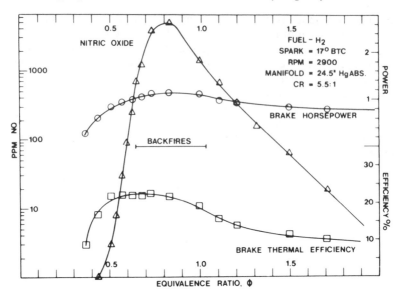

Fig. 12.9. Backfire and equivalence ratio.[65]

pound of hydrogen (equivalent to 51 mpg of gasoline).

Storage options are shown in Fig. 12.10.

Hydrogen engines may certainly be run with carburettors, but the carburettor design does have to be different from that for internal gas or gasoline, because the volumetric mixture ratio is unsuitable for use with hydrogen. The re-design needs a change in the area ratio of the gas and air passages. Apart from the ignition systems, other changes in engines are zero. Thus, it was demonstrated in 1948 that a carburettor engine free from carbon deposits will run on hydrogen with a compression ratio of 10:1.

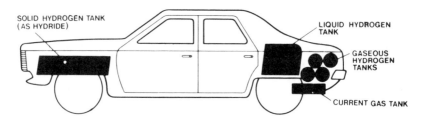

Fig. 12.10. Storage options for H_2 car.[56]

The remaining problems with hydrogen automobiles are with the handling and distribution system. The development of hardware to store and utilise hydrogen has still to be done, as well as the overcoming of public resistance to the use of hydrogen, because of lack of understanding that the passage and transport of hydrogen on highway and rail has long been a common practice.

The present hydrogen engine for cars

The Oklahoma State University engine uses direct cylinder gaseous hydrogen injection.[71] The engine is a modified 4-stroke cycle, air cooled, single cylinder, 3.5 hp engine. Air alone is compressed, which limits hydrogen infiltration past the piston rings and prevents pre-ignition. Use of air as the working fluid eliminates the possibility of an accumulation of an explosive mixture in the intake manifold or crankcase. When further co-ordinated with an injection means, as used in the design by Murray and Schoeppel, combustion commences at once. It continues smoothly without detonation, excessive pressure or temperature.

The brake horse power-torque and brake specific fuel consumption for wide-open throttle conditions are shown in Fig. 12.11. The engine requires about one-third the fuel mass flow rate of its fossil fuel counterpart.

Difficulties recently met have concerned heat transfer characteristics and cast-iron cylinders in the neighbourhood of the exhaust valve.[61,63,71] Localised hot spots in this area tend to produce cylinder distortion.[64] A cooling system is necessary. These difficulties have been overcome.

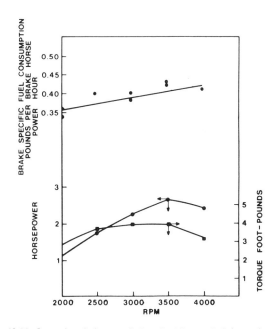

Fig. 12.11. Operational characteristics of a Murray & Schoepel engine.[71]

Safety

A number of safety devices will be required for hydrogen-driven cars to avoid obvious hazards. Most vehicles are left to stand for several days from time to time and (if the fuel is to be liquid) a safe venting system will have to be devised. The buoyancy of hydrogen is great and the diffusion rapid. It will be safe simply to vent it slowly into the air, so long as the space is not enclosed. Venting into enclosed spaces with ceiling ventilation will need testing. Other methods of dealing with the hydrogen which has to be vented during storage would be by various means of combustion to water, e.g. catalytic or electrochemical. The catalytic ignition will require some research, for instance into catalysts which are cheaper than platinum, but have the same effect.[72]

Leaks will have to be guarded against by regular checks: colouring or addition of an odorant have been suggested.

One difficulty is the heavy collision. The major consideration would be to locate the tank within the car in such a position as to minimise its involvement.[73] Fire resulting from piercing of the tank is possible, as with gasoline. *Explosion*, however, could not be expected, except in an enclosed space.

Characteristics of present hydrogen engines

An internal-combustion engine with fuel injection develops a higher output with hydrogen than is possible with gasoline. Carburetted engines produce about half the power. Its emission characteristics are in Fig. 12.12. They average 2.0 g of NOX per brake-hp per hr, 10% of that from gasoline. Ignition can be achieved using compression, glow or spark. Hydrogen engines are easy to start, respond rapidly to different rates of fuel injection and run cooler than their gasoline equivalent.[75]

Hydrogen engines could easily meet the 1978 Federal controls.

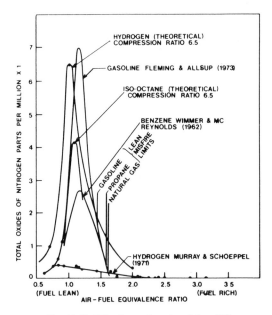

Fig. 12.12. NO$_X$ for various conditions.[51,74]

The development of a liquid-hydrogen car

FURUHAMA, HIRUMA AND ENOMOTO'S CAR[76]

Furuhama, Hiruma and Enomoto have shown how their Datsun B210 passenger car can be converted to liquid hydrogen. The car ran 400 miles for its test in a 1975 rally in the United States.

The authors note that the volume efficiency of the use of hydrogen is increased by using cold-hydrogen. NO control becomes better in this way.

The engine modifications which had to be made included the following:

1. To allow the introduction of cold-hydrogen gas: Hydrogen was conducted from the storage tank through a vacuum-insulated tube to the engine. It entered at $-130°$.
2. Fuel injection into the intake port: The mechanical fuel-injection method gave an intermittent injection of fuel to prevent backfire. The hydrogen was injected into the intake port of each cylinder at 4-5 kg cm^{-2} sec^{-1}.
3. Control of mixture ratio. The modified engine was tested by using cold-hydrogen fuel. Figure 12.13 shows the emissions of NO as a function of the excess air ratio. Thus, the air throttle valve was kept in the full-open position in the high-load position.

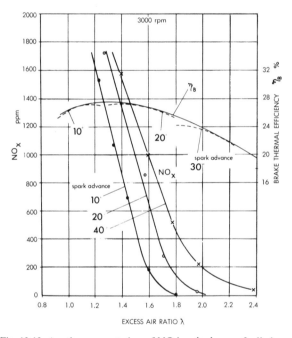

Fig. 12.13. Another presentation of NO in a hydrogen-fuelled car.[76]

4. Spark plug and timing. A special spark plug was used because its heat value was high enough to prevent backfire. Though the optimum spark time depended on the air ratio, it was controlled by the excess air ratio only as a factor.

FUEL TANK DESIGN FOR LIQUID HYDROGEN IN CARS

For the 650 kilometre range necessary, it was assumed in the Furuhama *et al.* work that the consumption would be 3.08 km/litre of LH$_2$. On this basis, and to allow for some reserve, a tank of 230 litres, or 15 kg, of liquid hydrogen was used.

In addition to this, a reserve volume for hydrogen gas was necessary to allow response in acceleration. The safety features were looked after by constructing the tank so that it could withstand the shock of 10 g. The inner shell of Furuhama *et al's* tank was of 800 mm diameter, 2.5 mm thickness, and 3 mm spherical end plates. It was about 600 mm in height, made of stainless steel, and had an internal volume of 230 litres. The weight of the tank was 120 kg. Blow-off was about 2.5% per day.

Difficulty was experienced with the level meter, measuring the pressure in the service tube.

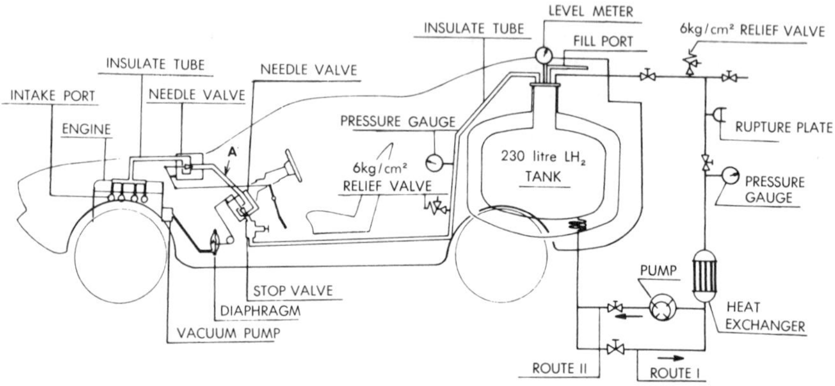

Fig. 12.14. General arrangement of the liquid-hydrogen-driven car of Furuhama *et al.*[76]

The general arrangement is shown in Fig. 12.14.

Some backfire was experienced later on in the rally and this was diagnosed as due to break-down of the mixture control due to wear.

The car was subject to emission testing and was excellent in respect to hydrocarbons and CO. However, the NO increased up to 4.1 grams per mile because of the poor condition of the engine in backfire.

THE FUTURE OF LIQUID HYDROGEN ENGINES

So long as the price of liquid hydrogen can be brought down to somewhere in the region of $10 per MBTU, liquid hydrogen has a bright future. Thus, the Furuhama *et al.* car drove with satisfying performance and acceleration. Fuel economy was superior to that of other cars on the basis of energy, although NO was too much, and this could easily be improved. LH_2 at about $7.50 per MBTU should be possible from coal.

The most important changes which should be made are the control of the backfire and to provide the tank and charging device with a more practical blow-off system.

The crash-testing of a liquid hydrogen vehicle

The present description, due to Weingold and van Vorst, concerns a small truck which was loaned to the hydrogen car project of the University College of Los Angeles by the U.S. Postal Service. The truck is shown in Fig. 12.15 and the liquid hydrogen fuel system for it is shown in Fig. 12.16.

Fig. 12.15. The vehicle used in the crash experiments.[77]

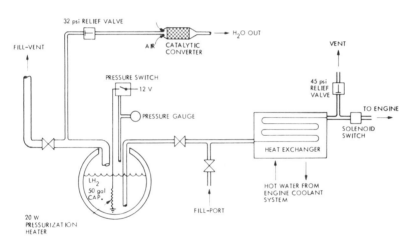

Fig. 12.16. Liquid hydrogen system for the car used by Weingold and van Vorst.[77]

The dewars weighed 94 lb when empty and 124 lb when filled with 50 gallons of liquid hydrogen. The boil-off was 0.8% per day. A relief valve set at 32 psi prevented over-pressurisation in the dewars. Refuelling was accomplished by coupling a liquid hydrogen transfer line to the fill-port using a ½-inch Linde bayonet fitting. A capacitance liquid level gauge was used to provide a continuous level indication. The capacitor was constructed from stainless steel tubing. The inner tube served as the liquid withdrawal tube.

The standard American Motors 6-cylinder engine was used *without internal modifications*. Emission control systems were rendered inoperative. The spark plugs were re-gapped at 0.012″ and the distributor advance mechanism modified to yield a spark advance appropriate for use with hydrogen.

For normal driving the throttle was left closed on the secondary system and power was controlled by regulating the throttle position of the primary hydrogen mixture. The equivalence ratio was set at approximately 0.45 to yield maximum break thermal efficiency and low NO. When more power is demanded it can be provided by the primary mixture at wide-open throttle.

Water induction was used to prevent backfires by lowering the combustion temperature and raising the ignition energy requirements for the inducted mixture. This lowers the emission of NO.

THE CRASH ITSELF

The mail truck reported on by Weingold and van Vorst was loaded onto a tandem Maxwell trailer.[77] The accident caused the mail truck, which had been mounted previously on a trailer, to turn on its side when the trailer was doing about 30 km/h. The truck finally slid to a stop, but turned upside down.

There was no injury to anyone and the liquid hydrogen fuel system remained intact. The mail truck was righted and driven away from the scene of the accident.

CONCLUSIONS FROM THE CRASH STUDIED

Some small modifications are perhaps desirable. The conclusions are, in general, rather positive. A larger vent-line and relief valve could be used for an extra margin of safety.

A mercury switch to detect rapid deceleration should be installed in series with the ground cable for the battery. This could be shut off when a crash had taken place, or if the vehicle rolled over (the mercury switch would detect a change in height). Hydrogen flow would then be shut off.

Thus, the crash of a liquid hydrogen-fuel vehicle is not more dangerous than would be the crash of a gasoline-fuel vehicle.

The use of automotive hydride tanks for hydrogen-driven cars[78]

The type of vehicle used is shown in Fig. 12.17. The hydride was contained in tubes of hydride shown in Fig. 12.18. The design shown in the figure has a number of advantages.

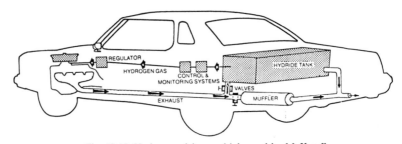

Fig. 12.17. Hydrogen-driven vehicle used by McKay.[72]

On the one hand it is simple with a few welds; it is compact, flexible and economical. There is a large external area of active hydride so that the time for taking up equilibrium of the hydrides is small.

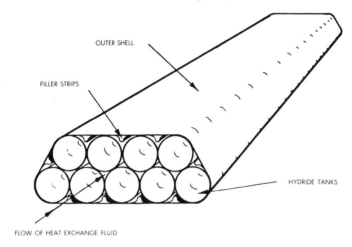

OUTER SHELL

FILLER STRIPS

HYDRIDE TANKS

FLOW OF HEAT EXCHANGE FLUID

Fig. 12.18. Tubes of hydride from McKay's car.[78]

The main point about the design of automotive hydride tanks is that they are both pressure vessels and heat exchangers. Until the work of McKay, there was little data concerning hydride heat-transfer properties. Heat exchange data and results obtained from theoretical investigations gave rise to the tubular design shown.

Heat transfer and hydride materials provide problems because of the granular nature of the hydrides. The absorption of large amounts of heat at the grain boundaries by grains located in the active zone is a factor. The inactivity of the material outside the reacting zone must also be taken into account. A tube bundle with hydride on the inside appears to be the logical configuration to satisfy these requirements. It is a matter of obtaining the optimal configuration.

The Billings' Bus[79]

The first hydrogen-engine bus programme uses a 21-passenger Winnebago mini-bus. The vehicle is shown in Fig. 12.19.[80]

The original bus engine was a Dodge 7-litre engine and was converted to hydrogen operation by removing the gasoline carburettor and replacing it with a gaseous fuel carburetion device. A water-injection system was also installed to control NO_x formation. To improve efficiency and power of the engine, the cylinder heads were milled down 1 mm.

The hydrogen storage capacity for the vehicle was obtained using two iron-titanium metal hydride vessels. These are shown in Fig. 12.19.[80] The iron-titanium hydride powder is located inside the cylinder and the hot exhaust gases pass through a manifold which surrounds the tank. The internal pressure of the containers is controlled and, when the hydrogen drops below a preset minimum, exhaust gases are directed through the metal hydride storage system to heat it and expel hydrogen. When the pressure reaches an upper limit, the exhaust gases are redirected through the muffler by-pass.

The bus has been operated up to 95 kilometres per hour, but this speed could not be maintained. At lower power-outputs, the engine runs well.

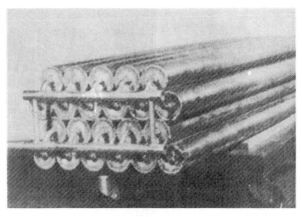

Fig. 12.19. (a) One of Billings' hydrogen-powered buses; (b) Fe-Ti storage for bus.[79]

In Fig. 12.20 (Billings) an important comparison is made in which coal is utilised imaginarily to generate hydrogen, gasoline, methanol and electricity. The production via hydrogen produces a larger vehicle range than any other possibility. This is due to the very high efficiency of the use of the hydrogen in the internal-combustion engine.

ECONOMIC CONSIDERATIONS OF THE USE OF HYDROGEN COMPARED WITH OTHER FUELS

Figure 12.21 (which uses 1974 dollars) shows that *hydrogen will be a cheaper fuel than gasoline* when both are produced from coal.

SAFETY ASPECTS IN BUSES

The bus contains a pressure switch located on the intake manifold of the engine, and this senses proper engine operation and opens a lock-off solenoid which stops hydrogen leaking out in an accident if a fuel line is damaged.

If an iron-titanium storage container were fractured, and a source of spark were present, hydrogen would burn. However, as the hydrogen is discharged the hydride material is cooled, and the amount of hydrogen dissociating

FUEL PRICE FORECAST
(COST / 10⁹ JOULES, 1974 U.S. DOLLARS)

	1974	1980	1985	1990
GASOLINE	$2.93	$3.32	$3.43	$3.43
HYDROGEN	$1.37	$2.32	$2.53	$2.53
(WITH EFFICIENCY CORRECTION)	($.90)	($1.53)	($1.69)	($1.69)

Fig. 12.20. Hydrogen and gasoline as vehicular fuels: the efficiency of the use of hydrogen is greater than that of gasoline.[81]

ANNUAL OPERATIONAL EXPENSES
(100 BUS FLEET, 480 km/DAY, 1974 U.S. DOLLARS)

	FUEL COST	ANNUAL SAVINGS	
GASOLINE	$580,000	INCREMENTAL FUEL COST	$410,000
HYDROGEN	$170,000	CREDIT FOR ENGINE OVERHAUL	5,000
DIFFERENCE	$410,000	ANNUAL SAVINGS	$405,000
		INITIAL CONVERSION COST	$400,000

Fig. 12.21. Hydrogen is already now a cheaper fuel for automotive transportation than gasoline or electricity.[79]

would then become smaller. Thus, metal hydride storage designs are safer than other types of storage of fuel, and much safer in respect to fire on collision than a conventional gasoline-fired system.

There is a significant potential for mass transport running on hydrogen from coal. This would decrease the pollutional difficulties of utilising coal if the hydrogen production facility could be associated with CO_2 and sulphur treatment.

The proposed use of hydrogen fuel in railroads

The concept of the use of hydrogen in railroads has been developed by H. L. Gier.[82]

Thus, Gier points out that it is desirable to have a large-scale test of hydrogen which will not dislocate present industry. The railways would provide one of the most convenient first applications of a Hydrogen Economy. Thus, several U.S. railroads already service liquid-hydrogen production plants so that they could utilise the hydrogen from them. Their safety record is excellent. There is a geographical independence of the railroads so that they could convert themselves individually to hydrogen. Little change will be needed in the whole railway system—only a small modification of the diesel motors on diesel-electric locomotives.

The total quantity of liquid hydrogen necessary to run all U.S. railroads would be 12,000 tons per day. This would be created by 50 atomic reactors at 1000 megawatt size, or the appropriate coal plants. The capital investment needed for conversion of the railways to hydrogen would be 30 billion dollars and would be supplied over 10 years. A liquid hydrogen system could thus be begun—and could be developed for other purposes.

Efficiency of burning hydrogen in internal-combustion engines and its effect upon relative cost considerations

The efficiency of burning with hydrogen is shown from Fig. 12.22 which indicates that typically the hydrogen engine burns at about 50% higher efficiency than that of the gasoline engine for the equivalence ratios in which we are interested.[81] Something else important happens, however, and that is that the only situation in which the gasoline engine burns efficiently is the equivalence ratio of about 0.9:1 (thus encouraging NO production) whereas the hydrogen engine burns efficiently at equivalence ratio of less than 0.6 (i.e. less NO production).

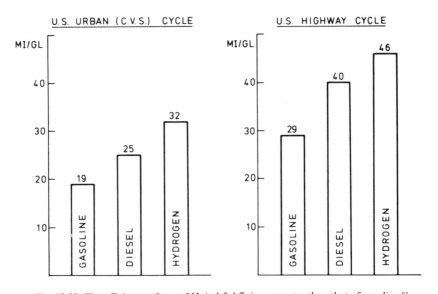

Fig. 12.22. The efficiency of use of H_2 is 1.5-1.7 times greater than that of gasoline.[83]

Thus, hydrogen can burn more efficiently and less pollutantly than the gasoline engine. These two facts have to be taken into consideration in weighing any extra *apparent* 1st Law cost of H_2 per MBTU compared with that of CH_4.

It is interesting to recall a price of around $4.50 (1976 dollars) per MBTU for H_2 from coal, estimated in an earlier chapter. The present information, then, indicates that the simplistic cost of H_2 from coal, or CH_4 from coal (little difference) is incorrect. Hydrogen would be, *per unit of distance driven*, 1.5 times cheaper, i.e. *equivalent* to about $3 per MBTU.

The recent work of Watson and Milkins clarifies these issues immensely.[75] They show that the relative efficiency of the use of hydrogen to gasoline can conservatively be taken as 1.5 for low and medium torque (Fig. 12.22). The

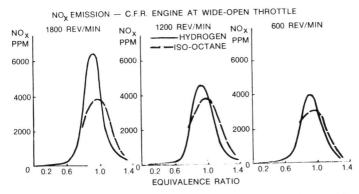

Fig. 12.23. The NO_x with hydrogen fuel as a function of engine speed.[83]

NOX emission for hydrogen is between 3 and 20 times less than with gasoline (Figs. 12.23 and 12.12).

Cost benefits from the lessened pollutional aspects of the use of hydrogen in transportation

AN INVALID COST COMPARISON

When we make a comparison of the cost of hydrogen compared with the cost of fossil fuels we usually work out the cost of producing 1 MBTU hydrogen, and the cost of producing 1 MBTU of fossil fuel, for example, natural gas or oil from coal. It has already been seen that the efficiency of mechanical energy is greater than that of the conversion of H_2 to conversion of methane and thus the price of one unit of energy of the two gases is an invalid one.

Another reason why such a comparison is invalid is because these fuels have damaging aspects in atmospheric pollution which cause emphysema and other health costs. This addition to the atmosphere of poisons, causing illness and death, apart from the resulting dirt and smog, are not counted in the cost. Every time a person buys a tank of gasoline, he is paying three extra amounts which he does not see. The first is the cost of the tax money used to support the Environmental Protection Agency and government anti-pollution measures. The second is the payment for any of his own illnesses, or those of his family, caused by the presence of atmospheric pollutants, including ageing effects produced by smog; and the last is in his share of all the other illness and death originating in fossil fuel effluents.

None of this would have to be paid if hydrogen were the fuel, and this aspect of the cost must be taken into account in comparing the cost of coal-origined fuel. Thus, the amount of money spent in the United States for health care is $547 per person per year. Zweig has invented the word 'smog-itis' to describe the diseases caused by polluting the air with fossil fuels.[84]

POLLUTION CAUSED BY FOSSIL FUELS

The primary pollutants are carbon monoxide, hydrocarbons and NO, together with the particulates formed from fossil-fuel combustion.

Sulphur-containing fuels when combusted produce oxides of sulphur, aerosols and, if a Pt catalyst is present to remove other pollutants, sulphuric acid.

The lead additives in gasoline produce microscopic particulate granules of lead found in 'smoke components'.

There are secondary pollutants, the photochemical oxidants, formed by chemical reactions of several of the primary pollutants (NO, HC, SO_2) in the presence of the ultra-violet light of sunlight.

The resultant oxidants consist of ozone, NO_2, and peroxyaclnitrate (PAN) which are toxic to human tissues.

Severe effects may be noted when these pollutants combine. In 1952, London suffered a 4,000 persons death from 100 hours of heavy smog.

HEALTH EFFECTS OF POLLUTANTS[84]

The physiology of these pollutants is interesting. The carbon monoxide reacts with haemoglobin in the blood to form carboxyhaemoglobin which reduces the oxygen-carrying possibilities of the blood. Hardening of the arteries continues from chronic exposure. Brain effects cause a stroke and myocardial infarction may occur as a result of a stroke in the brain.

Increased amounts of carboxyhaemoglobin will also cause inefficiency in the central nervous system which results in poor co-ordination.

The particulates which arise from the incomplete combustion of hydrocarbons cause respiratory troubles in the nose, sinus, throat and lungs. There is a decrease of the oxygen exchange as these particulates begin to coat the lining of the body. They may cause cancer.

The sulphur contaminants cause irritation of the respiratory epithelium and spasm of the small airways in the body. This was the largest cause of the 4,000 deaths in London in 1952. The SO_2 produced from each coal-fired electric generating plant producing 1000 megawatts will cause 100 deaths per year.

Lead, when inhaled as a particulate, gets absorbed through the epithelium and terminates in the red blood cells and in the bone marrow. Concentrations high enough cause difficulties of bone growth in children and a decrease in the function of the nervous tissues. Lead is difficult to remove and the excretion time may last several years.

Photochemical oxidants such as smog result in an increase in the ageing process. Patients with asthma, bronchitis and emphysema show increased symptoms of their disease when the smog level exceeds 0.2 parts per million.

The cost of the pollutional damage due to the use of fossil fuels

Detailed estimates have been discussed by Zweig.[84] Some questions are difficult to estimate, for example, the money equivalent for a human life has been estimated anywhere between $1,000 and $1,000,000. However, the Environmental Pollution Agency has suggested that the direct cost of air pollution was about 12 billion dollars in 1970. Assuming the cost has now risen to approximately 24 billion (1978 dollars), one can estimate the pollutional cost of the combustion of fossil fuels, in order of magnitude terms, by taking the energy output in the United States of 10 kilowatts per person and a population of the order of 250 million. Supposing that the cost per MBTU for the fuel averages $2.50, we obtain a cost of:

$$\frac{10.8760.250.10^6\ 2.50}{289}$$

This gives about 1.8×10^{11} dollars for the cost of fuels per year; with 2.410^{10} dollars for the cost of air pollution, the pollutional cost appears to be equivalent to about 13%.

This 13% estimate as the cost of fossil fuel pollution paid tacitly by the public is, however, not yet a rational estimate because it does not take into account the cost of the deaths caused. An estimate of a component of this is at the rate of 100 deaths per thousand megawatt coal-based electricity plant.

Let us take the fraction of the U.S. energy supply to be given in the form of electricity as 25% and assume this is all coal-powered.

With 10 kW per person and 250.10^6 people, the equivalent electrical kW are:

$$\frac{250.10^6\ .10}{4} = 6.3\ 10^8\ \text{kW}$$
$$= 6.3\ 10^5\ \text{MW}$$
$$= 6.3\ 10^2\ 1000\ \text{MW Plants}$$
$$= 63{,}000\ \text{deaths per year*}$$

The 75% of the energy supplied from oil, natural gas and uranium will cause different degrees of death per 1000 MW. It has been shown above that the degree arising from fission plants is likely to be greater than that from coal plants, per unit of energy produced. That from the use of natural gas is likely to be very small; and that from oil somewhat undetermined, but less than that from coal. In view of the fact that the future of the fossil fuels, in any worthwhile comparison with hydrogen, is bound to be from coal, it seems a reasonable first approximation to take the death rate for the whole energy supply (oil, natural gas, coal and uranium) as that for coal-electricity plants. In that case, the number of deaths totals 4 x 63,000 $\simeq$ 252,000 per year.

To reduce death to dollars must always be somewhat arbitrary. It is bound to neglect the cost of suffering. The life terminated at a normal age by emphysema should not be counted as a cost on the community. The life terminated near birth by leukaemia arising from air-borne radio-active pollutant should be counted fully. Statistics concerning the age-distribution of such deaths may always be difficult to get because of the lack of definiteness about the origin of death. At present it seems best to make a first approximation by assuming all deaths occur half-way through the earning span. The commercial value of a life is clearly a subject for discussion: it is more than the total earning capacity (educational and other tax-origined expenditure).

It is impractical to attempt a finer definition than to assume a certain earning life (40 years); and a certain untaxed income per year ($10,000). On this basis, each life is equivalent to $400,000; and with the arbitrary assumption of a pollution death cutting the earning in half, the income lost is $200,000. With 252,000 deaths per year, the sum is, thus, $5 10^{10}. It has been shown above that $2 10^{10} is the direct cost so that $7 10^{10} per year is a first approx-

---

*The automobile-caused deaths in the U.S. are about 100,000 per year.

imation estimate for the environmental cost of a coal-based economy in 1978.

Of course, this is an uncertain estimate, containing arbitrary assumptions. A better analysis may be possible even with available data. There would still have to be arbitrary assumptions. Some of these tend to make the present estimate too low. Thus, nothing has been allowed for difficulties arising from fossil-fuel illness not resulting in death;* for the dirt, and aggravation of smog; for the ageing effects of smog; and for the as yet negligible but potentially gargantuan costs from a change of weather patterns due to the growing CO_2 concentration, which, by, say, 2050, seem likely to hold a potential for damage greater than any other fuel-related cost.

Thus, with the figure of $7 10^{10}, the cost is likely to be about a third of the cost of the fossil fuel. In view of the intangible costs neglected, it seems reasonable to suggest 25%-50% as a reasonable range for the cost unpaid (i.e. the citizens' subsidy) when a unit of coal-based fossil fuel is purchased.

A realistic cost comparison of hydrogen as a fuel in transportation

The fuels with which hydrogen should be compared would be synthetic natural gas and a gasoline from coal.

The usual comparison made is one in which the cost of producing a certain unit of energy of the fuel concerned is made. Thereby, however, one neglects the efficiency of conversion; and the subsidy which is implicitly being given to the fuels which cause environmental and health damage.

Detailed comparisons will continue to be made as more evidence becomes available. The extra cost of storage of the H_2, compared with that for gasoline, or liquid synthetic natural gas, must also be accounted for. In respect to storage of liquid H_2, the cost is in the liquefaction. The cost of the cryogenic tank for automotive purposes would be about $500 per car and assuming a gasoline equivalent of 15 gallons ($\simeq$ 2 MBTU), and a life of 5 years, with a lifetime of the fuel in the tank of 1 day, the added cost is equivalent in terms of gasoline to 2 cents per gallon.

Figure 12.22 suggests that the efficiency of conversion of H_2 to mechanical energy is some 1.6 times that of gasoline.

It has been shown earlier that the cost of one unit of gaseous CH_4 and H_2 is about the same (hydrogen slightly cheaper); and that the cost of one energy unit of gasoline from coal and liquefied H_2 from coal would be such that the LH_2 would be about 25% more expensive (than the estimated costs of the gasoline from coal, which were taken as around $6 per MBTU).

But these are First Law comparisons, and effective, meaningful comparisons must take into account Second Law losses and pollutional costs for injection of CO_2 and other coal-related contaminants into the atmosphere.

---

*In particular, lead insult, the effect of threshold concentrations of lead, may well be an important part of the damage.

EFFECTIVE COST OF HYDROGEN FUEL IN TRANSPORTATION

Fossil Fuel:	Arbitrary Standard:	Comparative cost of H_2* per unit distance:	
		Max.	Min.
Gaseous CH_4 from coal	1	0.76	0.55
Gasoline from coal	1	0.49	0.35

Applications of hydrogen to aircraft

1. THE RELATIVE COSTS OF PRODUCING HYDROGEN FROM COAL, COMPARED WITH THAT OF PRODUCING METHANE AND KEROSENE

According to Wittkofski,[85] a comparison of the results of producing liquid hydrogen, liquid methane and synthetic aviation kerosene from coal shows that the coal-steam iron process has the highest thermal *efficiency* of the processes involved, and leads, of course, to hydrogen.

Gaseous methane from the Hygas process is slightly more costly than gaseous hydrogen from the steam-iron process. However, because of the cost of liquefying hydrogen, which is greater than that of liquefying methane, liquid hydrogen turns out to be *slightly* more expensive than liquid methane. (But the CO_2 emission is then localised to central plants.)

The thermal efficiency of producing synthetic aviation kerosene from coal is slightly less than that of producing liquid hydrogen from coal.

These conclusions involve two aspects which are doubtful. First of all the Hygas process for producing methane from coal is one which has not been found satisfactory in recent trials. It was first used in 1967 but has had a rather doubtful history since then.

Like other estimates of cost, in which hydrogen may be found to be slightly more expensive than that of other fuels, an error is made by not taking into account the environmental cost of the production of further hydrocarbons and injection of the impurities connected with their use into the atmosphere. Environmental damage of coal giving H_2 could be made less than those giving other fuels.

The basis to the figures in this table involve the following acceptances: Hydrogen burns 33% more efficiently than methane in internal-combustion motors; and 50% more efficiently than gasoline. Further, it is assumed that all three fuels come from coal, but that, for synthetic methane and gasoline, the fuels are used on board, and the pollution is the same as that of an electricity power plant burning coal. For hydrogen, it is assumed that there can be a rejection of polluting components from coal into the deep ocean, and that this reduces to zero the health hazards of burning coal. Also, it is assumed that the First Law Price of hydrogen and methane from coal is $4.50 and that of gasoline $6.00. All these assumptions are not only rough and subject to change with time, but they are to a degree arbitrary because, for example, the efficiency figures are taken for urban driving and would not be applicable, for example, to aircraft fuels. The difference between the figures called *Max.* and *Min.* is that in the *Max.* column, differences in First Law cost and efficiency only are used. In the second column, the pollutive differences which may favour hydrogen are taken account to it.

The following factors unfavourable to hydrogen have been neglected: the cost of storing and packing it. Thus, for distances of < 1000 km, transmission costs are probably < 4% of the First Law cost and storage could be largely line-pack.

Further, the pollutive and health-hazard costs which make the difference between the *Max.* and *Min.* figures are very uncertainly and roughly reasoned (see above) as 25%-50% of the First Law cost. In the *Min.* figure, the hydrogen price has been lowered by the mean of these percentages to allow for the environmental superiority of this fuel.

It seems safe to conclude that, from the point of view of those who use it, hydrogen from coal with deep-sea injection of CO_2, etc., would be between ½ and ¾ the cost of other fossil fuels developable from coal. Even LH_2 from coal (at about $8 MBTU[-1] First Law cost) would be cheaper than gasoline in real terms.

Hydrogen from the steam-iron process is the cheapest fuel available.[85]

2. A LIQUID-HYDROGEN BASE FOR AIR TRANSPORTATION

The first consideration is the cost of the hydrogen. The cost, in 1978 terms, of gaseous hydrogen from electrolysis for a 1985 technology would be around $8 per MBTU. However, along with the production of hydrogen goes the production of corresponding amounts of oxygen which can be used as a credit, thus reducing the cost of the hydrogen some 18%. The liquefaction process is a costly one. It is expensive, not only in capital investment but in energy. The requirement is 5.67 kWh per lb of hydrogen, although the theoretical liquefaction work is only 1.37 kWh per lb. The efficiency of the liquefaction process is some 23%.

It is possible with current technology to install units liquefying 250 tons per day. The compressors are the major equipment and contribute 53% of the overall thermodynamic losses. The Linde Corporation has examined these losses and there are some suggestions which would lead to their reduction were the market available to justify the necessary R and D.

The amount of liquid hydrogen which is being produced at present has peaked because of the turn-down in the Space Programme.

Electrolytic gas generation could be used to split water and provide liquid hydrogen, even at small airports. With liquid hydrogen, engine exhaust pollution is eliminated. The threat to stratospheric ozone would be reduced to negligible. There would be less noise generated by hydrogen-fuelled engines at airports.

There are about 2,600 aircraft in the U.S. commercial air transport fleet, and about 260 of these are wide-bodied jets. We should need a total of about 8,300 tons of liquid hydrogen per day to run the fleet.

The main point, of course, is the cost of liquid hydrogen. Elsewhere we have estimated it to be around $11 per MBTU in 1978 currency. A commonly estimated price in literature of $6 per MBTU appears to be too low. The price paid by NASA at the present time ($22 per MBTU) appears significantly above cost. The first Law cost from coal would be around $8 MBTU[-1].

In judging the contributions which the use of liquid-hydrogen technology could make to air transport, we have to take into account the added potentialities for combustion at high altitudes. Thus, hydrogen sustains combustion at altitudes higher than do hydrocarbon fuels. Hydrogen-fuelled aircraft could operate at higher altitudes, thus avoiding traffic congestion on heavily travelled routes.

The safety aspects of the situation can be dealt with simply. Jet fuelled airplanes are maintained and serviced by well-trained and experienced personnel. They could certainly be trained to handle liquid hydrogen-fuelled transportation.

Liquid hydrogen will be firstly used in the larger aircraft, with the extra volume for the fuel being contained in the present body, e.g. in the upstairs compartment of a Boeing 747.

There is concern in respect to the crash-worthiness of hydrogen-fuelled aircraft. It would be possible to make the fuel tanks crashproof.

A National Policy decision is needed to begin to off-load the growing demand for transportation fuels away from petroleum. The introduction of liquid hydrogen would be a major step, particularly for wide-bodied jets. On the other hand, such an introduction would require a re-thinking of the ground requirements for the wide-bodied jets.

A comparison of aircraft fuels with respect to costs

A detailed study of this by Wittcoffski is of interest.[85] It concludes that if the basic energy source is to be coal—thus *nuclear and solar sources neglected*—the production of hydrogen from coal via the steam–iron process is significantly cheaper than the cost of methane from coal. It is noteworthy that Wittcoffski concludes that the cost of a unit of energy in synthetic liquid aviation kerosene from coal would be about the same as that of liquid hydrogen.

However, it is clear that it is liquid methane which should be compared with liquid hydrogen. The cost of liquefaction of the latter is clearly more than that of methane. Thus, the costs would be:

Cost of L.N.G.*	Cost of LH$_2$*
(1 MBTU)	(1 MBTU)
$5.50	$6.50

At this point, therefore, it would be concluded that liquid methane from coal is the cheaper fuel. The cost advantage is about 18% in favour of methane.

However, it may not necessarily be that the cost per passenger mile would be cheaper. As has been shown above, in automotive engines there is an important efficiency difference which makes the LH$_2$ a cheaper fuel for cars than L.N.G. We do not as yet know the relative efficiency of aircraft engines running on methane compared with those running on hydrogen.

It seems unlikely that a carbonaceous fuel would burn as cleanly (in respect to deposits) in an engine as H$_2$.

By far the most important cost difference would be in the environmental. It may be that methane pollutes much less than gasoline when burned in an internal-combustion engine. However, the CO$_2$ from aviation CH$_4$ burning would, of course, have to be evolved into the atmosphere. Were H$_2$ to be the fuel, the CO$_2$ from the coal could be dissolved in the ocean.

How much extra cost should the insidious CO$_2$ damage put onto the cost of CH$_4$? It is much more difficult to answer this than to attempt an answer, as done above, for the environmental damage from automotive fossil-fuel burning. At first (until, say, > 2010) the effect would be small. Eventually (>2030), it would be stupendous (e.g. change most agricultural prospects in the U.S., etc.).

It is clear that aircraft will not be flown in the post-1990 future on synthetic kerosene, but either on L.N.G. or LH$_2$. If it is H$_2$ then, of course, one can continue to utilise the same fuel as the basic energy sources become solar and atomic. If it is L.N.G., the cost is likely to be greater than that of H$_2$ *if the long-term environmental damage cost is not neglected.*

Conclusions regarding the use of hydrogen as an aircraft fuel

1. The decisive reasons are economic. At some time in the 1980s, the real

---

*Wittcoffski's figures are 4.19 and 6.77 respectively but seem to assume a methane production figure well below that of other Hygas estimates.

cost of liquid hydrogen is likely to become less than that of gasoline.
2. The second most important reason is the improvement in aircraft performance which the use of liquid hydrogen would allow. It would mean a longer range and better payload. In particular, it would revolutionise the prospect for hypersonic transports by using airframe cooling to make lightweight-alloy use possible (Table 12.III).
3. Pollutional aspects of aircraft, both near airports and at high altitudes, would be reduced towards zero.

TABLE 12.III: AIRCRAFT CHARACTERISTICS (PRELIMINARY DATA)
Basis: 1981 Technology

Aerodynamic configuration	Arrow wing
Mach No. (cruise)	2.7
Payload	234 passengers
Range	4200 n mile
Engines	Turbofan, duct-burning
Fuel	Liquid hydrogen
Wing-loading (take off)	50 lb/ft²
Thrust/weight (sea level, static)	0.5
Gross take-off weight	379,000 lb
Fuel weight (total)	98,000 lb
Aircraft zero-fuel weight	280,000 lb
Operator's empty weight	232,000 lb
Payload weight	49,000 lb

To what extent could the use of hydrogen be commenced now?[86]

In considering the use of hydrogen from electrolysis at the present time, there are several factors to take into account, and the first of these is the cost of electrical energy. It *may* be better to utilise the off-peak power which is available for more than 25% of the time without seasonal interruption. However, the use of the low-use off-peak power is not necessarily better because the capital costs involved are considerable and, insofar as the equipment is standing idle, money is being wasted. The current costs of electrolysers are between $200-$450 per kilowatt.

The industrial markets for hydrogen in the late 1970s[86]

The present largest industrial markets using hydrogen are ammonia synthesis, petroleum refining, and methanol synthesis. The demand for these industries in the United States is two trillion SCF per year, and the largest user is the ammonia synthesis.

Whilst hydrogen from coal is available, electrolytic hydrogen *may* always be too expensive. However, this does depend on the size of the plant. If the plant is relatively small, electrolytic H_2 becomes competitive.

There are many needs which could be supplied by electrolytic hydrogen competitively at this time. A few of these are:

1. In the direct reduction of iron ore to produce pure iron.
2. In space travel.
3. In the hydrogenation of fats and oils.
4. In production of non-ferrous metals such as tungsten and molybdenum.
5. In use in some heat-treating atmospheres.
6. In welding, cutting and brazing.
7. In cooling electric generators.

The use as an automotive fuel, particularly for buses, could be carried out in isolated cases where captive hydro-electric energy is occasionally available in interrupted fashion at very low prices, e.g. 0.3 cents per kWh (for example, the Bonneville Dam in Oregon will supply municipal users of electrical energy for purposes where interruption is acceptable, at 0.3 cents per kWh.) Low-use-period power can be applied particularly easily with the production of electrolytic hydrogen because this process is interruptable without any corresponding penalty. Few other applications can use interruptable power with such a lack of disadvantage. It is for this reason that interruptable power is not easily marketed at this time. It is best applied in producing hydrogen which could then be used in driving bus systems.

Let us calculate the cost of this hydrogen. Utilising the more liberal formula:

$$\text{Cost of } 10^6 \text{ MBTU} = 2.29\text{Ec} + 1$$

and the current cost of the interruptable power from the Bonneville Dam (0.3c per kWh), the cost of the hydrogen becomes (utilising 1.6 volts for an advanced electrolyser) $2.10 per MBTU. The current cost of gasoline (no tax, dealer mark-up or transportation cost) is about $3 per MBTU in the U.S., so that in this case, even the First Law costs are in favour of H_2.

The commercial prices of hydrogen

A variable which controls the price of hydrogen is the scale upon which it is used, and unexpectedly large variations occur depending upon that scale.

Thus, variation in the commercial hydrogen *price* per unit of energy due to this scaling is up to an order of magnitude! It varies from $90 per MBTU for the supply of 20,000 SCF per month to $15 per MBTU for a supply of about 2 million SCF per month. Figure 12.24 shows these figures in competition with that of natural gas in 1974.[88]

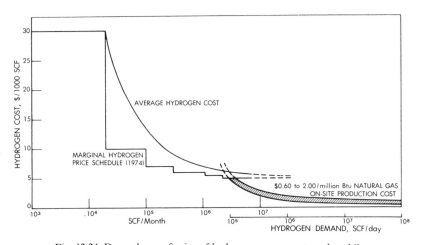

Fig. 12.24. Dependence of price of hydrogen on amount produced.[92]

The reduction in cost using modern electrolysers to using those of current technology would be equivalent to a reduction in cell voltage from 2.0 to 1.6, i.e. 25%. Thus, when the daily hydrogen requirement is a million SCF per day, electrolysis costs would sink to $5.50 per MBTU. Electrolytic hydrogen becomes competitive with steam reforming at demands of less than 1,000,000 SCF per day. *This is the area*, in which there is a competitive situation for hydrogen, which is not being exploited now.

Furthermore, this area could be extended. One extension could be made by changing from classical old electrolysers to (the as yet commercially unavailable) electrolysers, running at 1.6 volts with a current density of 200 m amps cm^{-2}.

Secondly, the above costs do not involve low-use-period power. Use of this would reduce costs by 30-40%, extending the area of cost competitiveness of hydrogen about another order of magnitude towards situations of ten million SCF per day.

Observations on costing in the production of hydrogen

There are factors which have to be taken into account in costing, apart from the basic costs of gaseous hydrogen, calculated according to an equation of the type

$$\text{cost of 1 MBTU in 1978 dollars} = 2.29\text{Ec} + 1$$

One such cost is that of pumping the hydrogen to a pressure suitable for transmission in pipelines. Increase of voltage in the electrolyser could achieve the same result and it seems likely that a costing of the increased electrolyser construction costs, and that arising from a larger voltage, would amount to less than those of the pumps.

Buying rectifying equipment is one cost which cannot be avoided. The plant has to have a building: there is the cost of land site preparation, etc.

In 1976 the total cost of electrolytic hydrogen technology was about $470 per kilowatt. The GE projection for 1980 in 1977 dollars is $212 per kilowatt.

The commercial calculations given by Darrow, Biederman and Knopka have been 60% debt financing at 9% interest and 40% equity financing at 15% after tax rated return.[86] This gives rise to a cost on capital of 11.4%.

Low-use period power

The availability of low-use period power is established, and the power costs from it are 0.5-0.65 times the full daytime cost. However, this does not mean that the cost of hydrogen would always be reduced by using this power, because when the plant factor (the time the plant is in operation) is reduced, the capital costs go up. This is shown well in Fig.12.25. Thus, for 5 mils per kilowatt hour, the cost of hydrogen at a plant utilisation factor of 100% would be about $5.50 per MBTU, but if the plant were utilised only one-third of the time the cost would rise to about double this, at the same power costs.

Thus, the increase in the amortisation factor has to be traded off against the cost reduction in the electricity price obtained on using low-use period power. This depends upon how expensive electrolysers are, so the cost cal-

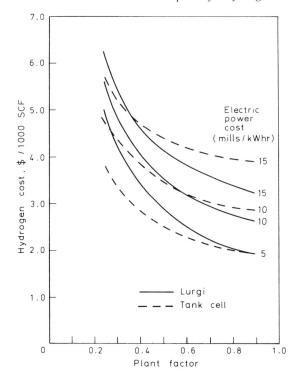

Fig. 12.25. Effect of use rate on capital cost.[92]

culation has to be made individually. However, a partial solution occurs in the fact that the electrolyser would probably be used 100% of the time. During the time it is used with normal power it produces hydrogen for demands where the higher cost may be met. The low-use period power can then be utilised for producing low-cost hydrogen for the amortisation figure is now that for 100% use.

Hydrogen in the home: A specific example

Billings has formed an H_2-driven home in Provo, Utah. The basic energy source is wind-driven (Fig.12.26).[87]

Electrolysis with a solid polymer electrolyte is used. The hydrogen is stored in a solid hydride. The H_2 pressure is 500 psi, the pressure for recharge equilibrium with the hydride, and the design output pressure of the electrolyser.

Hydride equilibrium is 55°C and the hydride bed is kept at that by heat liberated by the hydriding reaction and by solar-heated water. When the home demands more than the electrolyser can give, there is supply from the storage. The temperature drops as heat is used to release H_2 and more H_2 flows in.

The electrolyser delivers 3 lb (1.36 kg) of H_2 per day at 500 psi. It operates at 0.4 amps per sq cm.

The storage vessel is composed of two mild steel hemispheres welded to

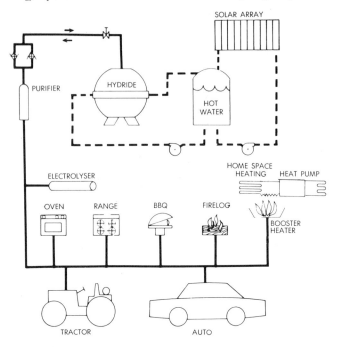

Fig. 12.26. The plan at Billings' place.[87]

a cylindrical center section. It is 3 feet in diameter and 4 feet in height. The wall thickness is 1 inch. 4000 lb of Ti-Fe alloy are loaded into it. The actual alloy used was $Ti_{54}Fe_{44}Mn_5$.

The household appliances run on hydrogen are an oven, a range, a barbeque, a fireplace log and a booster heater.

A new burner was used for the oven range and booster. It glows when combustion is occurring and decreases NO production. A mesh is used. It inhibits the mixing of H_2 and air and the combustion temperature is lowered.

Two vehicles are supplied. A Cadillac-Seville has two systems. It runs on H_2 held in Fe-Ti for local journeys and switches to gasoline for longer journeys.

A garden tractor is powered exclusively by H_2. Billings' picture of the tractor converted is shown in Fig.12.27.[87] Water induction into the engine intake valves was accomplished by two spray nozzles. Heat exchange with the hydride was achieved from a water/anti-freeze mixture, passing through an exhaust-gas heat exchanger. Centrifugal pumps circulate fluid between heat exchangers hydride tanks as shown.

Practical aspects of distributing hydrogen to residences and commercial properties[88]

During the 1950s and 1960s there was a degree of conversion in Europe from coal gas (50% hydrogen) to natural gas. We are conceiving now a turn-about from this procedure to the use of 'purified coal gas' (hydrogen) in place of natural gas. Thus, just as the burners, and to some extent the tubing, had

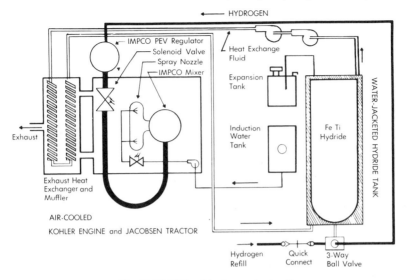

Fig. 12.27. Billings' hydrogen tractor.[87]

to be changed when the change came from coal gas to natural gas, so there will have to be a modification in burner design when the fuel is changed to hydrogen.

Thus, hydrogen would be combusted in appliances which would have to have modified burners. A change in the flow rate and pressures of a gas distribution system using hydrogen would be necessary compared with one using natural gas. There would be an increase in operating pressure because of the lesser amount of energy per unit volume in hydrogen. The leakage problem may not be severe. However, flashback has to be prevented.

Odorising the hydrogen will be necessary because of the need to notice leaks. Sulphur compounds, mercaptants, could be used.

An illuminant should be added. It seems necessary not only in respect to leaks but also in respect to the adjusting of flames. A small amount of organic sodium compound would burn with a yellow flame.

However, such a compound must be cautiously tested because of the possibility of its interaction with the burner; an experimental programme is necessary.

1. Leakage

The rate of leakage of hydrogen through orifices, corrosion pinholes or leaky seals will be three times greater on a volume basis than that for natural gas. Consequently, the rate of energy loss is the same as for natural gas. The examination suggests that loss through this cause will be negligible. One of the feared losses, permeation through plastic pipes, will be far less than the accepted loss of methane in the normal pipeline distribution.

2. Burner characteristics necessary for hydrogen

(a) The burners should be controllable over a wide range of turn-downs without danger of flashback.

(b) The distribution of heat should be uniform.

(c) The flames must not lift away from the burner ports. It should operate quietly on emission.

3. Burner velocity and flame stability

The burning velocity of natural gas using 100% theoretical air (namely air containing stoichiometric oxygen) is 1 ft per second. The burning velocity of hydrogen is 9 ft/sec using 57% theoretical air. Thus, the hydrogen flame is much faster than the methane flame and there is a danger of flashback: the propagation of the flame-front back through the burner ports and up to the metering orifice. The flame cannot travel through the orifice because the gas upstream is pure fuel and hence cannot sustain combustion. However, if combustion takes place at the metering orifices instead of the burner ports, the burner head may be damaged.

4. The flashback in the conversion of an appliance

The flashback problem is treatable in more than one way when converting from natural gas to H_2. One can increase the upstream pressure and decrease the port sides, which increases the flow velocity through the burner port so that it is greater than the flame speed. Alternatively, one can decrease the primary air to the point at which the upstream of the burner ports is not inflammable.

Another technique is to eliminate the primary area entirely. The present natural gas pipelines, where they exist in a suitable direction, seem fitted for utilising the hydrogen which will be transmitted to houses. There will be some differences. For example, the operating pressure of 75 psi, now used, will be maintained, but the flow rate will be increased. The hydrogen flow will be three times that of the natural gas flow.

On the other hand, if the flow of hydrogen is, say, 130% of that of natural gas, to maintain lamina flow, the energy will be only 40% that of natural gas. If turbulent flow is not reduced, the volumetric flow of hydrogen could be increased 260% that of natural gas, whereupon the delivery of the energy will be 80% that of natural gas. To deliver the same content of energy per unit time in the pipeline formerly used for natural gas, the hydrogen would have to be increased by increasing the operating pressure in the pipeline. Leakage would not be a problem. Measured volumetrically the leaks might be 2.5 times that of natural gas, but the energy loss would be less.

Modification in the appliance burners will be required. Increasing the pressure drop of flow rate increases the rate of energy delivery and retards flashback, also enhancing flame positions and height.

Apart from replacing the burners, it may be necessary to replace gas regulators, or at least the vents therein.[89]

Environmental

Introduction

One would not be complete in a presentation of the various energy possibilities if the pollutional pros and cons were not considered. There can be no doubt, as far as atmospheric pollution is concerned, that the Hydrogen Economy is an absolutely satisfactory economy, for the long term. However, in considering the environmental effects of an economy, it is not sufficient to consider only its effect upon the quality of air and water. We must also ask about the consumption of resources, and other effects upon the environment, which the introduction of such a technology would involve.

This type of analysis has been sparse, but it has been done recently in a preliminary way by Plass,[90] and it is his analysis which has been the main influence in the following considerations.

Resources and the hydrogen economy

There is a tendency in considering a Solar-Hydrogen Economy to regard it as using no resources, because it converts water to hydrogen and oxygen, which then come back to water. However, materials would be used for the construction of the system, that is for collectors, electrolysis plants, pipelines, storage tanks, etc. From a conservationist's viewpoint, as distinguished from the air and water pollutional viewpoint, a Hydrogen Economy based upon fossil or nuclear fuels should be compared with a conventional economy based on such fuels.

In doing this, Plass uses the following equation:

$$\frac{R}{T} = P \times \frac{H}{PT} \times \frac{R}{H} \tag{7}$$

where R = quantity of the resource in question (e.g. tons for minerals, Btu for energy resources)

T = time (years)
P = population
H = quantity of hydrogen consumed (Btu).

The second factor H/PT is the per capita demand for hydrogen per year. The third factor, R/H, is the resource cost per unit of hydrogen. These are both important. When conversion efficiencies from heat, etc., are high, H/PT is low. For low efficiencies, the reverse is true. If the hydrogen-manufacturing

TABLE 12.IV: ENERGY APPETITES OF FOUR SYSTEMS, TWO OF WHICH ARE HYDROGEN ECONOMIES[90]

System	User requirements (1970) Electricity E/T	Synthetic fuel F/T	Hydrogen H/T	R coal E	R coal F	R coal H	R nucl E	R nucl H	Total resource demand R/T
I (coal-hydrogen)	7.98	–	40.57	3.09	–	3.92	–	–	183.7
I (coal-synthetic fuels)	7.98	40.57	–	2.92	1.52	–	–	–	84.9
II (nuclear hydrogen)	7.98	–	40.57	–	–	–	3.56	4.52	211.8
II (nuclear all electric)	38.30	–	–	–	–	–	3.96	–	151.5

All of above x 10^{15} Btu/yr. Btu resource/Btu of E, F, or H x 10^{15} Btu/yr. Present energy economy, at 1970 levels, requires 64.6 x 10^{15} Btu/yr of raw energy from various sources.

design and distributing facility is good, R/H is small, whereas poor design will cause and increase in R/H. It is necessary in applying equation (7) to make reasonable estimates about the factors, H/PT and R/H.

The resources consumed in the production, transport and storage of hydrogen are the fuel (except for the solar case), iron, aluminium and copper, land occupied by collector farms, pipelines and storage facilities.

Plass studied several kinds of energy systems. The results obtained are summarised in Table 12.IV.

Thus, in spite of the environmental advantage of a Hydrogen Economy, it would consume more energy than other economies in the setting-up stage. This would not be so, however, were the economy to be based upon an inexhaustible source, such as the solar source (or, conceivably, fusion). However, even with these inexhaustible sources, caution must be taken that the introduction of hydrogen does not run away with too high a proportion of mineral resources, all of which must be regarded as limited in amount.

Environmental effects

The added resource costs which would come from hydrogen used along with coal and fission might be thought to be overcome by the environmental advantage of forming only water back from water. A simple equation which can be used for looking at the environmental effects of hydrogen is that given by Commoner:[91]

$$\frac{D}{T} = P \times \frac{H}{PT} \times \frac{D}{H} \qquad (8)$$

where P = population
H = quantity of hydrogen consumed (Btu)
T = time (years)
D = environmental damage (dollars).

The first two factors have been discussed. The third factor, D/H, is the amount of environmental damage per unit of hydrogen produced. Its value depends upon the technological process, for example, D/H for hydrogen produced by coal would be greater than for that produced were solar energy the origin of the hydrogen.

Plass considers alternatives for utilising coal, at the same time taking into account land destruction by strip-mining. Synthetic fuel plants, uranium mines, solar farms, and other means, are also considered.

To make a conclusion of relative pollutional effects, Plass utilises a classification of environmental matrix which classifies environmental problems, causative factors, character of the environmental insult, problem threshold, area affected and other allied considerations.[90]

The hydrogen situations are more advantageous environmentally than any other. However, in converting coal to hydrogen, more coal is needed to provide the necessary energy for the nation's economy, if hydrogen is used as a medium, and a correction has to be made for this.* *A solar-based*

---

*Plass' analysis did not involve the correctional concept of the reduction of coal-hydrogen pollution by injecting CO_2 into the sea. It seems likely that such a concept would allow the coal-hydrogen system to become cleaner than the coal-synthetic fuel one.

Hydrogen Economy is only about 40% as polluting as the corresponding nuclear-based hydrogen system.

If environmental damage alone were the criterion, then the optimal system is the solar-electric alternative. The final results are shown in Table 12.V.

Thus, the advantages of the solar systems come out well, and the solar-hydrogen systems excellently, particularly if utilised with wind power. Wind-utilising sea-borne stations would probably have a better index than even the solar-electrical company.

General discussion

Considering, then, the environmental contaminants produced by a Hydrogen Economy—rather than resource exhaustion—there could be only two pollutants, NO and water. The NO can be eliminated by using fuel cell conversion.

Contamination with water must be considered. Table 12.VI shows the relative production of water. Water production would be an advantage, not a difficulty, if it were condensed and then collected, because it would be produced free from other gases, and hence would be clean.

There is hydrogen peroxide production during internal combustion of hydrogen with air, and the amount is shown in Table 12.VII. This contaminant (0.02%) of H_2O in *condensed* water from internal combustion is probably not of importance because of the rapid decomposition of H_2O_2 in normal vessels and in the presence of light.[83]

TABLE 12.V: Environmental Damage Comparisons[90]

System	Environmental Damage Index (1970 levels)	Ratio of Damage to that of Present System
I (coal-hydrogen)	670	1.64
I (coal-synthetic fuel)	554	1.36
II (nuclear-hydrogen)	483	1.18
II (nuclear-electrical)	461	1.13
III (solar-hydrogen)	259	0.63
III (solar-electric)	173	0.42
Present mixed system (calculation omitted)	408	1.00

An advantage of a Hydrogen Economy will be its capacity for energy storage. The absence of overhead transmission lines will be an environmental bonus.

Electricity and hydrogen are both clean burning, but, at the generating plant, hydrogen has the environmental advantage. If transmitted by pipe, it is environmentally more acceptable than the transport of electricity via a wire grid. Underground electricity transmission is many times more expensive than overground.

In respect to transport, the limitation of hydrogen is in the storage technique. A cylindrical tank, 10in x 60in, would hold about 35 gallons of hydrogen, equivalent to 9 gallons of gasoline in energy. It would need special

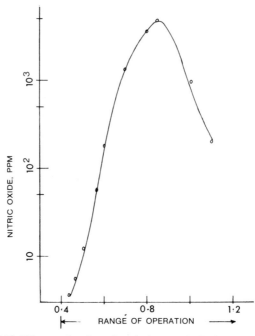

Fig. 12.28. NO_x as a function of equivalence ratio for H_2; the car can be operated at 0.4.[92]

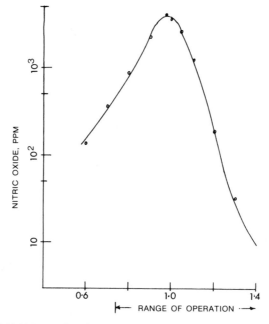

Fig. 12.29. NO_x as a function of equivalence ratio for gasoline; the car cannot be operated without NO_x production.[92,93]

TABLE 12.VI: Water Production for Various Energy Sources

Fuel	lbs water/Btu
Gasoline (C_8H_{18})	74×10^{-6}
Methane (CH_4)	105×10^{-6}
Hydrogen	174×10^{-6}

TABLE 12.VII: Concentration of H_2O_2 in the Exhaust of an Engine Using H_2 Gas as a Fuel[83]

Test No.	H_2O_2 in the exhaust (ppm)
1	230
2	220
3	220

handling techniques, but these seem well justified in view of the environmental advantage over methane.

Summary of environmental effects

In respect to air and water pollution, hydrogen is the ideal fuel, and its general use would lead to a radical reduction of air and water pollution. In respect to resource use-up, so long as one speaks of a Solar-Hydrogen Economy, the situation is excellent. A Solar-Electrochemical Economy would be, in respect to resource use-up, still better.

Could there be any pollutional difficulties with hydrogen?[92]

The only pollutant which can arise from the use of hydrogen is NO.[92] Everything is comparative, so what we must do is to compare the NO produced in the burning of hydrogen with that used in the burning of gasoline.

A principal difference in burning H_2 in air compared with burning CH_4 is that the ignition range with hydrogen is greater—*less oxygen is needed for the hydrogen to explode* so that we *can work with a leaner mixture*: in turn less nitric oxide is produced, as that occurring with the burning of gasoline. So long, therefore, as the mixture is kept lean, less nitric oxide will be produced in the burning of hydrogen, than with methane.

This is shown in Fig. 12.28, which predicts the NO emission for a hydrogen-fuelled engine. It can be from zero to quite high, depending on the equivalence ratio. Thus, it must be kept low, about 0.4. The *very great decrease* in the NO for lean burning with hydrogen compared with gasoline, as most recently recorded by Chakrevarty and Varde, is noteworthy. (Fig. 12.29).[93]

Such a comparison still avoids taking into account the pollutive costs of distributing products of combustion of coal randomly in the atmosphere by using methane or petroleum from coal, versus H_2 from coal, when such emissions may be dealt with in central plants.

SUMMARY OF CHAPTER

1. Suggestions of the use of hydrogen as a fuel were passingly made in a lecture at Cambridge University by Haldane in 1923. According to E.W. Justi, Lawaczeck 'in the 1930s' pointed out H_2 in pipes was the

cheapest way of transporting energy. In 1962, Bockris suggested H_2 as the fuel to be produced from floating solar reactors using sea electrolysis, and in 1965 Justi published suggestions of a desert-based scheme. In 1971 (*cf* Bockris & Appleby, 1972) the suggestion was published of an atomic and solar-hydrogen economy and in 1972, Gregory, Ng and Long quantified the suggestion said first to have been made by Lawaczeck. The term "A Hydrogen Economy" originated with Bockris and Triner in 1969. Marchetti (1972) and Lessing (1972) were early advocates of H_2 in modern times.

2. The transduction of H_2 to mechanical power was made by various forms of internal-combustion engines, by the external-combustion Aphodid engine, and by fuel cells.

3. The metallurgical processes of hydrogen reduction of Al_2O_3 Fe_2O_3, among others—would be feasible with H_2 directly, were the water-origined H_2 to become sufficiently cheap *compared* with other fuels available after 1990. A similar statement applies to many chemical and industrial processes.

4. Among futuristic notions connected with the massive availability of hydrogen is that of food production from atmospheric CO_2 and N_2.

5. Availability of O_2 on a massive scale would be useful for sewage, pollution reversal, and in the reduction of the cost of combustion equipment (because of the resulting reduction in size).

6. Erren and King were leaders in finding out how to use H_2 in internal combustion. At present, the technology is satisfactory except for the problem of storage and the economics of the available fuel. However, projections into the intermediate period where oil will be got from coal are that the economics of hydrogen is superior to that of liquid methane and gasoline from coal. This unexpected discovery arises from the greater efficiency of the combustion of hydrogen in internal-combustion than the fossil fuel.

7. The conclusion of (6) concerning the economics of the post-1990 fuel for transportation is independent of the taking account of the tacit subsidy to the fossil-fuel price paid by the U.S. government in the form of tax-based anti-pollution measures; in the cost of pollution-caused death (eventually, of CO_2 damage to the climate). Accounting for these costs is more difficult. One such accounting suggests they effectively increase the real cost of coal-based carbonaceous fuels by 50%. In such a case, the cost of hydrogen per unit distance becomes about half the cost of gasoline from coal.

8. *Liquid* hydrogen will become a practical automotive fuel at $10 per MBTU. Its present commercial price is $22 per MBTU. Its calculated cost from coal (1978) on a large scale should be around $8 per MBTU.

9. Crash studies of H_2 driven vehicles are very encouraging.

10. An argument has been made that the U.S. railroads represent a very suitable first conversion objective for LH_2 fuel.

11. All aircraft would have a better payload if run on liquid H_2. Hypersonic

aircraft will have to use LH_2 to get an acceptable range. Cooling the airframe with LH_2-based refrigerant would allow the use of lightweight alloys.

12. The use of H_2 fuel could be commenced now in numerous situations in which there is objection on pollutional grounds to the use of oil and coal as a fuel; and in specialist technologies.

13. The commercial price of small-scale tank H_2 may be up to an order of magnitude more expensive than the cost of large-scale H_2.

14. Electrolytic H_2 is cheaper than hydrogen from coal now for situations demanding less than 10^6 SCF of H_2 per day.

15. Application of low-use-period electric power may be economically helpful. However, the non-fuel component of the cost of the equipment increases with a low period of use.

16. Households have now been practically fuelled by hydrogen. The key is storage in Fe-Ti-Mn.

17. Utensils for H_2 use would have to be modified to avoid NO production, etc.

18. The environmental aspects of a solar-hydrogen system are exceeded only by those of a solar-electrochemical one. NO emissions from internal-combusion engines are very small if the engine is run lean, a procedure impractical with gasoline.

AUTHOR'S ARBITRARY CHOICE OF A MORE IMPORTANT CONCLUSION FROM CHAPTER

Hydride-stored hydrogen from coal would be cheaper than present gasoline (untaxed, zero dealer profit, at refinery) now in terms of costs per unit distance in (at least) urban transportation. LH_2 from coal *would* be cheaper on a similar basis than gasoline from coal.

REFERENCES

1. J. Verne, *Twenty Thousand Leagues Under the Sea* (Paris, 1869).
2. J. B. S. Haldane, in a lecture, 'Daedalus, or Science of the Future', at Cambridge, 4 February 1923.
3. A. T. Stuart, *Industrial and Engineering Chemistry* 1927, **19**, 1321.
4. R. A. Erren & W. A. Hastings-Campbell, *J. Inst. Fuel*, 1933, **VI**, 277, see also *Chem. Trade J.* **92**, 239 (1933).
5. F. Lawaczeck (1930), quoted by R. O. Lindstrom in ref. 33, and also quoted by E. W. Justi in ref. 74; also in private communication, 6 May 1974.
6. H. Niederreither, German Patent 21b, 648941, 1937.
7. I. I. Sikorski, Steinmitz Lecture on Aviation (1938).
8. J. S. Just, *Gas and Oil Power*, Annual Technical Review, 326 (1944).
9. R. O. King, W. A. Wallace & B. Mahapatra, *Can. J. Res.*, 1948, **26F**, 264.
10. F. T. Bacon & R. G. H. Watson, private communication, 1950.
11. F. T. Bacon, *BEAMA Journal* (January 1954), p. 2.
12. F. T. Bacon, *World Science Review* (April 1959), p. 21.
13. A. M. Weinberg, *Physics Today* (1959), p. 18.
14. L. Lessing, *Fortune* (May 1961), p. 152.
15. J. O'M. Bockris, Memorandum to Westinghouse Company (C. Zener), 1962.
16. R. O. Lindstrom, private communication to F. T. Bacon (1953).
17. R. O. Lindstrom, *ASEA Journal*, 1964, **37**, 1.

18. E. W. Justi, *Leitungsmechanismus and Energieunwandlung in Festkorpen* (Vandehoeck & Ruprecht, Gottingen, 1965).
19. H. R. Linden, *Gas Scope,* Institute of Gas Technology, publication 19, 1971.
20. J. O'M. Bockris, *Environment,* 1971, **13,** 51.
21. J. L. Dean & R. J. Schoeppel, paper presented to the 1971 Frontiers of Technology Conference, Oklahoma State University, 30 September-1 October, 1971.
22. J. O'M. Bockris & J. Appleby, *Environment this month* (July 1972), 29.
23. D. P. Gregory, D. Y. C. Ng & G. M. Long, in J. O'M. Bockris (ed.), *The Electrochemistry of Cleaner Environments* (Plenum Press, New York, 1972).
24. C. Marchetti, *Chemical Economic Engineering Review,* 1973, **5,** 7.
25. L. Lessing, *Fortune* (November 1972), p. 138.
26. J. O'M. Bockris & S. Srinivasan, *Fuel Cells: Their Electrochemistry* (McGraw-Hill, New York, 1969), Appendix A, p. 633.
27. C. Marchetti, *Chemical Engineering and Economic Review, 21973,* **5,** 1, 23.
28. W. L. Hughes & S. O. Brauser, 'Energy Storage Systems', U.S. Patent No. 3459953, 5 Aug. 1969.
29. J. O'M. Bockris & Z. Nagy, *Electrochemistry for Ecologists* (Plenum Press, New York, 1974).
30. J. O'M. Bockris & A. K. N. Reddy, *Modern Electrochemistry,* Rosetta Edition (Plenum Press, New York, 1973), p. 1361.
31. E. Justi & A. Winsel, *Kalte Verbrennung-Fuel Cells* (Steiner, 1962).
32. J. O'M. Bockris, *J. Chem. Ed.,* 1971, **48,** 352.
33. R. Henderson, private communication, 1966.
34. D. P. Gregory, assisted by P. J. Anderson, R. J. Dufour, R. J. Elkins, W. J. D. Escher, R. B. Foster, G. M. Long, J. Wurm & G. G. Yie, 'A Hydrogen-Energy System', prepared for the American Gas Association by the Institute of Gas Technology, Chicago, August 1972, p. VII-17.
35. H. F. Coward & G. W. Jenks, 'Limits of Flammability of Gases and Vapors', U.S. Bureau of Mines Bulletin, 503, 1952.
36. J. L. Schanz & E. K. Bullock, paper presented at the American Rocket Society, Santa Monica, California, 25-28 September 1962.
37. A. M. Squires, *Iron and Steel with Hydrogen* (The City College of the City University of New York, 1971).
38. A. S. Mann & C. Marchetti, paper presented at The Hydrogen Economy Miami Energy (THEME) Conference, March 1974.
39. 'An Electrochemical Carbon Dioxide Reduction–Oxygen Generation System having Only Liquid Waste Products', Phase I, prepared by F. B. Leitz & H. I. Viklund, Ionics Incorporated, February 1967.
40. 'An Electrochemical Carbon Dioxide Reduction–Oxygen Generation System having Only Liquid Waste Products', Phase II, prepared by F. H. Meller, Ionics Incorporated, April 1968.
41. M. Steinberg, M. Beller & J. R. Powell, 'A Survey of Applications of Fusion Power Technology to the Chemical and Material Processing Industry', Brookhaven National Laboratory, New York, May 1974.
42. R. L. Savage, L. Blank, T. Cady, K. Cox, R. Murray & R. D. Williams (edd.), *op. cit.* p. 94.
43. H. G. Schlegel, in *Fermentation Advances* (Academic Press, New York, 1969).
44. R. C. Corey, 'Pyrolysis, Hydrogenation and Incineration of Municipal Refuse–A Progress Report', Proceedings of the 2nd Mineral Waste Utilisation Symposium, ITT Research Institute, Chicago, Illinois, March 1970.
45. H. G. Schlegel & R. M. Lafferty, in *Advances in Biochemical Engineering* (Springer-Verlag, Germany, 1971), vol. 1.
46. L. O. Williams, *Astronautics and Aeronautics* (February 1972), p. 42.
47. M. D. Rickard & A. F. Gaudy, Jr., *Journal of Water Pollution Control* (May 1968).
48. W. F. Schaffer, Jr., 'Cost Study of the Treatment of Sewage Sludge by the Wet-Air Oxidation Process, using Oxygen Produced by Low-Cost Electricity from Large Nuclear Reactors', Oak Ridge National Laboratory, February 1968.
49. J. E. Browning, *Chemical Engineering* (26 February 1968), p. 88.
50. G. Eckland & E. Kestner, World Hydrogen Energy Conference, 1976, Vol. 2, 3B-22, Miami.

51. R. G. Murray, R. J. Schoeppel & C. L. Gray, paper presented at the 7th Intersociety Energy Conversion Engineering Conference, San Diego, September 1972.
52. E. H. Hietbrink, J. McBreen, S. M. Selis, S. B. Trickelbank & R. R. Witherspoon, in J. O'M. Bockris (ed.), *The Electrochemistry of Cleaner Environments* (Plenum Press, New York 1972), p. 47.
53. 'Automobile and Air Pollution: A Programme for Progress'—Part II, 'Subpanel Reports to the Panel on Electrically Powered Vehicles (R. S. Morse, Chairman), U.S. Department of Commerce, December 1967, p. 103.
54. E. H. Hietbrink, J. McBreen, S. M. Selis, S. B. Tricklebank & R. R. Witherspoon, *loc. cit.*
55. E. Hines, M. S. Mashikian & L. J. van Tuyl, SAE Publication—690441, Chicago, May 1969.
56. R. J. Schoeppel, *Chemtech* (August 1972), p. 476.
57. Recorded by R. A. Erren & W. H. Campbell, *J. Inst. Fuel*, 1933, **6**, 277; W. Cecil, Trans. Cambridge Phil. Soc. (1820), 1, part 2, ch. 14, pp. 217-239.
58. H. F. Ricardo, Report of the Empire Motor Fuels Committee, Proc. Inst. Automobile Engineers, 1923-24, 18.
59. A. F. Burstall, *Proc. Inst. Automobile Engineers*, 1927, **22**, 358.
60. R. A. Erren, 'Method for Driving Internal Combustion Engines', U.S. Patent No. 1.901.709, applied 15 March 1930.
61. R. A. Erren & W. H. Campbell, *J. Inst. Fuel*, 1933, **6**, 277.
62. R. A. Erren, 'Method of Charging Internal Combustion Engines', U.S. Patent No. 2.164.234, Application 17 September 1938.
63. R. O. King *et al.*, 'The Hydrogen Engine: Combustion Knock and Related Flame Velocity', Trans. E.I.C., Vol. 2, 1958.
64. R. O. King, W. A. Wallace & B. Mahapatra, *Can. J. of Res.*, 1978. **26**, Sec. F, 264.
65. R. E. Billings & F. E. Lynch, 'History of Hydrogen-Fueled Internal Combustion Engines', Publication No. 73001, Utah, 1973.
66. R. J. Schoeppel, paper presented at the Gas Symposium of the Society of Petroleum Engineers of AIME, Omaha, Nebraska, 21-22 May 1970.
67. R. G. Murray & R. J. Schoeppel, paper presented at the Intersociety Energy Conversion Engineering Proceedings, Boston, Massachusetts, 3-6 August 1971.
68. R. J. Schoeppel & R. G. Murray, paper presented at the Frontiers of Power Technology Conference, Stillwater, Oklahoma, 28-29 October 1968.
69. Perris Smogless Automobile Association, 'An Answer to the Air Pollution Problem: The Hydrogen and Oxygen Fueling Systems for Standard Internal Combustion Engines', First Annual Report, Perris, California, 1971.
70. M. R. Swain & R. R. Adt, Jr., paper presented at the 7th Intersociety Energy Conversion Engineering Conference, San Diego, California, 25-29 September 1972; paper presented at Intersociety Conference of Energy Conversion, University of Pennsylvania, 13-16 August 1973.
71. R. G. Murray & R. G. Schoeppel, paper presented at Intersociety Energy Conference, Boston, Mass., 3-6 August 1971.
72. W. F. Libby, *Science*, 1971, **171**, 499.
73. D. M. Miller, *Scientific American*, 1973, **228**, 78.
74. R. L. Savage, L. Blank, T. Cady, K. Cox, R. Murray & R. D. Williams (edd.), *A Hydrogen Energy Carrier*, Vol. II—Systems Analysis, NASA-ASEE, 1973.
75. H. C. Watson & E. E. Milkins, IECEC, 1978, in press.
76. A. Furuhama, B. Hiruma and Y. Enomoto, World Hydrogen Energy Conference, 1976, 6C 27.
77. P. Weingold & H. van Vorst, 1st World Hydrogen Energy Conference, 1976, 66-97.
78. D. B. McKay, 1st World Hydrogen Energy Conference, 1976, 7C-13.
79. R. Billings, *ibid.*, 7B-27.
80. *ibid.*, 7C-40.
81. C. Chakravarty & H. Varde, 1st World Hydrogen Energy Conference, 1976, 4C-17.
82. H. L. Gier, 1st World Hydrogen Energy Conference, 1976, 7C-41.
83. E. J. Griffith, *Nature*, 1974, **248**, 458.
84. R. M. Zweig, 1st World Hydrogen Energy Conference, 1976, 4C-19.
85. R. D. Wittkoffski, 1st World Hydrogen Energy Conference, 1976, 5C-3.
86. K. Darrow, N. Biedermann & A. Knopke, 1st World Hydrogen Energy Conference, 1976, 8C-17.
87. R. Billings, *Hydrogen Progress*, No. 1, Provo, Utah, 1977.
88. J. Pangborn, M. Scott & J. Sharer, 1st World Hydrogen Energy Conference, 1976, 8C-47.
89. B. Angur, K. Scott & H. Schewar, 1st World Hydrogen Energy Conference, 1976, 8C-47.

90. H. J. Plass, THEME Conference, Miami, March 18-20, 1974.
91. B. Commoner, 'The Environmental Cost of Economic Growth', in Schurr (ed.), *Energy, Growth & the Environment* (Johns Hopkins University Press, 1972).
92. S. P. Chakrevarty & K. S. Varde, 1st World Hydrogen Energy Conference, 1976, 4C-5.
93. W. L. Hughes & S. O. Brauser, 'Energy Storage Systems', U.S. Patent No. 3459953, 5 August, 1969.

13

THE SPLITTING OF WATER

Introduction

The production of hydrogen in recent years has been mainly from natural gas.[1] The price had been sinking. However, natural gas and oil are unlikely future sources of hydrogen on a large scale, because of the price increases which began in 1973, and will continue as the demand exceeds supply, due to the approaching turn-down of these supplies (late 1980s in the U.S.A.). A Hydrogen Economy must be understood mainly in respect to a coupling of hydrogen with one or more of the inexhaustible sources of energy. Methods of extracting hydrogen from water will be, therefore, the principal relevant methods (though, see Chapter 4).

Water

The reaction for the production of hydrogen from water is endothermic and hence heat has to be used to make hydrogen.

The enthalpy change in the reaction:

$$H_2O_{(g)} \rightarrow H_2 + \tfrac{1}{2}O_2 \qquad (13.1)$$

is (150°C):

$$+ 58.14 \text{ kcal mole}^{-1} \qquad (13.2)$$

and correspondingly the $\Delta G°$ at 150°C is:

$$+ 52.99 \text{ kcal mole}^{-1} \qquad (13.3)$$

and $\Delta S°$ at this temperature is 12.29 eu. $\Delta G°$ will become less positive as the temperature is increased, and the equilibrium of (1) shifts to the right. ΔG becomes negative at about 4700°K, the temperature, therefore, at which a hypothetical fuel cell containing H_2O at 1 atm, and producing H_2 and O_2 at 1 atm, would begin to function. At 2000°C, there is c. 1% H_2 in equilibrium with H_2O at 1 atm.

The difficulties of the *direct* thermal dissociation to obtain H_2 are not only the material difficulties arising from the high temperature at which appreciable amounts of hydrogen are in equilibrium with water (refractories over about 1600°C provide difficulties), but is due also to the lack of massive amount of heat at such temperatures. Nuclear heat could be available only up to about 800°.

Irradiation of water should be considered. The strength of the H-O bond in 104 kcals mole[-1]. Several reactions occur when water is irradiated. Ung and Back have used u.v. radiation at 1849 A° (*c.* 6 ev), and found hydrogen.[2] Photo-electrochemical dissociation occurs at room temperature if the electrodes of a cell are subject to energy greater than about 1.2 ev (because the products are H_2 and O_2, i.e. not hydrogen and oxygen radicals). The photo-electrochemical dissociation occurs when the radiant energy is greater than the band gap for the semiconductor electrode material.[3]

These parameters act as background to photo-oriented methods for the harvesting of hydrogen from water.

Seawater is a likely source of hydrogen in a Hydrogen Economy, because of the advantage of sea-borne collectors of solar and solar-gravitational energy; the cost has to have included in it an allowance for dealing with the Cl_2 which would be evolved (instead of O_2) on the electrolysis of seawater (see later section).

Production of hydrogen from fossil fuels

Methods using natural gas and oil are not of interest for innovatory considerations. (The cost of hydrogen from these sources will rise during the next decade, with fossil-fuel prices reaching more than four times the 1973 values in constant dollars by the early 1990s.)[4]

The only fossil fuel to be considered for hydrogen production on a large scale is coal. Some methods for obtaining hydrogen from coal have already been given in Chapter 4.

The direct thermal production of hydrogen

General

The concept of the *direct* use of heat to dissociate water, usually rejected because of the lack of availability of heat at the temperature required, has undergone a reawakening of interest with the prospect that heat at temperatures above 2000°K could become available from solar sources, e.g. from concentration available in solar-thermal power plants.

The thermodynamic position is, of course, unambiguous, and is summarised in Figure 13.I.[5] It shows that, at a pressure of 0.01 mm. of Hg, 10% of hydrogen would exist in an equilibrium mixture at 2200°K. At 1 At., the temperature needed for 20% hydrogen is 3000°K.

There are two main problems of implementation, assuming that an appropriate heat source is available.

Materials

Few materials are thermally stable at 2200°K. But to be acceptable here, they have to be stable in contact with the equilibrium mixture which contains hydrogen and oxygen with which they can react. There are few discussions of the materials available. Thus, the substances shown in Table 13.I have melting points above 3000°K.

The breakdown of these materials at 3000°K in the presence of water, hydrogen and oxygen (all of which would have immense effects on the stability of the materials) has not been studied, although could probably be

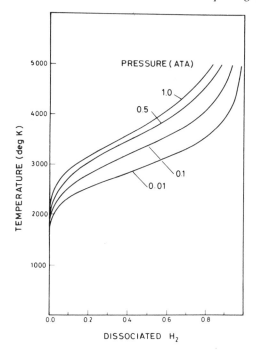

Fig. 13.1. Dependence of degree of dissociation of water on temperature
and pressure.[5]

TABLE 13.I: Materials Which Melt Above 3000°K

Substance	Melting point
Tantalum Boride, TaB_2	*c.* 3000°C
Niobium Boride, NbB_2	2900°C
Tantalum Carbide, TaC	3880°C
Tantalum Nitride, TaN	3360°C
Tungsten, W	3410°C
Tungsten Boride, WB_2	2900°C
Tungsten Carbide, WC	2870°C
Graphite, C	3550°C
Hafnium Oxide, HfO_2	2812°C
Hafnium Nitride, HfN	3305°C
Zirconium Boride, Z_3B_4	*c.* 3000°C
Zirconium Nitride, ZrN	2880°C

the subject of interesting thermodynamic calculations, using data from the
JANAF tables.

Graphite, tungsten and molybdenum, along with the compounds of zirconium and tantalum, are worth considering. It is a small choice, and until
the evidence is available that there is chemical stability in hydrogen-oxygen-
water mixtures at 3000°C, *no scheme for the practical realisation of direct
decomposition should be studied.*

Separation

The hydrogen remains 10% of gas mixture so long as there is heat at 2200°K available. Upon cooling, the hydrogen will recombine with the oxygen to form water. How does one separate the hydrogen and oxygen from the equilibrium mixture without recombination? Thus, such separations are easily possible if one of the two gases to be separated at high temperature forms a liquid at lower, but still practicable, temperatures. This is not so in the case of the separation of hydrogen and oxygen.

Methods of separation of hydrogen and oxygen after high temperature dissociation have been proposed by Ihara[6] and Nakamura.[7] Among the possibilities pointed out are the use of the paramagnetic moment of oxygen; and magneto-hydrodynamic separation. The authors do not suggest materials which might go along with these methods.

It might be possible (materials-wise) to use a membrane, involving zirconium oxide. However, in the absence of extra energy to be used to create a potential difference (steam electrolysis), the practicality of separation by oxygen ion diffusion seems dubious. Materials which diffuse hydrogen (palladium and some alloys of iron) are decomposed, or molten, below the temperature at which hydrogen would become available in this approach.

The availability of solar heat at 3000° K

The use of parabolic mirrors or Fresnel lenses allows one to get very high temperatures from solar heat. The concentration ratio has to be above 1000 to get temperatures of the order of 3000°K, and such temperatures have recently been obtained in the well-known French work on solar furnaces.[8] However, even discounting momentarily the large material difficulties, such concentration can only be upon a small volume. For example, the large expanse of concentrators in the famous Odeillo furnace produced more than 3000°K, but only over a volume corresponding to a large (laboratory) size metallurgical crucible.

Conclusion

The advantages of the direct thermal method are its relative simplicity and the possibility of going along with the solar-thermal devices. However, concepts in which the temperatures have to be above 3000°K seem to have no prospect whatsoever of becoming practical. If (*cf.* the difficulties with processes of fusion with hydrogen) the feasible temperature were dropped to 2000°K, where the material difficulties, although still severe, are not so overwhelming, there would be available only a few per cent hydrogen at 0.01 atmospheres, a pressure expensive to maintain at such temperatures.

In summary, the direct method still seems unlikely to become economic, and those who propose it ought to associate their support with suggestions for *chemical*, as well as thermal, stability in the temperature regions concerned.

Thermochemical cycles

Basic idea

It has been pointed out above that the thermal quantities involved in the reaction

$$H_2O \rightarrow H_2 + \tfrac{1}{2}O_2$$

are such that no significant amount of hydrogen occurs at 1 At. pressure and less than 2000°K. Even at 3000°K, it is necessary (at 1 atmosphere pressure), for copious amounts of hydrogen to be available in an equilibrium mixture to consider practical extraction; and that, further, *separation* of hydrogen and oxygen might be an expensive problem.

The equilibrium constant for the above process is:

$$K = e^{-\Delta G°/RT}$$

$$= \frac{P_{H_2}P_{O_2}^{\frac{1}{2}}}{P_{H_2O}}$$

Therefore, if positive values of $\Delta G°$ can be reduced, the hydrogen available in the equilibrium mixture at a given temperature can be increased, i.e. the temperature at which a substantial quantity of hydrogen could be available is decreased.

Were it possible to decrease $\Delta G°$ sufficiently so that the temperature at which there is sufficient hydrogen in the equilibrium mixture is 1000°K, then suitable heat could (perhaps) be available from atomic reactors. Consequently, hydrogen could, then, be produced on a large scale by the use of heat, to drive the endothermic reaction to the right.

In rough terms, we wish to reduce the value of $\Delta G°$ from the value which it has at, say, 2000°K, considering the one-step decomposition, to about one-half that value, so that a reasonable amount of H_2 can be obtained at about 1000°K.

According to Hess's Law, there is no change in the *heat* of reaction by making the reaction pass through various paths. However, suppose we consider that hydrogen is produced *by a cycle* such as:

$$A + H_2O \rightarrow H_2 + AO$$
$$AO \rightarrow A + \tfrac{1}{2}O_2$$

It may be possible to make each reaction occur in such a way (for example at different temperatures) that the net $\Delta G°$ is reduced.

Correspondingly, by not allowing equilibrium to be set up, i.e. by removing the hydrogen from the AO of the above equation, significant amounts of hydrogen could be produced at a (maximum) temperature of less than 1000°K.

If the second reaction in the cycle, that producing oxygen, say, also goes over to the right sufficiently as a result of removal of oxygen from the mixture, it may be possible to recover nearly all of the A, and recommence the cycle, with a fresh supply of water.

Neither reaction must need temperatures above those at which heat will be available on a larger scale (e.g. 1000°K).

As $\Delta G°$ is positive, it is advantageous to have a high temperature. Hence, among the cyclical steps, when there is a negative ΔS, the temperature could be made as low as is consistent with reactions still occurring at a rate which fits in with the rate of the other steps (for, in steady state, all the reaction steps must occur at the same velocity).

Thus, in the thermochemical-cycle method for water splitting,[9,10] a cycle is chosen which ends up with the provision of the hydrogen and oxygen and regeneration of the original material. It will tend to produce hydrogen at lower temperatures than those which would have to be used with water alone. This temperature lowering is important, not only because of improvements in the materials and economic prospects of a process if it can be made to occur at lower temperatures, especially below $1500°K$, but also because large quantities of heat are going to be available (from atomic reactors at only $1000°K$ or less). Thus, one tries to make an intelligent tuning of temperatures of the reactions in the cycle, so that their specific $T\triangle S°$ contributions are taken into account to lower the $\triangle G°$.

The hoped-for advantage behind the thermochemical-cycle method

The material given above explains how the positive $\triangle H°$ for the decomposition of water could possibly be reduced by the use of the entropy aspect of the various cyclical steps so that it reaches manageable proportions. However (and see below), although the reduction of the value of $\triangle G°$ from its high positive value for a one-step splitting of water towards the necessary less positive value could probably be achieved by the appropriate application of $T\triangle S$ terms, this is not to be regarded as the essential point of the method. The most important aspect of the thermochemical cycle method for the splitting of water was intended by its originators to be an increase in the efficiency of energy conversion.[11,12]

In the alternative, electrochemical, method for producing hydrogen, the efficiency of the electrochemical part of the process is high (in modern approaches, nearing 100%). However, and of course, it is the efficiency of the production of hydrogen referred to *an original source of energy* which is the important one. As the electrochemical method is based upon the use of electricity, the efficiency of the production of this from some heat source is what counts. If the efficiency of the electrolysis is, say, 0.95, and that of the production of electricity, say, 0.4, the efficiency of the electrochemical method for the production of hydrogen is 0.38 with respect to the original energy source. The reason is the Carnot Theorem, which states that in the conversion of heat to mechanical work by means of a heat engine then the maximum possible efficiency of such a conversion — to be reached only when it is carried out under conditions of limiting slowness, i.e. 'reversibility' — is:

$$\frac{T_H - T_L}{T_H}$$

where T_H and T_L are the high and low temperature limits of the process.

If hydrogen is to be produced by a method which involves a heat-to-mechanical work conversion, its efficiency will have to be in this region, less than 50%, because of the limitation put in practice by the Carnot Theorem upon the degree of the heat energy which can be converted to electricity — and thence, electrochemically, to hydrogen.

It was implied by the early proposer of the thermochemical-cycle method[11] that if one applied heat to reactants and obtained chemical reactions which produce hydrogen, then (apart, of course, from practical, extrinsic losses) one would produce the hydrogen at an efficiency which would approach 100%, because one had found a way of splitting water without the losses arising from the effect of Carnot's Theorem.

It seems that Marchetti and de Beni thought that they had made a fundamental advance in the direction of manufacturing hydrogen from water,[12] driving the endothermic reaction in a sense which would avoid the Carnot losses and be carried out at practical temperatures.

Examples of thermochemical cycles proposed

From the beginning of the Marchetti and de Beni concept of thermochemical cycles in 1972,[12] very many cycles have been proposed. In view of the discussion below, there is not much point in presenting many of them. A series of chemical reactions is generally devised which balance out so that the only net reaction is water decomposition. A consideration of the signs and magnitudes of the entropies involved is made, and it is proposed that a process be engineered, with the various steps – depending on the sign of the entropy – running at 'high temperature' (900-1000°K), or 'low temperature' ($\sim 500°K$).

Examples of some thermochemical cycles are presented in detail in Table 13.IIa and a summary of others is given in Table 13.IIb.

Many chemical cycles for obtaining hydrogen are now available in the chemical literature, and a good collection of the newest ones are given by Veziroglu and Kacke.[5] However, no thermochemical cycle has, through 1979, yielded continuously, any hydrogen.

The widespread-ness of the thermochemical work on the decomposition of water

The appearance of a New Idea for the splitting of water, along with a current emphasis in the early 1970s on the need to make this fuel, gave rise to widespread support for the thermochemical water cycle approach to hydrogen production. In many cases, however, the work was 'systems analysis' or a 'computerised study'. The computer was programmed to spot optimal entropy and temperature situations.

None of the proposals and studies apparently allowed for the increased materials losses of experiments at high temperatures, particularly in systems (as with most of them) involving steam and ionic salts. Thus, the book by Bockris, White and Mackenzie, *Physicochemical Measurements at High Temperature,* presents much relevant material not taken into account in the theoretical studies concerned.[13]

By 1978, in certain American Government research-funding agencies, a reconsideration of the degree of stress put on work on thermochemical cycles had begun. However, as much research supported by Government Agencies in countries outside the United States is that supported in the United States one or two years earlier, there seems at present to be a still-increasing effort in thermochemical water cycles in other countries, particularly in Germany and Italy.[14,15] The cycle of Russian work does not yet seem to have begun.

TABLE 13.IIa: THERMOCHEMICAL CYCLES SUGGESTED FOR PRODUCING HYDROGEN

Cycle title	Type	Thermochemical reactions	Maximum temperature (°K)	Thermal efficiency (%)	Reference
oxide-sulfate	Bicyclic	$SO_2 + H_2O + MO \text{ (M = Metal)} \xrightarrow{500°K} MSO_4 + H_2$ $MSO_4 \xrightarrow{1100°K} MO + SO_2 + \frac{1}{2}O_2$	1100	85	11
carbon-steam-iron	Tricyclic	$C + H_2O \rightarrow CO + H_2$ $CO + 2Fe_3O_4 \rightarrow C + 3Fe_2O_3$ $3Fe_2O_3 \rightarrow 2Fe_3O_4 + \frac{1}{2}O_2$	1673	75.5	12
calcium oxide-iodine	Tetracyclic	$6CaO + 6I_2 \xrightarrow{393°K} Ca(IO_3)_2 + 5CaI_2$ $5CaI_2 + 5H_2O \xrightarrow{800-1100°K} CaO + I_2 + \frac{5}{2}O_2$ $5CaI_2 + 10H_2O \xrightarrow{550-800°K} 5Ca(OH)_2 + 10HI$ $10HI \xrightarrow{550-1000°K} 5H_2 + 5I_2$	1100	30	13
calcium-bromide	Tetracyclic	$2CaBr_2 + 4H_2O \xrightarrow{1000°K} Ca(OH)_2 + 4HBr$ $4HBr + Cu_2O \xrightarrow{400°K} 2CuBr_2 + H_2O + H_2$ $2CuBr_2 + 2Ca(OH)_2 \xrightarrow{400°K} 2CuO + 2CaBr_2 + 2H_2O$ $2CuO \xrightarrow{1200°K} Cu_2O + \frac{1}{2}O_2$	1200	59	12

TABLE 13.IIb: OTHER THERMOCHEMICAL CYCLES WHICH MAY GENERATE HYDROGEN

Cycle title	Type	Maximum temperature °K	Thermal efficiency %	Reference
Iron chloride-iron oxide	Pentacyclic	923	53.0	14
Cesium oxide	Tetracyclic	1323	48.0	12
Steam-iron-carbon dioxide	Pentacyclic	923	24.6	15
Arsenic iodide-arsenic oxide	Tetracyclic	600	53.3	15
Copper chloride	Tricyclic	973	29.4	15
Euratom cycle MARK-9	Tricyclic	1000	17.5	16

A difficulty in the argument for the thermochemical approach to the production of hydrogen from water

There are intrinsic advantages in water electrolysis. It leads to the separation of the hydrogen and oxygen, evolved in different compartments at the two different electrodes. It works at or near to room temperature. It takes place in single modules and is not subject to scale-up difficulties. It does not need a complex plant. These advantages make the capital investment aspect of it more economic (in the absence of a counterweight) than a high-temperature method using many separate stages (i.e. several stages in plant design in a thermochemical cycle). The main point of the latter was the alleged presence of a method to split water without the energy loss implied by the Carnot cycle using a heat engine to make the electricity necessary to drive the electrolysers.

However, the absence of a Carnot-like efficiency expression in the thermochemical cycle is illusionary, and the reason is as follows. Were the heat supplied to the reactions at the same temperature and pressure in all the cycles of a sequence, then there could (ideally) be a complete absorption of heat applied to the reactants and its take-up into the heat content of a chemical reaction, so that the concept of Marchetti and de Beni might be realised.[12] However, in the thermochemical-cycle method, the idea involved is that the steps of the cycle are carried out at different temperatures, to make use of the different size in the $\Delta S°$ expressions (optimising the reduction of the $\Delta G°$). This means (for the same mass of gases) that the pressure must be changed. When it is necessary to change the pressure of a mass of gas, work has to be done. This work (or expenditure of energy) must come from the heat which had otherwise been assumed to be put into the reaction.[16]

When the various processes in the cycles are followed through, starting at the highest temperature of T_H, and ending at the temperature of the surroundings, T_o, it is possible to show that the loss of energy due to these extra work processes is:[17]

$$\frac{\Delta G}{\Delta H} \cdot \frac{T_H - T_o}{T_H} \tag{13.4}$$

ΔG and ΔH are not very different in numerical value for water-splitting, so that the expression for the efficiency of the use of the heat carrying out the chemical cycle reaction (when the steps are at different temperatures and pressures) is given by an expression which is near to that of the Carnot efficiency expression in the conversion of heat to mechanical energy—as in the production of electricity for the electrolysis situation.

Thus, though the thermochemical cycle method does not at first *appear* to involve the conversion of heat into mechanical work, with Carnot losses, there is, in fact, a near-Carnot expression governing the conversion of heat into hydrogen, i.e. *the intrinsic losses in the thermochemical cycle method* are similar to the losses in the conversion of a fuel to heat in the manufacture of electricity.[18] It could only be an advantage in this comparison to use the chemical-cycles method, if the value of the pseudo-Carnot factor were more than the Carnot factor which occurs in the manufacture of steam. But steam can be made at high temperatures, too, if high temperature heat is available from atomic reactors, and thus the efficiency of production of steam would be no less than that which exists in the thermochemical cycle.

Thus, the reasoning which seems to have encouraged so much work on the thermochemical cycle was to confuse the driving of a constant pressure, constant temperature chemical reaction with the heat needed to drive a chemical reaction (involving gases) when it goes through various stages *not* at the same temperature and *not* at the same pressure. Then, some of the heat is used up in the process of getting the reaction to occur, and does not go into driving the chemical reaction: what is lost in the work done in changing the pressure is near to what is lost in the conversion of heat to mechanical work in the making of electricity from heat.

Overheat

Another aspect intervenes in calculating the amount of energy needed to drive chemical water-splitting at a certain rate. The work which must be provided to make the reaction occur at a real rate (as opposed to the work needed for a hypothetical reversible change) is more than the enthalpy change between the reactants and the products. This change is the work which occurs when the reaction is caried out limitingly slowly. There is a certain *minimum* free energy which must be available to carry out a chemical reaction. As the real energy needed is compared for varying rates of carrying out the reaction, the energy decreases with a decrease of the rate of the reaction. If one extrapolates the energy needed to carry out the reaction at various rates, to the value needed to carry out the reaction at zero rate, then one would come to the value mentioned in calculations in thermodynamic text books, the free energy change under reversible conditions.

It is clear that in a practical, commercial sense, a reaction cannot be carried out infinitely slowly, but the amount of energy needed (apart from the pseudo-Carnot-cycle aspects of work needed to compress gases, change temperatures, etc.) is more than the energy supposed by workers who, between 1970 and 1978, have been concerned with chemical cycles. This extra energy has been named by Appleby and Bockris 'Overheat',[19] and one may write the following equations:

$$\Delta H_v = \Delta H_{v=0} + \Delta\Delta H \qquad (13.5)$$

where $\Delta\Delta H$ is the overheat for a certain reaction corresponding to the velocity, v.

Corresponding to this is the equation:

$$\Delta G_v = \Delta G_{v=o} + \Delta\Delta G \tag{13.6}$$

where $\Delta\Delta G$ is the overfree-energy.

The overfree-energy is analogous to the electrochemical concept of over-potential. In an electrochemical process, there is a reversible potential (analogous to the standard free energy of reversible thermodynamic reactions), the potential which represents the equilibrium situation of the reaction, and the work needed to carry out the reaction at limiting low rate. The real work done in carrying the reaction out, however, is different from this, and greater. It is the work corresponding to the reversible potential, plus an overpotential. Thus, in the electrochemical case, one has:

$$V = V_{v=o} + \eta \tag{13.7}$$

where η is the overpotential.

It is easy to show that the value of the overpotential, η, is:[20]

$$\eta = \frac{RT}{\alpha F} \ln \frac{i}{i_o} \tag{13.8}$$

In this expression, RT and F are well known; the subsequent quantity, α, is a characteristic electrochemical constant, the value of which is complex but around ½ in many practical cases, i is the current density (proportional to the rate of reaction) actually existing, and i_o is the rate of the reaction at the reversible potential, when the reaction is occurring in both directions at the same rate.

By analogy to this, then:[21,22]

$$\Delta\Delta G \simeq \frac{RT}{\alpha} \ln \frac{v}{v_o}$$

where v is the velocity corresponding to the overfree-energy, $\Delta\Delta G$, and v_o is the velocity of the rate-determining reaction occurring at equal velocities in both directions at the equilibrium situation.

There is no reason to believe that the value of overfree-energy in thermochemical reactions taking place between 200 and 1000°K is small enough to be neglected. Its presence adds to the energy cost for the process. It increases the cost of hydrogen above that which has been calculated by workers who have adopted the thermochemical hydrogen route.

Work necessary to make a thermochemical cycle occur

If the cycle occurs between T_H and T_L, and the heat available from atomic or chemical sources to apply to the cycle is Q, then:

$$Q\left[\frac{T_H - T_L}{T_L}\right] = (\Delta H_{v=o} + \Delta\Delta H_{v=v}) \tag{13.9}$$

The value of $\Delta H_{v=o}$ is the heat content change in the thermodynamically reversible chemical reaction.

Let us assume as an example that $\dfrac{T_H - T_L}{T_L}$ is 0.6 and that $\triangle\triangle H$ is $\frac{1}{2}$ $H_{v=0}$.

Then, for these circumstances,

$$Q = 2.5 \, \Delta H_{rev} \qquad (13.10)$$

Thus, with the equations we have derived, and with simple and realistic values, one would need more than twice the heat which would be necessary in a reversible cycle at one T and P. The above process would be equivalent to an efficiency of $\dfrac{1}{2.5}$. 100   40%.

In reality, of course, there will be extrinsic losses, too (analogous to IR drops in the electrolyser), and these will reduce the efficiency below the 40% calculated for the circumstances quoted.

Thus, we can write that, for thermochemical processes, one has

$$Q > T_H \left[\frac{\Delta H + \Delta\Delta H}{T_H + T_L} \right] \qquad (13.11)$$

Kinetic and logistical aspects of the chemical approach to water splitting

We have thought out some energy-conversion aspects of the thermochemical method of splitting water. One does not yet know the numerical values of the overheat.*

It is important to realise that in a process which is not at equilibrium, it will be the *rate constants* of the reaction which determine the predominant path the reaction takes.

This brings out a further obstacle to the application of the usual reasoning on the cyclical thermochemical path to hydrogen. It is generally assumed that when they write the free energies and entropies in steps within the proposed cycles, and decide upon the optimisation of a set of reactants, that the reactions follow the free energy gradients, as would be so if the situation followed the indications of *reversible* thermodynamic laws. However, insofar as a net velocity of production of hydrogen and oxygen at finite rate is occurring, the quantities are the rate constants for the possible reactions which may be undergone by the reactants in the individual steps. There may be several of these, both homogeneously or heterogeneously, or with the walls of the vessel, and with the products of such reactions. The real reaction path in a 1000°K reaction involving ionic constituents and water is likely to be complex.

As the temperature increases, there is a tendency for equilibrium to be more nearly attained.[23] For this reason, processes which are carried out at higher temperatures by the thermochemical cycle method are more likely to follow the path assumed than reactions in low-temperature cycles (v_o will

---

*Even if the v_o values were very high, with the result that the overfree energy and overheat would be small, the Carnot-like efficiency expression would still make it doubtful that the thermochemical cycle method could be economic compared with the electrochemical one.

also be raised and $\triangle\triangle H$ decreased). However, this point does little to encourage the chemical-cycle method because the higher temperature also extends the number of possible competitive side reactions.

Some problems in the thermochemical-cycle method arising from the temperatures involved

Three aspects of the breakdown of vessels, in which chemical reactions take place, are relevant:
1. The vessel walls become reactants in side reactions.
2. Corrosion reactions occur, above all when (as in most cycles) ionic constituents are present.
3. Erosion reactions occur.

Erosion depends upon the presence of solids striking the side of the vessel, and this condition would be present in the thermochemical cycle method involving inorganic solids.

The thermochemical-cycle method tends to set up circumstances which would lead to costly materials problems. These have been considered for high temperature reactions by Bockris, White and Mackenzie.[13] They will apply markedly to pumps, gauges and valves which would be involved in the transfers of reactants from one reaction vessel (at a given T and P) to the next (at another T and P).

The degree of cyclicity

The materials used in thermochemical cycles — those which are meant to be recycled — may be costly. In a plant corresponding, say, to 1000 MW, the amount of water processed per day would be some 5 million tons, and the materials lost from the cycle will be in the order of magnitude of thousands of tons at 0.1% lack of cyclicity.

A summary of the thermochemical-cycle method for the massive production of hydrogen

1. The fundamental idea of the thermochemical-cycle method was to avoid the Carnot loss in using heat energy to produce mechanical energy, electricity and hydrogen by electrolysis. The use of cycles with entropies of different signs had the objective of reducing the necessary temperature.
2. However, important matters have been omitted in the consideration of these matters: (a) because the cycles operate between two different temperatures and pressures, an energy-loss expression would enter which involved temperature in a way similar to that of Carnot; and (b) it was not realised that to drive an endothermic chemical reaction at a finite velocity needs more energy than is calculated in terms of the thermodynamics of reversible reactions. When they are brought into account, they bring the amount of heat energy needed for the production of a unit of H_2 from the thermochemical cycle method to the same level as that needed for electrolysis (around 2.5 times the ideal value).[24]
3. On the other hand, although the electrolysis method has small materials difficulties, and the fraction of costs of a unit of H_2 is in the region of 20% of the total cost, in the thermochemical-cycle method, maintenance and costs of equipment would be likely to be a much greater fraction of the whole.

4. Corrosion would contribute to such extra costs: the steam-ionic systems in contact with metals are corrosive.
5. It is doubtful whether the degree of cyclicity of the cycles would be enough to avoid having to recycle material; side reactions would lead to the production of impractical masses of materials to be removed from plants.

Should the present considerations lead to an abandoning of the thermochemical approach to hydrogen? Were a cycle to be found which did not involve water and ionic compounds, the corrosion difficulties would be reduced; and if it worked at relative high temperatures the Carnot efficiency could be correspondingly high. Cycles involving, say, CO, CO_2, CH_4, water and hydrogen could be derived and might be relatively effective. However, the iron-water reaction, which consumes coal, and which is therefore not a thermochemical cycle, is generally regarded as being able to give hydrogen at about \$4.50. Could a closed thermochemical cycle give a lower price?

Cost

The cost of one MBTU may be written as:

$$AEc + \Sigma D_i$$

where A is a factor depending only upon fundamental laws, units, and not dependent upon the efficiency or energy costs in the process, E is the factor involving the amount of energy needed to run the process, together with a factor governing the efficiency with which the electricity efficiency can be used to obtain the product, and c is the cost of a unit of the energy; D_i is the cost of an ith stage of the process. In the case of the simple one-step electrolytic process, the minimum cost of 1 MBTU is in \$:[25]

$$2.29\ Ec + 1$$

where the potential which runs the process is E in volts (representing the thermodynamic reversible component + the overpotential for operating the cell at a given overpotential), and the cost of the energy is given by cents per kWh; the 1 allows for depreciation, insurance, and maintenance.

For the various thermochemical-cycle proposals, the first term would represent the cost of the thermal energy needed in dollars per MBTU. The E in the electrochemical process corresponds to the thermochemical factor $\Sigma\Delta G_i + \Delta\Delta G_i$ and c would be replaced by a factor which would be the cost of the heat per MBTU needed to run the process divided by the Carnot-like efficiency factor which we have discussed. The first term for a thermochemical process would be about the same as that for the corresponding electrochemical process.

Now, for the thermochemical process, the term representing costs of 1 MBTU apart from energy would be the sum of several terms for the plants corresponding to the various steps of the thermochemical cycle. It seems likely that none of the plant costs for each stage would be as cheap as those for the one-step electrolysis situation because of the need for equipment to work at high temperature, and withstand changes of pressure; and for the materials to withstand corrosion. Furthermore, it would not be a single D_i, but would have to be expressed as $D_i + D_j + ...$, corresponding to plant for the various steps of the thermochemical process.

In most thermochemical processes at present proposed, there are three stages, and the cost of each would have to be on average one-third the non-electricity consuming costs of an electrolyser unit for the thermochemical method to be cost-competitive with the electrochemical.

It seems unlikely that such cost-competitiveness could occur. The economic viability of high-temperature thermochemical-cyclical processes for the production of hydrogen is hence to be doubted.

Electrochemical processes

For water dissociation, one can work at room temperatures, and drive the reaction $H_2O \rightarrow H_2 + \frac{1}{2}O_2$, so long as one has available the electrical energy.

The *electrosynthesis* of hydrogen is simple, may be achieved at low temperature, and the products are generated separately. The technology is established, but old. Although the fundamentals of electrode kinetics are now

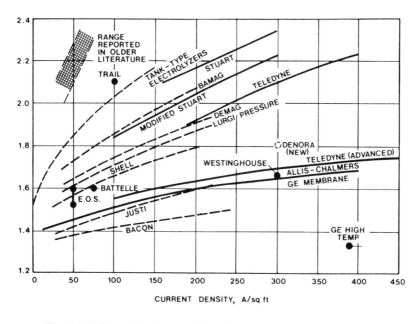

Fig. 13.2. Cell operating characteristics of various advanced electrolysers.[27]

understood,[26] and many laboratory improvements have been made (see Fig. 13.2), none have yet been incorporated in a large-scale plant. There is much to do in the way of new, and modified, methods for the production (and cost lowering) of electrolytic hydrogen.

The effect of temperature upon the electrochemical production of hydrogen

For $H_2O \rightarrow H_2 + \frac{1}{2}O_2$ at 25°C:

$$\Delta G° = 56.69 \text{ kcals mole}^{-1}$$
$$\Delta H = 68.32 \text{ kcals mole}^{-1}$$
$$\Delta S° = 39.13 \text{ eu}$$
$$E_{cell} (1 \text{ atm}) = 1.229$$

At the boiling point of water, the parameters change because ΔS and ΔH include a contribution due to the heat of vaporisation.

At 150°, the equivalent quantities have been given in the first section of this chapter.

The temperature coefficient of the standard reversible potential is:

$$\frac{dE}{dt} = 0.25 \text{ mv (°C)}^{-1} \qquad (13.12)$$

Also:[28]

$$\Delta G = -nFE \qquad (13.13)$$

so that, as the temperature rises, the *voltage* which must be applied to a cell to overcome the thermodynamically necessary energy is reduced. In a hypothetical state, for which $\Delta S = 0$, then:

$$\Delta G = \Delta H,$$

$$E = \frac{\Delta H}{nF} = \frac{68.32 \cdot 4.18}{2 \cdot 96500} = 1.47 \text{ volts} \qquad (13.14)$$

Under these hypothetical conditions, then, the manufacture of H_2 is carried out entirely by electricity, and there is no heat evolved to the surroundings, and no cooling effect on the cell (or corresponding heat picked up from the surroundings to contribute to the running of the reaction).

The reversible potential of a hydrogen-oxygen cell at 25°C is 1.23v.[28] Hence, under the hypothetical condition that a cell could work thermally with thermodynamic reversibility (no overpotential), 0.24 volts of the energy necessary would come from the $T\Delta S$ term. In this hypothetical situation, heat is withdrawn from the surroundings to be added to that needed for completing the reaction. The electrical energy used is less than the energy needed to decompose water to hydrogen and oxygen. If the potential falls below 1.23 volt, H_2 cannot be produced at 1 At pressure, and 298°K even at extremely low rates.[29]

Correspondingly, if the potential applied exceeds 1.47 volts at 25°, the electrical energy entering the cell with be greater than that needed—thermodynamically—to dissociate water to hydrogen and oxygen at 1 atm pressure, and the excess energy will be given off as heat.[27]

These relations of heat and electricity can be seen in Fig. 13.3.

Thermoneutral potential

Gregory called the potential at which heat was neither being taken from the surroundings to create hydrogen, nor being rejected to the surroundings, the 'thermoneutral potential' (see Fig. 13.3).[30]

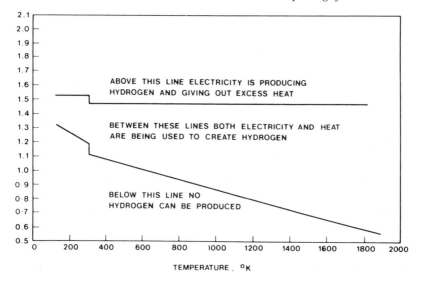

Fig. 13.3. Electricity and heat: gain and loss in electrosynthesis of
hydrogen.

Can ambient heat be converted to hydrogen?

Consideration of the conversion of heat to hydrogen via an electrochemical
cell can be divided into two ranges. Firstly, if no heat is applied to the cell
from outside, then, if electrolysis is occurring below the thermoneutral potential, the cell tends to cool, i.e. extract heat from the surroundings. The temperature could be restored by keeping the surroundings mobile, i.e. blowing
air over the cell, but a practical device for extracting energy from the surroundings could only be made with difficulty in this way for kinetic reasons.
Thus, at the thermoneutral potential, 1.47 volts, the overpotential of the cell
would be 1.47–1.23 at 25° = 0.24 volt. Assuming that this overpotential is
entirely on the oxygen anode, and that this is working on a planar electrode
which has an i_o (exchange current density) of 10^{-8} amp cm^{-2}, the current density would be given (at 25°C) by:

$$0.25 = \frac{RT}{\alpha F} \log \frac{i}{i_o}, \qquad (13.15)$$

or, with $\alpha = \frac{1}{2}$, i 2.10^{-6} amp cm^{-2}, i.e., $10^5 - 10^6$ times slower rate than what
is desirable. By the use of porous systems, this situation could perhaps be
improved by only *one to two* orders of magnitude. A hypothetical solution,
and perhaps a goal for research, would be a super-catalyst for the oxygen
anode. Were such a catalyst to give a real i_o of 10^{-4} amp cm^{-2}, and area effects
(porosity) to contribute a further ten to one hundred times to the rate of
production per apparent unit area,[19] then, working at a reasonable 10^{-1} amp
cm^{-2}, the overpotential would be:

$$\eta = \frac{RT}{\alpha F} \log \frac{10^{-1}}{10^{-3}} = 0.24 \qquad (13.16)$$

i.e. the loss of energy due to overpotential would compensate the gain in energy from the surroundings, neglecting I^2R loss, because the I would be very low. It follows that, by building a plant for the electrosynthesis of hydrogen which covered a cell area 10-100 times larger than used hitherto (building upwards?), one might begin to gain some energy from the atmosphere, for at, say, 10^{-2} amps cm^{-2}, the activation overpotential would be such that the cell potential would be 0.1 volt less than the thermoneutral potential.

However, any hope of an economically meaningful heat-to-electricity extraction to a cooled cell from normally warm surroundings should be abandoned for a variety of reasons: (a) Increased fixed costs for the land area in building extra large plants for working at low current densities; (b) Neglect of IR drop tends to make the above statements optimistic, even if, at low current densities, the ohmic drop is low; (c) Only gold in alkaline solutions has an i_o as high as 10^{-8} amp cm^{-2} for O_2 evolution, at $T \simeq 25°C$, has been reported. Seeking one remains a good research goal, but it would be foolish to rely upon its attainment in a relatively short time.

Analogous remarks apply to concepts of working in electrolytes below $T = 273°K$. The i_o value would drop with temperature and the energy losses due to polarisation would increase, wiping out the likelihood of a usable heat transfer to a cooled cell.

The conversion of high temperature heat to electricity and hydrogen

If the current density is increased, a hydrogen-oxygen reactor will experience an increased potential between the electrodes, due (among other sources of overpotential) to the ohmic drop, IR.[20] Such a potential difference produces heat, at a rate of I^2R, and the temperature of the cell tends to rise above that of the surroundings, so that no heat can flow to it from them.

However, due to the $T\Delta S$ term in the equation, $\Delta G = \Delta H - T\Delta S$, the electrical potential thermodynamically needed for the decomposition of water to hydrogen, is reduced as the temperature is increased. Further, activation overpotential is effectively the amount by which the heat of activation is dimished to achieve a certain rate. Increased temperature leads to an increased rate, and hence the activation overpotential, η, necessary to attain a given rate, is diminished at an increased T. If the temperature of a cell is raised several hundred degrees above room temperature, i.e. the electrolyte is a solid electrolyte with mobile 0^{--} ions, and the fuel is steam, there is a possibility of supplying the cell with heat from the surroundings (e.g. 1000° heat from an atomic reactor), and converting such heat directly to hydrogen.

To investigate this, consider the $T\Delta S$ term during the electrolysis of water to H_2 at above 1000°C. The value is for the conversion of 1 mole. The rate of production of hydrogen at a current density i is i/nF moles sec^{-1} cm^{-2}. Hence, the cell loses heat at the rate of:

$$4.18 \ T\Delta S \frac{i}{nF} \text{ joules } sec^{-1} \ cm^{-2} \qquad (13.17)$$

Thus, if at, say, 1000°C, $i \simeq 1$ amp cm^{-2}, and the resistance of the membrane (Fig. 13.4)[31] is < 0.01 ohms cm^2, then the IR drop is less than

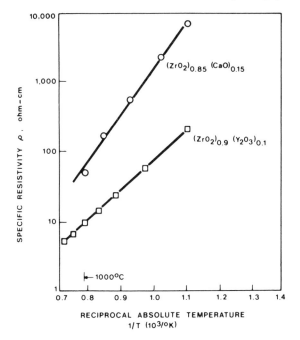

Fig. 13.4. The specific resistivity of solid electrolytes as a function of temperature.

0.01 v (i.e. negligible), although the *potential* needed for the production of hydrogen will be about 0.8 volt (Fig. 13.3). As the thermoneutral potential at $1273°K$ is about 1.49 v, 0.69 v or 46%, of the energy for the decomposition of water would be coming from the external heat source, which would then be compensating for the cooling tendency of the cell. The cell has become, therefore, a one-step heat-to-hydrogen converter which operates near to 1000°C. Such a converter of heat to hydrogen would be superior to a purely electrochemical process, because nuclear heat is cheaper than the same quantity of energy after conversion to electricity. But it is also to be preferred to cyclical *chemical* processes using heat, because these are thermally inefficient, complex to build, and would therefore involve high maintenance costs, and may not be 100% cyclical.

The approximations in the above argument are: negligible activation overpotential, a reasonable assumption at 1000°C, and negligible IR drop. The latter condition has not been achieved; but it has also not been desired because the concept of high-temperature cells for electrolysing water is usually that they provide their own heat from the I^2R of the passage of current through the solid electrolyte. Insofar as it were economic to utilise atomic- or solar-derived heat to convert to electricity and hydrogen, then solid electrolytes for function at $T > 1000°C$, with sufficiently small Rs, are probably feasible. The long-term chemical or thermal stability is not explored.

A cost estimate for the hydrogen produced in this way can be made by taking equation (13.33), i.e.

$$\text{Cost of MBTU of hydrogen (cents)} = 229 \text{ Ec} + 40 \qquad (13.18)$$

using E from the reduced value at 1000°C (about 0.8 volt in the absence of IR and η), and adding to the value obtained from equation (13.18) the necessary heat cost.

The electrosynthesis of hydrogen at high temperatures without an external heat source.

Let it be assumed an electrochemical cell for the production of hydrogen is working at a sufficiently high temperature so that the activation over-potential is negligible, and IR is the source of the heat which is equal to $T\Delta S$ cooling. As a first approximation, let it be supposed that there are zero radiational and convectional heat losses, then, just to compensate the cooling effects of the endothermic reaction:

$$I^2R = \frac{4.18 \ T\Delta SI}{nF} \qquad (13.19)$$

$$IR = \frac{T\Delta S}{nF} 4.18 \qquad (13.20)$$

Hence, the total applied potential must be:

$$E_{thermo} + IR = E_{thermo} + \frac{T\Delta S}{nF} 4.18 \qquad (13.21)$$

But $(T\Delta S/nF)$ 4.18 is the difference between the reversible thermodynamic potential and the thermoneutral potential. Thus, in the absence of an external heat source, one cannot, in practice, electrolyse water to produce H_2 at below the thermoneutral potential and above the temperature of the surroundings. It has sometimes been implied that this can be done with consequent decrease of E, and, from equation (13.33), lowering of costs.[32]

Electrolysis at high temperatures gives, then, no net *thermodynamic* advantage. The lowering of the thermodynamically reversible potential is nugatory, because the IR drop which has to be added to the reversible potential to provide the heat necessary to prevent the cell cooling (in the absence of an external source of heat) is equal to the voltage-lowering gained by the increase in temperature. However, a real gain may exist by electrolysis at higher temperatures, because of the reduction of the anodic activation over-potential. A considerable gain in necessary energy cost *is* available if external heat is used to maintain the cell at constant temperature, whilst electrolysing steam at high temperature, because now some of the energy for electrolysis comes from heat and not from electricity.

Heat to hydrogen and net electricity production

If one raised the temperature of a hydrogen-oxygen reactor to that at which $T\Delta S > \Delta H$, the cell would begin spontaneously to produce electricity as well as hydrogen, i.e. it would function as a hydrogen and oxygen-*producing* fuel cell. This would be of interest as a method of converting heat to electricity, but it is easy to show that the temperature at which the process would begin, even at low partial pressures of hydrogen and oxygen, is above 4000°C, and hence unfeasible.

It might be thought that a heat-to-electricity converter could still be made if one ran the high-temperature steam electrolyser at a temperature sufficiently high so that the necessary cell potential difference would be less than the potential of the fuel cell operating on the hydrogen produced. In fact, this is rather a pipe-dream. It can be assumed, for example, that 0.9 volt is the highest potential which a room-temperature fuel cell will produce. To obtain a net gain of 0.1 volt electrical potential (from heat), the high temperature cell will therefore have to work at 0.8 volt, or less, and reference to Fig. 13.3 shows that, even accepting the ideal condition of negligible IR and negligible overpotential, the steam-electrolyser would have to be run at 1300°K. This is certainly possible, but replacing the ideal by the still optimistic assumption of a total 0.1 loss in IR and overpotential, one has a minimum temperature of some 1500°K. Were a 2000°K cell feasible, one could expect a net potential source of 0.3 volt. Although attractive from the viewpoint of efficiency of electricity production from heat whilst avoiding Carnot losses, the temperatures are impossible from atomic sources and difficult for solar ones.

Conclusion concerning an optimal path for heat to hydrogen conversion

There is much to be said for using solar heat to keep an electrolysis cell at 1000°C, and to convert part of the heat electrochemically to hydrogen.

One could make a rough estimate of the cost of such hydrogen by taking the necessary cell potential as the ideal thermodynamic one at 1000°C (see Fig. 13.3), 0.82 volt, and adding 0.1 volt for polarisation losses. Then, if one takes the value of the cost of interruptible electricity at the plant site as 1.6 cents kWh^{-1},[33] the electricity cost is (see equation 13.31) 2.29 Ec per MBTU, i.e. $3.00. If one takes the cost of atomic heat as $2.50 per MBTU, and assumes that half the energy for the electrolysis under the endothermic conditions is thus supplied, one needs $1.25 per MBTU for the heat. It is more difficult to estimate the cost of the amortisation, maintenance and insurance, but a 1978 value for this per MBTU is $1 for a simple electrolyser (equation 13.33), so it seems reasonable to assume a doubling for the high temperature cell. With this poorly founded assumption, the cost of 1 MBTU of H_2 would be $6.25, in the low part of the range of $6-9 for 1978 costs of the long-scale production of H_2 from water.[33]

The electrode-kinetics of the electrochemical production of hydrogen from water

Although the first textbook on the kinetics of electrode processes was published in 1955,[28] most electrode kinetical equations are developed to apply to individual electrodes, and there has been little development of equations which are applicable to the overall cell. If the cathode and anode are of the same area, it is easy to show that:[29]

$$I = (i_o)_{cell}e^{(V-V_e)/q} \qquad (13.22)$$

where V = total potential to drive the cell at I; V_e = equilibrium potential; and $q = \lambda_1 + \lambda_2$, where $\lambda = RT/\alpha F$, 1 and 2 refer to the two electrode reactions, respectively; α is the so-called transfer coefficient of electrode kinetics. This coefficient is related in a complex way to the shape of the barrier at the electrode-solution interface,[34] and to its stoichiometry in practice, and is often near to ½. Detailed values are given elsewhere.[34]

Thus, as the value of the applied potential departs significantly from the equilibrium potential, i.e. as the overpotential, η, begins to be significant, the *rate* of production of the H_2 rises exponentially with the overpotential.

Overpotential is like inflation: it always leads one to spend more than one thought would be necessary (i.e. more than the price necessary, assuming electrolysis at V_e, i.e. electrolysis at zero overpotential). On the other hand, like inflation, the results are not all bad, because both give rise to an acceleration of the action; currents and economies, respectively, go faster. However, the overpotential of cells increases the price of the product just as inflation affects the price of goods. One has to pay more (compared with the price hypothetically available at very low rates when overpotential would be nearer to zero), per mole of product, for the electricity to drive the cell by the ratio:

$$1 + \frac{\eta}{V_e} \tag{13.23}$$

Conversely, cells occupy space and space costs. The *faster* the reaction (arising from a greater overpotential), the *less* the space is covered per unit mass and time of production. Hence, there will be an optimal value of overpotential to bring about a high current-density depending on the local price of electricity and land. However, i/i_o (see equation 13.22) should always be maximised, for the reaction rate, for a *given* overpotential (i.e. cost of fuel per mole of H_2) is proportional to it.

The overpotential needed to give a certain value of i, or rate of production of hydrogen, is proportional to log i/i_o. The overpotential can be broken down to:

$$V = V_e + \eta_{\substack{\text{anodic} \\ \text{activation}}} + \eta_{\substack{\text{cathodic} \\ \text{activation}}} + \eta_{\substack{\text{anodic} \\ \text{concentration}}}$$

$$+ \eta_{\substack{\text{cathodic} \\ \text{concentration}}} + IR, \tag{13.24}$$

where the activation η's refer to the overpotential associated with electro-catalysis, and the concentration η's to transport difficulties. A fuller development of equations for electrochemical cells is given in the book by Bockris and Reddy.[35]

Thus, equation (13.24) can be written:

$$V_{\text{working}} = V_e + \Sigma\eta \tag{13.25}$$

where $\Sigma\eta$ comprises the sum of the overpotentials at the two electrodes.

In the electrolysis of water, concentration overpotentials are negligible and the overpotentials are both activational and ohmic. Oxygen overpotential is a major problem for electrolysis at temperatures in aqueous solutions. Several tenths of a volt deviation from the reversible potential can be observed at current densities in the order of 100 milliamps per sq. cm. Where c_{elec} = 3 cents $(kWh)^{-1}$, 0.4v overpotential would increase the cost of an MBTU of hydrogen by c. \$2.75, i.e. around 33%.

The reduction of these overpotentials can be achieved by going to higher temperatures: above 500°C, the oxygen overvoltage problem is greatly reduced. Two approaches for reducing overpotential at low temperatures exist:

1. The use of platinum[36] as an electrode catalyst reduces the overpotential, but is too expensive, and there would not be enough.[37] However, *very* small amounts of platinum may be used,[38] the Pt being confined to the active zone within the pore. The cost of the Pt needed is about $10(kW)^{-1}$.

2. Small traces of platinum on tungsten bronze facilitate the evolution of oxygen and make the electrode per unit area have the same properties as Pt, although their costs are small compared with that needed if Pt electrodes were used. This work[39-41] is worthy of pursuit in respect to low temperature electrolysers. Analogous work to this in which the tungsten bronzes are replaced by more complex, but similar, materials, is of interest. Thus, Tseung[42] has reported electrodes which in oxygen evolution, at room temperatures, have overpotential of less than 100 mv at rates of hydrogen production equivalent to 100 milliamps cm^{-2}.

Classical electrolysers

Classical electrolysers have been little changed in design for many years. A series arrangement has an advantage because there is difficulty in obtaining the 2 volts per cell from the rectified AC. Conversely, large total potentials are used in the series arrangements and, if one cell fails, the whole bank ceases to operate. Hence, a parallel arrangement is also used.

In classical electrolysers, the potential applied is about 2 volts, and the current density about 100 amps ft^{-2}, i.e. 0.1 amps cm^{-2}.

The *cost* of H_2 produced in classical electrolysers is about 4.58c + 1 in dollars per MBTU, where c is the cost of electricity in cents per kWh. H_2 can be produced from coal at (1978) about \$4.50 per MBTU. Large-scale interruptible sources of electricity at the plant would have a 1978 value of about 1.6 cents kWh^{-1}. Hence, \$8.30 would be a minimum cost for large-scale electrolytic hydrogen production at the plant site using a classical electrolyser, and without cost of storage. Thus, whilst large-scale coal plants for the production of hydrogen are available, they will be a cheaper source of this substance than simple electrolysis from Carnot derived electricity.

Factors which may make hydrogen by electrolysis economic

1. When the hydrogen producible from coal is compared with hydrogen produced from electrolysers (based on atomic or solar electricity), it is not the same product. That from coal is only 97-98% pure, and contains CO, together with some H_2S. These impurities may *at a cost* be reduced to negligible concentrations. However, the cost has not yet been added to

the quoted price of H_2 from coal. Hydrogen from electrolysers is completely clean, without further treatments. Further, the vastly enhanced use
of coal as a basis to the production of the major fuel is associated with
the CO_2 hazards described in Chapter 4. It may be that the CO_2 may be
ocean-dissolved. But this cost, as well as that of the S removal and
disposal, would have to be costed to compare coal-based H_2 with that from
water-splitting.

2. Comparisons between the cost of hydrogen and that of fuels from fossil
   fuels is not too valid anyway. The entire concept of hydrogen is as a fuel
   to produce from sources other than fossil fuels. Its present relevance is
   that, *taking into account environmental factors,* the time period left before
   hydrogen fuel from atomic and solar-based water-splitting, will be shorter
   than the time needed to build a technology of large-scale hydrogen
   production.

3. The classical electrolysers—for which the price of more than $8 per MBTU
   has been calculated—have not been cost minimised. They have been
   engineered without use of the insight which modern electrode kinetics has
   given to the engineering of fuel cells, and hence of electrolysers. Thus, the
   present technology electrolysers:

   (a) Do not use an electrocatalyst to minimise overpotential;
   (b) Have no devices to reduce the effect of bubbles on IR drop between
       electrodes;
   (c) Do not use flow devices to reduce possible super-saturation hold up;
   (d) In fuel cell technology, current densities per external unit area are
       increased at least 10-100 times by the use of porous electrodes; but
       the use of porous electrodes has not been introduced into practical
       electrolyser technology (but see Reference 43).

       That a reduction can be achieved in the cost of electrolytic hydrogen,
       as a result of appropriate research and development of the above con-
       cepts, follows not only from the technical obsolescence of present elec-
       trolysers, but also from the performances of many new experimental
       electrolysers which have been demonstrated on the laboratory scale
       over the last decade. Current-potential curves are shown in Fig. 13.2.[44]
       They illustrate that, for the same price of electricity, the potential could
       be reduced from *c.* 2.2 to *c.* 1.5, i.e. reduced by some 33% for a given
       electricity cost. There could be a diminution of fixed costs, too, because
       higher current-densities possible with the emerging technology would
       give a reduction of area occupied by an electrolyser plant. With elec-
       tricity (interruptible, at the plant, very large scale) at 1.6 cents per
       kWh, and a potential of 1.6v, the cost of electrolytic H_2 would be
       around $6.80. There would be no environmental or health costs, as
       compared with the cheaper coal-based substance.

4. The cost foreseen in (3) does not take into account the application of
   known principles to the electrolytic process. Some of these results,
   described below, indicate a probability of lowering the cost to around $6
   per MBTU.

5. Photosynthetic and photo-electrochemical approaches are only in their
   laboratory stages. However, they could result in hydrogen at costs much
   less than $6 per MBTU. With Biomass production of H_2, costs comparable

with those of H_2 from coal seem reasonable to expect. The CO_2 difficulty would be eliminated.

Direct electrochemical water splitting

Introduction

By 'direct electrochemical water splitting' is meant the production of hydrogen from water by electrolysis without thermal assistance, or any other indirect process, e.g. acceleration with the aid of light.

The advantages of electrolysis are plain and clear. They include:

1. The basic technology has been known for many decades.
2. The present large scale electrolyser plants are old, both in practice and in concept; knowledge of electrode processes brought in during the last two decades has not been applied. There is room for the reduction of the presently necessary applied difference potential to cause a given rate of evolution of hydrogen.
3. The method is the only one which, by its nature, separates the hydrogen from the oxygen.
4. It can be produced at all plant sizes without significant scale-up problems.
5. It is easy to produce from it hydrogen at pressures of the order of thirty to one hundred atmospheres, suitable for leading directly to a pipeline (thus avoiding costly pressurisation attendant upon other methods).
6. Materials problems are limited to the separator material and are not great.
7. The temperature for most versions of the method is less than 100°C.
8. There are no environmental hazards.

Deduction of the cost of electricity to produce one MBTU of hydrogen by electrolysis

Let it be assumed that the hydrogen fuel will be combusted to produce steam. Then:

$$H_2 + \tfrac{1}{2}O_2 \rightarrow H_2O + 58.14 \text{ kcal} \tag{13.26}$$

1 BTU is the heat to raise the temperature of a lb of water 1°F. Hence, it is 450 x 5/9 calories = 250 calories. One needs, for 10^6 BTU, $2.5 \cdot 10^8$ calories and this is got from $\dfrac{2.5 \times 10^8}{5.814 \times 10^4}$ moles of H_2, from which the coulombs necessary are:

$$\frac{2.5 \cdot 10^8 \cdot 2 \cdot 9.6 \cdot 10^4}{5.814 \cdot 10^4} \tag{13.27}$$

Hence, if the cell voltage is E, the watts seconds are:

$$\frac{E. 2.5 \cdot 2 \cdot 9.6 \cdot 10^{12}}{5.814 \cdot 10^4} \tag{13.28}$$

so that the kWh are:

$$\text{E.} \quad \frac{2.5 \cdot 2 \cdot 9.6 \cdot 10^2}{5.814 \cdot 10^4 \cdot 10^3 \cdot 3.6 \cdot 10^3} \tag{13.29}$$

and the cost for the electricity to produce 1 MBTU, in cents, is:

$$\frac{2.5 \cdot 2 \cdot 9.6 \cdot 10^{12} \text{ Ec}}{5.814 \cdot 3.6 \cdot 10^{10}} \tag{13.30}$$

$$= 229\text{Ec} \tag{13.31}$$

where c is the electricity cost in cents $(kWh)^{-1}$.

The efficiency of an electrolytic plant is subject to ambiguity. If it is defined in respect to the ΔH needed for the dissociation of water, it is 75% in industrial practice; and 95% in laboratory work established in 1976; and is expected to be practical at 100% within a decade (Srinivasen *et al.*).[45-47] However, this definition, though consistent, must be related to another kind of efficiency, that of conversion from the source of energy which produces the energy needed, electricity, used in electrolysis. As the efficiency of this process is 35-40%, and the efficiency of electrolysis 75-100%, the efficiency of hydrogen production, related to the energy source (e.g. coal), is 26-40%. These are the efficiencies which should be thought of when relating the electrochemical method to that of the thermochemical cycle method.

We are looking to solar and atomic energy sources for hydrogen. Here, heat will be available in the region of 800°C from a nuclear reactor; and at such temperatures, or higher ones (by the use of concentrators), from solar. Thus, electricity could probably be made at efficiencies above the 40% achieved hitherto, because the higher the T_H in the Carnot expression, the larger is the efficiency of conversion.

If the production of electricity can be carried out at, say, 50% efficiency, and the efficiency of water electrolysis 100%, the efficiency could be 50% for direct, simple, water electrolysis.

There have been misunderstanding and confusion when one refers to the efficiency of water electrolysis. Even with old plants, it is an efficient process compared with many.[48] With advances discussed here, made in the Brookhaven Laboratories, it reaches an asymptotically high efficiency.

Advances in electrolysis technique during the 1960s were associated with the names of Justi and Bacon.[49,50] Because of the equation relating the cost of hydrogen to the cost of electricity in which the two principal variables are the cell potential, E, and the electricity cost, c, the *operational* point in research on electrolysers is the reduction of the value of E. This quantity consists of a thermodynamic part, E_{rev}, and an irreversible kinetic contribution, η, which increases with the current density at which electrolysis is occurring.

It is not acceptable to make the overvoltage, η, low by simply reducing the current density because, with a decrease in this, land area occupied by the plant for a given production of hydrogen becomes greater, and therefore the capital costs of the equipment higher.[51] There is an optimum situation of overpotential, and hence the magnitude of the current density, at some value below the maximum attainable, thus reducing electricity costs although raising the needed land area.

During the 1970s, work led by Srinivasen[45] and by Appleby[46] is particularly important in this field (see Fig. 13.5). Important developments have also been made by the General Electric and the Teledyne Companies.

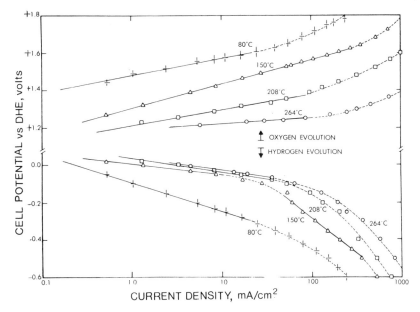

Fig. 13.5. Effect of increasing temperature on the cell voltage required to attain a desired current density.

The effect of temperature

Reduction of E, the potential needed for electrolysis at a given current density and temperature, implies a reduction of overpotential. This can be broken down into the electrode kinetic parameters of exchange current density and Tafel slope or a correlated factor called the transfer coefficient, α.

Miles, Kissel, Lu and Srinivasen[45] have shown that there is a substantial increase in exchange current density (i.e. a reduction in the necessary cell voltage) in 50% KOH if the temperature is increased from 80 through 264°C, and crosses the Neél temperature for nickel oxide (see Fig. 13.6).[52]

Electrocatalysis

Electrocatalysis increases the exchange current density: the larger the value of this is, the smaller the overpotential for a given current density.

The needs of the oxygen anode in respect to electrocatalysis are much greater than those of the hydrogen cathode. The problem of finding suitable catalysts, however, is more difficult for the anode than for the cathode because the anodic potentials are more positive and hence more in the range in which metals dissolve anodically (thus restricting consideration to all but

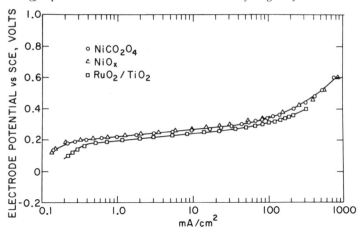

Fig. 13.6. Tafel's slopes for the 'mixed oxide' oxygen electrodes.

noble metals). At the cathode, the potential is more than 1 volt in the negative direction, and hence the danger of dissolution is slight. Electrocatalysis has been studied, therefore, more comprehensively for the hydrogen evolution reaction than for the oxygen evolution reaction, although its study for the latter is more necessary than for the former. Thus, the component of the cost of hydrogen due to cathodic overpotential is much less than that from the oxygen overpotential.

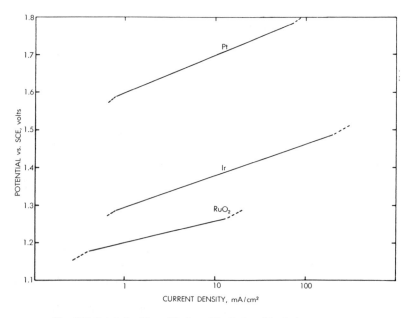

Fig. 13.7. Catalytic effect of Pt, Ir and RuO_2 in acid solution on oxygen overvoltage.

In acid solutions, ruthenium oxide, RuO_2, turns out to be both a better and a cheaper catalyst than platinum for oxygen evolution (this is shown in Figure 13.7).[52]

Alloys of nickel with iridium, ruthenium, tungsten, titanium, silver, copper and iron have been examined in alkaline solution.[53] Little improvement compared with the behaviour of plain nickel was noted. All these electrodes form oxide films and the electrocatalysis will depend on the electronic properties of the oxides rather than the metals.

In spinels, the mixed valency states of the cations help oxygen dissociation. Oxygen dissociation and adsorption by $NiCo_2O_4$ and RuO_2. TiO_2 have been investigated in OH^- between 25° and 100°C.[54] A decrease in the Tafel slope appears and an increase in the exchange current density for nickel cobaltate, $NiCo_2O_4$, is over 150 mv better than is nickel at 200 ma. cm^{-2}.

Interesting studies have been conducted by Tseung and Jasem on semi-conducting oxides supported on metallic screens (e.g. $NiCo_2O_4$ on Ni).[55] The effect of such a material on current densities is shown in Figure 13.8.

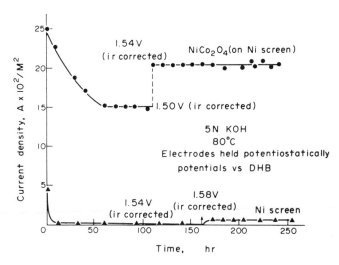

Fig. 13.8. Current density over long period for oxygen evolution on a semiconducting oxide compared with the same on a metal.[55]

The use of traces of platinum has been found to be advantageous on tungsten and bronze electrodes. Without the platinum, this substance is not a good electrocatalyst for oxygen evolution; but with traces of it, which are negligible in cost, it attains properties which, in oxygen *dissolution,* are better than those of platinum over certain current-density ranges. This appears to be the basis for new investigations in which synergicity effects are taken into account.[56]

There has been as yet little *basic* electrocatalytic work (a quantum mechanical approach has been suggested by Bockris[57]).

Separator materials

With the advantages found by Srinivasan *et al.,*[58] in going to higher temperatures (e.g. 150°C), it is desirable to find a separator more resistant to alkaline solutions at these temperatures than is asbestos. *Potassium titanate* works well (hydroxol ion transporting solid?).

The General Electric Company markets a polymer which allows 1 ma. cm^{-2} at 1.8 volts. It is proton transporting and acidic, so the electrode-catalyst used in conjunction with it have to be noble metals, thus reducing the desirability of the polymer. It would be advantageous if it were possible to develop an analogue which is effective in alkaline solutions. A polymer involving quaternary ammonium groups would be suitable.[59]

Corrosion

Some difficulties occur in hydrogen electrolysers due to corrosion even at 100°C. The corrosion is caused by inner stray currents and is little studied.

Anode depolarisation

The potential necessary to produce hydrogen electrolytically is contributed to by the O_2 electrode potential of 1.23 v (standard value). If one could avoid this reaction by substituting a material which is cheap, or a pollutant which can be made inert by oxidation at the anode, it would not only be possible to remove the pollutant but, if the anodic reaction of the pollutant removal occurs at a lesser potential than that of O_2 evolution, the oxidation of the pollutant (instead of water) will be accompanied by the necessary potential for electrolysis and hence a drop in the price of H_2 (see equation 13.30).

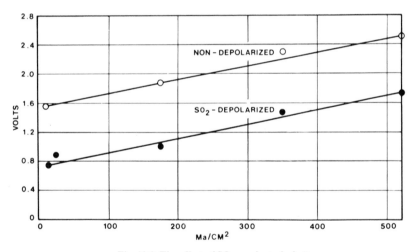

Fig. 13.9. The effect of SO_2 on electrolysis.[69]

Juda and Moulton experimented on these lines with SO_2.[60] They introduced this in the form of 6% H_2SO_3 into 30% H_2SO_4. The voltage for the electrolysis of water before SO_2 addition was 1.6-2.4 volts for the current density 1-500 ma. cm^{-2}, and with SO_2, 0.74 to 1.62 v for the same current density (Fig. 13.9).

SO_2 production from H_2SO_4 is possible; NO from stack gas could be converted to HNO_3; sewage could be oxidised to CO_2. Catalyst costs would be involved.*

Present large-scale electrolytic generators

Introduction

There are some ten organisations in the world today which produce large electrolysers.[61] Electrolysers developed by the Allis-Chalmers Company[62] (Fig. 13.10)[63] and the General Electric Company[64] (Fig. 13.11)[65] in the 1960s contained some new technology, but the more recent electrolysers are in general somewhat classical in concept.

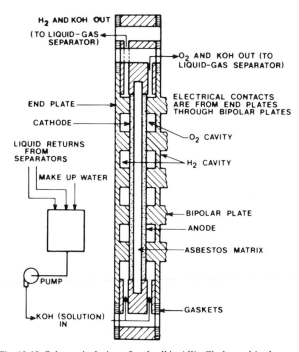

Fig. 13.10. Schematic design of end cell in Allis-Chalmers bipolar water electrolysis cell.[62]

In a pre-Hydrogen Economy time, whilst natural gas is allowed to remain available at less than $6 per MBTU[†], hydrogen from electrolysis based on electricity from fossil fuels is likely to be more expensive than hydrogen from natural gas or coal.[‡]

In Europe and Japan, larger-scale hydroelectric resources imply a greater

---

*Attempts to de-polarise with coal would be less good because the coal is not a waste product and would cost.

†However, 15 January 1978, *Los Angeles Times,* reported $7 per MBTU as the Mexican Government price for new natural gas.

‡But according to Dugger and Francis, hydrogen from OTEC could be economic for ammonia manufacture at the present time.[66]

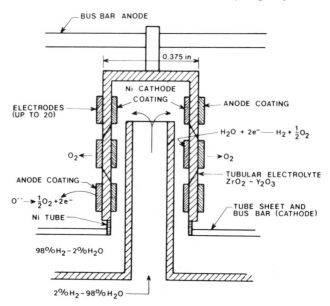

Fig. 13.11. Schematic diagram of single tube in proposed General Electric steam electrolysis cell.

availability of electrolytic hydrogen. Hydrogen from electrolysers is used there (as also in India and Africa) for manufacturing fertilisers. 25% KOH is used in a filter press module at about 7 atmospheres. A typical small plant produces 100 lb of hydrogen (2.5 MBTU) per hour. The block diagram is shown in Figure 13.12.[61] The electrolyte's temperature and flow are followed and connected to an alarm in case temperature should build up. Automated additions of de-ionised water are made. After the gas has been removed from the cell, it enters a demister to remove water. It continues through a molecular sieve catalyst purification set-up to remove traces of oxygen. The vessels and the piping are of stainless steel. Pumps are magnetic.

Optimisation considerations govern the design and working of a plant: as the applied potential falls, the energy costs of making hydrogen decrease. However, with the diminished values of E, there is a lessened value for the current density, and this in turn means less hydrogen per unit area of the electrode and plant; hence, the capital cost per unit of hydrogen increases. Mathematical models of each plant are used to optimise conditions.

Cost of industrial hydrogen in the late 1970s

Hydrogen costs are affected by a number of items. They are determined by the price of electricity and the characteristics of the E-i relationship. However, as the above remarks indicate, it is important to optimise capital cost and reduction of potential.

At high efficiencies, the plant costs start to rise again because of the use of larger amounts of metal in the electrode and supports, or for the catalyst. It is simplistic to assume that the cost of hydrogen will decrease with increased efficiency, though there will be a region in which this will be so.

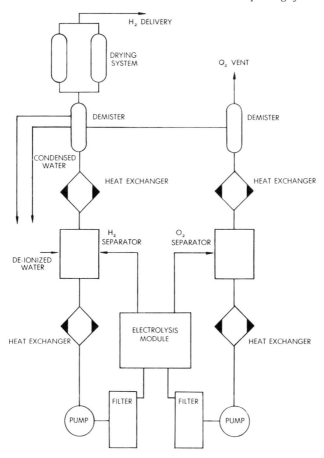

Fig. 13.12. Block diagram of 1.25 tons per day capacity hydrogen plant. A 25% KOH solution is forced, through filters, into the electrolysis module, the gases thus produced are separated and freed from KOH vapours in the primary separators. The hydrogen is lead through the heat exchanger and finally collected by drying in a molecular sieve system.

An example of cost ratios as a function of efficiency is shown in Fig. 13.13.[61]

Teledyne sells a small plant which would give hydrogen at about $8 per MBTU.

Delay in application of laboratory results to 1970s electrolyser technology

There seems to be a lag in applying research in hydrogen electrolysers, represented by the work of Srinivasan, Appleby[46] and Tseung[55] (Figs. 13.8, 13.14), and present commercial manufacture. Present electrolysers have not yet shown application of the knowledge on catalysis of the oxygen electrodes due to Tseung,[55] or Srinivasan.[58,59] Ruthenium oxide for acid solutions, and cobalt nickelate, $CoNi_2O_4$, in alkaline solutions, have not yet been introduced. Potassium titanate as a separator is not yet in use. Temperature

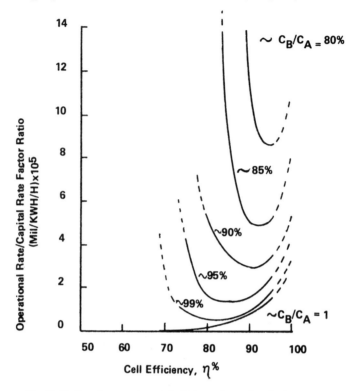

Fig. 13.13. Cost-factor ratio vs cell efficiency for various hydrogen cost reductions. C = cost of hydrogen. A and B refer to cells with different characteristics.

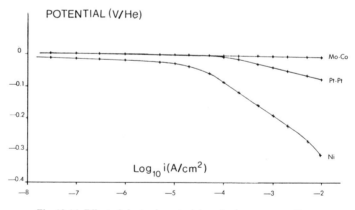

Fig. 13.14. Effect of electrode materials on hydrogen overvoltage.

has not yet been used in optimisation. The IR associated with bubbles is recognized but not yet analysed and taken into account. The concept of Tafel slope reduction has not yet been applied.

There is, thus, some way to go in the design of electrolysers, but in view of the trade-off of capital costs* versus electricity costs above, it would be unwise to suggest that all these potential improvements will *necessarily* reduce the cost of the final product. They may increase capital costs, and, depending on the price of money, this would add to the cost of hydrogen per MBTU. However, an excellent example of electrochemical innovation which reduced capital cost is the anode of RuO_2-TiO_2 which is used in Cl_2 evolution.

A new analysis for cost optimisation has to be made for each new plant.

Projections of the results of optimising present technology are shown in Fig. 13.15.[61] For a 1990 stage in the practice of a Hydrogen Economy, 1.6 volts is a reasonable value to use for E at 100 amps per ft².

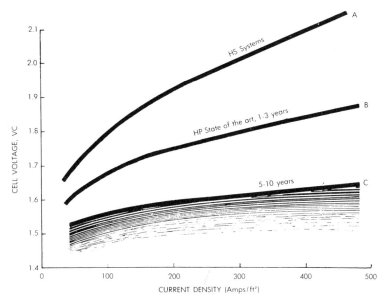

Fig. 13.15. Current-voltage characteristics of electrolysis modules of Teledyne energy systems.[61]

Forward concepts for electrolyser design

There are a number of new methods proposed for the production of hydrogen, e.g. the photoelectrochemical method, and a number of ways associated with thermal assistance. In this section, some concepts are suggested which might be realisable at the laboratory level during the 1980s.

Super-active catalyst

The field of electrocatalysis has remained poor in concept (see Bockris and McHardy).[56] Nevertheless, a steady improvement in the finding of new

---

*The importance of this would depend upon the price of money. In a highly inflationary economy it will be more important because of the high cost of money there, than in a low inflation rate economy with interest rates at, say 4%.

materials for oxygen electrodes has occurred since the pioneering work of Sepa, Damjanovic and Bockris on the tungsten bronzes.[67]

Thus, not only have conducting oxides, often reasonably catalytic, come into existence, but there is a knowledge of the theory of porous electrodes and the current distribution in them, which will be usable to optimise the area of electrodes.[68] Synergistic aspects in electrocatalysis have not yet been strongly developed, although a beginning has been made.[69]

However, it seems unlikely that the extensions of electrocatalysis would push the i_o (per *apparent* sq cm) for oxygen above, say, 10^{-2} amp/cm^{-2} at $100°$. With 100 ma. cm^{-2} for the delivery rate of hydrogen there would then, at 100°C, be an oxygen overpotential of:

$$(\eta_{O_2})100° = 0.18 \log 10^{-1}/10^{-2}$$

$$\simeq 0.18 \text{ volts}$$

Correspondingly, the hydrogen overvoltage at 100 ma. cm^{-2} will not be reduced below the very low value of 0.05 volts. With an E_{rev} of about 1.2, this means a possible minimum working potential of 1.43, without any contribution from an IR drop. The thermoneutral voltage is 1.47, so that one could state that a feasible goal for 100°C, 100 ma electrolysers would be 1.47 volt.

Another approach to lowering overpotential exists, the attainment of a higher transfer coefficient (say, 2) in the Tafel equation. It has been shown that this is possible in some cases (Srinivasan *et al*).[70] Thus, an exchange current density of 10^{-2} amp cm^{-2} would then contribute at 100 ma. cm^{-2}

$$0.045.\log.10^{-1}/10^{-2} \simeq 0.05 \text{ volts}$$

and the cell potential could then be as low as 1.4 as a final goal for 100°C and 100 ma. cm.$^{-2}$

Possible high-temperature electrode surfaces
The use of an increased temperature to raise the exchange current density and decrease the overpotential has several trade-off aspects. The advantages are counteracted by increasing costs of the separator and the significant costs of providing the heat.[71]

Further, if the electrolyte is to be heated over 100°C, one has to use high-pressure vessels, which again cause an increase in capital cost.

However, let it be supposed that the electrode material is deposited in thin layers upon a sufficiently low-heat conductivity base; and that a part of the electrical energy needed for the electrolysis is used to heat this layer to high temperatures, e.g. 250°C. The result would be rapid vaporisation of the layer of the solution next to the electrode, and this would increase desirable turbulence and mixing near to the electrode surface. The main effect would be a high exchange current density values at a cost less than attaining these through high-pressure vessels, and the use of heat to raise the temperatures in the solution as a whole.

Cost optimisation would have to be attained, but it is noteworthy that *cf.*

high local temperatures (e.g. 500°C) are attainable, some heat would be converted to electricity.[71] Electrode heating could perhaps be attained by a directed IR beam at the frequencies which utilised IR 'window' in water.

Removal of bubbles in gas evolution: no separator

A separator is used in most electrolysers, so that there will be no mixing of the gas stream from cathode and anode.

At first desirable, a separator has some negative effects. It adds to the potential necessary to drive the electrolysis at a certain rate by introducing a significant IR drop. It causes difficulties when it deteriorates with use, particularly when it begins to add unwanted particles to the gas stream. It adds to capital costs.

Several 'no separator' arrangements can be conceived. There are a few applications (e.g. welding torch fuel, and perhaps the direct provision of onboard automotive fuel), where the two gases could be pre-mixed. The hydrogen-oxygen combination, and the energy therefrom, per unit volume, will be greater if there is no diluting nitrogen present.

In the majority of cases, however, particularly when hydrogen has to be stored, there is a need to separate the gases:

(a) For a rapid vertical movement of electrolyte between the electrodes, there will be insufficient time for the bubbles which have just come into the moving layer from the electrode to grow and move toward each other. The stream may meet a metal, non-porous separator out of line of sight of the electrodes, and hence offering no IR resistance. In this way, two collectors of hydrogen and oxygen can be obtained with no IR drop due to a separator. Would the pumping and flow system cost be less than the IR loss and the separator costs? Would pumping system costs be less than the saving in the absence of an IR loss and the separator costs?

(b) It may be possible to arrange for a sucking-in of bubbles through the electrode to exit at the back, and thus allow a bubble-free stationary path for ions to flow.

Desirability of fast flow in KOH solution

The particles which undergo reaction at the electrodes are in fact water itself. However, in a stationary electrolyte the evolution of hydrogen and oxygen would cause a pH change in the vicinity of the electrodes. These are normally eliminated by the stirring arising from bubble formation. The more this becomes, the more it is necessary to remove further IR losses.

Hence, investigation of the economics of rapid-flow systems seems desirable, independently of what might be achieved in the direction of the elimination of separators.

Limitingly low IR drop

As the current density increases, the value of E increases, not only because of activation overpotential, but because of IR drop. This arises because of the resistance of the electrolyte, and because of bubble effects which tend to increase at high rates. Capital costs (per unit of hydrogen produced in unit time) go down with increases of current density. Ideally, electrodes should be limitingly near each other. However, mixing of gases and the presence of the membrane has limited this. One sees increasingly the advantages which could be attained by a removal of bubbles and an elimination of the separator.

Pulse and reverse electrolysis

There is a growth of overpotential with time and a decrease of catalytic property with time. It is worth considering what improvements could be made with various current-interruption regimes. These would include the chopping common to battery charging and discharging, but also reverse electrolysis for electrode activation.

Prospects here may become limited if the overpotential can be made so small that gains from its further reduction are not great. By contrast, in the operation of a battery, the conditions of diffusion and the Prandtl layers are important. However, pulse operation may be of benefit in catalytic activation.

The high price of small-scale electrolytic hydrogen in the United States (late 1970s)

An incorrect impression has been given to persons who have thought of the Hydrogen Economy in terms of prices given by a small-scale manufacturer of hydrogen: the prices of hydrogen contained in cylinders quoted is very much greater than those calculable from the cost equation:[33]

$$\text{Cost of 1 MBTU} = 2.29Ec + 1.$$

Thus, bottled hydrogen is so high in price that any consideration of the use of hydrogen as a fuel appears at once impossible. An example is given in the paper written by Campbell,[72] where he writes about the price of *bottled* gas. Campbell quotes the American firm, Lindy, as selling bottled hydrogen at $32 per 1,000 SCF (and therefore about $117 per MBTU), an order of magnitude greater than the cost based upon the unbottled material.

This *price* can be compared with the cost of unbottled electrolytic hydrogen. To obtain the largest reasonable cost, let us take the pessimistic figure of 2.2 v for the electrolyser voltage, and 4 cents per kWh for consumer-purchased electricity, and $1 per MBTU for amortisation, maintenance and insurance. Then, applying the equation cost of 1 MBTU (dollars) $=2.29Ec + 1.0$, one obtains $15.65.

Thus, either the mark-up is about 700% or the cost of bottling the gas is many times the gas cost.

When one looks into the cost of unbottled gas from small-scale electrolysers, there is a marked variety. These are given in Table 13.III, derived from Campbell's paper.[72]

TABLE 13.III: Campbell's Prices of Hydrogen From Small-Scale Electrolysers. United States, Late 1970s

Manufacturer	Characteristics	Cost $/MBTU
Teledyne Energy Systems	500 ml H_2 min^{-1}	4.00
Bendix 8814	500 ml H_2 min^{-1} Has Pd purifier.	7.83
Milton Roy	150 ml H_2 min^{-1}	9.00
	Cost per kWh of electricity taken as 2 cents.	

The costs from the small electrolysers are thus reasonable. They are in great contrast to those of hydrogen in bottled form.

Fixed costs in water electrolysis

The costs of production of hydrogen in dollars per MBTU are

$$\text{Cost of 1 MBTU in dollars} = Ac + B$$

where c is the cost of electricity in cents per kWh. Thus, Ac is the cost in dollars of the electricity to produce 1 MBTU, B is the cost of the sum of other items. It is necessary to rent the money by which one pays for the building of the plant, and then to pay the money back in a certain time. The cost of this financing can be expressed in terms of a certain figure per MBTU, on the assumption that the life of the electrolyser has a certain value. In such amortisations, the positive value of a high inflation rate should be noted, for the plant is financed to be economic at birth, and as the years grow the dollar figure for its product will increase whilst the amount to be paid on the financing will remain constant. The plant must be maintained and repaired. There is overhead to pay on the factory and floor space. There is depreciation of equipment. An estimate of some of these costs is shown in Table 13.IV.

TABLE 13.IV: Maintenance, Labour, Overhead, and Depreciation in an Electrolytic Hydrogen Plant (c. per MBTU)

Maintenance and operating supplies	2.08
Labour, $7.50 per hour	3.06
Overhead, at 60% of labour	1.35
Depreciation at 6.7%, local taxes, & insurance, 2.3%	37.65
	44.14

To this is added a capital cost amortisation figure. Taking the cost of the electrolyser as $200 per kW, 10% money, and 1.8v as the value of E, one obtains about 50 cents per MBTU for amortisation (if the electrolyser works continuously).

Hence, the total fixed costs are 94 cents per MBTU (1978).

This is a conservative figure for a reason first cited by Gregory.[27] In future large-scale electrolysers, there will be a higher current-density than the 100 amps per sq ft assumed here, and as the fixed costs are reduced with increasing current density, this would lead to a reduction of the value of 94 cents below the calculated one. It is better to lean towards the conservative cost estimates at present. This will be a compensation for the fact that no 'down-time' for the electrolyser has been allowed for in the above.

A comparison between rational fixed figures and ones quoted by various organisations is enlightening. These are shown in Table 13.V.

The extra price over the cost estimate of 0.94 (except for the Teledyne system) is partly due to the purification systems, which may not be necessary for some purposes. The price/cost ratio involved in the figures given is not known.

TABLE 13.V: Campbell's Estimates of Fixed Costs in U.S. Small Electrolyser Manufacture (1968)[72]

Company	Type of product	Fixed costs $ per MBTU
Teledyne Energy Systems, HS, 200	20 ml. min^{-1} of hydrogen	0.36
Bendix 8814-500	500 ml. min^{-1} (with palladium purifier)	6.30
Milton Roy	150 H_2 min^{-1} (palladium cathode and purifier)	10.00

Total rational cost of large scale electrolytic hydrogen for various electricity prices

From the above, a conservative equation in dollars per MBTU for the cost of electrolytic hydrogen is (in $).

$$\text{Cost} = 2.29 \ \text{Ec} + 1$$

TABLE 13.VI: Cost Values for Electrolytic Hydrogen (Dollars per MBTU)

$C = 2.29 \ \text{Ec} + 1$

Cell potential (volts)	Electricity price: interruptible power, massive purchase, plant next to generating station (cents)							
	0.3	0.5	1.0	1.5	2.0	3.0	4.0	6.0
1.3	1.89	2.48	3.97	4.46	6.94	9.93	12.90	18.86
1.4	1.96	2.60	4.26	5.81	7.41	10.62	13.82	20.23
1.5	2.03	2.71	4.44	6.15	7.87	11.31	14.74	21.61
1.6	2.09	2.83	4.66	6.50	8.32	11.99	15.65	22.98
1.7	2.16	2.95	4.89	6.83	8.79	12.67	16.57	24.35
1.8	2.24	3.06	5.12	7.18	9.06	13.36	17.48	25.73
2.0	2.37	3.29	5.58	7.87	10.16	14.74	19.32	28.48

Thermally assisted electrochemical production of hydrogen

Heat must be cheaper than electricity generated from it.

To counteract this, one could try to remove the hydrogen electrically from an aqueous solution, at a potential below that normally used to evolve hydrogen and oxygen.

There are many substances which could be electrolysed in aqueous solution to produce hydrogen at a lesser potential than the thermodynamic value used for the decomposition of water. For example, the standard reversible potential for HI electrolysis is 0.535 v, i.e. HI can be generated to 100 ma cm^{-2} at, say, a cell potential of 0.75 v, about half that of an optimistic prospect for water electrolysis. Thus, the electricity costs for the release of hydrogen by the electrolysis of HI would be less than half those in the electrolysis of, say, KOH, where both H_2 and O_2 are evolved.

Another reason for attempting to avoid the evolution of oxygen is that this reaction has particularly unfavourable rate constants.[73] For this reason—as is shown in terms of electrodekinetic theory—there will be a large overpotential (or 'polarisation loss'). The presence of this increases E, so that the cost is proportional to the development of overpotential. For a given rate of production of hydrogen (or current density), the overpotential is proportional to $\frac{2RT}{F} \log \frac{i}{i_o}$, where i_o is proportional to the rate constant.

In a process for hydrogen, which avoids the evolution of oxygen by evolving chlorine, it is necessary to recycle the chlorine back to oxygen and HCl, which is then rejected into the solution. However, heat is relatively cheap (say, one-third to half the cost of the cost of the same quantity of energy as electricity), so that the expenditure of some heat to achieve a recycling of, e.g. Cl_2, may be advantageous if the saving on the electrolysis (because of the decreased voltage) is sufficiently large.

This argument is valid but one must realise that it depends only on energy costs. It neglects the plant cost charges which would be increased.

It has been shown above that the fixed costs for a straight-forward electrolysis plant should be about $1 per MBTU. As the second plant is to be a high-temperature one, it will not be as cheap as a low-temperature electrolysis plant per unit of production. Let it be assumed that the costs are double those of the electrolysis plant. To save $2 per MBTU, the reduction in the cost of the electrical component of the net production, diminished by the costs of the heat in the heat cycle, would have to be $2. With nuclear heat at $2.50 per MBTU, and efficiency of the use of heat assumed to be 50%, the thermal part of the cycle would cost, say, $5 per MBTU. Hence

$$2.29 \ \Delta Ec - 5 = 2, \text{ or}$$
$$\Delta E > 7/2.29 \text{ c volt} \tag{13.32}$$

where ΔE is the reduction from the electrolysis potential from that used to electrolyse water, with evolution of oxygen, to that utilising the aqueous phase, with evolution of some other material, for example, chlorine, which has to be thermally regenerated. If $c = 3$ cents per kWh, the needed reduction in E would be ~ 1 volt (i.e. the alternative electrolysis would have to occur at about $1.23 - 1 = 0.23$ v).

The maximum reasonable value of ΔE would indeed be about 1 v. Hence, the cost of electricity would have to be 3 cents per kWh before it became advantageous to use nuclear heat in a two-step thermal-electrolytic cycle. In 1978, this is about twice times the cost at which large-scale interruptible power* next to the plant can be purchased.

The reason is an interesting one, and was not realised by those who firstly suggested the use of this heat. The efficiency (ε) of the use of the heat in a non-isothermal process is about

$$\frac{T_H - T_L}{T_H}$$

where T_H is the temperature at which the heat is given to the reactants, and T_L is the temperature of the surroundings, for

---

*The interruptibility of the electrolysis process, which is so feasible in the one-cycle electrolysis, is not necessarily so good in two or more step processes because the electrolysis has to be coupled to the thermal plant which cannot be shut on and shut off so easily as a water electrolysis plant. Straight one-step electrolysers can be used predominantly in the low-use-period situation.

$$T_H = 1100°K$$
$$T_L = 300, \text{ and}$$
$$\varepsilon = 0.73$$

However, extrinsic losses will bring the efficiency down further to around 0.5. On the other hand, water electrolysis cells can already be made to work at 90% efficiency, and the prospect of 100% efficient use of electricity in an electrolyser is a real one before 1983 (Srinivasan and Salzano).[52]

The likelihood of a thermal-electrochemical cycle having a lower cost than a one-step electrolysis plant using nuclear or solar heat to make electricity can be looked at in a different way. Let us relate the cost of nuclear heat to that of electricity by assuming that electricity costs 2.5 times as much as the heat used to generate it, and that the basic cost of the heat is H dollars per MBTU. Let the high-temperature conversion plant be F times the cost of the electrolysis plant. The cost of 1 MBTU of H_2 by straight electrolysis is:

$$\$(2.29 \, Ec + 1) \tag{13.33}$$

As there are 263 kWh in 10^6 BTU, and c is in cents, whilst H is in $, one obtains

$$2.29 \, (E-\Delta E) \, \frac{H \cdot 2.5 \cdot 100}{263} + 1 + F + \frac{H}{\varepsilon} \frac{\Delta H_{Therm}}{\Delta H_{H_2O}} < 2.29 \, E \, H \, 2.5 \frac{100}{263} \tag{13.31}$$

where $\dfrac{\Delta H_{Therm}}{\Delta H_{H_2O}}$ is the ratio of the heat of reaction of the thermal regenerative process to that of the thermal water dissociation; and ε is the efficiency with which heat is used in this one-step process.

Hence:

$$\Delta E > \frac{F}{2.2H} + \frac{1}{2.2\varepsilon} \frac{\Delta H_{Therm}}{\Delta H_{H_2O}} \tag{13.32}$$

Take $F = 2$; $H = \$2.50$; $\varepsilon = 0.7$; $\dfrac{\Delta H_{Therm}}{\Delta H_{H_2O}} = 1.$

Then, $\Delta E > 0.32 + 0.64 = 0.98$ volt for the dual process to be preferable. With $E > 1.6$, the new electrochemical process must therefore function at about 100 ma cm^{-2} at < 0.6 volt. This may be difficult to achieve.

Alternatively, one can take ΔE as a more reasonable 0.7 volt, and calculate F:

$$F < 2.2 \, \Delta E \, H - \frac{H}{\varepsilon} \tag{13.33}$$

With the same values of H and ε as before

$$F > 0.3 \tag{13.34}$$

This means that the cost of the thermal high-temperature part of the process would have to be 0.3 of that of the low-temperature electrolytic part of the plant and this is unlikely.

Finally, we can take $F = 2$, the other factors as before and work out the value of H at which it may become economically attractive to go in for a thermal-electrochemical two-step process.

Hence:

$$H > \frac{F}{2.2\Delta E - \frac{1}{\varepsilon}} \qquad (13.35)$$

$$> \$18$$

In fact, $H \simeq \$2.50$ at this time.

Such a sample of 'reasonable conditions' suggests it will be unlikely that a combination of conditions be found which makes the thermal-electrochemical two-step cycle yield hydrogen more cheaply than a one-step electrolysis.

In fact, further discussion shows that ΔE must be near to 1v; $\frac{\Delta H_{cyc}}{\Delta H_{H_2O}}$ must be < 1, and the thermal part of the plant would have to be constructed at less than 1.5 times the cost of the electrolyser plant for the two-step cycle to be more economic than the one-step electrolytic process.

The radiolytic production of hydrogen

Introduction

Radioactive substances emit high-energy particles, and if these are placed in water temporary dissociation of the water molecules occurs. Thus, particles from radioactive nucleii have an energy of 10^6 e.v. per particle and, as chemical bonds have an energy in the region of 1-10 e.v., the number which can be broken per particle is 10^5-10^6.

When one of the energetic particles passes near a water molecule it does not form O and H bonds, but ionises the atoms. Thus, some 10^{-14} sec after the passage of one of the energetic particles from radioactive emissions passes a water molecule, a proton faces an ionised oxygen ion. Application of the equation $\Delta^2 = 2D\tau$ with $D = 10^{-5}$ cm^2 sec^{-1} shows that a negligible distance can be travelled by diffusion in the time quoted, and the result is that the majority of the O^- and H^+ water fragments produced by means of dissociation recombine with each other, and do not form H_2 and O_2.

However—and perhaps remarkably—there *is* a significant hydrogen production from irradiated solutions, and it is enough (1% of the energy of the energy emitted) to be of interest. Without the interposition of some improved technology which changes the recombinative situation after ionisation, it would not be economic to use reactors just for the production of H_2. However, there are two reasons why we present the matter of the radiolytic hydrogen in this book:

1. One might indeed arrange circumstances where the recombination of the radical ions to water could be lessened. For example, suppose it were possible to exert high electrostatic fields on the system, the separation distance of the ions could be increased so that recombination of the water frag-

ments could be decreased and the possibility of H atom recombination (or reaction of H radicals with water to form H_2) is increased. Alternatively, one might carry out radiolysis with thin aqueous layers in contact with H-absorbing medium, and remove protons through a membrane.

2. In respect to nuclear waste, the volume of which is expected to increase, it may be possible to collect significant amounts of hydrogen from them to be interesting. Here, the lack of efficiency is of lesser importance.

Kerr and Majundar concepts for radiolytic hydrogen[74]

A reactor operating at a thermal power of P megawatts has f of the thermal output available to produce H_2. Thus Pf is the energy absorbed by the water in the reactor sec[-1]. It is simple to show that if G is the factor to allow for recombination, and is defined as the molecular yield of H_2 per 100 e.v. of the energy absorbed, then the rate of production of hydrogen is:

$$\text{Molecules sec}^{-1} \text{ reactor}^{-1} = 6.10^{22} \text{ PfG}$$

The value of G is 1.6 for uranyl solutions, and in this case one would produce 63lb of H_2 per MW of reactor power. This is equivalent to a yield of about 5% of the reactor energy. In fact, the efficiency is about 3G.

An increase in efficiency can occur if the reactor is arranged so that neutrons can leak into a blanket region and react with, e.g. Li^6 compounds. These, in turn, produce particles which would ionise water. In a type of reactor in which hydrogen is produced in the core, the blankets only act as a reflector. Uranium salts can be used as fuels. Large amounts of hydrogen and oxygen are thereby produced.

The possible value of the method depends to some extent upon the type of salts used and the corresponding corrosion situations. UO_2, SO_4, $UO_2(NO_3)_2$, UO_2F_2, etc., have been used. The nitrates are the best. Up to 300°C, Ti steels have the best corrosion resistance for the situation concerned.

One of the difficulties would be the extraction of hydrogen apart from the oxygen. One could pass the hydrogen-oxygen mixture over the anode in a fuel cell. There is no explosion under these conditions; hydrogen is electrochemically consumed. The oxygen may be used at the cathode to complete the reformation of water with the production of electricity.

In recent work, further systems analyses of radiolytic hydrogen have been made.[75] It may be possible to increase the G value by the addition of B^{10} and Li^6 to the solution.

The research future here is the increase in G; the possible engineering future is for an application to obtain hydrogen from radioactive waste products.

The massive production of hydrogen by a thermo-electrochemical method

The basis of this approach has been discussed above. The decomposition of water to hydrogen is endothermic. The variation of the cell potential with temperature is shown in Fig. 13.3.[76]

A cell can be made up of a solid electrolyte, for example, zirconia, and this would contain also CaO or Y_2O_3. It may be possible to advance such membranes by utilising the method of Bevan, Singh and Bockris,[77] to spray zirconia onto an electronically conducting high temperature oxide such as uranium oxide (Fig. 13.16).[77]

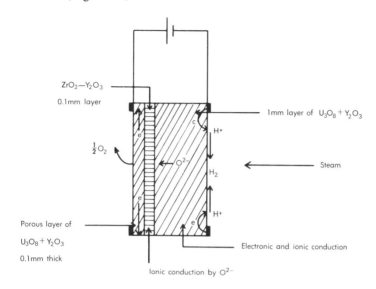

Fig. 13.16. A scheme for a high-temperature hydrogen-oxygen generator.[77]

Thus, the membrane thickness which has been used in such high temperature electrolysers is 10 ohms per cm^2 in resistance, and rather high.[78] A membrane would be about 10^{-2} mm in thickness.

If the internal I^2R loss in the cell is negligible, the heat which the cell needs to produce hydrogen at constant temperature (heat to compensate $T\Delta S$ cooling) will have to be supplied from an oxide source and this involves a Carnot loss. The electrochemical cell would be working at about 0.8 v; the working temperature would be 1200°K; so that about 54% ($= 0.8/1.47$) of the energy necessary for the dissociation of water would come from electricity and the other 46% would be supplied as heat.

The cost in cents of the electricity plus plant costs for 10^6 BTU would be, then:

$$2.29 \text{ Ec} + 1,$$

and if we make c 1.5 and E 0.8, we get $3.76 for the electricity part of the situation plus the use of heat at, say, $2.50 per MBTU, which gives us, then, $1.20 for the heat, so that the cost of the hydrogen will be in the region of $4.96 per MBTU, perhaps some 20-40% cheaper than that obtained by other methods.[33] But one is uncertain about long-term costs of the refractories.

Prospects for the high-temperature method

The prospects depend upon the properties of the zirconia-yttria membranes, together with the urania. The properties of yttrium-stabilised uranium oxide appear to be good for this kind of purpose, but the method is not yet out of the laboratory, and needs a considerable amount of work upon the stability of the membranes concerned.

High-intensity wind belts as massive sources of hydrogen

Introduction

It will be better to use seawater electrolysis. One could carry out the electrolysis at depth, producing immediately a pressure of 100 atmospheres for transmission. Venting chlorine at 1 kilometre may lead to equilibrium with water. Alternatively, one could pipe electricity from the seaborne wind farms to land, and use fresh water.

The concept is shown in Fig. 13.17.[80]

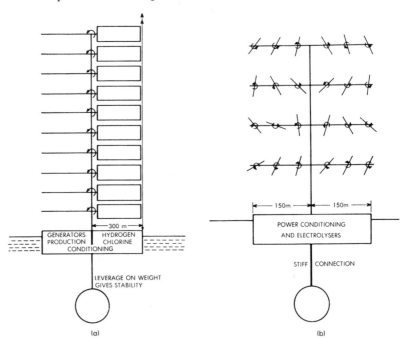

Fig. 13.17. A possible design for large-scale seaborne generators: (a) alternative possible arrangement, and (b) small rotor alternative.

Price of windborne hydrogen

The cost estimates for the wind generators cover a large range. The lower limit, achievable perhaps in mass production, is shown in Table 13.VII.

If one takes a value of $1,200 per kW, the costs would be 1.4 cents per kWh + maintenance. With E = 1.6, the H_2 cost would be 2.29 − 1.6. 1.4 + .1 = $6.12 per MBTU.

The prospect for the seaborne wind-generation of hydrogen

The need is for engineering work on the possibilities of having very large seaborne generators. The greatest difficulty would be the turning moment

TABLE 13.VII: Cost Estimates for Wind Based Hydrogen Energy Systems, 1978[81]

	$ per kW
Wind generators (per kW)	130-390
Electricity generators	45-190
Hydrogen production	195
Undersea storage	130
Fuel cells	325
Total	845-1230

of the wind on the situation, which would of course have to be balanced by large counterweights under the vessel.

There are many areas of the world, particularly in the Southern Hemisphere below the latitude of 40°, and the North East coast of the United States, which appear to be ideal for windborne electricity and hydrogen production.

Plasma torch photolysis

The solar spectrum is shown in Fig. 8.1. Water absorbs at several regions between 0.5 and 2 e.v. Thus, the frequences in solar radiation which would photolyse water have been partly absorbed when solar radiation passes through the atmosphere and photolysis of water from sunlight on earth is not an attractive proposition.

Eastlund and Gough have suggested that fusion reactors will make available photons from leakage plasma and these could be used to dissociate water on a large scale.[82] If certain elements are injected into the hydrogen plasma, optical and u.v. of various wavelengths can be produced,[83] e.g. if we add aluminium to the plasma, we obtain light in the region of 1800-1950A,° in which range water photolysis to hydrogen occurs.[84]

The leakage plasma, though very hot, is dilute (10^{10} atoms per cc). It would seem better to inject cool hydrogen and then give a stream with a high density (10^{13}-10^{14} per cc) at a lower temperature.

Using the data of Ung et al.,[2] 222,500 kWh of plasma energy would produce 1 ton of hydrogen. The main gain proposed in the method is that the thermal energy absorbed in the water cell could be converted to electricity at 30% efficiency in a heat engine. Then, 53,000 kWh of electricity could be produced per ton of hydrogen. The electricity could be used to provide hydrogen and then only 123,000 kWh of plasma energy would be required to produce 1 ton of hydrogen. As electrolysis requires 71,000 kWh to produce 1 ton of hydrogen; then, with a 40% efficiency reactor, 177,000 kWh is the thermal energy requirement, compared with 123,000 kWh of plasma energy.

Thus, the authors suggest that only about 70% of the energy needed to obtain H_2 by electrolysis would be needed in photolysis, but this is rough indeed, because it neglects both losses before the plasma reaches the cell and also gains from the use of the waste heat. The economic status of the method is unclear until the cost of the fusion heat is known. The recombination rate of H and OH radicals, and the absorption efficiency of the radiation, seem to have been neglected.

Seawater as a source of electrochemical hydrogen
Introduction

Large breeder reactors placed on the sea to reduce thermal pollution, solar collectors working from ocean thermal gradients and the use of constant wind belts to drive aero-generators on the sea, all indicate seawater, and its direct electrolysis, as the most convenient source of hydrogen on a very large scale.

There has been little consideration of the degree to which O_2 or Cl_2 respectively will be evolved, although Cl_2 can be prepared by the electrolysis of brine. There is a tacit assumption underlying some discussions of the Hydrogen Economy that O_2 alone is evolved in seawater electrolysis. An elucidation is necessary.

Thermodynamic properties of H_2-O_2 cells

The thermodynamic cell potential is:[85]

$$
\begin{aligned}
E &= \left[1.23 + \frac{RT}{F} \log (a_{H^+})_{an} + \frac{RT}{4F} \log p_{O_2} \right] \\
&\quad - \left[\frac{RT}{F} \log (a_{H^+})_{cath} - \frac{RT}{2F} \log p_{H_2} \right] \\
&= 1.23 + \frac{RT}{4F} \log p_{O_2} \, p^2_{H_2}
\end{aligned}
$$

(13.36)

Hence, if both electrodes are at the same pH, the cell potential is independent of the value of that pH. The pH of seawater will be near to seven. As electrolysis proceeds, and if it occurs in a confined space, the regions near the cathode become alkaline, and sodium hydroxide is locally produced, whereas the areas near the anode will have an excess of H^+ and HCl will be produced.

Thus, in an extreme case in which the anodic environment reaches a pH of 0, and the cathodic one a pH of 14, one has (for $p_{H_2} = p_{O_2} = 1$ atm):

$$
E = 1.23 + \frac{RT}{F} \ln 1 - \frac{RT}{F} \ln 10^{-14}
$$

(13.37)

$$
= 2.04 \text{ volts}
$$

(13.38)

$$
\therefore E_{cell} = 1.23 - 2.04
$$

(13.39)

thermo

Thermodynamic properties of $H_2 - Cl_2$ cells

The standard potential of the $Cl^- - Cl_2$ couple is 1.31 volt and at a concentration of Cl^- of 0.47, and 1 atm Cl_2, the thermodynamic potential is 1.35v. Thus, on the standard hydrogen scale:

$$
e_{REV/Cl_2 \text{ (sea)}} = 1.35
$$

(13.40)

The thermodynamic potential at which H_2 will be evolved is dependent on pH. Assuming pH $= 7$, the reversible hydrogen potential is 0.058 log a_{H^+} $= -0.406$. Thus, under the condition given, the thermodynamic potential of the $H_2 - Cl_2$ cell would be 1.76.

The potential near a cathode evolving H_2 will become alkaline. The pH attained will depend on agitation and the geometry of the situation. As an extreme let it be assumed that it reaches 14. Hence:

$$e_{REV/H_2 \; 1 \; atm} = -0.058 \times 14 = -0.812 \tag{13.41}$$

Hence, under circumstances which would lead to the high pH near the cathode,

$$E_{cell \; H_2 \; Cl_2} = 2.16 \; volt \tag{13.42}$$

The *thermodynamic* potential for an $H_2 - Cl_2$ cell in sea water will therefore be between:

$$1.8 \; to \; 2.2 \; volts \tag{13.43}$$

depending on current density, for, the higher this is, the larger the necessary applied potential, due to the increased pH.

Effect of kinetics[86]

As an approximation, one can assume the hydrogen electrode in water electrolysis to have a negligible polarisation, so that the polarisation is to be attributed to the anodic reaction. This is a good approximation for the hydrogen-oxygen cell, poor for $H_2 - Cl_2$. Using as order of magnitude parameters:

$$(i_o)_{H_2O \rightarrow O_2} = 10^{-10} \; amp \; cm^{-2} \tag{13.44}$$

$$(i_o)_{Cl^- \rightarrow Cl_2} = 10^{-3} \; amp \; cm^{-2} \tag{13.45}$$

the overpotential which must be added to the approximate thermodynamic potentials given is:[76]

$$\eta = \frac{RT}{\alpha F} \log \frac{i}{i_o} \tag{13.46}$$

for a current density, i, with $\alpha \simeq \frac{1}{2}$.

Thus, the actual cell potential needed to evolve H_2 from seawater at a current density, i, neglecting the effects of transport (which will become important only at higher current densities), will be:

$$E_{H_2} - Cl_2 = (1.8 - 2.2) + \frac{2RT}{F} \log \frac{i}{10^{-3}} \tag{13.47}$$

$$E_{H_2} - O_2 = 1.23 + \frac{2RT}{F} \log \frac{i}{10^{-10}} \tag{13.48}$$

Thus, the $H_2 - Cl_2$ cell begins to function at a higher applied potential difference than the $H_2 - O_2$ cell. However, once the thermodynamic conditions are reached whereby H_2 and Cl_2 can be evolved in seawater, the Cl_2 evolution rapidly becomes more favourable. This will occur for an applied potential cell potential between 1.8 and 2.2v. IR drop is neglected in the above calculation: the R can be reduced greatly by engineering design, but in any case at:

$$E_{cell,real} - IR > 1.8 \qquad (13.49)$$

the evolution of Cl_2 will start to displace the evolution of O_2 in the production of H_2 from seawater.

The course of the likely current-potential relations is shown in Fig. 13.18. The figure is approximate, though more than schematic. The values plotted are inexact because of the ambiguity of the reversible cell potential, which depends on the pH near to the electrodes. This latter quantity depending upon the degree to which free access of seawater is allowed.

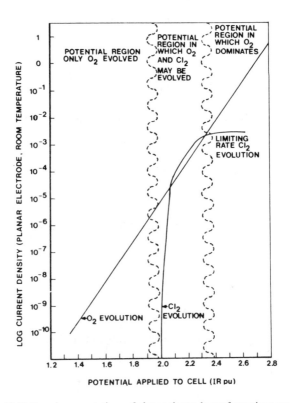

Fig. 13.18. Rough computations of planar electrode configurations suggest chlorine evolution from seawater exceeds O_2 evolution in a cell potential range (excluding IR) of about 2.0-2.2 volts (with possibility of competitive evolution beginning at 1.8 v).

Transport effects

Cl_2 evolution will replace O_2 evolution between 1.8 and 2.2 v. However, the transport of Cl^- ions to the electrode is limited, whereas there is no corresponding problem with the availability of water. Hence, there will be a potential sufficiently high at which there will be no further increase in the evolution rate of Cl_2, whereas that of O_2 will increase with potential. If ΔE is the increase in cell potential over that at which $i_{O_2} = (i_L)_{Cl_2}$, then:

$$\frac{2RT}{F} \ln \frac{i_{O_2}}{(i_L)_{Cl_2}} = \Delta E \qquad (13.50)$$

Thus, at sufficiently high cell potentials ($\Delta E > 0.2$ volt above that at which the limiting current for Cl^- sets in), the Cl_2 content of the evolved gas will be less than 1% (Fig. 13.18). A precise calculation of the transport control of Cl^- will depend (as with the pH at the interface) upon a knowledge of the transport conditions, e.g. natural and forced convection.[87] This, in turn, depends not only upon the flow of water in a macrosense, but in the diffusion and normal convection conditions in porous systems, apart, of course, from temperature, forced convection, etc. A calculation (which can be made[87]) implies knowledge of the system geometry. It is enough to use here a rough and simple calculation of the limiting current density,

$$i_L = 0.02 \, nC \qquad (13.51)$$

in which n is the number of electrons involved in the reaction, C the ionic concentration in moles 1^{-1}. The expression[88] implies zero agitation and gives the *minimum* limiting current, that due to diffusion and natural convection in the steady state at a planar electrode without pores. As agitation increases, the i_L increases until it is 10-100 times greater than the 'still' value. We arbitrarily take the factor as 25, whereupon, with n = 2, $C_{Cl} -$ 0.4M,

$$i_L = 0.4 \, amp \, cm^{-2} \qquad (13.52)$$

Assuming this as a limiting current for Cl_2 evolution from seawater in the considered geometry, there will develop, as the real current density approximates 0.04 amp cm^{-1} and above, a rapidly increasing extra overpotential (the concentration overpotential), according to:[89]

$$\eta_c = \frac{RT}{F} \ln \left[1 - \frac{i}{i_L} \right] \qquad (13.53)$$

As $i \to i_L$, η_c becomes very large and there will be no further increase in Cl_2 evolution as the applied potential increases.

Fig. 13.18 schematises these predictions. Reality would differ from Fig. 13.18 due to approximations made in respect to pH at the interface (it has been assumed that it is such as to displace the reversible potentials 0.2 v); neglect of H_2 overpotential; approximate values for i, η, Cl_2 and O_2 evolution; assumption of planar conditions for Cl_2 evolution, etc. One concludes that, up to about 1.8 v, Cl_2 evolution can be neglected, that after 2.2 it will predominate, but that after 2.6 volts it will become a rapidly decreasing component of the evolved gas.

However, the *higher* range of potentials in which Cl_2 evolution rates increase no more, but H_2 and O_2 evolution increase exponentially with the applied potential, is not a practical range. Thus, at > 1 amp cm^{-2}, IR drop and heating will be too large, and the applied potential uneconomic (see equation 13.30).

The aim will be, then, to achieve evolution at potentials < 1.8 volts. It is not possible, without more detailed transport calculation, and without knowledge of the degree of lowering of the anode potential (catalysis, depolarisation), to know the practicality of such a potential. Thus, the use of such measures, and special electrode structures, may achieve, or partly achieve, the desirable situation of negligible Cl_2 evolution (Fig. 13.18 has been calculated for planar electrodes, 25°C, and $i_o = 10^{-10}$ for O_2 evolution). Although the calculations on which Fig. 13.18 is based are limited and crude, it seems likely that, under practical conditions for seawater, a mixture of Cl_2 and O_2 would be evolved. The fact that electrode area is of less importance on or under the sea, makes a lower current density (and hence a cell potential nearer that at which Cl_2 does not evolve) acceptable.

Methods of dealing with chlorine evolution

Several methods may be available for preventing Cl_2 evolution into the atmosphere, which is, of course, unacceptable. Reactors on the sea are likely to be in deep water, because of the desirability of having cold water for cooling (ocean thermal gradient collectors would need deep water, too). Suppose the electricity manufactured on the surface was transmitted to a depth of 1 km, the pressure available would be *c.* 100 atm. H_2 could be evolved at this pressure for an extra potential (for H_2 and O_2) of about 0.1 volt, with a corresponding advantage for storage at depth.

(a) Assuming that the evolution is at depth, Cl_2 could be released into the sea. The reaction:

$$H_2O + Cl_2 \rightarrow HCl + HOCl \qquad (13.54)$$

is likely. The HCl would react with the NaOH produced and re-establish the original constituents of seawater. The hydrogen could be trapped and stored.

(b) The Cl_2 could be collected at the surface platform and the reaction:

$$Cl_2 + H_2O \rightarrow 2HCl + \tfrac{1}{2}O_2 \qquad (13.55)$$

performed, at 650°C. The process would add to the cost because heat would be needed to drive the reaction to the right. O_2 would then be vented and HCl re-dissolved. The HCl-NaOH reaction heat might be recoverable and used to provide fresh water.

(c) If these approaches are not economic, desalination would be necessary. In the presence of a nuclear reactor, on a floating platform, this would be the most acceptable method, because of the nuclear waste heat. The electrolysis might better be carried out in the sea depth for reasons of high-pressure storage. KOH would be the inexhaustible electrolyte. Solar platforms might have difficulty with economic large scale desalination; the costs of this hitherto have been placed 5-10 times above that of nuclear.

Untoward effects of seawater

A number of material difficulties will arise in seaborne plants and have been referred to in connection with seaborne platforms for solar sea power. Aluminium is the preferred material for anti-corrosion properties. Barnacles, etc., can be eliminated by means of a minute concentration of Cl_2 in the water, easily produced by making the plant materials anodic at very low current densities in sea water (an auxiliary cathode would be necessary). Storms can be faced either by careful anchoring or more likely by providing the platforms with a form of mobility, and manoeuvring it.

SUMMARY OF CHAPTER

1. The direct thermal decomposition of water to form hydrogen and oxygen is not likely to be successful due to the difficulty of maintaining refractories stable at the temperatures desired.

2. The method of thermochemical cycles had as its goal the avoidance of the Carnot cycle in the production of electricity from heat. Because the cycle method involves work to change the pressure of the system from p_1 to p_2, etc. there is effectively a Carnot cycle in the cyclical chemical method.

    Basically, therefore, the efficiency of the thermochemical cycle is of the same order as that of the normal electrochemical methods.

    However, there is a greater materials difficulty in the thermochemical cycle method so that the net cost of obtaining the hydrogen is likely to be greater than that of one of the newer electrochemical processes.

3. Classical electrolyzers work at 2.0 volts, and were built in times when the electricity costs of producing hydrogen were of lesser importance than at present.

4. The costs of 1 MBTU of hydrogen is given by the equation:

    $$\text{Costs 1 MBTU } H_2 = 2.29 \text{ Ec} + \text{C}$$

    where E is the potential in volts across the cell for a given rate of hydrogen production; c is the cost in cents of electricity under conditions of massive purchases and interruptibility of use (around half the normal cost); and C is the maintenance and monitoring costs, etc. of the electrolyzer.

5. Anode depolarization could provide low-cost hydrogen if the depolarizer is cost free (e.g. a pollutant).

6. Present large-scale electrolyzers do not involve application of knowledge available from electrode kinetic studies of the last decade.

7. Among forward concepts which should by now be introduced into electrolyzers are the following:

    (a) Super-active catalysts—for example, nickel cobaltate—in the anode. Correspondingly, a choice of catalyst which gives rise to low afel slopes should be made.

(b) High-temperature electrode surfaces should be used where heating is achieved by infrared beams.

(c) the introduction of devices for keeping cathode and anode streams without the presence of a separator.

(d) Attainment of a minimum IR drop situation by utilising a bubble retraction technique.

(e) Application of pulse and reverse electrolysis.

8. Small-scale electrolyzers give rise to prices which are several times the basic cost of hydrogen. This is due to considerations of scale and the cost of placing hydrogen in a cylinder.

9. The rational cost of large-scale electrolytic hydrogen is from around $3 per MBTU at 0.5c per kilowatt hour to about $15 per MBTU for 4c per kilowatt hour.

10. Thermal assisted electrolysis may give cheap hydrogen.

11. High-temperature (1000°C) electrolysis may be the cheapest method of decomposing water, because part of the energy used under these circumstances has not undergone the Carnot Cycle.

12. Windborn plans for the creation of hydrogen fuel from water seem to be feasible, with hydrogen costs in an acceptable realm ($< \$10$ per MBTU in 1979). Sea water electrolysis is not immediately feasible without research which would give rise to anodes which can evolve oxygen with less than 0.1 ppm of chlorine.

13. Light-oriented decomposition of water, particularly that of biomass, seems to be interesting and would give cheap hydrogen. There is a prospect of obtaining hydrogen from these methods at a cost less than that of gasoline in the late 1970s.

AUTHOR'S CHOICE OF TWO PARTICULAR CONCLUSIONS TO BE DRAWN FROM CHAPTER

1. When the work done in carrying out changes of state and over-free energy is accounted for, the chemical-cycles method does not promise efficiency of conversion of heat to hydrogen greater than those offered by electrochemical methods, which can, of themselves, approach 100% in efficiency.

2. Electrolyzers commercially available do not yet incorporate the results of the laboratory work of the 1970s, particularly that in electrocatalysis. A number of engineering improvements also seem feasible.

REFERENCES

1. A. J. Hammond, W. D. Metz & T. H. Maugh II, 'Energy and Future', American Association for the Advancement of Science, Washington, D.C. (1973).
2. A. Y. M. Ung & R. A. Back, *Can. J. Chem.*, 1964, **42**, 753.
3. A. Fujishima & H. Honda, *Nature*, 1972, **238**, 38.
4. G. H. Gough, paper presented at the Cornell National Symposium on the Hydrogen Economy, August 1973.
5. T. N. Verziroglu & S. Kakac in A. A. M. Sayigh (ed.), *Solar Energy Engineering* (Academic Press, New York, 1977), p. 389.
6. S. Ihara, First World Hydrogen Energy Conference, 5B-55, Miami, March 1976.
7. T. Nakamura, First World Hydrogen Energy Conference, 5B-71, Miami, March 1976.

8. F. Trombe, Applications Thermiques de l'Energy Solarie dans le Domaine de la Recherche et de l'Industrie, C.N.R.S., No. LXXXV (1961).
9. R. E. Chao, IEC, Prod. Res. Devel., 1974, **13,** 94.
10. R. E. Chao & K. E. Cox, in T. N. Veziroglu (ed.), *Hydrogen Energy* (Plenum Press, New York, 1976), Part A.
11. C. Marchetti, *Chemical Economy and Engineering Review,* 1973, **5,** 7.
12. G. de Beni & C. Marchetti, American Chemical Society Meeting, Boston, 9 April 1972.
13. J. O'M. Bockris, J. L. White & J. Mackenzie, *Physicochemical measurements at high temperatures* (Butterworths, London, 1959).
14. D. May & D. F. Rudd, First World Hydrogen Energy Conference, 6A-1, Miami, March 1976.
15. K. F. Knoche, H. Cremer, G. Steinborn & W. Schneider, First World Hydrogen Energy Conference, 5A-37, Miami, March 1976.
16. J. E. Funk, W. L. Conger & R. H. Cartey, in T. N. Veziroglu (ed.), *Hydrogen Energy* (Plenum Press, New York, 1976), Part A.
17. J. E. Funk, W. L. Conger, R. H. Carty, The Hydrogen Economy, Miami (THEME) Conference, March 1974, p. 511.
18. J. R. Pangoborn & J. C. Sharer, in T. N. Veziroglu (ed.), *Hydrogen Energy* (Plenum Press, New York, 1976), Part A.
19. J. Appleby & J. O'M. Bockris, 1979.
20. J. O'M. Bockris & A. K. N. Reddy, *Modern Electrochemistry* (Plenum Press, 1973, Vol. 2), p. 883.
21. J. O'M. Bockris & S. Srinivasan, *Fuel cells: Their Electrochemistry* (McGraw-Hill, New York, 1970).
22. J. O'M. Bockris & A. K. N. Reddy, *Modern Electrochemistry* (Plenum Press, New York, 1973), Rosetta Edition, p.1132.
23. K. J. Vetter, *Electrode Kinetics* (Springer, 1955).
24. J. O'M. Bockris in Bockris, Rand & Welch (edd.), *Trends in Electrochemistry* (Plenum Press, New York 1977), pp. 79-109.
25. J. O'M. Bockris & A. K. N. Reddy, *op. cit.,* Rosetta Edition, p. 1135.
26. J. O'M. Bockris & A. K. N. Reddy, *op. cit.,* Rosetta Edition.
27. D. Gregory, assisted by P. J. Anderson, R. J. Dufour, R. H. Elkins, W. J. D. Escher, R. B. Foster, G. M. Long, J. Wurm & G. G. Yie, 'The Hydrogen Energy System', p. III-3, prepared for American Gas Association by I.G.T. (1973).
28. J. O'M. Bockris, N. Bonicoat & F. Gutmann, *An Introduction to Electrochemical Sciences* (Wykeham Press, London, 1974), p. 78.
29. J. O'M. Bockris & D. Drazic, *Electrochemical Science* (Taylor & Francis, London, 1972), p. 7.
30. D. Gregory *et al., op. cit.,* p. III-4.
31. J. O'M. Bockris & S. Srinivasan, *op. cit.,* p. 541.
32. D. Gregory *et al., op. cit.,* p. III-16.
33. J. O'M. Bockris, *Int. J. Energy Res.,* 1978, **2,** 9-17.
34. J. O'M. Bockris & A. K. Reddy, *op. cit.,* Rosetta Edition, p. 1007.
35. *ibid.,* p. 1369.
36. J. O'M. Bockris & S. Srinivasan, *op. cit.,* p. 289.
37. *ibid.* p. 633.
38. B. Cahan, Thesis, University of Pennsylvania (1968).
39. A. Damjanovic, D. Sepa & J. O'M. Bockris, *J. Res. Inst. Catalysis,* Hokkaido Univ., 1968, **16,** 1.
40. J. McHardy & J. O'M. Bockris, 1973, **120.**
41. *ibid.,* p. 53.
42. A. Tseung & H. Bevan, 1973, **45, 429.**
43. J. O'M. Bockris & D. Drazic, *op. cit.,* p. 222.
44. D. Gregory *et al., op. cit.,* p. III-18.
45. M. H. Miles, G. Kissel, P. W. T. Lu & S. Srinivasan, *J. Electrochem Soc.,* 1976, **123,** 332.
46. A. J. Appleby & G. Crépy, ECS Meeting, Philla, May 1977.
47. A. J. Appleby, J. Jacquelin & G. Crépy, *Rev. Gen. Électricitié,* 1976, **85,** 551.
48. G. Kissel, F. Kulesa, G. Singh & S. Srinivasan, 10th IECEC Proceedings, 1975, 1194.
49. D. E. W. Just & H. H. Ewe, in S. K. Rangarajan (ed.) *Topics in Pure and Applied Electrochem.* (SAEST Karaikudi, India, 1975), pp. 201-15.
50. F. T. Bacon, *J. Inst. Fuel,* 1974, **47,** 147-62; F. T. Bacon & T. M. Fry, *Proc. Roy. Soc. London,* Ser. A. **334,** 427-52 (1973).
51. H. J. Allison, First World Hydrogen Energy Conference, Miami, March 1976.

52. S. Srinivasan & F. J. Salzano, 'Proceedings First World Hydrogen Energy Conference', Miami, March 1976.
53. S. Srinivasan, G. Kissel, P. W. T. Lu, F. Kulesa & C. Davidson, Brookhaven National Laboratory contribution No. 22163 (1977).
54. G. Singh, M. H. Miles & S. Srinivasan, Proceedings of Workshop on Electrocatalysis on Non Metallic Surfaces, NBS, 9-12 December 1975.
55. A.C.C. Tseung & S. Jasam, *Electrochim Acta,* 1977, **22,** 31-34.
56. J. O'M. Bockris, A. Damjanovic & J. McHardy, International Symposium on fuel cells, Brussels, 1969, p. 15; *J. Electrochem. Soc.,* 1973, **120,** 53, 61.
57. J. O'M. Bockris, Symposium on Electrocatalysis, San Francisco, May 1974.
58. P. W. T. Lu, S. Srinivasan, Extended Abstracts, 149th Meeting of the Electrochemical Society, pp. 821-823, Washington, D.C., May 1976.
59. S. Gottesfeld, S. Srinivasan, Extended Abstracts, 149th Meeting of the Electrochemical Society, pp. 907-909, Washington, D.C., May 1976.
60. W. Juda & D. McL. Moulton, *Chem. Eng. Symp. Series,* 1972, p. 59.
61. J. B. Laskin & R. D. Feldwick, First World Hydrogen Energy Conference, 3A-31, Miami, March 1976.
62. D. Gregory *et al., op. cit.,* p. III-16.
63. Figure from the Allis-Chalmers Manufacturing Co.
64. D. Gregory *et al., op. cit.,* p. III-16.
65. Figure from the General Electric Co.
66. G. L. Dugger & E. J. Francis, First World Hydrogen Energy Conference, 3A-31, Miami, March 1976.
67. D. B. Sepa, A. Damjanovic & J. O'M. Bockris, *Electrochim Acta,* 1967, **12,** 746.
68. J. O'M. Bockris & S. Srinivasan, *Fuel Cells* (McGraw-Hill, New York, 1969), pp. 289-356.
69. J. O'M. Bockris & J. McHardy, *Electrocatalysis of Fuel Cells,* Battelle, 385 (1972).
70. *cf.* ref. No. 45, p. 335.
71. J. O'M. Bockris, *Energy Conversion,* 1975, **14,** 81-85.
72. B. C. Campbell, First World Hydrogen Energy Conference, 7B-23, Miami, March 1976.
73. J. O'M. Bockris & A. K. N. Reddy, *Modern Electrochemistry* (Plenum Press, New York, 1973), p. 1141.
74. W. Kerr & D. P. Majumdar, in T. N. Veziroglu (ed.), *Hydrogen Energy* (Plenum Press, New York, 1975), Part A, pp. 167-181.
75. D. P. Majumdar, H. Ryes, W. Kerr, First World Hydrogen Energy Conference, Miami, March 1976.
76. J. O'M. Bockris, *Energy Conversion,* 1975, **14,** 81-85.
77. J. O'M. Bockris, in Bockris, Rand & Welch (edd.), *Trends in Electrochemistry* (Plenum Press, New York, 1977), p. 88.
78. R. E. Carter, W. E. Rocco, H. S. Spacil & W. E. Traget, General Electric Laboratory, Press release, 26 December 1962.
79. S. P. B. Singh, Ph.D. Thesis, Flinders University of S.A., 1977.
80. J. O'M. Bockris, *Energy Conversion,* 1975, **14,** 87-91.
81. J. O'M. Bockris, *Energy Conversion,* 1975, **2,** 283-288.
82. B. J. Eastlund & W. C. Gough, paper presented at the 163rd National Meeting of the American Chemical Society, Boston, Mass., 9-14 April 1972.
83. R. W. P. McWhirter, R. H. Huddlestone & S. L. Leonard (edd.), in *Plasma Diagnostics* (Academic Press, New York, 1965).
84. A. Y. M. Ung & R. A. Back, *op. cit.*
85. G. Kortum & J. O'M. Bockris, *Textbook of Electrochemistry* (Elsevier, 1959), Vol. 1, chapter VIII.
86. J. O'M. Bockris & A. K. N. Reddy, *op. cit.,* Rosetta Edition, p. 845.
87. V. G. Levich, in *Physical Hydrodynamics* (Prentice Hall, Englewood Cliffs, New Jersey, 1962), Chapter 6.
88. J. O'M. Bockris, in J. O'M. Bockris (ed.), *Modern Aspects of Electrochemistry* (Butterworths, London, 1954), Vol. 1, p. 243.
89. J. O'M. Bockris & A. K. N. Reddy, *op. cit.,* p. 1059.

14

MATERIALS ASPECTS

The effect of external pressure

The permeation of hydrogen into a metal—and thus its aggregation at voids—depends upon the hydrogen pressure in a well-known way.[1] The solubility is proportional to the square root of the external hydrogen pressure. It may be that, in pipes at pressures of several hundred atm, the hydrogen pressures would be large enough to cause a degree of embrittlement.

However, it seems unlikely that this would be the case, for most steels have breakdown points at room temperature which demand local pressures greater than 10^3 atm, if the stress is one-time and not cyclical.[2] If direct effects of hydrogen gas at room temperatures, and in the range of pressures expected within pipes, seem unlikely, indirect effects may occur. Hydrogen may combine with elements of an alloy, thus beginning to dissociate and breakdown the alloy at the surface, and change its properties. Internally, hydrogen diffusion may cause a build-up of methane as a result of the reaction of hydrogen and carbon in the iron. However, the most likely effects come from those associated with local stresses.

Thus, the solubility of hydrogen as a function of pressure stated above, refers to the zero stress situation.[2] There are usually local stresses. The effect of stress on solubility is important. Thus,[3] the equation which represents solubility as a function of stress under thermodynamic conditions is:

$$c_\sigma = c_0 e^{\overline{V}_H \sigma / RT} \tag{14.1}$$

where c_σ is the local solubility at an area at which the local stress is σ, and $\overline{V}_H$ is the partial molar volume of H in the metal.

Calculation shows that, in practical ranges of σ, the solubility may become very large.

For a given external stress, there is a larger local stress near dislocations.[4] For certain parameters, Bockris et al. calculated that the hydrogen solubility near a dislocation would be of the order of one hundred times more than the equilibrium solubility without stress.[4] Herein may originate some of the unexpected difficulties met in the embrittlement of steels with gaseous hydrogen at quite low pressures.

These remarks refer to a surface of iron or steel which is not oxide-covered. In so far as some coverage occurs, the surface may be protected, although the attack of hydrogen upon the oxide and its gradual, sometimes rapid, breakdown is a possibility. A thermodynamic calculation indicates whether surface oxides of iron are stable in the presence of hydrogen at various pressures, taking the surface and bulk oxides to have the same free energies, as a first approximation.

The effects of cracks and pits upon damage and embrittlement of steels by hydrogen

Pits and cracks occur in metals and these may induce special conditions which favour spreading and eventual fracture of the metal. The subject is well known in stress-corrosion cracking theory.[2]

The equation which relates solubility to stress is (14.1). However, the stress at the bottom of a pit must be distinguished from the macro stress put upon a sample; and from the stress which exists in the vicinity of dislocations.[4] Thus, the stress at the bottom of a pit, the radius of curvature of which is r, and the depth of which is l, is given by:[5]

$$\sigma_{tip} = \sigma_{macro} \, 2\left[\frac{l}{r}\right]\frac{1}{L} \qquad (14.2)$$

The solubility of hydrogen in iron has the order of magnitude of 10^{-6} moles hydrogen per mole of iron, so that if the exponential in equation (14.1) exceeds 10^6, about one hydrogen atom per iron atom can exist at the bottom of the pit and the iron-iron bond would then be greatly weakened. Utilising equation (14.2) and taking, as an example, $l=0.1$ cm, $r=10^{-6}$cm, $V_H = 2.67$ ccs mole^{-1} one finds that, if the stress is above 1.2×10^8 dynes per sq cm ($\simeq 1$ kg mm^{-2}), the H/Fe ratio in the surface layers of Fe at the bottom of the pit contains 1H to 1Fe. Thus, *even though the apparent external stress is relatively small*, the H concentration at the pit (or crack) head may be destructive.

The limits of the use of carbon steels in the presence of hydrogen

This has been discussed principally by Nelson, and he gives the curves of Fig. 14.1.[6]

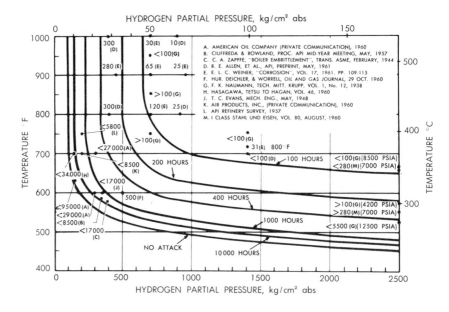

Fig. 14.1. Time for incipient attack of carbon steel in hydrogen service.[6]

Small amounts of carbide-stabilising limits, chromium and molybdenum, provide increased resistance to attack. A chart illustrating this has been published.[7] 2.25% chromium, 1% molybdenum steel has considerable strength in resisting hydrogen.

Difficulties arise in respect to temperature rises of sensitive parts. For example, some of the cooling facilities in a plant may go out of action. Temperatures may then rise locally in carbon steel equipment to a level where hydrogen attack will begin to occur (probably at the base of small invisible cracks).

Appearance of specimens during embrittlement

Hofmann and Rauls have made direct experiments upon the attack by high-pressure hydrogen and one of their pictures is shown in Fig. 14.2.[8] They observe that the cracks forming on the surface of specimens occur largely along grinding grooves or at notches. They quote a specimen of ARMCO iron, normalised CK22 and normalised C45. Specimens were 8 mm in diameter with a circumferential notch of 60° notch angle, 1 mm deep, and root radius of 0.1 mm, undergoing breakdown in 150 atm of hydrogen when the stress was lower than that in air.

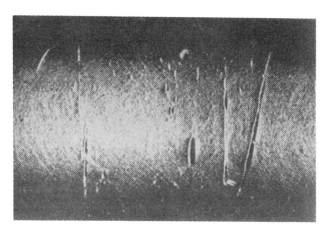

Fig. 14.2. Typical appearance of surface of a specimen suffering damage from plastic deformation during exposure to high pressure hydrogen.[8]

The effect of surface finish on embrittlement is important. Cracks in tensile specimens follow grooves formed in surface finishing. The notch effect of the grooves raises the local stress level. Cold working is an important influence, but is difficult to differentiate from geometric factors.[9]

Effects of high pressure storage upon vessels containing welds

This important subject has been examined particularly by Fairhurst. The effect of the ductility of unnotched specimens is shown in Fig. 14.3.[10]

Fairhurst comments upon the greater susceptibility to embrittlement of martensite rather than perlite; and the good resistance of high-alloy maraging steels. Austenitic steels are less sensitive, but they still embrittle.

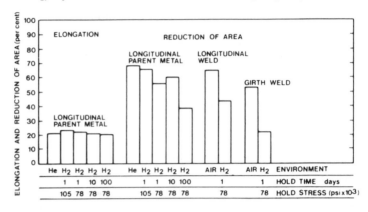

Fig. 14.3. Effect on the ductility of unnotched specimens of ASTM A-533 grade steel (quenched and tempered 1.3% Mn, 0.5% Mo, 0.5% Ni) when held at room temperature in high-pressure hydrogen (10,000 psi, or 700 kg$_r$/cm^2).[10]

There is definitely danger of situations in which the hydrogen pressure rises, as with some storage devices, above about 5,000 psi. Hydrogen causes a reduction of strength and the main problem areas are near welds and notches.

Thus, Walter and Chandler suggest that existing vessels should be used at lower pressures for hydrogen than for nitrogen or argon, and stress the importance of quality control to spot beginning surface flows.[11] However, many of these will be invisible at the beginning and damage may be spreading inside the metal.

The possibility of hydrogen damage to pressure vessels during operation has been examined by Whitman *et al.*[12] Vessels fabricated from low-alloy steels are less likely to undergo embrittlement, and carbon steels are more likely to fail.

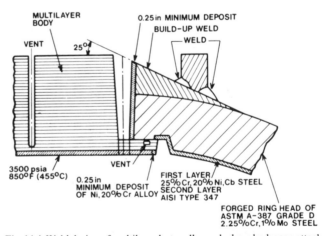

Fig. 14.4. Weld design of multilayer hot-wall vessel where hydrogen attack on the low-alloy weld metal is avoided by staggering the welds and by proper venting.[13]

A good practice is to use cold-wall pressure vessels. Refractory linings are used to lower the temperature of the vessel walls. Lower-alloy steels can be used to combat hydrogen attack. Multi-wall vessels may be used in the wall in contact with the hydrogen has a lower solubility for it than the second wall.

Special designs of welds and multi-layer hot wall vessels have been evolved and diagrammed. One such design is shown in Fig. 14.4.[13]

Hydrogen environmental embrittlement

The susceptibility of metals to hydrogen gas has been emphasised during recent times. Types of embrittlement are shown in Table 14.I,[14] and hydrogen environment embrittlement is the most relevant type to the Hydrogen Economy. Thus, storage tank failures which have occurred are interpreted in terms of hydrogen attack.[15,16] The phenomenon is characterised by the formation of growth of surface cracks and the metal becomes deformed in a high hydrogen-purity atmosphere. The disturbing feature is that the hydrogen may attack at even 1 atm.

The general solution is to use alloy steels, nickel, chromium and molybdenum being the important metals. There is no doubt that the difficulty can be avoided—the question is the cost of the steels.

Types of metals and their resistance to attack

The following indicates the groups of metals and their resistance to attack:

Very susceptible	High-strength steels
Susceptible	Nickel and nickel alloys; titanium alloys; low-strength steels
Fairly susceptible	Stainless steels
Non-susceptible	Monel; beryllium-copper alloys; aluminium and copper

Research is needed in developing an appropriate 100-year-lasting material for the hydrogen pipes. Perhaps aluminium (almost inexhaustible in quantity because of its existence in clay) will become sufficiently cheap to be used. Perhaps a suitable hydrogen-resistant aluminium cladding of steel can be developed.

Importance of oxygen impurity

Johnson has shown that hydrogen embrittlement will often propagate at the bottom of flaws or cracks, even at very low stresses, when the apparent stress (local stress?) is one-tenth of the yield stress.[17] High-strength steels are the worst. The most important positive aspect of such embrittlement is that it can be taken care of, not only by the use of carbon steels containing certain expensive additives, but by adding a small quantity of oxygen to the gaseous hydrogen.

It is likely that the oxygen absorbs at the crack tip, displacing hydrogen from the surface. Absorbed oxygen is a barrier which prevents access of potentially embrittling hydrogen.

The field of protection against hydrogen environment embrittlement by oxygen is new and requires research. Thus, for example 200 parts per million of oxygen is the suggested content.[18] However, other impurities such as car-

TABLE 14.I: Characteristics of the Types of Hydrogen Embrittlement[14]

Characteristics	Types of embrittlement		
	Hydrogen environment embrittlement	Internal reversible hydrogen embrittlement	Hydrogen Reaction Damage
Usual source of hydrogen	Gaseous (H_2)	Processing Electrolysis Corrosion	Gaseous or atomic hydrogen from any source
Typical conditions	10^{-6} to 10^8 N/m^2 gas pressure	0.1 to 10 ppm average H content	Heat treatment or service in hydrogen, usually at elevated temperatures
	Most severe near room temperature	Most severe near room temperature	
	Observed $-100°$ to $700°C$	Observed $-100°$ to $100°C$	
	Gas purity is important	Strain rate is important	
	Strain rate is important		
Crack initiation	(Surface or internal initiation)*	Internal crack initiation	Usually internal initiation from bubbles or flakes
Rate controlling step	Adsorption or* lattice diffusion = Embrittling step	Lattice diffusion to internal stress raisers	Chemical reaction to form hydrides (e.g. in titanium) or gas bubbles

*Unresolved

bon dioxide, water vapour, ammonium and sulphur dioxide also work, although the limits of their effectiveness are not known.

Particularly dangerous in causing hydrogen environment embrittlement is hydrogen from liquid-hydrogen storage, because this is hydrogen which is 'distilled off', and is particularly pure. With this hydrogen, an injection of impurities would have to be made before it is introduced into the pipeline.

Effect of cyclical stress

Walter and Chandler have examined the effect of cycling with pressure on the hydrogen embrittlement of iron, steel and some of their alloys.[19] The pressures were from 10MNm^{-2} (about 1400 psi) to 120 MNm^{-2} (about 1700 psi). Results on inconel are shown in Fig. 14.5.[19] At 4 cycles per sec, no environmental effects were noted on crack growth rate. The time per cycle must be at least 5 times greater for environmental effects. No influence on side grooves was shown.

If the results of Fig. 14.5[19] are extrapolated linearly down to 100 atm, 10^5 cycles would be needed to cause a 1 mm crack to grow. At 2 cycles of pressure change per day, this is 130 years. Low-alloy steel gives about 50 years.

The major result here is that 100 atm is perhaps the highest practical pressure for economically useful life.

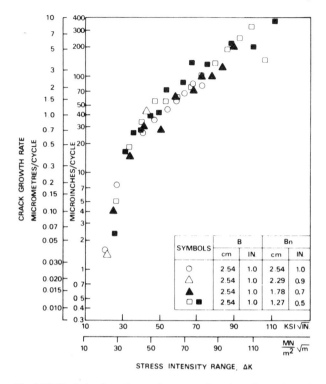

Fig. 14.5. Cyclic load crack growth rates as a function of stress intensity range for inconel 718 TDCB specimens with various side groove depths exposed to 34.5 MN/m² (5000 psi) hydrogen at ambient temperature R = 0.1, 1.0 cps.

Applications of liners

It has been assumed above that the hydrogen comes in contact with the metal. However, it is possible to interpose a material with a low permeation coefficient for hydrogen. The introduction of a liner, particularly on the material of a large spherical vessel, infers that the material must have good formability and make good welds. These needs determine what material can be used.

With all liner concepts, the possibility that the hydrogen may diffuse through the liner, and form a layer of increasing pressure between the liner and the vessel wall, must be faced. Eventually, this would cause detachment of the liner. Unfortunately, corrosion, particularly pitting-corrosion, makes it probable that some passage of hydrogen through a liner will occur. It may be possible to insert 'weep holes' in the vessel so that hydrogen which penetrated the liner cannot build up pressure and cause failure of the entire liner.

Among liner materials one should consider austenitic stainless steels which have a hydrogen permeability below that of ordinary steel.[20]

However, it must not be thought that the liner idea solves all problems. It introduces a cost problem and it is clear that the cost of putting liners into a long pipeline is too large. Further, it predicates the existence of a method of inspection which may have to be devised for the particular situation.

Potential material difficulties related to the method of production of hydrogen

Water is the desirable raw material for hydrogen production. From the material point of view the two main methods which are at present being considered for splitting water distinguish themselves enormously once it comes to the material side. In the electrochemical approach, the temperatures are mild, less than 120°C, and the resulting materials damage is easy to accept or deal with. It is mainly a matter of dealing with the possible attack of hydrogen on electrodes upon lengthy evolution at high temperatures, and it may be necessary to incorporate suitable alloying elements which stabilise carbon. A large variety of electrocatalysts are under consideration for hydrogen evolution work,[21] and these are seldom vetted from the point of view of hydrogen attack. This could become a factor in the choice among them. At sufficiently high current densities (~ 1 amp cm^{-2}) hydrogen permeation can be considerable for iron and nickel-based alloys and lead not only to reduction in ductility—less important because of the low stress on the electrode—but also to the spread of internal voids and their appearance on the surface of the electrode as 'craters'. Among the electrochemical methods for producing hydrogen is the high temperature electrolysis of steam at 1000° or more. In the past, this has involved ZrO_2-Y_2O_3 but now may involve the newer concept of Bevan, Badwall and Bockris,[22] involving U_3O_8-Y_2O_3. Thus, the uranium oxide is a high electronic conductor and is used as an electrode with zirconium oxide used as the electrolyte, yttrium oxide being the stabiliser. All the materials involved are thermodynamically stable until at least 1600°, and material attacked by hydrogen should not be a problem. However, it is not yet known what are the difficulties associated with the adherence of film of zirconium oxide, ZrO_2-Y_2O_3, on the surface of U_3O_8-Y_2O_3, and the possibility that this may peel off due to the development of a high-pressure hydrogen layer between the electrodes should be considered.

On the whole the electrochemical method, particularly that used in aqueous solutions, should provide few material difficulties.

When one comes to the production of hydrogen by the chemical cycles method, materials difficulties pass into a different situation.[23] Firstly, the temperatures reach up to 1250°K. Secondly, many of the systems involve hot aqueous electrolytes. The first condition is one which does offer considerable difficulties as far as hydrogen attack is concerned. Above about 500°K a new region is reached as far as attack on steels is concerned. The presence of high-temperature oxygen as well may provide difficulties with the metals present.

Electrochemical corrosion in steam at high temperatures is usually severe indeed, because the water present forms conducting pathways in the presence of ionic salts which add to the corrosional situation. Much is known about the attack of water in the region of 400-500°K on steel because of the presence of such attack in steam boilers. Under such conditions, attack can be considerable unless there is rigorous removal of all traces of electrolyte.

However, most thermochemical cycles involve water and ionic salts.

Thus, the temperature range over which the latter has been planned as possible lies between about 500° and 1250°K, and over all this range with water and steam in the presence of electrolytes, attack problems will be severe. No more specific statement can be made, short of discussing the individual cycles which have been proposed. The fact that many of these would involve the presence of several reacting vessels in contact, with valves, joints, and perhaps even welds, considerably increases the difficulties because of the likelihood of galvanic coupling between materials which may have different electrochemical properties.

Of course, these materials difficulties in the chemical cycles concept might be overcome in certain cases, in particular, for example, where only one high-temperature reaction is involved, and that perhaps at a lower temperature ($\sim <400°C$) in conjunction with an electrochemical step. Another situation in which the thermochemical cycle concept may have less material difficulties is when it involves only gases, and no ions, because of the reduced conductance and its helpful effect in inhibiting corrosion. However, the material difficulties proffered by most of the chemical cycles concept are such that they will certainly form a substantial cost-contribution to the economics of running such systems, although hitherto such costs have been totally neglected, or assumed to be equal to those of a much more simple concept, thus obfuscating the economic analysis for thermochemical cycle situations in comparison with alternative methods producing hydrogen (electricity- and light-oriented).

It is noteworthy that much work published hitherto on chemical cycles has referred to systems analysis, largely thermodynamic calculations. The deciding factors between one cycle and another—if indeed any of them are shown to have the requisite 100% cyclical property—seem likely to be the economics of the material components in the analysis, and that can be taken into account only after *real experiments* of several months' duration.

On the materials suitability of the existing gas lines for carrying hydrogen

It is an attractive thought that the combined network of transmission lines could be converted to lines carrying hydrogen.

Two considerations must be entertained. The first concerns the compatibility of the volume with the lower (one-quarter) volume density of hydrogen; and the second concerns the possibility of attack.

If one wished to pass the same amount of energy through the existing line at the same time, it would be necessary to increase the pressure. There is an increased compressibility and a lower viscosity when one changes from natural gas to hydrogen, and to some extent this decreases the amount of extra pressure needed. The net situation is that one would have to increase the pressure to about 140 atmospheres and this would be above the pressure at which most of the pipelines are rated for stability.[24]

It is of interest to note that a number of pipelines exist which have been carrying hydrogen for some time. They are mostly in the 20 centimetres diameter range and bear pressures of less than 70 atmospheres.[25,26] Two modern lines exist at a much higher pressure. One of them is at Los Alamos.

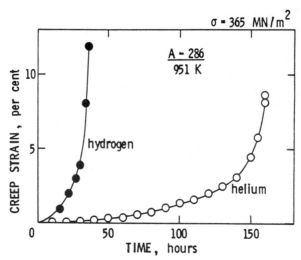

Fig. 14.6. Creep rupture for A-288 stainless steel at 951°K under constant stress at 365 MN/m², in 34.8 MPa pressure of He or H₂.[30]

It failed at 140 atmospheres. Another line is at the Kennedy Space Centre, operating at 420 atmospheres. It consists of AISI 316 austenitic stainless steel. The longest-lasting line (in operation since 1938) is in the Ruhr but operates in the 10-20 atmospheres region, and therefore does not give much information on the question of durability at the appropriately higher pressures.

There is little evidence on the effect of hydrogen on valves and pumps. A number of present ones have failed.[27] It is clear that materials research in these areas is much needed (see Fig. 14.6).

One very high pressure (1000 atmospheres) pipeline exists. It consists of a 21Cr, 6Ni, 9Mn steel.

The following is a general statement covering the situation to date: 100 atmospheres is the maximum pressure at which most of the ordinary pipeline material is safe. Up to 1000 atmospheres can be done but with the use of special steel, several times more expensive than the attackable steels.

One factor may be important: most failures so far observed occur near welds. The welding operation may use acetylene and it may use hydrogen (both with oxygen). However, it hardly matters from the point of view of this discussion because, at the welding temperature concerned, acetylene dissociates to give hydrogen. The weld, then, comes in contact with hydrogen at high temperatures (up to 1500°C) and this makes a highly embrittling situation, the hydrogen first permeating inside the metal and then, after cooling, attempting to come out again, leading to internal void formation of cracking. In non-welded pipes, it is possible that there would be a reduced tendency to failure.

Thompson suggests that the use of internal liners and stainless steel is the answer to these difficulties.[20] Returning, then, to the question of whether existing natural gas lines would be acceptable for hydrogen, the general answer is a cautious affirmative. However, a better definition of the maximum reliable pressure has to be given, and it seems probable that this would be less than 100 atmospheres, so that (see above) the energy per unit length and time in the pipe would be less than at present transporting with natural gas. The question of materials for the extra pumps necessary is at present open.

Direction of research for new line manufacture[20]

Optimum material properties to last a longer time and at higher pressures than 100 atmospheres along the lines already discussed is a research item: much has to be done to optimise to a strength which allows, say, 200 atmospheres or even 1000 atmospheres without becoming too expensive. The kind of alloy evolved could involve Cr, Ni, Ti. It would be low on carbon and manganese.[20] Liners would be acceptable for pressure vessels. Research on pumps, gauges and valves is urgently needed. 10-15 years would be the lead time.

The importance of an additive

Addition of an oxygen purity to pure hydrogen decreases material damage from H_2. The presence of small traces of several other materials (e.g. C_2H_2) in the hydrogen gas reduce cracking. Little is known about the dependence of the efficiency of the additive as a function of its partial pressure. Some evidence suggests that above one atmosphere the effect of inhibition is less, as would be expected on a Langmuir model.[28,29]

Thus, the additive obviously works by preferential adsorption of the formation of protective coating, i.e. it adsorbs preferentially to H. It will be necessary to keep up a low partial pressure of oxygen throughout the entire pipeline. It would not be possible to inject oxygen at one point—it would undergo diminution in concentration as adsorption increases and the effect would cease down the line.

SUMMARY OF CHAPTER

1. A thermodynamic analysis makes it probable that practical values of local mechanical stresses increase the H solubility by several orders of magnitude.

2. At the head of pits and cracks, theory indicates that very high concentrations of H may be dissolved.

3. Welds are the origin of most damage in H containers.

4. At high hydrogen-purity, an embrittlement may occur in terms of surface cracks, even at 1 atm pressure. However, the effect is reduced by addition of an impurity, e.g. oxygen, to the gas.

5. Liners of more expensive steels are an alternate to protect pipelines.

6. The chemical cycle method will present more severe materials problems than those of other methods.

7. The existing gas liners could carry hydrogen, but pumping work would have to be increased several times.

8. Some areas of needed research are: the mechanism of environmental embrittlement; of the cracking of welds; the material properties of pumps and valves; additives and their mechanism; the mechanical effect of diurnal pressure changes in pipes from solar farms.

AUTHOR'S SELECTION OF A MORE IMPORTANT CONCLUSION FROM CHAPTER

Hydrogen environmental embrittlement can be prevented by the presence of suitable trace additives, e.g. O_2, in the gas.

REFERENCES

1. E. Heyn, Stahl & Eisen, *Metallographist*, **20**, 837 (1900); **21**, 913 (1901); **6**, 39 (1903).
2. P. K. Subramanyan, 'Hydrogen in Metals', in J. O'M. Bockris (ed.), *Electrochemistry*. M.T.P. Review of Science (Butterworths, London, 1973), series 1, vol. 6, p.181.
3. W. Beck, J. O'M. Bockris, J. McBreen & L. Nanis, *Proceedings of the Royal Society, 1966*, A290, p.220.
4. J. O'M. Bockris, W. Beck. M. A. Genshaw, P. K. Subramanyan & F. S. Williams, *Acta Met.*, 1971, **19**, 1209.
5. R. Oriani, private communication.
6. G. A. Nelson, *Hydrocarbon Processing*, 1965, **44**, 5, p.185.
7. G. A. Nelson, *Werkstoff Korrosion*, 1963, **14**, 65.
8. W. Hofmann & W. Rauls, *Welding Research Supplement* (May 1965), p.225.
9. H. J. Wiester, W. Dahl & H. Henstenberg, *Arch. Eisenhuttenwes.*, 1963, **34**, 915.
10. W. Fairhurst, *Chemical & Process Engineering* (October 1970), p.66.
11. R. J. Walter & W. T. Chandler, Effects of High-Pressure Hydrogen on Storage Vessel Materials, paper W8-2.4, Westec (March 1968).
12. G. D. Whitman et al., 'Technology of Steel Pressure Vessels for Water-Cooled Nuclear Reactors'. ORNL-NSIC-21 (December 1967).
13. D. W. McDowell & J. D. Milligan, *Hydroc. Proc.*, 1965, **44**, 119.
14. R. L. Savage, L. Blank, T. Cady, K. Cox, R. Murray & R. D. Williams (edd.), 'A Hydrogen Energy Carrier', Vol. II—Systems Analysis, NASA-ASEE, September 1973, p.110.
15. W. B. McPherson & C. E. Cataldo, 'Recent Experience in High Pressure Gaseous Hydrogen Equipment at Room Temperature', Technical Report No. 8-14.1, American Society for Metals, Metals Park, Ohio, October 1968.
16. J. S. Laws, V. Frick & J. McConnel, 'Hydrogen Gas Pressure Vessel Problems in the M-1 Facilities', NASA CR-1305, Washington D.C., March 1969.
17. H. H. Johnson, paper presented at The Hydrogen Economy Miami Energy (THEME) Conference, Miami Beach, Florida, 18-20 March 1974.
18. R. L. Savage et al., *op. cit.*, p.67.
19. R. J. Walter & W. T. Chandler, 'The Influence of Hydrogen on the Fracture Mechanics Properties of Metals', Pub. 572-K-22, Rockwell International, Canoga Park, California 91304, 1974.
20. A. W. Thompson, in 'Hydrogen: Its Technology & Implications', Vol. II, Edition 1, K. F. Cox & K. D. Williams, C.R.C. Press, Inc., Cleveland, Ohio, 1976.
21. S. Srinivasen, R. W. T. Lu, G. Kissel, F. Kulesse, C. R. Davidson, H. Huang, S. Gottesfeld & J. Orehotzky, Department of Energy, Brookhaven National Laboratory, 1977, 23801.
22. D. J. M. Bevan, S. Badwall & J. O'M. Bockris, in course of publication, 1978.
23. See papers in 'Thermochemical Processes', Section 5A through 9A, Vol I, of the 1st World Hydrogen Energy Conference, Miami, March, 1976.
24. U.S. Code of Federal Regulations, Title 49, Part 192, revised October, 1974.
25. W. J. Glover & P. K. Roth, *Pipeline & Gas J.*, 1974, **46**, 201.
26. J. H. Swisher, S. C. Keeton, A. J. West & A. T. Jones, Report SAND 74-8219, Sandia Labs, Livermore, Cal., September 1974.
27. C. M. Hudgins, Interpretive Report on effect of Hydrogen on Pressure vessel steels, Bulletin No. 145, Welding Research Council, New York, October 1969, p.43.
28. G. G. Hancock & H. H. Johnson, 'Hydrogen, oxygen and subcritical crack growth in a high strength steel', Trans. TMS-ACME, 1966, **236**, 513.
29. H. W. Liu, Y. L. Hu, & P. J. Ficalora, *Eng. Frac. Mech.*, 1973, **5**, 281.
30. J. A. Harris & M. C. Wanderham, Report FR-5768, Pratt & Whitney, 1973.

15

SAFETY ASPECTS OF THE USE OF HYDROGEN

Introduction

One of the difficulties of the easy acceptance of hydrogen as a fuel, in particular of developing a Clean Hydrogen Energy Supply, is that two misleading and negative images come across the minds of the citizens when the subject is broached.

On the one hand, some persons recall an experiment carried out in High School Chemistry in which hydrogen is used in an enclosed space with oxygen to cause a 'popping' sound, i.e. the explosion caused by hydrogen and air.

Children never hear the corresponding explosion caused by gasoline or natural gas, under similar circumstances, but only that with hydrogen, which they remember. To them 'hydrogen is explosive'. The innate explosiveness of all fuels for internal-combustion engines, escapes the attention.

Correspondingly, the destruction of the airship *Hindenberg* in 1938 is recalled, and a recent film of the airship's journey has brought attention to the possibility of a hydrogen fire.

The *Hindenberg* fire is now thought to have been caused by sabotage (the case taken in the film). Another view is that the electrical storm through which the airship passed just before its landing made dangerous the method used to determine its height as it approached the landing mast: projection of a conductor to the ground.

Another psychological difficulty with the acceptance of hydrogen as a fuel by the public are the words 'hydrogen bomb' or 'hydrogen atomic weapons'.

The following chapter is based largely on the account given by Hord.[1] However, there are a number of technical publications (listed below) which pertain to hydrogen safety, and the use of hydrogen as a fuel in space-vehicle and rocket propulsion, particulary during the last 20 years, has made knowledge of the properties of hydrogen as a fuel, and the practice of dealing with it, a routine matter for those trained in the area.*

---

*Thus, Stamford H. Henry, Union Carbide's Manager for Hydrogen, is quoted (*Business Week*, 23 September 1972) as stating that handling hydrogen is *easier* than handling propane or gasoline.

With what should one compare hydrogen

The safety of a fuel is a comparative matter. If a substance is a fuel and it is used in internal-combustion engines, then, fundamentally, it must explode when mixed in a certain way with air or oxygen. Thus, in a sense, it is true that hydrogen is a dangerous substance in contact with oxygen, but all fuels must be similarly dangerous by being fuels.

It is only therefore possible to judge the degree of danger which would be incurred in using hydrogen as a fuel in place of fossil fuels by asking under what circumstances its use would be more dangerous than the dangers which are incurred (though unnoticeably, because we have worked out techniques of dealing with them) by the use of natural gas and gasoline.

In Table 15.I are given certain properties for a discussion of hydrogen, methane, and gasoline. Following the discussion by Hord, we divide the material into the following considerations.[1]

TABLE 15.I: SOME PROPERTIES OF HYDROGEN, NATURAL GAS AND GASOLINE[1]

Property	*Hydrogen*	*Methane*	*Gasoline*
Limits of flammability in air, vol %	4.0-7.6	5.3-15.0	1.0-7.6
Limits of detonability in air, vol %	18.3-59.0	6.3-13.5	1.1-3.3
Stoichiometric composition in air, vol %	29.53	9.48	1.76
Minimum energy for ignition in air, mJ	0.02	0.29	0.24
Auto-ignition temperature, °K	858	813	501-744
Hot air-jet ignition temperature	943	1493	1313
Flame temperature in air, °K	2318	2148	2470
Essential thermal energy, radiation flame to surroundings, %	17-25	23-33	30-42
Burning velocity in NTP air, cm/sec	265-325	23-33	30-40
Burning velocity in NTP air	265-325	37-45	37-43
Detonation velocity in NTP air, cm/sec	1.48-2.15	1.39-1.64	1.4-1.7
Diffusion coefficient in NTP air, cm²/sec	0.61	0.16	0.05
Diffusion velocity in NTP air, cm/sec	<2.0	<0.5	<0.2
Buoyant velocity in NTP air, m/sec	1.22-9	0.8-6	Non-buoyant
Maximum experimental safe gap in NTP air, cm	0.008	0.12	0.07
Quenching gap in NTP air, cm	0.06	0.2	0.2
Liquid pool without burning, cm/min	2.5-5.0	0.05-0.5	0.005-0.02
Burning rates of spilled liquid pools, cm/min	3.0-6.6	0.3-1.2	0.2-0.9
Flashpoint, °K	Gaseous	Gaseous	230
Toxicity	Non-toxic	Non-toxic	Slightly toxic
Energy of explosion, g TNT/g fuel	24	11	10
Energy of explosion, g TNT/cm³ NBP liquid fuel	1.71	4.56	7.04
Energy of explosion, kg of TNT/m³ NTP gaseous fuel	2.02	7.03	44.22

Fire hazards

The diffusion velocities of the vapours to be considered differ considerably, as can be seen from Table 15.I. The rate of mixing of the vapours with the air depends partly upon the buoyant effect, i.e. the buoyant velocity, but also upon the diffusion coefficient. The table shows that hydrogen will mix with air at a more rapid rate than the other two comparative substances.

Thus, on the basis of the buoyancy and diffusional properties, the fire hazard would be greater with hydrogen than with methane, and it would be, in terms of these effects, than with gasoline. However, the lastingness of the fire, once it has been set, would tend to be greatest with gasoline, then with methane, and then with hydrogen, because the hydrogen will disperse more quickly than the gasoline, and the dangers of a fire lasting over a longer time will thus be reduced.

Consider, for example, spilled liquid pools (methane and hydrogen will partly be used in the liquid form). Table 15.I shows that the volumetric vaporisation rates are highest for hydrogen, then methane, then gasoline. Thus, gasoline fires will last the longest, and the hydrogen fires the shortest. The fuels all burn at about the same flame temperature. The radiated thermal energy is more for a burning area of hydrogen than for methane, with that of gasoline being least. Thus, the scene of a hydrogen fire may be hotter than that for a hydrocarbon fire, but a hydrocarbon fire would last from 5 to 10 times longer than the hydrogen fire for the same fuel spilled.[1]

An important matter is the spark energy needed to set on fire hydrogen and air, and the actual energy is an order of magnitude less for hydrogen than for methane or gasoline. However, the comparative difference is not as bad as it sounds in effect, because the ignition energy for all three fuels is low and ignition will occur in the presence of sparks, matches, hot surfaces, etc., for all of them.

Hydrogen ignites at a somewhat higher temperature in auto-ignition than methane or gasoline, but the lower energy needed for the ignition makes it more readily ignitable than either of the other two fuels. In respect to a jet consisting of hot air and one of the fuels, the ignition temperature is highest for methane and lowest for hydrogen. Thus, hydrogen is easier to ignite by jets of hot combustion products emitted for an adjacent enclosure. The flash-point of gasoline is below room temperature, and all three fuels being considered here are volatile enough so that they will generate sufficient vapour to create a fire hazard at the earth's surface temperature.

There is one other hazard which must be discussed: detonation within long tubes. In such situations, hydrogen/air mixtures will proceed to detonate more rapidly than methane/air or gasoline/air, though these mixtures also detonate. Overpressure hazards in confined spaces are made worse when hydrogen is in the system. Industrial equipment is currently available to confine hydrogen explosions. However, such pipeline flame arresters are not yet reliable.[1]

Fire damage

The main types of fire damage are from thermal radiation, flame engulfment (fireball), smoke inhalation, fire detection, and extinguishment.

Fireball damage is the result of what happens when materials are engulfed by flames coming from one of the fuels which we are discussing. The fireball itself is an explosion which does not last long, but flames from it may last a long time.

Hord[2] quotes an unpublished report of 1972 in which he has developed an equation for the diameter of a fireball, namely:

$$D \simeq 7.93 \, W_f^{1/3}$$

where D is the diameter in metres, and W_f is the weight of fuel in kilograms.

The duration of the fireball is given by the equation

$$T = 0.47 \, W_f^{1/3}$$

where T is the time in seconds and W_f is the weight of fuel in kilograms.

The second danger of fire damage is from smoke inhalation, and it is this which causes direct deaths or injury from fire.

In the open air, only gasoline causes damage which would arise from smoke inhalation, because methane and hydrogen burn clean. Correspondingly, the products of combustion from hydrogen/air or methane/air fires are less damaging to health than those caused by gasoline because of the buoyancy effects from the two gaseous fuels which result in a larger degree of ingestion of air from the exterior into the buildings.[3] Clearly, sufficient inhalation of any of these fuels can cause asphyxiation.

The damage arising from detection must deal with the fact that hydrogen flames, though readily visible in darkness, are not visible in the daylight, although when they become big enough they cause convective heat ripples. Methane and gasoline flames are more easy to see.

Hydrogen fires are now detectable by ultra-violet or infra-red detection apparatus.[4] Another technique used is to paint the surface which would come into contact with the fire with paint which smells upon being heated. Providing an odoriferous substance in the hydrogen at low concentrations, so that a hydrogen leak would give rise to a noticeable odour, would be helpful.

The extinguishing of a hydrogen fire can be carried out with the normal water deluge or water spray method. It is, in fact, more effective for hydrogen and methane fires than for gasoline fires, because gasoline tends to get on top of the water and continue to burn.

Firefighting equipment for LNG fires now exist,[5] and firefighting equipment for liquid-hydrogen fires may be developed at the present time. CO_2 extinguishers may be used.

Explosion or fire?

When a fuel/air mixture is ignited, there can be either a fire or an explosion. An explosion is often accompanied by a fireball and a pressure wave ('overpressure'). This fireball may ignite combustibles in the surroundings, or fuel not yet exploded but released with the explosion, so that one often obtains an explosion first, followed by a fire later, as usually in aircraft accidents. Of course, the effect of the explosion depends largely upon whether the fuel/air mixture is enclosed at the time, because the overpressure resulting will then produce shrapnel from the rest of the enclosure.[1]

The limits of the detonatability are important in the judgement of the relative hazards from an explosion of a fuel/air mixture. The wider these limits, the greater is the probability of an explosion which may give overpressure sufficient to produce shrapnel hazards. Hydrogen has the largest detonatability of the three fuels considered, and does offer the greatest danger of explosion. However, this must be judged in respect to the potential damage which occurs after an explosion, which is different in all the fuels concerned.

The source of ignition may be many different things: spark, flame, impact, friction, etc.

The shape of the enclosure affects the difference between a deflagration and a detonation (detonation: explosion with attendant high explosion and shrapnel hazard; deflagration: low-order explosions with low overpressure).

U-shaped enclosures with the ground comprise confinement which supports relatively strong explosions in hydrogen-air mixtures, ignited by heat. Geometrical alterations in the walls which cause turbulence increase the likelihood of 'detonation'. Hydrogen is a rapidly burning fuel, and the flame front has a tendency to accelerate in long enclosures. Transition to detonation occurs more easily with hydrogen than with methane/air or gasoline/air, and flashback arrestors which stop combustion in hydrogen-rich mixtures or with methane and air in cylindrical pipes are difficult to design.[6,7,8] The detonation of hydrogen/air mixtures is more certain than that of gasoline or methane, but these mixtures also show danger in confined spaces.

Measures can be taken to reduce the threat from the detonation explosion of gasoline, methane or hydrogen. Forced ventilation stops the accumulation of gas within an enclosure. Build-up in an enclosure can be detected, monitored, and restricted. Weak walls can be used to relieve overpressure if it does occur. However, if a detonation occurs, there is not much help from the weak walls approach.[9] The main point in discussing an explosion, with its creation of overpressure and probably shrapnel if it takes place in an enclosed space, is to relate it to the energy that is released. This can be measured in units such as kJ, but conventionally it is expressed in the equivalent of a quantity of trinitrotoluene, TNT, a standard explosive.

The theoretical TNT equivalent of fuels is usually expressed in terms of the free energy of their reaction with oxygen. The results given in Table 15.I were obtained in this manner. Hydrogen is the most potent on a mass basis, and the least potent on a volumetric basis. Thus, for an equivalent amount of energy stored, hydrogen has the least explosive potential.[1]

Hydrogen disperses more rapidly than do methane and gasoline in the open, and this has to be taken into account in respect to the energy of the explosion given in Table 15.I.

The damage with an explosion depends upon overpressure, and this depends upon the degree and type of confinement. If there is an un-vented deflagration of hydrogen/air, or methane/air, the rise in static pressure is around eight times. The pressure exerted with gasoline/air is about 70-80% of those with hydrogen/air. The un-vented deflagration overpressure is 7 kPa, but only 3-4 causes structural damage to buildings, if confined. Thus, Hord quotes windows as fracturing between 3-7 kPa. Unreinforced masonry falls at 55. Eardrums rupture at 35.[1]

These quotes in kPa show how devastating confined deflagrations can be, for they will rise to pressures up to 8 atmospheres and this is 811 kPa. The unconfined deflagration will cause smaller damage, and any injury which may occur will be secondary, e.g. from flying glass-shrapnel from windows, etc.[1]

Detonations, of course, are much worse. They will cause damage even if unconfined, which may destroy buildings, as in the effects of bombs near buildings. The TNT pressure-distance data are used to find out how much overpressure would occur if there is a fuel/air detonation.[10] The static pressure rise would be round about 15:1 for hydrogen/air and methane/air, and about 12:1 for gasoline/air.

When a deflagration progresses to a detonation, it is a much worse one because the deflagration compresses the unburned fuel/air mixture before the detonation begins.

The engineering techniques for protection of personnel, from collapsing buildings and shrapnel, is reviewed by Hord, and the approximate calculations may be seen from his Fig. 15.1.[1]

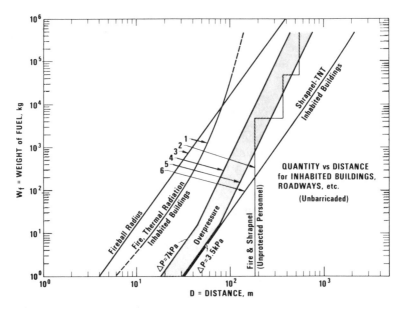

Fig. 15.1. Quantity-distance relationships for the protection of personnel near liquid-hydrogen storage and experimental areas: (1) Data from M. G. Zebetakis and D. S. Burgess, Research on the hazards associated with the production and handling of LH$_2$, Bureau of Mines Report 5707, 1961; (2) General Safety Engineering Design Criteria, Vol. 1, CPIA Publication 194, 1971; (3) (4) (5) From I. Hurd, unpublished report on explosion criteria for LH$_2$, National Bureau of Standards, 1972; (6) Same source as (2).

Comparison between the fuel storage standards in hydrogen, LNG and gasoline is seen in Fig. 15.2. The situation with hydrogen is less demanding than might have been thought. Industrial storage standards are the most restrictive for hydrogen, then for methane, and then for gasoline.

The main conclusion from all of this is that although industrial storage standards are less restrictive for gasoline than for LNG and hydrogen, the

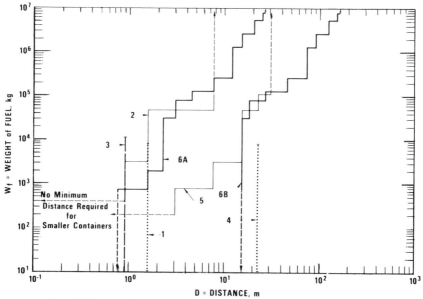

Fig. 15.2. Industrial storage standards (quantity/distance) for hydrogen, LNG and gasoline: (1) H$_2$ Dewar separation; (2) LNG container separation;. (3) Gasoline/Tank separation; (4) H$_2$ inhibited buildings; (5) LNG inhibited buildings; (6A) (6B) Gasoline inhibited buildings. From Hurd, *loc. cit.*

storage standards for hydrogen are not prohibitive and do not prevent their use.

Relative safety in respect to storage[1]

Gasoline is the easiest and the safest fuel to store of the three because of its lower volatility, and narrower detonable limits.

However, hydrogen and methane can also safely be stored, and the precise relative danger of these two and the various methods of storing them have to be re-assessed frequently as experience grows.

The various applications of hydrogen need their own safety precautions and codes worked out, as they have been worked out for fuels before. The long-term use of hydrogen in the aerospace industry, particularly by NASA, has given these codes. It must be recalled that gases 50-60% rich in H$_2$ in coal-gas, town-gas, and producer-gas, have been used for many decades, particularly in Europe, within the household.

Table 15.II summarises the situation.[1]

Hydrogen safety guidelines

There are now many documents which deal with the details of hydrogen safety in its handling, and the major technical note put out by Hord in 1976 gives a full summary of these.[1] The following is the collection gathered by Hord. For the actual technical use of hydrogen, his pamphlet should be further consulted.

TABLE 15.II: SUMMARY OF THE COMPARATIVE SAFETY SITUATION IN RESPECT TO HYDROGEN FUELS

Aspect	Hydrogen	Methane	Gasoline	Remarks
Confinement of liquid	Relatively difficult	Less difficult	Standard	All do-able routinely in Space program
Containment of vapour at NTP	Easy	Easy	Relatively difficult	
Danger in fuel spill				
(i) Ease of starting fire	Greatest	Intermediate	Less great	
(ii) Lastingness of fire once started	Shortest	Intermediate	Greatest	
(iii) Ignitibility in presence of weak sources, e.g. matches	Most easily ignited	Same as gasoline	Same as methane	
(iv) Detectability of fire	More difficult but can be done	O.K.	O.K.	
(v) Fire can be fought with?	Water	Water	Water	But gasoline difficult to fight with water
(vi) Health hazards by smoke inhalation	Least bad	Less bad than gasoline	Worst	
Ease of explosion	Greatest	Less bad	Least, but still considerable	Greater breadth of explosion limits for H_2
Danger from an explosion, once occurred	Small if unconfined. Devastating if confined, but less so for same volume than LNG or gasoline	See Hydrogen	See Hydrogen	
Safety in commercial and industrial use	No special problems	?	Routine	
Safety in transport and residential	At present greater risk than CH_4 of gas because routine methods for dealing with have not been worked out			Long-term use of 50% hydrogen gas in European households supports safety

Key to appendix on safety references (Hord)[1]

Safety Item	Reference
Handling procedures	(A1)-(A25)
Storage	(A1), (A16), (A17), (A21), (A22), (A23), (B1)
Explosive criteria	(A1), (C1), (C2), (C3)
Leak detection and control	(D1)-(D6), (A1), (G4)

Fire detection, prevention and control	(G5)
Facilities	(A1), (C1)
Mechanical equipment	(F1)-(F18)
Electrical equipment	(G1)-(G10)

APPENDIX REFERENCES[1]

NOTE: In the references that follow:

CGA = Compressed Gas Association, Inc., 500 Fifth Ave, New York, NY 10036.

ANSI = American National Standards Institute, 1430 Broadway, New York, NY 10018.

NFPA = National Fire Protection Association, Publication Sales Department, 470 Atlantic Ave, Boston, MA 02210.

ASME = American Society of Mechanical Engineers, United Engineering Centre, 345 East 47th Street, New York, NY 10017.

UL = Underwriters' Laboratories, Publication Stock, 333 Pfingsten Road, Northbrook, IL 60062.

ISA = Instrument Society of America, 400 Stanwix Street, Pittsburgh, PA 15222.

[A1]   General Safety Engineering Design Criteria, Vol. 1, CPIA public. 194 (October 1971); also Liquid Propellant Handling, Storage and Transportation, Vol. 3, CPIA publication 194 (May 1972)— documents prepared by the JANNAF propulsion committee of the JANNAF Hazards Working Group and are available from the Chemical Propulsion Information Agency (CPIA) of the Johns Hopkins University Applied Physics Laboratory, 8621 Georgia Ave, Silver Spring, MD 20910; (also available to the public through National Technical Information Service, Springfield, VA 22150: Vol. 1, Accession No. AD 889,763; Vol. 3, Accession No. AD 870,259).

[A2]   Hydrogen safety manual, NASA Lewis Research Centre, NASA Tech. Memo TM-X-52454 (1968).

[A3]   On an investigation of hazards associated with the storage and handling of liquid hydrogen, Final Report C-61092, Contract No. Af 18(600)-1687, prepared by Arthur D. Little, Inc., DDC Access No. AD 324194, 137 pp. (March 1960).

[A4]   Liquid hydrogen, a guide for the safe handling and storage of liquid hydrogen at LASL Facilities, Los Alamos Scientific Laboratory, P.O. Box 1663, Los Alamos, NM 87544.

[A5]   Weintraub, A.A., Control of liquid hydrogen hazards at experimental facilities: a review, health and safety laboratory, U.S. Atomic Energy Commission, New York, NY (May 1965); also, Grumer, J., Strasser, A., and Van Meter, R. A., Principles for safe handling of liquid hydrogen, Bureau of Mines Technical Report (June 1967).

[A6]   Chelton, D.B., 'Safety in the use of liquid hydrogen', in R.B. Scott, W. H. Denton & C. M. Nicholls (edd.), *Technology and Uses of*

Liquid Hydrogen (The Macmillan Co., New York, 1964), pp. 359-378.

[A7] Connolly, W. W., 'A practical safety standard for commercial handling of liquefied hydrogen', in K. D. Timmerhaus (ed.), *Advances in Cryogenic Engineering 12* (Plenum Press, New York, 1967), pp. 192-197.

[A8] Recommended materials and practices for use with cryogenic propellants, Aerospace Information Report, AIR 839B, 68 pp. (Soc. of Auto. Engrs., April 1969).

[A9] Cryogenics safety manual, a guide to good practice (British Cryogenics Council, 16 Belgrave Square, London, SW1X8PT, 1970).

[A10] Hernandez, H. P., Safety guidelines for accelerator installation, Lawrence Radiation Laboratory Rept. No. UCRL-18555 (February 1969).

[A11] Compressed Gas Association, Inc., *Handbook of Compressed Gases* (Reinhold Publishing Corp., New York, 1966).

[A12] Safe Handling of Compressed Gases in Containers, CGA Pamphlet P-1.

[A13] Method of Marking Portable Compressed Gas Containers to Identify the Material Contained, CGA Pamphlet C-4; [also ANSI Z48.1-1954 (R1971)].

[A14] Guide to the Preparation of Precautionary Labelling and Marking of Compressed Gas containers, CGA Pamphlet C-7.

[A15] Hydrogen, CGA Pamphlet G-5.

[A16] Standard for Gaseous Hydrogen at Consumer Sites, CGA Pamphlet G-5.1.

[A17] Standard for Liquefied Hydrogen Systems at Consumer Sites, CGA Pamphlet G-5.2.

[A18] Commodity Specification for Hydrogen, CGA Pamphlet G-5.3; see also, Hydrogen Commodity Specification, MIL-P-27201B (June 1971); (available from USN Supply Depot, 5801 Tabor Ave, Philadelphia, PA 19120).

[A19] Lightning Protection Code, NFPA Pamphlet No. 78 (ANSI C5.1).

[A20] Static Electricity, NFPA Pamphlet No. 77.

[A21] Standard for Gaseous Hydrogen Systems at Consumer Sites, NFPA Pamphlet No. 50A (ANSI Z292.2).

[A22] Standard for Liquefied Hydrogen Systems at Consumer Sites, NFPA Pamphlet No. 50B (ANSI Z292.3).

[A23] Standard for the Installation and Operation of Oxygen-Fuel Gas Systems for Welding and Cutting, NFPA Pamphlet No. 51; see also, Standard on Safety in Welding and Cutting, ANSI Z49.1.

[A24] Siewert, R. D., Evacuation areas for transportation accidents involving propellant tank pressure bursts, NASA TMX-68277 (November 1972).

[A25] Emergency services guide for selected hazardous materials (spills, fire, evacuation area), Department of Transportation, Office of the Secretary, Office of Hazardous Materials, Washington, D.C. 20590 (April 1974).

[B1] Zabetakis, M. G., & Burgess, D. S., Research on the hazards associated with the production and handling of liquid hydrogen, Bureau of Mines Report, RI-5707 (1961).

[C1] Hord, J., Explosion criteria for liquid hydrogen test facilities, Nat. Bur. Stand. (U.S.), NBS Report (February 1972).

[C2] Explosion Venting, NFPA Pamphlet No. 68.

[C3] Explosion Prevention Systems, NFPA Pamphlet No. 69.

[D1] Rosen, B., Dayan, V. H., & Proffit, R. L., Hydrogen leak and fire detection, NASA SP-5092 (1970).

[D2] Automatic Fire Detectors, NFPA Pamphlet No. 72E.

[D3] Fire Hazard Properties of Flammable Liquids, Gases, Volatile Solids, NFPA Pamphlet No. 325M.

[D4] National Fire Codes, NFPA Volumes 1 and 2 (general fire-fighting and fire control).

[D5] Donnini, J. M., Hydrogen fire blink detector, U.S. Patent Application S/N 51477 (July 1970).

[D6] Custer, R. L. P., & Bright, R. G., Fire detection: the state of the art, Nat. Bur. Stand. (U.S.) Tech. Note TN-839 (June 1974).

[F1] ASME Boiler and Pressure Vessel Code, Section VIII, Division 1, Pressure Vessels: this reference applies to gaseous and liquid containers for portable and stationary applications.

[F2] ASME Boiler and Pressure Vessel Code, Section VIII, Division 2, Pressure Vessels: Alternative Rules: this reference applies to gaseous and liquid containers for stationary applications only.

[F3] ASME Boiler and Pressure Vessel Code, Section IX, Welding and Brazing Qualifications.

[F4] ASME Boiler and Pressure Vessel Code, Section III, Nuclear Power Plant Components: a series of standards applicable to nuclear plants and installations.

[F5] American National Standard Code for Pressure Piping, Petroleum Refinery Piping, ANSI B31.3 (ASME, New York): this reference applies to gaseous and liquid piping.

[F6] American National Standard Code for Pressure Piping, Cryogenic Piping Systems, ANSI B31.10 (in preparation).

[F7] Vacuum insulated cryogenic pipes, some recommendations concerned with pipe and coupling design (British Cryogenics Council, 16 Belgrave Square, London SW1X8PT, 1972).

[F8] Safety Relief Device Standards, Part 1–Cylinders for Compressed Gases, CGA Pamphlet S-1.1; Part 2–Cargo and Portable Tanks for Compressed Gases, CGA Pamphlet S-1.2; Part 3–Compressed Gas Storage Containers, CGA Pamphlet S-1.3.

[F9] Recommended Practice for the Manufacture of Fusible Plugs, CGA Pamphlet S-4.

[F10] Frangible Disc Safety Device Assembly, CGA Pamphlet S-3.

[F11] Compressed Gas Cylinder Valve Outlet and Inlet Connections, CGA Pamphlet V-1 (also Canadian Standards Association CSA B96-1965 and American Standards Association ASA B57. 1-1965).

[F12] Methods for Hydrostatic Testing of Compressed Gas Cylinders, CGA

Pamphlet C-1.

[F13] Standards for Welding and Brazing on Thin Walled Containers, CGA Pamphlet C-3.

[F14] Cylinder Service Life, Seamless, High-Pressure Cylinder Specifications ICC-3, ICC-3A, ICC-3AA, CGA Pamphlet C-5.

[F15] Standards for Visual Inspection of Compressed Gas Cylinders, CGA Pamphlet C-6.

[F16] Standard for Requalification of DoT-3HT Cylinders, CGA Pamphlet C-8.

[F17] Tentative Standard for Insulated Tank Truck Specification for Cold Liquefied Gases, CGA Pamphlet CGA-341.

[F18] Voth, R. O., 'Safety of hydrogen pressure gauges' in K. D. Timmerhaus (ed.), *Advances in Cryogenic Engineering, 17* (Plenum Press, New York, 1972), pp. 182-187.

[G1]   Standard for Intrinsically Safe Process Control Equipment for Use in Class I Hazardous Locations, NFPA Pamphlet No. 493.

[G2]   Standard for Purged and Pressurized Enclosures for Electrical Equipment in Hazardous Locations, NFPA Pamphlet No. 496.

[G3]   National Electrical Code, Chap. 5, Articles 500-501, NFPA Pamphlet No. 70.

[G4]   Fire Protection Equipment List (January 1975), available from UL.

[G5]   Hazardous Location Equipment List (June 1974), available from UL.

[G6]   Electrical Instruments in Hazardous Atmospheres, ISA-RP 12.1 (1960).

[G7]   Intrinsically Safe and Non-Incendive Electrical Instruments, ISA-RP 12.2 (1965).

[G8]   Instrument Purging for Reduction of Hazardous Area Classification, ISA-S12.4 (1970).

[G9]   Electrical Safety Practices, ISA Monograph 113 (1972).

[G10] Magison, E. C., *Electrical Instruments in Hazardous Locations* (Instrument Society of America, Pittsburgh, Pennsylvania, 1972), 2nd edn., 321 pp.

[H1]   American National Standard Code for Pressure Piping, Gas Transmission and Distribution Piping Systems, ANSI B31.8.

[H2]   Code of Federal Regulations, Title 49, Transportation, Parts 100 to 199, U.S. Government Printing Office, Washington, D.C. 20402.

[H3]   Code of Federal Regulations, Title 46, Shipping, Parts 140 to 149, U.S. Government Printing Office, Washington, D.C. 20402.

[H4]   Code of Federal Regulations, Title 14, Aeronautics and Space, Parts 60 to 199, U.S. Government Printing Office, Washington, D.C. 20402.

[H5]   Occupational Safety and Health Act of 1970, PL 91-596 (29 December 1970) in United States Statutes at Large, 91st Congress, Second Session, *84*, Part 2, pp. 1590-1620 (U.S. Government Printing Office, Washington, D.C. 20402, 1971).

[H6]   Official Air Transport Restricted Articles Tariff No. 6-D, Civil Aeronautics Board (CAB) No. 82, Section I (pp. 14-15), Section

II (p. 53) and Section III—Part A (p. 94) issued by the Airline Tariff Publishing Company, Dulles International Airport, P.O. Box 17415, Washington, D.C. 20041.

SUMMARY OF CHAPTER

This is effectively Table 15.II. The many necessary practical details are in the references of the Appendix.[1]

AUTHOR'S CHOICE OF A MORE IMPORTANT CONCLUSION FROM THIS CHAPTER

Gasoline, methane and hydrogen are comparable in the danger which arises from potential ignition of an explosion when they are mixed with air. Hydrogen is more dangerous than the other two in some aspects (ignitability); and less dangerous than the others in other aspects (e.g. health hazard by smoke inhalation; violence of explosion from a given volume).

REFERENCES

1. J. Hord, Is Hydrogen Safe? National Bureau of Standards, Technical Note, 690, U.S. Department of Commerce, Washington, 1976.
2. J. Hord, National Bureau of Standards, Unpublished Report of February 1972.
3. R.L.P. Custer and R. G. Bright, NASA CR-134642, N.B.S., TN-839 (June 1974).
4. B. Rosen, V. H. Dayan, R. L. Proffit, NASA, SP5092, 1970.
5. L.N.G. Safety Program, Phase II, Consequences of LNG Spills on Land, American Gas Association, Project IS-3-1 Nov. 1973.
6. D. S. Burgess, Bureau of Mines, Pittsburgh, Pa., private communication to Hord, 1975.
7. M. G. Zepetakis, U.S. Bureau of Mines, private communication to Hord, 1975.
8. H. Carhart, Naval Research Lab., Washington, D.C., private communication to Hord, 1975.
9. J. Hord, National Bureau of Standards, Unpublished Report of February, 1972.
10. General Safety Engineering Design Criteria, Vol. 1, CPIA public 194, October, 1971.

16

PROSPECT

Introduction

At present, it is difficult to make out the shape of U.S. Energy policy. Thus, the initiative of the Carter plan of 1977 was minimised by the U.S. Congress to almost no change at all, i.e. the inertia of past movement carried through. Political factors hence still dominate the situation. There is an emphasis on short-term (1-2 year) thinking, whereas the appropriate time-scale is the several decades which would encompass the building of a New Energy System to use the renewable resources. There is a widespread impression that the situation is rate-determined by scientific inventiveness, and hence the funding of research; whereas a far greater difficulty is the provision of the capital needed for the building of machinery already in pilot plant scale (solar) or well known (coal, atomic).

Resources run out suddenly. By simply not making the capital investment needed to build the necessary machinery to convert the renewable resources to available fuels it would be possible to continue the normal high living standard engendered by the cheap sale of the remaining cache of fossil fuels until the last few years of their being able to supply demand (late 1980s). For up to a decade or so more, the Society could run unfettered and continue to expand. *The political attractiveness of that path is the principal danger* of the present situation: for, if the capital investment is not made *before* Downturn, it will be far more difficult to make when the tempo of the economy is forced continually lower by lack of fuel.

Thus, one necessary step in the evolution of energy policy is the presentation of the knowledge held by the energy scientists, and the rational part of the environmentalist groups, upon the electorate. Swayed as some of the members of Congress are said to be by their connections with the Corporations (to whom conservational decreases in the tempo of the Economy are unwelcome), they must eventually heed a sufficiently strong populist movement, or fall to rival candidates who will ride the electorate's sense of self-preservation.

But hitherto, the democratic voice has been free of a knowledge of the non-nuclear option, particularly in the economic and time aspects of what must be built before the exhaustion of the present fuels; and eager to hear promises of still further increases of living standards, the reverse of which now has to be offered, to ensure the possibility of increases later.

It is not possible to find a historical parallel to the social and economic aspects of the energy-exhaustion situation. The major changes which have hitherto threatened earth societies have been 'Acts of God' beyond control. What approaches, fully visible to those who have studied the position, is a

392

catastrophic energy exhaustion, in a time of about one generation. Action could be taken to avoid this Energy Exhaustion Catastrophe, but such actions would involve significant reduction in living standards (because of the magnitude—see Tables 16.II and 16.III—of the yearly capital investment needed) before these are forced upon us by energy exhaustion. To use the chemical idiom, the electorate is expected to make a *voluntary* decision to go *up* a free energy gradient, and not to follow the spontaneous driving force in the direction of comfort. Can that be expected?

The economic and time restraints

The cost of a new Energy Conversion System will be between about $(1-2) 10^{13} (1978 currency). It will be argued (below) that about 40 years is now available, i.e. an average national U.S. investment of $375 10^9 per year in 1978 dollars (1980 to 2020).

The present energy policy

The price of oil and oil imports

A desirable alteration in energy policy is to achieve, as soon as is feasible, a rise in the price of gasoline; and to achieve, correspondingly, a reduction (say, 10% per year over 10 years) in the amount of imported oil.

The need for the price increase is to encourage conservation and bring about, thereby, an extension of the present resources to allow time for the capital formation and building. Thus would be ameliorated the difficulties of a situation achieved by the dependence of the United States, and all the Western economies (including that of Australia from around 1985), upon OPEC oil. According to Hunter *et al.*,[1] the price of energy in the United States is 3-115 times cheaper than in other countries, if one takes into account the ability of the inhabitants to pay. One might start with a $1 per gallon price for gasoline and achieve, by 1990, a reduction to one-sixth of the 1978 oil imports, together with an increase in the gasoline price of up to $3 per gallon in 1978 money.

If one takes oil as supplying some 70% of the U.S. energy at this time, doubling of the price would produce some $200.$10^9$ per year. The amount gained per year, *if fed into a fund for the provision of the capital for the building of the New Energy Conversion System* (and not given to the group of investors who own the oil companies), would provide a substantial amount of the needed money.*

On the development of hydrogen from coal

The price of hydrogen developed from coal is marginally below that of methane, neglecting the environmental damage and temperature rise which would occur were we to continue to inject CO_2 from the burning of substantial amounts of coal into the atmosphere instead of, e.g. injecting it into the ocean—possible if H_2 and not CH_4 is the fuel extracted from coal.

---

*Would such an increase in the price of oil also increase unemployment and depress the economy (see Chapter 1) if it was devoted to the vigorous building programme needed? A war demands the same greatly increased capital investment in new goods and vastly increased spending rates which are not fed into the community but either destroyed by the enemy or scrapped after victory. Yet wars usually cause great prosperity in the U.S.

Thus, at present, the estimated cost of methane is about $4 per MBTU, but that of oil from coal about $6 per MBTU.[2] Liquid methane, the price of which would be about $5 per MBTU, is thus a much more attractive fuel than gasoline derived from coal.

The case against developing methane from coal, and in favour of developing hydrogen, arises from the possibility of injecting CO_2 into the ocean rather than the atmosphere. The difficulties include not only the CO_2 effect upon the atmosphere but the pollutive effects of SO_2 and the logistical difficulties of opening sufficient mines in time, training sufficient miners (about 2 million new miners would be necessary at 2000) to have an economy largely based on coal. The energy sources to follow coal are breeder reactors, solar converters (photovoltaic, solar-thermal and OTEC) and possibly fusion plants. All of these will produce electricity and hydrogen. Hence, over the period, say, 1990 to 2030, energy will be increasingly supplied by sources which will produce hydrogen and either methane or hydrogen. It is *less desirable to have two different fuels* for industry and commerce (for the apparatus to use each differs), and hence more economic (as well as cleaner) to produce hydrogen from coal rather than methane. Taking into account its comparative efficiency, it would be cheaper; taking into account the costly environmental damage, it would be much cheaper.

Conversely, hydrogen is more difficult to store and more expensive to liquefy than CH_4. The storage difficulty is in the process of being reduced.[3] Hydrogen for a 250 mile journey could be stored in fibreglass containers in several as yet unused spaces in a vehicle.

Fission and breeders

Only the development of plutonium breeders is a possible source of fissile-produced energy of sufficient longevity to be of interest. The difficulties of this source, presented in Chapter 5, are thought by many to be too great (air pollution; storing of wastes; hi-jacking potential) for the source to be viable.[4] However, the building of this plutonium economy is the present direction of U.S. energy policy.

Fusion

Until laboratory fusion has been achieved, including the production of electricity, it is difficult to estimate the economics. How will these economics compare with OTEC and solar-thermal energy plants, both of which have been systems-analysed to give electricity in the region of 4c per kWh? The competition is between the cost of large amounts of raw materials (steel and aluminium) needed for the solar plants, versus the cost of the high technology needed for the hypothetical fusion plants. However, fusion plants would continue to represent an environmental hazard (Chapter 6) absent in the large-scale collection of solar energy.

The building of solar-hydrogen systems

In view of the difficulties of coal and breeder paths, and the nebulous nature of the fusion path, the large-scale development of a solar technology now seems eventually inevitable. The difference between the solar and the nuclear prospects are clear: nuclear sources involve hazards, the degree of which can be converted into dollar terms, and breeder reactors seem to have unacceptable economics when the necessary safety measures, waste-storage and decommissioning costs are taken into account. Of the three solar options (Chapter 8), the photovoltaic one has been operational on a tiny scale, though too expensive. The estimated price of energy from it towards the late 1970s would be compatible with competing choices so long as there is the use of concentrating lenses. The solar-thermal and ocean-thermal prospects involve simple technology and the latter has been systems-analysed to give liquid hydrogen in the region of $8-16 per MBTU.[5] This is in the range of some estimates for gasoline from coal.[2] The solar approaches have no environmental or hi-jack problems. The main visible difficulty is the low degree of research and development put into these environmentally-satisfactory options in present Government Research programmes. Such programmes appear to have a viewpoint of an earlier time when the use of solar energy was thought to be mainly for household heating and the consequences of hydrogen as a storage and transmission medium had not been realised.

To spell out, with appropriate figures from recent estimates, the options for an energy future based upon solar-hydrogen systems, a summary of the two more likely possibilities will be reiterated (Chapter 8).

Solar-thermal production of electrical energy, with corresponding hydrogen production[6]

As described by Hildebrandt and Van't Hull for $100MW_e$, the area needed would be 1.5 × 1.8 km. The associated tower would be 330 m tall. No selective surfaces would be necessary. The boiler exterior would reach 1300°K. The mirrors would be 6.1 m octagonal assembled from 8 triangular facets. The peak power densities would be $1MW_e$ m^{-2}. This is 5 times greater than the density for a fossil fuel generator. The production could be, then, steam to give electricity, and the cost estimate of this (1977) would be about 1.7c per kWh. With electricity at this price, hydrogen could then be produced from water at some $7 per MBTU. The production of hydrogen from power towers would be important, not only because of its availability as a fuel for transportation and industry, but also because of the need for storage to smooth out the variations of sunlight (power towers can only be used when the solar disc is visible).

OTEC plants for hydrogen

G. L. Dugger and E. J. Francis have presented detailed designs for a $100MW_e$ OTEC ship producing liquid hydrogen and, if desired, ammonia.[7] The design is shown in Fig. 16.1 and, an artist's rendering in Fig. 16.2. Vast areas of the Atlantic Ocean exist in which a 24°C temperature difference is available, and in which OTEC boats could graze. OTEC hydrogen would be competitive with other fuels by 1990. For a 1985 technology in 1977 dollars, Dugger and Francis calculate a delivery price of $7.90 for *liquid* hydrogen at the port of entry of the ship. (Oil from coal $6-12 per MBTU.) Electricity which could be re-developed from hydrogen on land would cost 3c (kWh)$^{-1}$.

The development of ammonia would give this method an edge over the corresponding solar-thermal plant because of the immediate economic viability of such a plant, without waiting for the general development of a Hydrogen Economy. Industry would take up OTEC before government, because there is prospect of profit. Thus, Dugger and Francis quote a profit probability in the 50-60% range for NH_3, which would be attainable now.

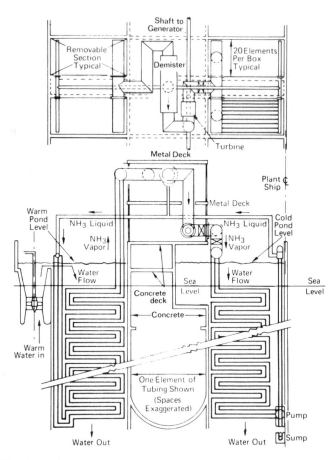

Fig. 16.1. Basic power unit on OTEC, comprising two each of evaporator and condenser modules powering one 6 MW gross-output turbine.

Potential stages in the development of a solar-hydrogen economy

There are some aspects of a hydrogen economy which will be developed independently of whether the energy source is solar or atomic. Thus:

1. *The uses of hydrogen as a fuel which offer economic viability at this time*

(a) WHERE CHEAP HYDRO-ELECTRIC POWER IS AVAILABLE
The cost of electricity from paid-off hydro plants is low, and coupling them to electrolysis in the low-use period (interruptable power) would give a price (E = 2 volt) of $2.07 per MBTU (gasoline about $3). Liquefaction based cost about $2.50 per MBTU, i.e. about $4.57 per MBTU for liquid H_2. If one takes into account a Second Law efficiency increment for hydrogen over gasoline of 1.5 (urban running), then the relevant price

Fig. 16.2. Dugger & Francis artist's sketch of OTEC.

ratios are no longer $\frac{2.07}{3} = 0.7$ and $\frac{4.57}{3} = 1.5$, but 0.5 and 1 respectively.

The competitiveness of some cheap H_2 available at this time with old electrolysers from such sources does not seem to be realised.

(b) USE OF SMALL HYDRO-ELECTRIC SOURCES

Hydro-electric possibilities on a small scale exist throughout the world. Their use to produce hydrogen as a fuel for remote districts is worth considering and this has been done by H. A. Wallace in respect to S.E. Asia. Mini-hydro-electric schemes have been discussed in respect to the U.S. by Brown and Gutmann.[8] They promise the cheapest of all the post-2000 energy sources (taking into account the cost of environmental damage) and could perhaps supply all transportation energy for under-developed countries.

(c) LOW USE-TIME POWER FROM FISSION REACTORS

About 64 fission reactors are operative in the United States in 1978. These are capital intensive. Water electrolysis with excess capacity during the low use-time period (9 p.m.-6 a.m.), and vacations and at week-ends, could be at about two-thirds the cost of the high use-time energy.

If this electricity were sold for large-scale use, water electrolysis plants at the site at 1.5 c (kWh)$^{-1}$ (1978) and the electrochemical reactor decomposing the water to hydrogen worked at 1.6 volts (already obtained in laboratory use), the resulting gaseous H_2 would cost about $6 per MBTU. However, the hydrogen has to be stored, and this involves utilisation of underground cavity or hydride storage, e.g. in iron-titanium-manganese.

There should be a possibility of use, at first for peaking cycles; and then for use when (as increasingly) environmental difficulties force the closing of oil-burning turbines.

(d) The synthesis of ammonia and oxygen

Where a hydrogen electrolysis plant to be placed near a reactor, and the low use-time power used to produce hydrogen and hence ammonia, the oxygen produced could be piped to a steel mill.[9]

Many water electrolysis plants work at 30-40 atmospheres and oxygen could easily be available from electrolysis at this pressure.

(e) Welding

Hydrogen-oxygen mixtures produced by electrolysis have been used for welding by Yull Brown.[10] If the stoichiometric mixture is produced (i.e. air is not the source of O_2), the welding flame reaches 3000°C. Because of the small and portable size of the practical unit (tap water, household electricity), there are considerable cost savings compared with the use of large-size acetylene and oxygen cylinders which have to be ported by truck to the location of use. The price of acetylene will rise with rises in the price of natural gas. Yull Brown's approach already shows great economic advantages and these should increase as the price of hydrocarbon gases rises.

(f) Anti-pollution devices on cars and planes

Jet aircraft pollute on take-off and landing. Injection of hydrogen into the fuel mix during this process would reduce pollution whilst the aircraft is near to the ground.

Recent experiments show that on-board production of hydrogen from gasoline, and burning this substance in the engine along with gasoline, reduces pollution in cars.[11] This seems to offer an immediate amelioration possibility in pollution from automobiles.

2. Household solar-hydrogen

The running of households on solar energy was begun by Boer at the University of Delaware in 1973. Cadmium sulphide panels were used for electricity production. Space heating is from air passed under the panels collecting solar electricity. The heat storage was in a bulky salt hydrate container stored in the basement. Electricity storage was in lead-acid batteries.

Billings built the first solar-hydrogen house in Provo, Utah, 1977 (Chapter 12).[12] Solar-hydrogen houses would provide house heating, cooling, and lighting, and might also allow (in sunnier climes) a fuelling of the family car. This would be possible in single-family homes, using collectors.

3. The solar-hydrogen farm

Before cheap oil, the provision of farm lighting from windmill electricity was commonplace. The major difference between a farm and house from the present viewpoint is that the farm has plenty of room for wind generators and for additional solar collecting surfaces.

Suppose one considers a wind-driven farm, then one might have the following:

1. Farm and building: 70 kWh per day.
2. Family car (100 miles per day at 20 kW): say, 40 kWh.
3. Tractors, 30 kWh each: 480 kWh per day.
4. Other machinery: say 200 kW per day.
   Total: 590 kWh per day.

If the mean annual wind has the modest value of 8 mph on the farm, about 80 windmills with 10 ft-radius blades would provide sufficient energy. This need not mean that one would have 80 separate windmills: the designs of Honnecker could be at, say, 10 separate towers, each containing 8 blades at a height of 100 feet above the ground.

Corresponding to these concepts are those of Tison and Viederman.[13] They project costs of stored power from wind energy on the farm as about 10c per kWh, higher than that estimated for OTEC or solar-thermal. An outline of their system is given in Fig. 16.3.[13]

Can the farm picture be enhanced by the joint use of a solar-thermal generator along with the wind generator?

The Tison and Viederman study was done with wind assumed at 7.95 mph.

4. Development of the solar-hydrogen economy on a large scale

A coal-bearing region would firstly be used to bring about gasification to hydrogen, passage through a pipe several km in length and the manufacture of electricity. This would be tried out over one year to examine the economics, starting in 1980. From there onwards, one possible schedule is suggested in Table 16.1.

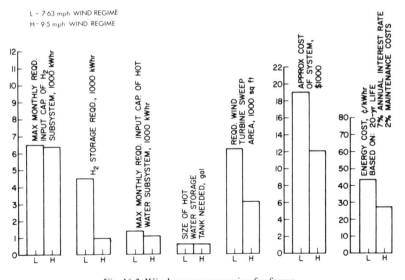

Fig. 16.3. Wind energy conversion for farms.

TABLE 16.I: Possible Stages in the Development of a U.S. Government-Sponsored Energy Programme Towards a Solar-Hydrogen Economy

Project	Date at which project should be operative	Energy source	Objective	Remarks
Municipal bus systems begin to run on hydrogen	1980	Old hydro-electric, or coal	Demonstrate practicability of hydrogen as automotive fuel	Portland, Oregon, using Bonneville Dam. Cost-savings to municipality by cheaper fuel
Coal-based plants on shore produce H_2, reject CO_2 to ocean	1981	Coal	Possible basis intermediate fuel for transportation	Coal-based H_2 competitive with gasoline on per km basis
Demonstration of an electricity production plant	1982	Coal	Show feasibility of concept guarantees plant income 10 years	Joliet, Illinois
Los Angeles, Public transportation on hydrogen	1985	Nuclear fission, off-shore plant. On-shore coal plant $\rightarrow H_2$ with CO_2	Would reduce smog in city	As electricity for water splitting would use low-use period power, cost saving in fuel for transportation
Tax advantages for small single-family homes to convert to partial solar production of energy	1985	Solar absorbers; photovoltaic	Save oil	Would have to use fossil-based electric power as standby
Convert isolated Government town to complete running hydrogen fuel	1990	Wind and solar-thermal	Demonstrate concept	Oahu Island in Hawaii (includes Honolulu industry)
Conversion period for whole country to common hydrogen medium with mixed energy base	2000-2030	Coal, fission, solar-thermal, OTEC, photovoltaic. Space-based photovoltaic? Fusion??	Energy sufficiency at 5kW per head	It is period of maximal capital investment
Gradual conversion to one energy source	–2030	Solar? Fusion?	Optimisation	

5. Final goal of 5 kW per person

The United States is using too much energy in the sense that the increase of the income per person is no longer linear with the increase of the energy per person, i.e. the worthwhileness of the rise of living standards which occurs with increase of the energy per head increase has fallen. With sufficient energy per head, negative feedbacks occur which (within the present structure of society) decrease the desirability of increasing the energy supply. For example, unemployment and crime (and the money spent to fight it) increase with the increase of the energy per head.[1] The willingness (and opportunity) to work is decreased. There is an increase in difficulties with mental health. In view of the living standards achieved by high-industry countries such as Sweden and France, at 5kW per head, it appears reasonable to aim the United States economy at an increased efficiency of energy use which would result in a 5kW economy. The capital investment needed to build the machinery for the New Energy System to replace the fossil fuels by collection from the renewable resources will be so great that an increase in efficiency must be aimed at to reduce the investment needed.

An analogy to addiction?

The difficulty of a too-early exhaustion of oil and natural gas arises from *expansion* and thus, from 'Prosperity'. For, if we could attain 'now', a constant energy economy, we *would* have more than 100 years of coal before us and that would decrease the rate of capital investment needed to build a machinery which converts the energy from renewable resources.

Why, then, is this way made to look so repulsive that, like the inevitability of death, it is seldom mentioned? Essentially, the answer seems to lie in the strength of materialism. It is this *addiction* to the immediate comforts of prosperity which blocks out a longer view which could change the situation. For, were we to think communally, what is wrong with stopping (at least energy) growth this year, now? The probability of exhaustion of the store of unrenewable fuels before sufficient renewable resource conversion machinery has been built would be then reduced. However, the analogy to drug-addiction holds, for the body-politics would as easily voluntarily give up its living standard as an addict will voluntarily renounce his habit (although, like a voluntary reduction in living standard, such a renunciation is seen rationally to be greatly to his long-term advantage). The nature of addiction involves a grip which overcomes rational considerations of long-term self advantage because the immediate pleasure is so sweet.

Difficulties arising from freedom of political choice

The practice of the democratic system is a choice by the population between two sets of representative officials. This choice is not a reasoned one with long-term optimisation for the community in mind (the choice which would be made if the voting population were ideal rationalists), but an emotion-filled choice, rationalised by the wish to increase the living standard of each individual voter *at the time.*

Building the New Energy System now would involve substantial tax increases, devaluation of the currency at an increased rate, and increased unemployment (though building solar plants, particularly photovoltaic farms and solar-thermal plants, is labour-intensive). Thus, the capacity of an *elected* government to carry through the measures to obtain the capital to invest in the new construction in time might be limited. If one political party introduces the necessary hard measures, the party out of power is bound by the nature of the System to present a rosier alternate picture which removes them, and power is restored to the set of officials who offer the easier path. Only increased living standard would result from the relaxation in needed measures for the time being. Thus, it will be very difficult to gather the capital to build a New Energy System under a multi-party system, before social suffering from economic decline has commenced. At some time between the present and 2000, a degree of 'Wartime Measures' will have to be introduced, i.e. a coalition government ('stopping the population rifling the remaining national fuel reserves') must be present until sufficient of the Energy Conversion Systems for using *renewable* systems has been built under the direction of an Energy Sources Executive Administration.

The difficulty of the democratic path is that the actions needed concern changes which will not be manifested in public life for a decade. Thus, gasoline prices have been declining in the U.S.A., in constant dollars, whilst the purchase of the most gasoline-consuming vehicles has been increasing. A democratic society will not deny itself the maximum degree of prosperity for a danger, the evidence for which is understood by a few thousand scientists and has been deeply studied by only a few hundred. A real war represents a traditional situation arousing immediate, simple fear and hence resolution arising out of imagined self-interest throughout the whole population. However, in the face of national emergency measures for the energy situation, the political party out of power can always point, with some degree of truth, to the *possibility* of a breakthrough in fusion, to the *possible* discovery of giant new oil deposits in Antarctica, etc. In this, they would be backed by the media power of the multi-national oil and coal companies, and their stockholders, eager to retain financial hegemony for the few remaining years, and able to offer the tremendous bait of continued (temporary) prosperity and high employment to the public.

A difficulty of an acceptance of a voluntary down-turn in consumer standards to give rise to the needed capital investment in time is the absence of knowledge of basics concerning the energy supply and its control of the living standards of society—in particular, the decades of lead-time needed for the building of the machinery for a changeover from non-renewable to renewable sources. Thus, 35% of the U.S. population was unaware in the late 1970s of the dependence of about half the U.S. oil supply upon the frequent arrival of the tankers from Saudi Arabia,[14] and the implied dependence of the Capitalist world's prosperity, on the attitude of a dozen of the one hundred Governing Saudi princes whose hegemony, like that of Iran's ruler, could be swept away at any moment.

Fossil fuels as basic capital

There is a lack of clarity in Energy discussions in the sense that, for many writers, the sources of Energy are distinguished only by quantitative economic factors.

This is not a good viewpoint. Fossil fuels are unique. They represent the *basic capital* which Man has been *spending* since the Industrial Revolution. No renewable resource will deliver energy to the consumer at prices as low as those at which the fossil fuels can be made available, for this is 'free' energy, the photosynthetic solar energy, from past aeons, stored in a form almost ready for use.

The price at which fossil fuels are sold is to some extent, arbitrary. It is analogous to the rate at which an executor of an estate sometimes allows the beneficiaries to take money from capital. It would be possible to produce a period of prosperity by selling the remaining fossil fuels at prices near to cost. The burst of increased expansion would threaten the relevant economies at an earlier date than that which exhaustion is foreseen at the present rate of expansion. Alternatively, it would be possible to stretch out the existence of the fossil fuels (thus increasing the possibility of building a New Energy System in time) by increasing their prices—but then only by diminishing expansion, and the standard of living, that is, by inducing depression.

Energy capital and energy income

Use of the renewable resources is equivalent to living on income; use-up of the fossil fuels is equivalent to living by spending capital. The difficulties to be faced in making a transfer to the use of renewable resources is easier to appreciate in terms of this equivalence.

Capitalism and the use-up of non-renewable resources

Capitalism is usually understood as the consequence of a *social* development arising out of the limitation of the power of the owners of land (feudalism). However, the pulse of capitalism has been contemporaneous with the industrial revolution, and this originated in the application of energy-conversion equipment to non-renewable energy resources.

Thus, the aggregation of capitalist wealth in the 18th and 19th centuries can be seen as a result of a dim realisation by a tiny fraction of the population that the one essential wealth was coal in the ground and that this could be converted to practically exchangeable and great wealth through the agency of energy-conversion machines.

Until the 1970s, the prosperity of the United States may have been based more upon the availability there of the most conveniently applicable form of fossil fuels (oil) than to any other factor.

Another aspect is that an essential aspect of capitalism is economic growth. One expects a unit of invested capital to become more than one in constant values, within a time short compared with one's lifetime, and without one's own *physical* effort. The present discussion suggests that this process has been occurring essentially by means of the use-up of the C-H bond energy gathered in photosynthesis at a rate greater than its arrival in the form of continued photosynthetic solar-energy storage.

Capitalism and growth may hence be one-time phenomena and terminate with the need to attain a steady state in economics in which the use-up of resources is equal to their rate of reformation, e.g. by recycling. The one *income* is energy—solar energy.

The end does not have to be catastrophic so long as, in the present terminal phase, the last part of the fossil-fuel capital wealth is used to purchase energy conversion machinery for the renewable resources.

New concepts as incipient capital creation?

Non-renewable fuel resources have been the basic capital hitherto. However, new ideas can be regarded as new capital. Thus, the concept of electromagnetism, when duly exploited, was equivalent to the donation of incalculable trillions to the community. If the concept of hydrogen pellet compression by laser impaction yields a path to mechanical energy at distant points at lower cost than any of the solar methods, this concept would prove to have been equivalent to capital of inestimably large value. In its present unachieved state, a concept such as laser fusion is analogous, e.g. to the existence of oil deposits at impractical depths under the sea.

New concepts may be seen as a form of information and thus as a show of disentropy arising from the ordering force of consciousness.

Social attitudes which make difficult the formation of an effective energy policy

Scientists advise legislators. However, in respect to Energy (changes in the policy concerning which feedback so rapidly on everyday life), there are difficulties in making the advice heeded.

1. There is a widespread opinion among the public that the concern for fossil-fuel exhaustion is contrived to keep price 'high'.
2. The times for exhaustion mentioned in this paper are *decades*. To legislators and even company executives, this is a period of time not of pressing interest. Stockholders will demand a good performance each year till it is no longer possible. They are most unlikely to agree to a voluntary reduction of share dividends over decades so that, twenty years later, they may prosper.
3. There is little consciousness in the minds of citizens and legislators that oil bears the same relation to a technological civilization which air and sunlight do to an agricultural one. Were the population informed that air would be gone in a few decades but that something could be done about it, by starting now, democracy might work, and dynamically.
4. Overwhelming attention to *present* matters is essential to personal survival in competition with one's fellows. Attention to matters 10-50 years away is the concern of dreamers. They will be poor and, hence, undesirable.
5. It is good to *get:* giving is for the nice guys who end last. Moves toward conservation are, thus, the concern of a very small (if vocal) proportion of the population.

In the presence of such attitudes, a politician who was conscious of the needed capital investment for building the New Energy Conversion Machinery in time (see Tables 16.II and 16.III) would have little chance of getting necessary legislation passed. The legislation would cause that reduced living standard called 'depression'. The democratic vote would go to him who promised continued good times, without focussing upon the effect this path would have upon the comparative degree of social pain at a later decade.

Is it justified to call a national emergency?

The situation of the exhaustion of oil and natural gas is unprecedented. It is possible to appreciate the situation by regarding it in the context of the time since the Industrial Revolution. The beginning of this can be identified with the Newcommen Engine of 1724. It was not until the early 1970s that the question of exhaustion was raised with concern.

Thus, for about 250 years the present world had been building up, based upon fossil-fuel energy sources, and expansion had gone on regardless of the

TABLE 16.II: Cost of Replacing (Non-Communist) Foreign Oil Shortfall as From 1993

Assumptions:
1. Foreign oil at 1993 $3.9 \ 10^{13}$ kWh/yr*.[15]
2. Cost of replacement equipment: 310^3 $/kW (1978 $) using cost-negligible fuel[+]

Period Considered	Cost of replacing shortfall, $/yr
1993-1995	$0.6 \ 10^{12}$
1995-2000	$0.5 \ 10^{12}$
2000-2005	$0.5 \ 10^{12}$
2005-2010	$0.3 \ 10^{12}$
2010-2015	$0.2 \ 10^{12}$

*This refers to the energy equivalent of the oil delivery-rate in kW, not to electricity generation.
[+]Thus, either using inexhaustible resources of wind, solar, etc., or the cost of atomic or coal converter equipment (but neglecting cost of fuel).

TABLE 16.III: A First Approximation Estimate of the Cost in $ per Yr of Replacing Oil and Natural Gas in the US After 1992*

Assumptions:
1. The economy is assumed to rise *linearly* after 1993.[15]
2. The supplies of oil and natural gas are assumed to fall linearly at 4% per year.[15]
3. The cost per kW is assumed to be $3000.
4. Currency is 1978 $ throughout.
5. Economy and energy per head is linear.
6. No changes in average conversion efficiency occur.

Economic Assumption (1992-2015)	Cost in $/yr of new energy machinery	Cost of new energy plant building per family of four, per yr	Cost of 1977 spending on defence, family of four per yr
Decline of economy averaged at 4%/yr	Zero	Zero	
Zero-growth	$0.3 \ 10^{12}$	$ 4,800	
1% growth	$0.4 \ 10^{12}$	$ 6,400	$1,920
3% growth	$0.5 \ 10^{12}$	$ 7,968	
5% growth	$0.7 \ 10^{12}$	$11,184	

*The precise year of maximum of the oil and natural gas supply is as yet uncertain: it is likely to occur in the 1990s.
[+]The yearly cost of a 90% mortgage on a house costing $40,000 at 9.75% interest is more than $3,510.

longevity of the resource which fuelled it. The concept of a 'renewable' energy resource, compared with non-renewable ones, the association of the first with *income,* and the second with energy *capital,* was not discussed, even among energy scientists.

The origin of the concern with exhaustion originated from the classic book of Meadows *et al., The Limits to Growth,* in 1972, when stress was placed upon the use-up of resources, including the remaining fuels.

From the Meadows book, there spread the concept of numerous types of Doom. The most discussed arise from over-population, and associated exhaustions (materials as well as energy).

The basic threat is an energy-exhaustion threat. This has not come over clearly because:
1. It is associated with numerous other threats, to an extent so great that there is now a public insensitivity to further warnings.
2. There is an overload of news without discrimination between the trivial

and the significant so that a sense of proportion has been lost.

Consequently, there is a continuation of old growth-mechanisms towards a situation where it may be too late to build resources needed, because of the great amounts of capital needed for the building. A number of true statements may be made by political leaders, but, as in the case of the Carter energy policy, these are washed away, not accepted seriously, and the politicians act in resonance with those on whom their power depends—the public and the companies. A conversational position—a less energised (lower income) one—gives rise only to psychological despondency.

At the same time, the pattern of life continues, as though a stable source of energy for continuation of normal life were available. The present economic system is geared to a situation (cheap and 'inexhaustible' resources) which no longer exists. For example, a number of countries have written energy scenarios in which they admit their inability to continue without greatly increased oil imports after 2000. These imports simply put down in white papers as though oil would be available from abroad, just at a time when foreign oil will be declining precipitously. It seems reasonable to coin the term 'struchion' (from *struchio*, the ostrich) for the present attitude.

With less than two decades to go before the liquid and gaseous fossil fuels pass through a maximum of production rate, it seems reasonable to consider the proclamation of a State of National Emergency.

Thus:

1. The present type of economics is not suitable to a country approaching energy exhaustion, with inadequate remaining time for the building of substitute energy-conversion machinery.

2. Much production at present is irrelevant to the winning of the fundamental battle between exhaustion of the present fuels and the building of machinery to extract energy from the surroundings. In a war, the exigencies of the situation are dealt with by appropriate methods. Thus, in 1941, Detroit was turned from the production of cars to military vehicles in a few months. It is necessary at this time to change the direction of normal production to the production of machinery which could be ready in time to provide the energy which the fading gaseous fuels will provide decreasingly after 1990.

3. *Capital investment:* Special means will have to be taken to obtain sufficient capital to build the new energy-conversion systems over a few decades.

4. *The actual building:* The building of the new energy-conversion systems will be the greatest individual engineering project ever undertaken. Yet, at present, the atomic energy industry is hamstrung with regulation: it takes *12 years* to build an atomic reactor. The real building time must be much less than this, perhaps 2-3 years. (The rest consists of legal hold-ups.)

The difference could be swept away under a dynamic policy arising from a state of national emergency.

Little of the needed dynamic can be obtained in the normal economy. Even in 1941 when the United States was fighting on the side of the allies and had (with them) a numerical superiority of 12:1, a suspension of normal economic life was considered necessary. The present situation appears to constitute an incomparably greater challenge than a war under conditions of vast numerical superiority.

Against the calling of a national emergency are the following:

1. The overwhelming reason is that the act would be politically unpopular. Wartime measures may have been unpopular, but 'war' makes the imposition of special measures acceptable.
2. The time of a national emergency is measured in years. The period of lengthy special investment and building of new energy sources will be decades.
3. Although there may be some differences from country to country, all technologically advanced countries will be in a similar situation as that of the United States. The calling of an emergency in the U.S. would be followed by the calling of national emergencies in the affluent countries within a few years. Would the relative situation of the United States be better than that of other countries because it acted firstly? The answer is in the affirmative: for the difficulties due to energy exhaustion will come anyway, and a few years may be gained by focusing attention upon the difficulty and starting a constructive activity as a model for what must surely become a united world effort, with corresponding business opportunity for those firstly with appropriate technology.

SUMMARY OF CHAPTER

1. The political attractiveness of being able to continue the economy more or less as in the past for a further decade, perhaps even two, provides the major danger that a massive building programme in energy machinery will not commence in time to avoid social suffering.
2. Reasonable assumptions concerning the cost per kW of new energy sources, and the time during which some liquid and gaseous fuels will be available, suggests an average needed rate of investment of the new energy machinery of several hundred billion dollars per year over some 40 years.
3. Raising the price of oil substantially would have numerous negative consequences. Does the extra building time this would give us justify the social pain?
4. If coal is to be used as a bridging resource, H_2, not CH_4, should be produced from it and CO_2 dumped in the deep ocean. Some of the environmental objections to the use of coal are thus removed.
5. It is re-emphasised and re-exemplified that solar-thermal ocean-thermal plants offer, in terms of systems analysis, hydrogen fuel at acceptable prices.
6. Several uses of hydrogen are economically viable now.
7. Some stages in the building of a Solar-Hydrogen Economy are proposed.
8. After some 5kW per person, the rate of increase of income per unit of energy increase per head declines.
9. Is the principal difficulty in a realistic adjustment to exhaustion an over-attachment to continuous increase in material living standards, regardless of concomitant consequences; would the present political and social sys-

tem make possible legislation which declined *present* living standards so that in the decade-future, standards could be maintained or increased? Is the concept of 'capital' dependent on having exhaustible resources to sell?

10. Is the prospect that the fossil fuel supply will begin to turn down (with attendant economic consequences), before the compensating machinery for energy conversion from renewable resources has been built, sufficiently negative in its image that the introduction of 'wartime' economic measures, *at this time*, would be politically possible within the present system?

AUTHOR'S CHOICE OF THE THREE MOST IMPORTANT CONCLUSIONS FROM THIS BOOK

1. On the basis that energy sources other than oil and natural gas will be the principal ones some *50* years from now, the average yearly spending rate on new energy-conversion machinery from 1980 to 2030 will be in the hundreds of billions of dollars per year (around $1000 per citizen per year) for around half a century.

2. The difficulties in attaining a new energy system before the fossil fuels exhaust is firstly due to lack of realisation that the burning of an exhaustible resource to energize the Society bears an analogy to living on capital; and secondly due to the formidable sums per year needed from the last of that capital to construct any new energy system, in the time in which it will be needed, even one built to burn up the residual coal.

3. In respect to which of the three available options (coal, breeders, solar), the apparent cost per unit of conversion machinery is as yet uncertain: each is in the order of magnitude $1000/kW. However, it is invalid to measure cost in that way. It should be measured as the cost of a unit of energy to the customer, taking into account the Second Law efficiencies, weighted for the various purposes for which the fuel is used; and the cost of the environmental and human damage which use of the fuel will cause, per unit used, should be attached to the selling price and recovered for use by Government Agencies. It is on this basis that the Solar-Hydrogen Alternative can be recognised not only as the likely ultimate but also as the cheapest among the near-future energy prospects.

REFERENCES

1. Y. Hunter, K. Walt, J. Flory, P. Hunter & N. Mosman, *Energy,* 1976, **1**, 375.
2. A. J. Weiss, World Conference on Alternative Energy Sources, Miami, 5-7 December, 1977.
3. R. Billings, World Conference on Alternative Energy Sources, Miami, 5-7 December, 1977.
4. G. C. Ferrel, International Institute for Applied Systems Analysis, Luxemburg, Austria.
5. J. O'M. Bockris, *International Journal for Energy Research,* 1978.
6. A. F. Hildebrandt & L. L. Van't Hull, First World Hydrogen Energy Conference, Miami, March, 1976.
7. G. L. Dugger & E. J. Francis, First World Hydrogen Energy Conference, Miami, Florida, 1976, 3A-63.
8. R. S. Brown & A. S. Gutmann, World Conference on Alternative Energy Sources, Miami, 5-7 December, 1977.

9. E. Hietbrink *et al.*, in J.O'M. Bockris (ed.); *Electrochemistry for Cleaner Environment* (Plenum, 1972).

10. Yul Brown, private communication, Sydney, 1978.

11. P. Quintevilla, private communication, 1978.

12. R. Billings, World Conference on Alternative Energy Resources, Miami, 5-7 December, 1977.

13. P. Tison & F. Wiedermann, First World Hydrogen Energy Conference, Miami, 1976, 4B-3.

14. F. N. Cotton, private communication, December, 1977.

15. Computed from a graph of total non-Communist oil production (excluding U.S. oil) as a function of time, provided by D. Root & F. Annatassi, private communication, 1978.

A NOTE ON NON-SOLAR-NON-NUCLEAR 'RENEWABLE' SOURCES OF ENERGY

Several other sources of energy should be considered. Corresponding to the title of this book, such considerations will be done briefly.

1. Solar-Gravitational Sources

Solar-Gravitational sources (i.e. hydro-electric power) have been mentioned above and in Chapter 8. Briefly, it is important to develop all which could be made available because it tends to be the cheapest source of energy. According to the present prospect, however, the total hydro-electric resources could not supply the economy, although the development of large resources underdeveloped at present, such as the potential Greenland resource (Chapter 8), would give a significant (small) amount of energy, available in the United States in the form of LH_2 at interesting prices.

It may be that our concepts of the hydro-electric resources have been too limited. For example, there has been neglect of those more than a few hundred km from use-centers. Such an attitude might be subject to revision if the transmission and storage possibilities of hydrogen are taken into account.

The advantages of hydro-electric power are so great that one might look not only at far-off resources such as the Victoria Falls in Rhodesia; and the possibilities available to hydro-electric engineering in the Amazon basin. It is interesting to enquire whether the potential use of atomic explosives could be made to provide substantial added hydro-electric capacity from the principal high places in the world, particularly from the vast Himalayan region.

2. Gravitational Sources

The gravitational source has the difficulty of being unidirectional in effect. It is only when solar evaporative forces reverse the flow of material against gravitation that the potential energy converted to kinetic in the fall of the water is regained.

It is of interest to enquire whether devices can be contrived for converting to useful energy the potential energy available in the various natural movements of water.

Thus, tides are often pointed to as potential energy sources. There might be many areas of the world in which there could be tidal energy stations.[1] To be economically attractive, one needs a tidal difference of about 10 metres; and coast-line geography which involves some inlet with a relatively narrow neck so that a large volume of water surges to and fro each day, thus operating appropriately placed rotors. A 500 MW station operated at Rance in Northern France from 1968.

Wave energy has recently come into a potential development situation in

411

the U.K. Essentially, the method depends on the oscillation of boat-like objects as moved by waves, these in turn cause movements which can be converted to electricity.[2] The energy wave-density of the Western Coasts of the U.K. is such that a single line of wave-transducer the whole length of the Western Coast, would provide the entire electricity supply for the U.K.

Both of these applications seem interesting in appropriate situations, and perhaps could be made economically attractive. However, there is little prospect that even their fullest development will fulfil the total needs of any country as could, e.g. wind and solar resources. It is clear that in certain situations, the tidal and wave energies may *contribute*. Again, the advantage of hydrogen as a common medium of energy is manifest. It would be possible to have, e.g. wave energy adding to, e.g. fuels from atomic and coal sources, if each produced hydrogen.

The force of buoyancy has been given little attention. It is of course gravitational and it seems reasonable to suggest that the name Archimedean be given to this potential energy source.

Thus, in principle, if an economic way could be found whereby salt which had been obtained from the evaporation of sea water could be used to sink a buoy; the salt then tapped onto the sea-bottom (there dissolving); the buoy would rise, thus producing usable energy. Were the salt produced by solar evaporation of sea water, the cost of the latter would determine the energy cost from this sort of approach. A preliminary cost calculation taking solar de-salinated water as 2 cents per gallon indicates an electricity cost in the region of 10 cents per kWh.

3. Geothermal Sources

The geothermal sources are of two kinds, those which come from a heat source near the surface; and those which, hypothetically, could arise by boring deeply into the rock (some tens of km in thickness) which separates the earth surface from the tremendous heat source of the magma (a molten silicate, the temperature of which is above 1000°C).

The exploitation of the surface geothermal resources has been carried out for many years, particularly in Southern California and New Zealand. The principal of exploitation is trivial: the heat is simply used to produce steam.

It is unlikely that use of the world's surface geothermal resources to form steam will have a significant effect on the world energy situation. However, two factors are as yet unexplored in this region:

(a) There may be many undiscovered hot springs sufficiently near the surface for them to be considered surface waters. They have not been sought.

(b) Hot water at, say, 60-70°C exists in abundance from natural sources. It could be used to boil organic liquids and the surrounding air used to cause condensation. The electricity thereby generated could be used to form pipeable hydrogen.

Apart from these possibilities, it would be *possible* to bore deep into the hot rock: at 2-3 km depth the temperature is 200-300°C. Thus, water would boil and it is easy to devise arrangements whereby the steam is channelled to the surface. After around 10-20 years, the walls of the rock will have cooled to below 100°C and there will be a need to rest a cavity for some years whilst another is opened.[4]

At first sight, the hot rock geothermal method seems attractive. Trivial calculation shows that there is enough total heat in the magma to run the present civilisation for a very long time without significant cooling. However, there are difficulties:

(a) The size of cavity which must be formed to supply a town of 10^6 people is several km in diameter, i.e. many cavities of much smaller diameter would have to be formed.

(b) The potential mode of formation of such cavities is uncertain. Atomic explosions are unsafe because of the possibility of causing widespreading earth disturbances.[5]

(c) The steam produced eats away at the rock and thousands of tons per day per energy station of rock fragments would be ejected on the surface and have to be removed.

A more-advantageous way to use the geo-thermal heat would avoid the need for large cavities, and also eliminate the ejection of rock fragments to the surface. Thus, thermo-electric couples could be sunk into bore holes several miles deep. The low voltage (1-2 volts) needed to electrolyze water would be developable by the use of series coupling. Electrolysis would occur at the earth's surface.

There might be a possibility of provoking an artificial and controlled volcano by drilling through to the magma and injecting water. This would form, at $1000°C$, a significant quantity of H_2 which could, perhaps, be extracted in significant amounts.

All in all, these non-solar and non-atomic sources are of interest for research, particularly the intriguing problem of whether one might find a way to use the Archimedean force. However, it seems that the direct solar and solar-gravitational sources look, at present, more certain in regard to the course of development.

REFERENCES

1. T. J. Gray & O. K. Gashus (edd.), *Tidal Power* (Plenum Publishing Corporation, New York, 1972).
2. See, e.g. Marshall F. Merriam, *Technology Review* **79** (1977), p. 28. (A general discussion, and comparison with other sources is in *Australian Science & Technology* **15** (1978), p. 4.)
3. J. O'M. Bockris, Patent Disclosure at Jet Propulsion Laboratory, 1 March 1978.
4. M. C. Smith, *Geothermal Power*, Publication LA-UR-74-233, Los Alamos Scientific Laboratory, 1974.
5. J. Banwell & T. Meidov, Geothermal Energy for the Future, 138th Meeting of the American Association for the Advancement of Science, Philadelphia, December 1971.

COST ESTIMATES

Unless otherwise stated, the costs which are referred to in this book are those which are calculated for the processes concerned, were they to be set up on a big scale, in 1979 money.

The following points should be noted:

1. The changes which will occur in the cost structure between the time of these estimates and the time the machinery is actually mass produced will depend not only on the inflational changes but also upon changes in technology. This may give rise to upwards or downwards movements, but they are likely to be downward in constant dollars.

2. When price estimates for 1973 or 1974 have been taken into the present book they have been corrected to 1978 values by assuming an overall inflation of 7% per year, if that referred to the purchase of capital goods. On the other hand if the item referred to was an energy cost (e.g. the price of a ton of coal, etc.) the actual changes since 1973 have been taken into account. Thus, for coal, this would be several hundred per cent over the last five years.

3. It is of course invalid to compare cost estimates with *prices* of alternative products, for these contain various additions above cost, probably some tax, and always some profit margin. The latter can be adjusted downwards if the costs of a competitive fuel challenges the price at which fossil fuels are being sold.

Note the difference in comparing the price of fossil fuels – capital in the ground – from the cost of fuel from income, e.g. hydrogen from solar energy. It is unlikely that new fuels, which will have to be got *ab initio,* could be as cheap as the fuels which were processed and stored in earlier aeons from the solar input. Much of the work and preparation of fossil fuels in a form nearly ready for use has been done by nature.

AN ENCAPSULATION

1. Our present economic policies and plans for the future assume that expansion of the economy (hence a growth in energy used per year) is desirable, and will continue. This view appears not to take into account the extremely large capital investment which will be needed, as from the 1990s, if the supply of energy is to be kept increasing at the same rate as at present (the close connection between the amount of energy per head and the living standard of the population appears to be little realised).

2. The time it will take to build the energy-conversion equipment to replace the diminishing oil and natural gas depends on the rate of capital investment possible, more than upon the ingenuity of persons who research and develop such devices. It is difficult to accept that sufficient capital will be available to build energy-conversion equipment to counteract the decrease in the oil and natural gas supply expected over the next fifty years (when these fuels will be available at only about one-quarter of the present production rate).

3. In view of (2), two alternatives stand before us between the end of the century and the middle of the next century: a substantial (tens of per cent) cutback in consumer standards which might then allow sufficient capital investment in the needed new energy-conversion devices; or a considerable enforced decline in the population caused directly by breakdown of city life which would occur if the energy supply per head declined sufficiently.

4. The potentialities of the development of coal to provide fuels to replace oil have been exaggerated. Gasoline from coal promises to be more expensive than synthetic liquid natural gas, so the latter is relatively far more attractive. However, the difficulties of pollution from sulphur and carbon dioxide mean either an unacceptable increase in atmospheric pollution or that extra cost must be allowed for to cover returning the sulphur for reburial. There appears to be a danger in the CO_2 problem if coal is viewed as a replacement to oil: the world temperature rise would be around $5°C$ before mid-century.

5. There is a misunderstanding in respect to the costing of energy from atomic fission. This has been based upon reactors which will not be of use to replace oil in the post-2000 future under consideration because of the exhaustion of uranium. What may be of use are breeder reactors. Safe breeder reactors, however, would provide electricity and hydrogen at costs several times those of fission reactors.

The hazards seen to be associated with nuclear reactors can probably all be overcome but only by increasing the cost of the product. It is not yet clear what that cost component may be.

6. There is agreement that fusion technology has so many unexplored

problems before it that it cannot be hoped in practice before 2050. (Many physicists doubt whether it will be available within the next century.) Oil and natural gas, and perhaps even coal, will be largely exhausted before fusion technology is likely to be available.

7. The challenge to conventional coal-nuclear thinking provided by solar-thermal and OTEC methods (also photovoltaics using concentrators) is considerable. Cost estimates indicate electricity and hydrogen by these methods at (only) around two times present values. The engineering problems are of a lesser order of magnitude than those of breeders or fusion. Pollutional problems are negligible.

The present views differ from the conventional views because:
(a) They take into account the effect of coupling solar energy with hydrogen on storage, transmission and the medium of application of solar energy in industry and transportation.
(b) They take account of the efficiencies of use upon the comparative economic value of the various fuels (Second Law efficiencies).
(c) They take into account the cost of environmental damage.

Second Law efficiency gives hydrogen an advantage of up to two times in respect to land transport compared with fossil-based fuels.

Cost estimates, taking into account the Second Law efficiencies of hydrogen, make hydrogen from coal potentially the cheapest available form of post oil and natural gas energy. Although the cost of environmental damage is difficult to estimate, conservative attempts to do this yield results which show a considerable net cost advantage to the public of hydrogen from coal compared with alternative post oil and natural gas fuels.

8. If hydrogen, instead of synthetic natural gas, were used as the synthetic fuel from coal during the interim period whilst breeder reactors and solar sources are being built, some of the environmental difficulties of using coal would disappear because the conversion plants could be shore based and reject CO_2 into the ocean. During the transitional stage of several decades, hydrogen could become the common fuel, fed by coal, nuclear and solar sources. However, sulphur pollution and the difficulty of building sufficient deep mines in the needed time suggest that coal's contribution would not be a lengthy one.

9. The transmission of hydrogen appears to be the cheapest way to send energy over distances between 1000-4000 kilometres on land. Barge transport of liquid hydrogen over the sea would increase the cost of the delivered fuel substantially.

10. Hydrogen can be stored *as a gas* in already-engineered systems using FeTi and Mg to an extent which would allow cars to go 400 kilometres without refuelling.

11. A noteworthy conclusion is that (because of a higher efficiency of conversion) hydrogen from coal, stored as a hydride, would drive cars at about the same cost as that of present U.S. gasoline (without tax, dealer mark-up). If environmental damage costs are accounted, hydrogen from coal would now be a cheaper fuel for transportation than gasoline or synthetic natural gas from coal.

12. There is misunderstanding concerning the efficiency of thermochemical cycles for the production of hydrogen compared with that of electrolysis. Such cycles are not likely to be more efficient than electrolysis, because of the pseudo-Carnot type of work which has to be done in carrying out the cycle, which has several steps at different T and P.

In respect to water electrolysis, research results at a laboratory level have not yet been applied to commercial electrolysers.

Bottled hydrogen is sold at a price of between 10 and 100 times that calculated for hydrogen from large-scale electrolysers.

13. Hydrogen environmental embrittlement can be removed by the addition of small quantities of oxygen.

14. Hydrogen is both less dangerous than methane (power of explosion per unit volume) and more dangerous (more easily ignitable).

15. To maintain the economy at a zero energy growth-rate after the mid-1990s will need the building of new energy-conversion or fuel-manufacturing plants which will cost more per year over several decades than the U.S. military budget. To make the economy grow (i.e. use more energy per head) at 5% per year, the cost of plant building would be between two and six times the 1978 military expenditure.

APPENDIX IV
A SUGGESTION FOR A NATIONAL ENERGY RESOURCES EXECUTIVE ('NERE')

There are so many aspects of the Energy situation that a difficulty is confusion, too many goals to attain at one time.

Among these, then, it is important to pick out the first in time: it is independence from overseas resources. Whilst the United States (and hence the non-Communist world) is dependent upon long sea lanes for its oil, under circumstances where the United States is not unchallenged at sea, the Western powers lie under a Damoclean sword.

The evolution to total Energy Independence in ten years would seem to be the most urgent objective to be attained, even if it meant the establishment of a war-time economy, as would seem to be indicated.

The second thing (time-wise) to decide upon is the situation of the remaining non-renewable resources, the remaining capital. Should we spend it, i.e., use the coal resources as a major source of hydrogen, or should we use these predominantly to build the new system and attempt to be on renewable resources by, say, 2030, rather than 2050-2060, by which period we shall *have* to be on the renewable resources (although by then should we not be too energy-poor to build the necessary conversion machinery)? Technological considerations have been discussed. A major uncertainty is the rate of development of fusion technology.

There is one message which comes through clearly from any study of the Energy situation: it is one in which the importance of the scientific and technological factors are heavily compounded with the sociological and economic ones. Even a dynamic programme of building breeder reactors, connected to water-splitting plants, would serve the situation, though with undesirable feed-backs, dangers which, however, seem trivial compared with the potential effect of autopharge. What lacks is COHERENCE OF VIEWPOINT. We are immured in comforts which arise from a comfort-giving technology fuelled by gasoline: all moves to decrease, even temporarily, the comfort level are understandably resisted with emotional fervour. But a sufficient degree of capital investment in renewable resources technology to be ready in time appears (see Chapter 16) to imply a diminution, generation-long, in living standards; this is the heart of the problem. Most people do not sufficiently realise the alternative, and there will always be politicians who will attempt, in the wisdom of a two-year viewpoint, to make injections into the body politic of comforting massage concerning the availability for another few years of the desired high income ($\equiv$ high energy consumption) state.

Why is the Department of Energy not yet associated with a programme on the development of renewable resources equal to or greater than the programme to develop further the non-renewable resources? Wind, solar-thermal, OTEC, perhaps photovoltaic–so long as they are coupled with a clean fuel–all seem to have acceptable economic prospects. Building of solar-thermal could begin in the 1980s. Research and development could go along with the building. In ten years' time, with a sufficiently dynamic programme, independence of potential foreign control of the national energy supply could be attained.

A coal-nuclear bias appears in those who have financial control of the direction of the Energy research spending apparatus (the members of the Committees of the Bureau of the Budget).

The pejorative part of the situation is the immurement of the body politic in the temporary comforts which come with the spending of capital. There must be an operative organ of cure. This is the appropriate political organisation to see that the body politic is in possession of sufficient information to allow the capital investment to build the equipment. What is needed is a National Energy Resources Executive (NERE). This would be an authority having war-time powers to gather capital and manpower, organise its building programmes. It would be set up after the declaration of a state of national emergency, the nub of which would be the vulnerability of the U.S.A. to foreign domination arising from the importing of amounts of oil in the region of 50% of total need.

What is the most appropriate part of the U.S. Government to house the National Energy Resources Executive? Is it not the Department of Defense? Is not defence primarily dependent upon an energy supply? NERE's central task would be: being ready in time with built plants to produce the energy to replace the short-fall in liquid and gaseous fuels, to be felt in the next decade.*

But should such a great enterprise be done nationally, alone? There has been talk of resource wars. Is a way to avoid such a situation to stimulate an international scheme for carrying out the construction of a resources network? One such collaboration is in being. Thus, PORSHE is the Plan for an Ocean Raft for a Solar-Hydrogen Economy, and involves American-Japanese collaboration in the building of a solar-thermal plant in the ocean, planned to produce 600 tons of liquid hydrogen a day.

The reader may think that much indicates the desirability, from a resource point of view, of multi-national co-ordination. There is much in the various national psyches which militates against such a system, but more in the Energy situation which suggests that its achievement has become essential.

---

*There will be apparent hold-up, and apparent signs of exhaustion before this as the suppliers restrict supply and force up the price, thus stressing their character as supra-governmental controllers of the economy. Of course, if Saudi-Arabia suffers revolution, drastic, and even catastrophic, down-turn would be immediate.

APPENDIX V
APPROPRIATE VOCABULARY

There are three new words which might be relevant in describing the energy situation in which we find ourselves. The first is autopharge (Hansen), and the second struchian. The latter describes a frequent reaction aroused by acquaintance with the situation, a wish not to look at it. The word corresponds to an ostrich's (Lat. *struchio*) alleged habit of placing its head beneath the sand when in danger.

Another useful word would appear to be an adjective relating to the collision of the 45,000 ton British Atlantic liner TITANIC with an iceberg in 1912: titanical. There are many parallels of the catastrophe with that which we appear to be approaching. The TITANIC epitomised the technological high of the time. The captain was given many pieces of warning information, in the hours before the accident, of the presence of icebergs on the route of the ship. He stated he could not slow down—*the passengers would not like* a late arrival.

Even after the ship struck (a glancing blow, hardly felt), great confidence was expressed among the passengers that everything would be all right. Some persons aroused by the ship warning bells actually went back to bed after they had found the ship had merely stopped. Persons treated the collision with little anxiety: the iceberg appeared to be small, and *nothing could be seen* of what had caused the ship to stop. By and large, passengers continued the amusements of the evening. The ship's officers—who understood the situation—*deemed it better to let the passengers go on dancing*. Only when the ship took on a visible forward tilt and sent off distress rockets did the passengers take some interest in the situation. Panic took hold only in the last few minutes, perhaps when it was realised that the Company had provided lifeboats for only one-third of the passengers. *Headquarters regarded it as absurd* to think that such a modern boat could sink.

About two-thirds of the passengers were floated off the decks* as the ship sank, a good example of a consequence of the sudden ending of a resource.

---

*Within the limitation of analogy, it is meaningful to report that, the disaster having occurred, and more than 2000 people being suddenly immersed into the Atlantic Ocean at 1°C, those who had occupied the lifeboats (many less than half full), in the disorderly last minute partial evacuation of the vessel, rowed away from the struggling, screaming mass as fast as they were able.

From a stationary vessel on the horizon, the tilting lights and distress rockets of the giant vessel were observed with equanimity. The radio officer had gone to sleep. The captain, in bed, was informed of the rockets from the bridge. His reply was: 'Is it a vessel of this Company?'. On being answered in the negative, he decided: *No Action*.

POLITICAL DIFFICULTIES IN FINANCING REPLACEMENT ENERGY-PLANTS BEFORE THE TURNDOWN IN THE FOSSIL FUEL SUPPLY

The Western-world fossil fuel supply is likely to turn down in the 1990s. Capital has to be invested in the building of new plants many years *before* the turndown begins, because *after* the turndown, it will be increasingly difficult to raise.

The logical, cold, unpolitical conclusion would be to raise the necessary funds (Chapter 16) by taxation or inflation, whilst restricting consumption, as in wartime. The difficulties are:

1. Confusion as to priorities

To scientists, engineers, and economists, it is obvious that the threatened reduction of the energy supply is a more basic problem than any other. As yet, the electorate does not see the fading of the energy supply a decade hence, as a topic as important as, e.g. cancer or the lowering of both inflation and taxes [sic.].

2. The declining credibility of the expert

There was a time when a Government Committee consisting of scientists knowledgeable in the field concerned would be convened to consider a problem; and, after a few weeks, would come up with a report, thereafter regarded as authoritative and a basis for action. Now, however, there are many more experts in most fields. Embarrassingly, they disagree publicly in loud voices. Each tends to speak with enthusiasm about his field. Many are consultants to companies. It is suspected that some scientists may lay more stress upon aspects of truth connected with their employment. Oil companies pay more consultants than companies with alternative energy schemes.

As a result of this, politicians and legislators tend to discount the advice of the expert.

3. Indifference

Only perhaps one-third of the electorate is politically interested. The active one-third is splintered into small groups, each pushing a special interest of immediate visible self-advantage.

If the voter votes, it will be out of some enthusiasm, not on a rational 'most probable best case' basis but for his *this year* advantage.

4. Lack of rational debate

The rules of scientists and engineers assume a rational debate between alternatives. The electorate regards such cold-blooded considerations as boring.

The consideration which is *felt* is a threat of a pejorative result if certain actions are not taken. If a scientist makes threats, he loses credibility among his peers. Hence, the scientist has no way of reaching people in a politically meaningful way.

5. Ecology in politics

Everything is interlocking: economy, society, technology. All would vote for measures to be taken so that the energy resources are ready in time; but preparing in time would seem to present many negative side-effects in the interim, and these would be vote-losing, and the measures therefore not obtainable within the system.

6. The two-year viewpoint

The politician has to fight day by day to maintain his position, paying attention to his image in publicity and the media. The probability of his re-election is only related to things people can *see*. Smog in Los Angeles is a powerful issue. The Fossil Fuel downturn predicted for the 1990s is not yet an issue.

Thus, although in this book the greatest difficulty in the Energy situation has been identified as the lack of economic resources to build the needed new plants, the underlying question is: can a populist politics prepare for a Great Storm seeable only by the few with powerful glasses?

APPENDIX VII
THE BIGGER VIEWPOINT

This book attempts to set out the alternative areas of technology to meet the coming exhaustion of the liquid and gaseous fossil fuels. The technology which is the main theme of the book is the collecting of solar light in suitable regions of the world upon a massive scale, applying the energy thus produced to split water and distribute the resulting hydrogen over large distances. This is seen as a final form of energy supply, giving the possibility of a steady state in the world economy, together with an eventual reasonably egalitarian distribution of energy among nations. The attainment of such a condition—possible within three generations—is seen as an evolutionary step of great magnitude—like the evolution of the biological energy storage system involving ATP and ADP. There are only two other possibilities (breeders and fusion), and reasons are given as to why the solar solution is to be preferred.

It would be better to convert as soon as possible to a solar-hydrogen energy base to the economy. However, for reasons of the structure of our society, it will be necessary to pass through a period in which some of the available coal is sold. Indeed, the energy from it would be cheaper—around one-third—than energy from alternative sources, for coal is already-collected-and-stored solar energy, energy *capital*.

It is advocated that coal should be used mainly as a fuel to build up atomic and solar sources, which can be seen, in the longer term, as escape systems, to allow the continuation of the civilisation after the fossil fuels are used.

A case is made that hydrogen would be a cheaper fuel from coal for transportation than gasoline and/or liquid methane. During the temporary coal-atomic-solar stage, the fuel likely to be the ultimate one would be increasingly used, and there would be no need to change the machinery later on.

These propositions and cost estimates are based upon a premise: that there is a wish among people to live at present standards of life, or better. However, it turns out that the act of replacing the use of the fossil fuels as an energy source ('living on capital') by machinery to exploit the renewable resources ('living on income'), has a tremendous price tag attached. The cost would be equivalent to the assumption of at least one extra mortgage by the average American family, and perhaps two. The optimistic view is that the living standards of the technologically based world will thus be temporarily lowered. 'Temporarily' here could mean for around two generations.

This conclusion seems forbidding and negative until viewed in the light of the alternative. This would be regression to a pre-technological society over a century or two, with an immense reduction of the population. Such a statement is not dependent upon any specific choice of system of energy conversion, for all replacements (coal fluidisation, breeders, fusion, solar) have the same order of magnitude in cost. At the end of the half-century which it would take to build machinery to use the renewable sources, we may come out into a halcyon era, with living standards not too much lower than those of our capital-spending phase.

The approach to this era of falling expectation is not being carried out by philosophers, calmly contemplating what might be regarded in terms of centuries, as a perturbation of mankind. We are going towards the end of the spending of our capital in a state lacking all consciousness of what lies just ahead. Attempts to translate the knowledge of the scientist to political consciousness are shucked off in ridicule and disbelief. We regard the standard of life we enjoy as 'the fruits of technology', but it appears to be as well described as a temporary spurt in the history of mankind, in which an unrealised splurging of the contents of the Middle Eastern Fuel Tank has given rise to a temporary living standard which should be at once inhibited, so that the already tenuous remaining resources can be used to build the renewable-resource energy-conversion machinery.

The over-riding difficulties are:
1. *The lack of consciousness of the facts among the population*
   The trouble is not only that the population does not wish to learn the unpleasant consequences of the approaching exhaustion: it is also true that the principal organisers of our society—producers and administrators—are not eager that the consciousness should spread. This does not imply a conspiracy—it is, essentially, an emotional bias against a view of the future other than the rosy one, that which promotes a contented stability.
2. *Sociological consequences of cut-backs*
   It has to be realised that the time and energy needed for the building of the machines for the new sources implies a cut-back in the degree of use of the present ones *before* they exhaust, and use them to build the new conversion machinery. If that way, then, is proved to lead to unemployment, it should at least lead to a new attitude to how money is distributed. Employment as the prerequisite of the distribution of wealth—the Protestant ethic—might consume too much energy to be viable. Resumption of manual labor for all would not maintain the technological society.

One may liken the present society to the groups of people still confidently dancing in the lounges of the TITANIC after the liner had struck. The Captain, who realizes the situation but thinks it is better not to tell the passengers, brings out some resonance to leading persons in our society, too. Others on the bridge know, but they are not beginning to do anything different from the comfortable things which they have been doing before realisation came.

It is best to end this book by creating a dialectical opposite view to that just espoused: it is concluded that the fossil fuels left do not allow continuation of an expanding economy but that adjustments (cut-backs) are necessary upon an unprecedented scale, so that sufficient energy (or capital—somewhat the same if the energy is to come from stored fossil energy) may be used to construct plants which convert solar (also gravitational and solar-gravitational) sources to useful forms of energy over a time long enough that the capital investment is reasonable.

A credible counter-view certainly cannot be created by a denial of the facts of exhaustion, for if, for example, much more coal should be removed from the resource classification to one of 'reserves', then it would change the situation only quantitatively—another few years added to our capital-spending life; and, in any case, there are other barriers to continued fossil-fuel burning, e.g. the CO_2 problem. But a case could be made that the whole system—the world economic and ecological system—could undergo a series of minor adjustments, each of which would be insignificant, the sum of which, however, could make a significant change. The United States is exceeded only by the United Kingdom in *in*-efficiency of energy use. Life in Europe is certainly on a lesser scale than that in the United States. It is not qualita· tively different; indeed, in another (but perhaps not unconnected) sense, it may be life at a higher quality. The *point* is that it is life at about one-half the rate of energy spending per head. Again, all of the time-calculations of exhaustion, of the dire capital investment rate which is needed to fulfil construction goals *in time*, are dependent upon assumptions about growth. Growth is a sacred-cow in our society. It seems our economic and social fabric is kept tough and healthy only if growth (3-4% real growth per year) occurs. Yet, in another sense, growth is the ghastly monster, the spirit of the autophage, that which is tending to make us eat ourselves up. Were it socially and economically possible to have a happy and prosperous nation at small or zero growth rates, the entire energy exhaustion problem is diminished and put off by at least a generation, and the capital aggregation rate needed significantly reduced.

This book is intended primarily for scientists and engineers. However, it is desirable for those who deal with energy-engineering to have a much wider perspective—an intellectual, and even philosophical, perspective. It is vital to see the longer and the larger view, to see man in terms, certainly not of a year or two, but not in terms of decades either—rather in terms of centuries, and, perhaps, if there be those who can retain credibility in such discussions, in terms of millenia. In *such* terms, therefore, in lucidity and calm, the situation is clear and can be summarised in one proposition and three questions.

The proposition is: the degree of energy per head (E/H), and the efficiency of energy conversions (ε) are the principal determinants of our standard of life, and hence of the materialistic component of our degree of happiness. Continued as in the United States at present, E/H and ε will lead to an untenable economic situation in a time of around one generation (though some consequences will be felt in a decade). However, with sufficient change in life-style, and social changes which make a zero growth economy acceptable, the burdens of building the renewable-resource energy-conversion machinery may become tolerable.

The questions are:

1. Can consciousness of the meaning of the fossil-fuel energy-exhaustion situation (of the concept of living on capital and living on income, in their energy meanings) spread in a sufficiently short time to make the necessary social changes possible?
2. If the consciousness spreads, will it then lead to a spontaneous disentropic

change in society towards massive conservation and zero or negative energy-growth?
3. If the answer to (2) is negative, are there latent political forces in the society which could have the power to impose the necessary controls?

APPENDIX VIII
CONCLUSION CONCERNING ACTION

1. As early as the 1980s, a new source of energy, apart from oil and natural gas, must begin to be introduced or the rate of world economic decline (caused partly by the increase in the price of energy) will increase.

2. In the plan of most countries, this new source is to be coal. However, it will be difficult to undergo a massive conversion to coal, because pollution would make coal unacceptable as a main source of energy, unless the plants are built on the shore, effluents led to the deep ocean, and hydrogen (rather than synthetic natural gas) distributed. Hence, renewable-resource conversion-machinery should be built during the forthcoming decades to take over from oil and natural gas. Massive solar energy conversion is the only practical choice. Breeders seem to be dangerous and would not be competitive with the (predicted) solar costs, if made safe. Fusion has little prospect of becoming a technology for 50 years: there is nothing yet to suggest economic competitiveness with massive solar.

3. If H_2 were used as the medium of energy, the storage, distributive and diurnal difficulties of solar energy would be greatly reduced.

4. The (as yet) hardly perceived principal difficulty of the Energy Future, (i.e. of the future), is the size of the capital investment which will be needed to transfer to the renewable sources (living on capital versus living on income). To build the renewable resource machinery in time, money would have to be taken out of general distribution, i.e. from money normally used to buy a life above that of the subsistence level.* The necessary measures will be difficult to take in a democracy because there is insufficient time for the spread of consciousness of the need for restrictive action among the voters. Politicians who advocated the necessary hard economic measures would be eliminated in the democratic process. This is, of course, why virtually nothing has yet been done to react to the difficulties of exhausting fossil fuels: all options lead to downturns.

5. Our most likely mode of Doom—continuing to use up the energy capital (coal) until there is not enough left to support the building of the renewable resource machinery—is only one of several Dooms which face the next generation. Another is resource exhaustion and the associated likely international stresses in the direction of resource (atomic) wars. Survival under these extremely difficult conditions would seem unlikely for societies which retain the slowly-reacting democratic system. Survival through 2050 might be possible with the introduction of a war-time, directed economy, in which the long-term good of the community transcends the short term advantage of individuals, and small groups.

---

*In the language of economics, 'Creating a Great Depression'.